SETTLEMENTS
TO
SOCIETY,
1607–1763

A Documentary History of Colonial America

SETTLEMENTS TO SOCIETY, 1607–1763

A Documentary History of Colonial America

Edited by
JACK P. GREENE

W· W· Norton & Company · Inc · New York

Selection 14*C* is reprinted with the permission of the Colonial Society of Massachusetts and the editor from Bernard Bailyn (ed.), "The Apologia of Robert Keayne," *Publications of the Colonial Society of Massachusetts, Transactions,* volume XLII (1952–1956), pages 293–294, 296–297, 300–302, 329–331.

Selection 31 is reprinted for the first time, by permission of the Harvard College Library, from the original manuscript in Papers concerning the Governorship of South Carolina, Item 9, b Ms Am 1455, Houghton Library, Harvard University.

Selection 36*A* is reprinted with the permission of Alfred A. Knopf, Inc., from Carl Bridenbaugh, *Cities in the Wilderness: The First Century of Urban Life in America, 1625–1742* (1938) and *Cities in Revolt: Urban Life in America, 1743–1776* (1955).

Selections 44*B* (1), 57*A,* and 57*B* are reprinted with the permission of Appleton-Century-Crofts, Inc., from Leonard Woods Labaree (ed.), *Royal Instructions to British Colonial Governors, 1670–1776* (1935), volume I, page 218; volume II, pages 748–749; and volume I, pages 190–193.

Selection 46*A* is reprinted with the permission of Columbia University Press from Herbert and Carol Schneider (eds.), *Samuel Johnson, President of King's College: His Career and Writings* (1929), volume II, pages 542–547, 555–560.

Selection 54 is reprinted with the permission of the Virginia Historical Society from Jack P. Greene (ed.), *The Diary of Colonel Landon Carter of Sabine Hall, 1752–1778* (two volumes, Charlottesville: The University Press of Virginia, 1965), volume I, pages 116–117.

Selection 55*A* is reprinted by permission of the Controller of H.M. Stationery Office from Colonial Office Papers, Class 5/372, ff. 80–87 (London: Public Record Office).

Copyright © 1975, 1966 by Ralph B. Greene, trustee for Granville Greene, and Ralph B. Greene, trustee for Jacqueline Megan Greene

Library of Congress Cataloging in Publication Data
Greene, Jack P   ed.
    Settlements to society, 1584-1763.
    Reprint of the 1966 ed. published by McGraw-Hill, New York, which was issued as v. 1 of A Documentary history of American life; with new pref.
    Includes bibliographical references.
    1. United States—History—Colonial period, ca. 1600-1775—Sources. I. Title. II. Series: A Documentary history of American life; 1.
E187.G8117   1975   973.2   74-34095
ISBN 0-393-09232-1

Published simultaneously in Canada by George J. McLeod Limited, Toronto

Printed in the United States of America

1   2   3   4   5   6   7   8   9   0

PART **TWO** Expansion and Adjustment, 1660–1713

PART **THREE**   The Emergence of American Society, 1 7 1 3 – 1 7 6 3

x   *Contents*

few straggling settlements planted along the Eastern seaboard of what is now the United States at the beginning of the seventeenth century developed over the next century and a half into a series of thirteen viable and vigorous societies. The first founders, though they were attempting to establish societies in a raw wilderness without any very clear precedents to guide them, did not start from scratch. They brought with them a considerable amount of cultural baggage in the form of ideas, values, traditions, and institutions, as well as relatively clear conceptions of what they hoped to accomplish. Very quickly, however, they found that they had to modify their conceptions to meet the conditions they found in the New World, to select out of their cultural inheritance those features which seemed most appropriate to their new situations. In the process they began to create societies that bore a close resemblance to that of their mother country but were yet markedly different. In the early years of settlement, and for nearly a century thereafter, the societies of the separate colonies differed almost as much from one another as they did from the society of their common parent, and these differences continued and were even accentuated in the eighteenth century. At the same time, however, significant similarities began to appear. Only faintly observable at first but becoming more and more obvious as the eighteenth century wore on, they make it possible, indeed necessary, to talk about a colonial American society—a society distinguished not just by the features the several colonies had in common but also, and more importantly, by their common cultural inheritance, which was refurbished and revitalized during the eighteenth century, and by a set of common experiences in the New World. It is with that process that the following collection of documents, obviously no more than a pallid sampling of the rich materials available, is concerned. Intended primarily for students, it will hopefully help to lead them to an enlarged understanding of the origins and early development of some of the central characteristics of American life. This volume was originally published in 1966 as the first volume in McGraw-Hill's multivolume *A Documentary History of American Life* under the general editorship of David Donald.

In the preparation of this volume, I depended upon the assistance of, and am extremely grateful to, David S. Shriver and Churchill E. Ward for helping me collect copies of documents; the staffs of the Western Reserve Historical Society, The Johns Hopkins University Library, the Library of Congress, the Public Record Office, Houghton Library of Harvard University, the Newberry Library, the Boston Athenaeum, and the William L. Clements Library for supplying me with Xerox copies of documents; Milton M. Klein, Darrett B. Rutman, and Alden T. Vaughan for valuable advice in choosing selections; Stuart Bruchey for suggesting the inclusion of Selection 36A; Michael Barlingame for doing a thorough check of facts and bibliographical citations; Judith Hope Reynolds for assisting in preparing the volume for the printer; and Sue N. Greene and, especially, David Donald for helpful editorial suggestions.

Jack P. Greene

SETTLEMENTS
TO
SOCIETY,
1607–1763

A Documentary History of Colonial America

PART ONE

The First Settlements, 1584–1660

Toward a Western Empire
Legal Foundations
From Outposts to Plantations on the Chesapeake
The Puritan Experiment in New England

he initial burst of English colonizing lasted roughly from 1584 to 1660. From Columbus's first voyage to the West Indies in 1492 until the 1560s, the Spanish and Portuguese had the Americas almost entirely to themselves, and it was only after the power of the Tudor monarchy had been consolidated and the religious situation stabilized under Queen Elizabeth I (1558–1603) that the English turned their attention to America. At first, they were interested primarily in taking Spanish treasure ships, selling slaves to the Spanish colonists, and seeking an easy passage to the East around the top of North America, but a number of prominent Elizabethans gradually began to advocate planting colonies along the vast stretch of the North American mainland not yet occupied by the Spanish. Between 1578 and 1583 Sir Humphrey Gilbert made two unsuccessful attempts to establish a colony in Newfoundland, and, after he was lost at sea in 1583, his half brother, Sir Walter Raleigh, twice tried and failed to plant a permanent settlement at Roanoke Island on the Carolina coast between 1585 and 1590. The expensive failures of Gilbert and Raleigh temporarily turned English interests away from colonization. Not until James I (1603–1625) had acceded to the throne and the conclusion of peace with Spain in 1604 had made privateering against Spanish shipping illegal did interest in colonization revive. Then, over the next three decades, the English proceeded to establish seven colonies on the North American mainland: Virginia (1607), Plymouth (1620), Massachusetts Bay (1628), Maryland (1634), Connecticut (1635), Rhode Island (1636), and New Haven (1638),

The first thrust in the colonizing process came from the English mercantile community. During the sixteenth century, while the Tudors were endeavoring to unify the country and expand its national power, English merchants had been slowly developing a vast overseas trading network, accumulating capital for investment, and acquiring experience with such useful business techniques as the joint stock company, which permitted individuals to pool their resources and limited their liability to the precise amount invested. After 1600 some of this capital and experience was directed into colonial enterprise, and Virginia, Plymouth, and Massachusetts Bay were each sponsored by English merchants organized into joint stock companies.

Discontent with religious conditions in England was a second source of colonizing energy. After 1580 there emerged several groups of Puritans who wanted to carry the reformation of the Anglican Church further than the Crown and Anglican establishment were willing to go, and they provided the majority of the settlers and most of the direction in the settlement of all the New England colonies. Plymouth and Massachusetts Bay were settled by Puritans migrating directly from England; Connecticut, Rhode Island, and New Haven were offshoots of Massachusetts Bay. Similarly, Maryland was in part the product of religious motives. The first colony to be settled under a proprietary grant and not by a joint stock company, it was intended by its founders, George and Cecilius Calvert, as a refuge for Catholics, though they were equally interested in securing a large landed estate for themselves and their heirs.

The central theme of this first period of English colonization is the attempt of the founders to establish viable societies in the wilderness. To find settlers, work out a set of social arrangements that would make it possible for them to live together in an orderly and stable society, and harness the resources of the new environment in such a way as to provide a sound economic base for their enterprises were, after the initial difficulties of simple survival had been overcome, the most important problems confronting the leaders of the early plantations. By mid-century, at least temporary solutions had been found, and two thriving settlements had been established on the North American mainland, one around the Chesapeake Bay and another in New England, each with a distinctive social and economic character of its own.

The outbreak of civil war in England in 1642 introduced a long lull in English colonizing activities. For almost two decades England was so rent by internal dissension that little energy and few resources were available for overseas enterprise. The result was that no new colonies were founded on the mainland, and existing colonies were left to fend for themselves. This neglect, which continued even after Parliament had asserted its jurisdiction over the colonies in the early 1650s, was in part responsible for driving all the New England colonies except Rhode Island to enter into the New England Confederation in 1643 to provide for their mutual defense against the Indians and potential European enemies. But it also intensified a natural tendency among the colonies toward local autonomy and independence from the mother country. Even Virginia, which had been a royal colony directly under the control of the Crown since 1624, maintained only a very tenuous connection with the parent state in the years just prior to the Restoration in 1660.

Throughout the civil war and the Interregnum, however, emigrants from England continued to augment the older settlements; by 1660 over seventy-five thousand Englishmen had migrated to the continental colonies, and the English had a firm hold upon both New England and the Chesapeake Bay region. At the same time, the French and the Dutch were also staking out claims in North America. Beginning in 1604, the French had proceeded to establish their hegemony over the entire St. Lawrence River region, and the Dutch, having planted the colony of New Netherlands at the mouth of the Hudson River in the early 1620s, had asserted their claim to the whole area between New England and the Chesapeake Bay by expanding eastward along Long Island Sound and by capturing New Sweden on the Delaware River in 1655. But the combined number of French and Dutch settlers was less than one-tenth of the total English population, and in the struggle for supremacy in North America, numbers and the effective control of territory that came with them would give the English an overwhelming advantage.

The First Settlements, 1584–1660:
Toward a Western Empire

SELECTION

Arguments for Planting English Colonies in America: Richard Hakluyt, "A Discourse concerning Western Planting" (1584)

The reasons that England entered the competition for colonies at the end of the sixteenth century and the beginning of the seventeenth century were many and diverse. No Englishman understood them better than Richard Hakluyt (1552?–1616), cleric, geographer, and one of the earliest and most persistent advocates of English colonial expansion. His famous tract, A Discourse concerning Western Planting, *written in 1584 to stir the interest of Queen Elizabeth I and other potential backers of the early colonizing ventures of Sir Walter Raleigh, was an inspired plea for the establishment of English plantations in America and is the clearest and most comprehensive statement of the motives—economic, patriotic, religious, and social—that impelled Englishmen to risk their lives and their fortunes in overseas enterprise. Howard Mumford Jones,* O Strange New World: American Culture, the Formative Years *(1964), is the best study of the English conception of America and of the psychology of the English migration. On Richard Hakluyt, see the superb introduction by E. G. R. Taylor in* The Original Writings & Correspondence of the Two Richard Hakluyts *(four volumes, 1935), volume I.*

The following excerpts from the summary chapter of Hakluyt's Discourse *are reprinted from* Collections of the Maine Historical Society, *(thirty-five volumes, 1831–1906), series 2, volume II, pages 152–161.*

1. The soyle yeldeth, and may be made to yelde, all the severall comodities of Europe, and of all kingdomes, domynions, and territories that England tradeth withe, that by trade of marchandize cometh into this realme.

2. The passage thither and home is neither to longe nor to shorte, but easie, and to be made twise in the yere.

3. The passage cutteth not nere the trade of any prince, nor nere any of their contries or territories, and is a safe passage, and not easie to be annoyed by prince or potentate whatsoever.

4. The passage is to be perfourmed at all times of the yere. . . .

5. And where England nowe for certen hundreth yeres last passed, by the peculiar comoditie of wolles, and of later yeres by clothinge of the same, hath raised it selfe from meaner state to greater wealthe and moche higher honour, mighte, and power then before, to the equallinge of the

princes of the same to the greatest potentates of this parte of the worlde; it cometh nowe so to passe, that by the greate endeavour of the increase of the trade of wolles in Spaine and in the West Indies, nowe daily more and more multiplienge, that the wolles of England, and the clothe made of the same, will become base, and every day more base then other; which, prudently weyed, yt behoveth this realme, yf it meane not to returne to former olde meanes and basenes, but to stande in present and late former honour, glorye, and force, and not negligently and sleepingly to slyde into beggery, to foresee and to plante at Norumbega or some like place, were it not for any thing els but for the hope of the vent of our woll indraped, the principall and in effecte the onely enrichinge contynueinge naturall comoditie of this realme. And effectually pursueinge that course, wee shall not onely finde on that tracte of lande, and especially in that firme northwarde (to whome warme clothe shallbe righte wellcome), an ample vente, but also shall, from the north side of that firme, finde oute knowen and unknowen ilandes and domynions replenished with people that may fully vent the aboundaunce of that our comoditie, that els will in fewe yeres waxe of none or of small value by forreine aboundaunce, &c.; so as by this enterprice wee shall shonne the ymmynent mischefe hanginge over our heades, that els muste nedes fall upon the realme, without breache of peace or sworde drawen againste this realme by any forreine state; and not offer our auncient riches to scornefull neighboures at home, nor sell the same in effecte for nothinge, as wee shall shortly, if presently it be not provaided for. The increase of the wolles of Spaine and America is of highe pollicie, with greate desire of our overthrowe, endevoured; and the goodnes of the forren wolles our people will not enter into the consideration of, nor will not beleve aughte, they be so sotted with opinion of their owne; and, yf it be not foresene and some such place of vent provided, farewell the goodd state of all degrees in this realme.

6. This enterprise may staye the Spanishe Kinge from flowinge over all the face of that waste firme of America, yf wee seate and plante there in time, in tyme I say, and wee by plantinge shall lett him from makinge more shorte and more safe returnes oute of the noble portes of the purposed places of our plantinge, then by any possibilitie he can from the parte of the firme that nowe his navies by ordinary courses come from, in this that there is no comparison betwene the portes of the coastes that the

Kinge of Spaine dothe nowe possesse and use and the portes of the coastes
that our nation is to possesse by plantinge at Norumbega, and on that
tracte faste by, more to the northe and northeaste, and in that there is from
thence a moche shorter course, and a course of more temperature and a
course that possesseth more contynuaunce of ordinary windes, then the
present course of the Spanishe Indian navies nowe dothe. And England
possessinge the purposed place of plantinge, her Majestie may, by the
benefete of the seate, havinge wonne goodd and royall havens, have plentie
of excellent trees for mastes, of goodly timber to builde shippes and to
make greate navies, of pitche, tarr, hempe, and all thinges incident for a
navie royall, and that for no price, and withoute money or request. Howe
easie a matter may yt be to this realme, swarminge at this day with valiant
youthes, rustinge and hurtfull by lacke of employment, and havinge goodd
makers of cable and of all sortes of cordage, and the best and moste con-
nynge shipwrights of the worlde, to be lordes of all those sees, and to spoile
Phillipps Indian navye, and to deprive him of yerely passage of his
treasure into Europe, and consequently to abate the pride of Spaine and
of the supporter of the greate Antechriste of Rome and to pull him downe
in equallitie to his neighbour princes, and consequently to cutt of the
common mischefes that come to all Europe by the peculiar aboundaunce
of his Indian treasure, and thiss withoute difficultie.

7. This voyadge, albeit it may be accomplished by barke or smallest
pynnesse for advise or for a necessitie, yet for the distaunce, for burden
and gaine in trade, the marchant will not for profitts sake use it but by
shippes of greate burden; so as this realme shall have by that meane
shippes of greate burden and of greate strengthe for the defence of this
realme, and for the defence of that newe seate, as nede shall require, and
withall greate increase of perfecte seamen, which greate princes in time
of warres wante, and which kinde of men are neither nourished in fewe
daies nor in fewe yeres.

8. This newe navie of mightie newe stronge shippes, so in trade to that
Norumbega and to the coastes there, shall never be subjecte to arreste of
any prince or potentate, as the navie of this realme from time to time
hath bene in the portes of thempire . . . but shall be alwayes free from
that bitter mischeefe, withoute grefe or hazarde to the marchaunte or to
the state, and so alwaies readie at the comaundement of the prince with
mariners, artillory, armor, and munition, ready to offende and defende
as shalbe required.

9. The greate masse of wealthe of the realme imbarqued in the marchantes shippes, caried oute in this newe course, shall not lightly, in so
farr distant a course from the coaste of Europe, be driven by windes and
tempestes into portes of any forren princes, as the Spanishe shippes of late
yeres have bene into our portes of the Weste Contries, &c.; and so our
marchantes in respecte of private state; and of the realme in respecte of
a generall safetie from venture of losse, are by this voyadge oute of one
greate mischefe.

10. No forren commoditie that comes into England comes withoute payment of custome once, twise, or thrise, before it come into the realme, and

so all forren comodities become derer to the subjectes of this realme; and by this course to Norumbega forren princes customes are avoided; and the forren comodities cheaply purchased, they become cheape to the subjectes of England, to the common benefite of the people, and to the savinge of greate treasure in the realme; whereas nowe the realme becomethe poore by the purchasinge of forreine comodities in so greate a masse at so excessive prices.

11. At the firste traficque with the people of those partes, the subjects of this realme for many yeres shall chaunge many cheape comodities of these partes for things of highe valor there not estemed; and this to the greate inrichinge of the realme, if common use faile not.

12. By the greate plentie of those regions the marchantes and their factors shall lye there cheape, buye and repaire their shippes cheape, and shall returne at pleasure withoute staye or restrainte of forreine prince; whereas upon staies and restraintes the marchaunte raiseth his chardge in sale over of his ware; and, buyenge his wares cheape, he may mainteine trade with smalle stocke, and withoute takinge upp money upon interest; and so he shalbe riche and not subjecte to many hazardes, but shalbe able to afforde the comodities for cheape prices to all subjectes of the realme.

13. By makinge of shippes and by preparinge of thinges for the same, by makinge of cables and cordage, by plantinge of vines and olive trees, and by makinge of wyne and oyle, by husbandrie, and by thousandes of thinges there to be done, infinite nombers of the Englishe nation may be set on worke, to the unburdenynge of the realme with many that nowe lyve chardgeable to the state at home.

14. If the sea coste serve for makinge of salte, and the inland for wine, oiles, oranges, lymons, figges, &c., and for makinge of yron, all which with moche more is hoped, withoute sworde drawen, wee shall cutt the combe of the Frenche, of the Spanishe, of the Portingale, and of enemies, and of doubtfull frendes, to the abatinge of their wealthe and force, and to the greater savinge of the wealthe of the realme.

15. The substaunces servinge, wee may oute of those partes receave the masse of wrought wares that now wee receave out of Fraunce, Flaunders, Germanye, &c.; and so we may daunte the pride of some enemies of this realme, or at the leaste in parte purchase those wares, that nowe wee buye derely of the Frenche and Flemynge, better cheape; and in the ende, for the parte that this realme was wonte to receave, dryve them oute of trade to idlenes for the settinge of our people on worke.

16. Wee shall by plantinge there inlarge the glory of the gospell, and from England plante sincere relligion, and provide a safe and a sure place to receave people from all partes of the worlde that are forced to flee for the truthe of Gods worde.

17. If frontier warres there chaunce to aryse, and if thereupon wee shall fortifie, yt will occasion the trayninge upp of our youthe in the discipline of warr, and make a nomber fitt for the service of the warres and for the defence of our people there and at home.

18. The Spaniardes governe in the Indies with all pride and tyranie; and like as when people of contrarie nature at the sea enter into gallies,

where men are tied as slaves, all yell and crye with one voice, *Liberta, liberta,* as desirous of libertie and freedome, so no doubte whensoever the Queene of England, a prince of such clemencie, shall seate upon that firme of America, and shalbe reported throughe oute all that tracte to use the naturall people there with all humanitie, curtesie, and freedome, they will yelde themselves to her government, and revolte cleane from the Spaniarde, and specially when they shall understande that she hathe a noble navie, and that she aboundeth with a people moste valiaunte for theyr defence. And her Majestie havinge Sir Fraunces Drake and other subjectes already in credite with the Symerons, a people or greate multitude alreadye revolted from the Spanishe governemente, she may with them and a fewe hundrethes of this nation, trayned upp in the late warres of Fraunce and Flaunders, bringe greate thinges to passe, and that with greate ease; and this broughte so aboute, her Majestie and her subjects may bothe enjoye the treasure of the mynes of golde and silver, and the whole trade and all the gaine of the trade of marchandize, that nowe passeth thither by the Spaniardes onely hande, of all the comodities of Europe; which trade of marchandize onely were of it selfe suffycient (withoute the benefite of the riche myne) to inriche the subjectes, and by customes to fill her Majesties coffers to the full. And if it be highe pollicie to mayneteyne the poore people of this realme in worke, I dare affirme that if the poore people of England were five times so many as they be, yet all mighte be sett on worke in and by workinge lynnen, and suche other thinges of marchandize as the trade into the Indies dothe require.

19. The present shorte trades causeth the maryner to be cast of, and ofte to be idle, and so by povertie to fall to piracie. But this course to Norumbega beinge longer, and a contynuaunce of themploymente of the maryner, dothe kepe the maryner from ydlenes and from necessitie; and so it cutteth of the principal actions of piracie, and the rather because no riche praye for them to take cometh directly in their course or any thing nere their course.

20. Many men of excellent wittes and of divers singuler giftes, overthrowen by suertishippe, by sea, or by some folly of youthe, that are not able to live in England, may there be raised againe, and doe their contrie goodd service; and many nedefull uses there may (to greate purpose) require the savinge of greate nombers, that for trifles may otherwise be devoured by the gallowes.

21. Many souldiers and servitours, in the ende of the warres, that mighte be hurtfull to this realme, may there be unladen, to the common profite and quiet of this realme, and to our forreine benefite there, as they may be employed.

22. The frye of the wandringe beggars of England, that growe upp ydly, and hurtefull and burdenous to this realme, may there be unladen, better bredd upp, and may people waste contries to the home and forreine benefite, and to their owne more happy state.

23. If Englande crie oute and affirme, that there is so many in all trades that one cannot live for another, as in all places they doe, this Norumbega (if it be thoughte so goodd) offreth the remedie.

SELECTION

Formula for Successful Plantations:
Francis Bacon, "Of Plantations" (1625)

The vast promises of the New World were not, of course, immediately realized, and the first settlers found that the visions of Hakluyt soon paled before the necessity of meeting the simple problems of day-to-day survival, of hanging on in an unfamiliar environment against the omnipresent enemies of disease, hunger, the elements, and the Indians. Both colonists in America and promoters at home quickly discovered that profits would be slight in the early years, that success would be slow and difficult, and that it would be a long time before English settlements would rival those of the Spanish. The new psychology and a practical formula for success were set forth by the philosopher-statesman Francis Bacon (1561–1626) in his essay "Of Plantations," an analysis of the lessons of the experiences of the Virginia colony during its first years. Written sometime between 1620 and 1624, the essay was first published in 1625. The foremost English philosopher of his day, Bacon was also a courtier, lawyer, member of Parliament, and successively solicitor general, attorney general, and Lord Chancellor under James I. The standard work on Bacon is James Spedding, An Account of the Life and Times of Francis Bacon *(two volumes, 1878).*

"Of Plantations" is reprinted in full from Samuel Harvey Reynolds (ed.), The Essays, or Counsels, Civil and Moral of Francis Bacon, *(1890), pages 237–240.*

Plantations are amongst ancient, primitive, and heroical works. When the world was young, it begat more children; but now it is old, it begets fewer: for I may justly account new plantations to be the children of former kingdoms. I like a plantation in a pure soil; that is, where people are not displanted, to the end to plant in others; for else it is rather an extirpation than a plantation. Planting of countries is like planting of woods; for you must make account to lose almost twenty years' profit, and expect your recompense in the end: for the principal thing that hath been the destruction of most plantations hath been the base and hasty drawing of profit in the first years. It is true, speedy profit is not to be neglected as far as may stand with the good of the plantation, but no further. It is a shameful and unblessed thing to take the scum of people and wicked condemned men to be the people with whom you plant; and not only so, but it spoileth the plantation; for they will ever live like rogues, and not fall to work, but be lazy, and do mischief, and spend victuals, and be quickly weary, and then certify over to their country to the discredit of the plantation. The people wherewith you plant ought to be gardeners, ploughmen, labourers, smiths, carpenters, joiners, fishermen, fowlers, with some few apothecaries, surgeons, cooks, and bakers. In a country of plantation, first look about what kind of victual the country yields of itself to hand: as chestnuts, walnuts, pine-apples, olives, dates, plums, cherries, wild honey, and the like; and make use of them. Then consider what victual or esculent things there are which grow speedily and within the year; as parsnips, carrots, turnips, onions, radish, artichokes of Hierusalem, maize, and the like: for wheat, barley, and oats, they ask too much labour; but with pease and beans you may begin, both because they ask less labour, and because they serve for meat as well as for bread; and of rice likewise cometh a great increase, and it is a kind of meat. Above all, there ought to be brought store of biscuit, oatmeal, flour, meal, and the like in the beginning till bread may be had. For beasts or birds take chiefly such as are least subject to diseases and multiply fastest; as swine, goats, cocks, hens, turkeys, geese, house-doves, and the like. The victual in plantations ought to be expended almost as in a besieged town; that is, with certain allowance: and let the main part of the ground employed to gardens or corn, be to a common stock; and to be laid in and stored up and then delivered out in proportion; besides some spots of ground that any particular person will manure for his own private. Consider likewise what commodities the soil where the plantation is doth naturally yield, that they may some way help to defray the charge of the plantation: so it be not, as was said, to the untimely prejudice of the main business, as it hath fared with tobacco in Virginia. Wood commonly aboundeth but too much; and therefore timber is fit to be one. If there be iron ore, and streams whereupon to set the mills, iron is a brave commodity where wood aboundeth. Making of bay-salt, if the climate be proper for it, would be put in experience: growing silk likewise, if any be, is a likely commodity: pitch and tar, where store of firs and pines are, will not fail; so drugs and sweet woods, where they are, cannot but yield great profit: soap-ashes likewise, and other things that may be thought of; but moil not too much under ground, for the hope of mines is very uncertain, and useth to make the planters lazy in other things. For government, let it be in the hands of one, assisted with some council; and let them have commission to exercise martial laws, with some limitation; and above all, let men make that profit of being in the wilderness, as they have God always and his service before their eyes: let not the government of the plantation depend upon too many counsellors and undertakers in the country that planteth, but upon a temperate number; and let those be rather noblemen and gentlemen than merchants; for they look ever to the present gain. Let there be freedoms from custom till the plantation be of strength; and not only freedom from custom, but freedom to carry their commodities where they may make their best of them, except there be some special cause of caution. Cram not in people by sending too fast company after company; but rather hearken how they waste, and send supplies proportionably; but so as the number may live well in the plantation, and not by surcharge be in penury. It hath been a great endangering to the health of some plantations that they have built along the sea and rivers, in marish and unwholesome grounds: therefore, though you begin there, to avoid carriage and other like discommodities, yet build still rather upwards from the streams than along. It concerneth likewise the health of the plantation that they have good store of salt with them, that they may use it in their victuals when it shall be necessary. If you plant where savages are, do not only entertain them with trifles and gingles, but use them justly and graciously, with sufficient guard nevertheless; and do not win their favour by helping them to invade their enemies, but for their defence it is not amiss; and send oft of them over to the country that plants, that they may see a better condition than their own, and commend it when they return. When the plantation grows to strength, then it is time to plant with women as well as with men; that the plantation may spread into generations, and not be ever pieced from without. It is the sinfullest thing in the world to forsake or destitute a plantation once in forwardness; for, besides the dishonour, it is the guiltiness of blood of many commiserable persons.

The First Settlements, 1584–1660: Legal Foundations

SELECTION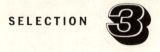

Charters

The men who planned and sponsored the English plantations derived their authority from royal charters. Granted by the Crown upon application to favored individuals or groups, these charters gave the grantees extensive and exclusive privileges in return for undertaking to develop trade and establish settlements in the New World. They were of two general types. The first kind, exemplified by the third Virginia charter (1612)—two earlier charters had proved unsatisfactory to the grantees—and the first Massachusetts charter (1629), was simply one of incorporation establishing a joint stock company with wide commercial privileges and title to a vast area of land with a generous measure of political authority over it. Similar charters had been granted to a number of overseas trading companies during the last years of the sixteenth century. Although the second type of charter, exemplified by the Maryland Charter (1632), had no precise or recent precedents, it was essentially similar to earlier feudal grants and conferred a tract of land with governing rights to a proprietor or group of proprietors.

Although the early trading-company charters were intended first of all to be commercial documents, they soon came to serve as frames of government for the colonies. Taken by the colonists with them to America, the Massachusetts Charter became the Bay Colony's constitution, and by the time of the Maryland grant in 1632, charters had come to be conceived of by English officials and colonists alike as the foundations of political authority and the chief bulwark against its abuse within the colonies. The numerous proprietary and corporate charters granted after the Restoration in 1660 were all primarily political and constitutional in character.

The standard work on the colonial charters is Louise P. Kellogg, "The American Colonial Charter: A Study of English Administration in Relation Thereto, Chiefly after 1688," American Historical Association, Annual Report, volume 1 (1903), pages 185–341.

A. THIRD VIRGINIA CHARTER (MAR. 12, 1612)*

JAMES, by the Grace of God, King of *England, Scotland, France,* and *Ireland,* Defender of the Faith; To all to whom these Presents shall come, Greeting. WHERAS at the humble Suit of divers sundry our loving Subjects, as well Adventurers as Planters of the first Colony in *Virginia,* and for the Propagation of *Christian* Religion, and Reclaiming of People barbarous,

* These excerpts are reprinted from Francis Newton Thorpe (ed.), *The Federal and State Constitutions, Colonial Charters, and Other Organic Laws* (7 vols., 1909), vol. VII, pp. 3802–3810.

to Civility and Humanity, We have, by our Letters-Patents, bearing Date at *Westminster,* the three-and-twentieth Day of *May,* in the seventh Year of our Reign of *England, France,* and *Ireland,* and the two-and-fortieth of *Scotland,* GIVEN and GRANTED unto them that they and all such and so many of our loving Subjects as should from time to time, for ever after, be joined with them as Planters or Adventurers in the said Plantation, and their Successors, for ever, shall be one Body politick, incorporated by the Name of *The Treasurer and Company of Adventurers and Planters of the City of London for the first Colony in Virginia:*

And whereas also for the greater Good and Benefit of the said Company, and for the better Furtherance, Strengthening, and Establishing of the said Plantation, we did further GIVE, GRANT and CONFIRM, by our Letters-Patents unto the said Company and their Successors, for ever, all those Lands, Countries or Territories, situate, lying and being in that Part of *America* called *Virginia,* from the Point of Land called *Cape* or *Point Comfort* all along the Sea Coasts to the Northward two hundred Miles; and from the said Point of *Cape Comfort* all along the Sea Coast to the Southward two hundred Miles; and all that Space and Circuit of Land lying from the Sea Coast of the Precinct aforesaid, up into the Land throughout from Sea to Sea West and North-west; and also all the Islands lying within one hundred Miles along the Coast of both the Seas of the Precinct aforesaid; with divers other Grants, Liberties, Franchises and Preheminences, Privileges, Profits, Benefits, and Commodities granted in and by our said Letters-patents to the said Treasurer and Company and their Successors for ever.

Now forasmuch as we are given to understand, that in those Seas adjoining to the said Coasts of *Virginia,* and without the Compass of those two hundred Miles by Us so granted unto the said Treasurer and Company as aforesaid, and yet not far distant from the said Colony in *Virginia,* there are or may be divers Islands lying desolate and uninhabited, some of which are already made known and discovered by the Industry, Travel, and Expences of the said Company, and others also are supposed to be and remain as yet unknown and undiscovered, all and every of which it may import the said Colony both in Safety and Policy of Trade to populate and plant; in Regard whereof, as well for the preventing of Peril, as for the better Commodity of the said Colony, they have been humble suitors unto Us, that We would be pleased to grant unto them an Enlargement of our said former Letters-patents, as well for a more ample Extent of their Limits and Territories into the Seas adjoining to and upon the Coast of *Virginia,* as also for some other Matters and Articles concerning the better government of the said Company and Colony, in which Point our said former Letters-Patents do not extend so far as Time and Experience hath found to be needful and convenient:

We therefore tendering the good and happy Success of the said Plantation, both in Regard of the General Weal of human Society, as in Respect of the Good of our own Estate and Kingdoms, and being willing to give Furtherance unto all good Means that may advance the Benefit of the said Company, and which may secure the Safety of our loving Subjects planted in our said Colony, under the Favour and Protection of God Almighty, and of our Royal Power and Authority, have therefore of our especial Grace, certain Knowledge, and mere Motion, given, granted, and confirmed, and for Us, our Heirs and Successors, we do by these Presents give, grant, and confirm to the said Treasurer and Company of Adventurers and Planters of the city of *London* for the first Colony in *Virginia,* and to their Heirs and Successors for ever, all and singular those Islands whatsoever situate and being in any Part of the Ocean Seas bordering upon the Coast of our said first Colony in *Virginia,* and being within three Hundred Leagues of any of the Parts heretofore granted to the said Treasurer and Company in our said former Letters-Patents as aforesaid, and being within or between the one-and-fortieth and thirtieth Degrees of Northerly Latitude; together with all and singular Soils, Lands, Grounds, Havens, Ports, Rivers, Waters, Fishings, Mines and Minerals, as well Royal Mines of Gold and Silver, as other Mines and Minerals, Pearls, precious Stones, Quarries, and all and singular other Commodities, Jurisdictions, Royalties, Privileges, Franchises, and Preheminences, both within the said Tract of Land upon the Main, and also within the said Islands and Seas adjoining whatsoever and thereunto or thereabouts, both by Sea and Land being or situate; And which, by our Letters-Patents we may or can grant, and in as ample Manner as We or any our noble Progenitors have heretofore granted to any Person or Persons, or to any Company, Body Politick or corporate, or to any Adventurer or Adventurers, Undertaker or Undertakers of any Discoveries, Plantations, or Traffick, of, in, or into any foreign Parts whatsoever, and in as large and ample Manner as if the same were herein particularly named, mentioned, and expressed. Provided always, that the said Islands or any Premises herein mentioned, or by these Presents intended or meant to be granted, be not actually possessed or inhabited by any other Christian Prince or Estate, nor be within the Bounds, Limits, or Territories of the Northern Colony heretofore by Us granted to be planted by divers of our loving Subjects in the North Parts of *Virginia.* To HAVE AND TO HOLD, possess and enjoy, all and singular the said Islands in the said Ocean Seas so lying and bordering upon the Coast and Coasts of the Territories of the first Colony in *Virginia,* as aforesaid. With all and singular the said Soils, Lands, Grounds, and all and singular other the Premises heretofore by these Presents granted or mentioned to be granted to them, the said Treasurer and Company of Adventurers and Planters of the City of *London* for the first Colony in *Virginia,* and to their Heirs, Successors, and Assigns, for ever, to the sole and proper Use and Behoof of them the said Treasurer and Company, and their Heirs and Successors and Assigns, for ever; TO BE HOLDEN OF US, our Heirs and Successors, as of our Manor of *East-Greenwich,* in Free and common Soccage, and not in *Capite;* YIELDING AND PAYING therefore to Us, our Heirs and Successors, the fifth Part of the Ore of all Gold and Silver which shall be there gotten, had, or obtained for all Manner of Services whatsoever. . . .

And we do hereby ordain and grant by these Presents, that the said Treasurer and Company of Adventurers and Planters aforesaid, shall and may, once every week, or oftener, at their Pleasure, hold, and keep a Court and Assembly for the better Order and Government of the said Plantation, and such Things as shall concern the same; And that any five Persons of our Council for the said first Colony in *Virginia,* for the Time being, of which Company the Treasure, or his Deputy, to be always one, and the Number of fifteen others, at the least, of the Generality of the said Company, assembled together in such Manner, as is and hath been heretofore used and accustomed, shall be said, taken, held, and reputed to be, and shall be a *sufficient Court* of the said Company, for the handling and ordering, and dispatching of all such casual and particular Occurrences, and accidental Matters, of less Consequence and Weight, as shall from Time to Time happen, touching and concerning the said Plantation.

And that nevertheless, for the handling, ordering, and disposing of Matters and Affairs of greater Weight and Importance, and such as shall or may, in any Sort, concern the Weal Publick and general Good of the said Company and Plantation, as namely, the Manner of Government from Time to Time to be used, the ordering and Disposing of the Lands and Possessions, and the settling and establishing of a Trade there, or such like, there shall be held and kept every Year, upon the last *Wednesday,* save one, of *Hillary* Term, *Easter, Trinity,* and *Michaelmas* Terms, for ever, one great, general, and solemn Assembly, which four Assemblies shall be stiled and called, *The four Great and General Courts of the Council and Company of Adventurers for Virginia;* In all and every of which said Great and General Courts, so assembled, our Will and Pleasure is, and we do, for Us, our Heirs and Successors, for ever, Give and Grant to the said Treasurer and Company, and their Successors for ever, by these Presents, that they, the said Treasurer and Company, or the greater Number of them, so assembled, shall and may have full Power and Authority, from Time to Time, and at all Times hereafter, to elect and chuse discreet Persons, to be of our said Council for the said first Colony in *Virginia,* and to nominate and appoint such Officers as they shall think fit and requisite, for the Government, managing, ordering, and dispatching of the Affairs of the said Company; And shall likewise have full Power and Authority, to ordain and make such Laws and Ordinances, for the Good and Welfare of the said Plantation, as to them from Time to Time, shall be thought requisite and meet: *So always,* as the same be not contrary to the Laws and Statutes of this our Realm of *England:* And shall, in like Manner, have Power and Authority, to expulse, disfranchise, and put out of and from their said Company and Society for ever, all and every such Person and Persons, as having either promised or subscribed

their Names to become Adventurers to the said Plantation, of the said
first Colony in *Virginia,* or having been nominated for Adventurers in
these or any other our Letters-Patents, or having been otherwise admitted
and nominated to be of the said Company, have nevertheless either not
put in any adventure at all for and towards the said Plantation, or else
have refused or neglected, or shall refuse and neglect to bring in his or
their Adventure, by Word or Writing, promised within six Months after
the same shall be so payable and due. And whereas, the Failing and not
Payment of such Monies as have been promised in Adventure, for the
Advancement of the said Plantation, hath been often by Experience found
to be dangerous and prejudicial to the same, and much to have hindered
the Progress and Proceeding of the said Plantation, and for that it seemeth
unto Us a Thing reasonable, that such Persons, as by their Hand Writing
have engaged themselves for the Payment of their Adventures, and afterwards neglecting their Faith and Promise, should be compelled to make
good and keep the same: Therefore, Our Will and Pleasure is, that in any
Suit or Suits commenced, or to be commenced in any of our Courts at
Westminister, or elsewhere, by the said Treasurer and Company, or otherwise against any such persons, that our Judges for the Time being, both
in our Court of Chancery, and at the Common Pleas do favour and
further the said Suits so far forth as Law and Equity will any wise further
and permit. And We do, for Us, our Heirs and Successors, further give
and grant to the said Treasurer and Company, or their Successors forever,
that the said Treasurer and Company, or the greater Part of them for the
Time being, so in a full and general Court assembled as aforesaid, shall
and may from Time to Time, and at all times forever hereafter, elect,
choose and admit into their Company, and Society, any Person or Persons,
as well Strangers and Aliens born in any Part beyond the Seas whereso-
ever, being in Amity with us, as our natural Liege Subjects born in any
our Realms and Dominions: And that all such Persons so elected, chosen,
and admitted to be of the said Company as aforesaid, shall thereupon be
taken, reputed, and held, and shall be free Members of the said Company,
and shall have, hold, and enjoy all and singular Freedoms, Liberties,
Franchises, Privileges, Immunities, Benefits, Profits, and Commodities
whatsoever, to the said Company in any Sort belonging or appertaining,
as fully, freely and amply as any other Adventurers now being, or which
hereafter at any Time shall be of the said Company, hath, have, shall may,
might, or ought to have and enjoy the same to all Intents and Purposes
whatsoever. And We do further of our especial Grace, certain Knowledge,
and mere Motion, for Us, our Heirs and Successors, give and grant unto
the said Treasurer and Company, and their Successors for ever, by these
Presents, that it shall be lawful and free for them and their Assigns, at
all and every Time and Times hereafter, out of any our Realms and
Dominions whatsoever, to take, lead, carry, and transport in and into the
said Voyage, and for and towards the said Plantation of our said first
Colony in *Virginia,* all such and so many of our loving Subjects, or any
other Strangers that will become our loving Subjects, and live under our
Allegiance, as shall willingly accompany them in the said Voyages and
Plantation, with Shipping, Armour, Weapons, Ordance, Munition, Powder,

Shot, Victuals, and all Manner of Merchandises and Wares, and all Manner of Clothing, Implements, Furniture, Beasts, Cattle, Horses, Mares, and all other Things necessary for the said Plantation, and for their Use and Defence, and for Trade with the People there, and in passing and returning to and from, without paying or yielding any Subsidy, Custom, or Imposition, either inward or outward, or any other Duty to Us, our Heirs and Successors, for the same, for the Space of Seven Years from the Date of these Presents.

And We do further, for Us, our Heirs and Successors, give and grant to the said Treasurer and Company, and their Successors forever, by these Presents, that the said Treasurer of that Company, or his Deputy for the Time being, or any two other of the said Council, for the said first Colony in *Virginia,* for the Time being, or any two other at all Times hereafter, and from Time to Time, have full Power and authority to minister and give the Oath and Oaths of Supremacy and Allegiance, or either of them, to all and every Person and Persons, which shall at any Time or Times hereafter, go or pass to the said Colony in *Virginia:*

And further, that it shall be lawful likewise for the said Treasurer, or his Deputy for the Time being, or any two or others of our said Council, for the said first Colony in *Virginia,* for the Time being, from Time to Time, and at all Times hereafter to minister such a formal Oath, as by their discretion shall be reasonably devised, as well unto any Person or Persons employed in, for, or touching the said Plantation, for their honest, faithful and just Discharge of their Service in all such Matters as shall be committed unto them, for the Good and Benefit of the said Company, Colony and Plantation; As also unto such other Person or Persons as the said Treasurer, or his Deputy, with two others of the said Council shall think meet, for the Examination or clearing of the Truth, in any Cause whatsoever, concerning the said Plantation, or any Business from thence proceeding, or thereunto belonging.

And furthermore, whereas We have been certified, That divers lewd and ill disposed Persons, both Sailors, Soldiers, Artificers, Husbandmen, Labourers and others, having received Wages, Apparel and other Entertainment, from the said Company, or having contracted and agreed with the said Company to go, or to serve, or to be employed in the said Plantation of the said first Colony in *Virginia,* have afterwards either withdrawn, hid, or concealed themselves, or have refused to go thither, after they have been so entertained and agreed withal: And that divers and sundry Persons also, which have been sent and employed in the said Plantation of the said first Colony in *Virginia,* at and upon the Charge of the said Company, and having there misbehaved themselves by Mutinies, Sedition, or other notorious Misdemeanors, or having been employed or sent abroad by the Governor of *Virginia,* or his Deputy, with some Ship or Pinnace, for our Provision of the said Colony, or for some Discovery, or other Business and Affairs concerning the same, have from thence most treacherously either come back again, and returned into our Realm of *England,* by Stealth, or without Licence of our Governor of our said Colony in *Virginia,* for the Time being, or have been sent thither as Misdoers and Offenders: And that many also of those Persons after their Return from thence, having been questioned by our Council here, for such their Misbehaviors and Offences, by their Insolent and Contemptuous Carriage in the Presence of our said Council, have shewed little Respect and Reverence either to the Place or Authority in which we have placed and appointed them; And others for the colouring of their Lewdness and Misdemeanors committed in *Virginia,* have endeavoured by most vile and slanderous Reports made and divulged, as well as the Country of *Virginia,* as also of the Government and Estate of the said Plantation and Colony, as much as in them lay, to bring the said Voyage and Plantation into Disgrace and Contempt: By Means whereof, not only the Adventurers and Planters already engaged in the said Plantation, have been exceedingly abused and hindered, and a great Number of other, our loving and well-disposed Subjects, otherwise well affected and inclined to join and adventure in so noble, Christian, and worthy an Action, have been discouraged from the same; but also the utter overthrow and Ruin of the said Enterprise hath been greatly endangered, which cannot miscarry without some Dishonour to Us, and our Kingdom.

Now, forasmuch as it appeareth unto us, that these Insolences, Misdemeanors, and Abuses, not to be tolerated in any civil Government, have, for the most part, grown and proceeded, in regard our said Council have not any direct Power and Authority, by any express Words in our former Letters-patents, to correct and chastise such Offenders; We therefore, for more speedy Reformation of so great and enormous Abuses and Misdemeanors heretofore practised and committed, and for the preventing of the like hereafter, do by these Presents for Us, our Heirs, and Successors, GIVE and GRANT, to the said Treasurer and Company, and their Successors for ever, that it shall, and may be lawful for our said Council for the first Colony in *Virginia,* or any two of them (whereof the said Treasurer or his Deputy for the Time being, to be always one) by Warrant under their Hands, to send for, or cause to be apprehended, all, and every such Person or Persons, who shall be noted, or accused, or found at any Time or Times hereafter, to offend or misbehave themselves in any the Offences before mentioned and expressed, and upon the Examination of any such Offender or Offenders, and just Proof made by Oath, taken before the said Council, of any such notorious Misdemeanors by them committed as aforesaid; And also upon any insolent and contemptuous, or indecent Carriage and Misbehavour, to, or against, any our said Council, shewed or used by any such Person or Persons so called, convented, and appearing before them as aforesaid; That in all such cases, they our said Council, or any two of them for the time being, shall, and may have full Power and Authority, either here to bind them over with good Sureties for their good Behaviour, and further therein, to proceed to all Intents and Purposes, as it is used in other like Cases, within our Realm of *England;* Or else, at their Discretions, to remand and send back the said Offenders, or any of them, unto the said Colony in *Virginia,* there to be proceeded against and punished, as the Governor, Deputy or Council there, for the Time being, shall think meet; Or otherwise, according to such Laws and Ordinances, as are and shall be in Use there, for the well-ordering and good Government of the said Colony.

And for the more effectual Advancing of the said Plantation, We do further, for Us, our Heirs, and Successors, of our especial Grace and Favour, by Virtue of our Prerogative Royal, and by the Assent and Consent of the Lords and others of our Privy Council, GIVE and GRANT, unto the said Treasurer and Company, full Power and Authority, free Leave, Liberty, and Licence, to set forth, erect, and publish, one or more Lottery or Lotteries, to have Continuance, and to endure and be held, for the Space of one whole Year, next after the opening of the same; And after the End and Expiration of the said Term, the said Lottery or Lotteries to continue and be further kept, during our Will and Pleasure only, and not otherwise. And yet nevertheless, we are contented and pleased, for the Good and Welfare of the said Plantation, that the said Treasurer and Company shall, for the Dispatch and Finishing of the said Lottery or Lotteries, have six Months Warning after the said Year ended, before our Will and Pleasure shall, for and on that Behalf, be construed, deemed, and adjudged, to be in any wise altered and determined.

And our further Will and Pleasure is, that the said Lottery and Lotteries shall and may be opened and held, within our City of *London,* or in any other City or Town, or elsewhere, within this our Realm of *England,* with such Prizes, Articles, Conditions, and Limitations, as to them, the said Treasurer and Company, in their Discretions, shall seem convenient:

And it shall and may be lawful, to and for the said Treasurer and Company, to elect and choose Receivers, Surveyors, Auditors, Commissioners, or any other Officers whatsoever, at their Will and Pleasure, for the better marshalling, disposing, guiding, and governing of the said Lottery and Lotteries; And that it shall likewise be lawful, to and for the said Treasurer and any two of the said Council, to minister to all and every such Person, so elected and chosen for Offices, as aforesaid, one or more Oaths, for their good Behaviour, just and true Dealing, in and about the said Lottery or Lotteries, to the Intent and Purpose, that none of our loving Subjects, putting in their Names, or otherwise adventuring in the said general Lottery or Lotteries, may be, in any wise, defrauded and deceived of their said Monies, or evil and indirectly dealt withal in their said Adventures.

And we further GRANT, in Manner and Form aforesaid, that it shall and may be lawful, to and for the said Treasurer and Company, under the Seal of our said Council for the Plantation, to publish, or to cause or procure to be published by Proclamation, or otherwise (the said Proclamation to be made in their Name, by Virtue of these Presents) the said Lottery or Lotteries, in all Cities, Towns, Burroughs, and other Places, within our said Realm of *England;* And we Will and Command all Mayors, Justices of the Peace, Sheriffs, Bailiffs, Constables, and other Officers and loving Subjects, whatsoever, that in no wise, they hinder or delay the Progress and Proceedings of the said Lottery or Lotteries, but be therein, touching the Premises, aiding and assisting, by all honest, good, and lawful Means and Endeavours.

And further, our Will and Pleasure is, that in all Questions and Doubts, that shall arise, upon any Difficulty of Construction or Interpretation of any Thing, contained in these, or any other our former Letters-patent, the same shall be taken and interpreted, in most ample and beneficial Manner for the said Treasurer and Company, and their Successors, and every Member thereof. . . .

B. FIRST MASSACHUSETTS CHARTER (MAR. 4, 1629)*

CHARLES, BY THE GRACE OF GOD . . . [does] give and graunte unto . . . Sir Henry Rosewell, Sir John Younge, Sir Richard Saltonstall, Thomas Southcott, John Humfrey, John Endecott, Symon Whetcombe, Isaack Johnson, Samuell Aldersey, John Ven, Mathewe Cradock, George Harwood, Increase Nowell, Richard Pery, Richard Bellingham, Nathaniel Wright, Samuell Vassall, Theophilus Eaton, Thomas Goffe, Thomas Adams, John Browne, Samuell Browne, Thomas Hutchins, William Vassall, William Pinchion, and George Foxcrofte, their Heires and Assignes, all that Parte of Newe England in America, which lyes and extendes betweene a great River there, comonlie called Monomack River, alias Merrimack River, and a certen other River there, called Charles River, being in the Bottome of a certen Bay there, commonly called Massachusetts, alias Mattachusetts, alias Massatusetts Bay; and also all and singuler those Landes and Hereditaments whatsoever, lying within the Space of Three Englishe Myles on the South Parte of the said River, called Charles River, or of any or every Parte thereof; and also all and singular the Landes and Hereditaments whatsoever, lying and being within the Space of Three Englishe Miles to the southward of the southermost Parte of the said Baye, called Massachusetts, alias Mattachusetts, alias Massatusets Bay: And also all those Landes and Hereditaments whatsoever, which lye and be within the Space of Three English Myles to the Northward of the saide River, called Monomack, alias Merrymack, or to the Norward of any and every Parte thereof, and all Landes and Hereditaments whatsoever, lyeing within the Lymitts aforesaide, North and South, in Latitude and Bredth, and in Length and Longitude, of and within all the Bredth aforesaide, throughout the mayne Landes there, from the Atlantick and Westerne Sea and Ocean on the East Parte, to the South Sea on the West Parte; and all Landes and Groundes, Place and Places, Soyles, Woodes, and Wood Groundes, Havens, Portes, Rivers, Waters, and Hereditaments whatsoever, lyeing within the said Boundes and Lymytts, and every Parte and Parcell thereof; and also all Islandes in America aforesaide, in the saide Seas, or either of them, on the Westerne or Easterne Coastes, or Partes of the saide Tracts of Landes hereby mentioned to be given and graunted, or any of them; and all Mynes and Mynerals as well Royal mynes of Gold and Silver and other mynes and mynerals, whatsoever, in the said Landes and Premisses, or any parte thereof, and free Libertie of fishing in or within any the Rivers or Waters within the Boundes and Lymytts aforesaid, and the Seas therevnto adjoining; and all Fishes, Royal Fishes, Whales, Balan, Sturgions, and other Fishes of what Kinde or Nature soever. . . . To BE HOLDEN of Vs, our

---

* These excerpts are reprinted from Thorpe, *Federal and State Constitutions, Colonial Charters, and Other Organic Laws,* vol. III, pp. 1846, 1849–1858.

Heires and Successors, as of our Manor of Eastgreenwich in our Countie of Kent, within our Realme of England, in free and comon Soccage, and not in Capite, nor by Knights Service; and also yeilding and paying therefore, to Vs, our Heires and Successors, the fifte Parte onlie of all Oare of Gould and Silver, which from tyme to tyme, and at all tymes hereafter, shall be there gotten, had, or obteyned, for all Services, Exactions, and Demaundes whatsoever. . . . WEE HAVE FURTHER hereby of our especial Grace, [&] certain Knowledge . . . Given, graunted and confirmed . . . vnto our said trustie and welbeloved subiects . . . and all such others as shall hereafter be admitted and made free of the Company and Society hereafter mentioned, shall from tyme to tyme, and att all tymes forever hereafter be, by Vertue of theis presents, one Body corporate and politique in Fact and Name, by the Name of the Governor and Company of the Mattachusetts Bay in Newe-England, and them by the Name of the Governour and Company of the Mattachusetts Bay in Newe-England, one Bodie politique and corporate, in Deede, Fact, and Name; Wee doe for vs, our Heires and Successors, make, ordeyne, constitute, and confirme by theis Presents, and that by that name they shall have perpetuall Succession, and that by the same Name they and their Successors shall and maie be capeable and enabled aswell to implead, and to be impleaded, and to prosecute, demaund, and aunswere, and be aunsweared vnto, in all and singuler Suites, Causes, Quarrells, and Actions, of what kinde or nature soever. And also to have, take, possesse, acquire, and purchase any Landes, Tenements, or Hereditaments, or any Goodes or Chattells, and the same to lease, graunte, demise, alien, bargaine, sell, and dispose of, as other our liege People of this our Realme of England, or any other corporacon or Body politique of the same may lawfully doe.

AND FURTHER, That the said Governour and Companye, and their Successors, maie have forever one comon Seale, to be vsed in all Causes and Occasions of the said Company, and the same Seale may alter, chaunge, breake, and newe make, from tyme to tyme, at their pleasures. And our Will and Pleasure is, and Wee doe hereby for Vs, our Heires and Successors, ordeyne and graunte, That from henceforth for ever, there shalbe one Governor, one Deputy Governor, and eighteene Assistants of the same Company, to be from tyme to tyme constituted, elected and chosen out of the Freemen of the saide Company, for the twyme being, in such Manner and Forme as hereafter in theis Presents is expressed, which said Officers shall applie themselves to take Care for the best disposeing and ordering of the generall buysines and Affaires of, for, and concerning the said Landes and Premisses hereby mentioned, to be graunted, and the Plantacion thereof, and the Government of the People there. AND FOR the better Execution of our Royall Pleasure and Graunte in this Behalf, WEE doe, by theis presents, for Vs, our Heires and Successors, nominate, ordeyne, make, & constitute; our welbeloved the saide Mathewe Cradocke, to be the first and present Governor of the said Company, and the saide Thomas Goffe, to be Deputy Governor of the saide Company, and the saide Sir Richard Saltonstall, Isaack Johnson, Samuell Aldersey, John Ven, John Humfrey, John Endecott, Simon Whetcombe, Increase Noell, Richard Pery, Nathaniell Wright, Samuell Vassall, Theophilus Eaton,

Thomas Adams, Thomas Hutchins, John Browne, George Foxcrofte, William Vassall, and William Pinchion, to be the present Assistants of the saide Company, to continue in the saide several Offices respectivelie for such tyme, and in such manner, as in and by theis Presents is hereafter declared and appointed.

AND FURTHER, Wee . . . doe ordeyne and graunte, That the Governor of the saide Company . . . shall have Authoritie from tyme to tyme vpon all Occasions, to give order for the assembling of the saide Company, and calling them together to consult and advise of the Bussinesses and Affaires of the saide Company, and that the said Governor, Deputie Governor, and Assistants of the saide Company, for the tyme being, shall or maie once every Moneth, or oftener at their Pleasures, assemble and houlde and keepe a Courte or Assemblie of themselves, for the better ordering and directing of their Affaires, and that any seaven or more persons of the Assistants, togither with the Governor, or Deputie Governor soe assembled, shalbe saide, taken, held, and reputed to be, and shalbe a full and sufficient Courte or Assemblie of the said Company, for the handling, ordering, and dispatching of all such Buysinesses and Occurrents as shall from tyme to tyme happen, touching or concerning the said Company or Plantation; and that there shall or maie be held and kept by the Governor, or Deputie Governor of the said Company, and seaven or more of the said Assistants for the tyme being, vpon every last Wednesday in Hillary, Easter, Trinity, and Michas Termes respectivelie forever, one greate generall and solempe assemblie, which foure generall assemblies shalbe stiled and called the foure greate and generall Courts of the saide Company; IN all and every, or any of which saide greate and generall Courts soe assembled, WEE DOE . . . give and graunte to the said Governor and Company, and their Successors, That the Governor, or in his absence, the Deputie Governor of the saide Company for the tyme being, and such of the Assistants and Freeman of the saide Company as shalbe present, or the greater nomber of them so assembled, whereof the Governor or Deputie Governor and six of the Assistants at the least to be seaven, shall have full Power and authoritie to choose, nominate, and appointe, such and soe many others as they shall thinke fitt, and that shall be willing to accept the same, to be free of the said Company and Body, and them into the same to admitt; and to elect and constitute such Officers as they shall thinke fitt and requisite, for the ordering, mannaging, and dispatching of the Affaires of the saide Govenor and Company, and their Successors; And to make Lawes and Ordinances for the Good and Welfare of the saide Company, and for the Government and ordering of the saide Landes and Plantation, and the People inhabiting and to inhabite the same, as to them from tyme to tyme shalbe thought meete, soe as such Lawes and Ordinances be not contrarie or repugnant to the Lawes and Statuts of this our Realme of England. AND, our Will and Pleasure is . . . That yearely once in the yeare, for ever hereafter, namely, the last Wednesday in Easter Tearme, yearely, the Governor, Deputy-Governor, and Assistants of the said Company and all other officers of the saide Company shalbe in the Generall Court or Assembly to be held for that Day or Tyme, newly chosen for the Yeare ensueing by such greater parte of the said Company, for the Tyme

being, then and there present as is aforesaide. . . . AND, Wee doe further
. . . give and graunte to the said Governor and Company, and their Successors for ever by theis Presents, That it shalbe lawfull and free for them
and their Assignes, at all and every Tyme and Tymes hereafter, out of
any our Realmes or Domynions whatsoever, to take, leade, carry, and
transport, for in and into their Voyages, and for and towardes the said
Plantation in Newe England, all such and soe many of our loving Subjects,
or any other strangers that will become our loving Subjects, and live
under our Allegiance, as shall willinglie accompany them in the same
Voyages and Plantation; and also Shipping, Armour, Weapons, Ordinance,
Municon, Powder, Shott, Corne, Victualls, and all Manner of Clothing,
Implements, Furniture, Beastes, Cattle, Horses, Mares, Merchandizes, and
all other Thinges necessarie for the said Plantation, and for their Vse and
Defence, and for Trade with the People there, and in passing and re-
turning to and fro, any Lawe or Statute to the contrarie hereof in any
wise notwithstanding; and without payeing or yeilding any Custome or
Subsidie, either inward or outward, to Vs, our Heires or Successors, for
the same, by the Space of seaven Yeares from the Day of the Date of theis
Presents. PROVIDED, that none of the saide Persons be such as shalbe
hereafter by especiall Name restrayned by Vs, our Heires or Successors.
AND, for their further Encouragement of our especiall Grace and Favor,
Wee . . . yeild and graunt to the saide Governor and Company, and their
Successors, and every of them, their Factors and Assignes, That they and
every of them shalbe free and quitt from all Taxes, Subsidies, and Customes, in Newe England, for the like Space of seaven Yeares, and from
all Taxes and Imposicons for the Space of twenty and one Yeares, vpon
all Goodes and Merchandizes at any Tyme or Tymes hereafter, either
vpon Importation thither, or Exportation from thence into our Realme
of England, or into any other our Domynions by the said Governor and
Company, and their Successors, their Deputies, Factors, and Assignes, or
any of them; EXCEPT onlie the five Pounds per Centum due for Custome
vpon all such Goodes and Merchandizes as after the saide seaven Yeares
shalbe expired, shalbe brought or imported into our Realme of England, or
any other of our Dominions, according to the auncient Trade of Merchants. . . .

AND, further our Will and Pleasure is . . . That all and every the
Subiects of Vs, our Heires or Successors, which shall goe to and inhabite
within the saide Landes and Premisses hereby mentioned to be graunted,
and every of their Children which shall happen to be borne there, or on
the Seas in goeing thither, or retorning from thence, shall have and enjoy
all liberties and Immunities of free and naturall Subiects within any of the
Domynions of Vs, our Heires or Successors, to all Intents, Constructions,
and Purposes whatsoever, as yf they and everie of them were borne within
the Realme of England. And that the Governor and Deputie Governor of
the said Company for the Tyme being, or either of them, and any two or
more of such of the saide Assistants as shalbe therevnto appointed by the
saide Governor and Company at any of their Courts or Assemblies to be
held as aforesaide, shall and maie at all Tymes, and from tyme to tyme
hereafter, have full Power and Authoritie to minister and give the Oathe

and Oathes of Supremacie and Allegiance, or either of them, to all and everie Person and Persons, which shall at any Tyme or Tymes hereafter goe or passe to the Landes and Premisses hereby mentioned to be graunted to inhabite in the same. AND, Wee doe of our further Grace, certen Knowledg and meere Motion, give and graunte to the saide Governor and Company, and their Successors, That it shall and maie be lawfull, to and for the Governor or Deputie Governor, and such of the Assistants and Freemen of the said Company for the Tyme being as shalbe assembled in any of their generall Courts aforesaide, or in any other Courtes to be specially sumoned and assembled for that Purpose, or the greater Parte of them (whereof the Governor or Deputie Governor, and six of the Assistants to be alwaies seaven) from tyme to tyme, to make, ordeine, and establishe all Manner of wholesome and reasonable Orders, Lawes, Statutes, and Ordinances, Directions, and Instructions, not contrairie to the Lawes of this our Realme of England, aswell for setling of the Formes and Ceremonies of Government and Magistracy, fitt and necessary for the said Plantation, and the Inhabitants there, and for nameing and setting of all sorts of Officers, both superior and inferior, which they shall finde needefull for that Government and Plantation, and the distinguishing and setting forth of the severall duties, Powers, and Lymytts of every such Office and Place, and the Formes of such Oathes warrantable by the Lawes and Statutes of this our Realme of England, as shalbe respectivelie ministered vnto them for the Execution of the said severall Offices and Places; as also, for the disposing and ordering of the Elections of such of the said Officers as shalbe annuall, and of such others as shalbe to succeede in Case of Death or Removeall, and ministring the said Oathes to the newe elected Officers, and for Imposicons of lawfull Fynes, Mulcts, Imprisonment, or other lawfull Correction, according to the Course of other Corporacons in this our Realme of England, and for the directing, ruling, and disposeing of all other Matters and Thinges, whereby our said People, Inhabitants there, may be soe religiously, peaceablie, and civilly governed, as their good Life and orderlie Conversacon, maie wynn and incite the Natives of Country, to the Knowledg and Obedience of the onlie true God and Sauior of Mankinde, and the Christian Fayth, which in our Royall Intention, and the Adventurers free Profession, is the principall Ende of this Plantation. WILLING, commanding, and requiring, and by theis Presents for Vs, our Heires, and Successors, ordeyning and appointing, that all such Orders, Lawes, Statuts and Ordinances, Instructions and Directions, as shal be soe made by the Governor, or Deputie Governor of the said Company, and such of the Assistants and Freemen as aforesaide, and published in Writing, vnder their comon Seale, shal be carefullie and dulie observed, kept, performed, and putt in Execution, according to the true Intent and Meaning of the same; and theis our Letters-patents, or the Duplicate or exemplification thereof, shal be to all and everie such Officers, superior and inferior, from Tyme to Tyme, for the putting of the same Orders, Lawes, Statutes, and Ordinances, Instructions, and Directions, in due Execution against Vs, our Heires and Successors, a sufficient Warrant and Discharge. . . .

C. MARYLAND CHARTER (JUNE 20, 1632)*

Whereas our well beloved and right trusty Subject Caecilius Calvert, Baron of Baltimore, in our Kingdom of Ireland, Son and Heir of George Calvert, Knight, late Baron of Baltimore, in our said Kingdom of Ireland, treading in the steps of his Father, being animated with a laudable, and pious Zeal for extending the Christian Religion, and also the Territories of our Empire, hath humbly besought Leave of us, that he may transport, by his own Industry, and Expense, a numerous Colony of the English Nation, to a certain Region, hereinafter described, in a Country hitherto uncultivated, in the Parts of America, and partly occupied by Savages, having no knowledge of the Divine Being, and that all that Region, with some certain Privileges, and Jurisdiction, appertaining unto the wholesome Government, and State of his Colony and Region aforesaid, may by our Royal Highness be given, granted and confirmed unto him, and his Heirs. . . .

Know Ye therefore, that We . . . by this our present Charter . . . do Give, Grant and Confirm, unto the aforesaid Caecilius, now Baron of Baltimore, his Heirs, and Assigns, all that Part of the Peninsula, or Chersonese, lying in the Parts of America, between the Ocean on the East and the Bay of Chesapeake on the West, divided from the Residue thereof by a Right Line drawn from the Promontory, or Head Land, called Watkin's Point, situate upon the Bay aforesaid, near the river Wigloo, on the West, unto the main Ocean on the East; and between that Boundary on the South, unto that Part of the Bay of Delaware on the North, which lieth under the Fortieth Degree of North Latitude from the Equinoctial, where New England is terminated: And all that Tract of Land within the Metes underwritten (that is to say) passing from the said Bay, called Delaware Bay, in a right Line, by the Degree aforesaid, unto the true meridian of the first Fountain of the River of Pottowmack, thence verging toward the South, unto the further Bank of the said River, and following the same on the West and South, unto a certain Place, called Cinquack, situate near the mouth of the said River, where it disembogues into the aforesaid Bay of Chesapeake, and thence by the shortest Line unto the aforesaid Promontory or Place, called Watkin's Point; so that the whole tract of land, divided by the Line aforesaid, between the main Ocean and Watkin's Point, unto the Promontory called Cape Charles, and every the Appendages thereof, may entirely remain excepted for ever to Us, our Heirs and Successors. . . .

Also We do grant . . . all Islands and Inlets within the Limits aforesaid, all and singular the Islands, and Islets, from the Eastern Shore of the aforesaid Region, towards the East, which had been, or shall be formed in the Sea, situate within Ten marine Leagues from the said shore; with all and singular the Ports, Harbours, Bays, Rivers, and Straits belonging to the Region or Islands aforesaid, and all the Soil, Plains, Woods,

* These excerpts are reprinted from Thorpe, *Federal and State Constitutions, Colonial Charters, and Other Organic Laws,* vol. III, pp. 1677–1681, 1684–1685.

Marshes, Lakes, Rivers, Bays, and Straits, situate, or being within the Metes, Bounds, and Limits aforesaid, with the Fishings of every kind of Fish, as well of Whales, Sturgeons, and other royal Fish, as of other Fish, in the Sea, Bays, Straits, or Rivers, within the Premises, and the fish there taken; And moreover all Veins, Mines, and Quarries, as well opened as hidden, already found, or that shall be found within the Region, Islands, or Limits aforesaid, of Gold, Silver, Gems, and precious Stones, and any other whatsoever, whether they be of Stones, or Metals, or of any other Thing, or Matter whatsoever: And furthermore the Patronages, and Advowsons of all Churches which (with the increasing Worship and Religion of Christ) within the Said Region, Islands, Islets, and Limits aforesaid, hereafter shall happen to be built, together with License and Faculty of erecting and founding Churches, Chapels, and Places of Worship, in convenient and suitable places, within the Premises, and of causing the same to be dedicated and consecrated according to the Ecclesiastical Laws of our Kingdom of England, with all, and singular such, and as ample Rights, Jurisdictions, Privileges, Prerogatives, Royalties, Liberties, Immunities, and royal Rights, and temporal Franchises whatsoever, as well by Sea as by Land, within the Region, Islands, Islets, and Limits aforesaid, to be had, exercised, used, and enjoyed, as any Bishop of Durham, within the Bishoprick or County Palatine of Durham, in our Kingdom of England, ever heretofore hath had, held, used, or enjoyed, or of right could, or ought to have, hold, use, or enjoy. . . .

And we do by these Presents, . . . Constitute Him, the now Baron of Baltimore, and his Heirs, the true and absolute Lords and Proprietaries of the Region aforesaid, and of all other Premises (except the before excepted) saving always the Faith and Allegiance and Sovereign Dominion due to Us. . . . To Hold of Us . . . as of our Castle of Windsor, in our County of Berks, in free and common Soccage, by Fealty only for all Services, and not in Capite, nor by Knight's Service, Yielding therefore unto Us . . . Two Indian Arrows of these Parts, to be delivered at the said Castle of Windsor, every Year, on Tuesday in Easter Week: And also the fifth Part of all Gold and Silver Ore, which shall happen from Time to Time, to be found within the aforesaid Limits. . . .

And . . . We . . . do grant unto the said now Baron . . . for the good and happy Government of the said Province, free, full, and absolute Power, by the Tenor of these Presents, to Ordain, Make, and Enact Laws, of what Kind soever, according to their sound Discretions, whether relating to the Public State of the said Province, or the private Utility of Individuals, of and with the Advice, Assent, and Approbation of the Free-Men of the same Province, or the greater Part of them, or of their Delegates or Deputies, whom We will shall be called together for the framing of Laws . . . in the Form which shall seem best . . . and the same to publish under the Seal of the aforesaid now Baron of Baltimore, and his Heirs, and duly to execute the same upon all Persons, for the time being, within the aforesaid Province, and the Limits thereof, or under his or their Government and Power . . . by the Imposition of Fines, Imprisonment, and other Punishment whatsoever: even if it be necessary, and the Quality of

the Offence require it, by Privation of Member, or Life. . . . So, nevertheless, that the Laws aforesaid be consonant to Reason, and be not repugnant or contrary, but (so far as conveniently may be) agreeable to the
Laws, Statutes, Customs, and Rights of this Our Kingdom of England. . . .

And forasmuch as, in the Government of so great a Province, sudden
accidents may frequently happen, to which it will be necessary to apply
a Remedy, before the Freeholders of the said Province, their Delegates,
or Deputies, can be called together for the framing of Laws; neither will
it be fit that so great a Number of People should immediately, on such
emergent Occasion, be called together, We therefore, for the better Government of so great a Province, do Will and Ordain . . . that the . . . Baron
of Baltimore . . . may . . . make and constitute fit and Wholesome Ordinances from Time to Time, to be Kept and observed within the Province
aforesaid, as well for the Conservation of the Peace, as for the better
Government of the People inhabiting therein, and publicly to notify the
same to all Persons whom the same in any wise do or may affect. . . . So
that the said Ordinances be consonant to Reason and be not repugnant nor
contrary, but (so far as conveniently may be done) agreeable to the Laws,
Statutes, or Rights of our Kingdom of England: And so that the same
Ordinances do not, in any Sort, extend to oblige, bind, charge, or take
away the Right or Interest of any Person or Persons, of, or in Member,
Life, Freehold, Goods or Chattels. . . .

We will also, and of our more abundant Grace, for Us, our Heirs and
Successors, do firmly charge, constitute, ordain, and command, that the
said Province be of our Allegiance . . . and in all Things shall be held,
treated, reputed, and esteemed as the faithful Liege-Men of Us . . . born
within our Kingdom of England; also Lands, Tenements, Revenues,
Services, and other Hereditaments whatsoever, within our Kingdom of
England, and other our Dominions, to inherit, or otherwise purchase, receive, take, have, hold, buy, and possess, and the same to use and enjoy,
and the same to give, sell, alien and bequeath; and likewise all Privileges,
Franchises and Liberties of this our Kingdom of England, freely, quietly,
and peaceably to have and possess, and the same may use and enjoy in
the same manner as our Liege-Men born, or to be born within our said
Kingdom of England, without Impediment, Molestation, Vexation, Im-
peachment, or Grievance of Us. . . .

Moreover, We will, appoint, and ordain . . . that the . . . Baron of
Baltimore . . . shall have, and enjoy the Taxes and Subsidies payable, or
arising within the Ports, Harbors, and other Creeks and Places aforesaid,
within the Province aforesaid, for Wares bought and sold, and Things
there to be laden, or unladen, to be reasonably assessed by them, and
the People there as aforesaid, on emergent Occasion; to whom We grant
Power by these Presents, for Us, our Heirs and Successors, to assess and
impose the said Taxes and Subsidies there, upon just Cause and in due
Proportion.

And furthermore . . . We . . . do give, grant and confirm, unto the said
now Baron of Baltimore . . . full and absolute License, Power, and Authority . . . [to] assign, alien, grant, demise, or enfeoff so many, such, and

proportionate Parts and Parcels of the Premises, to any Person or Persons willing to purchase the same, as they shall think convenient, to have and to hold to the same Person or Persons willing to take or purchase the same, and his and their Heirs and Assigns, in Fee-simple, or Fee-tail, or for Term of Life, Lives or Years; to hold of the aforesaid now Baron of Baltimore, his Heirs and Assigns, by so many, such, and so great Services, Customs and Rents of this Kind, as to the same now Baron of Baltimore, his Heirs, and Assigns, shall seem fit and agreeable. . . .

We also . . . do give and grant License to the same Baron of Baltimore, and to his Heirs, to erect any Parcels of Land within the Province aforesaid, into Manors, and in every of those Manors, to have and to hold a Court-Baron, and all Things which to a Court Baron do belong; and to have and to Keep View of Frank-Pledge, for the Conservation of the Peace and better Government of those Parts, by themselves and their Stewards, or by the Lords, for the Time being to be deputed, of other of those Manors when they shall be constituted, and in the same to exercise all Things to the View of Frank Pledge belong. . . .

And further We will, and do, by these Presents, for Us, our Heirs and Successors, covenant and grant to, and with the aforesaid now Baron of Baltimore, His Heirs and Assigns, that We, our Heirs, and Successors, at no Time heirafter, will impose, or make or cause to be imposed any Impositions, Customs, or other Taxations, Quotas, or Contributions whatsoever, in or upon the Residents or Inhabitants of the Province aforesaid for their Goods, Lands, or Tenements within the same Province, or upon any Tenements, Lands, Goods or Chattels within the Province aforesaid, or in or upon any Goods or Merchandizes within the Province aforesaid, or within the Ports or Harbors of the said Province, to be laden or unladen. . . .

SELECTION

Plantation Covenants

Not a few settlements were made, however, by colonists who either, like the Pilgrims, had tried and failed to obtain a charter or, like the settlers of Connecticut and Rhode Island, had ventured out on their own from an older colony. To give legitimacy to their proceedings and to establish sufficient order to enable them to live together in peace until they could obtain charters, they entered into covenants among themselves in which they agreed to bind themselves into a body politic and mutually promised to obey its laws. The first of these "plantation covenants" was the Mayflower Compact, adopted by the Pilgrims at Plymouth on November 11, 1620. Later covenants in Connecticut

and Rhode Island were more elaborate. specifying the details of the organiza-
tion of government as well as the distribution and limitations of power much in
the manner of modern constitutions. The first of these—reputedly the first
written constitution to create a government—was the Fundamental Orders of
Connecticut. adopted by the freemen of the Connecticut towns on January 14,
1639. On the nature and significance of these early covenants. see the provoca-
tive comments in Hannah Arendt. On Revolution *(1963). Also helpful is*
Benjamin F. Wright. Jr.. "The Early History of Written Constitutions in
America," in Carl Wittke (ed.), Essays in History and Political Theory in
Honor of Charles Howard McIlwain *(1936). pages 344–371.*

A. MAYFLOWER COMPACT (NOV. 11, 1620)*

IN THE NAME OF GOD, AMEN. We, whose names are underwritten, the
Loyal Subjects of our dread Sovereign Lord King *James,* by the Grace of
God, of *Great Britain, France,* and *Ireland,* King, *Defender of the Faith,*
&c. Having undertaken for the Glory of God, and Advancement of the
Christian Faith, and the Honour of our King and Country, a Voyage to
plant the first Colony in the northern Parts of Virginia; Do by these
Presents, solemnly and mutually, in the Presence of God and one another,
covenant and combine ourselves together into a civil Body Politick, for our
better Ordering and Preservation, and Furtherance of the Ends aforesaid:
And by Virtue hereof do enact, constitute, and frame, such just and equal
Laws, Ordinances, Acts, Constitutions, and Officers, from time to time, as
shall be thought most meet and convenient for the general Good of the
Colony; unto which we promise all due Submission and Obedience. IN
WITNESS whereof we have hereunto subscribed our names at *Cape-Cod* the
eleventh of *November,* in the Reign of our Sovereign Lord King *James,*
of *England, France,* and *Ireland,* the eighteenth, and of Scotland, the fifty-
fourth, *Anno Domini,* 1620.

MR. JOHN CARVER,	MR. SAMUEL FULLER,	EDWARD TILLY,
MR. WILLIAM BRADFORD,	MR. CHRISTOPHER MARTIN,	JOHN TILLY,
MR. EDWARD WINSLOW,	MR. WILLIAM MULLINS,	FRANCIS COOKE,
MR. WILLIAM BREWSTER,	MR. WILLIAM WHITE,	THOMAS ROGERS,
ISAAC ALLERTON,	MR. RICHARD WARREN,	THOMAS TINKER,
MYLES STANDISH,	JOHN HOWLAND,	JOHN RIDGDALE,
JOHN ALDEN,	MR. STEVEN HOPKINS,	EDWARD FULLER,
JOHN TURNER,	DIGERY PRIEST,	RICHARD CLARK,
FRANCIS EATON,	THOMAS WILLIAMS,	RICHARD GARDINER,
JAMES CHILTON,	GILBERT WINSLOW,	MR. JOHN ALLERTON,
JOHN CRAXTON,	EDMUND MARGESSON,	THOMAS ENGLISH,
JOHN BILLINGTON,	PETER BROWN,	EDWARD DOTEN,
JOSES FLETCHER,	RICHARD BRITTERIDGE,	EDWARD LIESTER.
JOHN GOODMAN,	GEORGE SOULE,	

* Reprinted in full from Francis Newton Thorpe (ed.), *Federal and State
Constitutions. Colonial Charters. and Other Organic Laws* (7 vols., 1909), vol.
III, p. 1841.

B. FUNDAMENTAL ORDERS OF CONNECTICUT (JAN. 14, 1639)*

FORASMUCH as it hath pleased the Allmighty God by the wise disposition of his diuyne prouidence so to Order and dispose of things that we the Inhabitants and Residents of Windsor, Harteford and Wethersfield are now cohabiting and dwelling in and vppon the River of Conectecotte and the Lands thereunto adioyneing; And well knowing where a people are gathered togather the word of God requires that to mayntayne the peace and vnion of such a people there should be an orderly and decent Gouerment established according to God, to order and dispose of the affayres of the people at all seasons as occation shall require; doe therefore assotiate and conioyne our selues to be as one Publike State or Commonwelth; and doe, for our selues and our Successors and such as shall be adioyned to vs att any tyme hereafter, enter into Combination and Confederation togather, to mayntayne and preserue the liberty and purity of the gospell of our Lord Jesus which we now profess, as also the disciplyne of the Churches, which according to the truth of the said gospell is now practised amongst vs; As also in our Ciuell Affairs to be guided and gouerned according to such Lawes, Rules, Orders and decrees as shall be made, ordered & decreed, as followeth:—

1. It is Ordered, sentenced and decreed, that there shall be yerely two generall Assemblies or Courts, the on the second thursday in Aprill, the other the second thursday in September, following; the first shall be called the Courte of Election, wherein shall be yerely Chosen from tyme to tyme soe many Magestrats and other publike Officers as shall be found requisitte: Whereof one to be chosen Gouernour for the yeare ensueing and vntill another be chosen, and noe other Magestrate to be chosen for more then one yeare; prouided allwayes there be sixe chosen besids the Gouernour; which being chosen and sworne according to an Oath recorded for that purpose shall haue power to administer iustice according to the Lawes here established, and for want thereof according to the rule of the word of God; which choise shall be made by all that are admitted freemen and haue taken the Oath of Fidellity, and doe cohabitte within this Jurisdiction, (hauing beene admitted Inhabitants by the maior part of the Towne wherein they liue,) or the mayor parte of such as shall be then present.

2. It is Ordered, sentensed and decreed, that the Election of the aforesaid Magestrats shall be on this manner: euery person present and quallified for choyse shall bring in (to the persons deputed to receaue them) one single paper with the name of him written in yt whom he desires to haue Gouernour, and he that hath the greatest number of papers shall be Gouernor for that yeare. And the rest of the Magestrats or publike Officers to be chosen in this manner: The Secretary for the tyme being shall first read the names of all that are to be put to choise and then shall seuerally

---

* These excerpts are reprinted from Thorpe, *Federal and State Constitutions, Colonial Charters, and Other Organic Laws*, vol. I, pp. 519–522.

nominate them distinctly, and euery one that would haue the person nominated to be chosen shall bring in one single paper written vppon, and he that would not haue him chosen shall bring in a blanke: and euery one that hath more written papers than blanks shall be a Magistrat for that yeare; which papers shall be receaued and told by one or more that shall be then chosen by the court and sworne to be faythfull therein; but in case there should not be sixe chosen as aforesaid, besids the Gouernor, out of those which are nominated, then he or they which haue the most written papers shall be a Magestrate or Magestrats for the ensueing yeare, to make vp the aforesaid number.

3. It is Ordered, sentenced and decreed, that the Secretary shall not nominate any person, nor shall any person be chosen newly into the Magestracy which was not propownded in some Generall Courte before, to be nominated the next Election; and to that end yt shall be lawfull for ech of the Townes aforesaid by their deputyes to nominate any two whom they conceaue fitte to be put to election; and the Courts may ad so many more as they iudge requisitt.

4. It is Ordered, sentenced and decreed that noe person be chosen Gouernor aboue once in two yeares, and that the Gouernor be always a member of some approved congregation, and formerly of the Magestracy within this Jurisdiction; and all the Magestrats Freemen of this Common-welth: and that no Magestrate or other publike officer shall execute any parte of his or their Office before they are seuerally sworne, which shall be done in the face of the Courte if they be present, and in case of absence by some deputed for that purpose.

5. It is Ordered, sentenced and decreed, that to the aforesaid Courte of Election the seuerall Townes shall send their deputyes, and when the Elections are ended they may proceed in any publike searuice as at other Courts. Also the other Generall Courte in September shall be for makeing of lawes, and any other publike occation, which conserns the good of the Commonwelth.

6. It is Ordered, sentenced and decreed, that the Gouernor ether by himselfe or by the secretary, send out summons to the Constables of euery Towne for the cauleing of these two standing Courts, on month at lest before their seuerall tymes: And also if the Gouernor and the gretest parte of the Magestrats see cause vppon any spetiall occation to call a generall Courte, they may giue order to the secretary soe to doe within fowerteene dayes warneing; and if vrgent necessity so require, vppon a shorter notice, giueing sufficient grownds for yt to the deputyes when they meete, or els be questioned for the same; And if the Gouernor and the Mayor parte of Magestrats shall ether neglect or refuse to call the two Generall standing Courts or ether of them, as also at other tymes when the occations of the Commonwelth require, the Freemen thereof, or the Mayor parte of them, shall petition to them soe to doe: if then yt be ether denyed or neglected the said Freemen or the Major parte of them shall haue power to giue order to the Constables of the seuerall Townes to doe the same, and so may meete togather, and chuse to themselues a Moderator, and may proceed to do any Acte of power, which any other Generall Courte may.

7. It is Ordered, sentenced and decreed that after there are warrants giuen out for any of the said Generall Courts, the Constable or Constables of ech Towne shall forthwith give notice distinctly to the inhabitants of the same, in some Publike Assembly or by goeing or sending from howse to howse, that at a place and tyme by him or them lymited and sett, they meet and assemble them selues togather to elect and chuse certen deputyes to be att the Generall Courte then following to agitate the afayres of the commonwelth; which said Deputyes shall be chosen by all that are admitted Inhabitants in the seurall Townes and haue taken the oath of fidellity; prouuided that non be chosen a Deputy for any Generall Courte which is not a Freeman of this Commonwelth.

The a-foresaid deputyes shall be chosen in manner following: euery person that is present and quallified as before expressed, shall bring the names of such, written in seuerall papers. as they desire to haue chosen for that Imployment, and these 3 or 4, more or lesse, being the number agreed on to be chosen for that tyme, that haue greatest number of papers written for them shall be deputyes for that Courte; whose names shall be endorsed on the backe side of the warrant and returned into the Courte, with the Constable or Constables hand vnto the same.

8. It is Ordered, sentenced and decreed, that Wyndsor, Hartford and Wethersfield shall haue power, ech Towne, to send fower of their freemen as deputyes to euery Generall Courte; and whatsoeuer other Townes shall be hereafter added to this Jurisdiction, they shall send so many deputyes as the Courte shall judge meete, a resonable proportion to the number of Freemen that are in the said Townes being to be attended therein; which deputyes shall have the power of the whole Towne to giue their voats and allowance to all such lawes and orders as may be for the publike good, and unto which the said Townes are to be bownd.

9. It is ordered and decreed, that the deputyes thus chosen shall haue power and liberty to appoynt a tyme and a place of meeting togather before any Generall Courte to aduise and consult of all such things as may Concerne the good of the publike, as also to examine their owne Elections, whether according to the order, and if they or the gretest parte of them find any election to be illegall they may seclud such for present from their meeting, and returne the same and their resons to the Courte; and if yt proue true, the Courte may fyne the party or partyres so intruding and the Towne, if they see cause, and giue out a warrant to goe to a newe election in a legall way, either *in whole or* in parte. Also the said deputyes shall haue power to fyne any that shall be disorderly at their meetings, or for not coming in due tyme or place according to appoyntment; and they may returne the said fynes into the Courtes if yt be refused to be paid, and the tresurer to take notice of yt, and to estreete or levy the same as he doth other fynes.

10. It is Ordered, sentenced and decreed, that euery Generall Courte except such as through neglecte of the Gouernor and the greatest parte of Magestrats the Freemen themselves doe call, shall consist of the Gouernor, or some one chosen to moderate the Court, and 4 other Magestrats at lest, with the mayor parte of the deputyes of the seuerall Townes legally

chosen; and in case the Freemen or mayor parte of them through neglect or refusall of the Gouernor and the mayor parte of the magestrats, shall call a Courte, that yt shall consist of the mayor parte of Freemen that are present or their deputyes, with a Moderator chosen by them: *In which said Generall Courts shall consist the supreme power of the Common-welth*, and they only shall haue power to make laws or repeale them, to graunt leuyes, to admitt of Freemen, dispose of lands vndisposed of,, to seuerall Townes or persons, and also shall haue power to call ether Courte or Magestrate or any other person whatsoeuer into question for any misdemeanour, and may for just causes displace or deale otherwise according to the nature of the offence; and also may deale in any other matter that concerns the good of this common welth, excepte election of Magestrats, which shall be done by the whole boddy of Freemen: In which Courte the Gouernour or Moderator shall haue power to order the Courte to giue liberty of spech, and silence vnceasonable and disorderly speakeings, to put all things to voate, and in case the vote be equall to haue the casting voice. But non of these Courts shall be adiorned or dis-solued without the consent of the maior parte of the Court.

11. It is ordered, sentenced and decreed, that when any Generall Courte vppon the occations of the Commonwelth haue agreed vppon any sume or soms of mony to be leuyed vppon the seuerall Townes within this Jurisdiction, that a Committee be chosen to sett out and appoynt what shall be the proportion of euery Towne to pay of the said leuy, provided the Committees be made vp of an equall number out of each Towne. . . .

The First Settlements, 1584–1660:
From Outposts to Plantations on the Chesapeake

SELECTION 5

The Problem of Survival: John Smith, "Generall Historie of Virginia, New-England, and the Summer Isles" (1624)

The first colony was the most difficult. English colonial adventurers had learned little from the abortive Roanoke enterprises of the 1580s, and a whole range of new and unexpected problems had to be met and solved by the Virginia Company and the first settlers. The physical environment was inhospitable and unfamiliar, most of the initial settlers were unsuited for the venture, and the methods of proceeding were tentative and unproved. Hard labor was necessary to build crude shelters and defense works, and disease, Indians, and hunger took a heavy toll. But these difficulties, grave though they were, only highlighted a more serious and fundamental one: how to preserve order and maintain discipline in an unstable environment far removed from the traditional sources of authority. To solve that problem, to keep the settlers at work for their own and the common welfare, Captain John Smith, the swashbuckling and immodest hero of the first years of settlement who became president of the colony in September, 1608, established what amounted to a military regime. The following passages from Smith's Generall Historie of Virginia, New-England, and the Summer Isles, *published in 1624 over a decade after Smith had returned to England, vividly describe the difficulties confronting the first settlers and the steps taken to cope with them. The excerpts below are reprinted from volume I of the two-volume Richmond edition of 1819, pages 154–155, 163–164, 168–169, 202–203, 241.*

Wesley Frank Craven, The Southern Colonies in the Seventeenth Century, 1607–1689 *(1949), is an excellent general treatment of the founding and early development of the Chesapeake colonies, though it should be supplemented for the early years by Sigmund Diamond, "From Organization to Society: Virginia in the Seventeenth Century,"* The American Journal of Sociology, *volume 63 (March, 1958), pages 457–475. On John Smith, see the recent study, Philip L. Barbour,* The Three Worlds of Captain John Smith *(1964).*

Trials of Settlement

. . . within ten dayes scarce ten amongst vs could either goe, or well stand, such extreame weaknes and sicknes oppressed vs. And thereat none need marvaile, if they consider the cause and reason, which was this; whilest the ships stayed, our allowance was somewhat bettered, by a daily proportion of Bisket, which the sailers would pilfer to sell, giue, or exchange with vs, for money, Saxefras, furres, or loue. But when they departed, there remained neither taverne, beere-house, nor place of reliefe, but the common Kettell. Had we beene as free from all sinnes as gluttony, and drunkennesse, we might haue beene canonized for Saints; But our President would never haue beene admitted, for ingrossing to his private, Oatmeale, Sacke, Oyle, *Aquavitæ*, Beefe, Egges, or what not, but the Kettell; that indeed he allowed equally to be distributed, and that was halfe a pint of wheat, and as much barley boyled with water for a man a day, and this having fryed some 26 weekes in the ships hold, contained as many wormes as graines; so that we might truely call it rather so much bran then corne, our drinke was water, our lodgings Castles in the ayre: with this lodging and dyet, our extreame toile in bearing and planting Pallisadoes, so strained and bruised vs, and our continual labour in the extremitie of the heat had so weakened vs, as were cause sufficient to haue made vs as miserable in our natiue Countrey, or any other place in the world. From May, to September, those that escaped, liued vpon Sturgeon and Sea-crabs, fiftie in this time we buried, the rest seeing the Presidents projects to escape these miseries in our Pinnace by flight (who all this time had neither felt want nor sicknes) so moved our dead spirits, as we deposed him; and established *Ratcliffe* in his place, *(Gosnoll* being dead) *Kendall* deposed, *Smith* newly recovered, *Martin* and *Ratcliffe* was by his care preserved and relieued, and the most of the souldiers recovered, with the skilfull diligence of Mr. *Thomas Wotton* our Chirurgian generall. But now was all our provision spent, the Sturgeon gone, all helps abandoned, each houre expecting the fury of the Salvages; when God the patron of all good indevours, in that desperate extremitie so changed the heart of the Salvages, that they brought such plenty of their fruits, and provision, as no man wanted.

And now where some affirmed it was ill done by the Councell to send forth men so badly provided, this incontradictable reason will shew them plainely they are too ill advised to nourish such ill conceits; first, the fault of our going was our owne, what could be thought fitting or necessary we had, but what we should find, or want, or where we should be, we were all ignorant, and supposing to make our passage in two moneths, with victuall to liue, and the advantage of the spring to worke; we were at Sea fiue moneths, where we both spent our victuall and lost the opportunitie of the time, and season to plant, by the vnskilfull presumption of our ignorant transporters, that vnderstood not at all, what they vndertooke.

35

Such actions haue ever since the worlds beginning beene subject to such accidents, and every thing of worth is found full of difficulties, but nothing so difficult as to establish a Common wealth so farre remote from men and meanes, and where mens mindes are so vntoward as neither doe well themselues, nor suffer others. . . .

Now in *Iames* Towne they were all in combustion, the strongest preparing once more to run away with the Pinnace; which with the hazzard of his life, with Sakre falcon and musket shot, *Smith* forced now the third time to stay or sinke. Some no better then they should be, had plotted with the President, the next day to haue put him to death by the Leviticall law, for the liues of *Robinson* and *Emry,* pretending the fault was his that had led them to their ends: but he quickly tooke such order with such Lawyers, that he layd them by the heeles till he sent some of them prisoners for *England.* Now ever once in foure or fiue dayes, *Pocahontas* with her attendants, brought him so much provision, that saved many of their liues, that els for all this had starved with hunger.

> Thus from numbe death our good God sent reliefe,
> The sweete asswager of all other griefe.

His relation of the plenty he had seene, especially at *Werawocomoco,* and of the state and bountie of *Powhatan,* (which till that time was vnknowne) so revived their dead spirits (especially the loue of *Pocahontas*) as all mens feare was abandoned. Thus you may see what difficulties still crossed any good indevour: and the good successe of the businesse being thus oft brought to the very period of destruction; yet you see by what strange means God hath still delivered it. As for the insufficiency of them admitted in Commission, that error could not be prevented by the Electors; there being no other choise, and all strangers to each others education, qualities, or disposition. And if any deeme it a shame to our Nation to haue any mention made of those inormities, let them pervse the Histories of the Spanyards Discoveries and Plantations, where they may see how many mutinies, disorders, and dissentions haue accompanied them, and crossed their attempts: which being knowne to be particular mens offences; doth take away the generall scorne and contempt, which malice, presumption, covetousnesse, or ignorance might produce; to the scandall and reproach of those, whose actions and valiant resolutions deserue a more worthy respect. . . .

. . . we returned all well to *Iames* towne, where this new supply being lodged with the rest, accidentally fired their quarters and so the towne, which being but thatched with reeds, the fire was so fierce as it burnt their Pallisado's, (though eight or ten yards distant) with their Armes, bedding, apparell, and much priuate prouision. Good Master *Hunt* our Preacher lost all his liberary and all he had but the cloathes on his backe: yet none neuer heard him repine at his losse. This happened in the winter in that extreame frost. 1607. Now though we had victuall sufficient I meane onely of Oatmeale, meale and corne, yet the Ship staying 14. weekes when shee might as wel haue beene gone in 14. dayes, spent a great part of that, and neare all the rest that was sent to be landed. When they

departed what their discretion could spare vs, to make a little poore meale
or two, we called feastes, to relish our mouthes: of each somwhat they
left vs, yet I must confesse, those that had either money, spare clothes
credit to giue billes of paiment, gold rings, furrs, or any such commodities,
were euer welcome to this remouing tauerne, such was our patience to
obay such vile commanders, and buy our owne provisions at 15. times the
value, suffering them feast (we bearing the charge) yet must not repine,
but fast, least we should incurre the censure of factious and seditious
persons: and then leakage, ship rats, and other casuallties occasioned them
losse, but the vessels and remnants (for totals) we were glad to receaue
with all our hearts to make vp the account, highly commending their
prouidence for preseruing that, least they should discourage any more to
come to vs. Now for all this plenty our ordynary was but meale and water,
so that this great charge little releeued our wants, whereby with the
extremitie of the bitter cold frost and those defects, more than halfe of vs
dyed; I cannot deny but both *Smith* and *Skriuener* did their best to amend
what was amisse, but with the President went the maior part, that there
hornes were to short. But the worst was our guilded refiners with their
golden promises made all men their slaues in hope of recompences; there
was no talke, no hope, no worke, but dig gold, wash gold, refine gold, loade
gold, such a bruit of gold, that one mad fellow desired to be buried in the
sands least they should by there art make gold of his bones, little neede
there was and lesse reason, the ship should stay, there wages run on, our
victualls consume 14. weekes, that the Mariners might say, they did helpe
to build such a golden Church that we can say the raine washed neere to
nothing in 14. dayes. Were it that captaine *Smith* would not applaude all
those golden inventions, because they admitted him not to the sight of
their trialls nor golden consultations; I know not, but I haue heard him
oft question with Captain *Martin* and tell him, except he could shew him
a more substantiall triall, he was not inamoured with their durty skill,
breathing out these and many other passions, neuer any thing did more
torment him, then to see all necessary busines neglected, to fraught such
a drunken ship with so much guilded durt. Till then we neuer accounted
Captaine *Newport* a refiner, who being ready to set saile for *England,*
and we not hauing any vse of Parliaments, Plaises, Petitions, Admiralls,
Recorders, Interpreters, Chronologers, Courts of Plea, nor Iustices of
peace sent Master *Wingfield* and Captaine Archer home with him, that
had ingrossed all those titles, to seeke some better place of imployment.

> Oh cursed gold those, hunger-starued movers,
> To what misfortunes lead'st thou all those lovers!
> For all the *China* wealth, nor *Indies* can
> Suffice the minde of an av'ritious man.

Prescription for Settlers

. . . When you send againe I entreat you rather send but thirty Carpenters,
husbandmen, gardiners, fisher men, blacksmiths, masons, and diggers vp of
trees' roots, well provided, then a thousaud of such as we haue: for except

wee be able both to lodge them, and feed them, the most will consume with want of necessaries before they can be made good for any thing. Thus if you please to consider this account, and the vnnecessary wages to Captaine *Newport,* or his ships so long lingering and staying here (for notwithstanding his boasting to leaue vs victuals for 12 moneths, though we had 89 by this discovery lame and sicke, and but a pinte of Corne a day for a man, we were constrained to giue him three hogsheads of that to victuall him homeward) or yet to send into *Germany* or *Poleland* for glasse-men and the rest, till we be able to sustaine ourselues, and releeue them when they come. It were better to giue fiue hundred pound a tun for those grosse Commodities in *Denmarke,* then send for them hither, till more necessary things be provided. For in over-toyling our weake and vnskilfull bodies, to satisfie this desire of present profit, we can scarce ever recover our selues from one Supply to another. And I humbly intreat you hereafter, let vs know what we should receive, and not stand to the Saylers courtesie to leaue vs what they please, els you may charge vs what you will, but we not you with any thing. These are the causes that haue kept vs in *Virginia,* from laying such a foundation, that ere this might haue given much better content and satisfaction; but as yet you must not looke for any profitable returnes. . . .

Accomplishments

Besides *Iames* towne that was strongly Pallizadoed, containing some fiftie or sixtie houses, he left fiue or sixe other severall Forts and Plantations: though they were not so sumptuous as our successors expected, they were better then they provided any for vs. All this time we had but one Carpenter in the Countrey, and three others that could doe little, but desired to be learners: two Blacksmiths; two saylers, and those we write labourers were for most part footmen, and such as they that were Adventurers brought to attend them, or such as they could perswade to goe with them, that neuer did know what a dayes worke was, except the *Dutch*-men and *Poles,* and some dozen other. For all the rest were poore Gentlemen, Tradsmen, Serving-men, libertines, and such like, ten times more fit to spoyle a Commonwealth, then either begin one, or but helpe to maintaine one. For when neither the feare of God, nor the law, nor shame, nor displeasure of their friends could rule them here, there is small hope ever to bring one in twentie of them ever to be good there. Notwithstanding, I confesse divers amongst them, had better mindes and grew much more industrious then was expected: yet ten good workemen would haue done more substantiall worke in a day, then ten of them in a weeke. Therefore men may rather wonder how we could doe so much, then vse vs so badly, because we did no more, but leaue those examples to make others beware, and the fruits of all, we know not for whom. . . .

Establishment of Discipline and Order:
Captain Thomas Dale's Laws (1611)

The military regime established by Captain John Smith was institutionalized and refined by Captain Thomas Dale (d. 1619), who became marshal of the colony in 1610. With full approval of company officials he devised a code, subsequently known as Dale's Laws, which not only set up a severe military regimen but also regulated in detail the daily conduct of every resident of the colony. This code was strictly enforced and remained in effect from May, 1611, to April, 1619. The nature of the code and the kind of social goals it sought to enforce may be surmised from the following selections reprinted from "Articles, Lawes, and Orders, Divine, Politique, and Martiall for the Colony in Virginea," in Peter Force (comp.), Tracts and Other Papers *(four volumes, 1836–1846), volume III, number 2, pages 9–13, 15–18. Darrett B. Rutman, "The Virginia Company and Its Military Regime," in Darrett B. Rutman (ed.),* The Old Dominion: Essays for Thomas Perkins Abernathy *(1964), 1–20, is a brief study of the code.*

Whereas his Maiestie like himselfe a most zealous Prince hath in his owne Realmes a principall care of true Religion, and reuerence to God, and hath alwaies strictly commaunded his Generals and Gouernours, with all his forces wheresoeuer, to let their waies be like his ends, for the glorie of God.

And forasmuch as no good seruice can be performed, or warre well managed, where militarie discipline is not obserued, and militarie discipline cannot be kept, where the rules or chiefe parts thereof, be not certainely set downe, and generally knowne, I haue . . . adhered vnto the lawes diuine, and orders politique, and martiall of his Lordship . . . an addition of such others, as I haue found either the necessitie of the present State of the Colonie to require, or the infancie, and weaknesse of the body thereof, as yet able to digest, and doe now publish them to all persons in the Colonie, that they may as well take knowledge of the Lawes themselues, as of the penaltie and punishment, which without partialitie shall be inflicted vpon the breakers of the same.

1. First since we owe our highest and supreme duty, our greatest, and all our allegeance to him, from whom all power and authoritie is deriued, and flowes as from the first, and onely fountaine, and being especiall souldiers emprest in this sacred cause, we must alone expect our successe from him, who is onely the blesser of all good attempts, the King of kings, the commaunder of commaunders, and Lord of Hostes, I do strictly commaund and charge all Captaines and Officers, of what qualitie or nature

soeuer, whether commanders in the field, or in towne, or townes, forts or fortresses, to haue a care that the Almightie God bee duly and daily serued, and that they call vpon their people to heare Sermons, as that also they diligently frequent Morning and Euening praier themselves by their owne exemplar and daily life, and dutie herein, encouraging others thereunto, and that such, who shall often and wilfully absent themselues, be duly punished according to the martiall law in that case prouided. . . .

6. Euerie man and woman duly twice a day vpon the first towling of the Bell shall vpon the working daies repaire vnto the Church, to hear diuine Service vpon pain of losing his or her dayes allowance for the first omission, for the second to be whipt, and for the third to be condemned to the Gallies for six Moneths. Likewise no man or woman shall dare to violate or breake the Sabboth by any gaming, publique, or priuate abroad, or at home, but duly sanctifie and obserue the same, both himselfe and his familie, by preparing themselues at home with private prayer, that they may be the better fitted for the publique, according to the commandements of God, and the orders of our Church, as also euery man and woman shall repaire in the morning to the diuine seruice, and Sermons preached vpon the Saboth day, and in the afternoon to diuine seruice, and Catechising, vpon paine for the first fault to lose their prouision, and allowance for the whole weeke following, for the second to lose the said allowance, and also to be whipt, and for the third to suffer death. . . .

12. No manner of person whatsoeuer, shall dare to detract, slaunder, calumniate, or vtter vnseemely, and vnfitting speeches, either against his Maiesties Honourable Councell for this Colony, resident in England, or against the Committies, Assistants vnto the said Councell, or against the zealous indeauors, & intentions of the whole body of Aduenturers for this pious and Christian Plantation, or against any publique booke, or bookes, which by their mature aduise, and graue wisdomes, shall be thought fit, to be set foorth and publisht, for the aduancement of the good of this Colony, and the felicity thereof, vpon paine for the first time so offending, to bee whipt three seuerall times, and vpon his knees to acknowledge his offence and to aske forgiuenesse vpon the Saboth day in the assembly of the congregation, and for the second time so offending to be condemned to the Galley for three yeares, and for the third time so offending to be punished with death.

13. No manner of Person whatsoeuer, contrarie to the word of God (which tyes euery particular and priuate man, for conscience sake to obedience, and duty of the Magistrate, and such as shall be placed in authoritie ouer them, shall detract, slaunder, calumniate, murmur, mutenie, resist, disobey, or neglect the commaundments, either of the Lord Gouernour, and Captaine Generall, the Lieutenant Generall, the Martiall, the Councell, or any authorised Captaine, Commaunder or publike Officer, vpon paine for the first time so offending to be whipt three seuerall times, and vpon his knees to acknowledge his offence, with asking forgiuenesse vpon the Saboth day in the assembly of the congregation, and for the second time so offending to be condemned to the Gally for three yeares: and for the third time so offending to be punished with death. . . .

15. No man of what condition soeuer shall barter, trucke, or trade with Indians, except he be thereunto appointed by lawful authority, vpon paine of death.

16. No man shall rifle or dispoile, by force or violence, take away any thing from any Indian comming to trade, or otherwise, vpon paine of death. . . .

22. There shall no man or woman, Launderer or Launderesse, dare to wash any vncleane Linnen, driue bucks, or throw out the water or suds of fowle cloathes, in the open streete, within the Pallizadoes, or within forty foote of the same, nor rench, and make cleane, any kettle, pot, or pan, or such like vessell within twenty foote of the olde well, or new Pumpe: nor shall any one aforesaid, within lesse then a quarter of one mile from the Pallizadoes, dare to doe the necessities of nature, since by these vnmanly, slothfull, and loathsome immodesties, the whole Fort may bee choaked, and poisoned with ill aires, and so corrupt (as in all reason cannot but much infect the same) and this shall they take notice of, and auoide, vpon paine of whipping and further punishment, as shall be thought meete, by the censure of a martiall Court. . . .

25. Euery man shall haue an especiall and due care, to keepe his house sweete and cleane, as also so much of the streete, as lieth before his door, and especially he shall so prouide, and set his bedstead whereon he lieth, that it may stand three foote at least from the ground, as he will answere the contrarie at a martiall Court.

26. Euery tradsman in their seuerall occupation, trade and function, shall duly and daily attend his worke vpon his said trade or occupation, vpon perill for his first fault, and negligence therein, to haue his entertainment checkt for one moneth, for his second fault three moneth, for his third one yeare, and if he continue still vnfaithful and negligent therein, to be condemned to the Gally for three yeare. . . .

28. No souldier or tradesman, but shall be readie, both in the morning, & in the afternoone, vpon the beating of the Drum, to goe out vnto his worke, nor shall hee return home, or from his worke, before the Drum beate againe, and the officer appointed for that businesse, bring him of, vpon perill for the first fault to lie vpon the Guard head and heeles together all night, for the second time so faulting to be whipt, and for the third time so offending to be condemned to the Gallies for a yeare. . . .

30. He that shall conspire any thing against the person of the Lord Gouernour, and Captaine Generall, against the Lieutenant Generall, or against the Marshall, or against any publike seruice commaunded by them, for the dignitie, and advancement of the good of the Colony, shall be punished with death: and he that shall haue knowledge of any such pretended act of disloyalty or treason, and shall not reveale the same vnto his Captaine, or vnto the Gouernour of that fort or towne wherein he is, within the space of one houre, shall for the concealing of the same after that time, be not onely held an accessary, but alike culpable as the principall traitor or conspirer, and for the same likewise he shall suffer death.

31. What man or woman soeuer, shall rob any garden, publike or priuate, being set to weed the same, or willfully pluck vp therein any roote, herbe,

or flower, to spoile and wast or steale the same, or robbe any vineyard, or gather vp the grapes, or steale any eares of the corne growing, whether in the ground belonging to the same fort or towne where he dwelleth, or in any other, shall be punished with death. . . .

36. No man or woman whatsoeuer, members of this Colonie, shall sell or giue vnto any Captaine, Marriner, Master, or Sailer, &c. any commoditie of this countrey, of what quality soeuer, to be transported out of the Colonie, for his or their owne priuate vses, vpon paine of death. . . .

SELECTION

Emergence of Virginia Society

Dale's Laws solved the immediate problem of discipline and gave the colony sufficient strength to meet the Indian menace. But Virginia was a commercial enterprise, and the Virginia Company still had to solve two other basic problems: how to make the colony attractive to prospective settlers under such a harsh regime and how to make it profitable. Initially, the company tried to solve the problem of recruitment by limiting the period of service to the company and promising a grant of land at the end of it. The failure of this policy to attract sufficient settlers, however, forced the company to make still greater concessions in 1618. By its instructions to Governor George Yeardley (1587–1627) in November of that year the company made it easier for settlers to acquire land, and by the so-called Great Charter, issued at the same time, it put an end to many of the harsher features of the military regime and authorized the convocation of a representative assembly. These concessions were the beginnings of the headright system and representative government, both of which became permanent features of the English colonial system. Between 1612 and 1617 a beginning had also been made toward the solution of the second problem. John Rolfe's experiments in growing and shipping tobacco had finally provided the colony with a potential cash crop. How successful tobacco had become by 1619 is indicated by a letter of John Pory (1572–1635). Pory had only just come to the colony as secretary of state and was speaker of the first General Assembly, which met at Jamestown on July 30, 1619.

In addition to the references cited in the introduction to Selection 5, see Sigmund Diamond (ed.), The Creation of Society in the New World *(1963), and Bernard Bailyn, "Politics and Social Structure in Virginia," in James Morton Smith (ed.),* Seventeenth-century America: Essays in Colonial History *(1959), pages 90–115.*

A. INCENTIVE OF THE LAND: INSTRUCTIONS
TO GEORGE YEARDLEY (NOV. 18, 1618)*

. . . that in all . . . Cities or Burroughs the ancient Adventurers and Planters which [were] transported thither with intent to inhabit at their own costs and charges before the coming away of Sir Thomas Dale Knight and have so continued during the space of three years shall have upon a first division to be afterward by us augmented one hundred Acres of land for their personal Adventure and as much for every single share of twelve pound ten Shillings paid [for such share] allotted and set out to be held by them their heirs and assigns forever And that for all such Planters as were brought thither at the Companies Charge to inhabit there before the coming away of the said Sir Thomas Dale after the time of their Service to the Company on the common Land agreed shall be expired there be set out One hundred Acres of Land for each of their personal Adventurers to be held by them their heirs and Assigns for ever. paying for every fifty Acres the yearly free Rent of one Shilling to the said treasurer and Company and their Successors at one Entire payment on the feast day of St. Michael the archangel for ever And in regard that by the singular indusary and virtue of the said Sir Thomas Dale the former difficulties and dangers were in greatest part overcome to the great ease and security of such as have been since that time transported thither We do therefore hereby ordain that all such persons as sithence the coming away of the said Sir Thomas Dale have at their own charges been transported thither to inhabit and so continued as aforesaid there be allotted and set upon a first division fifty acres of land to them and their heirs for ever for their personal Adventure paying a free rent of one Shilling yearly in manner aforesaid And that all persons which since the going away of the said Sir Thomas Dale have been transported thither at the Companies charges or which hereafter shall be so transported be placed as tenants on the Companies lands for term of seven years occupy the same to the half part of the profits as is abovesaid We therefore will and ordain that other three thousand Acres of Land be set out in the fields and territory of Charles City and other three thousand Acres of Land in the fields and territories of Henrico And other three thousand Acres of land in the fields and territory of Kiccowtan all which to be and be called the Companies lands and to be occupied by the Companies Tenants for half profits as afore said. . . . And for the better Encouragement of all sorts of necessary and laudable trades to be set up and exercised within the said four Cities or Burroughs We do hereby ordain that if any artizans or tradesmen shall be desirous rather to follow his particular Art or trade then to be imploied in husbandry or other rural business It shall be lawful for you the said Governor and Councel to alot and set out within any of the precincts aforesaid One dwelling house with four Acres of Land adjoining and held

* These excerpts are reprinted from Susan Myra Kingsbury (ed.), *The Records of the Virginia Company of London* (4 vols., 1906–1935), vol. III, pp. 100–103.

in fee simple to every said tradsman his heirs and Assigns for ever upon condition that the said tradesman his heirs and Assigns do continue and exercise his trade in the said house paying only a free rent of four pence by the year to us the said Treasurer and Company and our Successors at the feast of St. Michael the Archangel for ever. . . .

B. ESTABLISHMENT OF REPRESENTATIVE GOVERNMENT: ORDINANCE OF 1621*

I. To all people, to whom these presents shall come, be seen, or heard, the treasurer, council, and company of adventurers and planters for the city of London for the first colony of Virginia, send greeting. Know ye, that we, the said treasurer, council, and company, taking into our careful consideration the present state of the said colony of Virginia, and intending by the divine assistance, to settle such a form of government there, as may be to the greatest benefit and comfort of the people, and whereby all injustice, grievances, and oppression may be prevented and kept off as much as possible, from the said colony, have thought fit to make our entrance, by ordering and establishing such supreme councils, as may not only be assisting to the governor for the time being, in the administration of justice, and the executing of other duties to this office belonging, but also, by their vigilant care and prudence, may provide, as well for a remedy of all inconveniences, growing from time to time, as also for advancing of increase, strength, stability, and prosperity of the said colony;

II. We therefore, the said treasurer, council, and company, by authority directed to us from his majesty under the great seal, upon mature deliberation, do hereby order and declare, that, from hence forward, there shall be two supreme councils in Virginia, for the better government of the said colony aforesaid.

III. The one of which councils, to be called the council of state, (and whose office shall chiefly be assisting, with their care, advice, and circumspection, to the said governor) shall be chosen, nominated, placed, and displaced, from time to time, by us the said treasurer, council and company, and our successors: which council of state shall consist, for the present only of . . . persons . . . here inserted: . . . Which said counsellors and council we earnestly pray and desire, and in his majesty's name strictly charge and command, that (all factions, partialities, and sinister respect laid aside) they bend their care and endeavours to assist the said governor; first and principally, in the advancement of the honour and service of God, and the enlargement of his kingdom against the heathen people; and next, in erecting of the said colony in due obedience to his majesty, and all lawful authority from his majesty's directions; and lastly, in maintaining the said people in justice and christian conversation

* This ordinance is supposedly much the same as the now-missing Great Charter of 1618, which called for the convocation of the first Virginia Assembly in 1619. These excerpts are reprinted from William Waller Hening (ed.), *The Statutes at Large* (13 vols., 1809–1823), vol. I, pp. 110–113.

amongst themselves, and in strength and ability to withstand their enemies. And this council, to be always, or for the most part, residing about or near the governor.

IV. The other council, more generally to be called by the governor, once yearly, and no oftener, but for very extraordinary and important occasions, shall consist for the present, of the said council of state, and of two burgesses out of every town, hundred, or other particular plantation, to be respectively chosen by the inhabitants: which council shall be called The General Assembly, wherein (as also in the said council of state) all matters shall be decided, determined, and ordered by the greater part of the voices then present; reserving to the governor always a negative voice. And this general assembly shall have free power, to treat, consult, and conclude, as well of all emergent occasions concerning the publick weal of the said colony and every part thereof, as also to make, ordain, and enact such general laws and orders, for the behoof of the said colony, and the good government thereof, as shall, from time to time, appear necessary or requisite;

V. Whereas in all other things, we require the said general assembly, as also the said council of state, to imitate and follow the policy of the form of government, laws, customs, and manner of trial, and other administration of justice, used in the realm of England, as near as may be even as ourselves, by his majesty's letters patent, are required.

VI. Provided, that no law or ordinance, made in the said general assembly, shall be or continue in force or validity, unless the same shall be solemnly ratified and confirmed, in a general quarter court of the said company here in England, and so ratified, be returned to them under our seal; it being our intent to afford the like measure also unto the said colony, that after the government of the said colony shall once have been well framed, and settled accordingly, which is to be done by us, as by authority derived from his majesty, and the same shall have been so by us declared, no orders of court afterwards, shall bind the said colony, unless they be ratified in like manner in the general assemblies. . . .

C. DEVELOPMENT OF A PLANTATION ECONOMY: LETTER FROM JOHN PORY (SEPT. 30, 1619)*

. . . All our riches for the present doe consiste in Tobacco, wherein one man by his owne labour hath in one yeare raised to himselfe to the value of 200*l* sterling; and another by the meanes of six servants hath cleared at one crop a thousand pound English. These be true, yet indeed rare examples, yet possible to be done by others. Our principall wealth (I should have said) consisteth in servants: But they are chardgeable to be furnished with armes, apparell and bedding and for their transportation

* These excerpts are reprinted from Lyon Gardiner Tyler (ed.), *Narratives of Early Virginia, 1606–1625* (1907), pp. 284–285.

and casual, both at sea, and for their first yeare commonly at lande also:
But if they escape, they prove very hardy, and sound able men.

Nowe that your lordship may knowe, that we are not the veriest beggers
in the worlde, our cowekeeper here of James citty on Sundays goes ac-
cowtered all in freshe flaming silke; and a wife of one that in England
had professed the black arte, not of a scholler, but of a collier of Croydon,
weares her rough bever hatt with a faire perle hatband, and a silken suite
thereto correspondent. But to leave the Populace, and to come higher; the
Governour here, who at his first coming, besides a great deale of worth
in his person, brought onely his sword with him, was at his late being in
London, together with his lady, out of his meer gettings here, able to
disburse very near three thousand pounde to furnishe himselfe for his
voiage. And once within seven yeares, I am persuaded (*absit invidia
verbo*) that the Governors place here may be as profittable as the lord
Deputies of Irland. . . .

SELECTION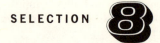

A Landed Estate and Religious Refuge

*Maryland had none of the early difficulties that beset Virginia. The first
settlers picked a site that was both healthy and distant from powerful Indian
neighbors. Its proximity to Virginia meant that they were in no danger of
starving. The easy adaptability of tobacco culture relieved them from the necessity of searching for a profitable economic staple. Maryland had its own
peculiar problems, however, deriving largely from the ambitions and convictions
of the proprietor, Cecilius Calvert (1605–1675), 2d Baron Baltimore. As indicated by his instructions to the initial settlers, Calvert, himself a Catholic,
hoped both to establish a religious refuge for members of his faith and to make
Maryland into a large and profitable family estate. Tensions developed early
between him and the settlers, a majority of whom were Protestant, over his
insistence upon maintaining his proprietary rights and the fact that he appointed only Catholics to government office. By the mid-1640s the Protestants
had become sufficiently strong to win significant concessions from Calvert. In
return, however, he forced them to consent to the famous "Toleration" Act of
1649, seeking thereby to protect the Catholic minority from persecution. Because it restricted toleration to believers in the divinity of Christ it established
only a very limited variety of toleration. Yet it probably covered all Mary-
landers at the time and is significant as one of the earliest legal guarantees of
toleration for Christians. The best treatment of the founding and early history
of Maryland is in Craven,* Southern Colonies in the Seventeenth Century.

A. OBJECTIVES AND PROCEDURES: LORD BALTIMORE'S INSTRUCTIONS TO THE FIRST SETTLERS OF MARYLAND (NOV. 15, 1633)*

1. . . . His Lordshipp requires his said Gouernor & Commissioners that in their voyage to Mary Land they be very carefull to preserue vnity & peace amongst all the passengers on Shipp-board, and that they suffer no scandall nor offence to be giuen to any of the Protestants, whereby any iust complaint may heereafter be made, by them, in Virginea or in England, and that for that end, they cause all Acts of Romane Catholique Religion to be done as priuately as may be, and that they instruct all the Romane Catholiques to be silent vpon all occasions of discourse concerning matters of Religion; and that the said Gouernor & Commissioners treate the Protestants with as much mildness and fauor as Justice will permitt. And this to be obserued at Land as well as at Sea. . . .

3. That . . . they come to an Anchor somewhere about Acomacke, so as it be not vnder the command of any fort; & to send ashoare there, to inquire if they cann find any to take with them, that cann giue them some good informatione of the Bay of Chesapeake and Pattawomeek Riuer, and that may giue them some light of a fitt place in his Lordshipp's Countrey to sett downe on; wherein their cheife care must be to make choice of a place first that is probable to be healthfull and fruitfull, next that it may be easily fortified, and thirdly that it may be convenient for trade both with the English and sauages. . . .

9. That where they intend to settle the Plantation they first make choice of a fitt place, and a competent quantity of ground for a fort within which or neere vnto it a convenient house, and a church or a chappel adiacent may be built, for the seate of his Lordshipp or his Gouernor or other Commissioners for the time being in his absence, both which his Lordshipp would haue them take care should in the first place be erected, in some proportion at least, as much as is necessary for present vse though not so compleate in euery part as in fine afterwards they may be and to send his Lordshipp a Platt of it and of the scituation, by the next oportunity, if it be done by that time, if not or but part of it neuertheless to send a Platt of what they intend to do in it. That they likewise make choise of a fitt place neere vnto it to seate a towne.

10. That they cause all the Planters to build their houses in as decent and vniforme a manner as their abilities and the place will afford, & neere adioyning one to an other, and for that purpose to cause streetes to be marked out where they intend to place the towne and to oblige euery man to buyld one by an other according to that rule and that they cause diuisions of Land to be made adioyning on the back sides of their houses and to be assigned vnto them for gardens and such vses according to the proportion of euery ones building and adventure and as the conveniency of the place will afford which his Lordshipp referreth to their discretion, but is desirous to haue a particuler account from them what they do in

---

* These excerpts are reprinted from "The Calvert Papers," *Maryland Historical Society Fund Publications,* no. 28 (1889), pp. 132–133, 138–140.

it, that his Lordshipp may be satisfied that euery man hath iustice done vnto him.

11. That as soone as conveniently they cann they cause his Lordshipp's surveyor Robert Simpson to survay out such a proportion of Land both in and about the intended towne as likewise within the Countrey adioyning as wilbe necessary to be assigned to the present aduenturers, and that they assigne euery adventurer his proportion of Land both in and about the intended towne, as alsoe within the Countrey adioyning, according to the proportion of his aduenture and the conditions of plantation propounded by his Lordshipp to the first aduenturers which his Lordshipp in his convenient time will confirme vnto them by Pattent. And heerein his Lordshipp wills his said Gouernor and Commissioners to take care that in each of the aforesaid places, that is to say in and about the first intended Towne and in the Countrey adiacent they cause in the first and most convenient places a proportion of Land to be sett out for his Lordshipp's owne proper vse and inheritance according to the number of men he sends this first yeare vpon his owne account; and as he alloweth vnto the aduenturers, before any other be assigned his part; with which (although his Lordshipp might very well make a difference of proportion between himself and the aduenturers) he will in this first colony, content himself, for the better encouragement and accomodation of the first aduenturers, vnto whom his Lordshipp conceiue himself more bound in honor and is therefore desirous to giue more satisfaction in euery thing then he intends to do vnto any that shall come heereafter. That they cause his Lordshipp's survayor likewise to drawe an exact mapp of as much of the countrey as they shall discouer together with the soundings of the riuers and Baye, and to send it to his Lordshipp.

12. That they cause all the planters to imploy their seruants in planting of sufficient quantity of corne and other prouision of victuall and that they do not suffer them to plant any other commodity whatsoeuer before that be done in a sufficient proportion which they are to obserue yearely.

13. That they cause all sorts of men in the plantation to be mustered and trained in military discispline and that there be days appoynted for that purpose either weekely or monthly according to the conueniency of other occasions; which are duly to be obserued and that they cause constant watch and ward to be kept in places necessary.

14. That they informe themselues whether there be any convenient place within his Lordshipp's precincts for the making of Salt whether there be proper earth for the making of saltpeeter and if there be in what quantity; whether there be probability of Iron oare or any other mines and that they be carefull to find out what other commodities may probably be made and that they giue his Lordshipp notice together with their opinions of them.

15. That In fine they bee very carefull to do iustice to euery man without partiality, and that they auoid any occasion of difference with those of Virginea and to haue as litle to do with them as they cann this first yeare that they conniue and suffer litle iniuryes from them rather then to engage themselues in a publique quarrell with them, which may disturbe the business much in England in the Infancy of it. . . .

B. FORMULA FOR SOCIAL STABILITY: AN ACT CONCERNING RELIGION (APR. 21, 1649)*

Forasmuch as in a well governed and Christian Common Weath matters concerning Religion and the honor of God ought in the first place to bee taken, into serious consideration and endeavoured to bee settled. Be it therefore ordered and enacted . . . That whatsoever person or persons within this Province and the Islands thereunto belonging shall from henceforth blaspheme God, that is Curse him, or deny our Saviour Jesus Christ to bee the sonne of God, or shall deny the holy Trinity the ffather sonne and holy Ghost, or the Godhead of any of the said Three persons of the Trinity or the Vnity of the Godhead, or shall use or utter any reproachfull Speeches, words or language concerning the said Holy Trinity, or any of the said three persons thereof, shalbe punished with death and confiscation or forfeiture of all his or her lands and goods to the Lord Proprietary and his heires. . . . And whereas the inforceing of the conscience in matters of Religion hath frequently fallen out to be of dangerous Consequence in those commonwealthes where it hath been practised, And for the more quiett and peaceable governement of this Province, and the better to preserve mutuall Love and amity amongst the Inhabitants thereof. Be it Therefore . . . enacted (except as in this present Act is before Declared and sett forth) that noe person or persons whatsoever within this Province, or the Islands, Ports, Harbors, Creekes, or havens thereunto belonging professing to beleive in Jesus Christ, shall from henceforth bee any waies troubled, Molested or discountenanced for or in respect of his or her religion nor in the free exercise thereof within this Province or the Islands thereunto belonging nor any way compelled to the beleife or exercise of any other Religion against his or her consent, soe as they be not unfaithfull to the Lord Proprietary, or molest or conspire against the civill Government established or to bee established in this Province vnder him or his heires. And that all & every person and persons that shall presume Contrary to this Act and the true intent and meaning thereof directly or indirectly either in person or estate willfully to wrong disturbe trouble or molest any person whatsoever within this Province professing to beleive in Jesus Christ for or in respect of his or her religion or the free exercise thereof within this Province other than is provided for in this Act that such person or persons soe offending, shalbe compelled to pay trebble damages to the party soe wronged or molested, and for every such offence shall also forfeit 20£ sterling in money or the value thereof, half thereof for the vse of the Lord Proprietary, and his heires Lords and Proprietaries of this Province, and the other half for the vse of the party soe wronged or molested as aforesaid, Or if the partie soe offending as aforesaid shall refuse or bee vnable to recompense the party soe wronged, or to satisfy such ffyne or forfeiture, then such Offender shalbe severely punished by publick whipping & imprisonment during the pleasure of the Lord Proprietary, or his Leivetenant or cheife Governor of this Province for the tyme being without baile or maineprise. . . .

* These excerpts are reprinted from William Hand Browne et al. (eds.), *Archives of Maryland* (70 vols., 1883–   ), vol. I, pp. 244, 246.

SELECTION

Society at Mid-century: John Hammond, "Leah and Rachel, or, the Two Fruitfull Sisters, Virginia and Mary-Land" (1656)

By 1660 Chesapeake society had assumed a definite character and was expanding rapidly. Tobacco was the chief staple, and free land the primary incentive to migration. Both the structure and the promise of Chesapeake society were described by John Hammond, an old resident and enthusiastic promoter of both Virginia and Maryland, in Leah *and* Rachel, *a promotional tract published in London in 1656 and reprinted in part below from Peter Force (comp.),* Tracts and Other Papers *(four volumes, 1836–1846), volume III, number 14, pages 14–16, 19–20. On Maryland at mid-century see Craven,* Southern Colonies in the Seventeenth Century, *and William A. Reavis, "The Maryland Gentry and Social Mobility, 1637–1676,"* William and Mary Quarterly, *third series, volume 14 (1957), pages 418–428.*

Those Servants that will be industrious may in their time of service gain a competent estate before their Freedomes, which is usually done by many, and they gaine esteeme and assistance that appear so industrious: There is no Master almost but will allow his Servant a parcell of clear ground to plant some Tobacco in for himself, which he may husband at those many idle times he hath allowed him and not prejudice, but rejoyce his Master to see it, which in time of Shipping he may lay out for commodities, and in Summer sell them again with advantage, and get a Sow-Pig or two, which any body almost will give him, and his Master suffer him to keep them with his own, which will be no charge to his Master, and with one years increase of them may purchase a Cow Calf or two, and by that time he is for himself; he may have Cattle, Hogs and Tobacco of his own, and come to live gallantly; but this must be gained (as I said) by Industry and affability, not by sloth nor churlish behaviour.

And whereas it is rumoured that Servants have no lodging other then on boards, or by the Fire side, it is contrary to reason to believe it: First, as we are Christians; next as people living under a law, which compels as well the Master as the Servant to perform his duty; nor can true labour be either expected or exacted without sufficient cloathing, diet, and lodging; all which both their Indentures (which most inviolably be observed) and the Justice of the Country requires.

But if any go thither, not in a condition of a Servant, but pay his or her passage, which is some six pounds: Let them not doubt but it is money well layed out (yet however, let them not fail) although they carry little else to take a Bed along with them, and then few Houses but will give them entertainment, either out of curtesie, or on reasonable tearms; and I think it better for any that goes over free, and but in a mean condition, to hire himself for reasonable wages of Tobacco and Provision, the first year, provided he happen in an honest house, and where the Mistresse is noted for a good Housewife, of which there are very many (notwithstanding the cry to the contrary) for by that means he will live free of disbursment, have something to help him the next year, and be carefully looked to in his sicknesse (if he chance to fall sick) and let him so covenant that exceptions may be made, that he work not much in the hot weather, a course we always take with our new hands (as they call them) the first year they come in.

If they are women that go after this manner, that is paying their own passages; I advise them to sojourn in a house of honest repute, for by their good carriage, they may advance themselves in marriage, by their ill, overthrow their fortunes; and although loose persons seldome live long unmarried if free; yet they match with as desolate as themselves, and never live handsomly or are ever respected. . . .

The Country is very full of sober, modest persons, both men and women, and many that truly fear God and follow that perfect rule of our blessed Saviour, to do as they would be done by; and of such a happy inclination is the Country, that many who in *England* have been lewd and idle, there in emulation or imitation (for example moves more then precept) of the industry of those they finde there, not onely grow ashamed of their former courses, but abhor to hear of them, and in small time wipe off those stains they have formerly been tainted with; yet I cannot but confesse, there are people wicked enough (as what Country is free) for we know some natures will never be reformed, but . . . if any be known, either to prophane the Lords day or his Name, be found drunk, commit whoredome, scandalize or disturb his neighbour, or give offence to the world by living suspiciously in any bad courses; there are for each of these, severe and wholsome laws and remedies made. . . .

The profit of the country is either by their labour, their stockes, or their trades.

By their labours is produced corne and Tobacco, and all other growing provisions, and this Tobacco however now low-rated, yet a good maintenance may be had out of it, (for they have nothing of necessity but cloathing to purchasse) or can this mean price of Tobacco long hold, for these reasons, First that in England it is prohibited, next that they have attained of late those sorts equall with the best Spanish, Thirdly that the sicknesse in Holland is decreasing, which hath been a great obstruction to the sail of Tobacco. . . .

Of the increase of cattle and hoggs, much advantage is made, by selling biefe, porke, and bacon, and butter &c. either to shipping, or to send to the Barbadoes, and other Islands, and he is a very poor man that hath not sometimes provision to put off.

By trading with Indians for Skine, Beaver, Furres and other commodi-

ties oftentimes good profits are raised; The Indians are in absolute subjection to the English, so that they both pay tribute to them and receive
all their severall king from them, and as one dies they repaire to the
English for a successor, so that none neede doubt it a place of securitie.

Several ways of advancement there are and imployments both for the
learned and laborer, recreation for the gentry, traffique for the adventurer,
congregations for the ministrie (and oh that God would stir, up the hearts
of more to go over, such as would teach good doctrine, and not paddle in
faction, or state matters; they could not want maintenance, they would
find an assisting, an imbracing, a conforming people.)

It is knowne (such preferment hath this Country rewarded the industrious with) that some from being wool-hoppers and of as mean and
meaner imployment in England have there grown great merchants, and
attained to the most eminent advancements the Country afforded. If men
cannot gaine (by diligence) states in those parts.) I speake not only
mine owne opinion, but divers others, and something by experience) it
will hardly be done (unlesse by meere lucke as gamsters thrive, and other
accidentals in any other part whatsoever. . . .

The First Settlements, 1584–1660:
The Puritan Experiment in New England

SELECTION

Foundations of Plymouth: William Bradford,
"History of Plymouth Plantation"

*What distinguished the New England settlements most sharply from the
plantations on the Chesapeake Bay was the predominance of Puritanism. More
than any other single factor, it was dissatisfaction with religious conditions in
England that drove the first settlers to New England and determined the shape
and orientation of the societies they established. There were, of course, several
strains of religious thought and practice in New England. One was represented
by the Separatists at Plymouth, who wanted little more than to disassociate
themselves from the Church of England and to worship together in the simplest
way possible without fear of interference from outside authorities. Coming
originally from Scrooby in Nottinghamshire, the Plymouth Separatists had fled
in 1608 first to Amsterdam and then to Leyden, in the Netherlands, to escape
possible persecution from their more orthodox neighbors. What determined
them to leave the Netherlands a decade later, the difficulties they had in
securing official permission and financial backing to migrate to America, and
their initial reaction to their new home are described by William Bradford
(1590–1657) in the following excerpts from his* History of Plymouth Plantation,
reprinted from William T. Davis, (ed.), Bradford's History of Plymouth
Plantation, 1606–1646 *(1908), pages 44–51, 63–64, 66–67, 78, 92, 95–97. Bradford
was one of the members of the Scrooby congregation who fled to the Netherlands in 1609, a chief organizer of the migration to America, and governor of
Plymouth for thirty of the first thirty-seven years of its existence. His* History,
*called by Perry Miller, the leading authority on American Puritanism, "the
pre-eminent work of art" among "all the writings by New England Puritans,"
was written between 1630 and 1650 but was not published until after Bradford's
death.*

On the Plymouth colony, see George F. Willison, Saints and Strangers:
Being the Lives of the Pilgrim Fathers & Their Families, with Their Friends &
Foes; & an Account of Their Posthumous Wanderings in Limbo, Their Final
Resurrection & Rise to Glory, & the Strange Pilgrimages of Plymouth Rock
(1945). A recent life of Bradford is Bradford Smith, Bradford of Plymouth
(1951).

Showing the Reasons and Causes of Their Remoovall

AFTER they had lived in this citie [Leyden] about some 11. or 12. years, (which is the more observable being the whole time of that famose truce between that state and the Spaniards,) and sundrie of them were taken away by death, and many others begane to be well striken in years, the grave mistris Experience haveing taught them many things, those prudent governours with sundrie of the sagest members begane both deeply to apprehend their present dangers, and wisely to foresee the future, and thinke of timly remedy. In the agitation of their thoughts, and much discours of things hear aboute, at length they began to incline to this conclusion, of remoovall to some other place. Not out of any newfangled-nes, or other such like giddie humor, by which men are oftentimes trans-ported to their great hurt and danger, but for sundrie weightie and solid reasons; some of the cheefe of which I will hear breefly touch. And first, they saw and found by experience the hardnes of the place and countrie to be such, as few in comparison would come to them, and fewer that would bide it out, and continew with them. For many that came to them, and many more that desired to be with them, could not endure that great labor and hard fare, with other inconveniences which they underwent and were contented with. . . . For many, though they desired to injoye the ordinances of God in their puritie, and the libertie of the gospell with them, yet, alass, they admitted of bondage, with danger of conscience, rather than to indure these hardships; yea, some preferred and chose the prisons in England, rather then this libertie in Holland, with these afflic-tions. But it was thought that if a better and easier place of living could be had, it would draw many, and take away these discouragments. Yea, their pastor would often say, that many of those who both wrote and preached now against them, if they were in a place wher they might have libertie and live comfortably, they would then practise as they did.

Secondly, they saw that though the people generally bore all these difficulties very cherfully, and with a resolute courage, being in the best and strength of their years, yet old age began to steale on many of them, (and their great and continuall labours, with other crosses and sorrows, hastened it before the time,) so as it was not only probably thought, but apparently seen, that within a few years more they would be in danger to scatter, by necessities pressing them, or sinke under their burdens, or both. And therefore according to the devine proverb, that a wise man seeth the plague when it cometh, and hideth him self, Pro. 22. 3., so they like skillfull and beaten souldiers were fearfull either to be intrapped or surrounded by their enimies, so as they should neither be able to fight nor flie; and therfor thought it better to dislodge betimes to some place of better advantage and less danger, if any such could be found. Thirdly; as necessitie was a taskmaster over them, so they were forced to be such, not only to their servants, but in a sorte, to their dearest children; the which as it did not a litle wound the tender harts of many a loving father and mother, so it produced likewise sundrie sad and sorowful effects. For many of their children, that were of best dispositions and gracious inclinations, haveing lernde to bear the yoake in their youth, and willing to bear parte of their parents burden, were, often times, so oppressed with their hevie labours, that though their minds were free and willing, yet their bodies bowed under the weight of the same, and became decreped in their early youth; the vigor of nature being consumed in the very budd as it were. But that which was more lamentable, and of all sorowes most heavie to be borne, was that many of their children, by these occasions, and the great licentiousness of youth in that countrie, and the manifold temptations of the place, were drawne away by evill examples into extravagante and dangerous courses, getting the raines off their neks, and departing from their parents. Some became souldiers, others tooke upon them farr viages by sea, and other some worse courses, tending to dissolutnes and the danger of their soules, to the great greefe of their parents and dishonour of God. So that they saw their posteritie would be in danger to degenerate and be corrupted.

Lastly, (and which was not least), a great hope and inward zeall they had of laying some good foundation, or at least to make some way therunto, for the propagating and advancing the gospell of the kingdom of Christ in those remote parts of the world; yea, though they should be but even as stepping-stones unto others for the performing of so great a work.

These, and some other like reasons, moved them to undertake this resolution of their removall; the which they afterward prosecuted with so great difficulties, as by the sequell will appeare.

The place they had thoughts on was some of those vast and unpeopled countries of America, which are frutfull and fitt for habitation, being devoyd of all civill inhabitants, wher ther are only salvage and brutish men, which range up and downe, litle otherwise then the wild beasts of the same. This proposition being made publike and coming to the scaning of all, it raised many variable opinions amongst men, and caused many fears and doubts amongst them selves. Some, from their reasons and hops conceived, laboured to stirr up and incourage the rest to undertake and prosecute the same; others, againe, out of their fears, objected against it, and sought to diverte from it, aledging many things, and those neither unreasonable nor unprobable; as that it was a great designe, and subjecte to many unconceivable perills and dangers; as, besids the casulties of the seas (which none can be freed from) the length of the vioage was such, as the weake bodys of women and other persons worne out with age and traville (as many of them were) could never be able to endure. And yet if they should, the miseries of the land which they should be exposed unto, would be to hard to be borne; and lickly, some or all of them togeither, to consume and utterly to ruinate them. For ther they should be liable to famine, and nakednes, and the wante, in a maner, of all things. The chang of aire, diate, and drinking of water, would infecte their bodies with sore sickneses, and greevous diseases. And also those which should escape or overcome these difficulties, should yett be in continuall danger of the salvage people, who are cruell, barbarous, and most trecherous, being most furious in their rage, and merciles wher they overcome; not being contente only to kill, and take away life, but delight to tormente men in the most bloodie manner that may be; fleaing some alive with the shells of fishes, cutting of the members and joynts of others by peesmeale, and broiling on the coles, eate the collops of their flesh in their sight whilst they live; with other cruelties horrible to be related. And surely it could not be thought but the very hearing of these things could not but move the very bowels of men to grate within them, and make the weake to quake and tremble. It was furder objected, that it would require greater summes of money to furnish such a voiage, and to fitt them with necessaries, then their consumed estats would amounte too; and yett they must as well looke to be seconded with supplies, as presently to be transported. Also many presidents of ill success, and lamentable misseries befalne others in the like designes, were easie to be found, and not forgotten to be aledged; besids their owne experience, in their former troubles and hardships in their removall into Holand, and how hard a thing it was for them to live in that strange place, though it was a neighbour countrie, and a civill and rich comone wealth.

It was answered, that all great and honourable actions are accompanied with great difficulties, and must be both enterprised and overcome with answerable courages. It was granted the dangers were great, but not desperate; the difficulties were many, but not invincible. For though their were many of them likly, yet they were not cartaine; it might be sundrie of the things feared might never befale; others by providente care and the use of good means, might in a great measure be prevented; and all of them, through the help of God, by fortitude and patience, might either be borne, or overcome. True it was, that such atempts were not to be made and undertaken without good ground and reason; not rashly or lightly as many have done for curiositie or hope of gaine, etc. But their condition was not ordinarie; their ends were good and honourable; their calling lawfull, and urgente; and therfore they might expecte the blessing of God in their proceding. Yea, though they should loose their lives in this action, yet might they have comforte in the same, and their endeavors would be honourable. They lived hear but as men in exile, and in a poore condition; and as great miseries might possibly befale them in this place, for the 12. years of truce were now out, and ther was nothing but beating of drumes, and preparing for warr, the events whereof are allway uncertaine. The Spaniard might prove as cruell as the salvages of America, and the famine and pestelence as sore hear as ther, and their libertie less to looke out for remedie. After many other perticuler things answered and aledged on both sids, it was fully concluded by the major parte, to put this designe in execution, and to prosecute it by the best means they could.

Shewing What Means They Used for Preparation to This Waightie Vioag

AND first after thir humble praiers unto God for his direction and assistance, and a generall conference held hear aboute, they consulted what perticuler place to pitch upon, and prepare for. Some (and none of the meanest) had thoughts and were ernest for Guiana, or some of those fertill places in those hott climats; others were for some parts of Virginia, wher the English had all ready made enterance, and begining. Those for Guiana aledged that the cuntrie was rich, frutfull, and blessed with a perpetuall spring, and a florishing greenes, where vigorous nature brought forth all things in abundance and plentie without any great labour or art of man. So as it must needs make the inhabitants rich, seing less provisions of clothing and other things would serve, then in more coulder and less frutfull countries must be had. As also that the Spaniards (having much more than they could possess) had not yet planted there, nor any where very near the same. But to this it was answered, that out of question the countrie was both frutfull and pleasante, and might yeeld riches and maintenance to the possessors, more easily then the other; yet, other things considered, it would not be so fitt for them. And first, that such hott countries are subject to greevous diseases, and many noysome impediments, which other more temperate places are freer from, and would not so well agree with our English bodys. Againe, if they should ther live, and doe well, the jealous Spaniard would never suffer them long, but would displante or overthrow them, as he did the French in Florida, who were seated furder from his richest countries; and the sooner because they should have none to protect them, and their owne strength would be too smale to resiste so potent an enemie, and so neare a neighbor.

On the other hand, for Virginia it was objected, that if they lived among the English which wear ther planted, or so near them as to be under their government, they should be in as great danger to be troubled and persecuted for the cause of religion, as if they lived in England, and it might be worse. And if they lived too farr of, they should neither have succour, nor defence from them.

But at length the conclusion was, to live as a distincte body by them selves, under the generall Government of Virginia; and by their freinds to sue to his majestie that he would be pleased to grant them freedome of Religion; and that this might be obtained, they wear putt in good hope by some great persons, of good ranke and qualitie, that were made their freinds. Whereupon 2. were chosen and sent in to England (at the charge of the rest) to sollicite this matter, who found the Virginia Company very desirous to have them goe thither, and willing to grante them a patent, with as ample priviliges as they had, or could grant to any, and to give them the best furderance they could. And some of the cheefe of that company doubted not to obtaine their suite of the king for liberty in Religion, and to have it confirmed under the kings broad seale, according to their desires. But it prooved a harder peece of worke then they tooke it for; for though many means were used to bring it aboute, yet it could not be effected; for ther were diverse of good worth laboured with the king to obtaine it, (amongst whom was one of his cheefe secretaries,) and some other wrought with the archbishop to give way therunto; but it proved all in vaine. Yet thus farr they prevailed, in sounding his majesties mind, that he would connive at them, and not molest them, provided they carried them selves peacably. But to allow or tolerate them by his publick authoritie, under his seale, they found it would not be. And this was all the cheefe of the Virginia companie or any other of their best freinds could doe in the case. Yet they perswaded them to goe on, for they presumed they should not be troubled. . . .

Conscerning the Agreements and Artickles between Them, and Such Marchants and Others as Adventured Moneys; with Other Things Falling out aboute Making Their Provissions

✻   ✻   ✻

It was . . . agreed on by mutuall consente and covenante, that those that went should be an absolute church of them selves, as well as those that staid; seing in such a dangrous vioage, and a removall to such a distance, it might come to pass they should (for the body of them) never meete againe in this world; yet with this proviso, that as any of the rest came over to them, or of the other returned upon occasion, they should be reputed as members without any further dismission or testimoniall. It was allso promised to those that wente first, by the body of the rest, that if the Lord gave them life, and means, and opportunitie, they would come to them as soone as they could. . . .

[The] conditions . . . are as foloweth.

1. The adventurers and planters doe agree, that every person that goeth being aged 16. years and upward, be rated at 10*li.*, and ten pounds to be accounted a single share.

2. That he that goeth in person, and furnisheth him selfe out with 10*li.* either in money or other provissions, be accounted as haveing 20*li.* in stock, and in the devission shall receive a double share.

3. The persons transported and the adventurers shall continue their joynt stock and partnership togeather, the space of 7. years, (excepte some unexpected impedimente doe cause the whole company to agree otherwise,) during which time, all profits and benifits that are gott by trade, traffick, trucking, working, fishing, or any other means of any person or persons, remaine still in the commone stock untill the division.

4. That at their comming ther, they chose out such a number of fitt persons, as may furnish their ships and boats for fishing upon the sea; imploying the rest in their severall faculties upon the land; as building houses, tilling, and planting the ground, and makeing shuch commodities as shall be most usefull for the collonie.

5. That at the end of the 7. years, the capitall and profits, viz. the houses, lands, goods and chatles, be equally devided betwixte the adventurers, and planters; which done, every man shall be free from other of them of any debt or detrimente concerning this adventure.

6. Whosoever cometh to the colonie herafter, or putteth any into the stock, shall at the ende of the 7. years be alowed proportionably to the time of his so doing.

7. He that shall carie his wife and children, or servants, shall be alowed for everie person now aged 16. years and upward, a single share in the devision, or if he provid them necessaries, a duble share, or if they be between 10. year

old and 16., then 2. of them to be reconed for a person, both in transportation and devision.

8. That such children as now goe, and are under the age of ten years, have noe other shar in the devision, but 50. acers of unmanured land.

9. That such persons as die before the 7. years be expired, their executors to have their parte or sharr at the devision, proportionably to the time of their life in the collonie.

10. That all such persons as are of this collonie, are to have their meate, drink, apparell, and all provissions out of the common stock and goods of the said collonie. . . .

I have bene the larger in these things, and so shall crave leave in some like passages following, (thoug in other things I shal labour to be more contrate,) that their children may see with what difficulties their fathers wrastled in going throug these things in their first beginnings, and how God brought them along notwithstanding all their weaknesses and infirmities. As allso that some use may be made hereof in after times by others in such like waightie imployment. . . .

Of Their Vioage, and How They Passed the Sea, and of Their Safe Arrival at Cape Codd

Being . . . arived in a good harbor and brought safe to land, they fell upon their knees and blessed the God of heaven, who had brought them over the vast and furious ocean, and delivered them from all the periles and miseries therof, againe to set their feete on the firme and stable earth, their proper elemente. . . .

But hear I cannot but stay and make a pause, and stand half amased at this poore peoples presente condition; and so I thinke will the reader too, when he well considers the same. Being thus passed the vast ocean, and a sea of troubles before in their preparation (as may be remembered by that which wente before), they had now no freinds to wellcome them, nor inns to entertaine or refresh their weatherbeaten bodys, no houses or much less townes to repaire too, to seeke for succoure. It is recorded in scripture as a mercie to the apostle and his shipwraked company, that the barbarians shewed them no smale kindnes in refreshing them, but these savage barbarians, when they mette with them (as after will appeare) were readier to fill their sids full of arrows then otherwise. And for the season it was winter, and they that know the winters of that cuntrie know them to be sharp and violent, and subjecte to cruell and feirce stormes, deangerous to travill to known places, much more to serch an unknown coast. Besids, what could they see but a hidious and desolate wildernes, full of wild beasts and willd men? and what multituds ther might be of them they knew not. Nether could they, as it were, goe up to the tope of Pisgah, to vew from this willdernes a more goodly cuntrie to feed their hops; for which way soever they turnd their eys (save upward to the heavens) they could have litle solace or content in respecte of any outward objects. For summer being done, all things stand upon them with a wetherbeaten face; and the whole countrie, full of woods and thickets, represented a wild and savage heiw. If they looked behind them, ther was the mighty ocean which they had passed, and was now as a maine barr and goulfe to seperate them from all the civill parts of the world. If it be said they had a ship to sucour them, it is trew; but what heard they daly from the marchant and company? but that with speede they should looke out a place with their shallop, wher they would be at some near distance; for the season was shuch as he would not stirr from thence till a safe harbor was discovered by them wher they would be, and he might goe without danger; and that victells consumed apace, but he must and would keepe sufficient for them selves and their returne. Yea, it was muttered by some, that if they gott not a place in time, they would turne them and their goods ashore and leave them. Let it also be considered what weake hopes of supply and succoure they left behinde them, that might bear up their minds in this sade condition and trialls they were under; and they could not but be very smale. It is true, indeed, the affections and love of their brethren at Leyden was cordiall and entire towards them, but they had litle power to help them, or them selves; and how the case stode betweene them and the marchants at their coming away, hath allready been declared. What could now sustaine them but the spirite of God and his grace? May not and ought not the children of these fathers rightly say: *Our faithers were Englishmen which came over this great ocean, and were ready to perish in this willdernes; but they cried unto the Lord, and he heard their voyce, and looked on their adversitie, etc. Let them therfore praise the Lord, because he is good, and his mercies endure for ever. Yea, let them which have been redeemed of the Lord, shew how he hath delivered them from the hand of the oppressour. When they wandered in the deserte willdernes out of the way, and found no citie to dwell in, both hungrie, and thirstie, their sowle was overwhelmed in them. Let them confess before the Lord his loving kindness, and his wonderfull works before the sons of men.*

SELECTION

The Vision of a Godly Society

Unlike the Plymouth settlers, the colonists at Massachusetts Bay were non-separating congregationalists who wanted to change the polity of the Church of England to a congregational form and to purify it in other respects without separating from it. They were bent on nothing less than discovering the "true way" in religion and establishing the "true church" in New England to serve as a model for the reformation of the Church of England at home and perhaps even for the entire Christian world. That such a work could not be undertaken in the Old World was clear to the Puritans. Sometime in early 1629 John Winthrop (1588–1649), scion of an important gentry family in Suffolk, director of the great migration to the Bay Colony in the spring of 1630, and governor of the colony for many of the rest of his remaining nineteen years, prepared and circulated in manuscript among his associates in the Massachusetts venture a paper entitled "Reasons to Be Considered for Justifieinge the . . . Plantation in New England." In this document he adduced a number of arguments for migration, but he put special stress upon what seemed to him to be deteriorating social conditions in England. That those conditions were inimical to the work and proper worship of God was also implicit in the Cambridge Agreement, a statement signed in August, 1629, by Winthrop and eleven others of the conditions under which they would move to New England. The very nature of their aspirations, the hope of contributing to "God's glory and the churches good" by finding and nurturing the true church, required them to flee the corruption of the Old World. That a strict devotion to the ordinances of God was the means by which they could avoid in the New World most of the social problems that so alarmed them in England was the message of both John Cotton (1584–1652)—later one of the foremost ministers in New England—in "God's Promise to His Plantations," a farewell sermon delivered at Southampton in the spring of 1630 to the expedition that carried Winthrop and over one thousand others to Massachusetts, and Winthrop in "A Modell of Christian Charity," a lay address that he gave aboard the Arbella during the voyage.

But the accomplishment of their divine mission, the establishment of the "citty upon a hill" envisioned by Winthrop, would require, the Puritans realized, not only a thorough and unrelenting devotion to the ways of God but also a strict adherence to a body of well-defined ideas about society, theology, and government which they brought with them from England. These ideas are succinctly summarized by Winthrop in "A Modell of Christian Charity." Among the most important of them were certain time-honored social values: cooperation and hard work by all individuals; acceptance of one's place in the social and religious order; stewardship of society by those marked out by God to be "high and eminent in power and dignitie"; and, above all, willingness to subordinate individual goals to the welfare of the community as a whole. Two separate covenants bound the inhabitants to adhere to these values and theoretically governed all social, religious, and political relationships within the colony. The first was between man and God and was the foundaton of society; the second was between the rulers and the ruled and was the basis for civil government.

The idea of the covenant was also the cornerstone of Puritan theology. The obligations between God and His chosen elect were regulated by covenant, and men entered into covenants with one another when they decided to establish a church. The covenant of the Charlestown-Boston Church, adopted by the subscribers soon after their arrival in Massachusetts, is an example of the covenant **idea in practice.** As it was elaborated by the Puritans over the next half-century, covenant theology was an important contribution to Protestant thought.

The best introductions to the study of New England Puritanism are Edmund S. Morgan, The Puritan Dilemma: The Story of John Winthrop *(1958); George Lee Haskins,* Law and Authority in Early Massachusetts: A Study in Tradition and Design *(1960); Alan Simpson,* Puritanism in Old and New England *(1955); and Perry Miller,* Errand into the Wilderness *(1956). For a deeper understanding, the works of Perry Miller—*Orthodoxy in Massachusetts, 1630–1650: A Genetic Study *(1933);* The New England Mind: The Seventeenth Century *(1939); and* The New England Mind: From Colony to Province *(1953)—and of Edmund S. Morgan—*The Puritan Family: Essays on Religious and Domestic Relations in Seventeenth-Century New England *(1944) and* Visible Saints: The History of a Puritan Idea *(1963)—are indispensable.*

A. UNDERLYING MOTIVES: JOHN WINTHROP, "REASONS TO BE CONSIDERED FOR JUSTIFIEINGE THE . . . PLANTATION IN NEW ENGLAND" (1629)*

First, It wilbe a service to the Church of great consequence to carry the Gospell into those parts of the world, to help on the cominge in of fulnesse of the Gentiles and to rayse a Bulworke against the kingdome of Antichrist, which the Jesuites labour to rear up in those parts.

2. All other Churches of Europe are brought to desolation and our sinnes for which the lord beginns already to frowne uppon us, doe threaten us fearfully, & who knowes but that god hath provided this place to be a refuge for many whom he meanes to save out of the generall callamitie, and seeinge the Church hath no place lefte to flie into but the wildernesse what better worke cann there be, then to goe before & provide Tabernacles, and food for her, against she cometh thither.

3. This land growes weary of her Inhabitants, soe as man whoe is ye most pretious of all creatures is heer more vile & base then the Earth we Tread uppon, & of lesse price among us, then a horse or a sheep, masters are forced by authoritie to entertaine servants, parents to maintaine their owne children, All Townes complaine of the burthen of their poore though we have taken up many unnecessary, yea unlawful trades to mainteine them. And we use the authoritie of the law to hinder the increase of people as urging the execution of the State against Cottages & Inmates & thus it is come to passe that children, servants & neighbors (especially if the be poore) are counted the greatest burthen which if things were right it would be the cheifest earthly blessinge.

4. The whole earth is the lords Garden & he hath given it to the sonnes of men, with a generall condition, Gen: 1. 28. Increase & multiply, replenish the earth & subdue it, which was againe renewed to Noah, the end is Double morall & naturall that man might injoy the fruites of the earth & god might have his due glory from the creature, why then should we stand hear striveing for places of habitation, (many men spending as

* Reprinted in full from "Winthrop's Conclusions for the Plantation in New England," *Old South Leaflets,* no. 50 (n.d.), pp. 4–6.

much labor & cost to recover or keep somtymes a Acre or two of land as would procure them many hundred as good or better in an other country) and in ye mean tyme suffer a whole Continent, as fruitfull & convenient for the use of man to lie waste without any improvement.

5. We are growne to that height of intemperance in all excesse of riot, as noe mans estate almost will suffice to keep saile with his equals, & he who failes herein must live in scorne & contempt, hence it comes that all arts & trades are carried in that deceiptfull & unrighteous course, as it is almost impossible for a good & upright man to maintaine his charge and live comfortably in any of them.

6. The fountaines of learning & religion are soe corrupted (as beside the unsupportable charge of the education) most Children (even the best witts & fairest hopes) are perverted corrupted and utterly overthrowen, by the multitude of evill examples and the licentious government of those Seminaries, where men straine at Gnats, & swallow Camells, use all severity for maintenance of cappes, & other accomplements but suffer all Ruffian-like fashion & disorder in manners to passe uncontrowled

7. What cann be a better worke & more honorable & worthy a Christian then to help rayse & support a particular church while it is in the infancy, & to Joyne his forces with such a company of faithfull people as by a tymely assistance may growe stronge and prosper, and for want of it may be put to great hazard, if not wholely ruined.

8. If any such whoe are knowen to be godly & live in wealth and prosperity here shall forsake all this to joyne themselves to this church & to runn a hazard with them of a hard & meane condition it wilbe an example of great use both for removeing the scandall of worldly & sinister respects which is cast uppon the adventurers to give more life to the faith of Gods people in their prayers for the plantation & to encourage other to joyne the more willingly in it.

9. It appeares to be a worke of god, for the good of his church in that he hath disposed the harts of soe many of his wise & faithfull servants (both ministers & others) not only to approve of the enterprise but to interest themselves in it, som in their persons & estates, others by their serious advise & helpe otherwise: And all by their prayers for the welfare of it, Amos 3. The lord revealeth his Secretts to his servants the Prophets, it is likely he hath some great worke in hand which he hath revealed to his prophets among us, whom he hath stirred upp to encourage his servants to this plantation for he doth not use to seduce his people by his owne Prophets, but committs that office to the ministery of false prophets and lyinge spirits. . . .

B. THE DECISION TO EMIGRATE: THE CAMBRIDGE AGREEMENT (AUG. 26, 1629)*

UPON due consideration of the state of the plantation now in hand for

* Reprinted in full from Thomas Hutchinson (ed.), *Collection of Original Papers Relative to the History of the Colony of Massachusetts-Bay* (1769), pp. 25–26.

New England, wherein wee (whose names are hereunto subscribed) have engaged ourselves: and having weighed the greatnes of the worke in regard of the consequence, God's glory and the churches good: As also in regard of the difficultyes and discouragements which in all probabilityes must be forecast upon the execution of this business: Considering withall that this whole adventure growes upon the joynt confidence we have in each others fidelity and resolution herein, so as no man of us would have adventured it without assurance of the rest: Now, for the better encouragement of ourselves and others that shall joyne with us in this action, and to the end that every man may without scruple dispose of his estate and afayres as may best fitt his preparation for this voyage, it is fully and faithfully agreed amongst us, and every of us doth hereby freely and sincerely promise and bind himselfe in the word of a christian and in the presence of God who is the searcher of all hearts, that we will so really endeavour the execution of this worke, as by God's assistance we will be ready in our persons, and with such of our severall familyes as are to go with us, and such provision as we are able conveniently to furnish ourselves withall, to embarke for the said plantation by the first of March next, at such port or ports of this land as shall be agreed upon by the Companie, to the end to passe the seas (under God's protection) to inhabite and continue in New England. Provided always, that before the last of September next the whole government together with the patent for the said plantation be first by an order of court legally transferred and established to remain with us and others which shall inhabite upon the said plantation. And provided also that if any shall be hindered by such just and inevitable lett or other cause to be allowed by 3 parts of foure of these whose names are hereunto subscribed, then such persons for such tymes and during such letts to be discharged of this bond. And we do further promise every one for himselfe; that shall fayle to be ready through his own default by the day appointed, to pay for every day's default the sum of 3*l.* to the use of the rest of the Companie who shall be ready by the same day and time.

This was done by order of court the 29th of August, 1629.

RICHARD SALTONSTALL	JOHN WINTHROP	ISAACK JOHNSON
THO: DUDLEY	WILL: PINCHON	JOHN HUMFREY
WILLIAM VASSALL	KELLAM BROWNE	THO: SHARP
NICKO: WEST	WILLIAM COLBRON.	INCREASE NOWELL

C. THE DIVINE MISSION: JOHN COTTON, "GOD'S PROMISE TO HIS PLANTATIONS" (1630)*

Moreover I will appoint a place for my people Israell, and I will plant them, that they may dwell in a place of their owne, and move no more.†

. . . Exhort all that are planted at home, or intend to plant abroad, to

---

* These excerpts are reprinted from *Old South Leaflets*, no. 53 (n.d.), pp. 4, 13–15.

† 2 Sam. 7. 10.

looke well to your plantation, as you desire that the sonnes of wickedness may not afflict you at home, nor enemies abroad, looke that you be right planted, and then you need not to feare, you are safe enough: God hath spoken it, I will plant them, and they shall not be moved, neither shall the sonnes of wickedness afflict them any more.

Quest. What course would you have us take?

Answ. Have speciall care that you ever have the Ordinances planted amongst you, or else never looke for security. As soone as Gods Ordinances cease, your security ceaseth likewise; but if God plant his Ordinances among you, feare not, he will maintaine them. . . .

Secondly, have a care to be implanted into the Ordinances, that the word may be ingrafted into you, and you into it: If you take rooting in the ordinances, grow up thereby, bring forth much fruite, continue and abide therein, then you are vineyard of red wine, and the Lord will keepe you, *Isay* 27. 2. 3. that no sonnes of violence shall destroy you. Looke into all the stories whether divine or humane, and you shall never finde that God ever rooted out a people that had the Ordinances planted amongst them, and themselves planted into the Ordinances: never did God suffer such plants to be plucked up; on all their glory shall be a defence.

Thirdly, be not unmindfull of our *Ierusalem* at home, whether you leave us, or stay at home with us. *Oh pray for the peace of Ierusalem, they shall prosper that love her. Psal.* 122. 6. *They shall all be confounded and turned backe that hate Sion, Psal.* 129. 5. As God continueth his presence with us, (blessed be his name) so be ye present in spirit with us, though absent in body: Forget not the wombe that bare you and the brest that gave you sucke. Even ducklings hatched under an henne, though they take the water, yet will still have recourse to the wing that hatched them: how much more should chickens of the same feather, and yolke? In the amity and unity of brethren, the Lord hath not onely promised, but commanded a blessing, even life forevermore: *Psal.* 133. 1, 2.

Fourthly, goe forth, every man that goeth, with a publick spirit, looking not on your owne things onely, but also on the things of others: *Phil.* 2. 4. This care of universall helpfullnesse was the prosperity of the first Plantation of the Primitive Church, *Acts* 4. 32.

Fifthly, have a tender care that you looke well to the plants that spring from you, that is, to your children, that they doe not degenerate as the Israelites did; after which they were vexed with afflictions on every hand. How came this to passe? *Ier.* 2. 21. *I planted them a noble Vine, holy, a right seede, how then art thou degenerate into a strange Vine before mee?* Your Ancestours were of a noble divine spirit, but if they suffer their children to degenerate, to take loose courses, then God will surely plucke you up: Otherwise if men have a care to propagate the Ordinances and Religion to their children after them, God will plant them and not roote them up. For want of this, the seede of the repenting *Ninivites* was rooted out.

Sixthly, and lastly, offend not the poore Natives, but as you partake in their land, so make them partakers of your precious faith: as you reape their temporalls, so feede them with your spirituals: winne them to the love of Christ, for whom Christ died. They never yet refused the Gospell, and therefore more hope they will now receive it. Who knoweth whether God have reared this whole Plantation for such an end:

. . . Secondly, for consolation to them that are planted by God in any place, that finde rooting and establishing from God, this is a cause of much encouragement unto you, that what hee hath planted he will maintaine, every plantation his right hand hath not planted shalbe rooted up, but his owne plantation shall prosper, & flourish. When he promiseth peace and safety, what enemies shalstbe able to make the promise of God of none effect? Neglect not walls, and bulwarkes, and fortifications for your owne defence; but

ever let the name of the Lord be your strong
Tower; and the word of his Promise the
Rocke of your refuge. His word
that made heaven and earth
will not faile, till hea-
ven and earth be
no more.

D. OBJECTIVES AND IDEALS: JOHN WINTHROP, "A MODELL OF CHRISTIAN CHARITY" (1630)*

A Modell Hereof

GOD ALMIGHTY in his most holy and wise providence, hath soe disposed of the condition of mankind, as in all times some must be rich, some poore, some high and eminent in power and dignite; others mean and in submission.

The Reason Hereof

1. Reas. First to hold conformity with the rest of his world, being delighted to show forth the glory of his wisdom in the variety and difference of the creatures, and the glory of his power in ordering all these differences for the preservation and good of the whole; and the glory of his greatness, that as it is the glory of princes to have many officers, soe this great king will haue many stewards, counting himself more honoured in dispensing his gifts to man by man, than if he did it by his owne immediate hands.

2. Reas. Secondly that he might haue the more occasion to manifest the work of his Spirit: first upon the wicked in moderating and restraining them: soe that the riche and mighty should not eate upp the poore nor the poore and dispised rise upp against and shake off theire yoake. 2ly

* These excerpts are reprinted from *Collections of the Massachusetts Historical Society,* 3d ser., vol. 7 (1838), pp. 33–34, 44–48.

In the regenerate, in exerciseing his graces in them, as in the grate ones, theire love, mercy, gentleness, temperance &c., in the poore and inferior sorte, theire faithe, patience, obedience &c.

3. Reas. Thirdly, that every man might have need of others, and from hence they might be all knitt more nearly together in the Bonds of brotherly affection. From hence it appears plainly that noe man is made more honourable than another or more wealthy &c., out of any particular and singular respect to himselfe, but for the glory of his creator and the common good of the creature, man. . . .

Herein are 4 things to be propounded; *first* the persons, 2ly the worke, 3ly the end, 4thly the meanes. 1. For *the persons.* Wee are a company professing ourselves fellow members of Christ, in which respect, onely though wee were absent from each other many miles, and had our imployments as farre distant, yet wee ought to account ourselves knitt together by this bond of loue, and, live in the exercise of it if wee would have comforte of our being in Christ. . . . 2nly for the *work* wee have in hand. It is by a mutuall consent, through a speciall overvaluing providence and a more than an ordinary approbation of the Churches of Christ, to seeke out a place of cohabitation and Consorteshipp under a due forme of Government both ciuill and ecclesiasticall. In such cases as this, the care of the publique must oversway all private respects, by which, not only conscience, but meare civill pollicy, dothe binde us. For it is a true rule that particular Estates cannot subsist in the ruin of the publique. 3ly The *end* is to improve our lives to doe more service to the Lord; the comforte and encrease of the body of Christe, whereof we are members; that ourselves and posterity may be the better preserved from the common corruptions of this evill world, to serve the Lord and worke out our Salvation under the power and purity of his holy ordinances. 4thly for the *meanes* whereby this must be effected. They are twofold, a conformity with the worke and end wee aime at. These wee see are extraordinary, therefore wee must not content ourselves with usuall ordinary meanes. Whatsoever wee did, or ought to have done, when wee liued in England, the same must wee doe, and more allsoe, where wee goe. That which the most in theire churches mainetaine as truthe in profession onely, wee must bring into familiar and constant practise; as in this duty of loue, wee must loue brotherly without dissimulation, wee must loue one another with a pure hearte fervently. Wee must beare one anothers burthens. We must not looke onely on our owne things, but alsoe on the things of our brethren. Neither must wee thinke that the Lord will beare with such faileings at our hands as he dothe from those among whome wee have lived; and that for these 3 Reasons; 1. In regard of the more neare bond of mariage between him and us, wherein hee hath taken us to be his, after a most strickt and peculiar manner, which will make them the more jealous of our loue and obedience. Soe he tells the people of Israell, *you onely have I knowne of all the families of the Earthe, therefore will I punish you for your Transgressions.* 2ly, because *the Lord will be sanctified in them that come neare him.* We know that there were many that corrupted the service of the Lord; some setting upp altars before his owne; others offering both strange fire and strange sacrifices allsoe; yet there came noe fire from heaven, or other sudden judgement upon them, as did upon Nadab and Abihu, whoe yet wee may think did not sinne presumptuously. 3ly When God gives a speciall commission he lookes to have it strictly observed in every article, When he gave Saule a commiss:on to destroy Amaleck, Hee indented with him upon certain articles, and because hee failed in one of the least, and that upon a faire pretense, it lost him the kingdom, which should have beene his reward, if hee had observed his commission. Thus stands the cause between God and us. We are entered into Covenant with Him for this worke. Wee haue taken out a commission. The Lord hath given us leave to drawe our own articles. Wee haue professed to enterprise these and those accounts, upon these and those ends. Wee have hereupon besought Him of favour and blessing. Now if the Lord shall please to heare us, and bring us in peace to the place we desire, then hath hee ratified this covenant and sealed our Commission, and will expect a strict performance of the articles contained in it; but if wee shall neglect the observation of these articles which are the ends wee have propounded, and, dissembling with our God, shall fall to embrace this present world and prosecute our carnall intentions seeking greate things for ourselves and our posterity, the Lord will surely breake out in wrathe against us; be revenged of such a [sinful] people and make us knowe the price of the breache of such a covenant.

Now the onely way to avoyde this shipwracke, and to provide for our posterity, is to followe the counsell of Micah, *to do justly, to love mercy, to walk humbly with our God.* For this end, wee must be knitt together, in this worke, as one man. Wee must entertaine each other in brotherly affection. Wee must be willing to abridge ourselves of our superfluities, for the supply of other's necessities. Wee must uphold a familiar commerce together in all meekeness, gentlenes, patience and liberality. Wee must delight in eache other; make other's conditions our oune; rejoice together, mourne together, labour and suffer together, allwayes haueving before our eyes and our commission and community in the worke, as members of the same body. Soe shall wee *keepe the unitie of the spirit in the bond of peace.* The Lord will be our God, and delight to dwell among us, as his oune people, and will command a blessing upon us in all our wayes. Soe that wee shall see much more of his wisdome, power, goodness and truthe, than formerly wee haue been acquainted with. Wee shall finde that the God of Israell is among us, when ten of us shall be able to resist a thousand of our enemies; when hee shall make us a prayse and glory that men shall say of succeeding plantations, "the Lord make it likely that of *New England.*" For wee must consider that wee shall be as a citty upon a hill. The eies of all people are uppon us. Soe that if wee shall deale falsely with our God in this worke wee haue undertaken, and soe cause him to withdrawe his present help from us, wee shall be made a story and a by-word through the world. Wee shall open the mouthes of enemies to speake evill of the wayes of God, and all professors for God's sake. Wee shall shame the faces of many of God's worthy servants, and cause theire prayers to be turned into curses upon us till wee be consumed out of the good land whither wee are a goeing. . . .

Therefore lett us choose life
that wee, and our seede
may liue, by obeyeing His
voyce and cleaveing to Him,
for Hee is our life and
our prosperity.

E. THE CONTRACTUAL BASIS OF THE CHURCH: COVENANT OF THE CHARLESTOWN- BOSTON CHURCH (JULY 30, 1630)*

In the Name of our Lord Jesus Christ, & in Obedience to His holy will & Divine Ordinaunce.

Wee whose names are herevnder written, being by His most wise, & good Providence brought together into this part of America in the Bay of Masachusetts, & desirous to vnite ourselves into one Congregation, or Church, vnder the Lord Jesus Christ our Head, in such sort as becometh all those whom He hath Redeemed, & Sanctifyed to Himselfe, do hereby solemnly, & religiously (as in His most holy Proesence) Promisse, & bind ourselves, to walke in all our wayes according to the Rule of the Gospell, & in all sincere Conformity to His holy Ordinaunces, & in mutuall love, & respect each to other, so neere as God shall give vs grace.

SELECTION

Theological Foundations

Most Puritan religious ideas were derivative. They drew upon the entire body of Western European Protestant beliefs and in particular upon the writings of such influential Puritan divines as William Perkins (1558–1602) and William Ames (1576–1633). Perkins was a fellow at Christ's College, Cambridge, and lecturer at Great St. Andrews. He was an effective preacher, and his reputation as a theologian was second only to that of John Calvin or Richard Hooker during the early seventeenth century. Greatly influenced by Perkins, Ames was also a fellow at Christ's College and later, after his suspension from that post, holder of a chair and rector at Francker in the Netherlands. The nature of such important Puritan doctrines as original sin, predestination, and salvation

* Reprinted in full from Arthur B. Ellis, *History of the First Church in Boston, 1630–1880* (1881), p. 3.

through grace can be seen most clearly in the works of William Ames. The Puritan ideal of learned and saintly ministers whose task was to explain the Scriptures and provide a model of conduct for their flocks was perhaps best stated by Perkins. A comprehensive study of the thought of English Puritans is William Haller, The Rise of Puritanism: or, the Way to the New Jerusalem as Set Forth in Pulpit and Press from Thomas Cartwright to John Lilburne and John Milton, 1570–1643 *(1938).*

A. THE MARROW OF PURITAN DIVINITY: WILLIAM AMES, ''SIN, SANCTIFICATION, AND PREDESTINATION''*

Of the State of Sinne

1. The state of man since the fall of *Adam* is twofold. A state of sinne, and a state of grace *Acts* 26.18. I *John* 3.10.14.

2. The state of sinne consists in the privation of spirituall life, and happinesse. From this estate therefore we are to fly, as from death and the greatest evill: Concerning this state of sin the first question is, how a man may discerne, whither he do still continue in it?

3. *Ans.* The signes, or arguments, whereby this state may certainly be discern'd, are in generall, all those which are opposite to a state of grace, and spirituall life. For if a man be not in the one state, he must necessarily be in the other.

4. The first signe is a grosse ignorance of those things, which belong to spirituall life, *Ep.* 4.18. for hereby men are strangers to the life of God. The reason is because it is impossible that any man should please God without faith, *Heb.* II.6. And for Faith it is impossible to be had without the knowledge of the will of God, which comes by the preaching and hearing of the Word. *Rom.* 10.14.

5. The second signe, is a perverse disposition of will, wherby it is in subjection to the rule, and dominion of sin, *Rom.* 6.12. The reason is because those who do yeild themselves servants to obey sin, are in a state of slavery to sin, unto death *Rom.* 6:16.

6. Now the signes of raiging sinne, are first if a man do not seriously, and in good earnest, make opposition against the lusts of sinne, but rather yeild up himselfe unto them. *Rom.* 6.13. Secondly, If in delibreate counsell either profit, or pleasure be preferred by him, and prevaile more with him, then either honesty and piety, *Phil.* 3.19. Thirdly, if the committing of sinne stir him up rather to pleasure, then griefe, *Pro.* 2.14. Fourthly, if he take delight in the company of the wicked, *Ps.* 50.18.2 *Cor.* 6.14.

7. The third signe, whereby it may be discerned whether a man be in the state of sinne, is the disposition of will, whereby a man opposeth himselfe, to the will of God, *Rom.* 8.7.

* These excerpts are reprinted from *Conscience with the Power and Cases Thereof,* bk. 2, pp. 4–5, 25–27; and "The Marrow of Sacred Divinity," in *The Works of William Ames (1643),* pp. 58–59, 103–109.

8. The signes of this perverse disposition are, I. To reject the knowledge of Gods wayes, *Iob.* 21.14, 15.16. 2. To hate correction, and instruction, *Psal.* 50.17. 3. To contemne the threatnings, and judgments of God, *Psalme* 36.1.2. *Deut.* 29.19.

9. The fourth signe, is perversnesse of the affections wherby men, turne away from God, and wholy cleave, and adhere, to worldly things, I *John.* 2.15.

10. The aversnesse of a man from God, is wont to be seene, 1. By his alination from the Word of God, especially when it is preacht to him powerfully 2 *Tim.* 4.3.4. 2. By a neglect of prayer, and other parts of Gods worship, *Psal.* 14.3.4. Psa. 79.6. *Ier.* 10.25. 3. By an alienation from the servants of God, *Pro.* 29.27. I *John* 3.10.

11. The signes of a man cleaving to and as it wer drownd in the things of this world are, 1. If he imploy his chiefest care, and diligence about these things *Mat.* 6.25.31.32. The reason is given *Verse* 21. & 24. for *where your treasure is, there will your heart be also.* 2. If he be ready rather to forsake God and his righteousnesse then these worldly things. *Mat.* 37.38. 3. If he do in his heart judge those men to be happy which have an abundance of these worldly goods. *Pro.* 11.28. & 18.11.

12. The fifth signe is the corruption of a mans life; or of the works of life *Rom.* 8.13. This corruption of life doth not consist in those sins which even the godly sometimes through infirmity fall into, but in a continued course, and tenour of, sinning. It is called in Scriptures *the way of sinne, Psal.* 1.1. *A working of iniquity,* Mat. 7.23. *A walking in sinne, Psal,* 1.1. Pro. 1.15. *A walking after sinne,* Jer. 9.14. And a *custome in sinne,* Jer. 13.23. These works of the flesh are manifest by themselves, *Gal.* 5.19.

13. The sixth and the most desperate signe is, obstinacy in evill, whereby a man shuts and stops up the way to all amendment, *Esay.* 6.9, 10, *Ier.* 6.10.

Of Sanctification

Concerning Sanctification the first question is, what a man ought to doe that he may be sanctified?

1. *Ans.* He ought, 1. wholy to submit himselfe to the word of God. For the word of God is that truth which sanctifies us. *Ioh* 17.17. *Ier.* 31.33. And it is effectuall to worke sanctification, 1. Because of that utter opposition which it hath against sinne, by reason whereof it repells sinne out of the heart, where it is seated, 2. Because it is the powerful instrument of God to regenerate men, I. *Pet.* 1.23.

2. He ought 2. By Faith to apply Christ unto himselfe, as in Sanctification, I *Cor.* 1.30. Hee ought therefore, 1. To suck as it were holinesse out of Christ, that is, Considering that Christ is the Fountaine of all spirituall life and Sanctifying grace, *Ioh.* 1.16 *Col.* 1.19. & 2.9. He ought to rely & put his confidence in Christ for the obtaining of Sanctification, and to draw it ought of that Fountaine, *Esa.* 12.3. He ought, 2. To provoke himselfe unto it by the meditation of Christ, that is, seriously weighing and

considering the blessings of God in Christ, he ought to stir up himselfe to such an endeavor after Sanctification as becometh such benefits.

3. Now because there are two parts of our Sanctification, namely *mortification,* whereby sinne or the old man is put off, and *vivification,* whereby grace or the new man is put on, *Eph.* 4.22.24. *Col.* 3.8.10. Therefore there are two parts of the application of it for Sanctification, the first is the application of his death, the second of his Resurrection and life, *Rom.* 6.

4. The application of the death of Christ to the mortifying of sinne, is when Faith doth effectually collect this mortification of sin, from the death of Christ, Rom. 6. 11.

5. By this application sin is said to bee crucified. *Romans* 6.6 *Gal.* 5.24. To be killed, *Romans* 6.2. And to be buried, *Rom.* 6.4.

6. The Nailes whereby in this application sinne is fastned to the Crosse, are the very same with those, whereby Christ was fastned to the Crosse. For there is nothing more effectuall, then if one would consider seriously, 1. The nature and desert of his sinnes. For he which seriously considers that his sins doe deserve, and will procure his death, and destruction, he cannot but seeke by all meanes to prevent it, by the mortification of sinne; for either sinne, or the sinner must needs die, *Rom.* 8.13. 2. The love and mercy of God the Father toward him a sinner, in sending Christ to take away his sin. For the love of God will constraine us to seeke that for our selves, which God so earnestly sought for us, I *John* 4.11. 3. The love of Jesus Christ in undergoing, and fulfilling all things that were required for the taking away of our sinnes. For this grace and love of Christ, if it worke but upon us as it ought, will constraine us to set about this worke, 2 *Cor.* 5. 14,15. Those were the very Nailes whereby Christ was fastned to the Crosse, and not those materiall ones, which his murtherers did use for this purpose.

7. The application of the resurrection and life of Christ unto vivification, is when Faith doth effectually collect this life of grace, from the resurrection and life of Christ. *Rom.* 6.11. Now it is effectually collected, by a meditation of the efficient cause, and end, the fruits of the resurrection of Christ, *Col.* 3.1. The meditation of the efficient cause affordeth this argument; If the said spirit which raised up Christ from the dead, dwell in me, it will also raise up my soule from the death of sinne, to the life of grace, *Rom.* 8.11. The meditation of the end, this; As Christ was raised up, that sinne might have no more dominion over him, but that he might for ever live to God, so also must we, *Rom.* 6.9.10. The meditation of the fruits yeilds this argument: As Christ being raised up sitteth at the right Hand of his Father in Heaven, so ought we also to live as Citizens of Heaven, *Phil.* 3.20.

8. He ought, 3. by a lively Faith, not onely to apprehend the generall promises of salvation, but those particular ones also, which doe in a singular manner pertaine to sanctification *Ex.* 30.24.

9. He ought, 4. To yeeld up himselfe wholly to the holy Ghost, to be acted and led by him in all things. *Ro.* 8.13.14.

10. *Ans.* If he consider, I. That without holinesse no man shall see God. *Heb.* 12.14. *Mat.* 5.20. 2 That holinesse is the Image of God, and that

perfection, wherein we were created at the beginning, *Eph.* 4.24. 3 That holinesse is the end of our election, redemption and vocation, *Eph.* 1.4. I *Tim.* 4.7. *Tit.* 2.14. I *Cor.* 1.2. 4 That it is not the least part of glory and eternall blisse. *Eph.* 5.27. 5 That there can be no true Faith or justification, or adoption without sanctification, *Iac.* 2.26. 2 *Pet.* 1.10. I *Cor.* 6.11.

The third Question, what are the signes of true sanctification.

Ans. 1. A reformation of all the powers, and faculties of the whole man, I *Thess.* 5.23. 2 A respect to all the Commandments of God, *Psal.* 11.6. *James* 2.10. 3 A constant care to avoid all sinne, *Pro.* 28.14. 4 A walking before God, *Gen.* 17.1. *Acts* 24.16. I *Cor.* 10.31. *Col.* 3.23. 5 A combat betwixt the flesh and the spirit.

Of Originall Sinne

1. The *Sinne* that followed upon the first Fall is either Originall, or Actuall.

2. Originall *Sinne*, is an habituall exorbitancy, of the whole nature of man, or it is a deviation from the Law of God.

3. Because it is the corruption of the whole man: hence it is called in the holy Scriptures. *The old man. Rom.* 6.6. *Eph.* 4.22 *Col.* 3.9. The body of *Sinne. Rom.* 6.7.24. A Law of the members. *Rom.* 7.23. And the members themselves. *Col.* 3.5. Flesh. *John* 3.6. *Rom.* 7.5 18.25.

4. Hence also it is that in Scripture, a *homogeneall* corruption is attributed not only generally to the whole man but also to every part of it: as to the understanding, *Gen.* 6.5. The imagination and thoughts only evill. *Rom.* 8.5, 6.7. They favour the things of the flesh. To the conscience. *Tit.* 1.15. Their mind and conscience is defiled. To the will, *Gen.* 8.21. The imagination of the heart of man is evill from his childhood. To the affections of every kind. *Rom.* 1.24. To un cleannesse in the lusts of their hearts. Lastly, to the body and all the members of it. *Rom.* 6.19. Your members servants to un cleannesse, and iniquity to commit iniquity.

5. This *Sinne* is said to be an exorbitancy, or deviation in man, because it is in man an habituall privation of that due conformity to the Law imposed on man by God, wherein he ought to walk as in his way.

6. Hence it is that that originall depravation is called in the Scriptures *Sinne* or that *Sinne*, by a certaine special appropriation. *Rom.* 6.12.7.17. . . . *Rom.* 7.8.20. The Law of *Sinne.* 7.23. *Sinne* dwelling in us, inhering, adhering and compassing us about. *Rom.* 7.17.20.7.21. *Heb.* 12.1.

7. This disorder in man, hath as it were two parts. One formall, and the other as it were materiall, *Ier.* 2.13. *My people have done two evills: they have forsaken me, etc.* That they might dig to themselves Cisternes. The description of actuall *Sin* doth containe the picture of originall, as the daughter doth containe the picture of the mother.

8. The formall part is an aversion from good. *Rom.* 3.12. There is none that doth good, no not one.

9. The materiall part is a turning and inclining to evill. *Rom.* 7.23. The Law of *Sin*.

10. By reason of this originall depravation, it commeth to passe, that although the will of man be free in the state of *Sinne*, at touching all acts which it doth exercise, yet it is captive and servile, as touching the manner of doing, because it is deprived of that power whereby it should will well, and that inclination is as it were a forme whereby it comes to passe that it willeth amisse, even when that thing is good about which it is exercised in willing. *Rom.* 3.12.7.14. 2 *Cor.* 3.5. *John* 8.34.2. *Pet.* 2.19. *Rom.* 6.16.

Of Predestination

1. Because this application of redemption is made to some certaine men, and not to all, so that it sheweth a manifest difference betweene men, in respect of the dispensation of grace; hence it doth make the predestination of God concerning men appeare to us in the first place.

2. Predestination indeed was from eternity, *Eph.* 1.4. He hath chosen us before the foundations of the World were laid 2. *Tim.* 1.9. Which grace was given us before all ages. And it did also worke from the beginning of the workes of God: but it makes no inward difference in the Predestinate themselves before the actuall dispensation of this application *Eph.* 2.3. And we were by nature the children of wrath as well as others. I *Cor.* 6.11. Thus yee were indeed. For predestination before the application of grace doth put nothing in the persons Predestinated, but it doth lie hid only in them that doth predestinate.

3. This Predestination is the decree of God of manifesting his speciall glory in the eternall condition of men. Willing to shew his .wrath and to make his power knowne he suffered with much long suffering the vessels of wrath, prepared to destruction. And to make knowne the riches of his glory towards the vessels of mercy which he hath prepared unto glory. I *Thess* 5.9. God hath not appointed us to wrath, but to obtaine mercy.

4. It is called destination: because it is a certaine determination of the order of meanes unto the end. But because God had determined this order with himselfe, before any actuall existence of things, therefore it is not simply called destination, but predestination.

5. It is called a decree: because it containes a definite sentence to be executed by certaine counsell. In the same sence also it is called a purpose, and counsell, because it propounds an end to be attained unto, as it were with an advised deliberation.

6. Hence predestination hath greatest wisdome, freedome, firmenesse, and immutability joyned with it: because these are found in all the decrees of God.

7. Therefore the reason of Predestination is unmoveable, and indissoluble, 2 *Tim.* 2.19. The foundation of God standeth sure having this seale. The Lord knoweth who are his. And under that respect the number of the predestinated (not only the formall number, or number numbering (as they speake) that is, how many men at length shall be saved, and how many not: but also the materiall number or number numbred, that is, who those severall men are) is certaine with God, not only by certainty of fore-

knowledge, but also by certainty of order of meanes. *Luc.* 10.20 Rejoyce
that your names are written in the Heavens.

8. For Predestination doth not necessarily presuppose either its limit,
or object as existing, but it maketh it to exist: so that by force of predestination it is ordered, that is should be I *Pet.* 1.20. *Of Christ fore-
knowne before the foundations of the world were laid.*

9. Hence also it depends upon no cause, reason or outward condition,
but it doth purely proceed from the will of him that predestinateth. *Mat.*
11.26. Even so Father, because it pleased thee. *Rom.* 9.16.18. It is not of
him that willeth, nor of him that runneth, but of God that sheweth mercy:
he hath mercy on whom he will, and whom he will he hardeneth.

10. Hence it is neither necessary nor agreeable to the Scriptures either
to appoint any fore-required quality in man, as it were the formall object
of Predestination: or so to assigne any certaine condition of man, that the
rest should be excluded: for it is sufficient to understand that men are
the object of this decree, so that the difference of the decree doth not
depend upon man, but that difference, which is found in men, doth follow
upon the decree.

11. In order of intention there is no fore-knowledge, fore-required, or
ought to be presupposed unto the decree of Predestination, besides that
simple intelligence which is of all possible things: because it depends not
upon any reason, or eternall condition, but doth purely proceed from the
will of him that doth predestinate. *Eph.* 1.5.9. He hath predestinated us
according to the good pleasure of his owne will. According to his free good
will which he had purposed in himselfe.

12. It is properly an act of Gods Will whereby it is exercised about a
certaine object which it determines to bring to a certaine end by certaine
meanes. *Eph.* 1.21. We were chosen, when we were predestinated, according to the purpose of him that worketh all things according to the pleasure
of his own will.

13. This decree as it doth exist in the mind of God presupposing an act
of the will is called fore-knowledge: whence It comes to passe that fore-
knowledge signifies as much doctrine as Predestination, but lesse properly,
Romans II.2. Hee hath not cast away his people whom hee fore-knew.

14. There is only one act of will in God properly, because all things in
him are together, and nothing before or after, and so there is only one
decree about the end and meanes: but after our manner of conceiving,
God in order of intention doth will the end before the meanes. *Rom.* 8.30.
Whom he hath predestinated, those he called: although in order of execution, he willeth the means first before their direction to the end. 2. *Thess.*
2. 13. He hath chosen us to salvation through sanctification, and faith.

15. Some things are the meanes, and the end, and the causes also of
other meanes. *Iohn* 6.37. Whatsoever the Father giveth me shall come
to me, and him that commeth to me I will in no wise cast away, yet they
are not causes of the act it selfe of Predestination, nor of all the effects
of it.

16. There are some meanes which of their own nature are ordered to
the end of Predestination: of which sort are all those things which pertaine

to the grace revealed in the Gospell; but other things in a certaine outward respect are subjected to this order: such as are naturall good or evill things which above or beyond their nature through the over-ruling direction of grace doe worke together to our salvation.

17. Of Predestination there are two kinds, Election and Reprobation.

18. Election is the predestination of some certaine men, that the glorious grace of God may be manifested in them. *Eph.* 1.4, 5, 6 He hath chosen us, he hath predestinated us to the praise of his glorious grace.

19. Election is an act of the will, which in God is only one and simple: yet after our manner of conceiving it sets forth (by Syncedoche) by divers acts.

20. The first act of election then is to will the glory of his grace in the salvation of some men. 2 *Thess.* 2.13. God hath chosed us from the beginning unto salvation.

21. The second act is to appoint some certaine men who shal be made partakers of this salvation. 2 *Tim.* 2.19. The Lord knoweth who are his.

22. But the proper reason of election is in this second act, which act containes these three things in the conceiving of it. 1. Love, *Rom.* 9.13. 2. Love with respect to a supernaturall and chiefe good. *Jer.* 31.3. *Eph.* 5.25. 3. Love with a separating from others: in which comparative manner, there is contained a certaine virtuall intention of love. *Rom.* 9.13 *Iohn* 17.6.1. *Cor.* 1.27, 28.

23. The third act of election is a purpose or intentione preparing and directing those meanes by which men elected are certainely lead through to salvation as to an end. But these meanes are properly redemption, and application of redemption. *Iohn* 6.37. 2 *Thess.* 2.13.

24. The third act in a special respect is called predestination: which is sometimes in the Scriptures distinguished from election, even as it respects the elect above, *Rom.* 8.29. *Eph.* 1, 4&5. Whom he did fore-know, those he also predestinated. As he hath chosen us. Who hath predestinated us. Although otherwise by a synecdoche it is used in the same sence with election.

25. Hence Predestination is sometime said to be according to his purpose. *Eph.* 1.11. And his purpose according to election, *Rom.* 9.11. And election also according to purpose, the counsell, and good pleasure of the Will of God, *Eph.* 1.5.

26. There doth a certaine knowledge particularly accompany the acts of will in election in the mind of God, whereby God doth most certainly know the heires of eternal life: whence also election it selfe is called, knowledge or fore-knowledge. *Rom.* 8.29. But this knowledge of God because with greatest firmnesse it retaines the distinct names of those that are to be saved, and the good things appointed for them, as if all were written in Gods Booke, therefore it is called the booke of Life. *Psalms* 69.29. *Revelations* 3.5. and 13.8.

27. This election was only one in God in respect of whole Christ mystically considered, that is, of Christ, and of those who are in Christ, as there was one Creation of all mankind; yet as a certaine distinction may be conceived according to reason, Christ was first elected as the Head, and then some men as members in him. *Eph.* 1.4.

28. Yet Christ is not the meritorious, or impulsive cause in respect of the election of men it selfe, although it hath the reason of a cause in respect of all the effects of election, which follow the sending of Christ himselfe.

29. Christ himselfe in the first act of election as touching the worke of redemption is rightly said to be an effect, and meanes ordained to the salvation of man, as the end, as this salvation is the action of God, *Iohn* 17.6. Thine they were, and thou gavest them me. Yet as this salvation is our good, Christ is not the effect, but the cause of it. So it may be rightly said in respect of the first act of election, that Christ the redeemer *was* the effect and subordinate meanes, but in the third act of election he is to be considered as a cause, *Eph.* 1.3. He hath blessed us with all spirituall blessings, in the Heavens, in Christ.

30. Reprobation is the predestinating of some certaine men, that the glory of Gods Justice might be manifested in them. *Rom.* 9.22.2 *Thess.* 2.12. *Iud.* 4.

31. Three acts are to be conceived in reprobation, as before in election.

32. The first act is to will the setting forth of Justice. Therefore the end of God in reprobation, is not properly the destruction of the Creature, but the Justice of God, which shines forth in deformed destruction.

33. Hence is the first difference in reason betweene election and reprobation, for in election not only the glorious grace of God hath the respect of an end: but also the salvation of men themselves: but in reprobation damnation in it selfe has not the respect of an end, or of good.

34. The second act is to appoint those certaine men in whom this Justice of GOD should be made manifest *Jude* 4.

35. That act cannot properly be called election: because it is not out of love, neither doth it bring the bestowing of any good, but the privation of it: Therefore it is properly called reprobation, because it doth reject or remove them about whom it is exercised, from that love wherewith the elect are appointed to salvation. . . .

36. But because this negative setting apart which is found in reprobation, doth depend upon that setting apart which is in election: hence the remote end of reprobation is the glory of that grace which is manifested in election. . . .

37. Because of this setting apart, whereby God will not communicate blessednesse upon some persons, he is therefore said to hate them. *Rom.* 9.13. This hatred is called negative, or privative, because it denies election: but it includes a positive act whereby God would that some should be deprived of life eternall.

38. Neverthelesse in this is the second difference of reason, between election and reprobation, that the love of election, doth bestow the good on the Creature immediately, but the hatred of reprobation, doth only deny good, doth not bring or inflict evill, but the desert of the Creature comming between.

39. The third act of reprobation is an intention to direct those meanes whereby Justice may be manifested in the reprobate.

The most proper meanes of this kind are permission of *sin,* and living in sin, *Rom.* 9.18. 2 *Thess.* 2.11, 12.

40. In this act there is the third difference of reason between election and reprobation, that election is the cause, not only of salvation, but also of all those things which have the consideration of a cause unto salvation: but reprobation is not properly a cause, either of damnation, or of sin which deserves damnation, but an antecedent only.

41. Hence also followes a fourth disparity, that the very meanes have not alwayes among themselves the respect of a cause and effect: for the permission of sin is not the cause of forsaking, hardning, punishing, but sin it selfe.

B. THE ROLE OF THE CLERGY: WILLIAM PERKINS, "OF THE CALLING OF THE MINISTRY"*

. . . Prophets and Ministers are Angels, in the very institution of their calling. Therefore thou must preach Gods word as *Gods word,* and deliuer it as thou receiuest it: for Angels, Embassadours, and Messengers, carry not their owne message, but the message of their Lords and Masters who sent them; and ministers cary the message of the Lord of hosts: therefore they are bound to deliuer it as *the Lords,* and not their owne.

In the first Epistle of *Peter,* 4.11. we are bid, *If any man speake, let him speake,* not onely the *word of God,* but *as the word of God.* Gods *word* must be spoken, and *as Gods word:* then shewe they faithfulnes to the Lord, in discharging thy hands sincerely of that message, which he hath honoured thee to carry: Gods word is pure, therefore purely to be thought vpon, and to be deliuered. Then let all that are Gods *Angels,* and would be honoured as his *Angels* and Embassadors, thinke it no lesse reason to doe the duty of Gods *Angels,* least (as many men marre a good tale in the telling) so they take away the power and maiestie of Gods word, in the manner of deliuering it.

The second vse concernes the Ministers also: are they *Gods Angels?* therfore they must preach Gods word in *euidence and demonstration of the spirit of God:* for he that is Gods Angel, the spirit of that God must speake in him: Now to speake in the demonstration of Gods spirit, is to speake in such a *plainenesse,* and yet such a *powerfulnesse,* as that the capacities of the simplest, may perceiue; not man, but God teaching them in that *plainenesse,* and the conscience of the mightiest may feele, not man, but God reproouing them in that *powerfulness.* That this is so, appeares by *S. Paul: If a man prophesie aright* (saith the holy Ghost) *the vnlearned or vnbeleeuing man comes in, hee thinkes his secret faults are disclosed and laid open, hee thinkes all men see his nakedness, and doe reprooue him for it; hee therefore falls downe, and saith, Surely God speakes in this man.*

In which words, obserue an *admirable plainenesse,* and an admirable *powerfulnesse* (which a man would thinke, could not so well stand to-

* These excerpts are reprinted from William Perkins, *Works* (1618), vol. III, pp. 430–431.

gether.) First, plainnesse: for whereas the vnlearned man perceiueth his faults discouered, it followes necessarily he must needs vnderstand; and if an vnlearned man vnderstand it, then consequently it must needs be plaine. Secondly, powerfulnesse; in that his conscience is so conuinced, his secret faults so disclosed, and his very heart so ript vp; that he saith, *Certainely God speakes in this man*. This is the euidence & demonstration of Gods spirit. It is thought good commendation before the world, when men say of a Preacher; Surely, this man hath showne himselfe a proper scholler, of good learning, great reading, strong memorie, and good de-liuere; and so it is, and such commendation (if iust) is not to be con-temned: but that that commends a man to the Lord his God, & to his owne conscience is, when he preacheth so plainely to the capacitie, and so *powerfully* to the conscience of a wicked man, as that he thinks, doubt-lesse God is within him. Art thou therefore an Angel of God, then magnifie the spirit of God, and not they selfe in the preaching of his word.

The next vse is for the hearers; and they are here taught, that if their Ministers be *Angels* sent them from God, then they are to heare them gladly, willingly, reuerently, and obediently: gladly and willingly because they are Ambassadours; reuerently and obediently, because they are sent from the high God, the King of Kings, and doe deliuer his embassage. God saith, the *people must seeke the Lawe at his mouth:* and good reason, for if the Law be the reuealed will of God, and the Minister the *Angel* of God, then where should they seeke the will of God, but at the mouth of his *Angel?* The reason therefore followeth well in that place: they should *seeke the Lawe at his mouth, for he is the messenger of the Lord of hostes:* and this must all Christians doe, not onely if their Doctrine be pleasing vnto them, but though it crosse their corruption, and be quite contrarie to their dispositions; yea, though it be neuer so vnsauoury and hard vnto nature, yet in as much as it is a message from thy God and King, and the teacher *the Angel or Messenger* of that God, therefore both he and it, must be receiued with all reuerence, and with the very obedience of the heart and soule. And this is the cause why a conuenient reuerence and honour is to be giuen of all good Christians, euen to the persons of Gods ministers (especially when they adorn their high calling with a holy life:) euen because they are Angels of *God.* Saint *Paul* teacheth *that women ought to bee modestly attired in the congregation, because of the Angels:* it is not onely, because *the holy Angels are present,* and alwayes beholders of our seruice of God, but euen because the Ministers which are *Angels* and Messengers sent from God, are there, deliuering their Message and Embassage receiued from God. And thus we haue the first title giuen to the Minister; he is an *Angell.*

Secondly, he is an *Interpreter:* that is, one that is able to deliuer aright the reconciliation made betwixt God and man: I say not, the *Author* of that *reconciliation,* for that is the Godhead it selfe; nor the *Worker* of this reconcilitation, for that is the second person, Christ Iesus nor the *Assurer* or *Ratifier,* for that is the holy Ghost: nor the *Instrument* of it, for that is the glad tidings of the Gospel; but I say, he is the *Interpreter* of it; that is, first one that can open and explaine the couenants of grace, & rightly lay downe the meanes how this reconciliation is wrought. Secondly, one that can *rightly and iustly* apply meanes, for the working of it out.

Thirdly, one that hath authoritie to publish and declare it when it is wrought: and by these three actions, hee is Gods *Interpreter* to the people.

Then hee is also the peoples *Interpreter* to God, by being able to speake to God for them, to lay open their wants and nakednesses, to confesse their sinnes, to craue pardon and forgiuenesse, to giue thanks in their names for mercies receiued: and in a word, to offer vp all their spirituall sacrifices vnto God for the: and so euery true Minister is a double *Interpreter,* Gods to the people, and the peoples to God. In which respects, he is properly called *Gods mouth* to the people, by preaching to them from God; and the peoples mouth to God, by praying for them to God: & this calling sheweth how great and glorious a calling this Ministery is, if it be rightly conceiued. Now then for the vse of it.

First, if euery true Minister must be Gods *Interpreter* to the people, & the peoples to God; then hence we learne, that euery one, who either is or intends to be a Minister, must haue that tongue *of the learned,* whereof is spoken in Esa 50.4. where the Prophet saith (first in the name of Christ, as he that is the great Prophet and Teacher of his Church; and secondarily, in the name of himselfe and all true Prophets, while the world endureth.) *The Lord God hath giuen me a tongue of the learned, that I should know to speake a word in season to him that is wearie:* where note the *weary soule,* or troubled conscience, must haue a word *in season* spoken to him for his comfort; and that cannot be spoken without the *tongue of the learned.* And lastly, that tongue of the learned must be *giuen of God.* Now to haue this tongue *of the learned,* which Esay speakes of, what is it but to be this *interpreter* which the holy Ghost here saith a Minister must be, But to be able to speake with this tongue is, First, to be *furnished with humane learning.* 2. *With diuine knowledge,* as it may by outward meanes be taught from man to man: but besides these, he that will speake *this tongue* aright, must be *inwardly learned,* and taught by the spirit of God: the two first he must learne from men, but the third from God: a true Minister must bee inwardly taught by the spirituall schoolemaster the holy Ghost. Saint *Iohn* in the Reuelation must take the booke, that is, the Scripture, and eate it; and when he had eaten it, *then* (saith the Angel) *he must goe preach to Nations, tongues, people, and to Kings:* which was done, not that Saint *Iohn* had not eaten that booke, in the comming *downe of the holy Ghost,* the very ende of whose comming was to teach them spiritually; but that in him Christ might teach his Church for euer, that no minister is so fit to preach to Nations and to Kings, *until they haue eaten the booke of God:* that is, til after and besides all the learning that man can teach them, they be also taught by the spirit of God himselfe: and this teaching is it that maketh a man a *true interpreter,* and without this he cannot be: for how can a man be Gods *interpreter* to his people, vnlesse hee knowe the minde of God himselfe; and how can he *knowe the minde of God, but by the teaching of the spirit of God?* For as no man knoweth the thought of a man, but the spirit of man that is in him: so the things of God knoweth no man, but the spirit of God. Indeed we may be mans *interpreter* by humane teaching, and may interpret the Scriptures truely and soundly as a humane booke or story, for the increase of knowledge; but the diuine and *spirituall interpreter,* which shall peirce the heart, and astonish the soule of man, must be taught by the inward teaching of the holy Ghost. . . .

SELECTION

The Role of the State:
John Cotton, Letter to Lord Say and Sele (1636)

The basic political ideas of the Puritans are succinctly summarized in portions of the letter written by John Cotton in 1636 to Lord Say and Sele, a Puritan nobleman interested in migrating to Massachusetts Bay. The excerpts reprinted below are from Thomas Hutchinson, The History of Massachusetts *(third edition, two volumes, 1795), volume I, pages 437–439. In their distrust of democracy and insistence upon the predominance of magisterial authority in the polity, the Puritans were only reaffirming traditional English political attitudes. But to a far greater extent than most of their contemporaries in England they thought that civil government and civil laws should be patterned as closely as possible after God's designs as they were revealed in the Bible, and such an emphasis inevitably led to a much closer relationship between civil and religious authorities than was common in England. As Cotton carefully points out, however, the role of the ministers was strictly advisory in Massachusetts. They could not hold civil office, and, although civil leaders were expected to support them in matters of religion, the authority of church and that of state were separate. Detailed treatments of Puritan political thought can be found in the references listed in the introduction to Selection 11. A recent study of Cotton is Larzer Ziff,* The Career of John Cotton: Puritanism and the American Experience *(1962).*

. . . I am very apt to believe, what Mr. Perkins hath, in one of his prefatory pages to his golden chaine, that the word and scripture of God doe conteyne a short *upoluposis* or platforme, not onely of theology, but also of other sacred sciences (as he calleth them) attendants, and hand maids thereunto, which he maketh ethicks, eoconomicks, politicks, church-government, prophecy, academy. It is very suitable to Gods all-sufficient wisdome, and to the fulnes and perfection of Holy Scriptures, not only to prescribe perfect rules for the right ordering of a private mans soule to everlasting blessednes with himself, but also for the right ordering of a mans family, yea, of the commonwealth too, so farre as both of them are subordinate to spiritual ends, and yet avoide both the churches usurpation upon civill jurisdictions, *in ordine ad spiritualia,* and the commonwealths invasion upon ecclesiasticall administrations, *in ordine* to civill peace, and conformity to the civill fate. Gods institutions (such as the government of church and of commonwealth be) may be close and compact, and co ordinate one to another, and yet not confounded. God hath so framed the state of church government and ordinances, that they may be compatible to any commonwealth, though never so much disordered in his frame. But yet when a commonwealth hath liberty to mould his owne frame *(scripture plenitudinem adoro)* I conceyve the scripture hath given full direction for the right ordering of the same, and that, in such sort as may best mainteyne the *euexia* of the church. Mr. Hooker doth often quote a saying out of Mr. Cartwright (though I have not read it in him) that noe man fashioneth his house to his hangings, but his hangings to his house. It is better that the commonwealth be fashioned to the setting forth of Gods house, which is his church, than to accommodate the church frame to the civil state. Democracy I do not conceyve that ever God did ordeyne as a fitt government eyther for church or commonwealth. If the people be governors, who shall be governed? As for monarchy, and aristocracy, they are both of them clearly approved, and directed in scripture, yet so as referreth the soveraigntie to himselfe, and setteth up Theocracy in both, as the best forme of government in the commonwealth, as well as in the church.

When your Lordship doubteth, that this corse will draw all things under the determination of the church, *in ordine ad spiritualia* (seeing the church is to determine who shall be members, and none but a member may have to doe in the government of a commonwealth) be pleased (I pray you) to conceyve, that magistrates are neyther chosen to office in the church, nor doe governe by directions from the church, but by civill lawes, and those enacted in generall corts, and executed in corts of justice, by the governors and assistants. In all which, the church (as the church) hath nothing to doe: onely, it prepareth fitt instruments both to rule, and to choose rulers, which is no ambition in the church, nor dishonor to the commonwealth; the apostle, on the contrary, thought it a great dishonor and reproach to the church of Christ, if it were not able to yield able judges to heare and determine all causes amongst their brethren. I Cor. vi. 1 to 5. which place alone seemeth to me fully to decide this question; for it plainely holdeth forth this argument: It is a shame to the church to want able judges of civill matters (as v. 5) and an audacious act in any church member voluntarily to go for judgment, other where than before the saints (as v. 1.) then it will be noe arrogance nor folly in church members, nor prejudice to the commonwealth, if voluntarily they never choose any civill judges but from amongst the saints, such as church members are called to be. But the former is cleare: and how then can the latter be avoyded? If this therefore be (as your Lordship rightly conceyveth) one of the maine objections if not the onely one which hindereth this commonwealth from the entertainment of the propositions of those worthy gentlemen, wee intreate then, in the name of the Lord Jesus, to consider, in meeknes of wisdome, it is not any conceite or will of ours, but the holy counsell and will of the Lord Jesus (whom they seeke to serve as well as wee) that overruleth us in this case; and we trust will ovverule them also, that the Lord onely may be exalted amongst all his servants. What pittie and griefe were it, that the observance of the will of Christ should hinder good things from us!

But your Lordship doubteth, that if such a rule were necessary, then the church estate and the best ordered commonwealth in the world were not compatible. But let not your Lordship so conceyve. For, the church sub-mitteth it selfe to all the lawes and ordinances of men, in what common-wealth soever they come to dwell. But it is one thing, to submit unto what they have noe calling to reforme; another thing, voluntarily to ordeyne a forme of government, which to the best discerning of many of us (for I speake not of my selfe) is expressly contrary to rule. Nor neede your Lordship feare (which yet I speake with submission to your Lordships better judgment) that this corse will lay such a foundation, as nothing but a mere democracy can be built upon it. Bodine confesseth, that though it be *status popularis,* where a people choose their owne governors; yet the government is not a democracy, whether one (for then it is a mon-archy, though elective) or by many, for then (as you know) it is aristoc-racy. In which respect it is, that church government is iustly denied (even by Mr. Robinson) to be democratical, though the people choose their owne officers and rulers.

Nor neede wee feare, that this course will, in time, cast the common-wealth into distractions, and popular confusions. For (under correction) these three things doe not undermine, but doe mutually and strongly mainteyne one another (even those three which wee principally amie at) authority in magistrates, liberty in people, purity in the church. Purity, preserved in the church, will preserve well ordered liberty in the people, and both of them establish well-balanced authority in the magistrates. God is the author of all these three, and neyther is himselfe the God of confusion, nor are his wayes the wayes of confusion, but of peace. . . .

SELECTION

Challenges from Within

The attempt to implement these ideas encountered opposition from the very beginning, and over the next decades Puritan leaders had to meet a series of challenges from within Massachusetts society. The first challenge came from Roger Williams (1603–1683), son of a merchant tailor, graduate of Cambridge, and gifted preacher, who arrived in the colony in 1631. An aggressive Separatist, he proceeded over the next five years to threaten the very foundations of the Puritan experiment by demanding that Massachusetts churches formally separate from the Church of England, questioning the King's and therefore the colony's title to lands in America, and denying the authority of civil officials over religious affairs. When persuasion and coercion failed to bring Williams into line, the authorities banished him from the colony in the winter of 1635–1636. This and other experiences eventually caused him to become an ardent advocate for religious toleration, and in 1644, while he was in England trying to secure a charter for Rhode Island, he published The Bloudy Tenent of Persecution, *in which he attacked the Massachusetts system and set forth his arguments in favor of toleration and against the exercise of magisterial authority in matters of religious belief.*

Shortly after Williams's banishment an equally serious challenge arose from the activities of the followers of Mrs. Anne Hutchinson (1591–1643), a brilliant and deeply religious woman who had come to the colony in 1634. In direct defiance of the Puritan contention that divine truth was revealed to men only indirectly through the Bible, she came to advocate the Antinomian position that God could reveal his wishes directly to men and that revealed truths were of a higher order than those found in the Bible. Further, she charged that among the entire Puritan clergy in the colony only John Cotton and her brother-in-law, John Wheelwright (ca. 1592–1679), were members of God's proved elect. The rest, she contended, were living under a covenant of works and leading a holy life and performing good works in order to appear as if they had God's grace. Pressure from an informal synod of all orthodox ministers only made her more intransigent, and in 1637 the General Court intervened with a sentence of banishment which was carried out the following year. Anne Hutchinson left behind no written statement of her beliefs, but Wheelwright, who supported her throughout and also suffered banishment in the same cause, summarized the Hutchinsonian position in a sermon delivered January 16, 1637, on the occasion of a general fast.

Over the next ten years equally serious challenges presented themselves in the behavior of Robert Keayne (1595–1656) and Dr. Robert Child (1613–1654). Keayne was a successful merchant and devout Puritan who had migrated to Boston in 1635 and was in general sympathetic to the direction of events in the Bay Colony. Yet, the threat he represented was in many ways the most serious Puritan leadership had to face. His immediate offense was taking excess profits, and for that he was convicted by the General Court in November, 1639, and subsequently censured by the Boston Church. But the real issue at stake was whether self always had to be subordinated to the interests of society. In passing sentence upon Keayne, the General Court answered in the affirmative. To merchants like Keayne, however, the answer was not so clear. For fifteen years he managed to contain his resentment at what he considered unjust treatment, but in his will, written in 1653, he attempted to vindicate himself by suggesting that a merchant ought to have regard for both his own and his community's welfare. Probably better than any other contemporary document,

Keayne's apologia thus reveals the tension between individual and community values that has been so fundamental to American life. The danger to the Puritan experiment, a danger that ultimately could not be entirely avoided, was that, given the opportunities of the American environment, this delicate balance could not be maintained, that individual enterprise could not be constrained, that the concern for the common good would give way to pursuit of individual happiness, and that social and religious anarchy would result.

Less fundamental, though more immediately dangerous, was the challenge of Dr. Robert Child, a presbyterian, and his associates in 1646–1647. Child had visited the colony earlier, and returned in 1645. Within a year he was seeking to utilize all varieties of local discontent to force basic changes in the organization of both church and government. With six others he presented a remonstrance in May, 1646, asking the General Court to enlarge the basis for church membership, extend political liberties to non-Puritan groups, and adhere more closely to English laws. Threatening to appeal to Parliament if their pleas went unheeded, the remonstrants, as Edmund S. Morgan has suggested, represented the "greatest challenge" the colony had to face from foreign intervention in its early days and a grave threat to its independence in both civil and religious matters. Their success could have meant the end of the Puritan experiment, and the General Court summarily rejected their plea; the remonstrants were arrested and convicted of sedition, and Child was prevented from going to England until his charges had been parried by dispatches favorable to the colony.

For fuller treatments of each of these episodes, see, in addition to the works cited in the introduction to Selection 11, Perry Miller, Roger Williams: His Contribution to the American Tradition *(1953), and Ola E. Winslow,* Master Roger Williams: A Biography *(1957), on Williams; Emery Battis,* Saints and Sectaries: Anne Hutchinson and the Antinomian Controversy in the Massachusetts Bay Colony *(1962), on the Hutchinson episode; Bernard Bailyn (ed.),* The Apologia of Robert Keayne *(1965), on Keayne; and George Lyman Kittredge, "Dr. Robert Child the Remonstrant,"* Publications of the Colonial Society of Massachusetts, Transactions, *volume 21 (1919), pages 1–146, on the Child affair.*

A. THE DEMAND FOR TOLERATION AND SEPARATION: ROGER WILLIAMS, "THE BLOUDY TENENT OF PERSECUTION" (1644)*

Propositions

First, That the blood of so many hundred thousand soules of *Protestants* and *Papists*, spilt in the *Wars* of *present* and *former Ages*, for their respective *Consciences*, is not *required* nor *accepted* by *Jesus Christ* the *Prince* of *Peace*.

* These excerpts are reprinted from Samuel L. Caldwell (ed.), *Publications of the Narragansett Club* (6 vols., 1866–1874), vol. III, pp. 3–4, 62–63, 72–73, 125–126, 132–133, 148–150, 217–219.

Secondly, Pregnant *Scripturs* and *Arguments* are throughout the Worke proposed against the *Doctrine* of *persecution* for *cause* of *Conscience*.

Thirdly, Satisfactorie Answers are given to *Scriptures*, and objections produced by Mr. *Calvin, Beza,* Mr. *Cotton,* and the Ministers of the New English Churches and others former and later, tending to prove the *Doctrine of persecution* for cause of *Conscience*.

Fourthly, The *Doctrine of persecution* for cause of *Conscience*, is proved guilty of all the *blood* of the *Soules* crying for *vengeance* under the *Altar*.

Fifthly, All *Civill States* with their *Officers* of *justice* in their respective *constitutions* and *adminstrations* are proved *essentially Civill,* and therefore not *Judges, Governours* or *Defendours* of the *Spirituall* or *Christian state* and *Worship*.

Sixtly, It is the will and command of *God,* that (since the coming of his Sonne the *Lord Jesus*) a *permission* of the most *Paganist, Jewish, Turkish,* or *Antichristian consciences* and *worships,* bee granted to *all* men in all *Nations* and *Countries*: and they are onely to bee *fought* against with that *Sword* which is only (in *Soule matters*) *able* to *conquer,* to wit, the *Sword of Gods Spirit,* the *Word of God*.

Seventhly, The *state* of the Land of *Israel,* the *Kings* and *people* thereof in *Peace & War,* is proved *figurative* and *ceremoniall,* and no *patterne* nor *president* for any *Kingdome* or *civill state* in the *world* to follow.

Eightly, God requireth not an *uniformity* of *Religion* to be *inacted* and *inforced* in any *civill state;* which inforced *uniformity* (sooner or later) is the greatest occasion of *civill Warre, ravishing* of *conscience, persecution* of *Christ Jesus* in his servants, and of the *hypocrite* and *destruction* of *millions* of *souls*.

Ninthly, In holding an inforced *uniformity* of *Religion* in a *civill state,* wee must necessarily *disclaime* our desires and hopes of the *Iewes conversion to Christ*.

Tenthly, An inforced *uniformity* of *Religion* throughout a *Nation* or *civill state,* confounds the *Civill* and *Religious,* denies the principles of Christianity and civility, and that *Jesus Christ* is come in the Flesh.

Eleventhly, The permission of other *consciences* and *worships* than a state professeth, only can (according to God) procure a firme and lasting *peace,* (good *assurance* being taken according to the *wisdome* of the *civill state* for *uniformity* of *civill obedience* from all sorts.)

Twelfthly, lastly, true *civility* and *Christianity* may both flourish in a *state* or *Kingdome,* notwithstanding the *permisson* of divers and contrary *consciences,* either of *Iew* or *Gentile*.

Dialogue

Truth. . . . Mr. *Cotton* . . . layes downe severall *distinctions* and conclusions of his owne, tending to prove persecution. . . .

Peace. The first distinction is this: By persecution for cause of Conscience, "I conceive you meane "either for professing some point of *doctrine* which "you beleeve in *conscience* to be the *truth,* or for "practicing some worke which you beleeve in "*conscience* to be a *religious* dutie.

Truth. I acknowledge that to molest any person, *Jew* or *Gentile,* for either professing *doctrine,* or practicing *worship* meerly *religious* or spirituall, it is to persecute him, and such a person (what ever his *doctrine* or *practice* be true of *false*) suffereth persecution for *conscience*.

But withall I desire it may bee well observed, that this *distinction* is not full and complete: For beside this that a man may be persecuted because he holdeth or practiseth what he beleeves in *conscience* to be a *Truth*, (as *Daniel* did, for which he was cast into the *Lyons* den, Dan. 6.) and many thousands of *Christians*, because they durst not cease to *preach* and *practice* what they beleeved was by *God* commanded, as the *Apostles* answered (*Acts* 4. & 5.) I say besides this a man may also be persecuted, because hee dares not be *constrained* to yeeld obedience to such *doctrines* and *worships* as are by men invented and appointed. So the three famous *Jewes* were cast into the fiery furnace for refusing to fall downe (in a *non-conformity* to the whole conforming world) before the golden *Image*, Dan. 3.21. So thousands of *Christs witnesses* (and of late in those bloudy *Marian* dayes) have rather chose to yeeld their *bodies* to all sorts of *torments*, then to subscribe to *doctrines*, or practice *worships*, unto which the States and Times (as *Nabuchadnezzar* to his golden *Image*) have compelled and urged them. . . .

Gods people were and ought to be *Nonconformitants*, not daring either to be *restrained* from the *true*, or *constrained* to *false Worship*, and yet without *breach* of the Civill or *Citie-peace*, properly so called.

Peace. Hence it is that so many glorious and flourishing *Cities* of the World maintaine their *Civill* peace, yea the very *Americans* & wildest *Pagans* keep the peace of their *Towns* or *Cities*; though neither in one nor the other can any man prove a true *Church* of God in those places, and consequently no spirituall and heavenly peace: The Peace *Spirituall* (whether true or false) being of a higher and farre different nature from the Peace of the place or people, being meerly and essentially *civill* and *humane*.

Truth. O how lost are the sonnes of men in this point? To illustrate this: The *Church* or *company* of *worshippers* (whether true or false) is like unto a Body of Colledge of *Physitians* in a *Citie*; like unto a *Corporation*, *Society*, or *Company* of *East-Indie* or *Turkie-Merchants*, or any other *Societie* or *Company* in *London*: which Companies may hold their *Courts*, keep their *Records*, hold *disputations*; and in matters concerning their *Societie*, may dissent, divide, break into *Schismes* and *Factions*, sue and implead each other at the *Law*, yea wholly breake up and dissolve into pieces and nothing, and yet the *peace* of the *Citie* not be in the least measure impaired or disturbed; because the *essence* or being of the *Citie*, and so the *well-being* and *peace* thereof is essentially distinct from those particular *Societies*; the *Citie-Courts*, *Citie-Lawes*, *Citie-punishments* distinct from theirs. The *Citie* was before them, and stands absolute and intire when such a *Corporation* or *Societie* is taken down. . . .

Peace. Yea but it is said that the blinde *Pharises* misguiding the subjects of a *Civill State*, greatly sinne against a *Civill State*, and therefore justly suffer *civill punishment;* for shall the *Civill Magistrate* take care of *outsides* only, to wit, of the bodies of men, and not of soules, in labouring to procure their everlasting welfare?

Truth. I answer, It is a *truth*, the mischiefe of a blinde *Pharises* blinde *guidance* is greater than if he acted Treasons, Murders, &c. and the losse of one soule by his seduction is a greater mischiefe then if he blew up Parliaments, and cuts the throats of Kings or Emperours, so pretious is that invaluable Jewell of a Soul, above all the present lives and bodies of all the men in the world! and therefore a firme Justice calling for *eye* for *eye, tooth* for *tooth, life* for *life;* calls also *soule* for *soule,* which the blind-guiding seducing *Pharisee* shall surely pay in that dreadfull Ditch, which the Lord Jesus speakes of, but this sentence against him the Lord Jesus only pronounceth in His *Church,* His *spirituall judicature,* and executes this *sentence* in part at present and hereafter to all eternity: Such a *sentence* no *Civill Judge* can passe, such a *Death* no *Civill sword* can inflict.

I answer secondly, *Dead men* cannot be infected, the *civill state,* the *world,* being in a naturall state dead in sin (what ever be the *State Religion* unto which *persons* are forced) it is impossible it should be infected: Indeed the *living,* the *beleeving,* the *Church* and *spirituall state,* that and that onely is capable of *infection;* for whose helpe we shall presently see what *preservatives,* and *remedies* the *Lord Jesus* hath appointed.

Moreover as we see in a *common plague* or *infection* the names are taken how many are to dye, and not one more shall be strucke, then the destroying *Angel* hath the names of. So here, what ever be the soule *infection* breathed out from they lying lips of a *plague-sicke Pharisee,* yet the names are taken, not one *elect* or chosen of God shall perish, *Gods sheep* are safe in His *eternall hand* and *counsell,* and he that knowes his *materiall,* knows also his *mysticall stars,* their *numbers,* and calls them every one by *name,* none fall into the *Ditch* on the blinde *Pharises* backe, but such as were *ordained* to that *condemnation,* both *guid* and *followers,* 1 *Pet.* 2. 8. *Jude* 4. The *vessels* of *wrath* shall breake and split, and only they to the praise of *Gods* eternal *justice, Rom.* 9. . . .

I observe that he implyes that beside the *censure* of the *Lord Jesus,* in the hands of his *spirituall governours,* for any spirituall evill in *life* or *doctrine,* the *Civill Magistrate* is also to inflict *corporall punishment* upon the contrary minded: whereas

First, if the *Civill Magistrate* be a *Christian,* a *Disciple* or follower of the meeke *Lambe* of *God,* he is bound to be far from destroying the *bodies of men,* for refusing to receive the *Lord Jesus Christ,* for otherwise hee should not know (according to this speech of the *Lord Jesus*) what *spirit* he was of, yea and to be ignorant of the sweet end of the comming of the *Son of Man,* which was not to destroy the *bodies of Men,* but to save both *bodies* and *soules, vers.* 55. 56.

Secondly, if the *Civill Magistrate,* being a *Christian,* gifted, *prophesie* in the *Church,* I *Corinth.* I. 14. although the *Lord Jesus Christ,* whom they in their owne persons hold forth, shall be refused, yet they are here forbidden to call for fire from *heaven,* that is, to procure or inflict any corporall *judgement* upon such *offenders,* remembring the end of the *Lord Iesus* his comming, not to *destroy* mens lives, but to *save* them.

Lastly, this also concernes the *conscience* of the *Civill Magistrate,* as he is bound to preserve the *civill peace* and quiet of the *place* and people under him, he is bound to suffer no man to breake the *Civill Peace,* by laying hands of *violence* upon any, though as vile as the *Samaritanes* for not receiving of the *Lord Iesus Christ.*

It is indeed the *ignorance* and blind *zeale* of the second *Beast,* the *false Prophet, Rev.* 13. 13. to perswade the *civill Powers* of the earth to persecute the Saints, that is, to bring fiery *judgements* upon men in a *judiciall way,* and to pronounce that such *judgements* of *imprisonment, banishment, death,* proceed from Gods righteous *vengeance* upon such *Hereticks.* So dealt divers *Bishops* in *France,* and *England* too in Queene *Maries* dayes with the Saints of God at their putting to death, declaiming against them in their Sermons to the people, and proclaiming that these persecutions even unto death were Gods *just judgements from heaven upon these Heretickes. . . .*

. . . To batter downe *Idolatry, false worship, heresie, schisme, blindnesse, hardnesse,* out of the *soule* and *spirit,* it is vaine, improper, and unsutable to bring those *weapons* which are used by *persecutors, stocks, whips, prisons, swords, gibbets, stakes,* &c. (where these seem to prevaile with some Cities or Kingdomes, a stronger force sets up againe, what a weaker pull'd downe) but against these *spirituall strong holds* in the soules of men, *Spirituall Artillery* and *weapons* are proper, which are mighty through *God* to subdue and bring under the very *thought* to *obedience,* or else to binde fast the soule with *chaines* of *darknesse,* and locke it up in the *prison* of *unbeleefe* and hardnesse to *eternity.*

2. I observe that as *civill weapons* are improper in this businesse, and never able to effect ought in the *soule:* So (although they were proper, yet) they are *unnecessary,* for if as the *Spirit* here saith (and the *Answerer* grants) *spirituall weapons* in the hand of *Church officers* are able and ready to take *vengeance* on all disobedience, that is *able* and mighty, sufficient and ready for the *Lords* worke either to *save* the soule, or to *kill* the soule of whomever, be the party or parties opposite, in which respect I may againe remember that speech of *Job,* How hast thou helped him that hath no power? *Job* 26. . . .

Will the *Lord Jesus* (did He ever in His owne Person practice, or did he appoint to) joyne to His *Breastplate of Righteousnesse,* the *breastplate* of *iron* and *steele?* to the *Helmet* of *righteousnesse* and *salvation* in *Christ,* an helmet and crest of *iron, brasse,* or *steel,* a target of wood to His shield of *Faith?* [to] His two *edged sword* comming forth of the mouth of *Jesus,* the *materiall sword,* the worke of Smiths and Cutlers? or a girdle of shooes leather to the girdle of truth, &c. Excellently fit and proper is that *alarme* and *item, Psal.* 2. Be *wise* therefore O ye *Kings* (especially those ten *Horns, Rev.* 17.) who under pretence of fighting for *Christ Jesus* give their power to the *Beast* against *Him,* and be warned ye *Judges* of the Earth: *Kisse the Son,* that is with *subjection* and *affection,* acknowledge Him only the *King* and *Judge* of *soules* (in that power bequeathed to His *Ministers* and *Churches*) lest if His wrath be kindled, yea but a little, then *blessed* are they that *trust* in Him. . . .

Peace. Yea but (say they) the *godly* will not persist in *Heresie* or turbulent *Schisme,* when they are convinced in *Conscience,* &c.

Truth. Sweet *Truth,* if the Civill Court and *Magistracy* must judge (as before I have written) and those Civill Courts are as lawfull, consisting of *naturall men* as of *godly* persons, then what *consequences* necessarily will follow, I have before mentioned. And I adde, according to this *conclusion* it must follow, that, if the most *godly* persons yeeld not to once or twice *Admonition* (as it maintained by the *Answerer*) they must necessarily be esteemed *obstinate* persons, for if they were *godly* (saith he) they would yeeld. Must it not then be said (as it was by one, passing sentence of *Banishment* upon some, whose godlinesse was acknowledged) that he that commanded the *Judge* not to respect the poore in the cause of *judgement,* commands him not to respect the holy or the godly person?

Hence I could name the place and time when a *godly* man, a most desirable person for his trade, &c. (yet something different in *conscience*) propounded his willingnesse and desire to come to dwell in a certaine *Towne* in *New England;* it was answered by the Chiefe of the place, This man differs from us, and wee desire not to be troubled. So that in conclusion (for no other reason in the world) the poore man, though godly, usefull and peaceable, could not be admitted to a Civill Being and Habitation on the Common Earth in that Wildernesse amongst them. . . .

Peace. Mr. *Cotton* concludes with a confident perswasion of having removed the grounds of that great *errour, viz.* that persons are not to be persecuted for cause of *conscience.*

Truth. And I beleeve (dear *Peace*) it shall appear to them that (with feare and trembling at the word of the Lord) examine these passages, that the charge of *errour* reboundeth backe [,] even such an *errour,* as may well be called the *bloody tenent,* so directly contradicting the *spirit* and *minde* and *practice* of the *Prince* of *Peace;* so deeply guilty of the *blood* of soules compelled and forced to *Hypocrite* in a *spirituall* and *soule rape;* so deeply guilty of the *blood* of the *Soules* under the *Altar,* persecuted in all *ages* for the *cause* of *Conscience,* and so destructive to the *civill peace* and *welfare* of all *Kingdomes, Countries,* and *Commonwealths.* . . .

B. THE ANTINOMIAN THREAT: JOHN WHEELWRIGHT, FAST-DAY SERMON (JAN. 16, 1637)*

. . . the only cause of the fasting of true beleeuers is the absence of Christ.

Either Christ he is present with his people, or els absent from his people; if he be present with his people, then they haue no cause to fast: therefore it must be his absence that is the true cause of fasting, when he is taken away then they must fast; If we take a view of all the fasts, that haue beene kept either in the old or new-Testament, we shall find the fasts that haue beene kept by true beleeuers, haue had this for the ground of them, the absence of the Lord. . . .

Reas: 1. The first reason is, when Jesus Christ is aboundantly present he doth make a supply of whatsoeuer the children of God can procure in this extraordinary way of fasting. . . .

Reas: 2. The second reason is, because when the Lord Jesus Christ cometh once to be absent, then cometh in matter of mourning & fasting,

* These excerpts are reprinted from *Publications of the Prince Society,* vol. 9 (1876), pp. 155–156, 158–165, 167–169, 174–175.

all misery followeth the absence of Christ, as you see darknes followeth the absence of the sunne. . . .

[There] are divers evills which wee may happily desire shold be remoued, both from forrayne Nations & from this place where we live, and divers good things we desire shold be procured both for them & ourselues. What is the course we must take? must we especially looke after the remouing those euill things, & procuring those good things? this an hipocrite will do, see the example of Ahab. I Kings 21:27.28.29. and the Lord will grant the desire of hipocrites: in this case, see 78 Ps. 34. for there the hipocriticall people of the Jewes, in their misery sought the Lord, and the Lord being full of compassion, he forgiueth their iniquities & destroyeth them not, in the 38 verse of that psalme, must we then do as they did? by no meanes: what must we do then? we must looke first, at the Lord Jesus Christ, & most desire now that Jesus Christ may be receaued in other Nations & other places, and may be more receaued amongst our selues, we must turne vnto the Lord, & then he will turne all into a right frame; . . . therefore if we meane to procure good things & remooue euill things, this will be our course, seeing the absence of the Lord is the cause of fasting, and the end of our fasting must be our turning to the Lord, & he will turne to vs, Joel. 2. and thus the Lord will turne all things for the good of his, Rom: 8.32. if we get the Lord Jesus Christ, we shall haue all things. . . .

. . . the Lord Jesus Christ is not only the author of life, but is the seat of the life of Gods children, and all their life is derived from Christ, for he is the roote, & he convayeth life to the branches, and those that are the children of God, they live by the faith of the sonne of God: Gal: 2.20. they haue faith to lay hold on the sonne of God, and the sonne of God convayeth life vnto them; therefore if we part with Christ, we part with our lives, therefore it standeth vs all in hand, to haue a care Christ be not taken from vs, if we belong to the election of grace, Christ cannot be taken wholy away from vs, yet he may be taken away in some degree, therefore let vs haue a care to keepe the Lord Jesus Christ.

Obiect: It may be here demanded, what course shall we take to keepe the Lord Jesus Christ?

Answ: The way we must take, if so be we will not haue the Lord Jesus Christ taken from vs, is this, we must all prepare for a spirituall combate, we must put on the whole armour of God, Ephes: 6. [11,] and must haue our loynes girt & be redy to fight; behold the bed that is Solomons, there is threescore valient men about it, valient men of Israell, euery one hath his sword in his hand & being expert in warre, & hath his sword girt on his thigh, because of feare in the night, if we will not fight for the Lord Jesus Christ, Christ may come to be surprised. Solomon lyeth in his bed, & there is such men about the bed of Solomon, & they watch ouer Solomon & will not suffer Solomon to be taken away, and who is this Solomon, but the Lord Jesus Christ, and what is the bed, but the Church of true beleeuers, aand who are those valient men of Israell, but all the children of God, they ought to shew themselues valient, they shold haue their swords redy, they must fight, & fight with spirituall weapons, for the

weapons of our warfare are not carnall but spirituall 2 Cor, 10. 4. & therefore wheresoeuer we liue, if we wold haue the Lord Jesus Christ to be
aboundantly present with vs, we must all of vs prepare for battell & come
out against the enimyes of the Lord, & if we do not strive, those vnder a
covenant of works will prevaile. . . .

Obiect: It may be demaunded what course must we take to prevaile in
this combate, for fight we must?

Answ: If we wold prevayle through the strength of the Lord (for of
our selues we can do nothing) then we must first contend for the faith
once deliued to the saynts. Jude. 3. that is the Gospell, it was but once
deliued for the substance, though many tymes in regard of the manner, we
must therefore striue for the faith of the Gospell, & striue together for the
Gospell. . . .

Obiect: It may be demaunded, what is the Gospell?

Answ: . . . The Gospell is a divine heauenly supernaturall doctrine,
contayning in it the revelation of Jesus Christ. to preach the Gospell is to
preach Christ, and the Apostle saith Gal: 6. 14. God forbidd that I shold
glory in any thing but in the crosse of Christ: so that the Gospell is such a
doctrine as doth hold forth Jesus Christ & nothing but Christ, when such
a doctrine is holden forth as doth reveale Jesus Christ to be our wisdome,
our righteousnes, our sanctification & our redemption I Cor. 1. 30. when
all is taken away from the creature, & all giuen to Christ, so that neither
before our conversion nor after, we are able to put forth one act of true
saving spirituall wisdome, but we must haue it put forth from the Lord
Jesus Christ, with whom we are made one; and such a doctrine holden
forth as declares, that we are not able to do any worke of sanctification,
further then we are acted by the Lord, nor able to procure our justification, but it must be the Lord Jesus Christ that must apply himselfe &
his righteousnes to vs; and we are not able to redeeme our selues from the
least euill, but he is our redemption; when Christ is thus holden forth to
be all in all, all in the roote, all in the branch, all in all, this is the
Gospell. . . .

Obiect: It may be demaunded, is there nothing to be holden forth in
poynt of iustification, but only the righteousnes of the Lord Jesus Christ,
may there not be a reuelation of some worke of sanctification, & from that,
may not we be caried to Christ Jesus, and so come to beleeue in the Lord
Jesus Christ, must Christ be all in Poynt of iustification?

Answ: Truly both in poynt of iustification, & the knowledg of this our
iustification by faith, there must be nothing in the world reuealed but
Christ Jesus, none other doctrine vnder heauen is able to iustify any, but
merely the revelation of the Lord Jesus Christ, I am not ashamed of the
Gospell faith Paul, for it is the power of God to saluation, I Rom: 16.
how? for in it, the righteousnes of God is revealed: so it cold not be a
doctrine with power to convert a soule if the righteousness of the Lord
were not revealed: therefore when the Lord is pleased to convert any soule
to him, he revealeth not to him some worke, & from that worke, carieth
him to Christ, but there is nothing revealed but Christ, when Christ is
lifted vp, he draweth all to him, that belongeth to the election of grace; if

men thinke to be saved, because the see some worke of sanctification in them, as hungring & thristing & the like: if they be saued, they are saued without the Gospell. No, no, this is a covenant of works, for in the covenant of grace, nothing is revealed but Christ for our righteousnes; and so for the knowledge of our iustification by faith, nothing is revealed to the soule but only Christ & his righteousnes freely giuen, it was the very grace of God that appeared, that same apparition whereby the soule cometh to know that he is iustified, the object of it is Christ freely giuen, when the louing kindnes of Christ appeared 3 Tit: 5. not by the works of righteousnes, they are layd aside, and the Lord revealeth only to them the righteousness of himselfe giuen freely to the soule; if men haue revealed to them some worke of righteousnes in them selues, as loue to the brethren & the like, & herevpon they come to be assured they are in a good estate, this is not the assurance of faith, for faith hath Christ revealed for the object, therefore [if] the assurance of ones iustification be by faith as a worke, it is not Gospell. . . .

Obiect: It may be obiected that there will be little hope of victorie for the servants of God, because the Children of God are but few, and those that are enimyes to the Lord & his truth are many?

Answ: True, I must confesse & acknowledge the saynts of God are few, they are but a little flocke, and those that are enemyes to the Lord, not onely Pagonish, but Antichristian, and those that run vnder a covenant of works are very strong: but be not afrayd, the battle is not yours but Gods. . . .

Object: It will be obiected, that divers of those who are oposite to the wayes of grace & free covenant of grace, they are wondrous holy people, therefore it shold seeme to be a very vncharitable thing in the seruants of God to condemne such, as if so be they were enimyes to the Lord & his truth, whilest they are so exceeding holy & strict in their way.

Answ: Brethren, those vnder a covenant of works, [the] more holy they are, the greater enimyes they are to Christ, Paul acknowledgeth as much in Gal: [1] he saith he was zealous acording to the Law & the more he went in a legall way, the more he persecuted the wayes of grace 13 Acts. 14. 50. where all the devout people were such, as did expell Paul out of Antioch & out of all the coasts, It maketh no matter how seemingly holy men be, according to the Law; if they do not know the worke of grace & wayes of God, they are such as trust to their owne righteousnes, they shall dye sayth the Lord. Ezek: 33. 13. what a cursed righteousnes is that, that thrusteth out the righteousnes of Christ, the Apostle speaketh, they shall transforme themselues into an Angell of Light, 2 Cor. 11. 14. therefore it maketh no matter how holy men be that haue no acquaintance with Christ. Seest thou a man wise in his owne conceit, more hope their is of a foole then of him. Pro: 26. 12. we know (through the mercy of God) assone as Christ cometh into the soule, he maketh the creature nothing: therefore if men be so holy & so strict & zealous, & trust to themselues & their righteousnes, & knoweth not the wayes of grace, but oppose free grace; such as these, haue not the Lord Jesus Christ, therefore set vpon such with the sword of the Spiritt, the word of God. . . .

. . . let vs haue a care to be holy as the Lord is holy, let vs not giue an ocasion to those that are coming on, or manifestly opposite to the wayes of grace, to suspect the way of grace, let vs cary our selues, that they may be ashamed to blame vs, let vs deale vprightly with those, with whom we haue occasion to deale, and haue a care to guide our familyes, & to performe duties that belong to vs, and let vs haue a care that we giue not ocasion to others to say we are libertines or Antinomians, but Christians, let vs expresse the vertue of him that hath called vs, and then he will manifest his presence amongst vs. John: 14. if you loue me I will manifest myselfe to you, he will crovne his owne worke with his presence, he will come into his garden & eate of the pleasant fruits; therefore let vs carry our selues, so that we may haue no cause of mourning, for if the Lord be absent, there is cause of mourning. . . .

C. INDIVIDUAL VERSUS COMMUNITY: THE APOLOGIA OF ROBERT KEAYNE (1653)*

It may be some on the other side may marvel (especially some who have been acquainted with some expressions or purposes of mine in former wills) that I should give away so much of my estate in private legacies and to private uses which might better have been spared and to give little or nothing to any public use for the general good of the country and commonwealth [except] what I have appropriated to our own town of Boston.

To answer this doubt or objection I must acknowledge that it hath been in my full purpose and resolution ever since God hath given me any comfortable estate to do good withal, not only before I came into New England but often since, to study and endeavor both in my life and at my death to do what I could do to help on any public, profitable, and general good here. . . . My thoughts and intents have been about the castle for public defense, the college and schools for learning, the setting up of a bridewell or workhouse for prisoners, malefactors, and some sort of poor people, stubborn, idle, and undutiful youth, as children and servants, to have been kept at work in either for correction or to get their living, and some other things that I need not mention. In which things, though I could not have done so much as I desired, yet so much I should have done as might have proved an example and encouragement to others of greater estates and willing minds to have done more and to have helped to carry them on to more perfection. For I have held it a great degree of unthankfulness to God that when He hath bestowed many blessings and a large or comfortable outward estate upon a man that he should leave all to his wife and children to advance them only by making them great and rich in the world or to bestow it upon some friends or kindred that it may be hath no great need of it and to dispose none or very little of it to public

* These excerpts are reprinted from Bernard Bailyn (ed.), "The Apologia of Robert Keayne," *Publications of the Colonial Society of Massachusetts, Transactions*, vol. 42 (1952–1956), pp. 293–294, 296–297, 300–302, 329–331.

charitable or good works such as may tend to His glory and the good of others in way of a thankful acknowledgment to Him for so great favors. . . .

I did submit to the censure, I paid the fine to the uttermost, which is not nor hath been done by many (nor so earnestly required as mine was) though for certain and not supposed offenses of far higher nature, which I can make good not by hearsay only but in my own knowledge, yea offenses of the same kind. [My own offense] was so greatly aggravated and with such indignation pursued by some, as if no censure could be too great or too severe, as if I had not been worthy to have lived upon the earth. [Such offenses] are not only now common almost in every shop and warehouse but even then and ever since with a higher measure of excess, yea even by some of them that were most zealous and had their hands and tongues deepest in my censure. [At that time] they were buyers, [but since then] they are turned sellers and peddling merchants themselves, so that they are become no offenses now nor worthy questioning nor taking notice of in others. Yet [they cried] oppression and excessive gains, [when] considering the time that they kept the goods bought in their hands before they could or would pay and the quality or rather the business of their pay for kind, yea contrary to their own promises, instead of gains there was apparent loss without any gains to the seller.

The oppression lay justly and truly on the buyer's hand rather than on the seller; but then the country was all buyers and few sellers, though it would not be seen on that side then. For if the lion will say the lamb is a fox, it must be so, the lamb must be content to leave it. But now the country hath got better experience in merchandise, and they have soundly paid for their experience since, so that it is now and was many years ago become a common proverb amongst most buyers that knew those times that my goods and prices were cheap pennyworths in comparison of what hath been taken since and especially [in comparison with] the prices of these times. Yet I have borne this patiently and without disturbance or troubling the Court with any petitions for remission or abatement of the fine, though I have been advised by many friends, yea and some of the same Court, so to do, as if they would be willing to embrace such an occasion to undo what was then done in a hurry and in displeasure, or at least would lessen or mitigate it in a great measure. But I have not been persuaded to it because the more innocently that I suffer, the more patiently have I borne it, leaving my cause therein to the Lord.

Yet I dare not subscribe to the justness of that time's proceeding against me, nor did my conscience to the best of my remembrance ever yet convince me that that censure was either equal or deserved by me. I speak not this to grieve any godly heart or to lay any misinterpretation or scandal upon the whole Court or all the magistrates in general whom I have ever thought myself bound to honor and esteem and submit to in lawful things. . . .

I did not then nor dare not now go about to justify all my actions. I know God is righteous and doth all upon just grounds, though men may mistake in their grounds and proceedings, counsel have erred and courts may err and a faction may be too hard and outvote the better or more discerning part. I know the errors of my life. The failings in my trade and otherwise have been many. Therefore from God [the censure] was most just. Though it had been much more severe I dare not so open my mouth against it, nor never did as I remember, [except to] justify Him. Yet I dare not say nor did I ever think (as far as I can call to mind) that the censure was just and righteous from men. Was the price of a bridle, not for taking but only asking, 2 s. for [what] cost here 20 d. such a heinous sin? [Such bridles] have since been commonly sold and still are for 2 s. 6 d. and 3 s. or more, though worse in kind. Was it such a heinonus sin to sell 2 or 3 dozen of great gold buttons for 2 s. 10 d. per dozen that cost 2 s. 2 d. ready money in London, bought at the best hand, as I showed to many by my invoice (though I could not find it at the instant when the Court desired to see it) and since was confirmed by special testimony from London? The buttons [were not even] paid for when the complaint was made, nor I think not yet; neither did the complaint come from him that bought and owed them nor with his knowledge or consent, as he hath since affirmed, but merely from the spleen and envy of another, whom it did nothing concern. Was this so great an offense? Indeed, that it might be made so, some out of their ignorance would needs say they were copper and not worth 9 d. per dozen. But these were weak grounds to pass heavy censures upon.

Was the selling of 6 d. nails for 8 d. per lb. and 8 d. nails for 10 d. per lb. such a crying and oppressing sin? And as I remember it was above two years before he that bought them paid me for them (and not paid for if I forget not) when he made that quarreling exception and unrighteous complaint in the Court against me, (he then being of the Court himself) that I had altered and corrupted my book in adding more to the price than I had set down for them at first delivery. If I had set down 8 d. after 2 years' forbearance for what I would have sold for 7 d. if he had paid me presently, I think it had been a more honest act in me than it was in him that promised or at least pretended to pay me presently that he might get them at a lower price than a man could well live upon, and when he had got my goods into his hands to keep me 2 or 3 years without my money. All that while there was no fault found at the prices, but when he could for shame keep the money no longer, yet he will requite it with a censure in the Court. For my own part, as I did ever think it an ungodly act in him, so I do think in my conscience that it had been more just in the Court to have censured him than me for this thing, though this was the chiefest crime alleged and most powerfully carried against me. Other things, as some farthing skeins of thread, etc., were drawn in to make this the more probable and to help to make up a censure. But the truth of the thing was this:

This man sent unto me for 2 or three thousand of 6 d. nails. I sent to him a bag full of that sort just as they came to me from Mr. Foote's in London, never opened nor altered by me. These I entered into my book at 8 d. per lb. thinking he would have paid me in a very short time. It fell out that these nails proved somewhat too little for his work. He sent them [back] again and desired me to let him have bigger [ones] for them. I took them and sent him a bag of 8 d. nails of the same quantity at 10 d. per lb. Now because I was loath to alter my book and to make a new charge I only altered the figures in my book and made the figure of "6" a figure of "8" for 8 d. nails and the figure of "8" that before stood for 8 d. a lb. I made "10 d." Now though he knew of the change of these 6 d. nails for 8 d. (which I had quite forgot through my many other occasions and the length of time that they had stood in the book unpaid) yet this he concealed from me and from the Court also. To make the matter more odious he challenged me and my book of falsehood, supposing that because he had kept me so long from my money therefore by altering the figures I had made the price higher than at first I had charged them down, and that I required 10 d. per lb. for 6 d. nails. And so carried it in the Court (where he was the more easily believed because he was a magistrate and of esteem therein, though it was a most unjust and untrue charge, and only from his own imagination), till I cleared it by good testimony from an honest man in his own town whom he sent for the first nails and [who] brought them back and received the bigger nails for them. [This man] came to me of his own accord and told me he heard there was a difference between such a man and I, which he said he could clear, and related the matter fully to me which I was very glad to hear. [His words] brought all things to my mind, [especially] what was the ground of altering the figures in the book, which before I had forgot though I saw it was done with my own hand. . . .

Now I leave it to the world or to any impartial man or any that hath understanding in trade to judge whether this was a just offense or so crying a sin for which I had such cause to be so penitent (this being the chief [accusation] and pressed on with so great aggravation by my opposers) [or whether] my actions, innocent in themselves, were misconstrued. I knew not how to help myself, especially considering it was no oppressing price but usual with others at that time to sell the like so and since [then] frequently for almost half as much more, as I think all know, and yet both given and taken without exception, or at least without public complaint. Yea, the same gentleman himself, since he had turned merchant and trader, seems to have lost his former tenderness of conscience that he had when he was a buyer and is not so scrupulous in his own gains. . . .

Now having thus cleared my intentions plainly and really in all things as far as I can remember, which hath occasioned my will to be far larger than I either intended or desired, there are 2 or 3 objections which doth lie in the way, which being answered or removed I shall draw to an end. For I desire in this my will to give an account of my actions and endeavor to remove all jealousies as near as I can, these being as it were my last words that will live to speak for me when I am dead and in my grave. . . .

The objections are these:

First, if I value my estate to be worth 4000 lb. or thereabouts, how could I get such an estate with a good conscience or without oppression in my calling, seeing it is known to some that I had no portion from my parents or friends to begin the world withal. If none did know of this I am bound to acknowledge [it,] that all may be attributed to the free mercy and kindness of God alone who raiseth up and pulleth down as He pleaseth, so that when I call to mind my first beginning or my first going to London I may with old Jacob thankfully say, with my staff came I over this Jordan and now the Lord hath given me two bands.

To which I answer, I have now traded for myself about 40 or 50 years and through the favor of God, though I had very little at first to begin with, yet I had good credit and good esteem and respect in the place where I lived so that I did ever drive a great trade not only since I came hither but especially in England.

Now to get 4000 lb. in 40 or 50 years is not 100 lb. a year clear gains, one year with another, which we account to be no great matter in driving but a small trade by an industrious and provident man, especially where there is no great trusting of chapmen or giving of credit which usually is subject to great hazards and losses. A tradesman or merchant that hath a full trade may get a 100 lb. a year above his expenses and a great deal more very honestly without hurting his own conscience or wronging those that he deals with at all.

Since I came into New England it is well known to some that I brought over with me two or 3000 lb. in good estate of my own, and I have been here in a way of trade and merchandise besides farming now this 18 years. He that hath a stock of his own of 2 or 3000 lb. to manage in a way of trade, I think he may very lawfully and honestly get 200 lb. a year by it clear if his expenses be not very great and large. And yet with turning and managing this stock of my own (besides what goods have been sent me from England by other men to a considerable value from time to time) I have not cleared near 100 lb. a year above my expenses since I came hither, which is not 5 lb. per cent clear gains. And yet I have been no prodigal spender as I have been no niggardly sparer in things needful, as the account of my daily and weekly expenses will testify for me when those books come to be viewed over, whether . . . [in] relation to my expenses in Old England or since I came hither.

For . . . I have undergone many censures since I came hither according to men's uncharitable and various apprehensions, some looking at me as an oppressor in trading and getting unconsciousably by what I sold and others as covetous and niggardly in housekeeping and not so liberal and bountiful as I should be. How those two contraries can justly be charged upon me and yet have increased my estate no more in so long a time I yet see not, [unless] it be [charged] by such as care not what they say of other men though never so false, so [long as] they may lay others under reproach and magnify themselves and their ways by disgracing of others. But it is nothing for me to be judged of men. I have labored to bear it with patience and to approve my heart and ways to God that judgeth righteously. . . .

D. THE THREAT OF OUTSIDE INTERVENTION: THE CHILD REMONSTRANCE (MAY 19, 1646)*

Humbly sheweth, That we cannot but with all thankfulnesse acknowledge your indefatigable pains, continuall care, and constant vigilancie, which

* Reprinted in full from *New-Englands Jonas Cast up at London,* in Peter Force (comp.), *Tracts and Other Papers* (4 vols., 1836–1846), vol. IV, no. 3, pp. 8–14.

(by the blessing of the Almighty) hath procured unto this Wildernesse the much desired fruits of Peace and Plenty; while our native Land, yea the Christian world is sharply afflicted with the devouring Sword, and the sad consequents of Intestine wars. And further, That you whom the Lord hath placed at the helm of these Plantations, and endowed with eminent gifts fit for such honourable callings, are best able to foresee the clouds which hang over our heads, the storms and tempests which threaten this poor Handfull here planted; and timously to amend them. Notwithstanding, those who are under decks, being at present unfit for higher imployments, may perceive those Leaks which will inevitably sink this weak and ill compacted Vessell, if not by your Wisdoms opportunely prevented.

We therefore in the behalf of our selves and divers of our Countrymen, laying our hands on our breasts, and seriously considering, That the hand of our good God who through his goodnesse hath safely brought us and ours through the great Ocean, and planted us here, seems not now to be with us, nay rather against us, blasting all our designs, though contrived with much deliberation, undertaken with great care, and proceeding with more than ordinary probability of successfull events; by which many of good estates are brought to the brinks of extreme poverty; yea, at this time laying His just hand upon our families, taking many away to himself, striking others with unwonted malignant sicknesses and noysome shamefull diseases: Have thought it convenient, with all respectivenesse, to present these our sincere requests and Remonstrance to this honoured Court, hoping we have found out the speciall Leaks, which concurring with the many and great Sins of this place, (which our Consciences know, and our Brethren of *England* are not ignorant of) are the speciall causes of the Lords turning his face from us, leaving us to our selves, and consequently to strife, contention, unfaithfulnesse, idlenesse, and other lamentable failings, not blessing us in any of our endeavours, so as to give us any great hopes of Staple-commodities, and consequently of comfortable subsistence; though we to the utmost of our powers these many years, even to the exhausting of our estates and spirits, have endeavoured the same: but contrariwise all things grow worse and worse, even to the threatning (in our apprehension) of no lesse than finall ruine. Not doubting but you will receive these our Requests and Remonstrance with the same candor of mind, which we, not aiming at novelty and disturbance, but at the glory of God, our allegiance to the State of *England,* and good of these poor Plantations, (if our hearts deceive us not) present them unto you; though for want of skill and other necessary helps roughly drawn up; and hope that you will be more diligent in amending, then we in the searching out the causes of these our present calamities, &c. Not to trouble you (who are imployed in the most serious affaires of these Plantations) with many words, wee shall briefly referre them to these Heads——

1. Whereas this place hath been planted by the incouragements (next under God) of Letters Patents given and granted by His Majesty of *England* to the Inhabitants hereof, with many priviledges and immunities, *viz.* Incorporation into a Company, liberty of choosing Governours, setling Government, making Laws not repugnant to the Laws of England, power

of administring the Oath of Allegiance to all, &c. as by the said Letters Patents more largely appeareth. Notwithstanding we cannot according to our judgements cleerly discern a setled form of Government according to the Fundamentall lawes of *England;* which may seem strange to our Country-men, yea to the whole World, especially considering we are all *English.* Neither do we so understand or perceive our own Lawes or Liberties, or any Body of Lawes here so established, as that thereby there may be a sure and comfortable enjoyment of our Lives, Liberties and Estates, according to our due Naturall rights, as Free-born subjects of the English nation. By which many inconveniences flow into these Plantations, *viz.* Jealousies of introducing Arbitrary Government, (which many are prone to believe) construing the procrastination of such setled Lawes, to proceed from an overgreedy spirit of Arbitrary power (which it may be is their weaknesse) such proceedings being most detestable to our English Nation, and to all good men, and at present a chief cause of the intestine War in our dear Country. Further it gives cause to many, to think themselves hardly dealt with, others too much favoured, and the scale of Justice too much bowed and unequally ballanced: From whence also proceedeth feares and jealousies of illegal Commitments, unjust Imprisonments, Taxes, Rates, Customes, Levies, of ungrounded and undoing Assesments, unjustifiable Presses, undue Fines, unmeasurable Expences and Charges, of unconceivable dangers through a Negative or destructive Vote unduly placed, or not well regulated; in a word, of a Non-certainty of all things we enjoy, whether lives, liberties or estates; as also of undue Oaths, being subject to exposition according to the will of him or them that gives them, and not according to a due and unbowed rule of Law, which is the true Interpreter of all Oaths to all men, whether Judge, or Judged.

Wherefore our humbled desire and request is. That you would be pleased to consider of our present condition, and upon what foundation we stand; and unanimously concurre to establish the Fundamentall and wholsome Lawes of our native Country, and such others as are no way repugnant to them, unto which all of us are most accustomed, and we suppose them best agreeable to our English tempers, and your selves obliged thereunto by the Generall Charter, and your Oaths of Allegiance: neither can we tell whether the Lord hath blest many in these Parts with such eminent Politicall gifts, so as to contrive better Lawes and Customes, than the Wisest of our Nation have with great consideration composed, and by many hundred years experience have found most equall and just; which have procured to the Nation much honour and renown amongst strangers, and long peace and tranquility amongst themselves. And for the more strict and due observation and execution of the said Lawes by all Ministers of Justice, that there may be a setled Rule for them to walk by in cases of Judicature, from which if they swerve, there may be some Power setled, according to the Lawes of *England,* that may call them to account for their Delinquencie, which may be a good means to prevent· divers unnecessary Appeals into *England.*

2. Whereas there are many thousands in these Plantations of the

English Nation free-born, quiet peacable men, righteous in their dealings, forward with hand, heart and purse to advance the publike good,
known friends to the honourable and victorious Houses of Parliament,
lovers of the Nation, &c. Who are debarred from all Civil imployment
(without any just cause that we know) not being permitted to beare the
least office (though it cannot be denied but some are well qualified.) No
not so much as to have any Vote in choosing Magistrates, Captains, or
other Civil or Military Officers; notwithstanding they have here expended
their youth, born the burthen of the day, wasted much of their estates for
the subsistence of these poor Plantations, paid all assessments, taxes,
rates, at least equal, if not exceeding others: Yea, when the late War was
denounced against the *Naraganset Indians,* without their consent; their
goods were seised on for the service, themselves and servants especially
forced and imprest to serve in that war, to the hazarding of all things most
neer and dear unto them. Whence issue forth many great inconveniences,
secret discontents, murmuring, rents in the Plantations, discouragements
in their callings, unsetlednesse of minde, strife, contention, (and the Lord
only knows to what a flame in time it may kindle) also jealousies of too
much unwarranted power and dominion on the one side, and of perpetuall
slavery and bondage to them and their posterity on the other, and which
is intolerable, even by them who ought to love and respect them as
brethren, &c.

We therefore desire, that Civil liberty and freedome be forthwith
granted to all truly *English,* equall to the rest of their Country-men, as in
all Plantations is accustomed to be done, and as all Free-borne enjoy in
our native Country; we hoping here in some things to enjoy greater
liberties then elswhere, counting it no small losse of liberty to be as it
were banished from our native home, and enforced to lay our bones in a
strange wildernesse. Without imposing any Oaths or Covenants on them,
which we suppose cannot be warranted by the Letters Patents, and seem
not to concurre with the Oath of Allegiance formerly enforced on all, and
later Covenants lately imposed on many here present by the honourable
Houses of Parliament; or at least to detract from our native Country, and
Laws, (which by some are stiled Foraign, and this Place termed rather a
Free State, then a Colony or Corporation of *England.)* All of us being
very willing to take such Oaths and Covenants, as are expressions of our
desires of advancing the glory of God and good of this place, of our duties
to the State of *England* and love to our Nation, being composed according
to the laws and customes of other Corporations of *England.* But all of us
are exceedingly unwilling, by any policies whatsoever, to be rent from our
Native country, though far distant from it; valuing our free Denizations,
the Immunities and Priviledges which we and our posterity do, and we
hope shall alwayes enjoy, above the greatest Honours of this Country
not cemented to the State of *England;* and glory to be accounted though
but as Rushes of that Land, and yet that we may continue to write, that
we and ours are *English.* Or at least we intreat, that the Bodies of us and
ours (English subjects possessing here on priviledges) may not be imprest,
nor Goods forcibly taken away; lest we not knowing the justnesse of the

war, may be ignorantly and unwillingly inforced upon our own destructions. And that all Assessments, Taxes, Impositions, (which are many and grievous) if Civil liberty be not granted) may be taken off, that in all things we may be Strangers: otherwise we suppose our selves in a worse case here, and lesse free, then the Natives amongst whom we live, or any Aliens. Further, that none of the English nation (who at this time are too forward to be gone, and very backward to come hither) be banished, unlesse they break the known Lawes of *England* in so high a manner, as to deserve so high a punishment. And that those few that come over, may settle here without having two Magistrates hands, which sometime not being possible to obtain, hath procured a kind of banishment to some, who might have been serviceable to this place, as they have been to the State of *England, &c.*

3. Whereas there are divers sober, righteous, and godly men, eminent for knowledge, and other gracious gifts of the Holy Spirit, no ways scandalous in their lives and conversations, Members of the Churches of *England* (in all Ages famous for piety and learning) not dissenting from the late and best Reformation of *English, Scotland, &c.* Yet they and their posterity are detained from the Seals of the Covenant of Free-grace, because (as it is supposed) they will not take these Churches Covenants, for which as yet they see no light in Gods word, neither can they cleerly perceive what they are, every Church having their covenant differing from anothers, at least in words, yea some Churches sometime adding, sometimes detracting, calling it sometime the Covenant of Grace, sometime a Branch of it, sometime a Profession of the Free-Covenant, &c. Notwithstanding they are compelled, under a severe Fine, every Lords day to appear at the Congregation, and notice is taken of such who stay not till Baptisme be administered to other mens children, though denied to their own; and in some places forced to contribute to the maintenance of those Ministers, who vouchsafe not to take them into their Flock, though desirous of the Ordinances of God, &c. yet they are not accounted so much as Brethren, nor publikely so called; nor is Christian vigilancie (commanded to all) any way exercised to them. Whence (as we conceive) abound an ocean of inconveniences; Dishonour to God and his Ordinances, little profit by the Ministery, increase of Anabaptism, and of those that totally contemn all Ordinances as vain, fading of Christian graces, decrease of Brotherly love, Heresies, Schisms, &c. The whole body of the Members of the Churches of *England,* like sheep scattered in the wildernesse without a shepherd, in a forlorne sad condition. We therefore humbly intreat you, in whose hands it is to help, and whose judicious eyes discern these great inconveniences; for the glory of God, and the comfort of your Brethren and Countrymen, to give liberty to the Members of the Churches of *England* not scandalous in their lives and conversations (as Members of those Churches) to be taken into your Congregations, and to enjoy with you all those liberties and ordinances Christ hath purchased for them, and into whose Name they are baptized; That the Lord may be one, and his Name one amongst us in this place; That the Seals of the Covenant may be applied to them and their posterity, as we conceive they

ought to be, till inconveniences hereby be found prejudiciall to the Churches, or Colonie (which we hope shall never be.) Not doubting but the same Christian favour will be shewed to all the Members of these Churches, when they shall retire to our deare native Country, (if their conversations be righteous and holy); Or otherwise to grant liberty to settle themselves here in a Church-way according to the best Reformations of *England* and *Scotland.* If not, we and they shall be necessitated to apply our humble desires to the Honourable Houses of Parliament, who we hope will take our sad conditions into their serious considerations, to provide able Ministers for us, (this place being not so well provided as to spare any); Or else out of their charity (many estates being wasted) to transport us to some other place, where we may live like Christians, and not be accounted burthens, but serviceable both to Church and State.

These things granted, by the blessing of God to us in Christ, we hope to see the now contemned Ordinances of God, highly prized; the Gospel much darkned, break forth as the sun at noon-day; Christian charity & brotherly love almost frozen, wax warm; Zeal and holy emulation, more fervent; Jealousies of Arbitrary Government, the bane of all Commonwealths, quite banished; The wicked, if any such be found, in their courses disheartned; The righteous actors, in their wayes encouraged; Secret discontents fretting like cankers, remedied; Merchandizing, shipping, by speciall Providence wasted, speedily increased; Mines undertaken with more cheerfulnesse, Fishing with more forwardnesse; Husbandry, now withering, forthwith flourishing; Villages and Plantations, much deserted, presently more populous; All mechanicall Trades, the great enrichers of all Commonwealths, bravely going on; Staple-commodities, the life of States, presently raised; Our almost lost credit regained; Our brethren of *England's* just indignation, and therefore as from a pest flying from us, turned to imbraces; The honourable Houses of Parliament, Patrons of Piety, under their wings, in these dangerous times, with all alacrity shrowding us; The Priviledges and Immunities which we and ours enjoy in our native Land, more firmly setled; Foraign enemies daily threatning, totally discouraged; Unsetled men now abounding, firmely planted, that the prosperity of *England* may not be the ruine of this Plantation, but the contrary; Hands, hearts, and purses now straightned, freely opened for publick and honorable services; Strife and contention now rife, abated; Taxes and sesses, lightned; The burthens of the State, but pleasure. To conclude, all businesses in Church and Common wealth which for many years have seemed to goe backward, beyound our desert, yea expectation, the good hand of our God going along with us, successfully thriving.

And shall alwayes pray the Almighty the only wise God, to guide you with his wisedome, strengthen you with his power, in all your undertakings, that all may be to his glory, and good of his people; and that he would blesse your Wisdomes with the blessings of peace, plenty, and long dayes, &c.

ROBERT CHILD, THO. FOWLE, SAMUEL MAVERICK,
THOMAS BURTON, DAVID YALE, JOHN SMITH, JOHN DAND.

SELECTION **15**

The Enforcement of Values

In response to these challenges, in the process of trying to enforce the social, religious, and political values they had brought with them, the leaders of the Bay Colony defined those values more precisely and elaborated what Perry Miller has called the "New England Way." Thus, although they, like almost all their contemporaries in both Europe and America, rejected the idea of religious toleration on the grounds that there was only one true way and that to permit any deviation from it was only to encourage error and promote wickedness, it was not until after Roger Williams had published his defense of toleration in 1644 that Nathaniel Ward (1578–1652), minister at Ipswich, or, as the Indians called it, Aggawam, prepared his classic statement of the Puritan argument against toleration in The Simple Cobler of Aggawam, *published in London in 1647. Similarly, Puritan ideas about the obligation of the merchant to the community were first worked out in detail by John Cotton in his observations on the Just Price during the trial of Robert Keayne, and many of the subtleties of Puritan political theory were first fully articulated to meet criticism from opponents of the existing regime. From the beginning Winthrop and the other leaders of the colony had assumed that government must be entrusted only to the virtuous and that the magistrates had a special responsibility both to God and to the people to see that government and society conformed as closely as possible to divine prescriptions. This assumption meant both that the magistrates were justified in removing from the colony any elements they considered inimical to that end and that the authority of the magistrates ultimately had to be supreme. These ideas were best expressed by John Winthrop. His "Defence of an Order of Court Made in the Year 1637," prepared during the Antinomian crisis to justify a law requiring immigrants to have the approval of the magistrates before settling in the colony, contains a full defense of the notion that the good of the community, as it is conceived by those in authority, must be the end of every decision of state. Winthrop's speech delivered to the General Court in 1645 following his acquittal on charges of exceeding his magisterial authority presents the argument that the magistrates, though elected by the people, derived their authority from God and offers the classic Puritan definition of the freedom to do "that only which is good, just and honest" in accordance with the will of God.*

Puritan ideas about church polity and the role of the church in the achievement of the divinely ordered commonwealth also developed in response to pressures from both without and within Puritan society. The fullest account of Puritan beliefs about church government and the basis for church membership is A Survey of the Summe of Church-Discipline, *by Thomas Hooker (1586–1647), one of the foremost Puritan divines in either England or New England;*

a former fellow of Emmanuel College, Cambridge; an associate of William Ames at Rotterdam; and a leading figure in the founding of Connecticut. The Survey was undertaken as a defense of the congregational church polity and the New England Way against its presbyterian opponents in New England. Similarly, the Puritan system for maintaining religious uniformity and congregational autonomy, for achieving doctrinal unity without outwardly encroaching upon the independence of the congregation, gradually emerged from the attempts of Puritan leaders to find ways to deal with the disruptive tendencies inherent in the challenges of Williams, the Hutchinsonites, Child and his followers, and others. The central elements in this system, which was institutionalized by the Cambridge Platform, an ecclesiastical constitution for the colony adopted in 1648 in the wake of the Child affair, were the synod—an informal meeting of all orthodox ministers—which could be used to bring the collective wisdom of the clergy to bear upon unorthodox ministers and congregations, and, for particularly difficult cases, the intervention of the civil magistrates to enforce uniformity by punishment, banishment, or execution.

State and church were not the only agencies of social control employed to enforce Puritan values. To ensure that there would be a constant supply of learned ministers to furnish intellectual and spiritual leadership to later generations, the Puritans founded Harvard College in 1636. Their respect for higher learning and the relationship of the college to the Puritan experiment are revealed in New England's First Fruits, an anonymous description of the college published in London in 1643. The same commitment to learning as well as the desire to perpetuate the ideals of Puritanism among the young prompted the General Court to pass laws in 1642 and 1647 requiring towns of a certain size to establish schools.

To defend Puritanism from outside attack while the mother country was distracted by civil war, the Bay Colony joined with Plymouth, Connecticut, and New Haven in 1643 to form the New England Confederation. Presided over by a commission with eight members, two from each colony, and having the authority to declare war and handle other matters of common interest, the Confederation lasted until 1684, though it never worked very well.

For further reading, see the works listed in the introductions to Selections 11 and 14.

A. THE LIMITS OF TOLERATION: NATHANIEL WARD, "THE SIMPLE COBLER OF AGGAWAM" (1645)*

. . . Satan is now in his passions, he feels his passion approaching; he loves to fish in royled waters. Though that Dragon cannot sting the vitals of the Elect mortally, yet that Beelzebub can fly-blow their Intellectuals miserably: The finer Religion grows, the finer he spins his Cobwebs, he will hold pace with Christ so long as his wits will serve him. He sees himself beaten out of gross Idolatries, Heresies, Ceremonies, where the

* These excerpts are reprinted from Peter Force (comp.), *Tracts and Other Papers* (4 vols., 1836–1846), vol. III, no. 8, pp. 5–10.

Light breaks forth with power; he will therefore bestir him to prevaricate Evangelical Truths, and Ordinances, that if they will needs be walking, yet they shall *laborare varicibus*, and not keep their path, he will put them out of time and place; Assassinating for his Engineers, men of Paracelsian parts; well complexioned for honesty; for such are fittest to Mountebank his Chimistry into sick Churches and weak Judgments.

Nor shall he need to stretch his strength overmuch in this work: Too many men having not laid their foundations sure, nor ballasted their Spirits deep with humility and fear, are prest enough of themselves to evaporate their own apprehensions. Those that are acquainted with Story know, it hath ever been so in new Editions of Churches: Such as are least able, are most busy to pudder in the rubbish, and to raise dust in the eyes of more steady Repayrers. Civil Commotions make room for uncivil practises: Religious mutations, for irreligious opinions: Change of Air, discovers corrupt bodies; Reformation of Religion, unsound minds. He that hath any well-faced phansy in his Crown, and doth not vent it now, fears the pride of his own heart will dub him dunce for ever. Such a one will trouble the whole *Israel* of God with his most untimely births, though he makes the bones of his vanity stick up, to the view and grief of all that are godly wise. The devil desires no better sport than to see light heads handle their heels, and fetch their carreers in a time, when the Roof of Liberty stands open.

The next perplexed Question, with pious and ponderous men, will be: What should be done for the healing of these comfortless exulcerations. I am the unablest adviser of a thousand, the unworthiest of ten thousand; yet I hope I may presume to assert what follows without just offence.

First, such as have given or taken any unfriendly reports of us *New-English*, should doe well to recollect themselves. We have been reputed a Colluvies of wild Opinionists, swarmed into a remote wilderness to find elbow-room for our Phanatic Doctrines and practises; I trust our diligence past, and constant sedulity against such persons and courses, will plead better things for us. I dare take upon me, to be the Herauld of *New-England* so far, as to proclaim to the World, in the name of our Colony, that all Familists, Antinomians, Anabaptists, and other Enthusiasts shall have free Liberty to keep away from us, and such as will come to be gone as fast as they can, the sooner the better.

Secondly, I dare aver, that God doth no where in his word tolerate Christian States, to give Tolerations to such adversaries of his Truth, if they have power in their hands to suppress them.

Here is lately brought us an Extract of a *Magna Charta*, so called, compiled between the Sub-planters of a *West-Indian* Island; whereof the first Article of constipulation, firmly provides free stable-room and litter for all kind of Consciences, be they never so dirty or jadish; making it actionable, yea, treasonable, to disturb any man in his Religion, or to discommend it, whatever it be. We are very sorry to see such professed Prophaneness in *English* Professors, as industriously to lay their Religious foundations on the ruine of true Religion; which strictly binds every Conscience *to contend earnestly for the Truth: to preserve unity of Spirit,*

Faith and Ordinances, to be all like minded, of one accord; every man to take his Brother into his Christian care, to stand fast with one spirit, with one mind, striving together for the faith of the Gospel; and by no means to permit Heresies or Erronious Opinions: But God abhorring such loathsome beverages, hath in his righteous judgment blasted that enterprize, which might otherwise have prospered well, for ought I know; I presume their case is generally known ere this.

If the Devil might have his free option, I believe he would ask nothing else, but liberty to enfranchize all false Religions, and to embondage the true; nor should he need: It is much to be feared that lax Tolerations upon State-pretences and planting necessities, will be the next subtle Strategem he will spread to distate the Truth of God, and supplant the Peace of the Churches. Tolerations in things tolerable, exquisitely drawn out by the lines of the Scripture, and pensil of the Spirit, are the sacred favours of Truth, the due latitudes of Love, the fair Compartments of Christian fraternity: but irregular dispensations, dealt forth by the facilities of men, are the frontiers of error, the redoubts of Schisme, the perillous irritaments of carnal and spiritual enmity. . . .

If the whole Creature should conspire to do the Creator a mischief, or offer him an insolency, it would be in nothing more, than in erecting untruths against his Truth, or by sophisticating his Truths with humane medleyes: the removing of some one iota in Scripture, may draw out all the life, and traverse all the Truth of the whole Bible: but to authorise an untruth, by a Toleration of State, is to build a sconce against the walls of Heaven, to batter God out of his Chair: To tell a practical lye, is a great Sin, but yet transient; but to set up a Theorical untruth, is to warrant every lye that lyes from its root to the top of every branch it hath, which are not a few. . . .

He that is willing to tolerate any Religion, or discrepant way of Religion, besides his own, unless it be in matters meerly indifferent, either doubts of his own, or is not sincere in it. . . .

That there is no Rule given by God for any State to give an affirmative Toleration to any false Religion, or Opinion whatsoever; they must connive in some Cases, but may not concede in any. . . .

That if the State of *England* shall either willingly Tolerate, or weakly connive at such Courses, the Church of that Kingdom will sooner become the Devils dancing-School, than Gods Temple: The Civil State a Beargarden, than an Exchange: The whole Realm a Pais base than an *England.* And what pity it is, that that Country which hath been the Staple of Truth to all Christendom, should now become the Aviary of Errors to the whole World, let every fearing heart judge.

I take Liberty of Conscience to be nothing but a freedom from Sin, and Error. . . . And Liberty of Error nothing but a Prison for Conscience. Then small will be the kindness of a State to build such Prisons for their Subjects.

The Scripture saith, there is nothing makes free but Truth, and Truth saith, there is no Truth but one: If the States of the World would make it their sum-operous Care to preserve this One Truth in its purity and

Authority, it would ease you of all other Political cares. I am sure Satan makes it his grand, if not only task, to adulterate Truth; Falshood is his sole Scepter, whereby he first ruffled, and ever since ruined the World. . . .

B. THE CASE AGAINST UNRESTRAINED ACQUISITIVENESS: JOHN COTTON, "ON THE JUST PRICE" (1639)*

Some false principles were these:—

1. That a man might sell as dear as he can, and buy as cheap as he can.
2. If a man lose by casualty of sea, etc., in some of his commodities, he may raise the price of the rest.
3. That he may sell as he bought, though he paid too dear, etc., and though the commodity be fallen, etc.
4. That, as a man may take the advantage of his own skill or ability, so he may of another's ignorance or necessity.
5. Where one gives time for payment, he is to take like recompense of one as of another.

The rules for trading were these:—

1. A man may not sell above the current price, i.e., such a price as is usual in the time and place, and as another (who knows the worth of the commodity) would give for it, if he had occasion to use it; as that is called current money, which every man will take, etc.
2. When a man loseth in his commodity for want of skill, etc., he must look at it as his own fault or cross, and therefore must not lay it upon another.
3. Where a man loseth by casualty of sea, or, etc., it is a loss cast upon himself by providence, and he may not ease himself of it by casting it upon another; for so a man should seem to provide against all providences, etc., that he should never lose; but where there is a scarcity of the commodity, there men may raise their price; for now it is a hand of God upon the commodity, and not the person.
4. A man may not ask any more for his commodity than his selling price, as Ephron to Abraham, the land is worth thus much. . . .

C. THE GOOD OF THE COMMUNITY AS THE END OF THE STATE: JOHN WINTHROP, "DEFENCE OF AN ORDER OF COURT" (1637)†

For clearing of such scruples as have arisen about this order, it is to be considered, first, what is the essentiall forme of a common weale or body

---

* Cotton's remarks on the Just Price are taken from James Kendall Hosmer (ed.), *Winthrop's Journal, 1630–1649* (2 vols., 1908), vol. I, pp. 317–318.

† These excerpts are reprinted from Thomas Hutchinson, *Collection of Original Papers*, pp. 67–71.

politic such as this is, which I conceive to be this—The consent of a certaine companie of people, to cohabite together, under one government for their mutual safety and welfare. . . .

It is clearly agreed, by all, that the care of safety and welfare was the original cause or occasion of common weales and of many familyes subjecting themselves to rulers and laws; for no man hath lawfull power over another, but by birth or consent, so likewise, by the law of proprietye, no man can have just interest in that which belongeth to another, without his consent.

From the premises will arise these conclusions.

1. No common weale can be founded but by free consent.

2. The persons so incorporating have a public and relative interest each in other, and in the place of their cohabitation and goods, and laws, &c. and in all the means of their welfare so as none other can claime priviledge with them but by free consent.

3. The nature of such an incorporation tyes every member therof to seeke out and entertaine all means that may conduce to the welfare of the bodye, and to keepe off whatsoever doth appeare to tend to theire damage.

4. The welfare of the whole is to be put to apparent hazard for the advantage of any particular members.

From these conclusions I thus reason.

1. If we heere be a corporation established by free consent, if the place of our cohabitation be our owne, then no man hath right to come into us &c. without our consent.

2. If no man hath right to our lands, our government priviledges, &c. but by our consent, then it is reason we should take notice of before we conferre any such upon them.

3. If we are bound to keepe off whatsoever appears to tend to our ruine or damage, then may we lawfully refuse to receive such whose dispositions suite not with ours and whose society (we know) will be hurtfull to us, and therefore it is lawfull to take knowledge of all men before we receive them.

4. The churches take liberty (as lawfully they may) to receive or reject at their discretion; yea particular towns make orders to the like effect; why then should the common weale be denied the like liberty and the whole more restrained than any parte? . . .

7. A family is a little common wealth, and a common wealth is a greate family. Now as a family is not bound to entertaine all comers, no not every good man (otherwise than by way of hospitality) no more is a common wealth.

8. It is a generall received rule, [that] . . . it is worse to receive a man whom we must cast out againe, than to denye him admittance.

9. The rule of the Apostle, John 2. 10. is, that such as come and bring not the true doctrine with them should not be received to house, and by the same reason not into the common weale.

10. Seeing it must be granted that there may come such persons (suppose Jesuits, &c.) which by consent of all ought to be rejected, it will follow that this law (being only for notice to be taken of all that come to us, without which we cannot avoyd such as indeed are to be kept out) is no other but just and needfull, and if any should be rejected that ought to be received, that is not to

be imputed to the law, but to those who are betrusted with the execution of it. And herein is to be considered, what the intent of the law is, and by consequence, by what rule they are to walke, who are betrusted with the keeping of it. The intent of the law is to preserve the welfare of the body; and for this ende to have none received into any fellowship with it who are likely to disturbe the same, and this intent (I am sure) is lawful and good. Now then, if such to whom the keeping of this law is committed, be persuaded in theire judgments that such a man is likely to disturbe and hinder the publick weale, but some others who are not in the same trust, judge otherwise, yet they are to follow theire owne judgments, rather then the judgments of others who are not alike interested: As in tryall of an offender by a jury; the twelve men are satisfied in their consciences, upon the evidence given, that the party deserves deserves death: but there are 20 or 40 standers by, who conceive otherwise, yet is the jury bound to condemn him according to their owne consciences, and not to acquit him upon the different opinion of other men, except theire reasons can convince them of the errour of theire consciences, and this is according to the rule of the Apostle, Rom. 14. 5. Let every man be fully persuaded in his own mynde. . . .

Lastly, Whereas it is objected that by this law, we reject good christians and so consequently Christ himselfe: I answer 1st, It is not knowne that any christian man hath beene rejected. 2, A man that is a true christian, may be denyed residence among us, in some cases, without rejecting Christ, as admitt a true christian should come over, and should maintaine community of goods, or that magistrates ought not to punish the breakers of the first table, or the members of churches for criminal offences: or that no man were bound to be subject to those lawes or magistrates to which they should not give an explicite consent, &c. I hope no man will say, that not to receive such an one, were to reject Christ; for such opinions (though being maintained in simple ignorance, they might stand with a state of grace yet) they may be so dangerous to the publick weale in many respects, as it would be our sinne and unfaithfullness to receive such among us, except it were for tryall of theire reformation, I would demand then in the case in question (for it is bootelesse curiosity to refrayne openesse in things publick) whereas it is sayd that this law was made of purpose to keepe away such as are of Mr. Wheelwright, his judgment (admit it were so which yet I cannot confesse) where is the evill of it? If we conceive and finde by sadd experience that his opinions are such, as by his own profession cannot stand with externall peace, may we not provide for our peace, by keeping of such as would strengthen him, and infect others with such dangerous tenets? and if we finde his opinions such as will cause divisions, and make people looke at their magistrates, ministers and brethren as enemies to Christ and Antichrists, &c. were it not sinne and unfaithfullness in us, to receive more of those opinions, which we allready finde the evill fruite of: Nay, why doe not those who now complayne joyne with us in keeping out of such, as well as formerly they did in expelling Mr. Williams for the like, though lesse dangerous? Where this change of theire judgments should arise I leave to themselves to examine, and I earnestly entreate them so to doe, and for this law let the equally mynded judge, what evill they finde in it, or in the practice of those who are betrusted with the execution of it.

D. THE RELATIONSHIP BETWEEN LIBERTY AND AUTHORITY: JOHN WINTHROP, SPEECH ON LIBERTY (JULY 3, 1645)*

. . . The great questions that have troubled the country, are about the authority of the magistrates and the liberty of the people. It is yourselves who have called us to this office, and being called by you, we have our authority from God, in way of an ordinance, such as hath the image of God eminently stamped upon it, the contempt and violation whereof hath been vindicated with examples of divine vengeance. I entreat you to consider, that when you choose magistrates, you take them from among yourselves, men subject to like passions as you are. Therefore when you see infirmities in us, you should reflect upon your own, and that would make you bear the more with us, and not be severe censurers of the failings of your magistrates, when you have continual experience of the like infirmities in yourselves and others. We account him a good servant, who breaks not his covenant. The covenant between you and us is the oath you have taken of us, which is to this purpose, that we shall govern you and judge your causes by the rules of God's laws and our own, according to our best skill. When you agree with a workman to build you a ship or house, etc., he undertakes as well for his skill as for his faithfulness, for it is his profession, and you pay him for both. But when you call one to be a magistrate, he doth not profess nor undertake to have sufficient skill for that office, nor can you furnish him with gifts, etc., therefore you must run the hazard of his skill and ability. But if he fail in faithfulness, which by his oath he is bound unto, that he must answer for. If it fall out that the case be clear to common apprehension, and the rule clear also, if he transgress here, the error is not in the skill, but in the evil of the will: it must be required of him. But if the case be doubtful, or the rule doubtful, to men of such understanding and parts as your magistrates are, if your magistrates should err here, yourselves must bear it.

For the other point concerning liberty, I observe a great mistake in the country about that. There is a twofold liberty, natural (I mean as our nature is now corrupt) and civil or federal. The first is common to man with beasts and other creatures. By this, man, as he stands in relation to man simply, hath liberty to do what he lists; it is a liberty to evil as well as to good. This liberty is incompatible and inconsistent with authority, and cannot endure the least restraint of the most just authority. The exercise and maintaining of this liberty makes men grow more evil, and in time to be worse than brute beasts: omnes sumus licentia deteriores.

* These excerpts are reprinted from John Winthrop, *The History of New England* (James Savage, ed., 1853), vol. II, pp. 280–282.

This is that great enemy of truth and peace, that wild beast, which all the ordinances of God are bent against, to restrain and subdue it. The other kind of liberty I call civil or federal, it may also be termed moral, in reference to the covenant between God and man, in the moral law, and the politic covenants and constitutions, amongst men themselves. This liberty is the proper end and object of authority, and cannot subsist without it; and it is a liberty to that only which is good, just, and honest. This liberty you are to stand for, with the hazard (not only of your goods, but) of your lives, if need be. Whatsoever crosseth this, is not authority, but a distemper thereof. This liberty is maintained and exercised in a way of subjection to authority; it is of the same kind of liberty wherewith Christ hath made us free. The woman's own choice makes such a man her husband; yet being so chosen, he is her lord, and she is to be subject to him, yet in a way of liberty, not of bondage; and a true wife accounts her subjection her honor and freedom, and would not think her condition safe and free, but in her subjection to her husband's authority. Such is the liberty of the Church under the authority of Christ, her king and husband; his yoke is so easy and sweet to her as a bride's ornaments; and if through frowardness or wantonness, etc., she shake it off, at any time, she is at no rest in her spirit, until she take it up again; and whether her lord smiles upon her, and embraceth her in his arms, or whether he frowns, or rebukes, or smites her, she apprehends the sweetness of his love in all, and is refreshed, supported, and instructed by every such dispensation of his authority over her. On the other side, ye know who they are that complain of this yoke and say, let us break their bands, etc., we will not have this man to rule over us. Even so, brethren, it will be between you and your magistrates. If you stand for your natural corrupt liberties, and will do what is good in your own eyes, you will not endure the least weight of authority, but will murmur, and oppose, and be always striving to shake off that yoke; but if you will be satisfied to enjoy such civil and lawful liberties, such as Christ allows you, then will you quietly and cheerfully submit unto that authority which is set over you, in all the administrations of it, for your good. Wherein, if we fail at any time, we hope we shall be willing (by God's assistance) to hearken to good advice from any of you, or in any other way of God; so shall your liberties be preserved, in upholding the honor and power of authority amongst you. . . .

E. THE TRUE CHURCH: THOMAS HOOKER, "SURVEY OF THE SUMME OF CHURCH-DISCIPLINE" (1648)*

That the people hath right to call their own officers, and that none must be imposed upon them by Patrons and Prelates.

That Scandalous persons are not fit to be members of a visible Church, nor should be admitted.

* These excerpts are reprinted from "The Way of the Churches of New England," *Old South Leaflets,* no. 55 (n.d.), pp. 8–12.

That the faithfull Congregations in England are true Churches: and therefore it is sinfull to separate from them as no Churches.

That the members which come commended from such Churches to ours here, so that it doth appear to the judgment of the Church, whence they come, that they are by them approved, and not scandalous, they ought to be received to Church communion with us, as members of other Churches with us in N.E. in like case so commended and approved.

To separate from Congregations for want of some Ordinances: Or,

To separate from the true worship of God, because of the sin of some worshippers, is unlawfull.

The Consociation of Churches is not only lawful, but in some cases necessary.

That when causes are difficult, and particular Churches want light and help, they should crave the Assistance of such a consociation.

That Churches so meeting have right to counsell, rebuke, &c. as the case doth require.

In case any particular Church shall walk pertinaciously, either in the profession of errour, or sinfull practice, and will not hear their counsell, they may and should renounce the right hand of fellowship with them.

That Infants of visible Churches, born of wicked parents, being members of the Church, ought to be baptized. . . .

If the Reader shall demand how far this way of Church-proceeding receives approbation by any common concurrence amongst us: I shall plainly and punctually expresse my self in a word of truth, in these following points, viz.

Visible Saints are the only true and meet matter, whereof a visible Church should be gathered, and confœderation is the form.

The Church as Totum essentiale, is, and may be, before Officers.

There is no Presbyteriall Church (*i.e.* A Church made up of the Elders of many Congregations appointed Classickwise, to rule all those Congregations) in the N.T.

A Church Congregationall is the first subject of the keys.

Each Congregation compleatly constituted of all Officers, hath sufficient power in her self, to exercise the power of the keyes, and all Church discipline, in all the censures thereof.

Ordination is not before election.

There ought to be no ordination of a Minister at large, Namely, such as should make him Pastour without a People.

The election of the people hath an instrumentall causall vertue under Christ, to give an outward call unto an Officer.

Ordination is only a solemn installing of an Officer into the Office, unto which he was formerly called.

Children of such, who are members of Congregations, ought only to be baptized.

The consent of the people gives a causall vertue to the compleating of the sentence of excommunication.

Whilst the Church remains a true Church of Christ, it doth not loose this power, nor can it lawfully be taken away.

Consociation of Churches should be used, as occasion doth require.

Such consociations and Synods have allowance to counsell and ad-monish other Churches, as the case may require.

And if they grow obstinate in errour or sinfull miscarriages, they should renounce the right hand of fellowship with them.

But they have no power to excommunicate.

Nor do their constitutions binde formalitèr & juridicè. . . .

F. AN ECCLESIASTICAL CONSTITUTION: THE CAMBRIDGE PLATFORM (1648)*

Of Synods

1. Synods orderly assembled, [Acts 15, 2, to 15.] and rightly proceed-ing according to the pattern, *Acts*. 15. we acknowledge as the ordinance of Christ: and tho' not absolutely necessary to the being, yet many times, thro' the iniquity of men, and perverseness of times, necessary to the well-being of churches, for the establishment of truth and peace therein.

2. Synods being spiritual and ecclesiastical assemblies, are therefore made up of spiritual and ecclesiastical causes. The next efficient cause of them under Christ, is the power of the churches sending forth their elders and other messengers, [Acts 15. 2, 3.] who being met together in the name of Christ, are the matter of a Synod; and they in arguing and de-bating and determining matters of religion, [verse 6.] according to the word and publishing the same to the churches it concerneth, [verse 7, to 23.] do put forth the proper and formal acts of a Synod, [verse 31.] to the conviction and errors, and heresies, and the establishment of truth and peace in the churches, which is the end of a Synod. [Acts 16. 4, 15.]

3. Magistrates have power to call a Synod, by calling to the churches to send forth their elders and other messengers to counsel and assist them in matters of religion; [2 Chron. 29. 4, 5. to 11.] but yet the constituting of a Synod is a church-act, and may be transacted by the churches, [Acts 15.] even when civil magistrates may be enemies to churches and to church-assemblies.

4. It belongeth unto Synods and councils to debate and determine controversies of faith, and cases of conscience; [Acts 15. 1, 2, 6, 7. 1 Chr. 15. 13. 2 Chr. 29, 6, 7. Acts 15. 24, 28, 29.] to clear from the word holy directions, for the holy worship of God and good government of the church: to bear witness against mal-administration and corruption in doc-trine or manners, in any particular church; and to give directions for the reformation thereof: not to exercise church-censures in way of discipline, nor any other act of church-authority or jurisdiction, which that presi-dential Synod did forbear.

5. The Synods directions and determinations, so far as consonant to the

---

* These excerpts consist of chaps. XVI–XVII of the Cambridge Platform and are reprinted from Cotton Mather, *Magnalia Christi Americana* (2 vols., 1820), vol. II, pp. 201–203.

word of God, are to be received with reverence and submission; not only for their agreement therewith, [Acts 15.] (which is the principal ground thereof, and without which they bind not at all) but also secondarily, for the power, whereby they are made, as being an ordinance of God appointed thereunto in his word.

6. Because it is difficult, if not impossible for many churches to come together in one place, in their members universally; therefore they may assemble by their delegates or messengers as the *church* at *Antioch* went not all to *Jerusalem*, but some select men for that purpose. [Acts 15. 2.] Because none are, or should be more fit to know the state of the churches, nor to advise of ways for the good thereof than elders: therefore it is fit, that in the choice of the messengers for such assemblies, they have special respect unto such: yet, inasmuch, as not only *Paul* and *Barnabas*, but certain others also, [Acts 15. 2, 22, 23.] were sent to *Jerusalem* from *Antioch*, *Acts* 15. and when they were come to *Jerusalem*, not only the apostles and elders, but other bretheren, also do assemble and meet about the matter: therefore Synods are to consist both of elders and other church-members, endued with gifts, and sent by the churches, not excluding the presence of any bretheren in the churches. . . .

Of the Civil Magistrates Power in Matters Ecclesiastical

1. It is lawful profitable and necessary for Christians to gather themselves together into church estate, and therein to exercise all the ordinances of Christ, according unto the word, [Acts 2. 41, 47. & 4. 1. 2. 3] altho' the consent of the magistrate could not be had thereunto; because the apostles and Christians in their time, did frequently thus practise, when the magistrates being all of them *Jewish* and *Pagan* and most persecuting enemies, would give no countenance or consent to such matters.

2. Church-government stands in no opposition to civil government of commonwealths, nor any way intrencheth upon the authority of civil magistrates in their jurisdictions; nor any whit weakeneth their hands in governing, but rather strengtheneth them, and furthereth the people in yielding more hearty and conscionable obedience to them, whatsoever some ill affected persons to the ways of Christ have suggested, to alienate the affections of kings and princes from the ordinances of Christ; as if the kingdom of Christ in his church, could not rise and stand, without the falling and weakening of their government, which is also of Christ: [Isa. 49, 23.] whereas the contrary is most true, that they may both stand together and flourish, the one being helpful unto the other, in their distinct and due administrations.

3. The power and authority of magistrates is not for the restraining of churches, [Rom. 13. 4. 1 Tim. 2.2.] or any other good works, but for helping in and furthering thereof; and therefore the consent and countenance of magistrates, when it may be had, is not to be slighted, or lightly esteemed: but, on the contrary, it is part of that honor *due* to Christian magistrates, to desire and crave their consent and approbation therein;

which being obtained, the *churches* may then proceed in their way, with much more encouragement and comfort.

4. It is not in the power of magistrates to compel their subjects to become church-members, and to partake of the Lord's supper; [Ezek. 44. 7,9.] for the priests are reproved, that brought unworthy ones into the sanctuary: [1 Cor. 5. 11.] then it was unlawful for the priests, so it is as unlawful to be done by civil magistrates, those whom the church is to cast out if they were in, the magistrate ought not to thrust them into the church, nor to hold them therein.

5. As it is unlawful for church-officers to meddle with the sword of the magistrate, [Mat. 2. 25, 26.] so it is unlawful for the magistrate to meddle with the work proper to church-officers. The acts of *Moses* and *David*, who were not only princes but prophets, were extraordinary, therefore not inimitable. Against such usurpation the Lord witnessed by smiting *Uzziah* with leprosie, for presuming to offer incense. [2 Chr. 26. 16,17.]

6. It is the duty of the magistrate to take care of matters of religion, and to improve his civil authority for the observing of the duties commanded in the first, as well as for observing of the duties commanded in the second table. They are called *Gods*. [Psa. 88.8.] The end of the magistrates office is not only the quiet and peaceable life of the subject in matters of righteousness and honesty, but also in matters of godliness, yea, of all godliness. [1 Tim. 2, 1,2. 1 Kings 15. 14. & 22. 43.2 Kings 12. 3. & 14.4. & 15. 35.] *Moses, Joshua, David, Solomon, Asa, Jehosaphat, Hezekiah, Josiah*, are much commended by the Holy Ghost, for the putting forth their authority in matters of religion: on the contrary, such kings as have been failing this way, are frequently taxed and reproved of the Lord. [1 Kings 20. 42. Job 29. 25. & 31, 26, 28. Neh. 13. Jonah 3. 7. Ezra 7. Dan. 3. 29.] And not only the kings of *Juda*, but also *Job, Nehemiah*, the king of *Nineveh, Darius, Artaxerxes, Nebuchadnezzar*, whom none looked at, as types of Christ, (tho' were it so, there were no place for any just objection) are commended in the books of God, for exercising their authority this way.

7. The objects of the power of the magistrate are not things meerly inward, and so not subject to his cognizance and view, as unbelief, hardness of heart, erroneous opinions not vented, but only such things as are acted by the outward man: neither their power to be exercised in commanding such acts of the outward man, and punishing the neglect thereof, as are but meer inventions and devices of men, [1 Kings 20. 28, 42.] but about such acts as are commanded and forbidden in the word: yea, such as the word doth clearly determine, tho' not always clearly to the judgment of the magistrate or others, yet clearly in its self. In these he, of right, ought to put forth his authority, tho' oft-times actually he doth it not.

8. Idolatry, blasphemy, heresie, [Deut. 13. 1 Kings 20. 28, 42.] venting corrupt and pernicious opinions, that destroy the foundation, [Dan. 3, 29.] open contempt of the word preached, [Zech. 13. 3.] prophanation of the Lord's Day, [Neh. 13. 31.] disturbing the peaceable administration and exercise of the worship and holy things of God, [1 Tim. 2 2.] and the like, [Rom. 13. 4.] are to be restrained and punished by civil authority.

9. If any church, one or more, shall grow schismatical, rending itself, from the communion of other churches, or shall walk incorrigibly and obstinately in any corrupt way of their own, contrary to the rule of the word; in such case the magistrate, [Josh. 22.] is to put forth his coercive power, as the matter shall require. The tribes on this side *Jordan* intended to- make war against the other tribes, for building the altar of witness, whom they suspected to have turned away therein, from following of the Lord.

G. THE FUNCTION OF HARVARD COLLEGE: "NEW ENGLAND'S FIRST FRUITS" (1643)*

After God had carried us safe to *New England,* and wee had builded our houses, provided necessaries for our liveli-hood, rear'd convenient places for Gods worship, and setled the Civill Government: One of the next things we longed for, and looked after was to advance *Learning,* and perpetuate it to Posterity, dreading to leave an illiterate Ministery to the Churches, when our present Ministers shall lie in the Dust. And as wee were thinking and consulting how to effect this great Work; it pleased God to stir up the heart of one Mr. *Harvard* (a godly Gentleman and a lover of Learning, there living amongst us) to give the one halfe of his Estate (it being in all about 1700. 1.) towards the erecting of a Colledge, and all his Library: after him another gave 300. 1. others after them cast in more, and the publique hand of the State added the rest: the Colledge was, by common consent, appointed to be at *Cambridge,* (a place very pleasant and accommodate and is called (according to the name of the first founder) *Harvard Colledge....*

Rules, and Precepts That Are Observed in the Colledge

1. When any Schollar is able to understand *Tully,* or such like classicall Latine Author *extempore,* and make and speake true Latine in Verse and Prose . . . And decline perfectly the Paradigim's of *Nounes* and *Verbes* in the *Greek* tongue: Let him then and not before be capable of admission into the Colledge.

2. Let every Student be plainly instructed, and earnestly pressed to consider well, the maine end of his life and studies is, *to know God and Iesus Christ which is eternall life,* Joh. 17.3. and therefore to lay *Christ* in the bottome, as the only foundation of all sound knowledge and Learning.

And seeing the Lord only giveth wisdome, Let every one seriously set him-selfe by prayer in secret to seeke it of him *Prov* 2, 3.

3. Every one shall so exercise himselfe in reading the Scriptures twice a day, that he shall be ready to give such account of his proficiency therein, both in *Theoreticall* observations of the Language, and *Logick,* and in *Practicall* and spirituall truths, as his Tutor shall require, according to his ability; seeing *the*

* These excerpts are reprinted from *Old South Leaflets.* no. 51 (n.d.), pp. 1–3.

entrance of the word giveth light, it giveth understanding to the simple, Psalm. 119. 130.

4. That they eschewing all profanation of Gods Name, Attributes, Word, Ordinances, and times of Worship, doe studie with good conscience, carefully to retaine God, and the love of his truth in their mindes else let them know, that (notwithstanding their Learning) God may give them up *to strong delusions,* and in the end *to a reprobate minde,* 2 Thes. 2. 11, 12. Rom. 1. 28.

5. That they studiously redeeme the time; observe the generall houres appointed for all the Students, and the speciall houres for their owne *Classis*: and then dilligently attend the Lectures without any disturbance by word or gesture. And if in any thing they doubt, they shall enquire as of their fellowes, so, (in case of *Non satisfaction*) modestly of their Tutors.

6. None shall under any pretence whatsoever, frequent the company and society of such men as lead an unfit, and dissolute life.

Nor shall any without his Tutors leave or (in his absence) the call of Parents or Guardians, goe abroad to other Townes.

7. Every Schollar shall be present in his Tutors chamber at the 7th. houre in the morning, immediately after the sound of the Bell, at his opening the Scripture and prayer, so also at the 5th houre at night, and then give account of his owne private reading, as aforesaid in Particular the third, and constantly attend Lectures in the Hall at the houres appointed? But if any (without necessary impediment) shall absent himselfe from prayer or Lectures, he shall bee lyable to Admonition, if he offend above once a weeke.

8. If any Schollar shall be found to transgresse any of the Lawes of God, or the Schoole, after twice Admonition, he shall be lyable, if not *adultus,* to correction, if *adultus,* his name shall be given up to the Overseers of the Colledge, that he may bee admonished at the publick monethly Act.

H. THE PERPETUATION OF PURITAN IDEALS: THE MASSACHUSETTS SCHOOL LAWS OF 1642 AND 1647*

1642

This Court, taking into consideration the great neglect in many parents & masters in training up their children in learning, & labor, & other imployments which may bee profitable to the common wealth, do hearupon order & decree, that in every towne the chosen men appointed for managing the prudenciall affaires of the same shall hencefourth stand charged with the care of the redresse of this evill, so as they shalbee liable to bee punished or fined for the neglect thereof, upon any presentment of the grand iurors, or other information or complaint in any plantations in this iurisdiction; & for this end they, or the greater part of them, shall have power to take accompt from time to time of their parents & masters, & of their children, concerning their calling & impliment of their children, especially of their ability to read & understand the principles of religion

* Reprinted in full from Nathaniel B. Shurtleff (ed.), *Records of the Governor and Company of the Massachusetts Bay* (6 vols., 1853–1854), vol. II, pp. 8–9, 203.

and the capital lawes of the country, & to impose fines upon all those who refuse to render such accompt to them when required; & they shall have power (with consent of any Court or magistrates) to put fourth apprentice the children of such as shall not be able & fitt to employ & bring them up, nor shall take course to dispose of them, of such as they shall find not to bee able & fit to imply & bring them up, nor shall take course to dispose of them themselues; & they are to take care that such as are set to keep cattle bee set to some other impliment withall, as spinning up on the rock, kniting, weveing tape, etc.; & that boyes & girles bee not suffered to converse together, so as may occasion any wanton, dishonest or immodest behavior; & for their better performance of this trust committed to them, they may divide the towne amongst them, appointing to every of the said townsmen a certeine number of families to have speciall oversight of; they are also to provide that a sufficient quantity of materialls, as hempe, flaxe, etc., may bee raised in their severall townes, & tooles & implements provided for working out the same; & for their assistance in this so needfull & beneficiall impliment, if they meete with any difficulty or opposition which they cannot well master by their owne power, they may have recourse to some of the magistrates, who shall take such course for their help & incuragment as the occasion shall require, according to iustice; & the said townsmen, at the next Court in those limits, after the end of their yeare, shall give a breife account in writing of their proceedings herein; provided, that they have bene so required by some Court or magistrate a month at least before; & this order to continue for two yeares, & till the Court shall take further order. . . .

1647

It being one cheife proiect of the ould deluder, Satan, to keepe men from the knowledge of the Scriptures, as in former times by keeping them in an unknowne tongue, so in these latter times by perswading from the use of tongues, that so at least the true sence & meaning of the originall might be clouded by false glosses of saint seeming deceivers, that learning may not be buried in the grave of our fathers in the church & commonwealth, the Lord assisting our endeavours.

It is therefore ordered, that every towneship in the iurisdiction, after the Lord hath increased them to the number of 50 housholders, shall then forthwith appoint one within their towne to teach all such children as shall resort to him to write & reade, whose wages shall be paid either by the parents or masters of such children, or by the inhabitants in generall, by way of supply, as the maior part of those that order the prudentials of the towne shall appoint; provided, those that send their children be not oppressed by paying much more than they can have them taught for in other townes; & it is further ordered, that where any towne shall increase to the number of 100 families or househoulders, they shall set up a grammer schoole, the master thereof being able to instruct youth so farr as they may be fited for the university, provided, that if any towne neglect the performance hereof above one yeare, that every such towne shall pay 5£ to the next schoole till they shall performe this order.

I. UNION AGAINST OUTSIDE ATTACK: THE NEW ENGLAND CONFEDERATION (MAY 19, 1643)*

Whereas we all came into these parts of America with one and the same end and aim, namely, to advance the Kingdom of our Lord Jesus Christ and to enjoy the liberties of the Gospel in purity with peace; and whereas in our settling (by a wise providence of God) we are further dispersed upon the sea coasts and rivers than was at first intended, so that we can not according to our desire with convenience communicate in one government and jurisdiction; and whereas we live encompassed with people of several nations and strange languages which hereafter may prove injurious to us or our posterity. And forasmuch as the natives have formerly committed sundry insolence and outrages upon several Plantations of the English and have of late combined themselves against us: and seeing by reason of those sad distractions in England which they have heard of, and by which they know we are hindered from that humble way of seeking advice, or reaping those comfortable fruits of protection, which at other times we might well expect. We therefore do conceive it our bounden duty, without delay to enter into a present Consociation amongst ourselves, for mutual help and strength in all our future concernments: That, as in nation and religion, so in other respects, we be and continue one according to the tenor and true meaning of the ensuing articles: Wherefore it is fully agreed and concluded by and between the parties or Jurisdictions above named, and they jointly and severally do by these presents agree and conclude that they all be and henceforth be called by the name of the United Colonies of New England.

2. The said United Colonies for themselves and their posterities do jointly and severally hereby enter into a firm and perpetual league of friendship and amity for offence and defence, mutual advice and succor upon all just occasions both for preserving and propagating the truth and liberties of the Gospel and for their own mutual safety and welfare. . . .

4. It is by these Confederates agreed that the charge of all just wars, whether offensive or defensive, upon what part or member of this Confederation soever they fall, shall both in men, provisions, and all other disbursements be borne by all the parts of this Confederation in different proportions according to their different ability in manner following, namely, that the Commissioners for each Jurisdiction from time to time, as there shall be occasion, bring a true account and number of all their males in every Plantation, or any way belonging to or under their several Jurisdictions, of what quality or condition soever they be, from sixteen

* These excerpts are reprinted from Francis Newton Thorpe (ed.), *Federal and State Constitutions, Colonial Charters, and Other Organic Laws* (7 vols., 1909), vol. I, pp. 77–81.

years old to three-score, being inhabitants there. And that according to the different numbers which from time to time shall be found in each Jurisdiction upon a true and just account, the service of men and all charges of the war be borne by the poll: each Jurisdiction or Plantation being left to their own just course and custom of rating themselves and people according to their different estates with due respects to their qualities and exemptions amongst themselves though the Confederation take no notice of any such privilege: and that according to their different charge of each Jurisdiction and Plantation the whole advantage of the war (if it please God so to bless their endeavors) whether it be in lands, goods, or persons, shall be proportionably divided among the said Confederates.

5. It is further agreed, that if any of these Jurisdictions or any Plantation under or in combination with them, be invaded by any enemy whomsoever, upon notice and request of any three magistrates of that Jurisdiction so invaded, the rest of the Confederates without any further meeting or expostulation shall forthwith send aid to the Confederate in danger but in different proportions; namely, the Massachusetts an hundred men sufficiently armed and provided for such a service and journey, and each of the rest, forty-five so armed and provided, or any less number, if less be required according to this proportion. But if such Confederate in danger may be supplied by their next Confederates, not exceeding the number hereby agreed, they may crave help there, and seek no further for the present: the charge to be borne as in this article is expressed: and at the return to be victualled and supplied with powder and shot for their journey (if there be need) by that Jurisdiction which employed or sent for them; but none of the Jurisdictions to exceed these numbers until by a meeting of the Commissioners for this Confederation a greater aid appear necessary. And this proportion to continue till upon knowledge of greater numbers in each Jurisdiction which shall be brought to the next meeting, some other proportion be ordered. But in any such case of sending men for present aid, whether before or after such order or alteration, it is agreed that at the meeting of the Commissioners for this Confederation, the cause of such war or invasion be duly considered: and if it appear that the fault lay in the parties so invaded then that Jurisdiction or Plantation make just satisfaction, both to the invaders whom they have injured, and bear all the charges of the war themselves, without requiring any allowance from the rest of the Confederates towards the same. And further that if any Jurisdiction see any danger of invasion approaching, and there be time for a meeting, that in such a case three magistrates of the Jurisdiction may summon a meeting at such convenient place as themselves shall think meet, to consider and provide against the threatened danger. . . .

6. It is also agreed, that for the managing and concluding of all affairs proper, and concerning the whole Confederation two Commissioners shall be chosen by and out of each of these four Jurisdictions: namely, two for the Massachusetts, two for Plymouth, two for Connecticut, and two for New Haven, being all in Church-fellowship with us, which shall bring full power from their several General Courts respectively to hear, examine,

weigh, and determine all affairs of our war, or peace, leagues, aids, charges, and numbers of men for war, division of spoils and whatsoever is gotten by conquest, receiving of more Confederates for Plantations into combination with any of the Confederates, and all things of like nature, which are the proper concomitants or consequents of such a Confederation for amity, offence, and defence: not intermeddling with the government of any of the Jurisdictions, which by the third article is preserved entirely to themselves. But if these eight Commissioners when they meet shall not all agree yet it [is] concluded that any six of the eight agreeing shall have power to settle and determine the business in question. But if six do not agree, that then such propositions with their reasons so far as they have been debated, be sent and referred to the four General Courts; namely, the Massachusetts, Plymouth, Connecticut, and New Haven; and if at all the said General Courts the business so referred be concluded, then to be prosecuted by the Confederates and all their members. It is further agreed that these eight Commissioners shall meet once every year besides extraordinary meetings (according to the fifth article) to consider, treat, and conclude of all affairs belonging to this Confederation. . . .

8. It is also agreed that the Commissioners for this Confederation hereafter at their meetings, whether ordinary or extraordinary, as they may have commission or opportunity, do endeavor to frame and establish agreements and orders in general cases of a civil nature, wherein all the Plantations are interested, for preserving of peace among themselves, for preventing as much as may be all occasion of war or differences with others, as about the free and speedy passage of justice in every Jurisdiction, to all the Confederates equally as to their own, receiving those that remove from one Plantation to another without due certificate, how all the Jurisdictions may carry it towards the Indians, that they neither grow insolent nor be injured without due satisfaction, lest war break in upon the Confederates through such miscarriages. It is also agreed that if any servant run away from his master into any other of these confederated Jurisdictions, that in such case, upon the certificate of one magistrate in the Jurisdiction out of which the said servant fled, or upon other due proof; the said servant shall be delivered, either to his master, or any other that pursues and brings such certificate or proof. And that upon the escape of any prisoner whatsoever, or fugitive for any criminal cause, whether breaking prison, or getting from the officer, or otherwise escaping, upon the certificate of two magistrates of the Jurisdiction out of which the escape is made, that he was a prisoner, or such an offender at the time of the escape, the magistrates, or some of them of that Jurisdiction where for the present the said prisoner or fugitive abideth, shall forthwith grant such a warrant as the case will bear, for the apprehending of any such person, and the delivery of him into the hands of the officer or other person who pursues him. And if there be help required, for the safe returning of any such offender, then it shall be granted to him that craves the same, he paying the charges thereof.

9. And for that the justest wars may be of dangerous consequence, especially to the smaller Plantations in these United Colonies, it is agreed

that neither the Massachusetts, Plymouth, Connecticut, nor New Haven, nor any of the members of them, shall at any time hereafter begin, undertake, or engage themselves, or this Confederation, or any part thereof in any war whatsoever (sudden exigencies, with the necessary consequents thereof excepted), which are also to be moderated as much as the case will permit, without the consent and agreement of the forementioned eight Commissioners, or at least six of them, as in the sixth article is provided: and that no charge be required of any of the Confederates, in case of a defensive war, till the said Commissioners have met, and approved the justice of the war, and have agreed upon the sum of money to be levied, which sum is then to be paid by the several Confederates in proportion according to the fourth article. . . .

11. It is further agreed that if any of the Confederates shall hereafter break any of these present articles, or be any other ways injurious to any one of the other Jurisdictions; such breach of agreement or injury shall be duly considered and ordered by the Commissioners for the other Jurisdictions, that both peace and this present Confederation may be entirely preserved without violation. . . .

SELECTION

The Failure of Enforcement and the Accommodation of Puritan Ideals

That it was impossible to enforce Puritan values strictly had already become apparent by the late 1650s. Economic prosperity and rapid expansion produced an increasing attention to secular matters, and the simultaneous decline of religious zeal, the falling away from old ideals, was deplored by preachers and magistrates alike. The explanation for this moral declension and a prediction of the dire consequences that would result if it was not reversed can be seen in "God's Controversy with New-England," a didactic poem by Michael Wigglesworth (1631–1705), minister of Malden and author of "The Day of Doom," probably the best-known Puritan poem. To shore up the crumbling foundations of Puritanism, a synod attempted to broaden its appeal in 1662 by adopting the Half-Way Covenant, which permitted baptism of children of parents who were halfway members of the church—that is, who had been baptized and had made a profession of faith but had not had any "experience" to indicate their membership in the elect. Previously, only children of "visible saints" could be baptized, and the Half-Way Covenant thus furnished some hope for the salvation of the children of the believers among the nonelect. Perry Miller, "The

Half-Way Covenant," New England Quarterly *volume 6 (1933), pages 676–715, is the fullest treatment of that subject, and* Kenneth B. *Murdock,* Literature and Theology in Colonial New England *(1949), provides further information on Wigglesworth and on Puritan prose and poetry.*

A. THE WAGES OF SIN: MICHAEL WIGGLESWORTH, ''GOD'S CONTROVERSY WITH NEW-ENGLAND'' (1662)*

✻ ✻ ✻

"Are these the men that erst at my command
  Forsook their ancient seats and native soile,
To follow me into a desart land,
  Contemning all the travell and the toile,
Whose love was such to purest ordinances
  As made them set at nought their fair inheritances?

"Are these the men that prized libertee
  To walk with God according to their light,
To be as good as he would have them bee,
  To serve and worship him with all their might,
Before the pleasures which a fruitful field,
  And country flowing-full of all good things, could yield,

"Are these the folk whom from the brittish Iles,
  Through the stern billows of the watry main,
I safely led so many thousand miles,
  As if their journey had been through a plain?
Whom having from all enemies protected,
  And through so many deaths and dangers well directed,

"I brought and planted on the western shore,
  Where nought but bruits and salvage wights did swarm
(Untaught, untrain'd, untam'd by vertue's lore)
  That sought their blood, yet could not do them harm?
My fury's flaile them thresht, my fatall broom
  Did sweep them hence, to make my people elbow-room.

"Are these the men whose gates with peace I crown'd,
  To whom for bulwarks I salvation gave,
Whilst all things else with rattling tumults sound,
  And mortall frayes send thousands to the grave?
Whilest their own brethren bloody hands embrewed
  In brothers blood, and fields with carcases bestrewed?

"Is this the people blest with bounteous store,
  By land and sea full richly clad and fed,

* These excerpts are reprinted from *Proceedings of the Massachusetts Historical Society,* 1st ser., vol. 12 (1873), pp. 86–91, 93.

Whom plenty's self stands waiting still before,
  And powreth out their cups well tempered?
For whose dear sake an howling wildernes
  I lately turned into a fruitful paradeis?

"Are these the people in whose hemisphere
  Such bright-beam'd, glist'ring, sun-like starrs I placed,
As by their influence did all things cheere,
  As by their light blind ignorance defaced,
As errours into lurking holes did fray,
  As turn'd the late dark night into a lightsome day?

"Are these the folk to whom I milked out
  And sweetnes stream'd from consolations brest;
Whose soules I fed and strengthened throughout
  With finest spirituall food most finely drest?
On whom I rained living bread from Heaven,
  Withouten Errour's bane, or Superstition's leaven?

"With whom I made a Covenant of peace,
  And unto whom I did most firmly plight
My faithfulness, If whilst I live I cease
  To be their Guide, their God, their full delight;
Since them with cords of love to me I drew,
  Enwrapping in my grace such as should them ensew.

"Are these the men, that now mine eyes behold,
  Concerning whom I thought, and whilome spake,
First Heaven shall pass away together scrold,
  Ere they my lawes and righteous wayes forsake,
Or that they slack to ruun their heavenly race?
  Are these the same? or are some others come in place?

"If these be they, how is it that I find
  In stead of holiness Carnality,
In stead of heavenly frames an Earthly mind,
  For burning zeal luke-warm Indifferency,
For flaming love, key-cold Dead-heartedness,
  For temperance (in meat, and drinke, and cloaths) excess?

"Whence cometh it, that Pride, and Luxurie
  Debate, Deceit, Contention, and Strife,
False-dealing, Covetousness, Hypocrisie
  (With such like Crimes) amongst them are so rife,
That one of them doth over-reach another?
  And that an honest man can hardly trust his Brother?

"How is it, that Security, and Sloth,
  Amongst the best are Common to be found?

That grosser sins, in stead of Graces growth,
   Amongst the many more and more abound?
I hate dissembling shews of Holiness.
   Or practise as you talk, or never more profess.

"Judge not, vain world, that all are hypocrites
   That do profess more holiness then thou:
All foster not dissembling, guilefull sprites,
   Nor love their lusts, though very many do.
Some sin through want of care and constant watch,
   Some with the sick converse, till they the sickness catch.

"Some, that maintain a reall root of grace,
   Are overgrown with many noysome weeds,
Whose heart, that those no longer may take place,
   The benefit of due correction needs.
And such as these however gone astray
   I shall by stripes reduce into a better way.

"Moreover some there be that still retain
   Their ancient vigour and sincerity;
Whom both their own, and others sins, constrain
   To sigh, and mourn, and weep, and wail, & cry:
And for their sakes I have forborn to powre
   My wrath upon Revolters to this present houre.

"To praying Saints I always have respect,
   And tender love, and pittifull regard:
Nor will I now in any wise neglect
   Their love and faithfull service to reward;
Although I deal with others for their folly,
   And turn their mirth to tears that have been too jolly.

"For thinke not, O Backsliders, in your heart,
   That I shall still your evill manners beare:
Your sinns me press as sheaves do load a cart,
   And therefore I will plague you for this geare
Except you seriously, and soon, repent,
   Ile not delay your pain and heavy punishment.

"And who be those themselves that yonder shew?
   The seed of such as name my dreadful Name!
On whom whilere compassions skirt I threw
   Whilest in their blood they were, to hide their shame!
Whom my preventing love did neer me take!
   Whom for mine own I mark't, lest they should me forsake!

"I look't that such as these to vertue's Lore
   (Though none but they) would have Enclin'd their ear:

That they at least mine image should have bore,
   And sanctify'd my name with awfull fear.
Let pagan's Bratts pursue their lusts, whose meed
   Is Death: For christians children are an holy seed.

"But hear O Heavens! Let Earth amazed stand;
   Ye Mountaines melt, and Hills come flowing down:
Let horror seize upon both Sea and Land;
   Let Natures self be cast into a stown.
I children nourisht, nurtur'd and upheld:
   But they against a tender father have rebell'd.

"What could have been by me performed more?
   Or wherein fell I short of your desire?
Had you but askt, I would have op't my store,
   And given what lawfull wishes could require.
For all this bounteous cost I lookt to see
   Heaven-reaching-hearts, & thoughts, Meekness, Humility. . . .

"Oft have I charg'd you by my ministers
   To gird your selves with sack cloth, and repent.
Oft have I warnd you by my messengers;
   That so you might my wrathfull ire prevent:
But who among you hath this warning taken?
   Who hath his crooked wayes, & wicked works forsaken?

"Yea many grow to more and more excess;
   More light and loose, more Carnall and prophane.
The sins of Sodom, Pride, and Wantonness,
   Among the multitude spring up amain.
Are these the fruits of Pious Education,
   To run with greater speed and Courage to Damnation? . . .

"Now therefore hearken and encline your ear,
   In judgment I will henceforth with you plead;
And if by that you will not learn to fear,
   But still go on a sensuall life to lead:
I'le strike at once an All-Consuming stroke;
   Nor cries nor tears shall then my fierce intent revoke. . . ."

Ah dear New England! dearest land to me;
   Which unto God hast hitherto been dear,
And mayst be still more dear than formerlie,
   If to his voice thou wilt incline thine ear.

Consider wel & wisely what the rod,
   Wherewith thou art from yeer to yeer chastized,
Instructeth thee. Repent, & turn to God,
   Who wil not have his nurture be despized.

Thou still hast in thee many praying saints,
   Of great account, and precious with the Lord,
Who dayly powre out unto him their plaints,
   And strive to please him both in deed & word.

Cheer on, sweet souls, my heart is with you all,
   And shall be with you, maugre Sathan's might:
And whereso'ere this body be a Thrall,
   Still in New-England shall be my delight.

B. THE HALF-WAY COVENANT (1662)*

1. They that, according to scripture, are members of the visible church, are the subjects of baptism.

2. The members of the visible church, according to scripture, are confederate visible believers, in particular churches, and their infant seed, *i.e.* children in minority, whose next parents, one or both, are in covenant.

3. The infant seed of confederate visible believers, are members of the same church with their parents, and when grown up are personally under the watch, discipline and government of that church.

4. These adult persons, are not therefore to be admitted to full communion, merely because they are, and continue members, without such further qualifications as the word of God requireth thereunto.

5. Church members who were admitted in minority, understanding the doctrine of faith, and publickly professing their assent thereto, not scandalous in life, and solemnly owning the covenant before the church, wherein they give up themselves and their children to the Lord, and subject themselves to the government of Christ in the church, their children are to be baptised.

6. Such church members, who either by death, or some other extraordinary providence, have been inevitably hindred from publick acting as aforesaid, yet have given the church cause in judgment of charity, to look at them as so qualified, and such as had they been called thereunto, would have so acted, their children are to be baptised.

7. The members of orthodox churches, being sound in the faith and not scandalous in life, and presenting due testimony thereof; these occasionally coming from one church to another may have their children baptised in the church, whither they come, by virtue of communion of churches: But if they remove their habitation, they ought orderly to covenant and subject themselves to the government of Christ in the church, where they settle their abode, and so their children to be baptised. It being the churche's duty to receive such into communion, so far, as they are regularly fit for the same.

* These excerpts are reprinted from Cotton Mather, *Magnalia Christi Americana* (1820), vol. II, pp. 239–240.

PART TWO

Expansion and Adjustment, 1660–1713

Foundations of a Colonial System
Countervailing Forces
Manifestation of Social Instability
The Revolutionary Settlement
Green Light for Expansion

The *Restoration of the Stuart monarchy in 1660 and the subsequent abatement of religious and political dissension within England were the signals for renewed activity by the English in America. More interested in overseas enterprise than any of his predecessors since Elizabeth, Charles II (1660–1685) made a series of proprietary grants on the Maryland model which served as rewards to some of his more loyal followers among the nobility during the Interregnum and led ultimately to the conquest of New Netherlands and the establishment of five new proprietary colonies: Carolina (1664), New York (1664), New Jersey (1665), Pennsylvania (1681), and Delaware (1682). Except for William Penn, who conceived of his colony in Pennsylvania as a refuge for Quakers as well as a source of revenue, the original proprietors of the Restoration colonies were primarily interested in the economic returns they hoped to derive from the sale of lands and collection of rents from settlers.*

Land-hungry proprietors were not the only Englishmen interested in the colonies after the Restoration, however. Though they had long since ceased to regard plantation founding as a potentially profitable enterprise, after 1650 the large overseas merchants came to value colonies as a source of raw materials and as a market for manufactured goods. Their resent-

ment of the successful engrossment by the Dutch of a large part of the carrying trade of the English colonies was primarily responsible for Parliament's passage of the first navigation acts in 1650 and 1651. The first comprehensive attempt to define the economic relationship between mother country and colonies, these acts were voided at the Restoration. At the merchants' insistence, however, Parliament reenacted their main provisions in the Navigation Act of 1660, which with several later acts theoretically established a national monopoly of colonial trade.

Increasing economic control was accompanied by closer political supervision as imperial officials sought to adjust the system of colonial administration to meet the demands of an expanding empire. Tentative steps toward the creation of a supervisory agency for the colonies during the 1650s and 1660s were followed in 1675 by the establishment of the Lords of Trade, a permanent committee of the Privy Council responsible for the administration of the colonies. During the twenty-year existence of the committee, the Lords vigorously attempted to systematize and centralize colonial administration, sending out special emissaries to investigate conditions in the colonies, establishing uniform instructions for all royal governors, expanding the size of the colonial bureaucracy in both England and the colonies, insisting upon a strict enforcement of the navigation acts and a firm maintenance of the royal prerogative, and advocating the conversion of all private colonies into royal colonies. Upon its recommendation, the New Hampshire towns were separated from Massachusetts Bay in 1679 and made a royal colony, and it was also responsible for legal proceedings that resulted in the forfeiture of the Charter of Massachusetts Bay in 1684. This movement toward centralization reached its culmination with the creation of the Dominion of New England in 1686 after the accession of James II (1685–1689). An experiment in colonial consolidation that was intended to include all the colonies from Maine south to Pennsylvania under one government with no representative assembly, the Dominion did not survive the flight of James II and the accession of William III (1689–1702) during the Glorious Revolution of 1688–1689.

Throughout the Restoration, in fact, powerful counterforces were working against the centralizing policies of the home government. Like the Virginia Company a half-century earlier, the Restoration proprietaries everywhere found it necessary to make generous concessions in the form of easy access to land, liberal conditions of land tenure, assurances of *religious toleration, and self-governing privileges both to recruit settlers and to keep them contented after they had migrated. Once such concessions had been made, they could not be withdrawn without risking disorder and rebellion in the colonies.*

That risk was all the greater because of the profound social instability that characterized colonial life during the last decades of the seventeenth century. Uncertainty about political conditions in England and about the nature of the relationship between the mother country and the colonies; uneasiness deriving from rapidly fluctuating social, economic, and political conditions within the colonies and especially from the inevitable dislocations of values which occurred when they were transferred from one environment to another; exposure to attack from Indians on the frontiers and rival European powers or pirates on the seaboard; and, particularly in New England, concern of the founders over the decline in religious zeal—all these factors combined to keep the colonists in a nearly perpetual state of anxiety and insecurity. The result was an unstable society subject to convulsion and upheaval at the slightest provocation. King Philip's War in New England, Bacon's Rebellion in Virginia, and Culpeper's Rebellion in North Carolina during the mid-1670s; the overthrow of Andros and the Dominion of New England in Massachusetts, Leisler's Rebellion in New York, and the seizure of authority by the Protestant Association in Maryland following the Glorious Revolution of 1688–1689 in England; the Salem witch trials between 1692 and 1693; and the more or less continuous unrest in the Carolinas from the mid-1680s until the revolution against the proprietors in South Carolina in 1719—almost every dramatic episode in colonial life at this time revealed and was to some extent the result of this instability.

The diminution of this condition required time, and it was only in the middle of the eighteenth century, only with the stabilizing of political arrangements within the empire, the clarifying of the lines of social and political authority and the conditions of economic life within the colonies, and the development of sufficient military potential to cope with the Indians, that colonial society achieved more equilibrium. In the meantime, developments which followed the Glorious Revolution both relieved and aggravated the situation. On the one hand, imperial acquiescence in the overthrow of the Dominion of New England and the restoration of the Massachusetts Charter tended to ensure that no further experiments of quite so drastic a nature would be repeated in the future. That the nature of the relationship between the colonies and the mother country was still not firmly fixed, however, was clearly indicated by a number of new measures designed to bring the colonies more closely under the control of the mother country.

The home government did not adopt even stronger measures largely because of its preoccupation with domestic problems arising out of the Glorious Revolution and its involvement first in King William's War (the War of the League of Augsburg in Europe), 1689 to 1697, and then in Queen Anne's War (the War of the Spanish Succession in Europe), 1702 to 1713. Thus at a time when constitutional relationships within the British Isles were undergoing significant changes and when some reordering of the imperial-colonial connection might logically have been expected, the home government made only minor adjustments rather than major alterations in the constitutional structure of the empire.

Expansion and Adjustment, 1660–1713:
Foundations of a Colonial System

SELECTION **17**

The Navigation System

The basic assumption behind English colonial policy as it gradually began to take shape in the years after 1650 was that the colonies existed for the benefit of the mother country. A central tenet of all aspects of mercantilistic thought concerning colonies, this assumption received expression in the economic realm in three navigation acts passed between 1660 and 1673. The Navigation Act of 1660 sought to establish an English monopoly over the carrying trade of the colonies by requiring that it be limited to English (including colonial) ships and by designating certain colonial products as "enumerated articles," which could be exported only to England or to another English colony. By stipulating that no goods—except salt for New England fisheries; wine from the Madeiras and the Azores; and servants, horses, and provisions from Ireland—could be shipped from any European country to the colonies without first passing through England, the Staple Act of 1663 attempted to secure as well an English monopoly over the export trade to the colonies. In placing duties on enumerated articles imported into England but not on those sent from one colony to another, the Navigation Act of 1660 had inadvertently favored the colonists by making it possible for them to obtain enumerated articles more cheaply than Englishmen. Moreover, there was no provision prohibiting the transshipment of such articles directly to Europe, where, because they had paid no duties, colonial merchants could undersell English merchants. To correct this situation, the Plantation Duties Act of 1673 levied duties to be collected in the plantations on all enumerated articles not bound for England. For the rest of the colonial period these three measures served as the basis for imperial economic policy toward the colonies.

Lawrence Harper, The English Navigation Laws: A Seventeenth-century Experiment in Social Engineering *(1939), and Oliver M. Dickerson,* The Navigation Acts and the American Revolution *(1951), are the standard works on the Navigation Acts. A short assessment of the effect of the Navigation Acts on the colonies and of the colonial reaction to them is Curtis P. Nettels, "British Mercantilism and the Economic Development of the Thirteen Colonies,"* The Journal of Economic History, volume 12 (1952), pages 105–114.

A. THE NAVIGATION ACT OF (SEPT. 13) 1660 *

Cap. XVIII

For *the increase of shipping and encouragement of the navigation of this nation, wherein, under the good providence and protection of God, the wealth, safety and strength of this kingdom is so much concerned;* (2) be it enacted by the King's most excellent majesty, and by the lords and commons in this present parliament assembled, and by the authority thereof, That from and after the first day of *December* one thousand six hundred and sixty, and from thenceforward, no goods or commodities whatsoever shall be imported into or exported out of any lands, islands, plantations or territories to his Majesty belonging or in his possession, or which may hereafter belong unto or be in the possession of his Majesty, his heirs and successors, in *Asia, Africa* or *America,* in any other ship or ships, vessel or vessels whatsoever, but in such ships or vessels as do truly and without fraud belong only to the people of *England* or *Ireland,* dominion of *Wales* or town of *Berwick* upon *Tweed,* or are of the built of and belonging to any the said lands, islands, plantations or territories, as the proprietors and right owners thereof, and whereof the matter and three fourths of the mariners at least are *English;* (3) under the penalty of the forfeiture and loss of all the goods and commodities which shall be imported into or exported out of any the aforesaid places in any other ship or vessel, as also of the ship or vessel . . . (4) and all admirals and other commanders at sea of any the ships of war or other ship having commission from his Majesty or from his heirs or successors, are hereby authorized and strictly required to seize and bring in as prize all such ships or vessels as shall have offended contrary hereunto, and deliver them to the court of admiralty, there to be proceeded against. . . .

II. And be it enacted, That no alien or person not born within the allegiance of our sovereign lord the King, his heirs and successors, or naturalized, or made a free denizen, shall from and after the first day of *February,* which will be in the year of our Lord one thousand six hundred sixty-one, exercise the trade or occupation of a merchant or factor in any the said places; (2) upon pain of the forfeiture and loss of all his goods and chattels, or which are in his possession . . . (3) and all governors of the said lands, islands, plantations or territories, and every of them, are hereby strictly required and commanded, and all who hereafter shall be made governors of any such islands, plantations or territories, by his Majesty, his heirs or successors, shall before their entrance into their government take a solemn oath, to do their utmost, that every the aforementioned clauses, and all the matters and things therein contained, shall be punctually and *bona fide* observed according to the true intent and meaning thereof: (4) and upon complaint and proof made before his Majesty, his heirs or successors, or such as shall be by him or them

---

* These excerpts are reprinted from Danby Pickering (ed.), *The Statutes at Large* (46 vols., 1762–1807), vol. VII, pp. 452–454, 459–460.

thereunto authorized and appointed, that any the said governors have been willingly and wittingly negligent in doing their duty accordingly, that the said governor so offending shall be removed from his government.

III. And it is further enacted by the authority aforesaid, That no goods or commodities whatsoever, of the growth, production or manufacture of *Africa, Asia* or *America,* or of any part thereof, or which are described or laid down in the usual maps or cards of those places, be imported into *England, Ireland* or *Wales,* islands of *Guernsey* and *Jersey,* or town of *Berwick* upon *Tweed,* in any other ship or ships, vessel or vessels whatsoever, but in such as do truly and without fraud belong only to the people of *England* or *Ireland,* dominion of *Wales,* or town of *Berwick* upon *Tweed,* or of the lands, islands, plantations or territories in *Asia, Africa* or *America,* to his Majesty belonging, as the proprietors and right owners thereof, and whereof the matter, and three fourths at least of the mariners are *English;* (2) under the penalty of the forfeiture of all such goods and commodities, and of the ship or vessel in which they were imported, with all her guns, tackle, furniture, ammunition and apparel. . . .

XVIII. And it is further enacted by the authority aforesaid, That from and after the first day of *April,* which shall be in the year of our Lord one thousand six hundred sixty-one, no sugars, tobacco, cotton-wool, indicoes, ginger, fustick, or other dying wood, of the growth, production or manufacture of any *English* plantations in *America, Asia* or *Africa,* shall be shipped, carried, conveyed or transported from any of the said *English* plantations to any land, island, territory, dominion, port or place whatsoever, other than to such other *English* plantations as do belong to his Majesty, his heirs and successors, or to the kingdom of *England* or *Ireland,* or principality of *Wales,* or town of *Berwick* upon *Tweed,* there to be laid on shore, (2) under the penalty of the forfeiture of the said goods, or the full value thereof, as also of the ship, with all her guns, tackle, apparel, ammunition and furniture. . . .

XIX. And be it further enacted by the authority aforesaid, That for every ship or vessel, which from and after the five and twentieth day of *December* in the year of our Lord one thousand six hundred and sixty shall set sail out of or from *England, Ireland, Wales,* or town of *Berwick* upon *Tweed,* for any *English* plantation in *America, Asia* or *Africa,* sufficient bond shall be given with one surety to the chief officers of the custom-house of such port or place from whence the said ship shall set sail, to the value of one thousand pounds, if the ship be of less burthen than one hundred tons; and of the sum of two thousand pounds, if the ship should be of greater burthen; that in case the said ship or vessel shall load any of the said commodities at any of the said *English* plantations, that the same commodities shall be by the said ship brought to some port of *England, Ireland, Wales,* or to the port or town of *Berwick* upon *Tweed,* and shall there unload and put on shore the same, the danger of the seas only excepted: (2) And for all ships coming from any other port or place to any of the aforesaid plantations, who by this act are permitted to trade there, that the governor of such *English* plantations shall before the said ship or vessel be permitted to load on board any of the said commodities, take bond in manner and to the value aforesaid, for each respective ship or vessel, that such ship or vessel shall carry all the aforesaid goods that shall be laden on board in the said ship to some other of his Majesty's *English* plantations, or to *England, Ireland, Wales,* or town of *Berwick* upon *Tweed:* (3) And that every ship or vessel which shall load or take on board any of the aforesaid goods, until such bond given to the said governor, or certificate produced from the officers of any custom-house of *England, Ireland, Wales,* or of the town of *Berwick,* that such bonds have been there duly given, shall be forfeited with all her guns, tackle, apparel and furniture, to be imployed and recovered in manner as aforesaid; and the said governors and every of them shall twice in every year after the first day of *January* one thousand six hundred and sixty, return true copies of all such bonds by him so taken, to the chief officers of the custom in *London.*

B. THE STAPLE ACT OF (JULY 27) 1663*

V. . . . *in regard his Majesty's plantations beyond the seas are inhabited and peopled by his subjects of this his kingdom of* England; *for the maintaining a greater correspondence and kindness between them, and keeping them in a firmer dependence upon it, and rendring them yet more beneficial and advantagious unto it in the further imployment and increase of* English *shipping and seamen, vent of* English *woolen and other manufacturers and commodities, rendring the navigation to and from the same more safe and cheap, and making this kingdom a staple, not only of the commodities of those plantations, but also of the commodities of other countries and places, for the supplying of them; and it being the usage of other nations to keep their plantations trade to themselves.*

VI. Be it enacted, and it is hereby enacted, That from and after the five and twentieth day of *March* one thousand six hundred sixty-four, no commodity of the growth, production or manufacture of *Europe,* shall be imported into any land, island, plantation, colony, territory or place to his Majesty belonging, or which shall hereafter belong unto or be in the possession of his Majesty, his heirs and successors, in *Asia, Africa* or *America,* (*Tangier* only excepted) but what shall be *bona fide,* and without fraud, laden and shipped in *England, Wales,* or the town of *Berwick* upon *Tweed,* and in *English* built shipping, or which were *bona fide* bought before the first day of *October* one thousand six hundred sixty and two, and had such certificate thereof as is directed in one act passed the last sessions of this present parliament, intituled, *An act for preventing frauds, and regulating abuses in his Majesty's customs;* and whereof the matter and three fourths of the mariners at least are *English,* and which shall be carried directly thence to the said lands, islands, plantations, colonies, territories or places, and from no other place or places

---

* These excerpts are reprinted from Pickering, *The Statutes at Large,* vol. VIII, pp. 161–163.

whatsoever; any law, statute or usage to the contrary notwithstanding; (2) under the penalty of the loss of all such commodities of the growth, production or manufacture of *Europe,* as shall be imported into any of them from any other place whatsoever, by land or water; and if by water, of the ship or vessel also in which they were imported, with all her guns, tackle, furniture, ammunition and apparel. . . .

VII. Provided always, and be it hereby enacted by the authority aforesaid, That it shall and may be lawful to ship and lade in such ships, and so navigated, as in the foregoing clause is set down and expressed, in any part of *Europe,* salt for the fisheries of *New-England* and *Newfoundland,* and to ship and lade in the *Madera's* wines of the growth thereof, and to ship and lade in the Western islands of *Azores* wines of the growth of the said islands, and to ship and take in servants or horses in *Scotland* or *Ireland,* and to ship or lade in *Scotland* all sorts of victual of the growth or production of *Scotland,* and to ship or lade in *Ireland* all sorts of victual of the growth or production of *Ireland,* and the same to transport into any of the said lands, islands, plantations, colonies, territories or places: any thing in the foregoing clause to the contrary in any wise notwithstanding.

VIII. And for the better prevention of frauds, be it enacted, and it is hereby enacted, That from and after the five and twentieth day of *March* one thousand six hundred sixty and four, every person or persons importing by land any goods or commodities whatsoever into any the said lands, islands, plantations, colonies, territories or places, shall deliver to the governor of such land, island, plantation, colony, territory or place, or to such person or officer as shall be by him thereunto authorized and appointed, within four and twenty hours after such importation, his and their names and surnames, and a true inventory and particular of all such goods or commodities: (2) and no ship or vessel coming to any such land, island, plantation, colony, territory or place, shall lade or unlade any goods or commodities whatsoever, until the master or commander of such ship or vessel shall first have made known to the governor of such land, island, plantation, colony, territory or place, or such other person or officer as shall be by him thereunto authorized and appointed, the arrival of the said ship or vessel, with her name, and the name and surname of her master or commander, and have shewn to him that she is an *English built* ship, or made good by producing such certificate, as abovesaid, that she is a ship or vessel *bona fide* belonging to *England, Wales,* or the town of *Berwick,* and navigated with an *English* master, and three fourth parts of the mariners at least *Englishmen,* and have delivered to such governor or other person or officer a true and perfect inventory or invoice of her lading, together with the place or places in which the said goods were laden or taken into the said ship or vessel; (3) under the pain of the loss of the ship or vessel, with all her guns, ammunition, tackle, furniture and apparel, and of all such goods of the growth, production or manufacture of *Europe,* as were not *bona fide* laden and taken in *England, Wales,* or the town of *Berwick,* to be recovered and divided in manner aforesaid; (4) and all such as are governors or commanders of any the said lands, islands, plantations, colonies, territories or places (*Tangier* only excepted) shall before the five and twentieth day of *March* one thousand six hundred sixty and four, and all such as shall hereafter be made governors or commanders of any of them, shall before their entrance upon the execution of such trust or charge, take a solemn oath before such person or persons as shall be authorized by his Majesty, his heirs and successors, to administer the same, to do their utmost within their respective governments or commands, to cause to be well and truly observed what is in this act enacted, in relation to the trade of such lands, islands, plantations, colonies, territories and places, under the penalty of being removed out of their respective governments and commands: (5) and if any of them shall be found, after the taking of such oath, to have wittingly and willingly offended contrary to what is by this act required of them, that they shall for such offence be turned out of their governments, and be uncapable of the government of any other land, island, plantation or colony; and moreover, forfeit the sum of one thousand pounds of lawful money of *England;* the one moiety to his Majesty, his heirs and successors; and the other moiety to him or them that shall inform or sue for the same in any of his Majesty's courts in any of the said plantations, or in any court of record in *England,* wherein no essoin, protection or wager of law shall be allowed. . . .

C.. THE PLANTATION DUTIES ACT OF (MAR. 29) 1673*

. . . And whereas by one act passed in this present parliament in the twelfth year of your Majesty's reign, intituled, An act for encouragement of shipping and navigation, *and by several other laws passed since that time, it is permitted to ship, carry, convey and transport sugar, tobacco, cotton-wool, indico, ginger, fustick and all other dying-wood of the growth, production and manufacture of any of your Majesty's plantations in* America, Asia *or* Africa, *from the places of their growth, production and manufacture, to any of your Majesty's plantations in those parts,* (Tangier only excepted) *and that without paying of custom for the same, either at the lading or unlading of the said commodities, by means whereof the trade and navigation in those commodities, from one plantation to another is greatly increased; (3) and the inhabitants of divers of those colonies, not contenting themselves with being supplied with those commodities for their own use, free from all customs, (while the subjects of this your kingdom of* England *have paid great customs and impositions for what of them hath been spent here) but contrary to the express letter of the aforesaid laws, have brought into divers parts of* Europe *great quantities thereof, and do also daily vend great quantities thereof, to the shipping of other nations who bring them into divers parts of* Europe, *to the great*

---

* These excerpts are reprinted from Pickering, *The Statutes at Large,* vol. VIII, pp. 398–399.

hurt and diminution of your Majesty's customs, and of the trade and navigation of this your kingdom; (4) for the prevention thereof, we your Majesty's commons in parliament assembled, do pray that it may be enacted; and be it enacted . . . That from and after the first day of *September* which shall be in the year of our Lord one thousand six hundred seventy and three, if any ship or vessel which by law may trade in any of your Majesty's plantations, shall come to any of them to ship and take on board any of the aforesaid commodities, and that bond shall not be first given with one sufficient surety to bring the same to *England* or *Wales,* or the town of *Berwick* upon *Tweed,* and to no other place, and there to unload and put the same on shore, (the danger of the seas only excepted) that there shall be answered and paid to your Majesty, your heirs and successors, for so much of the said commodities as shall be laded and put on board such ship or vessel, these following rates or duties: that is to say, for sugar white, the hundred weight containing one hundred and twelve pounds, five shillings; and brown sugar and muscovadoes, the hundred weight containing one hundred and twelve pounds, one shilling and six pence; (5) for tobacco, the pound one peny; for cotton wool, the pound one half-peny; for indico, the pound two pence; for ginger, the hundred weight containing two hundred and twelve pounds, one shilling; (6) for logwood, the hundred weight containing one hundred and twelve pounds, five pounds; for fustick and all other dying-wood, the hundred weight containing one hundred and twelve pounds, six pence: and also for every pound of cocoa-nuts, one peny; (7) to be levied, collected and paid at such places and to such collectors and other officers as shall be appointed in their respective plantations to collect, levy and receive the same, before the lading thereof, and under such penalties both to the officers and upon the goods, as for nonpayment of or defrauding his Majesty of his customs in *England.* . . .

SELECTION

Keeping Closer Reins on the Private Colonies

Enforcement of the Navigation Acts proved to be especially difficult in New England. The charters of Massachusetts, Rhode Island, and Connecticut gave the governments of those colonies such broad powers that they were almost impossible to control. A special royal commission sent out to New England between 1664 and 1666 did manage to persuade the governments of Rhode Island, Plymouth, and Connecticut to comply with the Navigation Acts and a series of regulations designed to bring legal and religious practices in New England into closer conformity with those of the mother country. But Massachusetts not only refused compliance but also defied a royal command to answer charges brought against it by the commission. The Lords of Trade dispatched Edward Randolph (ca. 1632–1703) to Boston in 1676 to investigate conditions in Massachusetts and to secure acquiescence to royal authority. Over the next few years Randolph produced a series of reports similar in tone to the representation of May 6, 1677, charging the Bay Colony with violations of the Navigation Acts and a variety of other misdeeds and urging greater exertion of royal authority over the colony. His reports were important in determining the Crown to initiate proceedings against the Massachusetts Charter in 1684.

Clearly, the extensive powers conferred on the proprietors and governing corporations by the charters made it extremely difficult to enforce the royal will in the colonies, and the Lords of Trade adamantly opposed the creation of additional proprietary colonies. Although it was unsuccessful in its attempt to block the grant to William Penn in 1681, it inserted a series of limitations and requirements in the Pennsylvania Charter that subjected Penn to much stricter controls than any of his predecessors.

One of the best studies of the movement to exert tighter controls over the private colonies is Michael Garibaldi Hall, Edward Randolph and the American Colonies, 1676–1703 *(1960), though Charles M. Andrews,* The Colonial Period of American History *(four volumes, 1934–1938), volume IV,* England's Colonial and Commercial Policy; *A. P. Thornton,* West-India Policy under the Restoration *(1956); and Philip S. Haffendon, "The Crown and the Colonial Charters, 1675–1688,"* William and Mary Quarterly, *third series, volume 15 (1958), pages 297–311, 452–466, should also be consulted.*

A. THE MISDEEDS OF NEW ENGLAND: EDWARD RANDOLPH'S REPRESENTATION (MAY 6, 1677)*

Representation of ye Affairs of N: England by Mr. Randolph

The present State of the affaires of New England depending before the Lords of the Committee for Plantations are reduced to Two heads Vizt. matter of Law and ffact.

Matter of Law ariseth from the Title of Lands and Government claimed by Mr Mason and Mr Gorges in their Several provinces of New Hampshire and Main, and also what right and Title the Massachusetts have to either Land or Government in any part of New England; these are referred to the Lords Cheif Justices of the Kings Bench and Common Pleas for their Opinion.

Matters of ffact concerne as well his Majestie as Mr Mason and Mr Gorges, and against the Government of the Massachusetts these following Articles will be proved.

* Reprinted in full from Robert Noxon Toppan (ed.), *Edward Randolph, Including His Letters and Official Papers* (1898–1899), vol. II, pp. 265–268.

1. That they have noe right either to Land or Government in any part of New England and have allwayes been Vsurpers.

2. That they have formed themselves into a Common Wealth, deneying any Appeals to England, and contrary to other Plantations doe not take the Oath of Allegiance.

3. They have protected the Late Kings Murtherers, directly contrary to his Majesties Royall Proclamation of the 6th of June 1660 and of his Letters of 28th June 1662.

4. They Coine money with their owne Impress.

5. They have put his Majesties Subjects to death for opinion in matters of Religion.

6. In the yeare 1665 they did violently oppose his Majesties Commissioners in the Settlement of New Hampshire and in 1668 by Armed fforces turned out his Majesties Justices of the peace in the Province of Main in Contempt of his Majesties Authority and Declaration of the 10th of Aprill 1666.

7. They impose an Oath of ffidelity upon all that inhabit within their Territoryes To be true and ffaithfull to their Government.

8. They violate all the Acts of Trade and navigation, by which they have ingrossed the greatest part of the West India Trade whereby his Majestie is damaged in his Customs above 100 000 i yearely and this Kingdome much more.

Reasons induceing a Speedy hearing and Determination.

1. His Majestie hath an oppertunity to Settle that Country under his Royall Authority with Little charge Sir John Berry being now at Virginia not farr distance from New England, and it Lyes in his way home, where are many good harbours free from the worms, convenient Townes for Quartering of Souldiers, and plentifull Accomidation for men and shipping.

2. The Earnest desire of most and best of the Inhabitants (wearied out with the Arbitrary proceedings of those in the present Government) to be under his Majesties Government and Laws.

3. The Indians upon the Settlement of that Country it is presumed would vnanimously Submitt and become very Servicable and vsefull for improveing that Country there being vpward of Three hundred Thousand English inhabiting therein.

Proposals for the Setling of that Country.

1. His Majesties Gratious and General pardon vpon their conviction of haveing acted without and in Contempt of his Majesties Authority will make the most refractory to comply to save their Estates.

2. His Majesties declaration of confirming vnto the Inhabitants the Lands and houses they now possess vpon payment of an Easie Quit rent and granting Libertie of Conscience in matters of Religion.

3. His Majesties Commission directed to the most Eminent persons for Estates and Loyalty in every Colony to meet consult and act for the present peace and Safety of that Country dureing his Majesties pleasure, and that Such of the present Magistrates be of the Councill as shall readily comply with his Majesties Commands in the Setleing of the Country and a pention to be allowed them out of the publicque Reuenue of the Country with Some Title of Honour to be conferred vpon the most deserveing of them, will cause a generall Submission.

B. THE CHARTER OF PENNSYLVANIA (MAR. 4, 1681)*

*   *   *

AND to the End the said *William Penn,* or his heires, or other the Planters, Owners, or Inhabitants of the said Province, may not att any time here-after by misconstruction of the powers aforesaid through inadvertencie or designe depart from that Faith and due allegiance, which by the lawes of this our Kingdom of *England,* they and all our subjects, in our Dominions and Territories, always owe unto us, Our heires and Successors, by colour of any Extent or largnesse of powers hereby given, or pretended to bee given, or by force or colour of any lawes hereafter to bee made in the said Province, by vertue of any such Powers; OUR further will and Pleasure is, that a transcript or Duplicate of all Lawes, which shall bee soe as afore-said made and published within the said Province, shall within five yeares after the makeing thereof, be transmitted and delivered to the Privy Councell, for the time being, of us, our heires and successors: And if any of the said Lawes, within the space of six moneths after that they shall be soe transmitted and delivered, bee declared by us, Our heires or Suc-cessors, in Our or their Privy Councell, inconsistent with the Sovereigntey or lawful Prerogative of us, our heires or Successors, or contrary to the Faith and Allegiance due by the legall government of this Realme, from the said *William Penn,* or his heires, or of the Planters and Inhabitants of the said Province, and that thereupon any of the said Lawes shall be adjudged and declared to bee void by us, our heires or Successors, under our or their Privy Seale, that then and from thenceforth, such Lawes, concerning which such Judgement and declaration shall bee made, shall become voyd: Otherwise the said Lawes soe transmitted, shall remaine, and stand in full force, according to the true intent and meaneing there-of. . . .

WE Will alsoe, and by these presents, for us, our heires and Successors, Wee doe Give and grant Licence by this our Charter, unto the said *William Penn,* his heires and assignes, and to all the inhabitants and dwellers in the Province aforesaid, both present and to come, to import or unlade, by themselves or theire servants, ffactors or assignes, all merchandizes and goods whatsoever, that shall arise of the fruites and comodities of the said Province, either by Land or Sea, into any of the ports of us, our heires and successors, in our Kingdome of *England,* and not into any other Countrey whatsoever: And wee give him full power to dispose of the said goods in the said ports; and if need bee, within one yeare next after the unladeing of the same, to lade the said Merchandizes and Goods again into the same or other shipps, and to export the same into any other Countreys, either of our Dominions or fforeigne, according to Lawe: Provided alwayes, that they pay such customes and impositions, subsidies and duties for the same, to us, our heires and Successors, as the

---

* These excerpts are reprinted from Francis Newton Thorpe (ed.), *Federal and State Constitutions, Colonial Charters, and Other Organic Laws* (7 vols., 1909), vol. V, pp. 3039–3041, 3043.

rest of our Subjects of our Kingdome of *England,* for the time being, shall be bound to pay, and doe observe the Acts of Navigation, and other Lawes in that behalfe made. . . .

AND Wee doe further appoint and ordaine, and by these presents, for us, our heires and Successors, Wee doe grant unto the said *William Penn,* his heires and assignes. That he, the said *William Penn,* his heires and assignes, may from time to time for ever, have and enjoy the Customes and Subsidies, in the Portes, Harbours, and other Creeks and Places aforesaid, within the Province aforesaid, payable or due for merchandizes and wares there to be laded and unladed, the said Customes and Subsidies to be reasonably assessed upon any occasion, by themselves and the People there as aforesaid to be assembled, to whom wee give power by these presents, for us, our heires and Successors, upon just cause and in dudue p'portion, to assesse and impose the same; Saveing unto us, our heires and Successors, such impositions and Customes, as by Act of Parliament are and shall be appointed.

AND it is Our further Will and plasure, that the said *William Penn,* his heires and assignes, shall from time to time constitute and appoint an Attorney or Agent, to Reside in or near our City of *London,* who shall make knowne the place where he shall dwell or may be found, unto the Clerks of our Privy Counsell for the time being, or one of them, and shall be ready to appeare in any of our Courts att *Westminster,* to Answer for any Misdemeanors that shall be committed, or by any wilful default or neglect permitted by the said *William Penn,* his heires or assignes, against our Lawes of Trade or Navigation: and after it shall be ascertained in any of our said Courts, what damages Wee or our heires or Successors shall have sustained by such default or neglect, the said William Penn, his heires and assignes shall pay the same within one yeare after such taxation, and demand thereof from such Attorney: or in case there shall be noe such Attorney by the space of a yeare, or such Attorney shall not make payment of such damages within the space of one yeare, and answer such other forfeitures and penalties within the said time, as by the Acts of Parliament in *England* are or shall be provided, according to the true intent and meaneing of these presents; then it shall be lawfull for us, our heires and Successors, to seize and Resume the government of the said Province or Countrey, and the same to retaine untill payment shall be made thereof: But notwithstanding any such Seizure or resumption of the government, nothing concerneing the propriety or ownership of any Lands, tenements, or other hereditaments, or goods or chattels of any the Adventurers, Planters, or owners, other then the respective Offenders there, shall be any way be affected or molested thereby. . . .

AND FURTHER our pleasure is, and by these presents, for us, our heires and Successors. Wee doe covenant and grant to and with the said *William Penn,* and his heires and assignes. That Wee, our heires and Successors, shall at no time hereafter sett or make, or cause to be sett, any imposition, custome or other taxation, rate or contribution whatsoever, in and upon the dwellers and inhabitants of the aforesaid Province, for their Lands, tenements, goods or chattells within the said Province, or in and upon any goods or merchandize within the said Province, or to be laden or unladen within the ports or harbours of the said Province, unless the same be with the consent of the Proprietary, or chiefe governor, or assembly, or by act of Parliament in *England.* . . .

AND Our further pleasure is, and wee doe hereby, for us, our heires and Successors, charge and require, that if any of the inhabitants of the said Province, to the number of Twenty shall at any time hereafter be desirous, and shall by any writeing, or by any person deputed for them, signify such their desire to the Bishop of *London* for the time being that any preacher or preachers, to be approved of by the said Bishop, may be sent unto them for their instruction, that then such preacher or preachers shall and may be and reside within the said Province, without any deniall or molestation whatsoever. . . .

SELECTION

The Dominion of New England: The Commission of Sir Edmund Andros as Governor (Apr. 7, 1688)

Following closely upon the forfeiture of the Massachusetts Charter, the accession in 1685 of James II, with his commitment to the principle that the Crown should exercise the predominant influence in both domestic and colonial affairs, set the stage for the Dominion experiment. The constitutional theory behind the Dominion was that colonies in forfeiting their charters lost all their former rights and that the Crown might thenceforth exercise unlimited authority over them. On the basis of this theory, the Crown conferred vast powers upon Sir Edmund Andros (1637–1714) as governor of the Dominion by a commission issued in 1688. The nature and extent of that power as well as the intentions and scope of the Dominion may be seen in the portions of the commission reprinted below from Francis Newton Thorpe (ed.), Federal and State Constitutions, Colonial Charters, and Other Organic Laws (seven volumes, 1909), volume III, pages 1863–1869. A favorite of James II, Andros had earlier been governor of New York, had served in the Army, had helped to put down Monmouth's Rebellion, and was later governor of Virginia. The standard work on the Dominion of New England is Viola F. Barnes, The Dominion of New England: A Study in British Colonial Policy (1923), though it should be read in conjunction with Hall, Edward Randolph and the American Colonies, and Richard S. Dunn, Puritans and Yankees: The Winthrop Dynasty of New England, 1630–1717 (1962), pages 212–257.

J ames the Second by the Grace of God King of England, Scotland France and Ireland Defender of the Faith &c. To our trusty and welbeloved Sir Edmund Andros Knight Greeting: Whereas by our Commission under our Great Seal of England, bearing date the third day of June in the second year of our reign wee have constituted and appointed you to be our Captain Generall and Governor in Chief in and over all that part of our territory and dominion of New England in America known by the names of our Colony of the Massachusetts Bay, our Colony of New Plymouth, our Provinces of New Hampshire and Main and the Narraganset Country or King's Province. And whereas since that time Wee have thought it necessary for our service and for the better protection and security of our subjects in those parts to join and annex to our said Government the neighboring Colonies of Road Island and Connecticutt, our Province of New York and East and West Jersey, with the territories thereunto belonging, as wee do hereby join annex and unite the same to our said government and dominion of New England. Wee therefore reposing especiall trust and confidence in the prudence courage and loyalty of you the said Sir Edmund Andros, out of our especiall grace certain knowledge and meer motion, have thought fit to constitute and appoint as wee do by these presents constitute and appoint you the said Sir Edmund Andros to be our Captain Generall and Governor in Cheif in and over our Colonies of the Massachusetts Bay and New Plymouth, our Provinces of New Hampshire and Main, the Narraganset country or King's Province, our Colonys of Road Island and Connecticutt, our Province of New York and East and West Jersey, and of all that tract of land circuit continent precincts and limits in America lying and being in breadth from forty degrees of Northern latitude from the Equinoctiall Line to the River of St. Croix Eastward, and from thence directly Northward to the river of Canada, and in length and longitude by all the breadth aforesaid and throughout the main land from the Atlantick or Western Sea or Ocean on the East part, to the South Sea on the West part, with all the Islands, Seas, Rivers, waters, rights, members, and appurtenances, thereunto belonging (our province of Pensilvania and country of Delaware only excepted), to be called and known as formerly by the name and title of our territory and dominion of New England in America.

And for your better guidance and direction Wee doe hereby require and command you to do & execute all things in due manner, that shall belong unto the said office and the trust wee have reposed in you, according to the severall powers instructions and authoritys mentioned in these presents, or such further powers instructions and authoritys mentioned in these presents, as you shall herewith receive or which shall at any time hereafter be granted or appointed you under our signet and sign manual or by our order in our Privy Councill and according to such reasonable lawes and statutes as are now in force or such others as shall hereafter be made and established within our territory & dominion aforesaid.

And our will and pleasure is that you the said Sir Edmund Andros having, after publication of these our Letters Patents, first taken the Oath of duly executing the office of our Captain Generall and Governor in Cheif of our said territory and dominion, which our Councill there or any three of them are hereby required authorized and impowered to give and administer unto you, you shall administer unto each of the members of our Councill the Oath for the due execution of their places and trusts.

And Wee do hereby give and grant unto you full power and authority to suspend any member of our Councill from sitting voting and assisting therein, as you shall find just cause for so doing.

And if it shall hereafter at any time happen that by the death, departure out of our said territory, or suspension of any of our Counselors, or otherwise, there shall be a vacancy in our said Council, (any five whereof wee do hereby appoint to be a Quorum) Our will and pleasure is that you signify the same unto us by the first oppurtunity, that Wee may under our Signet and Sign Manuall constitute and appoint others in their room.

And Wee do hereby give and grant unto you full power and authority, by and with the advise and consent of our said Councill or the major part of them, to make constitute and ordain lawes statutes and ordinances for the public peace welfare and good government of our said territory & dominion and of the people and inhabitants thereof, and such others as shall resort thereto, and for the benefit of us, our heires and successors. Which said lawes statutes and ordinances, are to be, as near as conveniently may be, agreeable to the lawes & statutes of this our kingdom of England: Provided that all such lawes statutes and ordinances of what nature or duration soever, be within three months, or sooner, after the making of the same, transmitted unto Us, under our Seal of New England, for our allowance or disapprobation of them, as also duplicates thereof by the next conveyance.

And Wee do by these presents give and grant unto you full power and authority by and with the advise and consent of our said Councill, or the major part of them, to impose assess and raise and levy rates and taxes as you shall find necessary for the support of the government within our territory and dominion of New England, to be collected and leveyed and to be imployed to the uses aforesaid in such manner as to you & our said Councill or the major part of them shall seem most equall and reasonable.

And for the better supporting the charge of the government of our said Territory and Dominion, our will and pleasure is and wee do by these presents authorize and impower you the said Sir Edmund Andros and our Councill, to continue such taxes and impositions as are now laid and imposed upon the Inhabitants thereof; and to levy and distribute or cause the same to be levyed and distributed to those ends in the best and most equall manner, until you shall by & with the advise and consent of our Councill agree on and settle such other taxes as shall be sufficient for the support of our government there, which are to be applied to that use and no other.

And our further will and pleasure is, that all publick money raised or to be raised or appointed for the support of the government within our said territory and dominion be issued out by warrant or order from you by & with the advise and consent of our Council as aforesaid.

And our will and pleasure is that you shall and may keep and use our Seal appointed by Us for our said territory and dominion.

And wee do by these presents ordain constitute and appoint you or the Commander in Cheif for the time being, and the Councill of our said territory & dominion for the time being, to be a constant and setled Court of Record for ye administration of justice to all our subjects inhabiting within our said Territory and Dominion, in all causes as well civill as Criminall with full power and authority to hold pleas in all cases, from time to time, as well in Pleas of the Crown and in all matters relating to the conservation of the peace and punishment of offenders, as in Civill causes and actions between party and party, or between us and any of our subjects there, whether the same do concerne the realty and relate to any right of freehold & inheritance or whether the same do concerne the personality and relate to matter of debt contract damage or other personall injury; and also in all mixt actions which may concern both realty and personality; and therein after due and orderly proceeding and deliberate hearing of both sides, to give judgement and to award execution, as well in criminall as in Civill cases as aforesaid, so as always that the forms of proceedings in such cases and the judgment thereupon to be given, be as consonant and agreeable to the lawes and statutes of this our realm of England as the present state and condition of our subjects inhabiting within our said Territory and Dominion and the circumstances of the place will admit.

And Wee do further hereby give and grant unto you full power and authority with the advise and consent of our said Councill to erect constitute and establish such and so many Courts of Judicature and public Justice within our said Territory and Dominion as you and they shall think fitt and necessary for the determining of all causes as well Criminall as Civill according to law and equity, and for awarding of execution thereupon, with all reasonable and necessary powers authorities fees and privileges belonging unto them.

And Wee do hereby give and grant unto you full power and authority to constitute and appoint Judges and in cases requisite Commissioners of Oyer and Terminer, Justices of the Peace, Sheriffs, & all other necessary Officers and Ministers within our said Territory, for the better administration of Justice and putting the lawes in execution, & to administer such oath and oaths as are usually given for the due execution and performance of offices and places and for the cleering of truth in judiciall causes.

And our further will and pleasure is and We doe hereby declare that all actings and proceedings at law or equity heretofore had or don or now depending within any of the courts of our said Territory, and all executions thereupon, be hereby confirmed and continued so farr forth as not to be avoided for want of any legall power in the said Courts; but that all and every such judiciall actings, proceeding and execution shall be of the same force effect and virtue as if such Courts had acted by a just and legall authority.

And wee do further by these presents will and require you to permit

Appeals to be made in cases of Error from our Courts in our said Territory and Dominion of New England unto you, or the Commander in Cheif for the time being and the Council, in Civill causes: Provided the value appealed for do exceed the sum of one hundred pounds sterling, and that security be first duly given by the Appellant to answer such charges as shall be awarded in case the first sentence shall be affirmed.

And whereas Wee judge it necessary that all our subjects may have liberty to Appeal to our Royall Person in cases that may require the same: Our will and pleasure is that if either party shall not rest satisfied with the judgment or sentence of you (or the Commander in Chief for the time being) and the Councill, they may Appeal unto Us in our Privy Councill: Provided the matter in difference exceed the value and summ of three hundred pounds sterling and that such Appeal be made within one fortnight after sentence, and that security be likewise duly given by the Appellant to answer such charges as shall be awarded in case the sentence of you (or the Commander in Cheif for the time being) and the Councill be confirmed; and provided also that execution be not suspended by reason of any such appeal unto us.

And Wee do hereby give and graunt unto you full power where you shall see cause and shall judge any offender or offenders in capitall and criminall matters, or for any fines or forfeitures due unto us, fit objects of our mercy, to parden such offenders and to remit such fines & forfeitures, treason and wilfull murder only excepted, in which case you shall likewise have power upon extraordinary occasions to grant reprieves to the offenders therein untill and to the intent our pleasure may be further known.

And Wee do hereby give and grant unto you the said Sir Edmund Andros by your self your Captains and Commanders, by you to be authorized, full power and authority to levy arme muster command or employ, all persons whatsoever residing within our said Territory and Dominion of New England, and, as occasion shall serve, them to transferr from one place to another for the resisting and withstanding all enemies pyrats and rebells, both at land and sea, and to transferr such forces to any of our Plantations in America or the Territories thereunto belonging, as occasion shall require for the defence of the same against the invasion or attempt of any of our enemies, and then, if occasion shall require to pursue and prosecute in or out of the limits of our said Territories and Plantations or any of them, And if it shall so please God, them to vanquish; and, being taken, according to the law of arms to put to death or keep and preserve alive, at your discretion. And also to execute martiall law in time of invasion insurrection or warr, and during the continuance of the same, and upon soldiers in pay, and to do and execute all and every other thing which to a Captain Generall doth or ought of right to belong, as fully and amply as any our Captain Generall doth or hath usually don.

And Wee do hereby give and grant unto you full power and authority to erect raise and build within our Territory and Dominion aforesaid, such and so many forts, platformes, Castles, cities, boroughs, towns, and fortifications as you shall judge necessary; and the same or any of them to fortify and furnish with ordnance ammunition and all sorts of armes, fit and necessary for the security & defence of our said territory; and the same again or any of them to demolish or dismantle as may be most convenient.

And Wee do hereby give and grant unto you the said Sir Edmund Andros full power and authority to erect one or more Court or Courts Admirall within our said Territory and Dominion, for the hearing and determining of all marine and other causes and matters proper herein to be heard & determined, with all reasonable and necessary powers, authorities fees and priviledges.

And you are to execute all powers belonging to the place and office of Vice Admirall of and in all the seas and coasts about your Government; according to such commission authority and instructions as you shall receive from ourself under the Seal of our Admiralty or from High Admirall of our Foreign Plantations for the time being.

And forasmuch as divers mutinies & disorders do happen by persons shipped and imployed at Sea, and to the end that such as shall be shipped or imployed at Sea may be better governed and ordered; Wee do hereby give and grant unto you the said Sir Edmund Andros our Captain Generall and Governor in Cheif, full power and authority to constitute and appoint Captains, Masters of Ships, and other Commanders, commissions to execute the law martial, and to use such proceedings authorities, punishment, correction and execution upon any offender or offenders who shall be mutinous seditious, disorderly or any way unruly either at sea or during the time of their abode or residence in any of the ports harbors or bays of our said Territory and Dominion, as the Cause shall be found to require, according to martial law. Provided that nothing herein conteined shall be construed to the enabling you or any by your authority to held plea or have jurisdiction of any offence cause matter or thing committed or don upon the sea or within any of the havens, rivers, or creeks of our said Territory and Dominion under your government, by any Captain Commander Lieutenant Master or other officer seaman soldier or person whatsoever, who shall be in actuall service and pay in and on board any of our ships of War or other vessels acting by immediat commission or warrant from our self under the Seal of our Admiralty, or from our High Admirall of England for the time being; but that such Captain Commander Lieutenant Master officer seaman soldier and other person so offending shall be left to be proceeded against and tryed, as the merit of their offences shall require, either by Commission under our Great Seal of England as the statute of 28 Henry VIII directs, or by commission from our said High Admirall, according to the Act of Parliament passed in the 13th year of the raign of the late King our most dear and most intirely beloved brother of ever blessed memory (entituled An Act for the establishing articles and Orders for the regulating and better government of His majestys navys, shipps or warr, and Forces by sea) and not otherwise. Saving only, that it shall and may be lawfull for you, upon such Captains and Commanders refusing or neglecting to execute, or upon his negligent or undue execution of any the written orders he shall receive from you for our service, & the service of our said Territory and Dominion, to suspend him the said Captain or Commander from the exercise of the said office of Commander and commit him safe custody, either on board his own ship or elsewhere, at the discretion of you, in order to his being brought to answer for the same by commission either under our Great Seal of England or from our said High Admirall as is before expressed. In which case our will and pleasure is that the Captain or Commander so by you suspended shall during his suspension and commitment be succeeded in his said office, by such commission or Warrant Officer of our said ship appointed by our self or our High Admirall for the time being, as by the known practice and discipline of our Navy doth and ought next to succeed him, as is case of death sickness of other ordinary disability hapning to the Commander of any of our ships & not otherwise; you standing also accountable to us for the truth & importance of the crimes and misdemeanors for which you shall so proceed to the suspending of such our said Captain or Commander. Provided also that all disorders and misdemeanors committed on shore by any Captain Commander, Lieutenant, Master, or other officer seaman soldier or person whatsoever belonging to any of our ships of warr or other vessel acting .by immediate commission or warrant from our self under the Great Seal of our Admiralty or from our High Admirallty from England for the time being may be tryed & punished according to the lawes of the place where any such disorders offences and misdemeanors shall be so committed on shore, notwithstanding such offender be in our actuall service and borne in our pay on board any such our shipps of warr or other vessels acting by immediate Commission or warrant from our self or our High Admirall as aforesaid; so as he shall not receive any protection (for the avoiding of justice for such offences committed on shore) from any pretence of his being imployed in our service at sea.

And Wee do likewise give and grant unto you full power and authority by and with the advice and consent of our said Councill to agree with the planters and inhabitants of our said Territory and Dominion concerning such lands, tenements & hereditaments as now are or hereafter shall be in our power to dispose of, and them to grant unto any person or persons for such terms and under such moderat Quit Rents, Services and acknowledgements to be thereupon reserved unto us as shall be appointed by us. Which said grants are to pass and be sealed by our Seal of New England and (being entred upon record by such officer or officers as you shall appoint thereunto, shall be good and effectual in law against us, our heires and successors.

And Wee do hereby give you full power and authority to appoint so many faires martes and markets as you with the advise of the said Councill shall think fitt.

As likewise to order and appoint within our said Territory such and so many ports harbors, bayes havens and other places for the convenience and security of shipping, and for the better loading and unloading of goods and merchandize as by you with the advice and consent of our Councill shall be thought fitt and necessary; and in them or any of them to erect nominat and appoint Cuxtom houses ware houses and officers relating thereto; and them to alter change, place, or displace from time to time, as with the advice aforesaid shall be thought fitt.

And forasmuch as pursuant to the lawes & customes of our Colony of the Massachusetts Bay and of our other Colonies and Provinces aforementioned, divers marriages have been made and performed by the Magistrats of our said territory; Our royall will and pleasure is hereby to confirm all the said marriages and to direct that they be held good and valid in the same manner to all intents and purposes whatsoever as if they had been made and contracted according to the lawes established within our kingdom of England.

And Wee do hereby require and command all officers and ministers, civill and military and all other inhabitants of our said Territory and Dominion to be obedient aiding and assisting unto you the said Sir Edmund Andros in the execution of this our commission and of the powers and authorityes therein conteined, and upon your death or absence out of our said Territory unto our Lieut. Governor, to whom wee do therefore by these presents give and grant all and singular the powers and authorityes aforesaid to be exercised and enjoyed by him in case of your death or absence during our pleasure, or untill your arrival within our said Territory and Dominion; as Wee do further hereby give and grant full power and authority to our Lieut. Governor to do and execute whatsoever he shall be by you authorized and appointed to do and execute, in pursuance of and according to the powers granted to you by this Commission.

And if in the case of your death or absence there be no person upon the place, appointed by us to be Commander in Cheif; our will and pleasure is, that the then present Councill of our Territory aforesaid, do take upon them the administration of the Government and execute this commission and the severall powers and authoritys herein conteined; and that the first Counselor who shall be at the time of your death or absence residing within the same, do preside in our said Councill, with such powers and preheminencies as any former President hath used and enjoyed within our said territory, or any other our plantations in America, untill our pleasure be further known, or your arrivall as aforesaid.

And lastly, our will and pleasure is that you the said Sir Edmund Andros shall and may hold exercise and enjoy the office and place of Captain Generall and Governor in Cheif in and over our Territory and Dominion aforesaid, with all its rights members and appurtenances whatsoever, together with all and singular the powers and authoryes hereby granted unto you, for and during our will and pleasure. . . .

Expansion and Adjustment, 1660–1713:
Countervailing Forces

SELECTION

The Recruitment of Colonists

*How successful their colonies were and how profitable they would ultimately
become depended in large measure on the ability of the proprietors to recruit
settlers. To make their colonies attractive to prospective emigrants, the Restoration proprietors offered very favorable conditions of settlement and published
tracts and broadsides extolling the virtues of their particular region. The kinds
of conditions they offered and the quality of the appeals they made may be
seen in the following two documents. The first, the "concessions and agreements" of the proprietors of New Jersey, was modeled on a similar document
issued six weeks earlier by the proprietors of Carolina and was published in
February, 1665. The second, A Brief Description of the Province of Carolina on
the Coasts of Floreda (1666), was a promotional tract sponsored by the Carolina proprietors which summarized the conditions offered in the Carolina concessions and agreements and described the benefits which various groups might
expect to derive from settling in Carolina. There is no comprehensive study of
colonial promotional literature or of the effort to recruit settlers, but John E.
Pomfret, The Province of East New Jersey, 1609–1702: The Rebellious
Proprietary (1962), discusses the New Jersey concessions and agreements in
some detail.*

A. CONCESSIONS AND AGREEMENTS OF THE PROPRIETORS OF NEW JERSEY (FEB. 10, 1665)*

. . . *Item* That all persons that are or shall become subjects to the King
of England and sweare or subscribe Allegiance to the King and faithfulness
to the Lords shalbe admitted to Plant and become ffreeman of the said
Province and enjoy the ffreedomes and Im'unities hereafter expressed
untill some stopp or contradiction bee made by us the Lords or else the
Governor Councell and Assemblie, which shalbe in force untill the Lords
see cause to the contrary, Provided that such stopp shall not any way
prejudice the right or continuance of any person that hath been received
before such stopp or order come from the Lords or generall Assemblie.

Item That noe person qualified as aforesaid within the said Province
at any time shalbe any waies molested punished disquieted or called in
Question for any difference in opinion or practice in matters of Religious

* These excerpts are reprinted from William A. Whitehead et al. (eds.),
Archives of the State of New Jersey (47 vols., 1880–1949), 1st ser., vol. 1,
pp. 30–35, 37–39.

concernements, who doe not actually disturbe the civill peace of the said Province, but that all and every such person and persons may from time to time and at all times truly and fully have and enjoy his and their Judgments and Conciences in matters of Religion throughout all the said Province: They behaveing themselves peaceably and quietly and not using this liberty to Licentiousnes, nor to the civill injury or outward disturbance of others, any Law Statute or clause conteyned or to be conteined usage or custome of this Realme of England to the contrary thereof in any wise notwithstanding.

Item That no pretence may be taken by us our heires or assignes for or by reason of our right of Patronage and power of Advowsen graunted by his Majesties Letters Patents unto his Royall Highnes James Duke of Yorke, and by his said Royall Highnes unto us, thereby to infringe the generall clause of Libertie of Conscience aforementioned WEE doe hereby graunt unto the Generall assembly of the said Province power by Act to Constitute and appoint such and soe many Ministers or Preachers as they shall think fitt, and to establish their maintenance, Giving liberty besides to any person or persons to keep and maintaine what Preachers or Ministers they please.

Item That the inhabitants being ffreemen or cheife Agents to others of the Province aforesaid doe as soone as this our Com'ission shall arrive by Virtue of a writt in our names by the Governor to be for the present (untill our Seale comes) sealed and signed make choice of Twelve Deputies or Representatives from amongst themselves who being chosen are to joine with the said Governor and Councell for the makeing of such Lawes Ordinances and Constitutions as shalbe necessary for the present good and welfare of the said Province, But so soone as Parishes Divisions Tribes or other distinctions are made That then the Inhabitants or ffreeholders of the severall and respective Parishes Tribes Devisions and distinctions aforesaid doe (by our writts under our seale which we engage shall be in due time issued) Annually meet on the first day of January and choose ffreeholders for each respective division Tribe or Parish to be the Deputies or Representatives of the same Which body of representatives or the major part of them shall with the Governor and Councell aforesaid bee the generall Assembly of the said Province, the Governor or his Deputy being present unless they shall wilfullee refuse, in which case they may appoint themselves a President dureing the absence of the Governor or his Deputy Governor.

WHICH Assemblies are to have power

1. To appoint their own times of meeting, and to adjorne their Sessions from time to time, to such times and places as they shall think convenient, As alsoe to ascertaine the number of their *Quorum* Provided that such numbers be not lesse than the third part of the whole in whom (or more) shall be the full power of the generall Assembly vizt.

2. To enact and make all such Lawes Acts and Constitutions as shalbe necessarie for the well Government of the said Province, and them to repeale: Provided that the same be consonant to reason, and, as neere as may be conveniently agreeable to the Lawes and Customes of his Majesties Kingdom of England Provided also that they be not against the interest of us the Lords Propriators our heires or assignes nor any of those our Concessions, especiallie that they be not repugnant to the Article for Libertie of Conscience abovementioned Which Lawes &c". soe made shall receive Publicacon from the Governor and Councell (but as the Lawes of us and our generall Assembly) and be in force for the space of one yeare and noe more unles contradicted by the Lords Propriators within which time they are to bee presented to us our heires &c. for our Ratificacon, and being confirmed by us they shall be in continuall force till expired by their own limitation or by Act of Repeale in like manner to be passed as aforesaid and confirmed.

3. By Act as aforesaid to constitute all Courts together with the limitts powers and Jurisdictions of the same, as alsoe the severall Offices and number of Officers belonging to each Court, with their respective Sallaries ffees and perquisits, their appellac'ons and dignities, with the penalties that shall be due to them for the breach of their severall and respective duties and Trusts.

4. By Act as aforesaid to lay equall taxes and assessments equally to raise moneys or goods upon all Lands (excepting the Lands of us the Lords Propriators before setling) or persons within the severall Precincts Hundreds Parishes, Manors or whatsoever other Divisions shall hereafter be made and etablished in the said Province as oft as necessity shall require and in such manner as to them shall seem most equall and easie for the said inhabitants in order to the better supporting of the publique charge of the said Government, and for the mutuall safetye defence and securitie of the said Province.

5. By Act as aforesaid to erect within the said Province such and soe many Manors with their necessarie Courts Jurisdictions ffreedoms and Priviledges as to them shall seem meet and convenient, as alsoe to devide the said Province into Hundreds Tribes Parishes or such other Divisions or distinctions as they shall think fitt, and the said Divisions to distinguish by what names wee shall order or direct, And in default thereof by such names as they please, As alsoe within the said Province to create and appoint such and soe many Ports Harbors Creekes and other places for the convenient lading and unlading of goods and Merchandizes out of Shipps Boates and other vessells as shalbe expedient, with such Jurisdictions priviledges and ffranchises to such Ports &c belonging as they shall judge most conducing to the generall good of the said Plantac'ons or Province.

6. By their Enacting to be confirmed as aforesaid to erect raise and build within the said Province or any part thereof such and soe many fforts ffortresses Castles Citties, Corporat'ons Burroughs, Towns, Villages, and other places of Strength and defence, and them or any of them to incorporate with such Charters and Priviledges as to them shall seem good and the Grant made unto us will permitt, and the same or any of them to ffortifie and furnish with such Provisions and proporc'ons of Ordinance powder shott Armour and all other weapons Amunition and Habiliments of Warr both offensive and deffen-

sive as shall be thought necessary and convenient for the safety and welfare of the said Province; But they may not at any time demolish dismantle or disfurnish the same without the consent of the Governor and the major part of the Councell of the said Province.

7. By Act as aforesaid to constitute Trained bands and companies with the number of Soldiers for the safety strength and defense of the said Province; and of the fforts Castles Citties &c. to suppresse all Mutinies and Rebellions, To make Warr Offensive and Defensive with all Indians Strangers and ffoureigners, as they shall see cause; And to pursue an Enemye by Sea as well as by Land if need be out of the limitts and Jurisdictions of the said Province, with the perticuler consent of the Governor or under his conduct or of our Com'ander in chiefe, or whom he shall appoint.

8. By Act as aforesaid to give unto all Strangers as to them shall seem meet A naturalization, and all such freedomes and priviledges within the said Province as to his Majesties subjects doe of right belong they Swearing or subscribeing as aforesaid Which said Strangers soe naturalized and priviledged shall be in all respects accompted in the said Province as the Kings naturall subjects.

9. By Act as aforesaid to prescribe the quantities of Land which shall be from time to time allotted to every head, free or Servant, Male or ffemale, and to make and ordeine rules for the casting of lotts for Land and the laying out of the same, Provided they doe not in their prescripc'ons exceed the severall proporc'ons which are hereby graunted by us to all persons arriving in the said Province or Adventuring thither.

10. The generally Assembly by Act as aforesaid shall make provision for the maintenance and support of the Governor, and for the defrayeing all necessarie charges of the Government As alsoe that the Constables of the said Province shall Collect the Lords Rent, and shall pay the same to, the Receiver that the Lords shall appoint to receive the same, unles the said generall assembly shall prescribe some other way whereby the Lords may have their Rents duely collected without charge or trouble to them.

11. *Lastlie* to enact constitute and ordeine all such other Lawes Acts and Constituc'ons as shall or may be necessary for the good property and settlement of the said Province (excepting what by these presents is excepted And conforming to the limitac'ons herein exprest. . . .

AND that the planting of the said Province may be the more speedily promoted.

1. WEE doe hereby Graunt unto all persons who have alreadie Adventured to the Province of New Cesaria or new Jersey or shall transport themselves or Servants before the first day of January which shall be in the yeare of our Lord 1665. These following proporc'ons vizt. to every ffreeman that shall goe with the first Governor from the Port when he imbarques (or shall meet him at the Randevouze hee appoints) for the Settlement of a Plantation there; armed with a good Muskett boare twelve bulletts to the Pound, with Tenn pounds of powder and Twenty pound of Bulletts, with bandeleers and match convenient, and with six months provision for his own person arriving there 150 acres of Land English measure And for every able man Servant that he shall carry with him armed and provided as aforesaid and arriving there, the like quantity of 150 acres of land English measure, And whoever shall send Servants at that time shall for every able man Servant hee or she soe sends armed and provided as aforesaid and arriving there the like quantity of 150 acres And for every weaker Servant or Slave male or female exceeding the age of ffourteen

yeares which any one shall send or carry arriveing there 75 acres of Land And to every Christian Servant exceeding the age aforesaid after the expiracon of their time of service 75 acres of Land for their own use.

2. *Item* to every Master or Mistres that shall goe before the first day of January which shalbe in the yeare of our Lord 1665, 120 acres of land and for every able man Servant that hee or she shall carry or send armed and provided as aforesaid and arriving within the time aforesaid the like quantity of 120 acres of land, and for every weaker Servant or Slave male or female exceeding the age of 14 yeares arriving there 60 acres of land, and to every Christian Servant to their owne use and behoofe 60 acres of land.

3. *Item* to every ffreeman and ffreewoman [who] shall arrive in the said Province armed and provided as aforesaid within the second year from the first day of January 1665 to the first of Jan'y 1666 with an intenc'on to plant 90 acres of land English measure, and for every able man Servant that hee or she shall carry or send armed and provided as aforesaid 90 acres of land like measure.

4. *Item* for every weaker Servant or slave aged as aforesaid that shall be soe carried or sent thither within the second yeare as aforesaid 45 acres of land of like measure And to every Christian Servant that shall arrive the second yeare 45 acres of land of like measure after the expiracon of his or their time of Service for their own use and behoofe.

5. *Item* to every ffreeman and ffreewoman Armed and provided as aforesaid That shall goe and arrive with an intencon to plant within the third yeare from January 1666 to January 1667 60 acres of land of like measure And for every able man Servant that he or they shall carry or send within the said time armed and provided as aforesaid the like quantitie of 60 acres of land, And for every weaker Servant or Slave aged as aforesaid that hee or they shall carry or send within the Third yeare 30 acres of land and to every Christian Servant soe carried or sent in the Third yeare 30 acres of land of like measure after the expiracon of his or their time of Service. All which Land and all other that shall be possessed in the said Province are to be held on the same termes and Condic'ons as is before menc'oned and as hereafter in the following Paragraphs is more at lar[g]e expressed. . . .

B. "A BRIEF DESCRIPTION OF THE PROVINCE OF CAROLINA ON THE COASTS OF FLOREDA" (1666)*

Carolina is a fair and spacious Province on the Continent of *America:* so called in honour of His Sacred Majesty that now is, *Charles the Second,* whom God preserve; and His Majesty hath been pleas'd to grant the same to certain Honourable Persons, who in order to the speedy planting of the same, have granted divers privileges and advantages to such as shall transport themselves and Servants in convenient time; This Province lying so neer *Virginia,* and yet more Southward, enjoys the fertility and advantages thereof; and yet is so far distant, as to be freed from the inconstancy of the Weather, which is a great cause of the unhealthfulness thereof; also, being in the latitude of the *Barmoodoes* may expect the like healthfulness which it hath hitherto enjoy'd, and doubtless there is no Plantation

---

* These excerpts are reprinted from B. R. Carroll (ed.), *Historical Collections of South Carolina* (2 vols., 1836), vol. II, pp. 10, 14–17.

that ever the *English* went upon, in all respects so good as this: for though *Barmoodoes* be wonderful healthy and fruitful, yet is it but a Prison to the Inhabitants, who are much streightned for want of room, and therefore many of them are come to *Carolina,* and more intend to follow. There is seated in this Province two Colonies already, one on the River *Roanoak* (now called *Albemarle* River) and borders on *Virginia;* the other at *Cape Feare,* two Degrees more Southerly; of which follows a more perticular Description. . . .

If therefore any industrious and ingenious persons shall be willing to pertake of the Felicites of this Country, let them imbrace the first opportunity, that they may obtain the greater advantages.

The chief of the Privileges are as follows.

First, There is full and free Liberty of Conscience granted to all, so that no man is to be molested or called in question for matters of Religious Concern; but every one to be obedient to the Civil Government, worshipping God after their own way.

Secondly, There is freedom from Custom, for all *Wine, Silk, Raisins, Currance, Oyl, Olives,* and *Almonds,* that shall be raised in the Province for 7. years, after 4 Ton of any of those commodities shall be imported in one Bottom.

Thirdly, Every Free-man and Free-woman that transport themselves and Servants by the 25 of *March* next, being 1667. shall have for Himself, Wife, Children, and Men-servants, for each 100 Acres of Land for him and his Heirs for ever, and for every Woman-servant and Slave 50 Acres, paying at most ½d. *per acre, per annum,* in lieu of all demands, to the Lords Proprietors: Provided always, That every Man be armed with a good Musquet full bore, 10l. Powder, and 20l. of Bullet, and six Months Provision for all, to serve them whilst they raise Provision in that Countrey.

Fourthly, Every Man-Servant at the expiration of their time, is to have of the Country a 100 Acres of Land to him and his heirs for ever, paying only ½d. *per Acre, per annum,* and the Women 50. Acres of Land on the same conditions; their Masters also are to allow them two Suits of Apparrel and Tools such as he is best able to work with, according to the Custom of the Countrey.

Fifthly, They are to have a Governour and Council appointed from among themselves, to see the Laws of the Assembly put in due execution; but the Governour is to rule but 3 years, and then learn to obey; also he hath no power to lay any Tax, or make or abrogate any Law, without the Consent of the Colony in their Assembly.

Sixthly, They are to choose annually from among themselves, a certain Number of Men, according to their divisions, which constitute the General Assembly with the Governour and his Council, and have the sole power of Making Laws, and Laying Taxes for the common good when need shall require.

These are the chief and Fundamental privileges, but the Right Honourable Lords Proprietors have promised (and it is their Interest so to do) to be ready to grant what other Privileges may be found advantageous for the good, of the Colony.

Is there therefore any younger Brother who is born of Gentile blood, and whose Spirit is elevated above the common sort, and yet the hard usage of our Country hath not allowed suitable fortune; he will not surely be afraid to leave his Native Soil to advance his Fortunes equal to his Blood and Spirit, and so he will avoid those unlawful ways too many of our young Gentlemen take to maintain themselves according to their high education, having but small Estates; here, with a few Servants and a small Stock a great Estate may be raised, although his Birth have not entitled him to any of the Land of his Ancestors, yet his Industry may supply him so, as to make him the head of as famous a family.

Such as are here tormented with much care how to get worth to gain a Livelyhood, or that with their labour can hardly get a comfortable subsistence, shall do well to go to this place, where any man what-ever, that is but willing to take moderate pains, may be assured of a most comfortable subsistance, and be in a way to raise his fortunes far beyond what he could ever hope for in *England.* Let no man be troubled at the thoughts of being a Servant for 4 or 5 year, for I can assure you, that many men give mony with their children to serve 7 years, to take more pains and fare nothing so well as the Servants in this Plantation will do. Then it is to be considered, that so soon as he is out of his time, he hath Land and Tools, and Clothes given him, and is in a way of advancement. Therefore all Artificers, as *Carpenters, Wheel-rights, Joyners, Coopers, Bricklayers, Smiths,* or diligent Husbandmen and Labourers, that are willing to advance their fortunes, and live in a most pleasant healthful and fruitful Country, where Artificers are of high esteem, and used with all Civility and Courtesie imaginable, may take notice, that,

There is an opportunity offers now by the *Virginia* Fleet, from whence *Cape Feare* is but 3 or 4 days sail, and then a small Stock carried to *Virginia* will purchase provisions at a far easier rate than to carry them from hence; also the freight of the said Provisions will be saved, and be more fresh, and there wanteth not conveyance from *Virginia* thither.

If any Maid or single woman have a desire to go over, they will think themselves in the Golden Age, when Men paid a Dowry for their Wives; for if they be but Civil, and under 50 years of Age, some honest Man or other, will purchase them for their Wives. . . .

SELECTION

The Demand for English Liberties in New York: The Charter of Liberties and Privileges (Oct. 30, 1683)

Unlike the Carolina and New Jersey proprietors, the Duke of York took over a going concern in New Netherlands in 1664. With large numbers already in the

colony, he did not feel their urgency to make generous concessions to prospective settlers. To pacify both the Dutch inhabitants in New York and the New Englanders on Long Island, he found it necessary, however, to confirm existing land titles, guarantee freedom of worship, and grant each a measure of self-government. Accordingly, he permitted the Dutch to retain control of the municipal government of New York, and by the Duke's Laws, derived by the Duke and his associates mostly from existing codes of the New England colonies and promulgated by a meeting of deputies from the towns in March, 1665, he extended local self-governing privileges to all the New England towns on Long Island. The only Restoration proprietor not expressly required by his charter to obtain the consent of the inhabitants in the passing of laws, the Duke insisted upon retaining his "full and absolute power and authority" and for over fifteen years adamantly refused to accede to the demands of the Long Islanders for a representative assembly to pass laws and secure redress of grievances. But after important New York merchants joined the Long Islanders in refusing to pay taxes levied without their consent, the Duke in 1683 authorized Governor Thomas Dongan to call a representative assembly, hoping that the assembly would assume the charges of government and defense. The assembly met on October 17, 1683, and promptly passed the Charter of Liberties and Privileges, in which it sought to ensure the continuance of representative government in the colony and to define the fundamental rights of the colonists as Englishmen. This document received the approval of the Duke in October, 1684. Before it could be returned to New York, however, Charles II died, the Duke became King, and the idea for the Dominion of New England was suggested. Although the assembly existed until January, 1687, the Privy Council officially disallowed the charter in May, 1686, and New York was subsequently incorporated into the Dominion. When New York finally did get a representative assembly on a permanent basis in 1691, it adopted a second charter of liberties, but that too was disallowed by the Privy Council. The events associated with the Charter of Liberties and Privileges are treated in Charles M. Andrews, The Colonial Period of American History, *volume III, chapter 3, and David S. Lovejoy, "Equality and Empire: The New York Charter of Libertyes, 1683,"* William and Mary Quarterly, *third series, volume 21 (1964), pages 493–515.*

The charter is reprinted in full from The Colonial Laws of New York *(1894), volume I, pages 111–116.*

ffOR The better Establishing the Government of this province of New Yorke and that Justice and Right may be Equally done to all persons within the same.

BEE It Enacted by the Governour Councell and Representatives now in Generall Assembly mett and assembled and by the authority of the same.

THAT The Supreme Legislative Authority under his Majesty and Royall Highnesse James Duke of Yorke Albany &c Lord proprietor of the said province shall forever be and reside in a Governour, Councell, and the people mett in General Assembly.

THAT The Exercise of the Cheife Magistracy and Administration of the

Government over the said province shall bee in the said Governour assisted by a Councell with whose advice and Consent or with at least four of them he is to rule and Governe the same according to the Lawes thereof. THAT in Case the Governour shall dye or be absent out of the province and that there be noe person within the said province Comissionated by his Royal Highnesse his heires or Successours to be Governour or Comander in Cheife there That then the Councell for the time being or Soe many of them as are in the Said province doe take upon them the Administration of the Governour and Execution of the Lawes thereof and powers and authorityes belonging to the Governour and Councell the first in nomination in which Councell is to preside untill the said Governour shall returne and arrive in the said province againe, or the pleasure of his Royall Highnesse his heires or Successours Shall be further knowne. THAT According to the usage Custome and practice of the Realme of England a sessions of a Generall Assembly be held in this province once in three yeares at least.

THAT Every ffreeholder within this province and ffreeman in any Corporation Shall have his free Choise and Vote in the Electing of the Representatives without any manner of constraint or Imposition. nd that in all Elections the Majority of Voices shall carry itt and by freeholders is understood every one who is Soe understood according to the Lawes of England.

THAT the persons to be Elected to sitt as representatives in the Generall Assembly from time to time for the severall Cittyes townes Countyes Shires or Divisions of this province and all places within the same shall be according to the proportion and number hereafter Expressed that is to say for the Citty, and County of New Yorke four, for the County of Suffolke two, for Queens County two, for Kings County two, for the County of Richmond two for the County of West Chester two.

for the County of Ulster two for the County of Albany two and for Schenectade within the said County one for Dukes County two, for the County of Cornwall two and as many more as his Royall Highnesse shall think fitt to Establish.

THAT All persons Chosen and Assembled in manner aforesaid or the Major part of them shall be deemed and accounted the Representatives of this province which said Representatives together with the Governour and his Councell Shall forever be the Supreame and only Legislative power under his Royall Highnesse of the said province.

THAT The said Representatives may appoint their owne Times of meeting dureing their sessions and may adjourne their house from time to time to such time as to them shall seeme meet and convenient.

THAT The said Representatives are the sole Judges of the Qualifications of their owne members, and likewise of all undue Elections and may from time to time purge their house as they shall see occasion dureing the said sessions.

THAT noe member of the general Assembly or their servants dureing the time of their Sessions and whilest they shall be goeing to and returning from the said Assembly shall be arrested sued imprisoned or any wayes molested or troubled nor be compelled to make answere to any suite, Bill, plaint, Declaration or otherwise, (Cases of High Treason and felony only Excepted) provided the number of the said servants shall not Exceed three.

THAT All bills agreed upon by the said Representatives or the Major part of them shall be presented unto the Governour and his Councell for their Approbation and Consent All and Every which Said Bills soe approved of Consented to by the Governour and his Councell shall be Esteemed and accounted the Lawes of the province, Which said Lawes shall continue and remaine of force untill they shall be repealed by the authority aforesaid that is to say the Governour Councell and Representatives in General Assembly by and with the Approbation of his Royal Highnesse or Expire by their owne Limittations.

THAT In all Cases of death or removall of any of the said Representatives The Governour shall issue out Sumons by Writt to the Respective Townes Cittyes Shires Countryes or Divisions for which he or they soe removed or deceased were Chosen willing and requireing the ffreeholders of the Same to Elect others in their place and stead.

THAT Noe freeman shall be taken and imprisoned or be disseized of his ffreehold or Libertye or ffree Customes or be outlawed or Exiled or any other wayes destroyed nor shall be passed upon adjudged or condemned But by the Lawfull Judgment of his peers and by the Law of this province. Justice nor Right shall be neither sold denyed or deferred to any man within this province.

THAT Noe aid, Tax, Tallage, Assessment, Custome, Loane, Benevolence or Imposition whatsoever shall be layed assessed imposed or levyed on any of his Majestyes Subjects within this province or their Estates upon any manner of Colour or pretence but by the act and Consent of the Governour Councell and Representatives of the people in Generall Assembly mett and Assembled.

THAT Noe man of what Estate or Condition soever shall be putt out of his Lands or Tenements, nor taken, nor imprisoned, nor disherited, nor banished nor any wayes distroyed without being brought to Answere by due Course of Law.

THAT A ffreeman Shall not be amerced for a small fault, but after the manner of his fault and for a great fault after the Greatnesse thereof Saveing to him his freehold, And a husbandman saveing to him his Wainage and a merchant likewise saveing to him his merchandize And none of the said Amerciaments shall be assessed but by the oath of twelve honest and Lawfull men of the Vicinage provided the faults and misdemeanours be not in Contempt of Courts of Judicature.

ALL Tryalls shall be by the verdict of twelve men, and as neer as may be peers or Equalls And of the neighbourhood and in the County Shire or Division where the fact Shall arise or grow Whether the Same be by Indictment Information Declaration or otherwise against the person Offender or Defendant.

THAT In all Cases Capitall or Criminall there shall be a grand Inquest who shall first present the offence and then twelve men of the neighbourhood to try the Offender who after his plea to the Indictment shall be allowed his reasonable Challenges.

THAT In all Cases whatsoever Bayle by sufficient Suretyes Shall be allowed and taken unlesse for treason or felony plainly and specially Expressed and menconed in the Warrant of Committment provided Always that nothing herein contained shall Extend to discharge out of prison upon bayle any person taken in Execution for debts or otherwise legally sentenced by the Judgment of any of the Courts of Record within the province.

THAT Noe ffreeman shall be compelled to receive any Marriners or Souldiers into his house and there suffer them to Sojourne, against their willes provided Always it be not in time of Actuall Warr within this province.

THAT Noe Comissions for proceeding by Marshall Law against any of his Majestyes Subjects within this province shall issue forth to any person or persons whatsoever Least by Colour of them any of his Majestyes Subjects bee destroyed or putt to death Except all such officers persons and Soldiers in pay throughout the Government.

THAT from hence forward Noe Lands Within this province shall be Esteemed or accounted a Chattle or personall Estate but an Estate of Inheritance according to the Custome and practice of his Majesties Realme of England.

THAT Noe Court or Courts within this province have or at any time hereafter Shall have any Jurisdiction power or authority to grant out any Execution or other writt whereby any mans Land may be sold or any other way disposed off without the owners Consent provided Always That the issues or meane proffitts of any mans Lands shall or may be Extended by Execution or otherwise to satisfye just debts Any thing to the Contrary hereof in any wise Notwithstanding.

THAT Noe Estate of a feme Covert shall be sold or conveyed But by Deed acknowledged by her in Some Court of Record the Woman being secretly Examined if She doth it freely without threats or Compulsion of her husband.

THAT All Wills in writing attested by two Credible Witnesses shall be of the same force to convey Lands as other Conveyances being registered in the Secretaryes Office within forty dayes after the testators death.

THAT A Widdow after the death of her husband shall have her Dower And shall and may tarry in the Cheife house of her husband forty dayes after the death of her husband within which forty dayes her Dower shall be assigned her And for her Dower shall be assigned unto her the third part of all the Lands of her husband dureing Coverture, Except shee were Endowed of Lesse before Marriage.

THAT All Lands and Heritages within this province and Dependencyes shall be free from all fines and Lycences upon Alienations, and from all Herriotts Ward Shipps Liveryes primer Seizins yeare day and Wast Escheats and forfeitures upon the death of parents and Ancestors naturall unaturall casuall or Judiciall, and that forever; Cases of High treason only Excepted.

THAT Noe person or persons which professe ffaith in God by Jesus Christ Shall at any time be any wayes molested punished disquieted or called in Question for any Difference in opinion or Matter of Religious Concernment, who doe not actually disturb the Civill peace of the province, But that all and Every such person or persons may from time to time and at all times freely have and fully enjoy his or their Judgments or Consciencyes in matters of Religion throughout all the province, they behaveing themselves peaceably and quietly and not useing this Liberty to Lycentiousnesse nor to the civill Injury or outward disturbance of others provided Always that this liberty or any thing contained therein to the Contrary shall never be Construed or improved to make void the Settlement of any publique Minister on Long Island Whether Such Settlement be by two thirds of the voices in any Towne thereon which shall alwayes include the Minor part Or by Subscriptions of perticuler Inhabitants in Said Townes provided they are the two thirds thereon Butt that all such agreements Covenants and Subscriptions that are there already made and had Or that hereafter shall bee in this Manner Consented to agreed and Subscribed shall at all time and times hereafter be firme and Stable And in Confirmation hereof It is Enacted by the Governour Councell and Representatives; That all Such Sumes of money soe agreed on Consented to or Subscribed as aforesaid for maintenance of said publick Ministers by the two thirds of any Towne on Long Island Shall alwayes include the Minor part who shall be regulated thereby And also Such Subscriptions and agreements as are before mentioned are and Shall be alwayes ratified performed and paid, And if any Towne on said Island in their publick Capacity of agreement with any Such minister or any perticuler persons by their private Subscriptions as aforesaid Shall make default deny or withdraw from Such payment Soe Covenanted to agreed upon and Subscribed That in Such Case upon Complaint of any Collector appointed and Chosen by two thirds of Such Towne upon Long Island unto any Justice of that County Upon his hearing the Same he is here by authorized impowered and required to issue out his warrant unto the Constable or his Deputy or any other person appointed for the Collection of Said Rates or agreement to Levy upon the goods and Chattles of the Said Delinquent or Defaulter all such Sumes of money Soe covenanted and agreed to be paid by distresse with Costs and Charges without any further Suite in Law Any Lawe Custome or usage to the Contrary in any wise Notwithstanding.

PROVIDED Always the said sume or sumes be under forty shillings otherwise to be recovered as the Law directs.

AND WHEREAS All the Respective Christian Churches now in practice within the City of New Yorke and the other places of this province doe appeare to be priviledged Churches and have beene Soe Established and Confirmed by the former authority of this Government BEE it hereby Enacted by this Generall Assembly and by the authority thereof That all the Said Respective Christian Churches be hereby Confirmed therein And that they and Every of them Shall from henceforth forever be held and reputed as priviledged Churches and Enjoy all their former freedomes of their Religion in Divine Worshipp and Church Discipline And that all former Contracts made and agreed upon for the maintenances of the severall ministers of the Said Churches shall stand and continue in full force and virtue And that all Contracts for the future to be made Shall bee of the same power And all persons that are unwilling to performe their part of the said Contract Shall be Constrained thereunto by a warrant from any Justice of the peace provided it be under forty Shillings Or otherwise as this Law directs provided allsoe that all Christian Churches that Shall hereafter come and settle within this province shall have the Same priviledges.

SELECTION

The Holy Experiment in Pennsylvania

Of all the late seventeenth-century proprietors, the Quaker William Penn (1644–1718) was probably the most idealistic, the most vigorous in promoting his colony, and the most generous in his treatment of colonists. His ambition was to make Pennsylvania a holy experiment free of religious and civil embroilments and solidly founded on the principles of religious toleration, good government, and social and individual morality. Inspired by this vision, he set about the task of seeking settlers with an avidity unknown to his predecessors. Almost immediately after receiving his charter in March, 1681, he published two promotional tracts. They were both circulated widely in the British Isles, and one, Some Account of the Province of Pennsylvania *(1681), was also translated into Dutch and German and distributed on the Continent. In that piece Penn offered liberal land grants, described the kinds of industrious and ambitious people he hoped to attract, and promised a constitution with a large measure of self-government.*

The nature of that constitution was revealed on May 5, 1682, with the issuance of Penn's first frame of government, which provided for a government composed of a governor, a seventy-two-member Council in which the governor had a triple vote, and a 200- to 500-member Assembly. The preface to this document, a succinct summary of Penn's basic ideas about government, expressed his willingness to alter the constitution to conform with existing conditions in Pennsylvania, and when it became immediately clear that his government was too unwieldy, he willingly joined with the Council and Assembly in 1683 to draw up a second frame of government, which reduced the number of councilors and assemblymen to eighteen and thirty-two, respectively. What

Penn would not accede to, however, was the persistent demand of the Assembly for the right to initiate laws. Strongly committed to the idea advanced by political philosopher James Harrington in his tract Oceana *that to maintain a proper balance between magistrates and people, the magistrates, represented in the Council, should propose laws, while the people, represented in the Assembly, should be limited to the function of either rejecting them or accepting them, he fought the Assembly on this issue until 1696, when he finally gave in and formally recognized the Assembly's right of initiative in legislation in a third frame of government. One of the results of this long controversy, however, was to persuade the Assembly that the Council ought to be eliminated from the legislative process altogether, and Penn eventually agreed to accept a constitution prepared by the Assembly as long as it did not interfere with his authority over proprietary lands. The result was the Charter of Privileges of 1701, a complete victory for the Assembly which made Pennsylvania the only colony with a unicameral legislature and severely limited proprietary power. This charter served as the constitution of Pennsylvania until 1776.*

On the first years of Pennsylvania, see Edwin B. Bronner, William Penn's "Holy Experiment": The Founding of Pennsylvania, 1681–1701 *(1962), and Roy Lokken,* David Lloyd, Colonial Lawmaker *(1959), a biography of one of Penn's chief antagonists. A recent life of Penn is Catherine Owens Peare,* William Penn. A Biography *(1957).*

A. WILLIAM PENN, "SOME ACCOUNT OF THE PROVINCE OF PENNSYLVANIA" (1681)*

The Constitutions

For the constitutions of the country, the patent shows,

[*1st.*] That the people and governour have a legislative power, so that no law can be made, nor money raised but by the peoples consent.

2dly. That the rights and freedoms of England (the best and largest in Europe) shall be in force there.

3dly. That making no law against allegiance (which should we, 'twere by the law of England void of it self that moment) we may enact what laws we please for the good prosperity and security of the said province.

4thly. That so soon as any are ingaged with me, we shall begin a scheam or draught together, such as shall give ample testimony of my sincere inclinations to encourage planters, and settle a free, just and industrious colony there.

The Conditions

My conditions will relate to three sorts of people: 1st. Those that will buy: 2dly. Those that take up land upon rent: 3dly. Servants. To the first, the shares I sell shall be certain as to number of acres; that is to say, every

* These excerpts are reprinted from Samuel Hazard (ed.), *The Register of Pennsylvania* (1828–1836), vol. I, pp. 307–308.

one shall contain five thousand acres, free from any *Indian* incumbrance, the price a hundred pounds, and for the quit-rent but one *English* shilling or the value of it yearly for a hundred acres; and the said quit-rent not to begin to be paid till 1684. To the second sort, that take up land upon rent, they shall have liberty so to do paying yearly *one penny* per acre, not exceeding two hundred acres. To the third sort, to wit, servants that are carried over, fifty acres shall be allowed to the master for every head, and fifty acres to every servant when their time is expired. And because some engage with me that may not be disposed to go, it were very advisable for every three adventurers to send an overseer with their servants, which would well pay the cost.

The dividend may be thus; if the persons concern'd please, a tract of land shall be survey'd; say *fifty thousand acres to a hundred adventurers;* in which some of the best shall be set out for towns or cities; and there shall be so much ground allotted to each in those towns as may maintain some cattel and produce some corn; then the remainder of the fifty thousand acres shall be shar'd among the said *adventurers* (casting up the barren for commons, and allowing for the same) whereby every *adventurer* will have a considerable quantity of land together; likewise every one a proportion by a navigable river, and then backward into the country.—The manner of dividend I shall not be strict in; we can but speak roughly of the matter here; but let men skilful in plantations be consulted, and I shall leave it to the majority of votes among the *adventurers* when it shall please God we come there, how to fix it to their own content.

Those persons that providence seems to have most fitted for Plantations, are,

1st. Industrious *husbandmen* and *day-labourers,* that are hardly able (with extreme labour) to maintain their families and portion their children.

2dly. Laborious handicrafts, especially carpenters, masons, smiths, weavers, taylors, tanners, shoemakers, shipwrights, &c. where they may be spared or low in the world: and as they shall want no encouragement, so their labour is worth more there than here, and there provision cheaper.

3dly. A plantation seems a fit place for those *ingenious spirits* that being low in the world, are much clogg'd and oppress'd about a livelyhood, for the means of subsisting being easie there, they may have time and opportunity to gratify their inclinations, and thereby improve science and help nurseries of people.

4thly. A fourth sort of men to whom a *plantation* would be proper, takes in those that are younger brothers of small inheritances; yet because they would live in sight of their kindred in some proportion to their quality, and can't do it without a labour that looks like farming, their condition is too strait for them; and if married, their children are often too numerous for the estate, and are frequently bred up to no trades, but are a kind of *hangers on or retainers to the elder brothers table and charity:* which is a mischief, as in it self to be lamented, so here to be remedied; for land they have for next to nothing, which with moderate labour produces plenty of all things necessary for life, and such an increase as by traffique may supply them with all conveniences.

Lastly, there are another sort of persons, not only fit for, but necessary in *plantations,* and that is, *men of universal spirits,* that have an eye to the good of posterity, and that both understand and delight to promote good discipline and just government among a plain and well intending people; such persons may find *room in colonies for their good counsel and contrivance,* who are shut out from being of much use or service to great nations under settl'd customs: these men deserve much esteem, and would be hearken'd to. Doubtless 'twas this (as I observ'd before) that put some of the famous *Greeks* and *Romans* upon transplanting and regulating *colonies* of people in divers parts of the world; whose names, for giving so great proof of their wisdom, virtue, labour and constancy, are with justice honourably delivered down by story to the praise of our own times; though the world, after all its higher pretences of religion, barbarously errs from their excellent example....

B. WILLIAM PENN, PREFACE TO THE FIRST FRAME OF GOVERNMENT (MAY 5, 1682)*

When the great and wise God had made the world, of all his creatures it pleased him to choose man his deputy to rule it; and to fit him for so great a charge and trust, he did not only qualify him with skill and power, but with integrity to use them justly. This native goodness was equally his honour and his happiness; and whilst he stood here, all went well; there was no need of coercive or compulsive means; the precept of divine love and truth in his bosom was the guide and keeper of his innocency. But lust prevailing against duty, made a lamentable breach upon it; and the law, that before had no power over him, took place upon him and his disobedient posterity, that such as would not live conformable to the holy law within, should fall under the reproof and correction, of the just law without, in a judicial administration.

This the apostle teaches us in divers of his epistles. The law (says he) was added because of transgression: In another place, knowing that the law was not made for the righteous man; but for the disobedient and ungodly, for sinners, for unholy and prophane, for murderers, for whoremongers, for them that defile themselves with mankind, and for menstealers, for liars, for perjured persons, &c. But this is not all, he opens and carries the matter of government a little further: Let every soul be subject to the higher powers, for there is no power but of God. The powers that be are ordained of God: whosoever therefore resisteth the power, resisteth the ordinance of God. For rulers are not a terror to good works, but to Evil: wilt thou then not be afraid of the power? Do that which is good, and thou shalt have praise of the same.—He is the minister of God to thee for good.—Wherefore ye must needs be subject, not only for wrath, but for conscience sake.

This settles the divine right of government beyond exception, and that for two ends; first, to terrify evil-doers; secondly, to cherish those that do well; which gives government a life beyond corruption, and makes it as

* Reprinted in full from *Minutes of the Provincial Council of Pennsylvania* (10 vols., 1851–1852), vol. I, pp. 29–32.

durable in the world, as good men shall be. So that government seems to me a part of religion itself, a thing sacred in its institution and end. For if it does not directly remove the cause, it crushes the effects of evil, and is as such (tho' a lower yet) an emanation of the same Divine Power, that is both author and object of pure religion; the difference lying here, that the one is more free and mental, the other more corporal and compulsive in its operations: but that is only to evil-doers; government itself being otherwise as capable of kindness, goodness and charity, as a more private society. They weekly err, that think there is no other use of government than correction, which is the coarsest part of it: daily experience tells us, that the care and regulation of many other affairs more soft and daily necessary, make up much the greatest part of government; and which must have followed the peopling of the world, had Adam never fell, and will continue among men on earth under the highest attainments they may arrive at, by the coming of the blessed second Adam, the Lord from Heaven. Thus much of government in general, as to its rise and end.

For particular frames and models, it will become me to say little; and comparatively I will say nothing. My reasons are: first, that the age is too nice and difficult for it; there being nothing the wits of men are more busy and divided upon. 'Tis true, they seem to agree in the end, to wit, happiness; but in the means they differ, as to divine, so to this human felicity; and the cause is much the same, not always want of light and knowledge, but want of using them rightly. Men side with their passions against their reason, and their sinister interests have so strong a bias upon their minds, that they lean to them against the good of the things they know.

Secondly, I do not find a model in the world, that time, place, and some singular emergences have not necessarily altered; nor is it easy to frame a civil government, that shall serve all places alike.

Thirdly, I know what is said by the several admirers of monarchy, aristocracy and democracy, which are the rule of one, a few, and many, and are the three common ideas of government, when men discourse on that subject. But I choose to solve the controversy with this small distinction, and it belongs to all three; any government is free to the people under it (whatever be the frame) where the laws rule, and the people are a party to those laws, and more than this is tyranny, oligarchy, and confusion.

But lastly, when all is said, there is hardly one frame of government in the world so ill designed by its first founders, that in good hands would not do well enough; and story tells us, the best in ill ones can do nothing that is great or good; witness the Jewish and Roman states. Governments, like clocks, go from the motion men give them, and as governments are made and moved by men, so by them they are ruined too. Wherefore governments rather depend upon men, than men upon governments. Let men be good, and the government cannot be bad; if it be ill, they will cure it. But if men be bad, let the government be never so good, they will endeavour to warp and spoil to their turn.

I know some say, let us have good laws, and no matter for the men that execute them: but let them consider, that though good laws do well, good men do better; for good laws may want good men, and be abolished or invaded by ill men; but good men will never want good laws, nor suffer ill ones. 'Tis true, good laws have some awe upon ill ministers, but that is where they have not power to escape or abolish them, and the people are generally wise and good: but a loose and depraved people (which is to the question) love laws and an administration like themselves. That therefore, which makes a good constitution, must keep it, viz: men of wisdom and virtue, qualities that because they descend not with worldly inheritances, must be carefully propagated by a virtuous education of youth, for which after ages will owe more to the care and prudence of founders, and the successive magistracy, than to their parents for their private patrimonies.

These considerations of the weight of government, and the nice and various opinions about it, made it uneasy to me to think of publishing the ensuing frame and conditional laws, foreseeing both the censures they will meet with from men of differing humours and engagements, and the occasion they may give of discourse beyond my design.

But next to the power of necessity (which is a solicitor that will take no denial) this induced me to a compliance, that we have (with reverence to God, and good conscience to men) to the best of our skill, contrived and composed the FRAME and LAWS of this government, to the great end of all government, viz: to support power in reverence with the people, and to secure the people from the abuse of power; that they may be free by their just obedience, and the magistrates honourable for their just administration: for liberty without obedience is confusion, and obedience without liberty is slavery. To carry this evenness is partly owing to the constitution, and partly to the magistracy; where either of these fail, government will be subject to convulsions; but where both are wanting, it must be totally subverted: then where both meet, the government is like to endure. Which I humbly pray and hope God will please to make the lot of this of Pennsylvania. Amen.

C. THE PENNSYLVANIA CHARTER OF PRIVILEGES (OCT. 28, 1701)*

WHEREAS, KING CHARLES THE SECOND . . . was Graciously pleased to Give and Grant unto me, my heirs & Assigns, forever, this Province of Pennsylvania . . . together with Powers and Jurisdictions for the good Government thereof . . . know ye therefore, that I, for the further well being and good Govrmt of the said Province and Territories, and in pursuance of the Rights and Powers before mentioned, I, the said WILLIAM PENN, do Declare, grant and Confirm unto all the freemen, Planters and adventurers, and other inhabitants in this Province and Territories, these following Liberties, ffranchises and Privileges, so far as in me lyeth, to be held, enjoyed and kept by the freemen, planters & ad-

* These excerpts are reprinted from *Minutes of the Provincial Council of Pennsylvania,* vol. II, pp. 56–59.

venturers, & other Inhabitants of and in the said Province and Territories thereunto Annexed, forever;

FIRST: Because no people can be truly happy, though under the greatest Enjoyment of Civil Liberties, if abridg'd of the freedom of their Consciences as to their Religious profession & Worship; and Almighty God being the only Lord of Conscience, ffather of Lights & Spirits, and the author as well as object of all Divine Knowledge, ffaith and Worship, who only doth Enlighten the Mind & perswade and Convince the Understandings of People, I do hereby Grant and Declare that no person or persons, inhabiting in this Province or Territories, who shall Confess and acknowledge one Almighty God, the Creator, Upholder and Ruler of the World, and Profess him or themselves obliged to Live Quietly under the Civil Government, shall be in any Case molested or prejudiced in his or their person or Estate because of his or their Consciencious perswasion or Practice, nor be Compelled to frequent or maintain any Religious Worship, place or ministry contrary to his or their mind, or to do or suffer any other act or thing Contrary to their Religious perswasion. And that all persons who also profess to believe in JESUS CHRIST the SAVIOUR of the World, shall be Capable (notwithstanding their other perswasions and Practices in Point of Conscience and Religion) to serve this Governmt in any Capacity, both Legislatively and Executively, he or they Solemnly promising, when Lawfully required, allegiance to the King as Sovereign, and fidelity to the Proprietor and Governour, and Taking ye attests as now Established, by the Law made at New Castle, in the Year One Thousand seven hundred, Intitled at act Directing the attests of several offices and ministers, as now amended and Confirmed by this present Assembly.

SECONDLY: for the well governing of this Province and Territories, there shall be an Assembly Yearly Chosen by the freemen thereof, to Consist of four persons out of each County of most note for Virtue, Wisdom & Ability, (or of a greater number at any time as the Governour and Assembly shall agree,) upon the first day of October, forever; and shall sitt on the fourteenth day of the said month, at Philadelphia, unless the Governour and Council for the time being shall see Cause to appoint another place within the said Province or Territories, which assembly shall have power to Choose a Speaker and other their officers, and shall be Judges of the Qualifications and Elections of their own members, sitt upon their own adjournments, appoint Committees, prepare bills in or to pass into Laws, Impeach Criminals and Redress Grievances; and shall have all other powers and Privileges of an Assembly, according to the Rights of the free born subjects of England, and as is usual in any of the King's Plantations in America. . . .

THIRDLY: that the freemen in each Respective County, at the time and place of meeting for Electing their Representatives to serve in Assembly, may, as often as there shall be occasion, Choose a Double number of persons to present to the Govr for Sherifs and Coroners, to serve for three years, if they so long behave themselves well, out of which respective Elections & Presentments The Gor shall nominate and Commissionate One for each of the said officers, The Third Day after such presentment, or else the first named in such presentment for Each office, as aforesaid, shall stand and serve in that office for the time before Respectively Limited; and in case of death or Default, such vacancies shall be supplied by ye Governour to serve to the End of the said Term. . . . And that ye Justices of the Respective Counties shall or may nominate & present to the Govr. three persons to serve for Clerk of the Peace for the said County when there is a vacancy, One of which the Governour shall Commissionate within Ten Days after such presentment, or else the first nominated shall serve in the said office During good behavior.

FOURTHLY: that the Laws of this Govrmt shall be in this stile, vizt: [By the Governour with the Consent and approbation of the freemen in General Assembly mett,] and shall be, after Confirmation by the Governour, forthwith Recorded in the Rolls office, and kept at Philadia, unless the Govr and Assembly shall agree to appoint another place.

FIFTHLY; That all Criminals shall have the same Privileges of Witnesses and Council as their Prosecutors.

SIXTHLY: That no person or persons shall or may, at any time hereafter, be obliged to answer any Complaint, matter or thing Whatsoever Relating to Property before the Governr and Council, or in any other place but in the ordinary Courts of Justice, unless appeals thereunto shall be hereafter by Law appointed.

SEVENTHLY: That no person within this Governmt shall be Licensed by the Governor to keep Ordinary, Tavern, or House of Publick Entertainment, but such who are first Recommended to him under the hand of the Justice of the Respective Counties, signed in open Court, wch Justices are and shall be hereby Impowered to suppress & forbid any person keeping such Publick House, as aforesaid, upon their misbehaviour, on such Penalties as the law doth or shall direct, and to Recommend others from time to time as they shall see occasion.

EIGHTHLY: . . . But because the happiness of mankind depends so much upon the Enjoying of Liberty of their Consciences, as aforesaid, I do hereby Solemnly Declare, promise and Grant for me, my heirs and assigns, that the first article of this Charter, Relating to Liberty of Conscience, and Every part and Clause therein, according to the true Intent and meaning thereof, shall be kept and remain without any alteration, Inviobly forever.

And LASTLY, I, the said William Penn, Proprietor & Govr of th Province of Pennsylvania and Territories thereunto belonging, for my self, my heirs and Assigns, have solemnly Declared, Granted and Confirmed, and do hereby Solemnly Declare, Grant and Confirm, that neither I, my heirs or Assigns, shall procure or do any thing or things whereby the Liberties in this Charter Contained and Exprest, nor any part thereof, shall be infringed or Broken; and if any thing shall be procured or done by any person or persons, Contrary to these presents, it shall be held of no force or effect. . . .

Expansion and Adjustment, 1660–1713:
Manifestations of Social Instability

SELECTION

The Indian Threat

In 1675–1676 both New England, for the first time in nearly forty years, and Virginia, for the first time in over thirty years, were besieged by hostile Indians. Pressed on all sides by a rapidly expanding white population, the southern New England tribes under the leadership of Philip, chief of the Wampanoags, unleashed a furious onslaught against the southern and western New England frontier in the summer of 1675. For nearly a year after the initial attack on Swansea on June 20, 1675, the New Englanders were on the defensive. The Indians struck at will, completely destroying a dozen towns and severely damaging many others, and the morale of the white settlers declined steadily. In Virginia, the Susquehannock Indians of Maryland, forced south to the Potomac River by the powerful Seneca Nation and indiscriminately attacked by a Virginia punitive expedition against some Doegs who had raided plantations in northern Virginia, fell upon the Virginia frontier in early 1676. Ranging as far south as the James River, they had killed thirty-six people by the end of March and had forced many Virginians to abandon their homes on the frontier.

The response to these events differed markedly in New England and Virginia. In Massachusetts, where there was a high degree of social unity built upon a coherent structure of ideas that corresponded reasonably closely to the actual conditions of social life, King Philip's War caused Puritan leaders to look within themselves and the society for an explanation of their difficulties. Already laboring under a deep sense of guilt over the obvious decline in religious zeal during the previous generation, they could interpret the Indian troubles only as a mark of God's wrath. This was the verdict of the Massachusetts General Court, and on November 3, 1675, it enacted a measure which coupled a series of regulations intended to force the citizenry to adhere more closely to the ways of God with provisions for prosecuting the war.

This conviction that it was the general sins of the community rather than the behavior of specific individuals or groups that had brought about the war tended to unify all groups in the effort to purge the colony of its corruption and thereby win God's help in the fight against the Indians. The identification of preservation with purification produced a vigorous effort in behalf of both during the late spring and early summer of 1676 and finally turned the tide in favor of the Puritans. Defeated in several battles in the Connecticut River Valley in May and June and suffering from hunger, the Indians surrendered in large numbers during the summer. Philip himself was captured and killed on August 12, 1676, and Indian resistance quickly collapsed except on the Maine frontier, where it continued sporadically until April, 1678. The subjugation of the Indians could be and was widely interpreted by the Puritans as evidence of their successful regeneration, of their reinstatement in the favor of God.

In Virginia, where—in contrast to Massachusetts Bay—there were unmistakable signs of social disunity deriving from dissatisfaction over high taxes and falling tobacco prices and from rumors of widespread political corruption and favoritism, the Indian attacks were followed by Bacon's Rebellion. The most serious uprising against constituted authority in the English colonies up to that time, the rebellion revealed basic tensions between the frontier and older, settled regions over Indian policy as well as extensive discontent with the regime of Governor Sir William Berkeley (1601–1677).

What set the rebellion off was Berkeley's attempt to restrain an aggressive frontier army under Nathaniel Bacon, Jr. (1647–1676), a twenty-nine-year-old ne'er-do-well nobleman who had recently settled in Henrico County near the western edge of settlement, from annihilating friendly Indians along with enemy ones. Having already once been declared a traitor and pardoned by Berkeley for leading an unauthorized expedition against the Indians in the spring, Bacon marched to Jamestown in June, 1676, with a force of 500 men and forced Berkeley to give him a commission and the legislature to pass acts making him commander in chief of a force to be sent against the Indians and pardoning all crimes committed by him and his men against friendly Indians in the previous months. Before Bacon marched on Jamestown, the legislature had also enacted a series of reform laws designed to remedy a number of grievances brought out in the open by the political ferment produced by the Indian raids and the debate over how they should be handled. But Bacon, as yet uninterested in political reforms, was primarily concerned with removing the Indian menace and promptly returned with his new commission to the frontier.

Only after Bacon had left Jamestown, and Berkeley, increasingly alarmed by the whole situation, had again proclaimed Bacon a rebel and had begun to raise a force to go against him did Bacon begin to show any interest in general social and political grievances. Abandoning his pursuit of the Indians, he issued on July 30, 1676, the "Manifesto concerning the Present Troubles in Virginia"—a vigorous defense of his own behavior and a catalogue of grievances against Berkeley that provides a clear picture of the sources and nature of political discontent and social instability in Virginia. On August 3 a number of leading men in the colony endorsed the charges made in the manifesto and took an oath to support Bacon after Berkeley, to avoid capture, had fled to the

Eastern Shore. *The Indian problem then became secondary to the domestic tumult as Berkeley gathered a large force of loyal supporters and offered battle. After defeating Berkeley at Jamestown and burning the town on September 18, Bacon appeared to be in a strong position, but his sudden death on October 18 left the rebels leaderless and enabled Berkeley to reassert his authority. By the time of his formal removal by the English government in April, 1677, he had crushed the rebellion and in the process had secured the execution of twenty-three rebel leaders.*

Bacon's death resulted in defeat for his Indian policy, but the political reforms associated with the rebellion were more lasting. In 1677 the legislature reenacted many of the reform laws passed in June, 1676, and they provided the foundation for a more stable political environment in succeeding decades.

Douglas E. Leach, Flintlock and Tomahawk: New England in King Philip's War *(1958), and Wilcomb E. Washburn,* The Governor and the Rebel: A History of Bacon's Rebellion in Virginia *(1957), are recent detailed treatments of these events.*

A. KING PHILIP'S WAR: THE PURITAN EXPLANATION (NOV. 3, 1675)*

WHEREAS the most wise & holy God, for seuerall yeares past, hath not only warned us by his word, but chastized us with his rods, inflicting vpon vs many generall (though lesser) judgments, but we haue neither heard the word nor rod as wee ought, so as to be effectually humbled for our sinns to repent of them, reforme, and amend our wayes; hence it is the righteous God hath heightened our calamjty, and given commission to the barbarous heathen to rise vp against us, and to become a smart rod and seuere scourge to us, in burning & depopulating seuerall hopefull plantations, murdering many of our people of all sorts, and seeming as it were to cast us off, and putting us to shame, and not going forth with our armjes, heereby speaking aloud to us to search and try our wayes, and turne againe vnto the Lord our God, from whom wee have departed with a great backsliding.

1. The Court, apprehending there is too great a neglect of discipline in the churches, and especially respecting those that are their children, through the non acknowledgment of them according to the order of the gospell; in watching ouer them, as well as chattechising of them, inquireing into theire spirittuall estates, that, being brought to take hold of the couenant, they may acknouledge & be acknouledged according to theire relations to God & to his church, and theire obligations to be the Lords, and to approove themselues so to be by a suiteable profession & conuersa-

---

* The following law passed by the Massachusetts General Court identified the sins of the colony, called for a general humiliation and repentance before God, and established measures calculated to begin the work of reformation and to meet the challenge of King Philip and his warriors. It is reprinted in full from Nathaniel B. Shurtleff (ed.), *Records of the Governor and Company of the Massachusetts Bay* (6 vols., 1853–1854), vol. V, pp. 59–64.

tion; and doe therefore solemnly recommend it vnto the respective elders and brethren of the seuerall churches throughout this jurisdiction to take effectuall course for reformation herein.

2. Whereas there is manifest pride openly appearing amongst us in that long haire, like weomens haire, is worne by some men, either their oune or others haire made into perewiggs, and by some weomen wearing borders of hajre, and theire cutting, curling, & immodest laying out theire haire, which practise doeth prevayle & increase, especially amongst the younger sort,—

This Court doeth declare against this ill custome as offenciue to them, and diuers sober christians amongst us, and therefore doe hereby exhort and advise all persons to vse moderation in this respect; and further, doe impower all grand jurjes to present to the County Court such persons, whither male or female, whom they shall judge to exceede in the premisses; and the County Courts are hereby authorized to proceed against such delinquents either by admonition, fine, or correction, according to theire good discretion.

3. Notwithstanding the wholesome lawes already made by this Court for restreyning excesse in apparrell, yet through corruption in many, and neglect of due execution of those lawes, the euill of pride in apparrell, both for costljnes in the poorer sort, & vajne, new, strainge fashions, both in poore & rich, with naked breasts and armes, or, as it were, pinioned with the addition of superstitious ribbons both on hajre & apparrell; for redresse whereof, it is ordered by this Court, that the County Courts, from time to time, doe giue strict charge to present all such persons as they shall judge to exceede in that kinde, and if the grand jury shall neglect theire duty herein, the County Court shall impose a fine vpon them at their discretion.

And it is further ordered, that the County Court, single magistrate, Commissioners Court in Boston, haue heereby power to summon all such persons so offending before them, and for the first offence to admonish them, and for each offence of that kinde afterwards to impose a fine of tenn shillings vpon them, or, if vnable to pay, to inflict such punishment as shall be by them thought most suiteable to the nature of the offence; and the same judges aboue named are heereby impowred to judge of and execute the lawes already extant against such excesse.

Whereas it may be found amongst us, that mens thresholds are sett vp by Gods thresholds, and mans posts besides Gods posts, espeacially in the open meetings of Quakers, whose damnable hæresies, abominable idolatrys, are hereby promoted, embraced, and practised, to the scandall of religion, hazard of souls, and provocation of divine jealousie against this people, for prevention & reformation whereof, it is ordered by this Court and the authority thereof, that euery person found at a Quakers meeting shall be apprehended, ex officio, by the constable, and by warrant from a magistrate or commissioner shall be committed to the house of correction, and there to haue the discipline of the house applied to them, and to be kept to worke, with bread & water, for three days, and then released, or else shall pay fiue pounds in money as a fine to the county for such offence; and all constables neglecting their duty in not faithfully executing this order shall incurr the pœnalty of four pounds, vpon conviction, one third whereof to the informer.

And touching the law of importation of Quakers, that it may be more strictly executed, and none transgressing to escape punishment, —

It is heereby ordered, that the penalty to that law averred be in no case abated to lesse than twenty pounds.

5. Whereas there is so mutch profanes amongst us in persons turning their backs vpon the publick worship before it be finished and the blessing pronounced, —

It is ordered by this Court, that the officers of the churches, or select-men, shall take care to prevent such disorders, by appointing persons to shutt the meeting house doores, or any other meete way to attajne the end.

6. Whereas there is much disorder & rudenes in youth in many congregations in time of the worship of God, whereby sin & prophaness is greately increased, for reformation whereof, —

It is ordered by this Court, that the select men doe appoint such place or places in the meeting house for children or youth to sit in where they may be most together and in publick vejw, and that the officers of the churches, or selectmen, doe appoint some graue & sober person or persons to take a particcular care of and inspection ouer them, who are heereby required to present a list of the names of such, who, by their oune observ-ance or the information of others, shallbe found delinquent, to the next magistrate or Court, who are impowred for the first offence to admonish them, for the second offence to impose a fine of fiue shillings on theire parents or gouernors, or order the children to be whipt, and if incorrigible, to be whipt with ten stripes, or sent to the house of correction for three dayes.

7. Whereas the name of God is prophaned by common swearing and cursing in ordinary communication, which is a sin that growes amongst us, and many heare such oathes and curses, and conceales the same from authority, for reformation whereof, it is ordered by this Court, that the lawes already in force against this sin be vigorously prosecuted; and, as addition therevnto, it is further ordered, that all such persons who shall at any time heare prophane oathes and curses spoken by any person or persons, and shall neglect to disclose the same to some magistrate, com-missioner, or constable, such persons shall incurr the same pœnalty pro-uided in that law against swearers.

8. Whereas the shamefull and scandelous sin of excessive drinking, tipling, & company keeping in tavernes, &c, ordinarys, grows vpon us, for reformation whereof, —

It is commended to the care of the respective County Courts not to license any more publick houses then are absolutely necessary in any toune, and to take care that none be licenst but persons of approoved sobriety and fidelity to law and good order; and that licensed houses be regulated in theire improovement for the refreshing & enterteynment of travajlers & strangers only, and all toune dwellers are heereby strictly enjoyned & required to forbeare spending their time or estates in such common houses of enterteynment, to drincke & tiple, vpon pœnalty of fiue shillings for euery offence, or, if poore, to be whipt, at the discretion of the judge, not exceeding fiue stripes; and euery ordinary keeper, permitting persons to transgress as aboue sajd, shall incurr the pœnalty of fiue shillings for each offence in that kinde; and any magistrate, commissioner, or selectmen are impowred & required vigorously to putt the abouesajd law in execution.

And, ffurther, it is ordered, that all private, unlicensed houses of enterteinment be diligently searched out, and the pœnalty of this law strictly imposed; and that all such houses may be the better discouered, the selectmen of euery toune shall choose some sober and discreete persons, to be authorized from the County Court, each of whom shall take the charge of ten or twelue familjes of his neighbourhood, and shall diligently inspect them, and present the names of such persons so transgressing to the magistrate, commissioners, or selectmen of the toune, who shall returne the same to be proceeded with by the next County Court as the law directs; and the persons so chosen and authorized, and attending theire duty ffaithfully therein, shall haue one third of the fines allowed them; but, if neglect of their duty, and shall be so judged by authority, they shall incurr the same pœnalty provided against vnlicensed houses.

9. Whereas there is a wofull breach of the fifth comandment to be found amongst us, in contempt of authority, civil, ecclesiasticall, and domesticall, this Court doeth declare, that sin is highly provoaking to the Lord, against which he hath borne seuere testimony in his word, especially in that remarkeable judgments vpon Chorah and his company, and therefore doe strictly require & comand all persons vnder this gouernment to reforme so great an evil, least God from heauen punish offenders heerin by some remarkeable judgments. And it is further ordered, that all County Courts, magistrates, commissioners, selectmen, and grand jurors, according to theire seuerall capacitjes, doe take strict care that the lawes already made & provided in this case be duely executed, and particcularly that evil of inferiours absenting themselues out of the familjes wherevnto they belong in the night, and meeting with corrupt company without leaue, and against the minde & to the great greife of theire superiours, which euil practise is of a very perrillous nature, and the roote of much disorder.

It is therefore ordered by this Court, that whateuer inferiour shallbe legally convicted of such an euil practise, such persons shall be punished with admonition for the first offence, with fine not exceeding ten shillings, or whipping not exceeding fiue stripes, for all offences of like nature afterwards.

10. Whereas the sin of idlenes (which is a sin of Sodom) doeth greatly increase, notwithstanding the wholesome lawes in force against the same, as an addition to that law, —

This Court doeth order, that the constable, with such other person or persons whom the selectmen shall appoint, shall inspect particcular familjes, and present a lyst of the names of all idle persons to the selectmen, who are heereby strictly required to proceed with them as already the law directs, and in case of obstinacy, by charging the constable with them, who shall convey them to some magistrate, by him to be committed to the house of correction.

11. Whereas there is oppression in the midst of us, not only by such

shopkeepers and merchants who set excessive prizes on their goods, also by mechanicks but *also by mechanicks* and day labourers, who are dayly guilty of that euill, for redress whereoff, & as an adition to ye law, title Oppression, itt is ordered by this Court, that any person that judgeth himself oppressed by shopkeepers or merchants in setting excessive prizes on their goods, haue heereby liberty to make theire complaint to the grand jurors, or otherwise by petition to the County Court immediately, who shall send to the person accused, and if the Court, vpon examination, judge the person complayning injuried, they shall cause the offendor to returne double the ouerplus, or more then the æquall price, to the injured person, and also impose a fine on the offendors at the discretion of the Court; and if any person judge himself oppressed by mechanicks or day labourers, they may make complaint thereof to the selectmen of the toune, who if vpon the examination doe find such complaint just, hauing respect to the quality of the pay, and the length or shortnes of ye day labour, they shall cause the offendor to make double restitution to the party injurjed, and pay a fine of double the value exceeding the due price.

12. Whereas there is a loose & sinfull custome of going or riding from toune to toune, and that oft times men & weomen together, vpon pretence of going to lecture, but it appeares to be meerely to drincke & reuell in ordinarys & tavernes, which is in itself scandalous, and it is to be feared a notable meanes to debauch our youth and hazard the chastity of such as are draune forth therevnto, for prevention whereof, —

It is ordered by this Court, that all single persons who, meerly for their pleasure, take such journeyes, & frequent such ordinaryes, shall be reputed and accounted riotous & unsober persons, and of ill behauiour, and shall be ljable to be summoned to appeare before any County Court, magistrate, or commissioner, & being thereof convicted, shall give bond & sufficjent suretjes for the good behauiour in twenty pounds, and vpon refusall so to doe, shall be committed to prison for ten days, or pay a fine of forty shillings for each offence.

It is ordered by this Court, that euery toune in this jurisdiction shall prouide, as an addition to their toune stocke of ammunition, sixe hundred of flints for one hundred of lysted souldjers, and so proportionably for a lesser or greater number, to be constantly mainteyned & fitted for publick service.

14. This Court, considering the great abuse & scandall that hath arisen by the license of trading houses with the Indians, whereby drunkenes and other crimes haue binn, as it were, sold vnto them, —

It is ordered by this Court, that all such trading houses, from the publication hereof, shall wholly cease, and none to presume to make any sale vnto them, except in open shops and tounes where goods are sold vnto the English, vpon the pœnalty of ten pounds for euery conviction before laufall authority, one third to the informers, the remainder to the country, any law, vsage, or custome to the contrary notwithstanding.

This Court, hauing ordered two watchmen from Dorchester and Milton to watch at Dorchester mill, and vnderstanding the vndertakers of the pouder mill, for better deffence thereof, are errecting a smale stone watch house at their oune charges, on theire request, as being of publicke concernment, this Court declares, that the vndertakers of the pouder mill may repaire to any one majestrate, who, by the law, are impowred to give warrant to impresse workmen to carry on publick works, of which sort this is.

This Court, considering the inconvenience & damage that may arise to particcular tounes by such as, being forced from theire habitations through the present calamity of the warr, doe repajre vnto them for succour, doe order and declare, that such persons (being inhabitants of this jurisdiction) who are so forced from theire habitations & repaire to other plantations for releife, shall not, by virtue of theire residenc in sajd plantations they repaire vnto, be accounted or reputed inhabitants thereof, or imposed on them, according to law, title Poore; but in such case, and where necessity requires, (by reason of inability of relations, &c,) they shall be suppljed out of the publicke treasury; and that the selectmen of each toune inspect this matter; and doe likeuise carefully prouide, that such men or weomen may be so imployed, and children disposed of, that, as much as may be, publick charge may be avoyed.

Whereas this Court haue, for weighty reasons, placed sundry Indians (that haue subjected to our gouernment) vpon some islands for their and our security, —

It is ordered, that none of the sajd Indians shall presume to goe off the sajd islands voluntarily, vpon pajne of death; and it shallbe laufull for the English to destroy those that they shall finde stragling off from the sajd places of theire confinement, vnlesse taken of by order from authorjty, and vnder an English guard. And it is further ordered, that if any person or persons shall presume to take, steale, or carry away either man, woeman, or child of the sajd Indians, off from any the sajd islands where they are placed, without order from the Generall Court or council, he or they shall be accounted breakers of the capitall law printed & published against man stealing; and this order to be forthuith posted and published.

The whole Court being mett, it is ordered, that the country Treasurer take care for ye provission of those Indians that are sent doune to Deare Island, so as to prevent their perishing by any extremity that they may be put vnto for want of absolute necessaries, and for that end he is to appoint meet persons to vissit them from time to time.

B. BACON'S REBELLION: NATHANIEL BACON'S MANIFESTO CONCERNING THE TROUBLES IN VIRGINIA (JULY 30, 1676)*

If vertue be a sin, if Piety be giult, all the Principles of morality goodness and Justice be perverted, Wee must confesse That those who are now called Rebells may be in danger of those high imputations, Those loud

* Reprinted in full from *The Virginia Magazine of History and Biography*, vol. 1 (1893–1894), pp. 55–61.

and severall Bulls would affright Innocents and render the defence of our Brethren and the enquiry into our sad and heavy oppressions, Treason. But if there bee as sure there is, a just God to appeal too, if Religion and Justice be a sanctuary here, If to plead ye cause of the oppressed, If sincerely to aime at his Majesties Honour and the Publick good without any reservation or by Interest, If to stand in the Gap after soe much blood of our dear Brethren bought and sold, If after the losse of a great part of his Majesties Colony deserted and dispeopled, freely with our lives and estates to indeavor to save the remaynders bee Treason God Almighty Judge and lett guilty dye, But since wee cannot in our hearts find one single spott of Rebellion or Treason or that wee have in any manner aimed at the subverting ye setled Government or attempting of the Person of any either magistrate or private man not with standing the severall Reproaches and Threats of some who for sinister ends were disaffected to us and censured our ino[cent] and honest designes, and since all people in all places where wee have yet bin can attest our civill quiet peaseable behaviour farre different from that of Rebellion and tumultuous persons let Trueth be bold and all the world know the real Foundations of pretended giult, Wee appeale to the Country itselfe what and of what nature their Oppressions have bin or by what Caball and mistery the designes of many of those whom wee call great men have bin transacted and caryed on, but let us trace these men in Authority and Favour to whose hands the dispensation of the Countries wealth has been commited; let us observe the sudden Rise of their Estates composed with the Quality in which they first entered this Country Or the Reputation they have held here amongst wise and discerning men, And lett us see wither their extractions and Education have not bin vile, And by what pretence of learning and vertue they could soe soon into Imployments of so great Trust and consequence, let us consider their sudden advancement and let us also consider wither any Publick work for our safety and defence or for the Advancement and propogation of Trade, liberall Arts or sciences is here Extant in any [way] adaquate to our vast chardg, now let us compare these things togit [her] and see what spounges have suckt up the Publique Treasure and wither it hath not bin privately contrived away by unworthy Favourites and juggling Parasites whose tottering Fortunes have bin repaired and supported at the Publique chardg, now if it be so Judg what greater giult can bee then to offer to pry into these and to unriddle the misterious wiles of a powerful Cabal let all people Judge what can be of more dangerous Import then to suspect the soe long Safe proceedings of Some of our Grandees and wither People may with safety open their Eyes in soe nice a Concerne.

Another main article of our Giult is our open and manifest aversion of all, not onely the Foreign but the protected and Darling Indians, this wee are informed is Rebellion of a deep dye For that both the Governour and Councell are by Colonell Coales Assertion bound to defend the Queen and the Appamatocks with their blood Now whereas we doe declare and can prove that they have bin for these Many years enemies to the King and Country, Robbers and Theeves and Invaders of his Majesties Right and our Interest and Estates, but yet have by persons in Authority bin defended and protected even against His Majesties loyall Subjects and that in soe high a Nature that even the Complaints and oaths of his Majesties Most loyall Subjects in a lawfull Manner proffered by them afainst those barborous Outlaws have bin by ye right honourable Governour rejected and ye Delinquents from his presence dismissed not only with pardon and indemnitye but with all incouragement and favour, Their Fire Arms soe destructfull to us and by our lawes prohibited, Commanded to be restored them, and open Declaration before Witness made That they must have Ammunition although directly contrary to our law, Now what greater giult can be then to oppose and indeavour the destruction of these Honest quiet neighbours of ours.

Another main article of our Giult is our Design not only to ruine and extirpate all Indians in Generall but all Manner of Trade and Commerce with them, Judge who can be innocent that strike at this tender Eye of Interest; Since the Right honourable the Governour hath bin pleased by his Commission to warrant this Trade who dare oppose it, or opposing it can be innocent, Although Plantations be deserted, the blood of our dear Brethren Spilt, on all Sides our complaints, continually Murder upon Murder renewed upon us, who may or dare think of the generall Subversion of all Mannor of Trade and Commerce with our enemies who can or dare impeach any of * * * Traders at the Heades of the Rivers if contrary to the wholesome provision made by lawes for the countries safety, they dare continue their illegall practises and dare asperse ye right honourable Governours wisdome and Justice soe highly to pretend to have his warrant to break that law which himself made, who dare say That these Men at the Heads of the Rivers buy and sell our blood, and doe still notwithstanding the late Act made to the contrary, admit Indians painted and continue to Commerce, although these things can be proved yet who dare bee soe giulty as to doe it.

Another Article of our Giult is To Assert all those neighbour Indians as well as others to be outlawed, wholly unqualifyed for the benefitt and Protection of the law, For that the law does reciprocally protect and punish, and that all people offending must either in person or Estate make equivalent satisfaction or Restitution according to the manner and merit of ye Offences Debts or Trespasses; Now since the Indians cannot according to the tenure and forme of any law to us known be prosecuted, Seised or Complained against, Their Persons being difficulty distinguished or known, Their many nations languages, and their subterfuges such as makes them incapeable to make us Restitution or satisfaction would it not be very giulty to say They have bin unjustly defended and protected these many years.

If it should be said that the very foundation of all these disasters the Grant of the Beaver trade to the Right Honourable Governour was illegall and not granteable by any power here present as being a monopoly, were not this to deserve the name of Rebell and Traytor.

Judge therefore all wise and unprejudiced men who may or can faithfully or truely with an honest heart attempt ye country's good, their vindication and libertie without the aspersion of Traitor and Rebell, since as soe doing they must of necessity gall such tender and dear concernes, But to manifest Sincerity [*sic*] and loyalty to the World, and how much wee abhorre those bitter names, may all the world know that we doe unanimously desire to represent our sad and heavy grievances to his most sacred Majestie as our Refuge and Sanctuary, where wee doe well know that all our Causes will be impartially heard and Equall Justice administered to all men.

The Declaration of the People

For having upon specious pretences of Publick works raised unjust Taxes upon the Commonalty for the advancement of private Favourits and other sinnister ends but noe visible effects in any measure adequate.

For not having dureing the long time of his Government in any measure advanced this hopefull Colony either by Fortification, Townes or Trade.

For having abused and rendered Contemptible the Majesty of Justice, of advancing to places of judicature scandalous and Ignorant favourits.

For having wronged his Majesties Prerogative and Interest by assuming the monopoley of the Beaver Trade.

By having in that unjust gaine Bartered and sould his Majesties Country and the lives of his Loyal Subjects to the Barbarous Heathen.

For haveing protected favoured and Imboldened the Indians against his Majesties most Loyall subjects never contriveing requireing or appointing any due or proper meanes of satisfaction for their many Invasions Murthers and Robberies Committed upon us.

For having when the Army of the English was Just upon the Track of the Indians, which now in all places Burne Spoyle and Murder, and when wee might with ease have destroyed them who then were in open Hostility for having expresly Countermanded and sent back our Army by passing his word for the peaceable demeanour of the said Indians, who imediately prosecuted their evill Intentions Committing horrid Murders and Robberies in all places being protected by the said Engagement and word pass'd of him the said S'r William Berkley having ruined and made desolate a great part of his Majesties Country, have now drawne themselves into such obscure and remote places and are by their successes soe imboldened and confirmed and by their Confederacy soe strengthened that the cryes of Bloud are in all places and the Terrour and consternation of the People soe great, that they are now become not only a difficult, but a very formidable Enemy who might with Ease have been destroyed &c. When upon the Loud Outcries of Blood the Assembly had with all care raised and framed an Army for the prevention of future Mischiefs and safeguard of his Majesties Colony.

For having with only the privacy of some few favourits without acquainting the People, only by the Alteration of a Figure forged a Commission by wee know not what hand, not only without but against the Consent of the People, for raising and effecting of Civill Warrs and distractions, which being happily and without Bloodshedd prevented.

For haveing the second tyme attempted the same thereby, calling downe our Forces from the defence of the Frontiers, and most weake Exposed Places, for the prevention of civill Mischief and Ruine amongst ourselves, whilst the barbarous Enemy in all places did Invade murder and spoyle us his Majesties most faithfull subjects.

Of these the aforesaid Articles wee accuse S'r William Berkely, as guilty of each and every one of the same, and as one, who hath Traiterously attempted, violated and Injured his Majesties Interest here, by the losse of a great Part of his Colony, and many of his Faithfull and Loyall subjects by him betrayed, and in a barbarous and shamefull manner exposed to the Incursions and murthers of the Heathen.

And we further declare these the Ensueing Persons in this List, to have been his wicked, and pernitious Councellors, Aiders and Assisters against the Commonalty in these our Cruell Commotions

SIR HENRY CHICHERLY, KNT.,	JOS. BRIDGER,
COL. CHARLES WORMLEY,	WM. CLABOURNE,
PHIL. DALOWELL,	THOS. HAWKINS, JUNI'R,
ROBERT BEVERLY,	WILLIAM SHERWOOD,
ROBERT LEE,	JOS. PAGE, CLERK,
THOS. BALLARD,	JO. CLIFFE, "
WILLIAM COLE,	HUBBERD FARRELL,
RICHARD WHITACRE,	JOHN WEST,
NICHOLAS SPENCER,	THOS. READE.
MATHEW KEMP,	

And wee doe further demand, That the said S'r William Berkley, with all the Persons in this List, be forthwith delivered upp, or surrender themselves, within foure dayes, after the notice hereof, or otherwise wee declare, as followeth, That in whatsoever house, place, or shipp, any of the said Persons shall reside, be hide, or protected, Wee doe declare, that the Owners, masters, or Inhabitants of the said places, to be Confederates, and Traitors to the People, and the Estates of them, as alsoe of all the aforesaid Persons to be Confiscated, This wee the Commons of Virginia doe declare desiring a prime Union among ourselves, that wee may Joyntly, and with one Accord defend ourselves against the Common Enemye. And Let not the Faults of the guilty, be the Reproach of the Innocent, or the Faults or Crimes of ye Oppressors divide and separate us, who have suffered by theire oppressions.

These are therefore in his Majesties name, to Command you forthwith to seize, the Persons above mentioned, as Traytors to ye King and Countrey, and them to bring to Middle Plantation, and there to secure them, till further Order, and in Case of opposition, if you want any other Assistance, you are forthwith to demand it in the Name of the People of all the Counties of Virginia

[signed]   NATH BACON, Gen'l.
                            By the Consent of ye People.

SELECTION **24**

Unsettled Conditions at Home:
The Glorious Revolution in America

News of the Glorious Revolution in England triggered a series of revolts in the colonies, the most important of which were in Massachusetts, New York, and Maryland. The common denominators in these uprisings were dislike of the colonial policy of James II and especially of the Dominion of New England, resentment of his Catholicism, and fear of a plot among James II, his lieutenants in America, the Catholics in Maryland, and his French protectors to hold the colonies for him by unleashing a combined French and Indian attack upon them. Behind each of these rebellions, however, there were peculiar local grievances arising out of the unstable and rapidly fluctuating conditions of colonial political life and fundamental social tensions within each of the colonies involved.

Massachusetts Puritans were the first to act. Embittered over the loss of their charter, alarmed at the loss of representative government, and resentful of the efforts of Andros to levy taxes without the consent of a legislature, to alter the system of land tenure so that property titles would be held by a grant from the Crown, to encourage the growth of Anglicanism in the colony, and to enforce the Navigations Acts strictly, the Puritans were ripe for revolt. Like King Philip's war, the Dominion of New England and all the grievances associated with it could be regarded as additional evidence of God's displeasure with the Puritans. But such an explanation only encouraged the determination of the Puritans to atone for their sins and rid themselves of the Dominion system. In the summer of 1688 Increase Mather (1639–1723), the leading Boston divine, went to England to seek an end to the Dominion. Just as he appeared to be making some progress, however, William invaded England and James fled to France.

When word of events in England arrived in Boston in early April, 1689, it appeared as a heaven-sent opportunity to strike a blow for Protestantism and liberty by removing Andros and bringing down the Dominion of New England. Still, Puritan leaders did not act hastily. Andros already knew about the Glorious Revolution, but was waiting to proclaim William and Mary as the rightful sovereigns until he had received official directions from home, in the meantime taking all possible precautions to keep the news from the Puritans. Andros's hesitation as well as his lenient treatment of the Indians in previous months gave some plausibility to charges that he was conniving with the French and Indians to save the colony for the Stuarts and encouraged the Puritans to take the initiative. On April 18 they seized the Boston Town House, drew up a declaration of grievances in which they sought to identify their behavior with that of William in England, jailed Andros and his associates, and the following day secured the surrender of the English soldiers in Fort Hill and His Majesty's frigate Rose, *which was anchored in Boston Harbor. This bloodless revolution was followed by the reinstatement of the pre-Dominion government operating under the old charter.*

Just six weeks later a group of New Yorkers followed the lead of the Puritans. The peculiar ingredients of discontent in New York were economic distress, high taxes, dissatisfaction over the abolition of representative government, and resentment of the monopolization of political power by a dominant group of merchants and landowners who had succeeded in securing political office, commercial monopolies, and large landed estates from James II and his lieutenants. In combination with the rumors of a French-Catholic plot, to which New Yorkers because of the exposed condition of their frontier were especially susceptible, these elements were more than sufficient to produce a revolt when Andros's lieutenant governor, Francis Nicholson, hesitated to declare for William and Mary. On May 31, after an intemperate outburst from Nicholson, the militia rebelled and seized the fort. Nicholson then left for England, and Jacob Leisler (1640–1691), a merchant representative of a wealthy group who had previously been excluded from political office, emerged as the leader of the rebels.

Unlike the Puritan leaders in Massachusetts, Leisler and his supporters did not have the nearly unanimous support of the social and economic leaders of the colony, and members of the old political elite did everything they could to thwart the rebels. Leisler countered by arresting many of them, and the result was open political warfare between his advocates and opponents throughout his twenty-two-month government. When Henry Sloughter, the new royal governor, arrived in the colony, he sided with Leisler's opponents. Charged with treason because of his refusal to surrender the colony to Major Richard Ingoldsby, commander of a royal regiment who had preceded Sloughter to the colony by a few weeks, Leisler and six of his supporters were convicted, and Leisler himself along with his son-in-law, Jacob Milborne, put to death. The repercussions of this episode rent New York political life for the next thirty years.

In Maryland, where there were already deep-seated tensions between the Protestant majority and the ruling Catholic minority as well as a large number of accumulated grievances against the proprietary government, the rumor of a Catholic plot was especially credible to the Protestants. Alarm grew during the spring of 1689 after Governor William Joseph and the proprietary Council prorogued the Assembly before it had met. Joseph's continued delay in proclaiming the new sovereigns finally decided the Protestants to act in the summer of 1689. Under the leadership of John Coode (d. 1709), a member of the Maryland Assembly, they formed the Protestant Association, drawing up a justificatory declaration of their intentions on July 25; seizing the capital, St. Mary's City, on August 1; and petitioning the Crown to establish royal government in the colony. This petition, coinciding as it did with the desires of imperial officials to royalize all the colonies, was successful, and in June, 1691, Maryland was made a royal colony—a status it was to occupy until 1715, when it was restored to the Calverts. Coode and his associates governed the colony until the new royal governor, Sir Lionel Copley, arrived in early 1692.

The anonymous tract by A. B., An Account of the Late Revolution in New-England, describes the background to, motives for, and course of the Massa-chusetts revolt. Published in Boston in 1689, it was sent to England to justify the actions of the Puritans. The memorial of Benjamin Blagge, one of Leisler's main supporters and envoy to England to secure royal approval of Leisler's actions, explains the considerations that led to the rebels' seizure of authority in New York and seeks to vindicate and explain the behavior of the Leislerian government during its first six months in power. The declaration of the Protes-tant Association is the formal statement of the reasons behind the revolt of the Maryland Protestants.

For further reading see especially two documentary collections, Charles M. Andrews (ed.), Narratives of the Insurrections, 1675–1690 (1915), and Michael Garibaldi Hall, Lawrence H. Leder, and Michael G. Kammen (eds.), The Glorious Revolution in America: Documents on the Colonial Crisis of 1689 (1964). Other useful supplementary studies include Bernard Bailyn, The New England Merchants in the Seventeenth Century (1955); Lawrence H. Leder, Robert Livingston, 1654–1728, and the Politics of Colonial New York (1961); Jerome R. Reich, Leisler's Rebellion: A Study of Democracy in New York 1664–1720 (1953); Michael G. Kammen, "The Causes of the Maryland Revolu-tion of 1689," Maryland Historical Magazine, volume 55 (1960), pages 293–333; and the works cited in the introduction to Selection 19.

A. THE OVERTHROW OF THE DOMINION OF NEW ENGLAND: A. B., ''AN ACCOUNT OF THE LATE REVOLUTION IN NEW-ENGLAND'' (JUNE 6, 1689)*

. . . Since the *Illegal* Subversion of our Ancient Government, this *Great,* but *poor* people have been in the Hands of *men skilful to destroy,* and all our Concerns both Civil and Sacred, have suffered by the Arbitrary Op-pressions of *Unreasonable Men.* I believe, no part of the *English America,* so powerful and united as *New-England* was, could have endured half so many Abuses as we have bin harrassed withal, with a tenth part of our *Patience;* but our *Conscience* was that which gave metal to our *Patience,* and kept us Quiet; for though our foul-mouth'd Enemies have treated us a *Rebellious,* because we are a *Religious* people, they may be pleased now to understand, That if we had not been *Religious,* we had long since been what they would, if they durst, have called *Rebellious.* The very *Form* of Government imposed upon us, was among the *worst of Treasons,* even a Treasonable Invasion of the Rights which the whole *English* Nation lays claim unto; every true *English-man* must justifie our Dissatisfaction at it, and believe that we have not so much *Resisted the Ordinance of God,* as we have Resisted an intollerable Violation of His *Ordinance.*

But Sir, be pleased now to reflect upon our Declaration, and consider whether the Administration of this Government was not as Vexatious, as

* These excerpts are reprinted from W. H. Whitmore (ed.), *The Andros Tracts* (1868–1874), vol. II, pp. 191–201.

the *Constitution* of it was Illegal. Consider whether the whole Government was not become a meer *Engine,* a sort of *Machin* contriv'd only to enrich a crew of Abject Strangers, upon the Ruines of a miserable people. And yet, I am to tell you, That *scarce one half is told you.* The *Declaration* was composed so much in the Hurry of Action that it comprehends not all our *Grievances;* However, you may guess from the *Clawes* there pourtray'd, what sort of Creatures were devouring of us.

Sir, I own, that we *Argue simply* about the Affairs of Government; but we *Feel True.* I have sometimes challenged any man to mention so much as *One Thing* done by our Late Superiors for the welfare of the Country; a thousand things we all *Felt* every day doing for the Ruine of it; and as 'tis said, once when they had Divine Service among them, he that read it, being to read that Epistle, where, according to their Translation 'tis said, *Be Harbarous one to another:* By an unhappy mistake read it *Be Barbarous one to another:* So we thought we *Felt* their continual Actings upon that mistaken Rule. However I confess (and I know not whether you will count it our *Honour* or our *Blemish*) we should have born the Grievances without any Attempts for our own Relief, but our own Supplications to the Great God; for our Applications to the Late King, our only remaining Remedy on earth, we had found ineffectual. But there happened one Provocation to our people more, which had more than an hundred in it, and such was their *Infirmity* if you will call it so, that this they could not bear. A small Body of our *Eastern* Indians had begun a *War* upon us: the *Occasion* of which was as doubtful to us all at first, as the whole *Management* of it was afterwards mysterious. A Party of Indians which were affirm'd to belong unto that crew of Murderers were seiz'd by the *English;* but Governour *Andros* with many favours to them, ordered them to be set at Liberty again: and it's affirmed *Those* very men have great part of the mischief sustained by us. An Army of near a *Thousand English* (and the flower of our Youth) was raised for the subduing of our Enemies, which I believe were much fewer than an *Hundred Indians.* This Army goes through the tedious Fatigues of a long and cold Winter, many scores of miles to the Northward; and underwent such Hardships that very many of our poor Souldiers perished on the Spot; and it is justly fear'd, That not a few more of them have got their bane, that they will never be strong men again: but not one Indian killed all the while: only Garrisons were here and there planted in the wild woods on a pretence, *To keep the Indians from Fishing;* which project of *Hedging in the Cuckow's,* our dull *New-Englanders* could not understand. It was further admirable to us, that though the Governour had been importun'd to take a much more *expedient,* and far less *Expensive* way of subduing our *Indian Enemies,* he was there to wholly unperswadeable. In the meantime the Country was wonderfully surprised, with Evidences coming in, from Indians and others, in several parts, which very Strangely concurred in their Testimonies, *That there was a Plot to bring in the Indians upon us;* and it was easy unto us to conceive. How *serviceable* another *Indian* War might have been to the Designs which we saw working for us. These Evidences were so far from being duly enquired into, that the *English-*

men,—who had been inquisitive after them, were put unto all manner of trouble, and must have been destroyed if a Turn had not happend,— though nothing in the World was more natural than the Agreement between such a *Plot* and the whole conduct of our *Eastern Affairs;* nor is there any contradiction in it in one of *Randolph's* Letters to *Blaithwait* which says *Nothing has been wanting in his Excellency to bring all things to a good posture; but this people are Rivetted in their Way, and I fear nothing but Necessity or Force will otherwise dispose them.* While these things were going on, by way of the *West Indies* there arrived unto us a few small Intimations, That the Prince of *Orange* had prospered in his Noble undertaking to reseue the *English* Nation from imminent POPERY and SLAVERY. But Sir *Edomond Andross* took all imaginable care to keep us ignorant of the News, which yet he himself could not be unacquainted with; and one that brought the Princess *Declaration* with him, was imprisoned for bringing Seditious and Treasonable Papers into the Country with him; and our Oppressors went on without *Fear* or *Wit,* in all the methods that could inflame the people to the highest exasperation. The Reports continually coming in from our *Eastern Army* now caused the Relations of those that were there perishing, here a little to bestir themselves; and they could not forbear forming themselves here and there in the Country unto some Body, that they might consider what should be done for their poor Children, whom they thought bound for a bloody Sacrifice. While this was doing, the people of *Boston* were Alarmed with Suspicions buzz'd about the *Town,* by some belonging to the Ship, That the *Rose Frigat* now in our Harbour was intended to carry off our Late *Governour* for *France,* & to take any of our *English* Vessels that might be coming in unto us; and we apprehended our selves in the mean time very ill provided, if an Attacque from any of the *French* Fleet in the *West Indies* were perfidiously made upon us. 'T is impossible to express the Agonies which filled the minds of both Town and Country; but the consideration of the extream Ferment which we were boiling in, caused several very deserving Gentlemen in *Boston,* about the middle of *April,* to enter into a Consultation, how they might best serve the Distressed Land in its present Discomposures. They considered the *Directions* given in the Princes *Declarations* (of which at last we had stolen a sight) and the *Examples* which the whole Kingdom of *England* (as far as we could learn) had set before us. They also considered, that the Governour being mov'd to call a General Council in this extraordinary juncture, instead of this, he never so much as called his Council here at hand to communicate unto them any part of the *Intelligence relating* to the Late Affairs in *England.* They likewise considered, That though they were above all things inclinable *to stay a little,* hoping that every day might bring some Orders from *England* for our safety, yet they could not undertake for such a Temper in all their provoked Neighbours. Wherefore they Resolved, That if either the outragious madness of our Foes, or the impatient motion of our *Friends,* did necessitate any Action, they would put themselves in the Head of it, and endeavour to prevent what ill effects an *Unform'd Tumult* might produce.

By that time the Eighteenth of *April* had given a few Hours of Light unto us, things were push'd on to such extremities that *Bostons* part in Action seem'd loudly enough and hastily called for. Accordingly, the Captain of the Frigat being then on Shoar, it was determined that he must be made incapable either to *Obstruct*, or to *Revenge* the Action, by *Firing* on, or *Sailing* from the Town; him therefore they immediately seized. There were not very many acquainted with the measures that were to be taken; but the Action was now begun, and the Rumour of it running like Lightning through the Town, all sorts of people were presently inspired with the most unanimous Resolution, I believe, that was ever seen. *Drums* were beaten, and the whole Town was immediately up in *Arms*.

The first work done, was by small parties here and there about the *Town* to seize upon these unworthy Men who by repeated Extortions and Abuses had made themselves the objects of *Universal Hatred* and Indignation. *These* were many of them secured and confined; but the principal of them, at the *First Noise* of the Action, fled into the Garrison on *Fort-Hill*, where the *Governours* Lodgings were; a place *very* Commodiously *Scituated* to Command the whole Town, but not sufficiently Fortify'd.

The Army had no sooner got well together, but a Declaration was Read unto them, unto which they gave an Assent by a very considerable Shout. And upon this, the Gentlemen with such as had come in to their Assistance in the *Town-house*, apprehending the Resolutions of the people, drew up a short Letter to Sir *Edmond Andross*, and dispatched away a couple of their Number with it; the whole armed Body attend them unto the *Fortification*, whither they Marched with all the Alacrity in the world, and yet with so composed a *Sobriety*, that I question whether *America* has ever seen what might equal it. It was expected, That the *Garrison* might make some Resistance: but they intended to be Owners of it within one-half hour, or perish in the Attempt. When they were just come to beset the Fort, they met the Governour and his Creatures, going down the Hill to the Man-of-Wars *Pinace*, which was come to fetch them off; had they not come thither just at that Neck of time, our Adversaries would have got down to the Castle, which is a League below the Town; and in spite of us all, the Frigat would have gone unto them: but our *Houses* on shore and our *Vessels* at Sea, must have paid all the satisfaction they could have demanded of us. However, now at the sight of our Forces, the Gentlemen ran back into their Hold; whither the two Gentlemen our Messengers, now advancing, were presented at by the Red-coat Centinels; our Souldiers warned them on pain of Death, to forbear firing; upon which they fled into the Fort, and (as 'tis affirmed) had very terrible Reprimands, *for not firing on them*. The Gentlemen being admitted, Sir *Edmond Andross* read what was written to him, and now better understanding his own circumstances, there was a safe conduct given to him, and he with his Associates were brought into the Chamber where he had formerly himself been hatching the Things that now procur'd his more humble Appearance there. *He* was treated with all the Respect that could be due unto his Character; but he was confined for that Night unto the House of the Late Treasurer, with Guards upon him; and the *Rest* had their several confinements alotted unto them in such places as were most agreeable to their Quality. With much ado, the Governour gave Order for the surrender of the Fort; and the ceremonies of the surrender were performed by Secretary *Randolph,* the very man whose lyes and clamours and malicious unwearied Applications had the greatest influence in the overthrow of our former Government.

All the Country round about now began to flock in, and by the next day some Thousands of Horse and Foot were come in from the Towns Adjacent, to express the unanimous content they took in the *Action,* and offer their utmost Assistance in what yet remained for the compleating of it. The obtaining of the Castle was the main thing that yet called for our cares; but after some stomachful Reluctances the Late Governour gave Order also for the surrender of *That,* and himself was by the people removed unto the Fort to be kept as a Prisoner there. Thus was the Action managed; and through the singular Providence of God, not one mans Life was lost in the whole Undertaking: There was no *Bloodshed,* nor so much as any *Plunder* committed in all the *Action;* and setting aside the intemperate Speeches of some inconsiderable men (if there were any such) the people generally gave a Demonstration, That they designed nothing but the securing of some great Malefactors, for the Justice which a course of Law would expose them to, and they were loath to treate them with any incivility beyond the bare keeping of them in sufficient custody. No man underwent any Confinement, but such as the people counted the Enemies of the *Prince* of *Orange,* and of our *English Liberties;* it was not any passion for the Service of *the Church of England,* that exposed any man to hardship; no, even some of that Communion did appear in their Arms to assist the enterprize; tho' the Worship of the Church of *England* had the disadvantage with us, that most of our Late Oppressors were the great and sole Pillars of it there. The principal Delinquents being now in durance, and the Frigat secured for the Crown of *England,* our main difficulty was yet behind: Namely what Form we should put our selves into, that the Peace might be kept among us.

A great part of the *Country* was for an immediate Reassumption of our old Government, conceiving that the vacating of our *Charter* was a most illegal and injurious thing, and that tho' *a Form of Law* had cast us out of it, yet we might now return to it at least as a *Vacuum Domicilium.* Others were of the Opinion, That since Judgment was entred against our *Charter,* and we did not know what Consequence a *wrong step* at this time might have, therefore 'twas best for the Affairs of the Country to continue in the Hands of a *Committee for the Conservation of the Peace,* till the daily expected Directions from *England* should arrive unto us. The latter Expedient was condescended unto, but the Sword yet continued in every man's hands, and for divers weeks the Colony continued without any pretence to *Civil Government;* yet thro' the mercy of God, all things were under such good Inclinations among us, that every man gave himself the Laws of good Neighbourhood, and little or nothing extravagant was all that while done, besides the seizure of a few more persons who had made themselves obnoxious to the Displeasure of the People. The Gentlemen of the Committee laid their Country under great Oblightions by their Studies for *the Conservation of our Peace,* and it mostly consisted of such as were ever worthy of our esteem. It was made up of them whose Hap 'twas to be in the Head of the late Action; but there were added unto them the most of our old Magistrates, who had not so far concerned themselves in the Affair. Our former Governour, the Honourable *Simon Bradford,* Esq: was Chosen by them for their President: Who tho' he be well towards Ninety Years of Age, has his *Intellectual Force hardly abated,* but retains a vigour and Wisdom that would recommend a younger man to the Government of a greater Colony.

But when the Day which our ancient *Charter* appoints for our Anniversary *Election* drew near, our people grew more and more set upon a Return to the *Basis* on which our *Charter* formerly had placed us; and of those who were thus disposed, some were for an *Election* on the proper Day; others judged that could not be so honestly attended, because a whole County in the *Colony* was too far to have a *Vote* in it, and they therefore were for a Re-assumption the Day following. These *Two* Opinions, with a *Third* which was for the continuing of their *Committee* just as it was, filled the Country; and very potent Numbers espoused each of these three opinions: only we all agreed in joyful expectations of having our *Charter* restored unto us. This Variety of Apprehension was the occasion of much needless Discourse and of many Heart burnings that might as well have been spared. But the Towns on the Eighth and Ninth of May sent in their Representatives at the Desire of the *Committee* to adjust the matters that concerned a further Necessary Settlement; and after many Debates and some Delays they came to this Temper: That our Ancient *Magistrates* should apply themselves unto the *Conservation of our Peace,* and exercise what acts of *Government* the Emergencies might make needful for us, and thus wait for further Directions from the Authority of *England.*

The Country being put into this posture, all things tended unto a good settlement both of *Minds* and *Things;* which were again too much disturbed by a Fire, too justly fear'd to be maliciously kindled (by some that made themselves parties to our Late Enemies) in the N * * * * * * * * * * * * * * * * whereby *Four Houses were* consumed, but perhaps more than * * * * * Thousand *Spirits* inflamed into an Heat that was hardly Governable. But our people being in a good measure again composed, the World mov'd on in its old orderly pace, until the last week in May when two Ships arrived unto us from *England* with more perfect *News* than we had yet been owners of; the first effect thereof was, our Proclaiming of King *William* and Queen *Mary,* with such a Joy, Splendour, Appearance and Unanimity, as had never before been seen in these Territories. The other Colonies are now settling on their old Foundations; and *We,* according to the Advice now brought us, hasten to put our selves into such a condition as may best answer the performance of our Allegiance to their Majesties.

B. LEISLER'S REBELLION: BENJAMIN BLAGGE'S MEMORIAL (DECEMBER, 1689)*

A Memoriall of What Has Occurred in Their Majesties Province of New: York since the News of Their Majesties Happy Arrivall in England

Setting forth the necessity of removing Capt. Fran: Nicholson (late Lieut. Govr. of the said Province) and putting the command thereof into [the] hands of such persons, of whose fidelity and good Inclination to their present Majesties the aforesaid Province is well assured.

The said Capt. Nicholson (in imitation of his Predecessor Coll Dungan) wholly neglected to repair the Fort and Fortifications of the city, and that not without a vehement suspicion, thereby the more easily to betray the same into the enemies hands, of which he gave the said Province sufficient grounds of apprehensions by discovering both by words and actions, his disaffection to the happy Revolution in England, and also to the inhabitants of the City by threatening to fire the same about their ears.

Whereupon the Inhabitants in order to secure the said Fort and City for their Majesties use and to repair and fortify the same & to place the government of the Province in the hands of some of undoubted loyalty and affection to their present Majesties Did remove the said Capt: Nicholson, and made choice of Capt: Jacob Leisler with a Committee (who were also chosen by the people) to take into their hands the Care and Charge of the Government until Their Majesties Pleasure should be further known.

Shortly after arrived their Majesties Proclamation to Proclaim them King and Queen of England, France and Ireland, notice whereof was given to those of the former Councill, and to the Mayor and Aldrmen of the City to assist in proclaiming thereof with the proper ceremonies for that solemnity, who desired an hours time to consider of it, which time being expired and no complyance yielded, but on the contrary an aversion discovered thereto, The said Capt. Leisler accompanyed with the Committee & most part of the Inhabitants, did with all the Demonstrations of Joy and affection they were capable of celebrate the same.

Whereupon the Mayor and Aldermen were suspended and some persons confined, who were the most eminent in opposing Their Majesties Interest and this Revolution, and some short time after this Their Majesties Letter arrived Directed to Capt Francis Nicholson Esqr Lieut. Governor of Their Majesties Province of New York and in his absence, to such as for the time being do take care for the preservation of their Majesties Peace, and Administring the Laws in that Their Majesties Province, Ordering such to take upon them the Place of Lieut Governor and Commander in Chief of the said Province, and to proclaim King William & Queen Mary King & Queen of England Scotland France and Ireland and Supreme Lord and Lady of the Province of New York, if not already done, which was accordingly performed.

* Reprinted in full from E. B. O'Callaghan (ed.), *The Documentary History of the State of New-York* (1850–1851), vol. II, pp. 55–58.

The Inhabitants of the said City and Province conceiving that by vertue of Their Majesties said Letter, the said Capt Leisler was sufficiently Im-powered to Receive the same and to act accordingly It gave them a generall satisfaction, whereupon the said Committee were immediately dismissed and a Councill chosen by whose assistance Capt Leisler acts in the said Government pursuant to His Majesties Order.

The members of the former Government notwithstanding gave all the opposition they could to this Reformation & have created a ffaction in the said Province to the endangering the loss thereof, since it happens at a time that we are under continuall alarms from the frequent attacks the French make upon our Frontiers, so that without the care and pre-caution aforesaid this Their Majesties Province was in apparent hazard of being delivered up to the Canada Forces belonging to the French King, whereby Their present Majesties most loyall protestant subjects of this Province would have been rendered miserable, equall to their fears, and this Province became a Colony of the French.

And to that height of insolence was that disaffected Party growne, that in a riotous manner in the day time they besett and surrounded the Capt. Leisler our Lievt. Govr. in the street treating him will ill Language & threats & had undoubtedly done violence to his person, had they not been apprehensive of danger to themselves from the people, who immediately gathered together and rescued the Governor out of their hands, seizing some of the principall actors and Ringleaders in that Ryott and com-mitting them to prison, and their ffriends and confederates sending them provisions to the prison in a superabundant and extraordinary manner, designedly to affront and insult the Government: thereupon it was thought fit to order, that no provisions should be permitted to be brought them, and they should only be allowed Bread and water, but that severity was continued towards them only for two daies, and afterwards they had the Liberty to have what Provisions they pleased.

This riotous Action of the Male-Contents occasioned a further Tumult of ill consequence to themselves for the Country people upon a rumour that the Government was in danger by the Rising of the disaffected party, flockt into the City armed in great numbers, and notwithstanding the endeavours of the Magistrates to appease them, they took the liberty (as is too usuall with an enraged multitude) to perpetrate revenge on those which were the occasion of their coming, Quartering themselves in their houses for two daies and committing divers Insolences upon them, much to the dissatisfaction of the Magistrates till they could persuade them to return in quiet to their houses, however it was thought requisite by the Government for the preventing such disorders for the future and to secure the publick peace, to detein severall of the disaffected in Prison for a time, some whereof were since fined, but all ordered to be discharged from Prison upon paying their Fines and entering into Recognizance to be of good Behaviour for the future.

The Fort and City are therefore now in a good posture wanting only Ammunition.

The Commissions are called in from those of the former Militia, who acted under Coll Dungan and Sir Edmond Andros, and other Commissions granted in the name of their present Majesties to such as are well affected to their Majesties Interest.

Upon these our actings for the Securing Their Majesties Interest in this Province and conserving the publick Peace our enemys have endeavoured all they can to misrepresent us and load us with Reproach, by terming our aforesaid proceedings a *Dutch Plott,* because indeed three quarter parts of the Inhabitants are descended from the Dutch & speak that language, and they also threaten our ruine, if ever the Government come into their hands again.

Which that it may not doe, and Their Majesties most loyal and dutiful subjects in this province may reap the benefit and blessing of this most happy Revolution, and not be made a Prey to most implacable and Insulting enemies on our Borders, who are ready to enter and devour us— humbly Submitting ourselves to your Majesties most Royall Will and Pleasure.

C. COODE'S REBELLION: THE DECLARATION OF THE PROTESTANT ASSOCIATION (JULY 25, 1689)*

Although the nature and state of Affairs relating to the government of this Province is so well and notoriously known to all persons any way concerned in the same, as to the people Inhabitants here, who are more imediately interested, as might excuse any declaration or apologie for this present inevitable appearance; Yet forasmuch as (by the plotte contrivances insinuations remonstrances and subscriptions carryed on, suggested, extorted and obtained, by the Lord Baltemore, his Deputys Representatives and officers here) the injustice and tyranny under which we groan, is palliated and most if not all the particulars of our grievances shrowded from the eyes of observation and the hand of redress, Wee thought fitt for general satisfaction, and particularly to undeceive those that may have a sinister account of our proceedings to publish this Declaration of the reasons and motives inducing us thereunto. His Lordships right and title to the Government is by virtue of a Charter to his father Cecilius from King Charles the first of blessed memory how his present Lordship has managed the power and authority given and granted in the same wee could mourn and lament onely in silence, would our duty to God, our allegiance to his Vicegerent, and the care & welfare of ourselves and posterity permit us.

In the first place in the said Charter is a reservation of the fayth and allegiance due to the Crown of England (the Province and Inhabitants being imediately subject thereunto) but how little that is manifested is too obvious, to all unbyasted persons that ever had anything to do here the very name and owning of that Sovereign power is some times crime enough to incurr the frownes of our superiors and to render our persons

---

* Reprinted in full from *Archives of Maryland,* vol. VIII, pp. 101–107.

obnoxious and suspected to be ill-affected to the government The ill usage of and affronts to the Kings Officers belonging to the customes here, were a sufficient argument of this. Wee need but instance the business of Mr. Badcock and Mr. Rousby, of whom the former was terribly detained by his Lordshipp from going home to make his just complaints in England upon which he was soon taken sick, and t'was more then probably conjectur'd that the conceit of his confinement was the chief cause of his death which soon after happened. The latter was barbarously murthered upon the execution of his office by one that was an Irish papist and our Cheif Governor.

Allegiance here by those persons under whom wee suffer is little talked of, other then what they would have done and sworn to, to his Lordship the Lord Proprietary, for it was very lately owned by the President himselfe, openly enough in the Upper House of Assembly, that fidelity to his Lordshipp was allegiance and that the denying of the One was the same thing with the refusall or denyall of the other. In that very Oath of Fidelity, that was then imposed under the penalty of banishment there is not so much as the least word or intimation of any duty, fayth or allegiance to be reserved to our Sovereign Lord the King of England.

How the jus regale is improved here, and made the prorogative of his Lordshipp, is so sensibly felt by us all in that absolute authority exercised over us, and by the greatest part of the Inhabitants in the service of their persons, forfeiture and loss of their goods, chatteles, freeholders and inheritances.

In the next place Churches and Chappels, which by the said Charter should be built and consecrated according to the Ecclesiastical lawes of the Kingdom of England, to our greate regrett and discouragement of our religion, are erected and converted to the use of popish Idolatary and superstition, Jesuits and seminarie preists are the only incumbents; (for which there is a supply provided by sending our popish youth to be educated at St. Omers) as also the Chief Advisers and Councellors in affaires of Government, and the richest and most fertile land sett apart for their use and maintenance, while other lands that are piously intended, and given for the maintenance of the Protestant Ministry, become escheats, and are taken as forfeit, the ministers themselves discouraged, and noe care taken for their subsistence.

The power to enact Laws is another branch of his Lordshipp's authority, but how well that has been executed and circumstances is too notorious. His present Lordshipp, upon the death of his father, in order thereunto, sent out writts for four (as was over the usage) for each County to serve as Representatives of the people, but when elected there were two of each respective four pickt out and sumoned to that convention, whereby many Laws were made, and the greatest leavy yet known layd upon the Inhabitants. The next Session the house was filled up, with the remaining two that was left out of the former in which there were many and the best of our Laws enacted to the great benefit and satisfaction of the people but his Lordship soon after dissolved and declared the best of these Laws, such as he thought fit, null and voyd by Proclamation: Notwithstanding they were assented to in his Lordshipps name, by the Governor in his absence, and he himselfe some time personally acted and governed by the same, soe that the question in our Courts of Judicature, in any point that relates to many of our Laws, is not so much the relation it has to the said Laws, but whether the Laws themselves be agreable to the pleasure and approbation of his Lordshipp. Whereby our liberty and property is become uncertain and under the arbitrary disposition of the Judge and Commissioners of our Courts of Justice.

The said Assembly being some time after dissolved by proclamation another was elected and mett consisting only of two members for each County, directly opposite to an Act of Assembly for four (in which severall laws with his Lordships personal assent were enacted, among the which one for the Encouragement of Trade and erecting of Towns, but the Execution of that Act was soon after the Proclamation from his Lordshipp out of England suspended the last year, and all officers Military and Civil severely prohibited executing and inflicting the penaltys of the same. Notwithstanding which suspension being in effect a dissolution and abrogateing of the whole Act, the income of three pence per hoggshead to the government (by the said Act payable for every hogshead of tobacco exported is carefully exacted & collected. How fatall and of what pernicious consequence that unlimited and arbitary pretended authority may be to the Inhabitants, is too apparent, but by considering that by the same reason all the use of the laws whereby our liberties and properties subsiste are subject to the same arbitary disposition, and if timely remedy be not had must stand or fall according to his Lordshipps good will and pleasure.

Nor is this nullyfyeing and suspending power the only grievance that doth perplex and burthen us in relation to Laws, but these laws that are of a certain and unquestioned acceptation are executed and countenanced, as they are more or less agreable to the good liking of our Govr in particular, one very good lawe provides that orphan children should be disposed of to persons of the same religion with that of their dead parents. In direct opposition to which several children of protestants have been committed to the tutlage of papists, and brought up in the Romish Superstition. Wee could instance in a young woman that has been lately forced by order of Council from her husband committed to the custody of a papist, and brought up in his religion.

T'is endless to enumerate the particulars of this nature, while on the contrary those laws that enhance the grandeur and income of his said Lordshipp are severely imposed and executed especially one that is against all sense, equity, reason and law punishes all speeches, practices and attempts relating to his Lordship and Government that shall be thought mutinous and seditious by the Judge of the provincial Court, with either whipping, branding, boreing through the Tongue, fines, imprisonments, banishment or death, all or either of the said punishments at the discretion of the said Judges, who have given a very recent and remarkable proof of their authority in each particular punishment aforesaid, upon several the good people of this Province, while the rest are in the same danger to have their words and actions lyable to the construction & punishment of the said Judges, and their lives and fortunes to the mercy of their arbitary fancies, opinions and sentences.

To these Grievances are added

Excessive Officers Fees, and that too under Execution directly against the Law made & provided to redress the same, wherein there is no probability of a legall remedy, the Officers themselves that are partys and culpable being Judges. The like Fee being imposed upon and extorted from Masters and Owners of Vessels trading into this Province, without any Law to justifie the same, and directly against the plaine words of the said Charter that say there shall be no imposition or assessment without the consent of the Freemen in the Assembly to the great obstruction of trade and prejudice of the Inhabitants.

The like excessive Fees imposed upon and extorted from the owners of Vessels that are built here or do really belong to the Inhabitants contrary to an Act of Assembly made and provided for the same, wherein moderate and reasonable Fees are ascertained for the promoting and incouragement of Shipping and navigation amongst ourselves.

The frequent pressing of men, horses, boats, provisions and other necessarys in time of peace and often to gratifie private designs and occations, to the great burthen and regrett of the Inhabitants contrary to Law and several Acts of Assembly in that case made and provided.

The seirvice and apprehending of Protestants in their houses with armed force consisting of Papists and that in time of peace, thence hurrying them away to Prisons without Warrant or cause of comittment these kept and confined with popish guards a long time without tryall.

Not only private but publick outrages, & murthers committed and done by papists upon Protestants without redress, but rather conived at and tolerated by the cheif in authority, and indeed it were in vain to desire or expect any help or other measures from them being papists and guided by the Councills and instigation of the Jesuits, either in these or any other grievances or oppresions, and yet these are the men that are our Cheif Judges at the Comon Law in Chancery of the Probat of Wills and the Affairs of Administration in the Upper House of Assembly, and Chief military Officers and Commanders of our forces, being still the same individuall persons, in all these particular qualifications & places.

These and many more even infinit pressures and Calamitys, wee have hitherto layne with patience under and submitted to, hoping that the same hand of providence that hath sustained us under them would at length in due time release us. And now at length for as much as it hath pleased Almighty God, by meanes of the great prudence and conduct of the best of Princes our most gracious King William to putt a check to that great inudation of Slavery and Popery, that had like to overwhelm their Majestys Protestant Subjects in all their Territorys and Dominions (of which none have suffered more or are in greater danger than ourselves) Wee hoped and expected in our particular Stations and qualifications, a proportionable shew in soe great a blessing.

But our greatest grief and consternation, upon the first news of the great overture and happy change in England, wee found ourselves surrounded with strong and violent endeavours from our Governors here (being the Lord Baltemores Deputys and Representatives) to defeat us of the same.

Wee still find all the meanes used by these very persons and their Agents, Jesuits, Priests, and lay papists that are of malice can suggest to devise the obedience and loyalty of the inhabitants from their most sacred Majestys to that height of impudence that solemn masses and prayers are used (as we have very good information) in their Chappells and Oratorys for the prosperous success of the popish forces in Ireland, and the French designs against England, whereby they would involve us, in the same crime of disloyalty with themselves and render us obnoxious to the insupportable displeasure of their Majesties.

Wee every where have not only publick protestations against their Majesties rights and possessions of the Crown of England, but their most illustrious persons vilefied and aspected with the worst and most trayterous expressions of obloquie and detraction.

Wee are every day threatened with the loss of our lives, libertys and Estates of which we have great reason to think ourselves in eminent danger by the practises and machinations that are on foot to betray us to the French, Northern and other Indians of which some have been dealt withall, and others invited to assist in our distruction, well remembering the incursion and invade of the said Northern Indians in the year 1681, who were conducted into the heart of this Province by French Jesuits, and lay sore upon us while the Representatives of the Country, then in the Assembly were severely prest upon by our superiours to yield them an unlimited and tyrannicall power in the Affairs of the Militia As so great a piece of villany cannot be the result but of the worst of principles, soe wee should with the greatest difficulty believe it to be true if undeniable evidence and circumstances did not convince Us.

Together with the promises we have with all due thinking and deliberation considered the endeavours that are making to disunite us among ourselves, to make and inflame differences in our neighbour Collony of Virginia, from those friendshipp, vicinity great loyalty and sameness of Religion wee may expect assistance in our great necessity. Wee have considered that all the other branches of their Majesty's Dominions in this part of the world (as well as wee could be informed) have done their duty in proclaiming and asserting their undoubted right in these & all other their Majesties Territoryes & Countys.

But above all with due and mature deliberation wee have reflected upon that vast gratitude and duty incumbent likewise upon us, to our Sovereign Lord and Lady the King and Queene's most Excellent Majesty's in which as it would not be safe for us, soe it will not suffer us to be silent in soe great and general a Jubilee, withall considering and looking upon ourselves, discharged, dissolved and free from all manner of duty, obligation or fidelity to the Deputy Govr or Chief Magistrate here as such they having departed from their Allegiance (upon which alone our said duty and fidelity to them depends) and by their Complices and Agents aforesaid endeavoured the destruction of our religion, lives, libertys, and propertys all which they are bound to protect.

These are the reasons, motives and considerrations which we doe declare have induced us to take up Arms to preserve, vindicate and assert the sovereign Dominion and right of King William and Queen Mary to this Province; to defend the Protestant Religion among us, and to protect and chelter the Inhabitants from all manner of violence, oppression and destruction that is plotted and designed against them, the which wee doe solemnly declare and protest wee have noe designes or intentions whatsoever.

For the more effectual Accomplishment of which, wee will take due care that a full and free Assembly be called and conven'd with all possible expedition by whom we may likewise have our condition circumstances, and our most dutyfull addresses represented and tendered to their Majesties, from whose great wisdom, justice and special care of the protestant religion wee may reasonably and comfortably hope to be delivered from our present calamity and for the future be secured under a just and legall Administration from being ever more subjected to the yoke of arbitrary government of tyranny and popery. . . .

Wee will take care, and doe promise that no person now in armes with us, or that shall come to assist us shall committ any outrage or doe any violence to any person whatsoever that shall be found peaceable and quiet and not oppose us in our said just and necessary designes, and that there shall be a just and due satisfaction made for provisions and other necessarys had and received from the Inhabitants and the souldiers punctually and duely payed in such wayes and methods as have been formerly accustomed or by Law ought to bee.

And wee doe lastly invite and require all manner of persons whatsoever residing or Inhabiting in this Province, as they tender their Allegiance, the Protestant Religion, their Lives, fortunes and Families, to ayd and assist us in this our undertaking. . . .

SELECTION

Visitations from Hell—The Salem Witchcraft Episode: Deodat Lawson, "Christ's Fidelity: The Only Shield against Satan's Malignity" (1693)

Until well after the end of the seventeenth century, belief in witchcraft was almost universal throughout Western European society, and convicted witches were normally put to death to preserve the community from their evil machinations. In Massachusetts there had been a number of witch trials and six executions prior to the difficulties at Salem Village (Danvers) beginning in Feb-

ruary, 1692. Then over the next eleven months twenty persons were executed as witches and two others died in jail, as the Salem community fell into a state of hysteria which did not subside until January, 1693, after some of the more important people in the colony had been accused. Like dozens of other similar outbursts that had occurred spasmodically all over Western Europe both before and after, the Salem excitement can be attributed to what George Lyman Kittredge called a "perturbed condition of the public mind" brought on by "crises in politics or religion." Massachusetts had just gone through nearly a decade of political uncertainty, beginning with the revocation of the charter in 1684 and continuing through the Dominion of New England, the overthrow of Andros, and the tentative beginnings of political life under the new, more restrictive charter of 1691. Much more important, however, New England was undergoing a spiritual crisis of grave proportions produced by the continuing decline of religious zeal and the decay of Puritan morality. That it was the moral declension of Puritan society that was primarily responsible for the devil's visitations in Salem and that only a spiritual reformation would induce God to drive the devil out was the message of the Reverend Deodat Lawson, minister at Scituate and former minister at Salem Village (1684–1688), in the following sermon, delivered at Salem Village on March 24, 1692, during the height of the panic. The excerpts here reprinted are from the second edition (1704), pages 54–64, 90–92. Kittredge's Witchcraft in Old and New England *(1929) attempts to place the episode in its general context; Marion L. Starkey,* The Devil in Massachusetts: A Modern Inquiry into the Salem Witchcraft Trials *(1949), is a readable popular account; and Perry Miller,* The New England Mind: From Colony to Province *(1953), evaluates the Lawson sermon and points out its significance as a contemporary analysis of the delusion.*

. . . 1. Let *Regenerate Souls,* that are in good hope of their Interest in GOD, and his Covenant, stir up themselves to *Confirm* and *Improve, that Interest to the Utmost.* Under shaking Dispensations, we should take the faster hold of GOD by Faith, and cleave the closer to him, that *Satan* may not, by any of his Devices or Operations, draw us from our steadfastness of Hope, and Dependence on the GOD of our Salvation. We would hope we are Interested in the Everlasting Covenant of GOD, and Delivered from the *Raging* Tyranny of the *Rearing* Lyon. It is good to be sure, and too sure we cannot be at any time, much less at such a time as this: That it may appear before *Angels* and *Men,* that we are Chosen unto Salvation by the GOD of *Jerusalem,* and are accordingly *Devoted* to him and to his service in an *Unviolable Covenant* against which the Gates of *Hell* shall never have any power. And the clearing up that we are in Covenant with GOD, is a Sovereign *Antidote* against all Attempts of *Satan,* to bring us into Covenant *With* him or subjection *To* him. And in order to this, let us be Awakened.

First, *To put our selves upon Faithful and Thorow Tryal and* Examination, *what hath been amiss.* We all, even the Best of us, have by sin a hand and share, in *Provoking* GOD thus to let *Satan Loose,* in an unusual Manner, WHO *can say he is Clean?* This is a time then, for *Solemn-Self-Examination.*

In this time of *Sore Affliction,* there should be great *Searchings of Heart,* as there was for the *Divisions of Reuben,* Judg. 5. 19. GOD is a GOD of Wisdom, A *Righteous* and *Holy* GOD, and he never Afflicts the People of his Covenant without a *Cause,* and *that Cause* is always Just: We should go as far as we can in the Search, by the Light of Conscience, Conducted by the *Rule* of the Word, and when we can go no farther, we should Pray that Prayer of *Job.,* Chap. 10. 2. *Do not Condemn me; shew me wherefore thou Contendest with me.* Yet was he Upright, and (even in GOD's Account;) *One that Feared* GOD, *and Eschewed Evil* Chap. 1. 8. The like Prayer *David* makes, Psal. 139. 23, 24. *Search me Oh GOD, and know my Heart, try me and know my thoughts. And see if there be any wicked way in me,* &c. These malicious operations of *Satan,* are the sorest afflictions can befal a person or people: And if under the Consideration of *Grievous* Calamities, upon the People of GOD, the Nations round about, will *Inquire* with amazement *after the Cause:* Then surely the People themselves, ought strictly to Examine, as Deut. 29. 24. *What meaneth the heat of this Great Anger?* And to the making this improvement of remarkable Afflictions, we are *directed* by the Example of the *Church,* Lam. 3.40. *Let us Search and Try our ways, and Turn again unto the Lord.* Which leads to the second thing.

2. Add to the former, *True and Unfeigned Reformation, of whatsoever appears to be the Provoking Evils we fall into.* He or They that to *Serious Examination,* (which must be supposed to include *Hearty Confession* of what hath been done amiss) Adds *Thorow Reformation,* may only hope to obtain Pardoning Mercy at the Hands of God, *Prov.* 28. 13. And may it not be said, even to the *Purest Churches,* as he said to them, 2 Chron. 28. 10. *But are there not with You, even with You, Sins against the* LORD *your God.* And certainly, no *Provokings* are so Abhorred of the Lord, as those of *his Sons* and *Daughters, Deut.* 32. 19. This Returning and Reforming then, is the Duty *Required* of, and *Pressed* upon *Israel,* or the visible Covenant People of God, when by sin they had *departed from* him, Hosea 14. 1. O ISRAEL, *Return unto the Lord thy God, for thou hast fallen by thine Iniquity.* Hence the neglect of this Returning, in those that are under many and great Afflictions, is very displeasing unto God, Amos 4. 11. *And ye were as a Firebrand pluckt out of the Burning, yet have ye not returned unto me, saith the Lord.* Insomuch, that *obstinate persisting,* in the neglect of it after *Frequent Warnings,* provokes the Lord to punish those that are guilty thereof, *Seven and seven times more,* Lev. 26. 23, 24. If we would then, *avoid* the Displeasure, and *obtain* the Covenant Favour of GOD, we must both in Profession, and Practice, fall in with the Example, of the formerly Degenerous, but afterwards Reformed *Ephraim,* Jer. 31. 18, 19. *Turn thou me, and I shall be turned; for thou are the Lord my God. Surely after that I was turned, I Repented, and after that I was instructed, I smote upon my Thigh,* &c. Then, and not till then, will the *Bowels* of the LORD, *be turned within him, and his Repentings kindled together* for us. Now that our Reformation may be unto Divine Acceptation, it must be,

First, *Personal* and particular. We commonly say, *that which is every Bodies work, is no Bodies work.* Every one is Guilty, in the *Provocation,* and therefore every one should apply themselves to *Reformation*. Every one of us should set our selves to do our *Own Duty*, and Repent of our *Own Sins*. There is an inclination in the best, to Charge the *Sins of others*, as the procuring cause of GOD's Judgments, and to reflect severely on the *Pride, Lukewarmness, Covetousness, Contention, Intemperance*, and *Uneven Conversation* of others; but we can hardly be brought, to smite upon our *own Breast*, and say, *What have I done?* Unless we be, in particular *Charged*, and *Convicted*, as *David* was by the Prophet *Nathan*, in 2 Sam. 12. 7. *Thou art the man*. Thou art he (q. d.) that art concerned in this Povocation by thy Transgressions.

Secondly, *Reformation*, (by which we may clear up, that we are the Covenant People of God) must be *Universal*. We must turn from *All* and *Every* sin which hath been *committed*, and apply our selves to the *discharge* of *Every* Duty, which hath been *neglected*. We must have no sinful Reserves, as he, 2 Kings 5. 18. *In this thing pardon thy Servant*, &c. He was Convicted it was a *Sin*, that needed *Pardon*, and yet would fain be Excused in the Commission thereof. Thus *Junius*, and *Trem*. and the *Dutch* Annotators translate it, and *Pisc*. Interprets it of his desire to continue in that Office, which he could not with good Conscience discharge. Though some Learned and Judicious understand it as a craving of pardon for what he had therein done amiss in time past. In short, so far as we are guilty of *Reservations* in our Reformation, so far will there remain a *Cloud* upon the Evidences of our *Covenant Interest* in GOD *that hath Chosen Jerusalem*. This to Regenerate Souls. Secondly then

Let *Unregenerate Sinners, be* warned *and* awakened, to *get out of that Miserable state of sin, and consequently of subjection to Satan, (That* Tyrannical, Implacable, and Indefatigable, Enemy of *Souls) in which you are*. O break off your sins by Repentence, and your Iniquities by a saving closure with the LORD JESUS CHRIST, for *Justification, Sanctification* and *Salvation*, That ye may be delivered, from the Power, and Dominion of *Satan*, under which you are ensnared, to do his will, altho' utterly cross to the will of GOD, and may be *Translated*, into the Kingdom of the Lord Jesus; the *Dear Son of God*, and Blessed Saviour of the Souls of men, *Col*. 1. 13. Being by infinite mercy, *Recovered* out of the snare of the Devil, who are (now) taken Captive by him at his will. 2 Tim. 2. 26. *Awake, Awake* then, I beseech you, and remain no longer under the Dominion of that *Prince of Cruelty* and Malice, whose Tyrannical Fury, we see thus exerted, against the *Bodies* and *Minds* of these afflicted persons. Surely no Sinner in this Congregation, who is *sensible* of his Bondage to *Satan*, that cruel (and worse than Egyptian) *Task-master*, and *Tyrant*, can be willing, to continue quietly, in subjection to him one day or hour longer. Thus much in respect of the Spiritual State of men.

Secondly, This *Warning* is directed to all *manner of persons*, according to their condition of life, both in *Civil* and *Sacred* Order: Both *High* and *Low, Rich* and *Poor, Old* and *Young, Bond* and *Free*. O let the observation of these amazing Dispensations of GOD's unusual and strange Providence, *quicken* us to our *Duty* at such a time as this, in our respective *Places* and *Stations, Relations*, and *Capacities*. The GREAT GOD, hath done such things amongst us, as *do make the Ears of those that hear them to Tingle;* Jer. 1. 3. and serious Souls, are at a *loss* to what these things *may grow;* and what we shall find to be the end, of this dreadful visitation, in the permission whereof the *Provoked* GOD *as a Lyon hath Roared; who can but Fear? The* LORD *hath spoken, who can but Prophecy?* Amos 3. 8. The Loud *Trumpet* of God, in this Thundering Providence, is *Blown in the City,* and the Eccho of it, heard through the *Country,* surely then, the *People* must, and ought to be afraid, Amos 3. 6. . . . Let it be for DEEP HUMILIATION, *to the people of this place, which is in special under the Influence of this Fearful Judgment of GOD.* The *LORD* doth at this day, manage a great controversy with You, to the astonishment of your selves and others, You are therefore to be deeply humbled, and sit in the dust Considering.

First, *The signal hand of God, in singling out this place, this poor Village, for the first seat of Satans Tyranny,* and to make it (as 'twere) the Rendezvous of Devils, where they *Muster* their infernal forces appearing to the afflicted, as coming Armed, to carry on their malicious designs, against the Bodies, and if God in mercy prevent not, against the Souls of many in this place. *Great Afflictions,* attended with Remarkable Circumstances, do surely call for more than ordinary degrees of Humiliation.

But Secondly be humbled also, *That so many Members of this Church, of the* LORD JESUS CHRIST, *should be under the Influences of Satans malice, in these his Operations;* some as the Objects of his Tyranny, on their Bodies to that degree of *Distress,* which none can be sensible of, but those that see and feel it, who are in the meantime also, sorely distressed in their Minds, by frightful Representations, made by the *Devils* unto them. Other professors, and visible Members of this Church, are under the awful *Accusations,* and imputations of being the *Instruments* of *Satan* in his mischevious actings. It cannot but be matter of deep humiliation, to such as are Innocent, that the Righteous and Holy GOD, should permit them to be named, in such pernicious and unheard of practices, and not only so, but that HE who cannot but do right, should suffer the stain of suspected Guilt, to be as it were *Rubbed on,* and *Soaked in,* by many sore and amazing Circumstances; and it is matter of soul abasement, to all that are in the Bond of GOD's Holy Covenant in this place, that *Satans* seat should be amongst them, where he attempts to set up *his* Kingdom, in opposition to *Christ's* Kingdom, and to take some of the Visible Subjects of our LORD JESUS, and use at least their shapes and appearances, instrumentally, to *Afflict* and *Torture, other* Visible Subjects of the same Kingdom. Surely his design is, that CHRIST's Kingdom, may be *Divided against it self,* that being thereby weakened, he may the better take Opportunity to set up his own *Accursed powers* and Dominions. It calls aloud then, to all in this place, in the Name of the Blessed JESUS and words of his Holy Apostle; 1 Pet. 5. 6. *Humble your selves under the mighty hand of God,* thus thru up in the midst of you, *and he shall Exalt, Save, and Deliver you, in due time.* . . .

To Conclude; *The Lord is known by the Judgments which he Executes in the midst of us.* The Dispensations of his Providence, appear to be unsearchable, and his Doings past finding out. He seems to have allowed *Satan,* to afflict many of our People, and that thereupon he is come down in *Great Wrath,* threatning the Destruction of the *Bodies,* (and if the Infinite Mercy of GOD prevent not) of the *Souls* of many in this place. Yet may we say, in the midst of all the *Terrible* things which he doth in Righteousness; He alone is the GOD of our Salvation, who represents himself, as the Saviour of all that are in a low and distressed Condition, because he is good, and *His Mercie endureth for ever.*

Let us then Return and Repent, rent our Hearts, and not our Garments. Who can tell if the LORD will *Return* in Mercy unto us? And by his Spirit lift up a Standard, against the GRAND *Enemy* who threatens to come in like a Flood, among us, and overthrow all that is *Holy,* and *Just,* and *Good.* It is no small comfort to consider, that *Job's* Exercise of Patience, had it's Beginning from the *Devil;* but we have seen the end to be from the LORD, *James* 5. 11. That We also, may find by experience, the same Blessed Issue, of our present Distress, by *Satan's* Malice. Let us repent of every Sin, that hath been Committed, and Labour to practice, every *Duty* which hath been Neglected. And when we are Humbled, and Proved for our good in the latter end: Then we shall assuredly, and speedily find, that the Kingly Power of Our LORD and SAVIOUR, shall be Magnifyed, in delivering his Poor Sheep and Lambs, out of the *Jaws* and *Paws* of the Roaring Lyon.

Then will JESUS the Blessed Antitype of *Joshua,* the Redeemer, and Chooser of *Jerusalem, Quell, Suppress,* and utterly *Vanquish,* this *Adversary* of ours, with *Irresistable* Power and Authority, according to our Text. *And the* LORD *said unto Satan, the* LORD *Rebuke thee O Satan, Even the* LORD *that hath Chosen Jerusalem, Rebuke thee: Is not this a Brand pluckt out of the* FIRE?

Expansion and Adjustment, 1660–1713:
The Revolutionary Settlement

SELECTION

The Second Massachusetts Charter (Oct. 7, 1691)

Following the overthrow of the Dominion of New England, Increase Mather with three other agents sent by the revolutionary government in Massachusetts conducted an intensive campaign in London to secure the restoration of the old Massachusetts charter. The best they could do, however, was to obtain a new charter which differed materially from the old one and made Massachusetts a semiroyal colony. The new charter, issued on October 7, 1691, designated both Plymouth and Maine as part of Massachusetts Bay and confirmed the right of the colony to enjoy representative government. By stipulating that the governor be a royal appointee, establishing a number of restrictions upon the General Court's legislative powers, and substituting a property for a religious qualification for the franchise, imperial officials sought to break the power of the Puritans and to weaken the authority of the legislature. The new restrictions, most of which are reprinted below from Francis Newton Thorpe (ed.), The Federal and State Constitutions, Colonial Charters, and Other Organic Laws (seven volumes, 1909), volume III, pages 1877–1883, served notice that imperial officials had not abandoned their efforts to achieve tighter controls over the colonies.

. . . And Wee doe further for Vs Our Heires and Successors Will Establish and ordeyne that from henceforth for ever there shall be one Governour One Leivtent or Deputy Governour and One Secretary of Our said Province or Territory to be from time to time appointed and Commissionated by Vs Our Heires and Successors and Eight and Twenty Assistants or Councillors to be advising and assisting to the Governour of Our said Province or Territory for the time being as by these presents is hereafter directed and appointed which said Councillors or Assistants are to be Constituted Elected and Chosen in such forme and manner as hereafter in these presents is expressed. . . . And Our Will and Pleasure is that the Governour of Our said Province from the time being shall have Authority from time to time at his discretion to assemble and call together the Councillors or Assistants of Our said Province for the time being and that the said Governour with the said Assistants or Councillors or Seaven of them at the least shall and may from time to time hold and keep a Council for the ordering and directing the Affaires of Our said Province *And further* Wee Will and by these presents for Vs Our Heires and Successors doe ordeyne and Grant that there shall and may be convened held and kept by the Governour for the time being vpon every last Wednesday in the Moneth of May every yeare for ever and at all such other times as the Governour of Our said Province shall think fitt and appoint a great and Generall Court of Assembly Which said Great and Generall Court of Assembly shall consist of the Governour and Councill or Assistants for the time being and of such Freeholders of Our said Province or Territory as shall be from time to time elected or deputed by the Major parte of the Freeholders and other Inhabitants of the respective Townes or Places who shall be present at such Elections Each of the said Townes and Places being hereby impowered to Elect and Depute Two Persons and noe more to serve for and represent them respectively in the said Great and Generall Court or Assembly To which Great and Generall Court or Assembly to be held as aforesaid Wee do hereby for Vs Our Heires and Successors give and grant full power and authority from time to time to direct appoint and declare what Number each County Towne and Place shall Elect and Depute to serve for and represent them respectively in the said Great and Generall Court or Assembly *Provided* alwayes that noe Freeholder or other Person shall have a Vote in the Election of Members to serve in any Greate and Generall Court or Assembly to be held as aforesaid who at the time of such Election shall not have an estate of Freehold in Land within Our said Province or Territory to the value of Forty Shillings per Annum at the least or other estate to the value of Forty pounds Sterl' And that every Person who shall be soe elected shall before he sitt or Act in the said Great and Generall Court or Assembly take the Oaths mentioned in an Act of Parliament made in the first yeare of Our Reigne Entituled an Act for abrogateing of the Oaths of Allegiance and Supremacy and appointing other Oaths and thereby appointed to be taken instead of the Oaths of Allegiance and Supremacy and shall make Repeat and Subscribe the Declaration mentioned in the said Act before the Governour and Lievtenant or Deputy Governour or any two of the Assistants for the time being who shall be therevnto authorized and Appointed by Our said Governour and that the Governour for the time being shall have full power and Authority from time to time as he shall Judge necessary to adjourne Prorogue and dissolve all Great and Generall Courts or Assemblyes met and convened as aforesaid And Our Will and Pleasure is and Wee doe hereby for Vs Our Heires and Successors Grant Establish and Ordeyne that yearly once in every yeare for ever hereafter the aforesaid Number of Eight and Twenty Councillors or Assistants shall be by the Generall Court or Assembly newly chosen that is to say Eighteen at least of the Inhabitants of or Proprietors of Lands within the Territory formerly called the Collony of the Massachusetts Bay and four at the least of the Inhabitants of or Proprietors of Lands within the Territory formerly called New Plymouth and three at the least of the Inhabitants of or Proprietors of Land within the Territory formerly called the Province of Main and one at the least of the Inhabitants of or Proprietors of Land within the Territory lying between the River of Sagadahoc and Nova Scotia And that the said Councillors or Assistants or any of them shall or may at any time hereafter be removed or displaced from their respective Places or Trust of Councillors or Assistants by any Great or Generall Court or Assembly And that if any of the said Councillors or Assistants shall happen to dye or be removed as aforesaid before the Generall day of Election That then and in every such Case the Great and Generall Court or Assembly at their first sitting may proceed to a New Election of one or more Councillors or Assistants in the roome or place of such Councillors or Assistants soe dying or removed And Wee doe further Grant and Ordeyne that it shall and may be lawfull for the said Governour with the advice and consent of the Councill or Assistants from time to time to nominate and appoint Judges Commissioners of Oyer and Terminer Sheriffs Provosts Marshalls Justices of the Peace and other Officers to Our Council and Courts of Justice belonging *Provided* always that noe such Nomination or Appointment of Officers be made without notice first given or summons yssued out seaven dayes before such Nomination or Appointment vnto such of the said Councillors or Assistants as shall be at that time resideing within Our said Province *And Our* Will and Pleasure is that the Governour and Leivtenant or Deputy Governour and Councillors or Assistants for the time being and all other Officers to be appointed or Chosen as aforesaid shall before the Vndertaking the Execution of their Offices and Places respectively take their severall and respective Oaths for the due and faithfull performance of their duties in their severall and respective Offices and Places and alsoe the Oaths appointed by the said Act of Parliament made in the first yeare of Our Reigne to be taken instead of the Oaths of Allegiance and Supremacy and shall make repeate and subscribe the Declaration mentioned in the said Act before such Person or Persons as are by these presents herein after appointed. . . . *And further* Our Will and Pleasure is and Wee doe hereby for Vs Our Heires and Successors Grant Establish and Ordaine That all and every of the Subjects of Vs Our Heires and Successors which shall goe to and Inhabit within Our said Province and Territory and every of their Children which shall happen to be born there or on the Seas in goeing thither or returning from thence shall have and enjoy all Libertyes and Immunities of Free and naturall Subjects within any of the Dominions of Vs Our Heires and Successors to all Intents Constructions and purposes whatsoever as if they and every of them were borne within this Our *Realme* of England and for the greater Ease and Encouragement of Our Loveing Subjects Inhabiting our said Province or Territory of the Massachusetts Bay and of such as shall come to Inhabit there Wee doe by these presents for vs Our heires and Successors Grant Establish and Ordaine that for ever hereafter there shall be a liberty of Conscience allowed in the Worshipp of God to all Christians (Except Papists) Inhabiting or which shall Inhabit or be Resident within our said Province or Territory . . . *And whereas* Wee judge it necessary that all our Subjects should have liberty to Appeale to vs our heires and Successors in Cases that may deserve the same Wee doe by these presents Ordaine that incase either party shall not rest satisfied with the Judgement or Sentence of any Judicatories or Courts within our said Province or Territory in any Personall Action wherein the matter in difference doth exceed the value of three hundred Pounds Sterling that then he or they may appeale to vs Our heires and Successors in our or their Privy Councill Provided such Appeale be made within Fourteen dayes after the Sentence or Judgement given and that before such Appeale be allowed Security be given by the party or parties appealing in the value of the matter in Difference to pay or Answer the Debt or Damages for the which Judgement or Sentence is given With such Costs and Damages as shall be Awarded by vs Our Heires or Successors incase the Judgement or Sentence be affirmed . . . *And* wee doe for vs our Heires and Successors Giue and grant that the said Generall Court or Assembly shall have full power and Authority to name and settle annually all Civill Officers within the said Province such Officers Excepted the Election and Constitution of whome wee have by these presents reserved to vs Our Heires and Successors or to the Governor of our said Province for the time being and to Settforth the severall Duties Powers and Lymitts of every such Officer to be appointed by the said Generall Court or Assembly and the formes of such Oathes not repugnant to the Lawes and Statutes of this our Realme of England as shall be respectiuely Administered vnto them for the Execution of their severall Offices and places And alsoe to impose Fines mulcts Imprisonments and other Punishments And to impose and leavy proportionable and reasonable Assessments Rates and Taxes vpon the Estates and Persons of all and every the Proprietors and Inhabitants of our said Province or Territory to be Issued and disposed of by Warrant vnder the hand of the Governor of our said Province for the time being with the advice and Consent of the Councill for Our service in the necessary defence and support of our Government of our said Province or Territory and the Protection and Preservation of the Inhabitants there according to such Acts as are or shall be in force within our said Province and to dispose of matters and things whereby our Subjects inhabitants of our said Province may be Religously peaceably and Civilly Governed Protected and Defended soe as their good life and orderly Conversation may win the Indians Natives of the Country to the knowledge and obedience of the onely true God and Saviour of Mankinde and the Christian Faith which his Royall Majestie our Royall Grandfather king Charles the first in his said Letters Patents declared was his Royall Intentions And the Adventurers free Possession to be the Princepall end of the said Plantation And for the better secureing and maintaining Liberty of Conscience hereby granted to all persons at any time being and resideing within our said Province or Territory as aforesaid *Willing* Commanding and Requireing and by these presents for vs Our heires and Successors Ordaining and appointing that all such Orders Lawes Statutes and Ordinances Instructions and Directions as shall be soe made and published vnder our Seale of our said Province or Territory shall be Carefully and duely observed kept and performed and put in Execution according to the true intent and meaning of these presents *Provided* alwaies and Wee doe by these presents for vs Our Heires and Successors Establish and Ordaine that in the frameing and passing of all such Orders Laws Statutes and Ordinances and in all Elections and Acts of Government whatsoever to be passed or done by the said Generall Court or Assembly or in Councill the Governor of our said Province or Territory of the Massachusetts Bay in New England for the time being shall have the Negative voice and that without his consent or Approbation signified and declared in Writeing no such Orders Laws Statutes Ordinances Elections or other Acts of Government whatsoever soe to be made passed or done by the said Generall Assembly or in Councill shall be of any Force effect or validity anything herein contained to the contrary in anywise notwithstanding *And* wee doe for vs Our Heires and Successors Establish and Ordaine that the said Orders Laws Statutes and Ordinances be by the first opportunity after the makeing thereof sent or Transmitted vnto vs Our Heires and Successors vnder the Publique Seale to be appointed by vs for Our or their approbation or Disallowance And that incase all or any of them shall at any time within the space of three years next after the same shall have presented to vs our Heires and Successors in Our or their Privy Council be disallowed and rejected and soe signified by vs Our Heires and Successors vnder our or their Signe Manuall and Signett or by or in our or their Privy Councill vnto the Governor for the time being then such and soe many of them as shall be soe disallowed and riected shall thenceforth cease and determine and become vtterly void and of none effect *Provided* alwais that incase Wee our Heires or Successors shall not within the Terme of Three Yeares after the presenting of such Orders Lawes Statutes or Ordinances as aforesaid signifie our or their Disallowance of the same Then the said orders Lawes Statutes or Ordinances shall be and continue in full force and effect according to the true Intent and meaneing of the same vntill the Expiracon thereof or that the same shall be Repealed by the Generall Assembly of our said Province for the time being. . . .

SELECTION

Refinements in the Navigation System

In the decades immediately following the Glorious Revolution, three important new laws were added to the navigation system. The first was the Navigation Act of 1696. Passed in response to continued reports of colonial violations of the earlier navigation acts and to intense competition from the Scots for the trade of the colonies beginning in 1694, this measure was intended to tighten up the enforcement of the old acts rather than to introduce any major change in policy. To that end, it required all colonial governors, in private as well as in royal colonies, to take an oath to enforce the Navigation Acts, reorganized the customs service in the colonies, established penalties upon both governors and customs officials for failure to enforce the acts, gave customs officials broad powers of search and seizure, made possible the establishment of juryless vice-admiralty courts to try cases arising under the acts, declared null and void all colonial laws contrary to the acts, and set down a number of other regulations.

Both the second and third acts represented major additions to existing policy. Although it was aimed primarily at Ireland and seems to have had little effect in the colonies, the Woolen Act of 1699 was the first of a series of acts that sought to curtail the manufacture of certain products in the colonies by limiting their sale to purely local markets. Seeking to encourage production of items for which England was otherwise dependent upon the Baltic, the Naval Stores Act of 1705 established a series of bounties upon pitch, tar, rosin, turpentine, hemp, masts, yards, and bowsprits and prohibited the destruction of pine trees suitable for the production of those goods. Although these bounties did not produce the goal for which they had been introduced—the reorientation of the New England economy from trade and commerce to the production of naval stores— they did help to stimulate a thriving naval-stores industry in the Carolinas, and the bounty system was extended to indigo in 1748 after that commodity had successfully been introduced into South Carolina.

The major provisions affecting the colonies of each of these acts are reprinted below. For further reading see the references listed in the introduction to Selection 17 and Joseph J. Malone, Pine Trees and Politics: The Naval Stores and Forest Policy in Colonial New England, 1691–1775 *(1964).*

A. THE NAVIGATION ACT OF (APR. 10) 1696*

Whereas notwithstanding divers acts made for the encouragement of the navigation of this kingdom, and for the better securing and regulating the plantation trade . . . great abuses are daily committed to the prejudice of the English *navigation, and the loss of a great part of the plantation trade to this kingdom, by the artifice and cunning of ill-disposed persons:* For remedy whereof for the future,

II. Be it enacted, and it is hereby enacted and ordained by the King's most excellent majesty, by and with the advice and consent of the lords spiritual and temporal, and commons, in parliament assembled, and by the authority of the same, That after the five and twentieth day of *March*, one thousand six hundred ninety-eight, no goods or merchandizes whatsoever shall be imported into, or exported out of, any colony or plantation to his Majesty, in *Asia*, *Africa* or *America*, belonging, or in his possession, or which may hereafter belong unto, or be in the possession of his Majesty,

---

* These excerpts are reprinted from Danby Pickering (ed.), *The Statutes at Large* (46 vols., 1762–1807), vol. IX, pp. 428–437.

his heirs or successors, or shall be laden in, or carried from any one port or place in the said colonies or plantations to any other port or place in the said colonies or plantations to any other port or place in the same, the kingdom of *England,* dominion of *Wales,* or town of *Berwick* upon *Tweed,* in any ship or bottom, but what is or shall be of the built of *England,* or of the built of *Ireland,* or the said colonies or plantations, and wholly owned by the people thereof, or any of them, and navigated with the masters and three fourths of the mariners of the said places only (except such ships only as are or shall be taken as prize and condemnation thereof made in one of the courts of admiralty in *England, Ireland,* or the said colonies or plantations, to be navigated by the master and three fourths of the mariners *English,* or of the said plantations as aforesaid, and whereof the property doth belong to *English* men; and also except for the space of three years, such foreign built ships as shall be employed by the commissioners of his Majesty's navy for the time being, or upon contract with them, in bringing only masts, timber, and other naval stores for the King's service from his Majesty's colonies or plantations to this kingdom, to be navigated as aforesaid, and whereof the property doth belong to *English* men) under the pain of forfeiture of ship and goods. . . . That all the present governors and commanders in chief of any *English* colonies or plantations . . . take a solemn oath to do their utmost, that all the clauses, matters and things, contained in the . . . acts of parliament heretofore passed, and now in force, relating to the said colonies and plantations, and that all and every the clauses contained in this present act, be punctually and *bona fide* observed, according to the true intent and meaning thereof (which oath shall be taken before such person or persons as shall be appointed by his Majesty, his heirs and successors, who are hereby authorized to administer the same) so far as appertains unto the said governors or commanders in chief respectively; and upon complaint and proof made before his Majesty, his heirs and successors, or such as shall be by him or them thereunto authorized and appointed by the oath of two or more credible witnesses, that any of the said governors or commanders in chief have neglected to take the said oath at the times aforesaid, or have been wittingly or willingly negligent in doing their duty accordingly, the said governor so neglecting or offending shall be removed from his government, and forfeit the sum of one thousand pounds sterling. . . .

V. . . . That all and every . . . [naval] officers already appointed shall, within two months after notice of this act in the respective plantations, or as soon as conveniently it may be, give security to the commissioners of the customs in *England* for the time being, or such as shall be appointed by them, for his Majesty's use, for the true and faithful performance of their duty; and all and every person or persons, who shall hereafter be appointed to the said office or employment, shall within two months, or as soon as conveniently it may be, after his or their entrance upon the said office or employment, give sufficient security to the commissioners of the customs as aforesaid, for his Majesty's use, for the true and faithful performance of his or their duty; and in default thereof, the person or persons neglecting or refusing to give such security, shall be disabled to execute the said office or employment; and until such security given, and the person appointed to the said office or employment be approved by the commissioners of the customs as aforesaid, the respective governor or governors shall be answerable for any the offences, neglects or misdemeanors, of the person or persons so by him or them appointed.

VI. And for the more effectual preventing of frauds, and regulating abuses in the plantation trade in *America,* be it further enacted by the authority aforesaid, That all ships coming into, or going out of, any of the said plantations, and lading or unlading any goods or commodities, whether the same be his Majesty's ships of war, or merchants ships, and the masters and commanders thereof, and their ladings, shall be subject and liable to the same rules, visitations, searches, penalties and forfeitures, as to the entring, lading or discharging their respective ships and ladings, as ships and their ladings, and the commanders and masters of ships, are subject and liable unto in this kingdom, by virtue of an act of parliament made in the fourteenth year of the reign of King *Charles* the Second, intituled, *An act for preventing frauds, and regulating abuses in his Majesty's customs:* and that the officers for collecting and managing his Majesty's revenue, and inspecting the plantation trade, in any of the said plantations, shall have the same powers and authorities, for visiting and searching of ships, and taking their entries, and for seizing and securing or bringing on shore any of the goods prohibited to be imported or exported into or out of any the said plantations, or for which any duties are payable, or ought to have been paid, by any of the before mentioned acts, as are provided for the officers of the customs in *England* by the said last mentioned act made in the fourteenth year of the reign of King *Charles* the Second, and also to enter houses or warehouses, to search for and seize any such goods; and that all the wharfingers, and owners of keys and wharfs, or any lightermen, bargemen, watermen, porters, or other persons assisting in the conveyance, concealment or rescue of any of the said goods, or in the hindring or resistance of any of the said officers in the performance of their duty, and the boats, barges, lighters or other vessels, employed in the conveyance of such goods, shall be subject to the like pains and penalties as are provided by the same act made in the fourteenth year of the reign of King *Charles* the Second, in relation to prohibited or uncustomed goods in this kingdom; and that the like assistance shall be given to the said officers in the execution of their office, as by the said last mentioned act is provided for the officers in *England;* and also that the said officers shall be subject to the same penalties and forfeitures, for any corruptions, frauds, connivances, or concealments, in violation of any the before mentioned laws, as any officers of the customs in *England* are liable to, by virtue of the said last mentioned act; and also that in case any officer or officers in the plantations shall be sued or molested for any thing done in the execution of their office, the said officer shall and may plead the general issue, and shall give this or other custom acts in evidence, and the judge to allow thereof, have and enjoy the like privileges and advantages, as are allowed by law to the officers of his Majesty's customs in *England.*

VII. And it is hereby further enacted, That all the penalties and forfeitures before mentioned, not in this act particularly disposed of, shall be one third part to the use of his Majesty, his heirs and successors, and one third part to the governor of the colony or plantation where the offence shall be committed, and the other third part to such person or persons as shall sue for the same, to be recovered in any of his Majesty's courts at *Westminster,* or in the kingdom of *Ireland,* or in the court of admiralty held in his Majesty's plantations respectively, where such offence shall be committed, at the pleasure of the officer or informer, or in any other plantation belonging to any subject of *England,* wherein no essoin, protection, or wager of law, shall be allowed; and that where any question shall arise concerning the importation or exportation of any goods into or out of the said plantations, in such case the proof shall lie upon the owner or claimer, and the claimer shall be reputed the importer or owner thereof.

VIII. *And whereas in some of his Majesty's* American *plantations, a doubt or misconstruction has arisen upon the before mentioned act, made in the five and twentieth year of the reign of King* Charles *the Second, whereby certain duties are laid upon the commodities therein enumerated (which by law may be transported from one plantation to another for the supply of each others wants) as if the same were by the payment of those duties in one plantation, discharged from giving the securities intended by the aforesaid acts, made in the twelfth, two and twentieth, and three and twentieth years of the reign of King* Charles *the Second, and consequently be at liberty to go to any foreign market in* Europe, *without coming to* England, Wales, *or* Berwick: it is hereby further enacted and declared, That notwithstanding the payment of the aforesaid duties in any of the said plantations, none of the said goods shall be shipped or laden on board, until such security shall be given as is required by the said acts, made in the twelfth, two and twentieth and three and twentieth years of the reign of King *Charles* the second, to carry the same to *England, Wales,* or *Berwick,* or to some other of his Majesty's plantations, and to *toties quoties,* as any of the said goods shall be brought to be re-shipped or laden in any of the said plantations, under the penalty and forfeiture of ship and goods, to be divided and disposed of as aforesaid.

IX. And it is further enacted and declared by the authority aforesaid, That all laws, by-laws, usages or customs, at this time, or which hereafter shall be in practice, or endeavoured or pretended to be in force or practice, in any of the said plantations, which are in any wise repugnant to the before mentioned laws, or any of them, so far as they do relate to the said plantations, or any of them, or which are any ways repugnant to this present act, or to any other law hereafter to be made in this kingdom, so far as such law shall relate to and mention the said plantations, are illegal, null and void, to all intents and purposes whatsoever. . . .

XI. And for the better executing the several acts of parliament relating to the plantation trade, be it enacted by the authority aforesaid, That the lord treasurer, commissioners of the treasury, and the commissioners of the customs in *England* for the time being, shall and may constitute and appoint such and so many officers of the customs in any city, town, river, port, harbour, or creek, of or belonging to any of the islands, tracts of land and proprieties, when and as often as to them shall seem needful; be it further also enacted, That upon any actions, suits, and informations that shall be brought, commenced or entred in the said plantations, upon any law or statute concerning his Majesty's duties, or ships or goods to be forfeited by reason of any unlawful importations or exportations, there shall not be any jury, but of such only as are natives of *England* or *Ireland,* or are born in his Majesty's said plantations; and also that upon all such actions, suits and informations, the offences may be laid or alledged in any colony, province, county, precinct or division of any of the said plantations where such offences are alledged to be committed, at the pleasure of the officer or informer.

XII. Provided always, That all places of trust in the courts of law, or what relates to the treasury of the said islands, shall, from the making of this act, be in the hands of the native-born subjects of *England* or *Ireland,* or of the said islands. . . .

XIV. *And whereas several ships and vessels laden with tobacco, sugars, and other goods of the growth and product of his Majesty's plantations in* America, *have been discharged in several ports of the kingdoms of* Scotland *and* Ireland, *contrary to the laws and statutes now in being, under pretence that the said ships and vessels were driven in thither by stress of weather, or far want of provisions, and other disabilities could not proceed on their voyage:* for remedy whereof be it enacted by the authority aforesaid, That from and after the first day of *December,* one thousand six hundred ninety six, it shall not be lawful, on any pretence whatsoever, to put on shore in the said kingdoms of *Scotland* or *Ireland,* any goods or merchandize of the growth or product of any of his Majesty's plantations aforesaid, unless the same have been first landed in the kingdom of *England,* dominion of *Wales,* or town of *Berwick* upon *Tweed,* and paid the rates and duties wherewith they are chargeable by law, under the penalty of the forfeiture of the ship and goods; three fourths without composition to his Majesty, his heirs and successors, and the other fourth to him or them that shall sue for the same. . . .

XVI. And be it further enacted by the authority aforesaid, That all persons and their assignees, claiming any right or propriety in any islands or tracts of land upon the continent of *America,* by charter or letters patents, shall not at any time hereafter aliene, fell or dispose of any of the said islands, tracts of lands or proprieties, other than to the natural-born subjects of *England, Ireland,* dominion of *Wales,* and town of *Berwick* upon *Tweed,* without the licence and consent of his Majesty, his heirs and successors, signified by his or their order in council, first had and obtained; and all governors nominated and appointed by any such persons or proprietors, who shall be intitled to make such nomination, shall be allowed and approved of by his Majesty, his heirs and successors, as aforesaid, and shall take the oaths injoined by this or any other act to be taken by the governors or commanders in chief in other his Majesty's colonies and plantations, before their entring upon their respective governments, under the like penalty, as his Majesty's governors and commanders in chief are by the said acts liable to.

XVII. And for a more effectual prevention of frauds which may be used to elude the intention of this act, by colouring foreign ships under *English* names; be it further enacted by the authority aforesaid, That from and after the five and twentieth day of *March,* which shall be in the year of our Lord one thousand six hundred ninety eight, no ship or vessel whatsoever shall be deemed or pass as a ship of the built of *England, Ireland, Wales, Berwick, Guernsey, Jersey,* or any of his Majesty's plantations in *America,* so as to be qualified to trade to, from or in any of the plantations, until the person or persons claiming property in such ship or vessel shall register the same. . . .

XX. Provided also, That nothing in this act shall be construed to require the registering any fisher-boats, hoys, lighters, barges, or any open boats or other vessels (though of *English* or plantation built) whose navigation is confined to the rivers or coasts of the same plantation or place where they trade respectively, but only of such of them as cross the seas to or from any of the lands, islands, places or territories, in this act before recited, or from one plantation to another. . . .

B. THE WOOLEN ACT (MAY 4, 1699)*

Cap. X

FORASMUCH *as wooll and the woollen manufactures of cloth, serge, bays, kerseys, and other stuffs made or mixed with wooll, and the greatest and most profitable commodities of this kingdom, on which the value of lands, and the trade of the nation do chiefly depend: and whereas great quantities of the like manufactures have of late been made, and are daily increasing in the kingdom of* Ireland, *and in the* English *plantations in* America, *and are exported from thence to foreign markets, heretofore supplied from* England, *which will inevitably sink the value of lands, and tend to the ruin of the trade, and the woollen manufactures of this realm:* for the prevention whereof, and for the encouragement of the woollen manufactures within this kingdom. . . .

XIX. And for the more effectual encouragement of the woollen manufacture of this kingdom; be it further enacted by the authority aforesaid, That from and after the first day of *December,* in the year of our Lord one thousand six hundred ninety nine, no wool, wolfells, shortlings, mortlings, woolstocks, worsted, bay, or woollen yarn, cloth, serge, bays, kerseys, fays, frizes, druggets, cloth-serges, shalloons, or any other drapery stuffs or woollen manufactures whatsoever, made or mixed with wool or woolstocks, being of the product or manufacture of any of the *English* plantations in *America,* shall be loaden or laid on board in any ship or vessel,

---

* Only those portions of the act relating to the colonies are reprinted. They are taken from Pickering, *Statutes at Large,* vol. X, pp. 249, 256.

in any place or parts within any of the said *English* plantations, upon any pretence whatsoever; as likewise that no such wool, woolfells, shortlings, mortlings, woolstocks, worsted, bay, or woollen yarn, cloth, serge, bays, kerseys, fays, frizes, druggets, cloth-serges, shalloons, or any other drapery stuffs, or woollen manufactures whatsoever, made up or mixt with wool or woolstocks, being of the product or manufacture of any of the *English* plantations in *America* as aforesaid, shall be loaden upon any horse, cart, or other carriage, to the intent and purpose to be exported, transported, carried or conveyed out of the said *English* plantations to any other of the said plantations, or to any other place whatsoever. . . .

C. THE NAVAL STORES ACT (MAR. 14, 1705)*

WHEREAS the royal navy, and the navigation of England, wherein, under God, the wealth, safety and strength of this kingdom is so much concerned, depends on the due supply of stores necessary for the same, which being now brought in mostly from foreign parts, in foreign shipping, at exorbitant and arbitrary rates, to the great prejudice and discouragement of the trade and navigation of this kingdom, may be provided in a more certain and beneficial manner from her Majesty's own dominions: and whereas her Majesty's colonies and plantations in America were at first settled, and are still maintained and protected, at a great expence of the treasure of this kingdom, with a design to render them as useful as may be to England, and the labour and industry of the people there, profitable to themselves: and in regard the said colonies and plantations, by the vast tracts of land therein, lying near the sea, and upon navigable rivers, may commodiously afford great quantities of all sorts of naval stores, if due encouragement be given for carrying on so great and advantageous an undertaking, which will likewise tend, not only to the further imployment and increase of English shipping and seamen, but also to the enlarging, in a great measure, the trade and vent of the woollen and other manufactures and commodities of this kingdom, and of another her Majesty's dominions, in exchange for such naval stores, which are now purchased from foreign countries with money or bullion: and for enabling her Majesty's subjects, in the said colonies and plantations, to continue to make due and sufficient returns in the course of their trade; be it therefore enacted by the Queen's most excellent majesty, by and with the advice and consent of the lords spiritual and temporal, and commons, in this present parliament assembled, and by the authority of the same, That every person or persons that shall, within the time appointed by this act, import or cause to be imported into this kingdom, directly from any of her Majesty's *English* colonies or plantations in *America,* in any ship or ships that may lawfully trade to her Majesty's plantations, manned as by law is required, any of the naval stores, here-

* These excerpts are reprinted from Pickering, *Statutes at Large,* vol. XI, pp. 109–111.

after mentioned, shall have and enjoy, as a reward or *premium* for such importation, after and according to the several rates for such naval stores. . . .

II. [List of rates.]

III. Which several rewards for *prœminums,* for each species afore-mentioned, shall be paid and answered by the commissioners or principal officers of her Majesty's navy, who are hereby impowered and required to make out bill or bills, to be paid in course for the same, upon certificate of the respective chief officer or officers of the customs, in any port of this kingdom, where such naval stores shall be imported, as aforesaid; such bill or bills to be made out and given to the person or persons importing the same. . . .

VI. And for the better preservation of all timber fit for the uses afore-said; be it further enacted and ordained by the authority aforesaid, That no person or persons within her Majesty's colonies of *New Hampshire,* the *Massachusets Bay, Rhode Island,* and *Providence Plantation,* the *Narraganset Country,* or *Kings Province,* and *Connecticut* in *New England,* and *New York,* and *New Jersey,* do or shall presume to cut, fell, or destroy any pitch, pine trees, or tar trees, not being within any fence or actual inclosure, under the growth of twelve inches diameter, at three foot from the earth, on the penalty or forfeiture of five pounds for each offence, on proof thereof to be made by one or more credible witnesses or oath, before one or more justice or justices of the peace within or nearest to such place where such offence shall be committed; one moiety of such penalty or forfeiture to be to her Majesty, her heirs or successors, the other moiety to the informer or informers. . . .

SELECTION

A New Supervisory Agency: The Commission of the Board of Trade (May 15, 1696)

Accompanying the Navigation Act of 1696 was a new administrative agency for the colonies, the Board of Trade. Under James II and William III, the old Lords of Trade had gradually lost its power over the colonies to a committee of the Privy Council, and the Council was so preoccupied with other matters that the colonies received scant attention. The Board of Trade was intended to remedy that situation, and although it had only advisory powers during most of its existence, it was the only governmental agency concerned primarily with the colonies from 1696 until the creation of a special secretary of state for the colonies in 1768. Thereafter, the Board was distinctly secondary to the new secretary, though it continued in operation until it was abolished in 1782 at the end of the American Revolution. The organization and functions of the Board were spelled out in the commission which created it. That commission is reprinted below from E. B. O'Callaghan and B. Fernqw (eds.), Documents Relative to the Colonial History of the State of New-York (fifteen volumes, 1853–1887), volume IV, pages 145–148. Oliver M. Dickerson, American Colonial Government, 1696–1765: A Study of the British Board of Trade (1912), and Arthur H. Basye, The Lords Commissioners for Trade and Plantations, 1748–1782 (1925), are the standard works on the Board.

William the Third by the Grace of God King of England, Scotland, France and Ireland, Defender of the Faith &a. To our Keeper of oure Seale of England or Chancellor of England for the time being, Our President of Our Privy Council for the time being, Our first Commissioner of Our Treasury And our Treasurer of England for the time being, Our first Commissioner of our Admiralty and Our Admirall of England for the time being, And our principall Secretarys of State for the time being, And the Chancellor of Our Exchequer for the time being, To Our Right Trusty and Right Well beloved Cousin and Councillor John Earl of Bridgewater, and Ford Earl of Tankerville, To our trusty and Well beloved Sir Philip Meadows, Knt, William Blaithwayte, John Pollexfen, John Locke, Abraham Hill, and John Methwen, Esquires, Greeting:

Whereas We are extreamly desirous that the Trade of Our Kingdom of England, upon which the strength and riches thereof do in a great measure depend, should by all proper means be promoted and advanced; And Whereas We are perswaded that nothing will more effectually contribute thereto than the appointing of knowing and fitt persons to inspect and examin into the general Trade of our said Kingdom and the severall parts thereof, and to enquire into the severall matters and things herein after mentioned relating thereunto, with such Powers and Directions as are herein after specified and contained.

KNOW YEE therefor that We reposing espetiall Trust and Confidence in your Discretions, Abilityes and Integrities, Have nominated, authorized and constituted, and do by these presents nominate authorize and appoint the said Keeper of Our Great Seale or Chancellor for the time being, The President of Our Privy Council for the time being, The Keeper of our Privy Seale for the time being, The first Commissioner of Our Treasury or Treasurer for the time being, The First Commissioner for executing the Office of Admirall and Our Admirall for the time being, Our Principall Secretarys of State for the time being, And Our Chancellor of the Exchequer for the time being, And you John Earl of Bridgewater, Ford Earl of Tankerville, Sir Philip Meadows, William Blathwayte, John Pollexfen, John Locke, Abraham Hill, and John Methwen, or any other three or more of you, to be Our Commissioners during our Royal Pleasure, for promoting the Trade of our Kingdome, and for Inspecting and Improving our Plantations in America and elsewhere.

And to the end that Our Royall purpose and intention herein may the better take effect OUR WILL and PLEASURE is, and We do hereby order, direct and appoint, That you do diligently and constantly as the nature of the service may require, meet togeather at some convenient Place in Our Palace of Whitehall which we shall assigne for that purpose, or at any other place which we shall appoint for the execution of this Our Commission.

And We do by these presents authorize and impower you Our said Commissioners, or any Three or more of you, to enquire, examin into and take an Account of the state and condition of the general Trade of England, and also of the several particular Trades in all Forreigne parts, and how the same respectively are advanced or decayed, and the causes or occasions thereof; and to enquire into and examine what Trades are or may prove hurtfull, or are or may be made beneficiall to our Kingdom of England, and by what ways and means the profitable and advantageous Trades may be more improved and extended and such as are hurtfull and prejudiciall rectifyed or discouraged; and to enquire into the several obstructions of Trade and the means of removing the same. And also in what manner and by what proper methods the Trade of our said Kingdom may be most effectually protected, and secured, in all the parts thereof; And to consider by what means the severall usefull and profitable manufactures already settled in Our said Kingdom may be further improved, and how and in what manner new and profitable Manufactures may be introduced.

And we do further by these presents Authorize and require you Our said Commissioners, or any three or more of you, to consider of some proper methods for setting on worke and employing the Poore of Our said Kingdome, and makeing them usefull to the Publick, and thereby easeing Our Subjects of that Burthen; and by what ways and means such designe may be made most effectuall; and in generall, by all such methods and ways as you in your Discretions shall think best, to inform your selves of all things relating to Trade and the promoting and encouraging thereof; As also to consider of the best and most effectual means to regaine, encourage and establish the Fishery of this Kingdom.

AND OUR FURTHER WILL AND PLEASURE is, that you Our said Commissioners, or any Five or more of you, do from time to time make representations touching the Premisses to Us, or to Our Privy Council, as the nature of the Business shall require, which said Representations are to be in writing, and to be signed by Five or more of you.

And We do hereby further Impower and require you Our said Commissioners to take into your care all Records, Grants and Papers remaining in the Plantation Office or thereunto belonging.

And likewise to inform your selves of the present condition of Our respective Plantations, as well with regard to the Administration of the Government and Justice in those places, as in relation to the Commerce thereof; And also to inquire into the Limits of Soyle and Product of Our severall Plantations and how the same may be improved, and of the best means for easing and securing Our Colonies there, and how the same may be rendred most usefull and beneficiall to our said Kingdom of England.

And We do hereby further impower and require you Our said Commissioners, more particularly and in a principal manner to inform yourselves what Navall Stores may be furnished from Our Plantations, and in what Quantities, and by what methods Our Royall purpose of having our Kingdom supplied with Navall Stores from thence may be made practicable and promoted; And also to inquire into and inform your selves of the best and most proper methods of settling and improving in Our Plantations, such other Staples and other Manuufactures as Our subjects of England are now obliged to fetch and supply themselves withall from other Princes and States; And also what Staples and Manufactures may be best encouraged there, and what Trades are taken up and exercised there, which are or may prove prejudiciall to England, by furnishing themselves or other Our Colonies with what has been usually supplied from England; And to finde out proper means of diverting them from such Trades, and whatsoever else may turne to the hurt of Our Kingdom of England.

And to examin and looke into the usuall Instructions given to the Governors of Our Plantations, and to see if any thing may be added, omitted or changed therein to advantage; To take an Account yearly by way of Journall of the Administration of Our Governors there, and to draw out what is proper to be observed and represented unto Us; And as often as occasion shall require to consider of proper persons to be Governors or Deputy Governors, or to be of Our Councill or of Our Councill at Law, or Secretarys, in Our respective Plantations, in order to present their Names to Us in Councill.

And We do hereby further Authorize and impower you Our said Commissioners, to examin into and weigh such Acts of the Assemblies of the Plantations respectively as shall from time to time be sent or transmitted hither for Our Approbation; And to set down and represent as aforesaid the Usefulness or Mischeif thereof to Our Crown, and to Our said Kingdom of England, or to the Plantations themselves, in case the same should be established for Lawes there; And also to consider what matters may be recommended as fitt to be passed in the Assemblys there, To heare complaints of Oppressions and maleadministrations, in Our Plantations, in order to represent as aforesaid what you in your Discretions shall thinke proper; And also to require an Account of all Monies given for Publick uses by the Assemblies in Our Plantations, and how the same are and have been expended or laid out.

And We do by these Presents Authorize and impower you Our said Commissioners or any Three of you, to send for Persons and Papers, for your better Information in the Premisses; and as Occasion shall require to examin Witnesses upon Oath, which Oath you are hereby impowred to Administer in order to the matters aforesaid.

And We do declare Our further Will and Pleasure to be, That you Our said Commissioners do from time to time report all your doeings in relation to the Premisses in writing under the hands of any Five of you, as aforesaid, to Us, or to Our Privy Council, as the nature of the thing shall require.

And We do hereby further Authorize and impower you Our said Commissioners to execute and perform all other things necessary or proper for answering our Royall Intentions in the Premisses.

And We do further give power to you Our said Commissioners, or any three or more of you, as aforesaid, from time to time, and as occasion shall require, to send for and desire the advice and assistance of Our Atturney or Sollicitor Generall or other Our Councill at Law:

And We do hereby further declare Our Royall Will and Pleasure to be, that We do not hereby intend that Our Chancellor of England or Keeper of Our great Seale for the time being, The President of Our Privy Councill for the time being, The Keeper of Our Privy Seale for the time being, The Treasurer or first Commissioner of Our Treasury for the time being, Our Admirall or first Commissioner for executing the Office of Admirall for the time being, Our Principall Secretarys of State for the time being, or Our Chancellor of the Exchequer for the time being, should be obliged to give constant attendance at the meeting of Our said Commissioners, but only so often and when the presence of them or any of them shall be necessary and requisite, and as their other Publick service will permitt. . . .

SELECTION

The Movement against the Private Colonies: Report of the Board of Trade (Mar. 26, 1701)

The Board of Trade entered into its task with gusto. Within five years it decided that the Lords of Trade had been right: the private colonies had to be brought under the direct supervision of the Crown if they were ever going to be properly subordinate to the imperial government. The Board set forth its case against the private colonies in the report of March 26, 1701. Reprinted in full below from William L. Saunders (ed.), The Colonial Records of North Carolina *(ten volumes, 1886–1890), volume I, pages 535–537, this report led to the introduction of bills into Parliament in 1701 and 1702 to reunite the proprietary and corporate colonies to the Crown, but the opposition of the colonial proprietors was strong, and neither bill got a full hearing. Similar bills introduced in 1706 and 1715 also failed to pass, and, although the idea continued to be fostered by the Board of Trade, it did not thereafter receive serious consideration from Parliament. The best account of the Board's efforts to recall the charters is in Charles M. Andrews, Colonial Period of American History 1931, volume IV, chapter xi.*

Having formerly on severall occasions humbly represented to your Majesty the state of the Government under Proprietors and Charters in America; and perceiving the irregularities of these Governments dayly to increase, to the prejudice of Trade, and of your Majesties other Plantations in America, as well as of your Majesties Revenue arising from the Customes here, we find ourselves obliged at present humbly to represent to your Majesty;

That those Colonies in general have no ways answered the chief design for which such large Tracts of Land and such Priviledges and Immunities were granted by the Crown.

That they have not conformed themselves to the severall acts of Parliament for regulating Trade and Navigation, to which they ought to pay the same obedience, and submit to the same Restrictions as the other Plantations, which are subject to your Majesties immediate Government, on the contrary in most of these Proprieties and Charter Governments, the Governours have not applyed themselves to your Majesty for your approbation, nor have taken the Oaths required by the acts of Trade, both which Qualifications are made necessary by the late Act for preventing frauds and regulating abuses in the Plantation Trade.

That they have assumed to themselves a power to make Laws contrary and repugnant to the Laws of England, and directly prejudicial to Trade, some of them having refused to send hither such Laws as they had enacted, and others having sent them but very imperfectly.

That diverse of them have denied appeals to your Majesty in Councill, by which not only the Inhabitants of those Colonies but others your Majesties subjects are deprived of that benefit, enjoyed in the Plantations, under your Majesties immediate Government, and the Parties agrieved are left without remedy from the arbitrary and Illegal proceedings of their Courts.

That these Colonies continue to be the refuge and retreat of Pirates & Illegal Traders, and the receptacle of Goods imported thither from forreign parts contrary to Law: In return of which Commodities those of the growth of these Colonies are likewise contrary to Law exported to Forreign parts; All which is likewise much incouraged by their not admitting appeals as aforesaide.

That by raising and lowering their coin from time to time, to their particular advantage, and to the prejudice of other Colonies, By exempting their Inhabitants from Duties and Customes to which the other Colonies are subject, and by Harbouring of Servants and fugitives, these Governments tend greatly to the undermining the Trade and Welfare of the other Plantations, and seduce and draw away the People thereof; By which Diminution of Hands the rest of the Colonies more beneficial to England do very much suffer

That these Independent Colonies do turn the Course of Trade to the Promoting and proprogating woolen and other Manufactures proper to England, instead of applying their thoughts and Endeavours to the production of such commodities as are fit to be encouraged in these parts according to the true design and intention of such settlements.

That they do not in general take any due care for their own defence and security against an Enemy, either in Building Forts or providing their Inhabitants with sufficient Armes and Amunition, in case they should be attacked, which is every day more and more to be apprehended, considering how the French power encreases in those parts.

That this cheifly arises from the ill use they make of the powers entrusted to them by their Charters, and the Independency which they pretend to, and that each Government is obliged only to defend its self without any consideration had of their Neighbours, or of the general preservation of the whole.

That many of them have not a regular militia and some (particularly the Colonies of East and West New Jersey) are no otherwise at present than in a state of Anarchy and confusion.

And because the care of these and other great mischiefs in your Majesties Plantations and Colonies aforesaid, and the introducing such an administration of Government and fit regulation of Trade as may put them into a better State of Security and make them duly subservient and usefull to England, does every day become more and more necessary, and that your Majesties frequent Commands to them have not met with due complyance: We humbly conceive it may be expedient that the Charters of the severall Proprietors and others intitling them to absolute Government be reassumed to the Crown and these Colonies put into the same State and dependency as those of your Majesties other Plantations, without prejudice to any man's particular property and freehold. Which being no otherwise so well to be effected as by the Legislative power of this Kingdome. . . .

Expansion and Adjustment, 1660–1713: Green Light for Expansion

SELECTION **30**

The Utrecht Settlement: Treaty of Peace between England and France (Mar. 31, 1713)

In general, the first two intercolonial wars ended quite favorably for the British colonies. The major theater of operations in both wars was Europe, and the fighting in America had been only a sideshow. Still, what had begun as a struggle for national power in Europe could not avoid becoming as well a battle for dominion over North America and the West Indies, and there was sporadic fighting in the West Indies and on the northern frontier between Canada and New England in both wars and along the Carolina-Florida frontier in the second conflict. The settlement at Utrecht in March, 1713, was a major triumph for Great Britain. In view of the significant concessions made by the Spanish and the French in separate treaties, there could no longer be any doubt that Britain had established itself as a major colonial power. British colonists in America could look forward to twenty-five years of peaceful expansion, uninterrupted by major threats from either their French or their Spanish neighbors. The nature of the territorial concessions made by the French can be seen in the excerpts printed below from Charles Jenkinson (comp.), A Collection of All the Treaties of Peace, Alliance, and Commerce between Great-Britain and Other Powers *(three volumes, 1785), volume II, pages 34–37.*

On the diplomatic background to the intercolonial wars, see Max Savelle, "The American Balance of Power and European Diplomacy, 1713–78," in Richard B. Morris (ed.), The Era of the American Revolution *(1939) pages 140–169; on the intercolonial wars, see Howard H. Peckham,* The Colonial Wars, 1689–1762 *(1964).*

X. The said most Christian King shall restore to the kingdom and Queen of Great Britain, to be possessed in full right for ever, the bay and streights of Hudson, together with all lands, seas, sea-coasts, rivers, and places situate in the said bay, and streights, and which belong thereunto, no tracts of land or of sea being excepted, which are at present possessed by the subjects of France. All which, as well as any buildings there made, in the condition they now are, and likewise all fortresses there erected, either before or since the French seized the same, shall within six months from the ratification of the present treaty, or sooner, if possible, be well and truly delivered to the British subjects, having commission from the Queen of Great Britain, to demand and receive the same, entire and un-demolished, together with all the cannon and cannonball which are therein, as also with a quantity of powder, if it be there found, in proportion to the cannon ball, and with the other provision of war usually belonging to cannon. . . .

XI. The abovementioned most Christian King shall take care that satisfaction be given, according to the rule of justice and equity, to the English company trading to the Bay of Hudson, for all damages and spoil done to their colonies, ships, persons, and goods, by the hostile incursions and depredations of the French, in time of peace, an estimate being made thereof by commissaries to be named at the requisition of each party. . . .

XII. The most Christian King shall take care to have delivered to the Queen of Great Britain, on the same day that the ratifications of this treaty shall be exchanged, solemn and authentic letters, or instruments, by virtue whereof it shall appear, that the island of St. Christophers is to be possessed alone hereafter by British subjects, likewise all Nova Scotia or Acadia, with its ancient boundaries, as also the city of Port Royal, now called Annapolis Royal, and all other things in those parts, which depend on the said lands and islands, together with the dominion, propriety, and possession of the said islands, lands, and places, and all right whatsoever, by treaties, or by any other way obtained, which the most Christian King, the crown of France, or any the subjects thereof, have hitherto had to the said islands, lands, and places, and the inhabitants of the same, are yielded and make over to the Queen of Great Britain, and to her crown for ever, as the most Christian King does at present yield and make over all the particulars abovesaid; and that in such ample manner and form, that the subjects of the most Christian King shall hereafter be excluded from all kind of fishing in the said seas, bays, and other places, on the coasts of Nova Scotia, that is to say, on those which lie towards the East, within 30 leagues, beginning from the island commonly called Sable, inclusively, and thence stretching along towards the South west.

XIII. The island called Newfoundland, with the adjacent islands, shall from this time forward, belong of right wholly to Britain; and to that end the town and fortress of Placentia, and whatever other places in the said island, are in the possession of the French, shall be yielded and given up, within seven months from the exchange of the ratifications of this treaty, **225** or sooner if possible, by the most Christian King, to those who have a commission from the Queen of Great Britain, for that purpose. Nor shall the most Christian King, his heirs and successors, or any of their subjects, at any time hereafter, lay claim to any right to the said island and islands, or to any part of it, or them. Moreover, it shall not be lawful for the subjects of France, to fortify any place in the said island of Newfoundland, or to erect any buildings there, besides stages made of boards, and huts necessary and usual for drying of fish; or to resort to the said island, beyond the time necessary for fishing, and drying of fish. But it shall be allowed to the subjects of France, to catch fish, and to dry them on land, in that part only, and in no other besides that, of the said island of Newfoundland, which stretches from the place called cape Bonavista, to the northern point of the said island, and from thence running down by the western side, reaches as far as the place called Point Riche. But the island called Cape Breton, as also all others, both in the mouth of the river of St. Lawrence, and in the gulph of the same name, shall hereafter belong of right to the French, and the most Christian King shall have all manner of liberty to fortify any place, or places there.

XIV. It is expressly provided, that in all the said places and colonies to be yielded and restored by the most Christian King, in persuance of this treaty, the subjects of the said King may have liberty to remove themselves within a year to any other place, as they shall think fit, together with all their moveable effects. But those who are willing to remain there, and to be subjects to the kingdom of Great Britain, are to enjoy the free exercise of their religion, according to the usage of the church of Rome, as far as the laws of Great Britain do allow the same.

XV. The subjects of France inhabiting Canada, and others, shall hereafter give no hindrance or molestation to the five nations or cantons of Indians, subject to the dominion of Great Britain, nor to the other natives of America, who are friends to the same. In like manner, the subjects of Great Britain shall behave themselves peaceably towards the Americans who are subjects or friends to France; and on both sides they shall enjoy full liberty of going and coming on account of trade. As also the natives of those countries shall, with the same liberty, resort, as they please, to the British and French colonies, for promoting trade on one side, and the other, without any molestation or hindrance, either on the part of the British subjects, or of the French. But it is to be exactly and distinctly settled by commissaries, who are, and who ought to be accounted the subjects and friends of Britain or of France. . . .

PART THREE

The Emergence of American Society, 1713–1763

Salutary Neglect
Expansion
The Way to Wealth: The Opportunities
and Problems of Economic Life
The Nature and Ideals of Society
Religion in Flux
Assumptions and Ideals of Politics
Constitutional Tensions
Aspirations, Accomplishments, and Loyalties

he Utrecht settlement in 1713 and the Hanoverian accession in 1714 ushered in a new era for Great Britain and its colonies. For twenty-one years, between 1721 and 1742, George I (1714–1727) and George II (1727–1760) entrusted the administration of government to First Minister Sir Robert Walpole. A brilliant politician, he managed to achieve a high degree of domestic stability, maintain harmonious relations with the colonies, and, until the outbreak of the War of Jenkins's Ear with Spain in 1739, preserve the peace. His formula for dealing with the colonies was to let them proceed on their own with a minimum of imperial interference, and during his administration home officials concerned themselves primarily only with colonial matters that were of serious and pressing concern to powerful interest groups in Great Britain and made only a few minor modifications in the colonial system that had been worked out between 1660 and 1713. Nor was there any immediate change in policy after the fall of Walpole in 1742. The War of Jenkins's Ear—which after France's entry on the side of Spain in 1744 merged into a general European War (War of the Austrian Succession in Europe, or King George's War in America) that had been in progress since 1740 and lasted until 1748— prevented imperial officials from undertaking any serious consideration of the internal affairs of the colonies.

For thirty-five years, then, imperial control weighed lightly upon the British colonies in America, and, especially during the long interlude of peace between 1713 and 1739, their expansive energies were permitted free rein. Only one new colony, Georgia (1733), was founded during these years, but thousands of immigrants from not only England but also Scotland, Ireland, and Germany poured into the older colonies, occupied much of the unsettled lands, and contributed to the development of a society that was becoming at once increasingly more diverse and more coherent. Land continued to be the principal economic resource, the means by which the vast majority of colonists secured their livelihoods and sought to increase their fortunes; but with the general expansion of population, settled areas, and towns, there were increasing opportunities in commerce, the crafts, and the professions. Only a chronic shortage of circulating currency and the high cost of labor seemed to limit the degree of economic expansion within the colonies, and the expedient of paper money and the institutions of indentured servitude and, particularly in the colonies south of Pennsylvania, Negro slavery seemed to provide reasonably satisfactory solutions to those problems.

With the reduction of imperial-colonial tensions and the general expansion of economic opportunity came a decrease in the social and psychological instability that had fraught colonial life during the last decades of the seventeenth century. The emergence in every colony of wealthy groups with both the capacity and the desire to assume social and political leadership clarified the lines of social and political authority within the colonies and led to the reaffirmation and cultivation of traditional English individual, social, and political values that helped to give coherence and order to colonial life even when they did not correspond precisely with conditions in the colonies. Moreover, an unusually high rate of social mobility and an open class structure prevented the increasing social differentiation from becoming burdensome to men at the lower end of the social scale, with the result that intracolonial conflict, wherever and whenever it occurred, tended to be between rival groups of wealthy men rather than between social classes. The new American elites expressed their cultural aspirations through the foundation of libraries, colleges, learned societies, theaters, and clubs and their political aspirations through the expansion of the influence of colonial political institutions. Chief among these were

the lower houses of assembly, the representative portions of the legisla-
tures, which existed in every colony, were dominated by the new colonial
elites and steadily acquired prestige and authority in all the colonies
through the middle decades of the eighteenth century.

The reaction among colonials to this phenomenal economic, social, and
political growth was ambivalent. Because it seemed to be accompanied
by a decline in religious zeal and a general weakening of the old theologi-
cal order—especially in such religious centers as New England and Penn-
sylvania—it tended to produce a sense of guilt that was an important
element in stimulating the Great Awakening, the first great American
religious revival, which began in the 1730s and lasted for nearly three
decades. At the same time, it contributed to a growing confidence in the
future of America, a heightened awareness of the importance of the col-
onies to the British Empire, and increasing aspirations for a greater role
within the empire.

But these aspirations came into direct conflict with a new movement for
reforming the empire that gathered momentum in the years immediately
following the conclusion of King George's War. The relaxation of colonial
policy under Walpole did not mean that imperial officials had abandoned
any of the traditional ideals of British colonial policy, and, when it became
clear in the late 1740s that colonial lower houses had acquired sufficient
power to alter the nature of the constitutional relationship between Britain
and the colonies, they embarked upon an intensive, if piecemeal, campaign
to enforce the old ideals. No sooner had this campaign gotten under way,
however, than the outbreak of the French and Indian War (the Seven
Years' War in Europe) in 1754 forced imperial officials to suspend it for
the duration. That the war began in America rather than in Europe was
symbolic of the growing importance of the colonies in the empire as a
whole, and its final outcome—the expulsion of the French from North
America and of the Spanish from Florida as well as the establishment of
British hegemony in Europe, India, and the West Indies—and the colonial
conviction that the colonies had played a major part in the victory con-
spired to produce among colonials both an expanded sense of self-impor-
tance and a surge of British nationalism. In the glow of the great British
victories in 1758 and 1759 and the final conclusion of hostilities by the
Treaty of Paris in 1763, the colonists scarcely noticed that in 1759, as soon

229

*as the victory over the French in Canada had been won and colonial sup-
port for the war effort was no longer vital, imperial authorities had renewed the campaign to bring the colonies under a tighter control and
reduce the power of the lower houses.*

The Emergence of American Society, 1713–1763: Salutary Neglect

SELECTION

A New Tone of Administration:
Charles Delafaye to Francis Nicholson (Jan. 26, 1722)

The new leniency in colonial administration associated with the government of Sir Robert Walpole is illustrated by the advice proffered by Charles Delafaye, secretary to the lords justices in Great Britain, to Francis Nicholson, by this time governor of South Carolina. The letter is reprinted here, with permission, for the first time from the original manuscript in Papers concerning the Governorship of South Carolina, *item 9, b Ms Am 1455, Houghton Library, Harvard University. For additional information, see the references listed in the introduction to Selection 29.*

Dear Sir:

I should not act consistently with the Friendship I always professed for you, should I conceal from you the Complaints I hear among Our Merchants who trade to your parts; 1. That you are depriving the Dissenters under your Government of Priviledges they enjoy by the Original Constitution, by the Laws and by the Customs of that Colony; 2. That you have established Bills of Credit, to the great prejudice of the Merchants here; and 3. That a Sloop being sent in June and another in October last from the Bahama Islands to Carolina, You Seized them in an illegal manner aggravated by Arbitrary and passionate proceedings as forcibly taking away and opening People's Letters and casting Reflections upon persons of Distinction on this Side the Water.

Whatever you are enjoyned by the Laws and by your Instructions, I never doubted but you would perform without respect of Persons, and in That you are certainly Right. But one would not Strain any point where it can be of no Service to our King or Country, and will create Ennemys to one's Self. The Dissenters here are a powerful Body and will you may believe be always ready to represent any Injury done to their Brethen abroad; as to the Bahama Settlement, You know there are People in the Chief Stations in the Admiralty and Board of Trade concerned in it, and one would not personally affront them. I do not mean that in the one case one should give the Dissenters more Encouragement than they have a Right to, or in the other one should countenance or connive at an illegal clandestine Commerce. But on the other hand where it may be done with a due Complyance with the Laws and with His Majesty's Instructions, it is certainly best to keep up Friendship and good Neighbourhood among the Inhabitants of a Colony and between one Plantation and another. The Maxim does in itself proceed from good nature and is certainly Right in politicks especially in the Plantations where the Government should be as Easy and mild as possible to invite people to Settle under it, and where a good understanding should be cultivated between the Several Colonies that they may be better disposed mutually to defend and Assist each other.

CHARLES DELAFAYE

SELECTION

Further Refinements in the Navigation System

Between 1713 and 1763 there were three notable additions to the battery of navigation acts passed during the previous half-century. Like most of the earlier acts, each was both an ad hoc *response to a specific problem and an expression of the imperial conviction that colonial interests had to give way before those of the home country. Two of them followed the example of the Woolen Act of 1699 in trying to limit colonial manufacturing. Passed at the request of British hat makers, the Hat Act of 1732 was designed to stem the rise of a thriving hat industry in the colonies, where, because of their proximity to the sources of beaver skins, hat makers had begun to produce beaver hats more cheaply than their English counterparts. Similarly, the Iron Act of 1750 was intended to channel an old and growing iron industry in the middle colonies into activities that would complement rather than conflict with British manufacturing interests. To that end it sought to discourage colonials from making finished iron products and encourage them to produce raw iron for shipment to the mother country. A victory for British manufacturers of finished iron, this measure was passed over the objections of British manufacturers of raw iron, who wanted to prohibit iron manufacturing in the colonies altogether. The Iron Act was, then, a concession to existing colonial iron manufacturers, who manufactured almost entirely raw-iron products. The Hat Act was effective, but the Iron Act was not.*

A third measure, the Molasses Act of 1733, was without precedent inasmuch as it sought to promote the prosperity of one group of colonies at the expense of another. Since the middle of the seventeenth century, imperial officials had regarded the West Indian colonies as the jewels of the empire. From the mercantilistic point of view they were ideal colonies. Producing mostly sugar and a few other tropical items otherwise available to Britain only from foreign rivals, they annually imported large quantities of British manufactures. During the early years of the eighteenth century, however, the foreign West Indies began to produce sugar more cheaply than the British West Indies and to undersell them on the world market, and New England merchants, who had developed a brisk trade with the West Indies exchanging foodstuffs, forest products, and slaves for sugar and molasses, began to trade increasingly with the foreign islands. The result was that the economic fortunes of the British islands began to decline, and West Indian interests in Britain began to clamor for protection from foreign competition. The Molasses Act was Parliament's response to this situation. Intended to discourage New England trade with the foreign islands by placing prohibitive duties on foreign sugar products, the act would have seriously affected the New England economy had it been enforced. It was not, however, and for the next thirty years it did no more than accustom New England merchants to illicit trade.

Further reading is provided by the references in the introduction to Selection 17.

A. THE HAT ACT (JUNE 1, 1732)*

Cap. XXII

WHEREAS the art and mystery of making hats in Great Britain *hath arrived to great perfection, and considerable quantities of hats manufactured in this kingdom have heretofore been exported to his Majesty's plantations or colonies in America, who have been wholly supplied with hats from* Great Britain; *and whereas great quantities of hats have of late years been made, and the said manufacture is daily increasing in the* British *plantations in* America, *and is from thence exported to foreign markets, which were heretofore supplied from* Great Britain, *and the hatmakers in the said plantations take many apprentices for very small terms, to the discouragement of the said trade, and debasing the said manufacture:* wherefore for preventing the said ill practices for the future, and for promoting and encouraging the trade of making hats in *Great Britain,* be it enacted by the King's most excellent majesty, by and with the advice and consent of the lords spiritual and temporal and commons in this present parliament assembled, and by the authority of the same, That from and after the twenty ninth day of *September* in the year of our Lord one thousand seven hundred and thirty two, no hats or felts whatsoever, dyed or undyed, finished or unfinished, shall be shipt, loaden or put on board any ship or vessel in any place or parts within any of the *British* plantations, upon any pretence whatsoever, by any person or persons whatsoever, and also that no hats or felts, either dyed or undyed, finished

---

* These excerpts are reprinted from Danby Pickering (ed.), *Statutes at Large* (46 vols., 1762–1807), vol. XVI, pp. 304–305, 307–308.

or unfinished, shall be loaden upon any horse, cart or other carriage, to the intent or purpose to be exported, transported, shipped off, carried or conveyed out of any of the said *British* plantations to any other of the *British* plantations, or to any other place whatsoever, by any person or persons whatsoever. . . .

VII. And it is hereby further enacted by the authority aforesaid, That no person residing in any of his Majesty's plantations in *America* shall, from and after the said twenty ninth day of *September* one thousand seven hundred and thirty two, make or cause to be made, any felt or hat of or with any wool or stuff whatsoever, unless he shall have first served as an apprentice in the trade or art of felt-making during the space of seven years at the least; neither shall any felt-maker or hat-maker in any of the said plantations imploy, retain or set to work, in the said art or trade, any person as a journeyman or hired servant, other than such as shall have lawfully served an apprenticeship in the said trade for the space of seven years. . . .

IX. Provided always, That nothing in this act contained shall extend to charge any person or persons lawfully exercising the said art, with any penalty or forfeiture for setting or using his or their own son or sons to the making or working hats or felts in his or their own house or houses, so as every such son or sons be bound by indenture of apprenticeship, for the term of seven years at the least, which term shall not be to expire before he shall be of the full age of twenty one years. . . .

X. Provided also, and be it enacted by the authority aforesaid, That every felt-maker residing in the said plantations, who at the beginning of this present session of parliament was a maker or worker of hats or felts, and being an householder, and likewise all such as were at the beginning of this present session apprentices, covenant servants, or journeymen in the same art or mystery of felt-making so as such apprentices serve or make up their respective apprenticeships, shall and may continue and exercise the trade or art of making hats and felts in the said plantations, although the same persons were not bound apprentices to the same art for the term of seven years; any thing in this act to the contrary notwithstanding. . . .

B. THE MOLASSES ACT (MAY 17, 1733)*

WHEREAS the welfare and prosperity of your Majesty's sugar colonies in America *are of the greatest consequence and importance to the trade, navigation and strength of this kingdom: and whereas the planters of the said sugar colonies have of late years fallen under such great discouragements, that they are unable to improve or carry on the sugar trade upon an equal footing with the foreign sugar colonies, without some advantage and relief be given to them from* Great Britain: *for remedy whereof, and*

* These excerpts are reprinted from Pickering *Statutes at Large,* vol. XVI, p. 374.

for the good and welfare of your Majesty's subjects . . . be it enacted . . . That from and after the twenty fifth day of *December* one thousand seven hundred and thirty three, there shall be raised, levied, collected and paid, unto and for the use of his Majesty . . . upon all rum or spirits of the produce or manufacture of any of the colonies or plantations in *America*, not in the possession or under the dominion of his Majesty . . . which at any time or times within or during the continuance of this act, shall be imported or brought into any of the colonies or plantations in *America*, which now are or hereafter may be in the possession or under the dominion of his Majesty . . . the sum of nine pence, money of *Great Britain*, to be paid according to the proportion and value of five shillings and six pence the ounce in silver, for every gallon thereof, and after that rate for any greater or lesser quantity; and upon all molasses or syrups of such foreign produce or manufacture as aforesaid, which shall be imported or brought into any of the said colonies or plantations of or belonging to his Majesty, the sum of six pence of like money for every gallon thereof, and after that rate for any greater or lesser quantity; and upon all sugars and paneles of such foreign growth, produce or manufacture as aforesaid, which shall be imported into any of the said colonies or plantations of or belonging to his Majesty, a duty after the rate of five shillings of like money, for every hundred weight *Avoirdupoize,* of the said sugar and paneles, and after that rate for a greater or lesser quantity. . . .

C. THE IRON ACT (APR. 12, 1750)*

WHEREAS the importation of bar iron from his Majesty's colonies in America, into the port of London, *and the importation of pig iron from the said colonies, into any port of* Great Britain, *and the manufacture of such bar and pig iron in* Great Britain, *will be a great advantage not only to the said colonies, but also to this kingdom, by furnishing the manufacturers of iron with a supply of that useful and necessary commodity, and by means thereof large sums of money, now annually paid for iron to foreigners, will be saved to this kingdom, and a greater quantity of the woollen, and other manufactures of* Great Britain, *will be exported to* America, *in exchange for such iron so imported;* be it therefore enacted by the King's most excellent Majesty, by and with the advice and consent of the lords spiritual and temporal, and commons, in this present parliament assembled, and by the authority of the same, That from and after the twenty fourth day of *June,* one thousand seven hundred and fifty, the several and respective subsidies, customs, impositions, rates, and duties, now payable on pig iron, made in and imported from his Majesty's colonies in *America,* into any port of *Great Britain,* shall cease, determine, and be no longer paid; and that from and after the said twenty fourth day of *June,* no subsidy, custom, imposition, rate, or duty whatsoever, shall be payable

* These excerpts are reprinted from Pickering, *Statutes at Large,* vol. XX, pp. 97, 99–100.

upon bar iron made in and imported from the said colonies into the port of *London;* any law, statute, or usage to the contrary thereof in any wise notwithstanding. . . .

IX. And, that pig and bar iron made in his Majesty's colonies in *America* may be further manufactured in this kingdom, be it further enacted by the authority aforesaid, That from and after the twenty fourth day of *June,* one thousand seven hundred and fifty, no mill or other engine for slitting or rolling of iron, or any plateing-forge to work with a tilt hammer, or any furnace for making steel, shall be erected, or after such creation, continued, in any of his Majesty's colonies in *America;* and if any person or persons shall erect, or cause to be erected, or after such erection, continue, or cause to be continued, in any of the said colonies, any such mill, engine, forge, or furnace, every person or persons so offending, shall, for every such mill, engine, forge, or furnace, forfeit the sum of two hundred pounds of lawful money of *Great Britain.*

X. And it is hereby further enacted by the authority aforesaid, That every such mill, engine, forge, or furnace, so erected or continued, contrary to the directions of this act, shall be deemed a common nuisance; and that every governor, lieutenant governor, or commander in chief of any of his Majesty's colonies in *America,* where any such mill, engine, forge, or furnace, shall be erected or continued, shall, upon information to him made and given, upon the oath of any two or more credible witnesses, that any such mill, engine, forge, or furnace, hath been so erected or continued (which oath such governor, lieutenant governor, or commander in chief, is hereby authorized and required to administer) order and cause every such mill, engine, forge, or furnace, to be abated within the space of thirty days next after such information given and made as aforesaid; and if any governor, lieutenant governor, or commander in chief, shall neglect or refuse so to do, within the time herein before limited for that purpose, every such governor, lieutenant governor, or commander in chief, so offending, shall, for every such offence, forfeit the sum of five hundred pounds of lawful money of *Great Britain,* and shall from thenceforth be disabled to hold or enjoy any office of trust or profit under his Majesty, his heirs or successors. . . .

The Emergence of American Society, 1713–1763:
Expansion

SELECTION

Population

*In the early decades of the eighteenth century, two long-term trends in popula-
tion development began to emerge. The first was a phenomenally rapid growth
rate, and the second was the appearance of an increasing number of non-
English immigrants. As Table A indicates, after 1700 the population doubled
roughly every twenty years. A large part of this increase was natural, but there
was also a constant stream of immigrants from England, Scotland, Ireland, and
Germany as the imperial government officially began to encourage foreigners
to settle in America and as the British colonies acquired a wide reputation
among Protestant Europeans as a haven for the poor. The extent and importance of the non-English immigration can be judged from Table B, an analysis
of the 1790 census by nationality.*

On population see especially Evarts B. Greene and Virginia D. Harrington,
American Population before the Federal Census of 1790 *(1932), and Stella
Helen Sutherland,* Population Distribution in Colonial America *(1936). Carl
Wittke,* We Who Built America: The Saga of the Immigrant *(second edition,
1964), is the standard work on the non-English immigration.*

TABLE A. ESTIMATED POPULATION OF AMERICAN COLONIES: 1610–1780

Series No.	Colony	1780	1770	1760	1750	1740	1730	1720	1710	1700	1690	1680	1670	1660	1650	1640	1630
1	Total	2,780,369	2,148,076	1,593,625	1,170,760	905,563	629,445	466,185	331,711	250,888	210,372	151,507	111,935	75,058	50,368	26,634	4,646
	WHITE AND NEGRO																
2	Maine (counties)*	49,133	31,257												1,000	900	400
3	New Hampshire	87,802	62,396	39,093	27,505	23,256	10,755	9,375	5,681	4,958	4,164	2,047	1,805	1,555	1,305	1,055	500
4	Vermont	47,620	10,000														
5	Plymouth†										7,424	6,400	5,333	1,980	1,566	1,020	390
6	Massachusetts*†	268,627	235,308	222,600	188,000	151,613	114,116	91,008	62,390	55,941	49,504	39,752	30,000	20,082	14,037	8,932	506
7	Rhode Island	52,946	58,196	45,471	33,226	25,255	16,950	11,680	7,573	5,894	4,224	3,017	2,155	1,539	785	300	
8	Connecticut	206,701	183,881	142,470	111,280	89,580	75,530	58,830	39,450	25,970	21,645	17,246	12,603	7,980	4,139	1,472	
9	New York	210,541	162,920	117,138	76,696	63,665	48,594	36,919	21,625	19,107	13,909	9,830	5,754	4,936	4,116	1,930	350
10	New Jersey	139,627	117,431	93,813	71,393	51,373	37,510	29,818	19,872	14,010	8,000	3,400	1,000				
11	Pennsylvania	327,305	240,057	183,703	119,666	85,637	51,707	30,962	24,450	17,950	11,450	680					
12	Delaware	45,385	35,496	33,250	28,704	19,870	9,170	5,385	3,645	2,470	1,482	1,005	700	540	185		
13	Maryland	245,474	202,599	162,267	141,073	116,093	91,113	66,133	42,741	29,604	24,024	17,904	13,226	8,426	4,504	583	
14	Virginia	538,004	447,016	339,726	231,033	180,440	114,000	87,757	78,281	58,560	53,046	43,596	35,309	27,020	18,731	10,442	2,500
15	North Carolina	270,133	197,200	110,442	72,984	51,760	30,000	21,270	15,120	10,720	7,600	5,430	3,850	1,000			
16	South Carolina	180,000	124,244	94,074	64,000	45,000	30,000	17,048	10,883	5,704	3,900	1,200	200				
17	Georgia	56,071	23,375	9,578	5,200	2,021											
18	Kentucky	45,000	15,700														
19	Tennessee	10,000	1,000														

NEGRO

No.		Total 575,420	459,822	325,806	236,420	150,024	91,021	68,839	44,866	27,817	16,729	6,971	4,535	2,920	1,600	597	60
2	Maine (counties)*	458	475														
3	New Hampshire	541	654	600	550	500	200	170	150	130	100	75	65	50	40	30	
4	Vermont	50	25														
6	Massachusetts*	4,822	4,754	4,866	4,075	3,035	2,780	2,150	1,310	800	400	170	160	422	295	150	‑
7	Rhode Island	‡2,671	3,761	3,468	3,347	2,408	1,648	543	375	300	250	175	115	65	25	15	
8	Connecticut	‡5,885	5,698	3,783	3,010	2,598	1,490	1,093	750	450	200	50	35	25	20		10
9	New York	21,054	19,112	16,340	11,014	8,996	6,956	5,740	2,811	2,256	1,670	1,200	690	600	500	232	
10	New Jersey	10,460	8,220	6,567	5,354	4,366	3,008	2,385	1,332	840	450	200	60				
11	Pennsylvania	7,855	5,761	4,409	2,872	2,055	1,241	2,000	1,575	430	270	25					
12	Delaware	2,996	1,836	1,733	1,496	1,035	478	700	500	135	82	55	40	30	15		
13	Maryland	80,515	63,818	49,004	43,450	24,031	17,220	12,499	7,945	3,227	2,162	1,611	1,190	758	300	20	
14	Virginia	220,582	187,605	140,570	101,452	60,000	30,000	26,559	23,118	16,390	9,345	3,000	2,000	950	405	150	50
15	North Carolina	91,000	69,600	33,554	19,800	11,000	6,000	3,000	900	415	300	210	150	20			
16	South Carolina	97,000	75,178	57,334	39,000	30,000	20,000	12,000	4,100	2,444	1,500	200	30				
17	Georgia	20,831	10,625	3,578	1,000												
18	Kentucky	7,200	2,500														
19	Tennessee	1,500	200														

Series No.	Colony	WHITE AND NEGRO	1620	1610
5	Plymouth		102	
14	Virginia		§2,200	350

*For 1660–1760, Maine Counties included with Massachusetts.
†Plymouth became a part of the Province of Massachusetts in 1691.
‡Includes some Indians.
§Includes 20 Negroes.

SOURCE: *Historical Statistics of the United States, Colonial Times to 1957* (1960), p. 756.

TABLE B. PERCENT DISTRIBUTION OF THE WHITE POPULATION, BY NATIONALITY: 1790

Area	Total	English	Scotch	Irish		German	Dutch	French	Swedish	Spanish	Unassigned
				Ulster	Free State						
Total colonies	100.0	60.9	8.3	6.0	3.7	8.7	3.4	1.7	0.7		6.6
Maine	100.0	60.0	4.5	8.0	3.7	1.3	0.1	1.3			21.1
New Hampshire	100.0	61.0	6.2	4.6	2.9	0.4	0.1	0.7			24.1
Vermont	100.0	76.0	5.1	3.2	1.9	0.2	0.6	0.4			12.6
Massachusetts	100.0	82.0	4.4	2.6	1.3	0.3	0.2	0.8			8.4
Rhode Island	100.0	71.0	5.8	2.0	0.8	0.5	0.4	0.8	0.1		18.6
Connecticut	100.0	67.0	2.2	1.8	1.1	0.3	0.3	0.9			26.4
New York	100.0	52.0	7.0	5.1	3.0	8.2	17.5	3.8	0.5		2.9
New Jersey	100.0	47.0	7.7	6.3	3.2	9.2	16.6	2.4	3.9		3.7
Pennsylvania	100.0	35.3	8.6	11.0	3.5	33.3	1.8	1.8	0.8		3.9
Delaware	100.0	60.0	8.0	6.3	5.4	1.1	4.3	1.6	8.9		*4.4
Maryland and District of Columbia	100.0	64.5	7.6	5.8	6.5	11.7	0.5	1.2	0.5		1.7
Virginia and West Virginia	100.0	68.5	10.2	6.2	5.5	6.8	0.3	1.5	0.6		.9
North Carolina	100.0	66.0	14.8	5.7	5.4	4.7	0.3	1.7	0.2		1.2
South Carolina	100.0	60.2	15.1	9.4	4.4	5.0	0.4	3.9	0.2		1.4
Georgia	100.0	57.4	15.5	11.5	3.8	7.6	0.2	2.3	0.6		1.1
Kentucky and Tennessee	100.0	57.9	10.0	7.0	5.2	14.0	1.3	2.2	0.5		1.9
OTHER AREAS											
Northwest Territory	100.0	29.8	4.1	2.9	1.8	4.3		57.1			1.7
Spanish, United States	100.0	2.5	0.3	0.2	0.1	0.4				96.5	
French, United States	100.0	11.2	1.6	1.1	0.7	8.7		64.2		12.5	

*Corrected figure; does not agree with source.
SOURCE: *Historical Statistics of the United States, Colonial Times to 1957* (1960), p. 756.

SELECTION

The Process of Americanization:
Michel-Guillaume Jean de Crèvecoeur,
"Letters from an American Farmer" (1782)

*What British America meant to new immigrants, how they were transformed
from Europeans into Americans, and how such a heterogeneous mixture became one people are movingly described in the following passages by Michel-
Guillaume Jean de Crèvecoeur (1735–1813), a Frenchman who came with the
French Army to America during the French and Indian War and subsequently
settled in New York. His* Letters from an American Farmer *was first published
in London in 1782, although his remarks are applicable to both earlier and later
periods. The following excerpts from his third letter are reprinted from the
edition edited by Ludwig Lewisohn (1904), pages 48–56. For further reading,
see the references listed in the introduction to Selection 33.*

I wish I could be acquainted with the feelings and thoughts which
must agitate the heart and present themselves to the mind of an
enlightened Englishman, when he first lands on this continent. He must
greatly rejoice that he lived at a time to see this fair country discovered
and settled; he must necessarily feel a share of national pride, when he
views the chain of settlements which embellishes these extended shores.
When he says to himself, this is the work of my countrymen, who, when
convulsed by factions, afflicted by a variety of miseries and wants, restless
and impatient, took refuge here. They brought along with them their national genius, to which they principally owe what liberty they enjoy, and
what substance they possess. Here he sees the industry of his native country displayed in a new manner, and traces in their works the embrios of
all the arts, sciences, and ingenuity which flourish in Europe. Here he
beholds fair cities, substantial villages, extensive fields, an immense country filled with decent houses, good roads, orchards, meadows, and bridges,
where an hundred years ago all was wild, woody and uncultivated! What
a train of pleasing ideas this fair spectacle must suggest; it is a prospect
which must inspire a good citizen with the most heartfelt pleasure. The
difficulty consists in the manner of viewing so extensive a scene. He is
arrived on a new continent; a modern society offers itself to his contemplation, different from what he had hitherto seen. It is not composed, as in
Europe, of great lords who possess every thing, and of a herd of people

who have nothing. Here are no aristocratical families, no courts, no kings, no bishops, no ecclesiastical dominion, no invisible power giving to a few a very visible one; no great manufacturers employing thousands, no great refinements of luxury. The rich and the poor are not so far removed from each other as they are in Europe. Some few towns excepted, we are all tillers of the earth, from Nova Scotia to West Florida. We are a people of cultivators, scattered over an immense territory, communicating with each other by means of good roads and navigable rivers, united by the silken bands of mild government, all respecting the laws, without dreading their power, because they are equitable. We are all animated with the spirit of an industry which is unfettered and unrestrained, because each person works for himself. If he travels through our rural districts he views not the hostile castle, and the haughty mansion, contrasted with the clay-built hut and miserable cabbin, where cattle and men help to keep each other warm, and dwell in meanness, smoke, and indigence. A pleasing uniformity of decent competence appears throughout our habitations. The meanest of our log-houses is a dry and comfortable habitation. Lawyer or merchant are the fairest titles our towns afford; that of a farmer is the only appellation of the rural inhabitants of our country. It must take some time ere he can reconcile himself to our dictionary, which is but short in words of dignity, and names of honour. There, on a Sunday, he sees a congregation of respectable farmers and their wives, all clad in neat homespun, well mounted, or riding in their own humble wagons. There is not among them an esquire, saving the unlettered magistrate. There he sees a parson as simple as his flock, a farmer who does not riot on the labour of others. We have no princes, for whom we toil, starve, and bleed: we are the most perfect society now existing in the world. Here man is free as he ought to be; nor is this pleasing equality so transitory as many others are. Many ages will not see the shores of our great lakes replenished with inland nations, nor the unknown bounds of North America entirely peopled. Who can tell how far it extends? Who can tell the millions of men whom it will feed and contain? for no European foot has as yet travelled half the extent of this mighty continent!

The next wish of this traveller will be to know whence came all these people? they are a mixture of English, Scotch, Irish, French, Dutch, Germans, and Swedes. From this promiscuous breed, that race now called Americans have arisen. The eastern provinces must indeed be excepted, as being the unmixed descendents of Englishmen. I have heard many wish that they had been more intermixed also: for my part, I am no wisher, and think it much better as it has happened. They exhibit a most conspicuous figure in this great and variegated picture; they too enter for a great share in the pleasing perspective displayed in these thirteen provinces. I know it is fashionable to reflect on them, but I respect them for what they have done; for the accuracy and wisdom with which they have settled their territory; for the decency of their manners; for their early love of letters; their ancient college, the first in this hemisphere; for their industry; which to me who am but a farmer, is the criterion of everything.

There never was a people, situated as they are, who with so ungrateful a soil have done more in so short a time. Do you think that the monarchical ingredients which are more prevalent in other governments, have purged them from all foul stains? Their histories assert the contrary.

In this great American asylum, the poor of Europe have by some means met together, and in consequence of various causes; to what purpose should they ask one another what countrymen they are? Alas, two thirds of them had no country. Can a wretch who wanders about, who works and starves, whose life is a continual scene of sore affliction or pinching penury; can that man call England or any other kingdom his country? A country that had no bread for him, whose fields procured him no harvest, who met with nothing but the frowns of the rich, the severity of the laws, with jails and punishments; who owned not a single foot of the extensive surface of this planet? No! urged by a variety of motives, here they came. Every thing has tended to regenerate them; new laws, a new mode of living, a new social system; here they are become men: in Europe they were as so many useless plants, wanting vegitative mould, and refreshing showers; they withered, and were mowed down by want, hunger, and war; but now by the power of transplantation, like all other plants they have taken root and flourished! Formerly they were not numbered in any civil lists of their country, except in those of the poor; here they rank as citizens. By what invisible power has this surprising metamorphosis been performed? By that of the laws and that of their industry. The laws, the indulgent laws, protect them as they arrive, stamping on them the symbol of adoption; they receive ample rewards for their labours; these accumulated rewards procure them lands; those lands confer on them the title of freemen, and to that title every benefit is affixed which men can possibly require. This is the great operation daily performed by our laws. From whence proceed these laws? From our government. Whence the government? It is derived from the original genius and strong desire of the people ratified and confirmed by the crown. . . .

What attachment can a poor European emigrant have for a country where he had nothing? The knowledge of the language, the love of a few kindred as poor as himself, were the only cords that tied him: his country is now that which gives him land, bread, protection, and consequence: *Ubi panis ibi patria*, is the motto of all emigrants. What then is the American, this new man? He is either an European, or the descendant of an European, hence that strange mixture of blood, which you will find in no other country. I could point out to you a family whose grandfather was an Englishman, whose wife was Dutch, whose son married a French woman, and whose present four sons have now four wives of different nations. *He* is an American, who leaving behind him all his ancient prejudices and manners, receives new ones from the new mode of life he has embraced, the new government he obeys, and the new rank he holds. He becomes an American by being received in the broad lap of our great *Alma Mater.* Here individuals of all nations are melted into a new race of men, whose labours and posterity will one day cause great changes in the world. Americans are the western pilgrims, who are carrying along with them that great mass of arts, sciences, vigour, and industry which began long since in the east; they will finish the great circle. The Americans were once scattered all over Europe; here they are incorporated into one of the finest systems of population which has ever appeared, and which will hereafter become distinct by the power of the different climates they inhabit. The American ought therefore to love this country much better than that wherein either he or his forefathers were born. Here the rewards of his industry follow with equal steps the progress of his labour; his labour is founded on the basis of nature, *self-interest;* can it want a stronger allurement? Wives and children, who before in vain demanded of him a morsel of bread, now, fat and frolicsome, gladly help their father to clear those fields whence exuberant crops are to arise to feed and to clothe them all; without any part being claimed, either by a despotic prince, a rich abbot, or a mighty lord. Here religion demands but little of him; a small voluntary salary to the minister, and gratitude to God; can he refuse these? The American is a new man, who acts upon new principles; he must therefore entertain new ideas, and form new opinions. From involuntary idleness, servile dependence, penury, and useless labour, he has passed to toils of a very different nature, rewarded by ample subsistence.—This is an American. . . .

SELECTION

A Charitable Project: James Oglethorpe, "Some Account of the Designs of the Trustees for Establishing the Colony of Georgia" (1733)

Georgia was the only new colony founded on the North American mainland between 1713 and 1763. Carved out of an unsettled area between the Savannah and Altamaha Rivers that had formerly been part of Carolina, it was conceived of by imperial officials as a buffer colony, a defensive outpost between South Carolina and Spanish Florida, and it was largely with this end in mind that Parliament broke all precedents and poured large sums of money into the colony for defense and development. Never before had the British government contributed directly to the expenses of establishing colonies. For the trustees of Georgia, humanitarian motives weighed much more heavily than strategic ones. They thought of the colony largely as a philanthropic undertaking, a haven for debtors and other unfortunates in which there would be no rum, slaves, or large estates. Their intentions as well as their general conception of what the colony should be may be seen from the following excerpts from a promotional pamphlet, Some Account of the Designs of the Trustees for Establishing the Colony of Georgia, *reprinted from Peter Force (comp.),* Tracts and Other Papers *(four volumes, 1836–1846), volume I, number 2, pages 4–7. First published in London in 1733, it was written by James Oglethorpe (1696–1785), a trustee and leading figure in the first settlement of the colony. By the charter of June 20, 1732, the trustees were to hold the colony in trust for tweny-one years, at the end of which time it was to revert to the Crown. Although they worked diligently to make the colony a success, their efforts must be regarded as a failure. Only after Georgia had passed into the hands of the Crown in 1752 did the colony begin to prosper.*

On the founding and early history of Georgia, see especially Trevor Reese, Colonial Georgia: A Study in British Imperial Policy in the Eighteenth Century *(1963), and W. W. Abbot,* The Royal Governors of Georgia, 1754–1775 *(1959).*

I**n** *America* there are fertile lands sufficient to subsist all the useless Poor in *England,* and distressed Protestants in Europe; yet Thousands starve for want of mere sustenance. The distance makes it difficult to get thither. The same want that renders men useless here, prevents their paying their passage; and if others pay it for 'em, they become servants, or rather slaves for years to those who have defrayed the expense. Therefore, money for passage is necessary, but is not the only want; for if people were set down in America, and the land before them, they must cut down trees, build houses, fortify towns, dig and sow the land before they can get in a harvest; and till then, they must be provided with food, and kept together, that they may be assistant to each other for their natural support and protection.

The Romans esteemed the sending forth of Colonies, among their noblest works; they observed that Rome, as she increased in power and empire, drew together such a conflux of people from all parts that she found herself over-burdened with their number, and the government brought under an incapacity to provide for them, or keep them in order. Necessity, the mother of invention, suggested to them an expedient, which at once gave ease to the capital, and increased the wealth and number of industrious citizens, by lessening the useless and unruly multitude; and by planting them in colonies on the frontiers of their empire, gave a new strength to the whole; and *This* they looked upon to be so considerable a service to the commonwealth, that they created peculiar officers for the establishment of such colonies, and the expence was defrayed out of the public treasury.

From the Charter. His Majesty having taken into his consideration, the miserable circumstances of many of his own poor subjects, ready to perish for want: as likewise the distresses of many poor foreigners, who would take refuge here from persecution; and having a Princely regard to the great danger the southern frontiers of South Carolina are exposed to, by reason of the small number of white inhabitants there, hath, out of his Fatherly compassion towards his subjects, been graciously pleased to grant a charter for incorporating a number of gentlemen by the name of *The Trustees for establishing the Colony of Georgia in America.* They are impowered to collect benefactions; and lay them out in cloathing, arming, sending over, and supporting colonies of the poor, whether subjects or foreigners, in Georgia. And his Majesty farther grants all his lands between the rivers *Savannah and Alatamaha,* which he erects into a Province by the name of GEORGIA, unto the Trustees, in trust for the poor, and for the better support of the Colony. At the desire of the Gentlemen, there are clauses in the Charter, restraining them and their successors from receiving any salary, fee, perquisite, or profit, whatsoever, by or from this undertaking; and also from receiving any grant of lands within the said district, to themselves, or in trust for them. There are farther clauses granting to the Trustees proper powers for establishing and governing the Colony, and liberty of conscience to all who shall settle there.

The Trustees intend to relieve such unfortunate persons as cannot subsist here, and establish them in an orderly manner, so as to form a well regulated town. As far as their fund goes, they will defray the charge of their passage to Georgia; give them necessaries, cattle, land, and subsistence, till such time as they can build their houses and clear some of their land. They rely for success, first on the goodness of Providence, next on the compassionate disposition of the people of England; and, they doubt not, that much will be spared from luxury, and superfluous expenses, by generous tempers, when such an opportunity is offered them by the giving of £20 to provide for a man or woman, or £10 to a child for ever.

In order to prevent the benefaction given to this purpose, from ever being misapplied; and to keep up, as far as human Precaution can, a spirit of Disinterestedness, the Trustees have established the following method: That, each Benefactor may know what he has contributed is safely lodged, and justly accounted for, all money given will be deposited in the Bank of England; and entries made of every benefaction, in a book to be kept for that purpose by the Trustees; or, if concealed, the names of those, by whose hands they sent their money. There are to be annual accounts of all the money received, and how the same has been disposed of, laid before the Lord High Chancellor, the Lord Chief Justice of the King's Bench, the Master of the Rolls, the Lord Chief Justice of the Common Pleas, and the Lord Chief Baron of the Exchequer, or two of them, will be transmitted to every considerable Benefactor.

By such a Colony, many families, who would otherwise starve, will be provided for, and made masters of houses and lands; the people in Great Britain to whom these necessitous families were a burthen, will be relieved; numbers of manufacturers will be here employed, for supplying them with clothes, working tools, and other necessaries; and by giving refuge to the distressed Saltzburghers, and other persecuted Protestants, the power of Britain, as a reward for its hospitality, will be encreased by the addition of so many religious and industrious subjects.

The Colony of *Georgia* lying about the same latitude with part of *China, Persia, Palestine,* and the *Madeiras,* it is highly probable that when hereafter it shall be well-peopled and rightly cultivated, ENGLAND may be supplied from thence with raw Silk, Wine, Oil, Dyes, Drugs, and many other materials for manufactures, which she is obliged to purchase from Southern countries. As towns are established and grow populous along the rivers Savannah and Alatamaha, they will make such a barrier as will render the southern frontier of the British Colonies on the Continent of America, safe from Indian and other enemies.

All human affairs are so subject to chance, that there is no answering for events; yet from reason and the nature of things, it may be concluded, that the riches and also the number of the inhabitants in *Great Britain* will be increased, by importing at a cheap rate from this new Colony, the materials requisite for carrying on in Britain several manufactures. For our Manufacturers will be encouraged to marry and multiply, when they find themselves in circumstances to provide for their families, which must necessarily be the happy effect of the increase and cheapness of our materials of those Manufactures, which at present we purchase with our money from foreign countries, at dear rates; and also many people will find employment here, on account such farther demands by the people of this Colony, for those manufactures which are made for the produce of our own country; and, as has been justly observed, the people will always abound where there is full employment for them.

CHRISTIANITY will be extended by the execution of this design; since, the good discipline established by the Society, will reform the manners of those miserable objects, who shall be by them subsisted; and the example of a whole Colony, who shall behave in a just, moral, and religious manner, will contribute greatly towards the conversion of the Indians, and taking off the prejudices received from the profligate lives of such who have scarce any thing of Christianity but the name.

The Trustees in their general meetings, will consider of the most prudent methods for effectually establishing a regular Colony; and that it may be done, is demonstrable. Under what difficulties, was *Virginia* planted?—the coast and climate then unknown; the Indians numerous, and at enmity with the first Planters, who were forced to fetch all provisions from England; yet it is grown a mighty Province, and the Revenue receives £100,000 for duties upon the goods that they send yearly home. Within this 50 years, *Pennsylvania* was as much a forest as *Georgia* is now; and in these few years, by the wise œconomy of William Penn, and those who assisted him, it now gives food to 80,000 inhabitants, and can boast of as fine a City as most in Europe.

This new Colony is more likely to succeed than either of the former were, since Carolina abounds with provisions, the climate is known, and there are men to instruct in the seasons and nature of cultivating the soil. There are but few *Indian* families within 400 miles; and those, in perfect amity with the English:—*Port Royal* (the station of his Majesty's ships) is within 30, and *Charlestown* (a great mart) is within 120 miles. If the Colony is attacked, it may be relieved by sea, from Port Royal, or the Bahamas; and the Militia of South Carolina is ready to support it, by land.

For the continuing the relief which is now given, there will be lands reserved in the Colony; and the benefit arising from them is to go to the carrying on of the trust. So that, at the same time, the money by being laid out preserves the lives of the poor, and makes a comfortable provision for those whose expenses are by it defrayed; their labor in improving their own lands, will make the adjoining reserved lands valuable; and the rents of those reserved lands will be a perpetual fund for the relieving more poor people. So that instead of laying out the money upon lands, with the income thereof to support the poor, this is laying out money upon the poor; and by relieving those who are now unfortunate, raises a fund for the perpetual relief of those who shall be so hereafter.

There is an occasion now offered for every one, to help forward this design; the smallest benefaction will be received, and applied with the utmost care:—every little will do something; and a great number of small benefactions will amount to a sum capable of doing a great deal of good. . . .

SELECTION

The Rise of Cities

With the expansion in population and in the area of occupied land in the colonies came the rise of bustling commercial centers. The growth of the five major cities—Philadelphia, New York, Boston, Charleston, and Newport—can be followed from 1630 to 1775 in Table A. By the end of the colonial period Philadelphia had become the second city in the British Empire. What it looked like and its general character in 1759–1760 are described by Andrew Burnaby (1734–1812), a young English traveler. His Travels through North America *was first published in London in 1775. The most important works on the development of colonial cities are Carl Bridenbaugh,* Cities in the Wilderness: The First Century of Urban Life in America, 1625–1742 *(1938), and* Cities in Revolt: Urban Life in America, 1743–1776 *(1955).*

TABLE A. ESTIMATED POPULATION OF
FIVE LEADING CITIES: 1630–1775

Date	Philadelphia	New York	Boston	Charleston	Newport
1630		300			
1640		400	1,200		96
1650		1,000	2,000		300
1660		2,400	3,000		700
1680		3,200	4,500	700	2,500
1690	4,000	3,900	7,000	1,100	2,600
1700	5,000	5,000	6,700	2,000	2,600
1710	6,500	5,700	9,000	3,000	2,800
1720	10,000	7,000	12,000	3,500	3,800
1730	11,500	8,622	13,000	4,500	4,640
1742	13,000	11,000	16,382	6,800	6,200
1760	23,750	18,000	15,631	8,000	7,500
1775	40,000	25,000	16,000	12,000	11,000

SOURCE: Carl Bridenbaugh, *Cities in the Wilderness* (1938), pages 6, 143, 303, and *Cities in Revolt* (1955), pages 5, 216.

B. A DESCRIPTION OF PHILADELPHIA:
ANDREW BURNABY, "TRAVELS THROUGH
NORTH AMERICA" (1759–1760)*

. . . Philadelphia, if we consider that not eighty years ago the place where it now stands was a wild and uncultivated desert, inhabited by nothing but ravenous beasts, and a savage people, must certainly be the object of every one's wonder and admiration. It is situated upon a tongue of land, a few miles above the confluence of the Delaware and Schuylkill; and contains about 3,000 houses, and 18 or 20,000 inhabitants. It is built north and south upon the banks of the Delaware; and is nearly two miles in length, and three quarters of one in breadth. The streets are laid out with great regularity in parallel lines, intersected by others at right angles, and are handsomely built: on each side there is a pavement of broad stones for foot passengers; and in most of them a causeway in the middle for carriages. Upon dark nights it is well lighted, and watched by a patrol: there are many fair houses, and public edifices in it. The stadt-house is a large, handsome, though heavy building; in this are held the councils, the assemblies, and supreme courts; there are apartments in it also for the accommodation of Indian chiefs or sachems; likewise two libraries, one belonging to the province, the other to a society, which was incorporated about ten years ago, and consists of sixty members. Each member upon admission, subscribed forty shillings; and afterward annually ten. They can alienate their shares, by will or deed, to any person approved by the society. They have a small collection of medals and medallions, and a few other curiosities, such as the skin of a rattle-snake killed at Surinam

* These excerpts are reprinted from the edition edited by Rufus Rockwell Wilson (1904), pp. 88–91.

twelve feet long; and several Northern Indian habits made of furs and skins. At a small distance from the stadt-house, there is another fine library, consisting of a very valuable and chosen collection of books, left by a Mr. Logan; they are chiefly in the learned languages. Near this there is also a noble hospital for lunatics, and other sick persons. Besides these buildings, there are spacious barracks for 17 or 1800 men; a good assembly-room belonging to the society of Free Masons; and eight or ten places of religious worship; viz. two churches, three Quaker meeting-houses, two Presbyterian ditto, one Lutheran church, one Dutch Calvinist ditto, one Swedish ditto, one Romish chapel, one Anabaptist meeting-house, one Moravian ditto: there is also an academy or college, originally built for a tabernacle for Mr. Whitefield. At the south end of the town, upon the river, there is a battery mounting thirty guns, but it is in a state of decay. It was designed to be a check upon privateers. These, with a few alms-houses, and a school-house belonging to the Quakers, are the chief public buildings in Philadelphia. The city is in a very flourishing state, and inhabited by merchants, artists, tradesmen, and persons of all occupations. There is a public market held twice a week, upon Wednesday and Satur-day, almost equal to that of Leadenhall, and a tolerable one every day besides. The streets are crowded with people, and the river with vessels. Houses are so dear, that they will let for 100 l. currency per annum; and lots, not above thirty feet in breadth, and a hundred in length, in advan-tageous situations, will sell for 1,000 l. sterling. There are several docks upon the river, and about twenty-five vessels are built there annually. I counted upon the stocks at one time no less than seventeen, many of them three-masted vessels.

Can the mind have a greater pleasure than in contemplating the rise and progress of cities and kingdoms? Than in perceiving a rich and opulent state arising out of a small settlement or colony? . . .

SELECTION

The Promises and Consequences of Growth: Benjamin Franklin, "Observations concerning the Increase of Mankind and the Peopling of Countries" (1751)

Better than any of his contemporaries, Benjamin Franklin (1706–1790), who somehow among his extensive business, political, and cultural activities found time to comment on just about every aspect of American life, understood the meaning of the colonies' rapid population growth for the future of both the colonies and the British Empire as a whole. Franklin's thoughts on the subject are presented in his essay Observations concerning the Increase of Mankind and the Peopling of Countries, *written in 1751 to convince imperial officials not to prohibit colonial manufactures and first published in 1755 anonymously as an appendix to a pamphlet written by William Clarke,* Observations on the Late and Present Conduct of the French. *The following excerpts from the essay are reprinted from Jared Sparks (ed.),* The Works of Benjamin Franklin *(ten volumes, 1840), volume II, pages 311–314, 319–320. For further reading, see Alfred Owen Aldridge, "Franklin as Demographer,"* Journal of Economic History, *volume 9 (1949), pages 25–44, and Norman E. Hines, "Benjamin Franklin on Population: A Reexamination,"* Economic History, *volume 3 (1934–1937), pages 388–398. A full biography of Franklin is Carl Van Doren,* Benjamin Franklin *(1938); a shorter study is Verner W. Crane,* Benjamin Franklin and a Rising People *(1954).*

1. TABLES of the proportion of marriages to births, of deaths to births, of marriages to the number of inhabitants, &c., formed on observations made upon the bills of mortality, christenings, &c., of populous cities, will not suit countries; nor will tables formed on observations, made on full-settled old countries, as Europe, suit new countries, as America.

2. For people increase in proportion to the number of marriages, and that is greater in proportion to the ease and convenience of supporting a family. When families can be easily supported, more persons marry, and earlier in life.

3. In cities, where all trades, occupations, and offices are full, many delay marrying till they can see how to bear the charges of a family; which charges are greater in cities, as luxury is more common; many live single during life, and continue servants to families, journeymen to trades, &c.; hence cities do not, by natural generation, supply themselves with inhabitants; the deaths are more than the births.

4. In countries full settled, the case must be nearly the same; all lands being occupied and improved to the height, those who cannot get land must labor for others that have it; when laborers are plenty their wages will be low; by low wages a family is supported with difficulty; this difficulty deters many from marriage, who therefore long continue servants and single. Only as the cities take supplies of people from the country, and thereby make a little more room in the country, marriage is a little more encouraged there, and the births exceed the deaths.

5. Europe is generally full settled with husbandmen, manufacturers, &c., and therefore cannot now much increase in people. America is chiefly occupied by Indians, who subsist mostly by hunting. But as the hunter, of all men, requires the greatest quantity of land from whence to draw his subsistence, (the husbandman subsisting on much less, the gardener on still less, and the manufacturer requiring least of all,) the Europeans found America as fully settled as it well could be by hunters; yet these, having large tracts, were easily prevailed on to part with portions of terri-

tory to the new comers, who did not much interfere with the natives in hunting, and furnished them with many things they wanted.

6. Land being thus plenty in America, and so cheap as that a laboring man, that understands husbandry, can in a short time save money enough to purchase a piece of new land sufficient for a plantation, whereon he may subsist a family, such are not afraid to marry; for, if they even look far enough forward to consider how their children, when grown up, are to be provided for, they see that more land is to be had at rates equally easy, all circumstances considered.

7. Hence marriages in America are more general, and more generally early than in Europe. And if it is reckoned there, that there is but one marriage per annum among one hundred persons, perhaps we may here reckon two; and if in Europe they have but four births to a marriage (many of their marriages being late), we may here reckon eight, of which, if one half grow up, and our marriages are made, reckoning one with another, at twenty years of age, our people must at least be doubled every twenty years.

8. But notwithstanding this increase, so vast is the territory of North America, that it will require many ages to settle it fully; and, till it is fully settled, labor will never be cheap here, where no man continues long a laborer for others, but gets a plantation of his own, no man continues long a journeyman to a trade, but goes among those new settlers, and sets up for himself, &c. Hence labor is no cheaper now in Pennsylvania, than it was thirty years ago, though so many thousand laboring people have been imported.

9. The danger therefore of these colonies interfering with their mother country in trades that depend on labor, manufactures, &c., is too remote to require the attention of Great Britain.

10. But in proportion to the increase of the colonies, a vast demand is growing for British manufactures, a glorious market wholly in the power of Britain, in which foreigners cannot interfere, which will increase in a short time even beyond her power of supplying, though her whole trade should be to her colonies; therefore Britain should not too much restrain manufactures in her colonies. A wise and good mother will not do it. To distress is to weaken, and weakening the children weakens the whole family. . . .

22. There is . . . no bound to the prolific nature of plants or animals, but what is made by their crowding and interfering with each other's means of subsistence. Was the face of the earth vacant of other plants, it might be gradually sowed and overspread with one kind only, as, for instance, with fennel; and, were it empty of other inhabitants, it might in a few ages be replenished from one nation only, as, for instance, with Englishmen. Thus, there are supposed to be now upwards of one million English souls in North America, (though it is thought scarce eighty thousand has been brought over sea,) and yet perhaps there is not one the fewer in Britain, but rather many more, on account of the employment the colonies afford to manufacturers at home. This million doubling, suppose but once in twenty-five years, will, in another century, be more

than the people of England, and the greatest number of Englishmen will be on this side the water. What an accession of power to the British empire by sea as well as land! What increase of trade and navigation! What numbers of ships and seamen! We have been here but little more than one hundred years, and yet the force of our privateers in the late war, united, was greater, both in men and guns, than that of the whole British navy in Queen Elizabeth's time. How important an affair then to Britain is the present treaty for settling the bounds between her colonies and the French, and how careful should she be to secure room enough, since on the room depends so much the increase of her people.

23. In fine, a nation well regulated is like a polypus; take away a limb, its place is soon supplied; cut it in two, and each deficient part shall speedily grow out of the part remaining. Thus, if you have room and subsistence enough, as you may, by dividing, make ten polypuses out of one, you may of one make ten nations, equally populous and powerful; or rather increase a nation ten fold in numbers and strength. . . .

The Emergence of American Society, 1713–1763: The Way to Wealth: The Opportunities and Problems of Economic Life

SELECTION **38**

The Catechism of Success: Benjamin Franklin, "The Way to Wealth" (1758)

In the tradition of the early Puritans, ambitious colonial Americans placed enormous importance upon success, and the formula for success, the way to wealth, was, it was widely held, through ceaseless striving and a strict adherence to such traditional individual values as hard work, careful use of time, attention to business, frugality, humility, simplicity, honesty, prudence, and sobriety. The classic statement of this belief, which was at the heart of colonial economic activity, came from the pen of Benjamin Franklin, first appeared as the preface to his Almanack, Poor Richard Improved *for 1758, and is reprinted below in full from Jared Sparks (ed.),* The Works of Benjamin Franklin *(ten volumes, 1840), volume II, pages 94–103. An excellent case study of the colonial economic ethic as it was manifested among Pennsylvania Quakers is Frederick B. Tolles,* Meeting House and Counting House: The Quaker Merchants of Colonial Philadelphia, 1682–1763 *(1948).*

Courteous Reader,

I HAVE heard, that nothing gives an author so great pleasure as to find his works respectfully quoted by others. Judge, then, how much I must have been gratified by an incident I am going to relate to you. I stopped my horse lately, where a great number of people were collected at an auction of merchants' goods. The hour of the sale not being come, they were conversing on the badness of the times; and one of the company called to a plain, clean, old man, with white locks, "Pray, Father Abraham, what think you of the times? Will not these heavy taxes quite ruin the country? How shall we ever be able to pay them? What would you advise us to?" Father Abraham stood up, and replied, "If you would have my advice, I will give it you in short; for *A word to the wise is enough*, as Poor Richard says." They joined in desiring him to speak his mind, and gathering round him, he proceeded as follows.

"Friends," said he, "the taxes are indeed very heavy, and, if those laid on by the government were the only ones we had to pay, we might more easily discharge them; but we have many others, and much more grievous to some of us. We are taxed twice as much by our idleness,

254

three times as much by our pride, and four times as much by our folly; and from these taxes the commissioners cannot ease or deliver us, by allowing an abatement. However, let us hearken to good advice, and something may be done for us; *God helps them that helps themselves,* as Poor Richard says.

"I. It would be thought a hard government, that should tax its people one-tenth part of their time, to be employed in its service; but idleness taxes many of us much more; sloth, by bringing on diseases, absolutely shortens life. *Sloth, like rust, consumes faster than labor wears; while the used key is always bright,* as Poor Richard says. *But dost thou love life, then do not squander time, for that is the stuff life is made of,* as Poor Richard says. How much more than is necessary do we spend in sleep, forgetting, that *The sleeping fox catches no poultry,* and that *There will be sleeping enough in the grave,* as Poor Richard says.

"*If time be of all things the most precious, wasting time must be,* as Poor Richard says, *the greatest prodigality;* since, as he elsewhere tells us, *Lost time is never found again; and what we call time enough, always proves little enough.* Let us then up and be doing, and doing to the purpose; so by diligence shall we do more with less perplexity. *Sloth makes all things difficult, but industry all easy;* and *He that riseth late must trot all day, and shall scarce overtake his business at night;* while *Laziness travels so slowly, that Poverty soon overtakes him. Drive thy business, let not that drive thee;* and *Early to bed, and early to rise, makes a man healthy, wealthy, and wise,* as Poor Richard says.

"So what signifies wishing and hoping for better times? We may make these times better, if we bestir ourselves. *Industry need not wish, and he that lives upon hopes will die fasting. There are no gains without pains; then help, hands, for I have no lands;* or, if I have, they are smartly taxed. *He that hath a trade hath an estate; and he that hath a calling, hath an office of profit and honor,* as Poor Richard says; but then the trade must be worked at, and the calling followed, or neither the estate nor the office will enable us to pay our taxes. If we are industrious, we shall never starve; for, *At the working man's house hunger looks in, but dares not enter.* Nor will the bailiff or the constable enter, for *Industry pays debts, while despair increaseth them.* What though you have found no treasure, nor has any rich relation left you a legacy, *Diligence is the mother of good luck, and God gives all things to industry. Then plough deep while sluggards sleep, and you shall have corn to sell and to keep.* Work while it is called to-day, for you know not how much you may be hindered to-morrow. *One to-day is worth two to-morrows,* as Poor Richard says; and further, *Never leave that till to-morrow, which you can do to-day.* If you were a servant, would you not be ashamed that a good master should catch you idle? Are you then your own master? Be ashamed to catch yourself idle, when there is so much to be done for yourself, your family, your country, and your king. Handle your tools without mittens; remember, that *The cat in gloves catches no mice,* as Poor Richard says. It is true there is much to be done, and perhaps you are weak-handed; but stick to it steadily, and you will see great effects; for *Constant dropping wears away stones;* and *By diligence and patience the mouse ate in two the cable;* and *Little strokes fell great oaks.*

"Methinks I hear some of you say, 'Must a man afford himself no leisure?' I will tell thee, my friend, what Poor Richard says, *Employ thy time well, if thou meanest to gain leisure; and, since thou art not sure of a minute, throw not away an hour.* Leisure is time for doing something useful; this leisure the diligent man will obtain, but the lazy man never; for *A life of leisure and a life of laziness are two things. Many, without labor, would live by their wits only, but they break for want of stock;* whereas industry gives comfort, and plenty, and respect. *Fly pleasures, and they will follow you. The diligent spinner has a large shift; and now I have a sheep and a cow, everybody bids me good morrow.*

"II. But with our industry we must likewise be steady, settled, and careful, and oversee our own affairs with our own eyes, and not trust too much to others; for, as Poor Richard says,

> *I never saw an oft-removed tree,*
> *Nor yet an oft-removed family,*
> *That throve so well as those that settled be.*

And again, *Three removes are as bad as a fire;* and again, *Keep thy shop, and thy shop will keep thee;* and again, *If you would have your business done, go; if not, send.* And again,

> *He that by the plough would thrive,*
> *Himself must either hold or drive.*

And again, *The eye of a master will do more work than both his hands;* and again, *Want of care does us more damage than want of knowledge;* and again, *Not to oversee workmen, is to leave them your purse open.* Trusting too much to others' care is the ruin of many; for *In the affairs of this world men are saved, not by faith, but by the want of it;* but a man's own care is profitable; for, *If you would have a faithful servant, and one that you like, serve yourself. A little neglect may breed great mischief; for want of a nail the shoe was lost; for want of a shoe the horse was lost; and for want of a horse the rider was lost, being over-taken and slain by the enemy; all for want of a little care about a horse-shoe nail.*

"III. So much for industry, my friends, and attention to one's own business; but to these we must add frugality, if we would make our industry more certainly successful. A man may, if he knows not how to have as he gets, keep his nose all his life to the grindstone, and die not worth a groat at last. *A fat kitchen makes a lean will;* and

> *Many estates are spent in the getting,*
> *Since women for tea forsook spinning and knitting,*
> *And men for punch forsook hewing and splitting.*

If you would be wealthy, think of saving as well as of getting. The Indies have not made Spain rich, because her outgoes are greater than her incomes.

"Away then with your expensive follies, and you will not then have so much cause to complain of hard times, heavy taxes, and chargeable families; for

> *Women and wine, game and deceit,*
> *Make the wealth small and the want great.*

And further, *What maintains one vice would bring up two children.* You may think, perhaps, that a little tea, or a little punch now and then, diet a little more costly, clothes a little finer, and a little entertainment now and then, can be no great matter; but remember, *Many a little makes a mickle.* Beware of little expenses; *A small leak will sink a great ship,* as Poor Richard says; and again, *Who dainties love, shall beggars prove;* and moreover, *Fools make feasts, and wise men eat them.*

"Here you are all got together at this sale of fineries and knick-knacks. You call them *goods;* but, if you do not take care, they will prove *evils* to some of you. You expect they will be sold cheap, and perhaps they may for less than they cost; but, if you have no occasion for them, they must be dear to you. Remember what Poor Richard says; *Buy what thou hast no need of, and ere long thou shalt sell thy necessaries.* And again, *At a great pennyworth pause a while.* He means, that perhaps the cheapness is apparent only, and not real; or the bargain, by straitening thee in thy business, may do thee more harm than good. For in another place he says, *Many have been ruined by buying good penny-worths.* Again, *It is foolish to lay out money in a purchase of repentence;* and yet this folly is practised every day at auctions, for want of minding the Almanac. Many a one, for the sake of finery on the back, have gone with a hungry belly and half-starved their families. *Silks and satins, scarlet and velvets, put out the kitchen fire,* as Poor Richard says.

"These are not the necessaries of life; they can scarcely be called the conveniences; and yet, only because they look pretty, how many want to have them! By these, and other extravagances, the genteel are reduced to poverty, and forced to borrow of those whom they formerly despised, but who, through industry and frugality, have maintained their standing; in which case it appears plainly, that *A ploughman on his legs is higher than a gentleman on his knees,* as Poor Richard says. Perhaps they have had a small estate left them, which they knew not the getting of; they think, *It is day, and will never be night;* that a little to be spent out of so much is not worth minding; but *Always taking out of the meal-tub, and never putting in, soon comes to the bottom,* as Poor Richard says; and then, *When the well is dry, they know the worth of water.* But this they might have known before, if they had taken his advice. *If you would know the value of money, go and try to borrow some; for he that goes a borrowing goes a sorrowing,* as Poor Richard says; and indeed so does he that lends to such people, when he goes to get it in again. Poor Dick further advises, and says,

> *Fond pride of dress is sure a very curse;*
> *Ere fancy you consult, consult your purse.*

And again, *Pride is as loud a beggar as Want, and a great deal more saucy.* When you have bought one fine thing, you must buy ten more, that your appearance may be all of a piece; but Poor Dick says, *It is easier to suppress the first desire, than to satisfy all that follow it.* And it is as truly folly for the poor to ape the rich, as for the frog to swell in order to equal the ox.

> *Vessels large may venture more,*
> *But little boats should keep near shore.*

It is, however, a folly soon punished; for, as Poor Richard says, *Pride that dines on vanity, sups on contempt. Pride breakfasted with Plenty, dined with Poverty, and supped with Infamy.* And, after all, of what use is this pride of appearance, for which so much is risked, so much is suffered? It cannot promote health, nor ease pains; it makes no increase of merit in the person; it creates envy; it hastens misfortune.

"But what madness must it be to *run in debt* for these superfluities? We are offered by the terms of this sale, six months' credit; and that, perhaps, has induced some of us to attend it, because we cannot spare the ready money, and hope now to be fine without it. But, ah! think what you do when you run in debt; you give to another power over your liberty. If you cannot pay at the time, you will be ashamed to see your creditor; you will be in fear when you speak to him; you will make poor, pitiful, sneaking excuses, and, by degrees, come to lose your veracity, and sink into base, downright lying; for *The second vice is lying, the first is running in debt,* as Poor Richard says; and again, to the same purpose, *Lying rides upon Debt's back;* whereas a free-born Englishman ought not to be ashamed nor afraid to see or speak to any man living. But poverty often deprives a man of all spirit and virtue. *It is hard for an empty bag to stand upright.*

"What would you think of that prince, or of that government, who should issue an edict forbidding you to dress like a gentleman or gentlewoman, on pain of imprisonment or servitude? Would you not say that you were free, have a right to dress as you please, and that such an edict would be a breach of your privileges, and such a government tyrannical? And yet you are about to put yourself under such tyranny, when you run in debt for such dress! Your creditor has authority, at his pleasure, to deprive you of your liberty, by confining you in gaol till you shall be able to pay him. When you have got your bargain, you may, perhaps, think little of payment; but, as Poor Richard says, *Creditors have better memories than debtors; creditors are a superstitious sect, great observers of set days and times.* The day comes round before you are aware, and the demand is made before you are prepared to satisfy it; or, if you bear your debt in mind, the term, which at first seemed so long, will, as it lessens, appear extremely short. Time will seem to have added wings to his heels as well as his shoulders. *Those have a short Lent, who owe money to be paid at Easter.* At present, perhaps, you may think yourselves in thriving circumstances, and that you can bear a little extravagance without injury; but

> *For age and want save while you may;*
> *No morning sun lasts a whole day.*

Gain may be temporary and uncertain, but ever, while you live, expense is constant and certain; and *It is easier to build two chimneys, than to keep one in fuel,* as Poor Richard says; so, *Rather go to bed supperless, than rise in debt.*

> *Get what you can, and what you get hold;*
> *'Tis the stone that will turn all your lead into gold.*

And, when you have got the Philosopher's stone, sure you will no longer complain of bad times, or the difficulty of paying taxes.

"IV. This doctrine, my friends, is reason and wisdom; but, after all, do not depend too much upon your own industry, and frugality, and prudence, though excellent things; for they may all be blasted, without the blessing of Heaven; and, therefore, ask that blessing humbly, and be not uncharitable to those that at present seem to want it, but comfort and help them. Remember, Job suffered, and was afterwards prosperous.

"And now, to conclude, *Experience keeps a dear school, but fools will learn in no other,* as Poor Richard says, and scarce in that; for, it is true, *We may give advice, but we cannot give conduct.* However, remember this, *They that will not be counselled, cannot be helped;* and further, that, *If you will not hear Reason, she will surely rap your knuckles,* as Poor Richard says."

Thus the old gentleman ended his harangue. The people heard it, and approved the doctrine; and immediately practised the contrary, just as if it had been a common sermon; for the auction opened, and they began to buy extravagantly. I found the good man had thoroughly studied my Almanacs, and digested all I had dropped on these topics during the course of twenty-five years. The frequent mention he made of me must have tired any one else; but my vanity was wonderfully delighted with it, though I was conscious that not a tenth part of the wisdom was my own, which he ascribed to me, but rather the gleanings that I had made of the sense of all ages and nations. However, I resolved to be the better for the echo of it; and, though I had at first determined to buy stuff for a new coat, I went away resolved to wear my old one a little longer. Reader, if thou wilt do the same, thy profit will be as great as mine. I am, as ever, thine to serve thee,

                                                                RICHARD SAUNDERS.

SELECTION

The Promise of the Land: "American Husbandry" (1775)

Over 90 per cent of colonial Americans made their living directly from the soil. Land was, at least initially, the greatest resource of Britain's North American mainland colonies. The availability of land was chiefly responsible for the absence of extreme poverty and a permanent landless class in the colonies as well as for a high rate of social mobility. Individuals could count on the land to bring them a measure of personal independence, social standing, and perhaps even wealth and membership in the highest level of colonial society. Uses made of the land varied of course from one section to another. The character of agricultural activity and the kinds of opportunities offered by the land in each of the four major areas—New England, the middle colonies, the Chesapeake colonies, and South Carolina—are described in the following passages from an anonymous treatise, American Husbandry, *published in two volumes in London in 1775. The following excerpts are reprinted from the original London edition, volume I, pages 61–67, 69–71, 73, 184–187, 189, 237–246, 249–251, 426–429. Percy Wells Bidwell and John I. Falconer,* History of Agriculture in the Northern United States, 1620–1860 *(1925), and Lewis Cecil Gray,* History of Agriculture in the Southern United States to 1860 *(two volumes, 1933), are the standard works on colonial agriculture.*

New England

THERE is in many respects a great resemblance between New England and Great Britain. In the best cultivated parts of it, you would not in travelling through the country, know, from its appearance, that you were from home. The face of the country has in general a cultivated, inclosed, and chearful prospect; the farm-houses are well and substantially built, and stand thick; gentlemen's houses appear every where, and have an air of a wealthy and contented people. Poor, strolling, and ragged beggars are scarcely ever to be seen; all the inhabitants of the country appear to be well fed, cloathed, and lodged, nor is any where a greater degree of independency, and liberty to be met with: nor is that distinction of the ranks and classes to be found which we see in Britain, but which is infinitely more apparent in France and other arbitrary countries. . . .

Here therefore we see a sketch of one class of people, that has a minute resemblance to the gentlemen in England who live upon their own estates, but they have in some respects a great superiority: they have more liberty in many instances, and are quite exempt from the overbearing influence of any neighbouring nobleman, which in England is very mischievous to many gentlemen of small fortunes. Further, they pay what may be almost called no taxes; for the increase of people and farms is so great, that the public burthens are constantly dividing; besides their being in all instances remarkably low. This is an advantage to be found no where but in America, for all the rest of the world groans under the oppressive weight which bad governments and absolute monarchs have laid on mankind. They have also the advantage of living in a country where their property is constantly on the increase of value. Trade, navigation, fisheries, increasing population, with other causes, have operated strongly to raise the value of all the estates under cultivation, whose situation is favourable, for in proportion as the wild country is taken up good lands and convenient situations rise in value; till we see they come, near the great towns, to as high a value as in the best parts of Great Britain, for near Boston there are lands worth twenty shillings an acre. Another circumstance, in which the estates of the gentlemen in New England have a great advantage, is that of being exempted from the payment of tythes, and rates for the support of the poor, which in Britain make a vast deduction from the product of an estate. The plenty of timber, and the cheapness of iron, and all materials for building, are also advantages to all country estates of a most valuable nature; in England this article, which is what goes under the general name of repairs, swallows up a large portion of rent, and with those already mentioned, and land-tax, leaves him, out of a large nominal rental, but a small neat income.

With these advantages, the New England gentlemen are enabled to live upon their estates in a genteel, hospitable, and agreeable manner; for the plenty of the necessaries of life makes housekeeping remarkably cheap, and counter-balances the small rents they get for such parts of their estates as they let. This circumstance is owing to the ease of every man setting up for a farmer himself on the unsettled lands: this makes a scarcity of tenants; for those who have money enough to settle a tract of waste land, which is much more flattering than being the tenant of another: one would suppose that such a circumstance would prevent their being a tenant in the country; but this is not the case, low rents and accidents sometimes induce them to live rather than to settle: nor, upon the whole are tenants common in New England, there are more estates that are under the management of over-seers than that are let to tenants.

Upon the whole, we may determine that the country gentlemen of New England are in many respects very fortunately situated, and as well stationed in all respects for living comfortably and at their ease, as any set of people can be: and this circumstance does not extend merely to the points which I have now mentioned, but to another which deserves attention; it is the growth of timber and increased value of forest land: in New-England, any gentlemen may have a grant of whatever land he pleases upon complying with the common terms of settlement, which are the grant of fifty acres for every white person fixed on the estate; this to a person in the country, is a condition so easily performed that they have it in their power to command almost what part of the ungranted land they please: this is an advantage unparalleled in any country of the world except our other colonies. By this means the gentlemen of New England have an opportunity of constantly encreasing their estates. Those of fortune erect saw mills on their new grants, by which means they are enabled to make a very considerable profit by the woods at the same time that they lay the foundation of future estates for their posterity. . . .

The next class of the country inhabitants of which I am to describe is the farmers; but I must previously observe, that by farmers we are to understand not only the men who rent lands of others, but also the little freeholders who live upon their own property, and make much the most considerable part of the whole province. There are the posterity of former settlers, who having taken in tracts of waste land proportioned to their ability, have died and left it to their descendants equally divided among all the children, by the gravelkind custom, which is prevalent throughout this province. These countrymen in general are a very happy people; they enjoy many of the necessaries of life upon their own farms, and what they do not so gain, they have from the sale of their surplus products: it is remarkable to see such numbers of these men in a state of great ease and content, possessing all the necessaries of life, but few of the luxuries of it: they make no distinction in their agriculture from the tenants of the gentlemen, only live more at their ease, and labour with less assiduity. . . .

It is very rarely that any families from the country make a winter residence at Boston for the sake of the small degree of pleasure which that capital affords. I know there are instances of it, but in general the thing is otherwise. The country gentlemen live the year round upon their estates, going to town only when business calls them. And thereby they escape an expence which is equally useless and consuming.

The new settlers upon fixing themselves in their plantations enter at once into the class of these freeholders; but from poverty in the beginning of their undertakings fall naturally into a class below them, unless they begin with a considerable sum of money that raises them in the consideration of their neighbours. There are many of these who begin with such small possessions, that they are some years before they can gain the least exemption from a diligence and active industry that equals any of the farmers of Great Britain. Such men, although they may be in the road of gaining as comfortable a living as any of the old freeholders, yet rather fall into an inferiority to them; not from the manners or constitution of the colony, but from modesty and the natural exertions of a domestic industry.

Respecting the lower classes in New England, there is scarcely any part of the world in which they are better off. The price of labour is very high, and they have with this advantage another no less valuable, of being able to take up a tract of land whenever they are able to settle it. In Britain a servant or labourer may be master of thirty or forty pounds without having it in their power to lay it out in one useful or advantageous purpose; it must be a much larger sum to enable them to hire a farm, but in New England there is no such thing as a man procuring such a sum of money by his industry without his taking a farm and settling upon it. The daily instances of this give an emulation to all the lower classes, and make them point their endeavours with peculiar industry to gain an end which they all esteem so particularly flattering.

This great ease of gaining a farm, renders the lower class of people very industrious; which, with the high price of labour, banishes every thing that has the least appearance of begging, or that wandering, destitute state of poverty, which we see so common in England. A traveller might pass half through the colony without finding, from the appearance of the people, that there was such a thing as a want of money among them. . . .

I have more than once mentioned the high price of labour: this article depends on the circumstance I have now named; where families are so far from being burthensome, men marry very young, and where land is in such plenty, men very soon become farmers, however low they set out in life. Where this is the case, it must at once be evident that the price of labour must be very dear; nothing but a high price will induce men to labour at all, and at the same time it presently puts a conclusion to it by so soon enabling them to take a piece of waste land. By day labourers, which are not common in the colonies, one shilling will do as much in England as half a crown in New England. This makes it necessary to depend principally on servants, and on labourers who article themselves to serve three, five, or seven years, which is always the case with new comers who are in poverty.

Pennsylvania

THIS country is peopled by as happy and free a set of men as any in America. Out of trade there is not much wealth to be found, but at the same time there is very little poverty, and hardly such a thing as a beggar in the province. This is not only a consequence of the plenty of land, and the rate of labour, but also of the principles of the Quakers, who have a considerable share in the government of the country. It is much to the honour of this sect that they support their own poor in all countries, in a manner much more respectable than known in any other religion.

There are some country gentlemen in Pensylvania, who live on their estates in a genteel and expensive manner, but the number is but small; many are found, who make much such a figure as gentlemen in England of three or four hundred pounds a year, but without such a rental; for money is scarce in this country, and all the necessaries and conveniences of life cheap, except labour. But in general the province is inhabited by small freeholders, who live upon a par with great farmers in England; and many little ones who have the necessaries of life and nothing more.

In the settled parts of the colony, there are few situations to be found that are without such a neighbourhood as would satisfy country gentlemen of small estates, or country parsons in Britain. There are, besides Philadelphia, many small towns in which are found societies that render the country agreeable; and the country itself is scattered with gentlemen at moderate distances, who have a social intercourse with each other, besides occasional parties to Philadelphia.

The most considerable of the freeholders that do not however rank with gentlemen, are a set of very sensible, intelligent, and hospitable people, whose company, in one that is mixed, improves rather than lessens the agreeableness of it; a circumstance owing to many of them being foreigners, which even gives something of a polish to the manners when we find ourselves in the midst of a country principally inhabited by another people. The little freeholders (there are not many farmers, except near Philadelphia) are in ease and circumstances much superior to the little farmers in England.

The method of living in Pensylvania in country gentlemen's families, is nearly like that of England: the only business is to ride about the plantation now and then, to see that the overseers are attentive to it; all the rest of the time is filled up with entertaining themselves; country sports, in the parts of the province not fully settled, are in great perfection; they have hunting, but their horses are unequal to those of England; shooting and fishing are much more followed, and are in greater perfection than in England, though every man is allowed both to shoot and fish throughout the province, except the latter in cultivated grounds. . . . It must be at once apparent, that a given income would go much further here than in Britain; this is so strongly a truth, that an income of four or five hundred pounds a year, and a plantation, can hardly be spent without extravagance, or indulging some peculiar expence; whereas that income from an estate in Britain will hardly give a man the appearance of a gentleman. . . .

Virginia and Maryland

The tobacco planters live more like country gentlemen of fortune than any other settlers in America; all of them are spread about the country, their labour being mostly by slaves, who are left to overseers; and the masters live in a state of emulation with one another in buildings, (many of their houses would make no slight figure in the English counties) furniture, wines, dress, diversions, &c. and this to such a degree, that it is rather amazing they should be able to go on with their plantations at all, than they should not make additions to them: such a country life as they lead, in the midst of a profusion of rural sports and diversions, with little to do themselves, and in a climate that seems to create rather than check pleasure, must almost naturally have a strong effect in bringing them to be just such planters, as foxhunters in England make farmers. To live within compass, and to lay out their savings in an annual addition to their culture, requires in the conduct a fixed and settled economy, and a firm determination not to depart from it, at least till a handsome fortune was made. This would not be long, as a slight calculation will shew.

	First year of increase		
	l.	s.	d.
Saving of the last,	175	0	0
Four negroes at 50l.	200	0	0
Implements,	10	0	0
Expences on negroes,	12	0	0
Addition to buildings,	20	0	0
Sundries,	8	0	0
	250	0	0
Produce 20l. a head,	80	0	0
Annual saving,	175	0	0
	255	0	0

	Second year		
Six negroes at 50l.	300	0	0
Implements,	20	0	0
Negroe expences,	30	0	0
Sundries,	10	0	0
	360	0	0
Produce 10 at 20l.	200	0	0
Annual saving,	175	0	0
	375	0	0

	Third year		
Eight negroes at 50l.	400	0	0
Expences on 18, at 3l.	54	0	0
Implements bought, and additional repairs,	30	0	0
Sundries,	16	0	0
Building,	10	0	0
	510	0	0
Produce 18 at 20l.	360	0	0
Annual saving,	175	0	0
	535	0	0

	Fourth year		
Ten negroes at 50l.	500	0	0
Expences, &c. 28 at 3l.	84	0	0
Implements,	40	0	0
Building,	30	0	0
Sundries,	20	0	0
Clearing land,	26	0	0
	600	0	0
Produce 28 at 20l.	560	0	0
Annual saving,	175	0	0
	735	0	0

	Fifth year		
	l.	s.	d.
2000 acres more land patent fees,	40	0	0
Another overseer,	40	0	0
Buildings,	50	0	0
Clearing land,	100	0	0
Implements,	50	0	0
Sundries,	30	0	0
8 negroes at 50l.	400	0	0
Expences on them,	102	0	0
Allow the planter,	48	0	0
	860	0	0
Produce 34 at 20l.	680	0	0
Annual saving,	175	0	0
	855	0	0

	Sixth year		
Overseer,	40	0	0
Clearing land,	50	0	0
Implements,	50	0	0
Sundries,	40	0	0
15 negroes at 50l.	750	0	0
Expences, &c. 49, at 3l.	147	0	0
Allow the planter,	28	0	0
	1095	0	0
Produce 49 at 20l.	980	0	0
Annual saving,	190	0	0
	1170	0	0

	Seventh year: account of the whole plantation		
Province taxes,	40	0	0
Expences on 72 negroes at 3l.	216	0	0
Repairs of implements,	50	0	0
Housekeeping,	300	0	0
Building and furniture,	50	0	0
Overseers,	80	0	0
House servants,	30	0	0
Incidents,	50	0	0
Interest,	94	5	0
	910	5	0

	Produce		
72 negroes at 20l.	1440	0	0
Cattle,	150	0	0
Fruit and sundries,	50	0	0
	1640	0	0
Expences,	910	5	0
Remains,	729	15	0

Hence it appears, that he can either continue the increase of culture, with a view to grow rich as soon as possible; or he may stop, and at the same time that he spends 300l. a year in manufactures, and foreign luxuries, may lay up 729l. 15s. a year: or else he may here begin a second system of increase; taking the annual sum of 729l. for the foundation in the manner before explained, which would soon accumulate into a great income.

To all accounts of that sort, there may be many objections made, in all countries, and in all branches of culture—and it would be the same if the account had been actually realized by a planter; but slight variations should not be attented to: and the greatness of this profit will admit of deductions, according to more accurate ideas, and yet the remainder be far more than sufficient to prove that the poverty of the planters is not necessary to their condition, but merely owing to their extravagant way of living. In most articles of life, a great Virginia planter makes a greater show, and lives more luxuriously than a country gentleman in England, on an estate of three or four thousand pounds a year. The great object I labour to prove, is, that this branch of agriculture, under its present circumstances, of price of negroes, and price of product, is such as will admit of great profit—to the capability of making a considerable fortune; and this advantage to be gained while the planter shall live in the midst of all the conveniences of life, and most of its agreeableness!

The poverty of the planters here, many of them at least, is much talked off, and from thence there has arisen a notion that their husbandry is not profitable: this false idea I have endeavoured to obviate, and to shew that the cause of it has little or no reference to their culture, but to the general luxury, and extravagant way of living which obtains among the planters—a circumstance which ought rather to occasion a contrary conclusion;—a supposition that their agriculture was very valuable; for men without some rich article of product cannot afford, even with the assistance of credit, to live in such a manner: it must be upon the face of it a profitable culture, that will support such luxury, and pay eight per cent. interest on their debts. What common culture in Europe will do this?

The observation I made on settlements in Pensylvania, are applicable in the present instance. It is not so much the profit which the farmer makes on his land, as the ability he has of extending his culture, in proportion to the money he makes. This cannot be done in Britain, nor in any cultivated country, but is the glory of America. If a man makes twenty per cent. on his agriculture in England, and lays by 500l. a year; he can get only four or five per cent. for that saving of 500l. he cannot lay it out in an increase of culture. But let him do the same in America, and he is able every year to increase his husbandry in whatever proportion his money will allow: this is making compound interest of his savings, and will, under a thousand disadvantages, accumulate presently into a considerable fortune, in comparison with the sum the planter first began with. This is a point which should never be forgotten, and in which consists the great superiority of America. It is not sufficiently considered by those who decry the profit of the Virginia planters, because they are not rich. They enjoy advantages which would make any set of men rich; but if instead of applying their money to making use of those advantages, he spends it in temporal enjoyments of living, dress, and equipage, he, nor the by-stander cannot, with any degree of propriety, charge that to the agriculture of the province, which is in fact owing to the private expences of individuals. . . .

In the plantations every man, however low his condition and rank in life, can obtain on demand, and paying the settled fees, whatever land he pleases, provided he engages to settle on it in ten years a certain number of white persons; and when he has got his grant, it is a freehold to him and his posterity for ever. In this circumstance nothing can be more different, or in more direct opposition than the two cases. The wastes in Britain are all private property, generally belonging to men of fortune, who, so far from being ready to make presents of them to whoever demands them, will scarce be prevailed on to let them on long leases: but suppose they gave leases at a trifling rent, they would not build and enclose them, and that is too great an expence here for a new settler, who could build a handsome house in Virginia for less than a beggarly cottage would cost in England. Thus therefore there are many essential reasons for mens preferring the wilds of America to the wastes of Britain, in relation to the state of the land; and the ease and plenty of living makes another object highly advantageous in Virginia, but by no means so in Britain.

The pleasures of being a land owner are so great, and in America the real advantages so numerous, that it is not to be wondered at, that men are so eager to enjoy, that they cross the Atlantic ocean in order to possess them; nor is it judicious to draw comparisons between our British wastes and these, between which there is no analogy in those essential circumstances that are the foundation of the great population of America; and at the same time that this is the case with our waste lands, it is the same with our cultivated ones which are equally different. . . .

South Carolina

. . . no husbandry in Europe can equal this of Carolina; we have no agriculture in England, where larger fortunes are made by it than in any other country, that will pay any thing like this, owing to several circumstances which deserve attention. First, land is so plentiful in America, that the purchase of a very large estate costs but a trifle, and all the annual taxes paid afterwards for ten thousand acres, do not amount to what the window duty in England comes to on a moderate house; no land-tax, no poor's rate, no tythe. This plenty of land, which is at the same time so excellent, enables the planter to proportion his culture every year, to the saving of the preceding, which is the grand circumstance in the increase of his fortune; since it is this which converts simple interest at 5 per cent. with an English farmer, to compound interest at 100 per cent. with an American planter. Were the waste lands of Britain in the same situation as those of America, to be granted to whoever would settle and engage to cultivate them, this would be the case with them; but the profit from the inferiority of the land, and the dearness of labour, would not equal that above stated. As these wastes are private property, and cannot be gained by other people, there is no comparison remains between them; and as to common agriculture, the profit of 20 or 30 per cent. without any ability of increasing the business annually, it cannot be named with this of America. Secondly, the price of labour is incomparably cheaper in Carolina than in Britain: a negro costs 2l. 13s. per annum, to which if we had 2l. 10s. the interest of his prime cost, the total is only 5l. 3s. and as the common calculation is, that one English labourer does as much work as two negroes, a labourer to the planter costs 10l. 6s. a year, whereas to an English farmer he costs from 20l. to 25l. The difference is 125 per cent. this article therefore is very decisive in favour of the planter. Thirdly, we are to remember the peculiar circumstance of the prices of the planter's products and consumptions: his crops, whether of indigo, tobacco, &c. are of a constant high value, the price rising, as it has done indeed for these fifty years; but his consumption of corn, meat, fruit, fowls, game, fish, &c. being chiefly the produce of his own plantation, stand him in little or nothing for his family. The common idea of the article game and fish is, that one Indian, or dextrous negro, will, with his gun and nets, get as much game and fish as five families can eat; and the slaves support themselves in provisions, besides raising the staples mentioned above; but in Britain the servants kept in the house cost the farmers 12l or 15l. a head in board, besides his own housekeeping being in the same articles as those he sells from his farm; so that he cannot in his sale have the advantage of high prices, without being proportionally taxed in his consumption. This point in a large family is of great importance, and would, if calculated for a course of years, be found to amount to a very considerable sum. Besides this great superiority in respect of profit, the pleasing circumstance of being a considerable freeholder, and living in a most plentiful, and even luxurious manner, is a point that has nothing among British farmers for opposition to it.

These three grand articles, plenty of good land free from taxes—cheapness of labour—and dearness of product sold, with cheapness of that consumed, are, united, sufficient to explain the causes of a Carolina planter having such vastly superior opportunities of making a fortune than a British farmer can possibly enjoy. . . .

SELECTION

The Function of Commerce: Amicus Reipublicae, "Trade and Commerce Inculcated" (1731)

If it was the land that provided most colonial Americans with an ample living, it was commerce that made possible the accumulation of great wealth and the rapid growth of the colonial economy. As the anonymous writer Amicus Reipublicae explains in Trade and Commerce Inculcated, *published in Boston in 1731, it was trade that enabled colonials to distribute surplus products to British, European, and West Indian markets; to increase their profits; and to acquire in exchange, goods or items necessary for colonial economic expansion—servants, slaves, crude sugar products, agricultural implements, craftsmen's tools—as well as European luxury manufactures. Much colonial commerce was handled, of course, by British merchants, but especially after 1660 an increasing number of colonials sought their fortunes in trade. By the early decades of the eighteenth century, there were wealthy mercantile communities in all the major colonial seaports in the northern colonies and in Charleston in the South, and colonial merchants operated within vast transatlantic trading networks stretching to Britain, continental Europe, Africa, and the West Indies and handled a sizable proportion of colonial trade. The excerpts reprinted here are from the original edition, pages 2–7. Emory R. Johnson et al.,* History of Domestic and Foreign Commerce of the United States *(two volumes, 1915), is the only comprehensive study of early American commerce, but it should be supplemented by a number of recent case studies, especially Bernard Bailyn,* The New England Merchants in the Seventeenth Century *(1955); James B. Hedges,* The Browns of Providence Plantations: Colonial Years *(1952); and Philip L. White,* The Beekmans of New York in Politics and Commerce, 1647–1877 *(1956).*

. . . Trade or Commerce is principally necessary to a Peoples flourishing in the World.

Altho' the Wealth and Flourishing of a People depends upon Diligent Labour as the Efficient of its Substance, or as a Cause without which it cannot be; yet Labour will not be improved to any considerable degree of Wealth, without the advantage & encouragement of a profitable *Commerce.* In all Labour there is profit, because none will Labour, but with a foresight of Profit; for Profit it the final Cause of Labour; and as there cannot be much profit by Labour without *Commerce,* so *Commerce* is the Cause of Profit by Labour, and consequently the cause of Labour, that is of the abundant Labour in order to Wealth and Flourishing.

The various constitutions and circumstances not only of Countries but also of particular Persons in the same Country, calls for a mutual communication of Goods or useful Commodities to supply each other with what the one wants and the other has to spare.

No Country has in it every thing that is useful and conducive to the comfortable Subsistance of its Inhabitants, independent of exchange or communication with other Countries; nor will the Accommodations, Faculty or Means of any particular Persons, afford them the same but by *Commerce.* And since each Country has but its peculiar Commodities to be raised in abundance, *Commerce* is necessary to a suitable distribution and digesture of it, holding it in value, and therefore necessary to the encouragement and support of Labour.

Trade or *Commerce,* is an Engine of State, to draw men in to business, for the advancing and enobling of the Rich, for the support of the Poor, for the strengthning and fortifying the State; and when it is wisely conducted and vigorously carried on, it is the King of Business for increasing the Wealth, Civil Strength, and Temporal Glory of a People.

Solomon the wise King of *Israel,* by his policy in *Trade,* advanced the Business & Wealth of his Kingdom, filling it with Riches, Strength, Beauty and Magnificence, above all the Kingdoms of the Earth.

Tyrus, the Crowning City, being situate at the entry of the Sea, became the Merchant of the People for many Isles; although seated upon a meer Rock, yet she became Renowned for Temporal Glory & Beauty; many Kingdoms and Countries occupied in her fairs; the Ships of *Tarshish* did sing of her in her markets, for that she was replenished and made very glorious in the midst of the Seas.

Holland (by relation) was such an obscure spot of Earth, as though GOD had reserved it only for a place to dig Turf in for the accommodating of those Countries wherein he hoards up the miseries of the winter. It naturally affording scarcely any one Commodity of use; yet by *Merchandize* and *Trade* it is now become the Storehouse of all those *Merchandizes* that may be collected from the rising to the setting of the Sun, and gives those People a name as large and as high as any Monarch this day on Earth; and this their Glory is owing to their peculiar Policy, good Regulations, Customs, and Restrictions in *Trade;* that being the principal object of their Care and Protection, having little besides to depend upon for their Support; whereas in other Countries, being well accommodated for other business, the *Trade* has been sometimes carelessly neglected and left to private discretion, which has proved the Ruin of all.

It is observable, that such Countries who have had the least dependencies upon other means, have gained such Policy in *Trade,* as to outvie the more Fertile and Productive Countries in Strength, Riches, and Worldly Grandeur.

Hence it is, that *Trade, Merchandize* and *Commerce,* are become the only object and care of the great Princes and Potentates of the Earth, as knowing that the Returns and Effects of Commerce is Riches, and the plenty of all things conducing to the benefit of humane life, for the Supporting of their Crowns and Grandeur, and Fortifying their Countries and Kingdoms with Reputation and Strength. . . .

It is the Bounty, Pomp, and Grandeur, peculiar to a free and vigorous carrying on in *Trade,* that ordinarily makes good Business for Labouring men.

The proper Fees and Immunities of a free and liberal *Commerce,* are very enriching to the Common-Wealth, naturally providing Stores and Plenty for a commodious and profitable carrying on; when with a dull *Trade* plenty makes little profit, but rather a discouragement in business; but as a People advances in Wealth and Worldly Magnificence, so the demand for all kinds of business will be enlarged. It requires much labour and business to furnish the Rich and Noble with their magnificent Buildings, rich Furniture, costly Apparel, and sumptuous Fare; also to provide for and replenish the Store-houses of the rich Merchants, and also for the effecting a Product to exchange for Money to line their Purses, Bags, Coffers, etc. in order for an able carrying on, all which must be produced by Labour and good Business. And then,

According to the demand for Labour, so will Labour be undertaken and carried on.

Men are ordinarily allowed to work six Days in a Week for their support; but yet one or two Days in a Week, will serve well for an *Indian*, or one that will live like an *Indian*, or an Hermite. Now if all were disposed to live mean, saving and plain, there would be but a small demand for the produce of those who effect great Stores for the Market, more than to purchase what they have occasion to expend; there would then be more Sellers than Buyers; which would soon discourage the Industry of the Laborious & Prudent.

Sometimes the Charges of Religion, as Tythes, Offerrings, Magnificent Buildings, and costly Preparations, Dedicated to Religious Services, as also a great part of time set apart for Holy Exercises, greatly enlarges and quickens the demand for Labour.

Sometimes the Charges of War, Military Service, Building of Fortifications and other Warlike Provisions, greatly enlarges and quickens the demand for Labour; as also does any great and notable Works or Undertakings of the Publick Charge. But,

The most wealthy and liberal demand is, when there is valuable Riches, Silver and Gold as well as other precious Substance to be had in exchange for Labour to a plentiful degree, advancing of the Common-wealth, enabling Men to improve and dispense with Labour in an able and forehanded way of living.

Now either of these occasions hinted at, may serve greatly to draw a people out of an Idle habit, encouraging Industry, Virtue, &c. being Profitable to Labouring Men, and a support to Poor Men; but when a People have no Business but only to provide for Common Occasions, or Necessities in a poor declining Reipublick that have no means to Convert their produce into that which shall enable and set them before hand for Business, (tho' this demand is apt to swell into many Extravagancies in an active fruitful Country) yet this is most oppressive to Poor Men, and ruining to the Common-Wealth, being an Inlet to Idleness and almost every other Ill-habit.

Had *Sodom* and *Gomorrah* been Politick in *Trade* and accustomed to Manners of Civility & Magnificence according as the fertillity of their Soil, would have endured it, they might have been diverted from the Sins of Idleness, fulness of Bread, etc.

But what I would have understood, is this, that any People whatsoever considered as a Common-Wealth, have Rich Mines in their Capacity of Labour, and carrying on Business, and with suitable policy in *Trade*, it may be drawn out and refined to a wealthy & flourishing State, altho' of but mean advantages, as to the produce of their Soil; and when quick profit lies ready to embrace the *Business* and *Trade* in general, as it may be undertaken and enlarged, the Business will be undertaken & carried on to very great degrees, and by continuance will do more to reduce a People to a habit of Prudence and Industry than is possible to be effected by Whip, or Hunger or by all the penal Laws that can be Invented for the Suppressing of Idleness, etc.

And contrarywise, a People may be possessed of a Fruitful Rich Country, and yet for want of good Regulations, and Policy in *Trade*, the business of the Country (considered in the mean) will be rendered greatly disadvantagious and unprofitable, as to any enlarged undertaking. However some through their better means may enlarge their Business with Profit, yet it must be upon the disadvantage and discouragement of some others, which disposition in a Publick State will inevitably in continuance reduce the most industrious Generation of People to an habit of Idleness, etc. And the more fruitful the Country, the more Intolerable the Consequence, as Idleness is the leader of most kinds of Vices. . . .

SELECTION

The Volume and Character of Colonial Trade

Throughout the eighteenth century the volume of colonial trade grew steadily. Table A gives the annual value of exports to, and imports from, England between 1697 and 1776. An examination of the figures for any given year will reveal that all the colonies imported large quantities of English goods but that the vast bulk of colonial exports to England came from the southern staple colonies. Of course, not all colonial trade went to England, and a better notion of the extent and character of the total trade for the middle years of the eighteenth century can be obtained from the 1740 report to the Board of Trade by Robert Dinwiddie (1693–1770), surveyor general of customs for the southern district (Maryland to Georgia and the West Indies) and later (1751 to 1758) lieutenant governor of Virginia. Dinwiddie's estimates include not only the annual value of the produce of each colony and the total worth of British goods imported into the colonies but also the number and value of vessels belonging to each colony and the amount of colonial trade with the French and Spanish colonies. For a more detailed and more accurate breakdown of colonial trade statistics, see Series Z in Historical Statistics of the United States *(1960).*

TABLE A. VALUE OF EXPORTS TO, AND IMPORTS FROM, ENGLAND: 1697–1776

Year	Total		New England		New York		Pennsylvania		Virginia and Maryland		Carolina		Georgia	
	Exports	Imports	Exports	Imports	Exports	Imports	Exports	Imports	Exports	Imports	Exports	Imports	Exports	Imports
	21	22	23	24	25	26	27	28	29	30	31	32	33	34
1776	103,964	55,415	762	55,050	2,318	1,228	1,421	365	73,226	1,921	13,668	6,245	12,569	113,777
1775	1,920,950	196,162	116,588	71,625	187,018	437,937	175,962	1,366	758,356	528,738	579,549	378,116	103,477	57,518
1774	1,373,846	2,590,437	112,248	562,476	80,008	289,214	69,611	625,652	612,030	328,904	432,302	344,859		67,647
1773	1,369,229	1,979,412	124,624	527,055	76,246	343,970	36,652	426,448	589,803	793,910	456,513	449,610	85,391	62,932
1772	1,258,515	3,012,635	126,265	824,830	82,707	653,621	29,133	507,909	528,404	920,326	425,923	409,169	66,083	92,406
1771	1,339,840	4,202,472	150,381	1,420,119	95,875		31,615	728,744	577,848		420,311		63,810	70,493
1770	1,015,535	1,925,571	148,011	394,451	69,882	475,991	28,109	134,881	435,094	717,782	278,907	146,273	55,532	56,193
1769	1,060,206	1,336,122	129,353	207,993	73,466	74,918	26,111	199,909	361,892	488,362	387,114	306,600	82,270	58,340
1768	1,251,454	2,157,218	148,375	419,797	87,115	482,930	59,406	432,107	406,048	475,954	508,108	289,868	42,402	56,562
1767	1,096,079	1,900,923	128,207	406,081	61,422	417,957	37,641	371,830	437,926	437,628	395,027	244,093	35,856	23,334
1766	1,043,958	1,804,333	141,733	409,642	67,020	330,829	26,851	327,314	461,693	372,548	293,587	296,732	53,074	67,268
1765	1,151,698	1,944,114	145,819	451,299	54,959	382,349	25,148	363,368	505,671	383,224	385,918	334,709	34,183	29,165
1764	1,110,572	2,249,710	88,157	459,765	53,697	515,416	36,258	435,191	559,408	515,192	341,727	305,808	31,325	18,338
1763	1,106,170	1,631,997	74,815	258,854	53,998	238,560	38,228	284,152	642,294	555,391	282,366	250,132	14,469	44,908
1762	742,632	1,377,160	41,783	247,385	58,882	288,046	38,091	206,199	415,709	417,599	181,695	194,170	6,522	23,761
1761	847,892	1,652,078	46,225	334,225	48,648	289,570	39,170	204,067	455,083	545,350	253,002	254,587	5,764	24,279
1760	761,099	2,611,764	37,802	599,647	21,125	480,106	22,754	707,998	504,451	605,882	162,769	218,131	12,198	15,178
1759	639,909	2,345,463	25,985	527,067	21,684	630,785	22,404	498,161	357,228	459,007	206,534	215,255	6,074	10,212
1758	670,720	1,712,887	30,204	465,694	14,260	356,555	21,383	260,953	454,362	438,471	150,511	181,002		2,571
1757	610,684	1,628,348	27,556	363,404	19,168	353,311	14,190	268,426	418,881	426,687	130,889	213,949		536
1756	659,356	1,352,178	47,359	384,371	24,073	250,425	20,095	200,169	337,759	334,897	222,915	181,780	7,155	
1755	939,553	1,112,997	59,533	341,796	28,054	151,071	32,336	144,456	489,668	285,157	325,525	187,887	4,437	2,630
1754	1,007,759	1,176,279	66,538	329,433	26,663	127,497	30,649	244,647	573,435	323,513	307,238	149,215	3,236	1,974
1753	972,740	1,452,944	83,395	345,523	50,553	277,864	38,527	245,644	632,574	356,776	164,634	213,009	3,057	14,128
1752	1,004,182	1,148,127	74,313	273,340	40,648	194,030	29,978	201,666	569,453	325,151	288,264	150,777	1,526	3,163
1751	835,651	1,233,168	63,287	305,974	42,363	248,941	23,870	190,917	460,085	347,027	245,491	138,244	555	2,065
1750	814,768	1,313,083	48,455	343,659	35,634	267,130	28,191	217,713	508,939	349,419	191,607	133,037	1,942	2,125
1749	663,524	1,230,386	39,999	238,286	23,413	265,773	14,944	238,637	434,618	323,600	150,499	164,085	51	5
1748	716,626	830,483	29,748	197,682	12,358	143,311	12,363	75,330	494,852	252,624	167,305	160,172		1,314
1747	660,715	726,669	41,771	210,640	14,992	137,984	3,832	82,404	492,619	200,088	167,500	95,529		24
1746	569,500	755,926	38,612	209,177	8,841	86,712	15,779	73,699	419,371	282,545	76,897	102,809		984
1745	554,431	535,253	38,948	140,463	14,083	54,957	10,130	54,280	399,423	197,799	91,847	86,815		939
1744	667,524	640,881	50,248	143,982	14,527	119,920	7,446	62,214	402,709	234,855	192,594	79,141		769
1743	880,807	829,273	63,185	172,461	15,067	135,487	9,596	79,340	557,822	328,195	235,136	111,499	2	2,291
1742	659,227	800,052	53,166	148,899	13,536	167,591	8,527	75,295	427,769	264,186	154,607	127,063		17,018
1741	912,291	885,492	60,052	198,147	21,142	140,430	17,158	91,010	577,109	248,582	236,830	204,770	1,622	2,533
1740	718,416	813,382	72,389	171,081	21,498	118,777	15,048	56,751	341,997	281,428	266,560	181,821	924	3,524

Year	(1)	(2)	(3)	(4)	(5)	(6)	(7)	(8)	(9)	(10)	(11)	(12)	(13)	(14)
1739	754,276	695,869	46,604	220,378	18,459	106,070	8,134	54,452	217,200	444,654	236,192	94,445	233	3,324
1738	620,212	751,270	59,116	203,233	16,228	133,438	11,918	61,450	258,860	391,814	141,119	87,793	17	6,496
1737	775,382	682,434	63,347	223,923	16,833	125,833	15,198	56,690	211,301	492,246	187,758	58,986	....	5,701
1736	699,764	677,624	66,788	222,158	17,944	86,000	20,786	61,513	204,794	380,163	214,083	101,147	....	2,012
1735	652,326	668,664	72,899	189,125	14,155	80,405	21,919	48,804	220,381	394,995	145,348	117,837	3,010	12,112
1734	611,350	556,275	82,252	146,460	15,307	81,758	20,217	54,392	172,086	373,090	120,646	99,658	18	1,921
1733	669,633	548,890	61,983	184,570	11,626	65,417	14,776	40,565	186,177	403,198	177,845	70,466	203	1,695
1732	519,036	531,253	64,095	216,600	9,411	65,540	8,524	41,698	148,289	310,799	126,207	58,298	....	828
1731	650,863	536,266	49,048	183,467	20,756	66,116	12,786	44,260	171,278	408,502	159,771	71,145	....	....
1730	572,585	536,860	54,701	208,196	8,740	64,356	10,582	48,592	150,931	346,823	151,739	64,785	....	....
1729	575,282	422,958	52,512	161,102	15,833	64,760	7,434	29,799	108,931	386,174	113,329	58,366	....	....
1728	605,324	517,861	64,689	194,590	21,141	81,634	15,230	37,478	171,092	413,089	91,175	33,067	....	....
1727	637,135	502,927	75,052	187,277	21,617	67,452	12,823	31,979	192,965	421,588	96,055	23,254	....	....
1726	526,303	553,297	63,816	200,882	38,307	84,866	5,960	37,634	185,981	324,767	93,453	43,934	....	....
1725	415,650	549,693	72,021	201,768	24,976	70,650	11,981	42,209	195,884	214,730	91,942	39,182	....	....
1724	462,681	461,584	69,585	168,507	21,191	63,020	4,057	30,324	161,894	277,344	90,504	37,839	....	....
1723	461,761	411,590	59,337	176,486	27,992	53,013	8,332	25,992	123,853	287,997	78,103	42,246	....	....
1722	437,696	424,725	47,955	133,722	20,118	57,478	6,882	26,397	172,754	283,091	79,650	34,374	....	....
1721	493,871	331,905	50,483	114,524	15,681	50,754	8,037	21,548	127,376	357,812	61,858	17,703	....	....
1720	468,188	319,702	49,206	128,767	16,836	37,397	7,928	24,531	110,717	331,482	62,736	18,290	....	....
1719	463,054	393,000	54,452	125,317	19,596	56,355	6,564	27,068	164,630	332,069	50,373	19,630	....	....
1718	*457,471	*425,333	61,591	131,885	27,331	62,966	5,588	22,716	191,925	316,576	46,385	15,841	....	....
1717	*426,090	*439,666	58,898	132,001	24,534	44,140	4,499	22,505	215,962	296,884	41,275	25,058	....	....
1716	*424,389	*402,042	69,595	121,156	21,971	52,173	5,193	21,842	179,599	281,343	46,287	27,272	....	....
1715	*297,246	*452,366	66,555	164,650	21,316	54,643	5,461	17,182	199,274	174,756	29,158	16,631	....	....
1714	*395,774	*333,443	51,541	121,288	29,810	44,643	2,663	14,927	128,873	280,470	31,290	23,712	....	....
1713	*303,222	*284,356	49,904	120,778	14,428	46,470	178	17,037	76,304	206,263	32,449	23,967	....	....
1712	*365,971	*309,691	24,699	128,105	12,466	18,524	1,471	8,464	134,583	297,941	29,394	20,015	....	....
1711	*324,698	*297,626	26,415	137,421	12,193	28,856	38	19,408	91,535	273,181	12,871	20,406	....	....
1710	*249,814	*293,659	31,112	106,338	8,203	31,475	1,277	8,594	127,639	188,429	20,793	19,613	....	....
1709	*324,534	*269,596	29,559	120,349	12,259	34,577	617	5,881	80,268	261,668	20,431	28,521	....	....
1708	286,435	240,183	49,635	115,505	10,847	26,899	2,120	6,722	79,061	213,493	20,340	11,996	....	....
1707	284,798	413,244	38,793	120,631	14,283	29,855	786	14,365	237,901	207,625	23,311	10,492	....	....
1706	187,073	161,691	22,210	57,050	2,849	31,588	4,210	11,037	58,015	149,152	8,652	4,001	....	....
1705	150,961	291,722	22,793	62,504	7,393	27,902	1,309	7,206	174,322	116,768	2,698	19,788	....	....
1704	321,972	176,088	30,823	74,896	10,540	22,294	2,430	11,819	60,458	264,112	14,067	6,621	....	....
1703	204,295	296,210	33,539	59,608	7,471	17,562	5,160	9,899	196,713	144,928	13,197	12,428	....	....
1702	335,788	186,809	37,026	64,625	7,965	29,991	4,145	9,342	72,391	274,782	11,870	10,460	....	....
1701	309,134	343,826	32,656	86,322	18,547	31,910	5,220	12,003	199,683	235,738	16,973	13,908	....	....
1700	395,021	344,341	41,486	91,918	17,567	49,410	4,608	18,529	173,481	317,302	14,058	11,003	....	....
1699*	255,397	403,614	26,660	127,279	16,818	42,792	1,477	17,064	205,078	198,115	12,327	11,401	....	....
1698*	226,055	458,097	31,254	93,517	8,763	25,279	2,720	10,704	310,135	174,053	9,265	18,462	....	....
1697*	279,852	140,129	26,282	68,468	10,093	4,579	3,347	2,997	58,796	227,756	12,374	5,289	....	....

*Corrected figures. Figures shown in source for 1709–1718 incorrectly presented totals of components.
†For years ending Sept. 28.
SOURCE: Historical Statistics of the United States, Colonial Times to 1957 (1960), p. 737.

B. ROBERT DINWIDDIE: REPORT TO BOARD OF TRADE ON THE TRADE OF THE BRITISH EMPIRE (APR. 29, 1740)*

My Lords'

I have been at a great deal of Trouble and Expence to inform Myself of the Trade of his Majesty's American Empire, and the annuall amount of the National Produce of each Colony or Plantation: I give You the following Thoughts, Observations and Calculations, which is partly from my own knowledge and from the best informations I possibly could get; If it's thought worthy your Notice, it will fully answer my hopes. I shall therefore, to make it Somewhat regular, first,

First—Give You an Account of the number of Vessells belonging to his Majesty's Subjects in America, distinguished by each respective Colony, beginning with Newfoundland and ending with Barbados.

Secondly—An Account of the number of Vessells belonging to Great Britain and Ireland trading to the American Colonys and Plantations.

Thirdly—An Estimate of the Value of the Vessells belonging to America, and those trading from Great Britain and Ireland thereto.

Fourthly—An Account of the Amount of the naturall Produce of each Plantation by the improvement and manufacturing of the British Subjects in those Parts.

Fifthly—An Estimate of the amount of Goods from Great Britain and Ireland annually carried to the Plantations in America, and to the Coast of Guinea.

Sixthly—the amount of Cash, Dye Woods, Druggs, Cacoa &c: brought into our Plantations, being the Consequence of a Trade with Spanish and French Colonys.

Seventhly—The whole brought into an Account, by which You will be able to observe the considerable Value of our American Trade. . . .

First—Is Account of the Vessels belonging to his Majestys Subjects in America distinguished by each Colony, beginning at Newfoundland and ending at Barbados

	Vessells
Belonging to Newfoundland, - - - - - - -	25
The Government of New England Vessels of different Denominations used in foreign Trade - - - - - - -	750
In the Same Government intirely employed in Fishing and Coasting being Sloops & Schooners - - - - - - -	350
In Connecticutt and Rhode Island in foreign Trade - - - -	260
In Ditto used in Fishing and Coasting Sloops and Schooners - - -	150
In New York and Jerseys, in foreign Trade and in Coasting &c: - -	60
In Pensylvania and the lower Countys - - - - - -	70
In Maryland - - - - - - - - - -	60
In Virginia - - - - - - - - - - -	80
In North Carolina - - - - - - - - -	25

* These excerpts are reprinted from *Archives of the State of New Jersey,* 1st ser., vol. 6, pp. 83–89.

In South Carolina - - - - - - - - - 25
In Bermuda - - - - - - - - - - 75
In Providence and Bahama Islands - - - - - - - 20
In Jamaica - - - - - - - - - - 30
In Leeward and Virgin Islands - - - - - - - 35
In Barbados - - - - - - - - - - 20
2035

✻ ✻ ✻

Secondly—Here follows the Account from information of the Ships &c: Trading to and from America belonging to Great Britain and Ireland distinguished by the Trade they are concerned in.

Vessells

To Newfoundland with the Fisherman and those employed in carrying } 80
Fish to the different Markets - - - - - - }
To New England and Nova Scotia - - - - - - 20
To Connecticutt and Rhode Island - - - - - - - 6
To New York and the Jerseys - - - - - - - 8
To Pensylvania - - - - - - - - - 10
To Maryland - - - - - - - - - - 95
To Virginia - - - - - - - - - - 120
To North Carolina - - - - - - - - - 30
To South Carolina - - - - - - - - - 200
To Jamaica - - - - - - - - - - 100
To Leeward Islands - - - - - - - - - 151
To Barbados - - - - - - - - - - 80
900

Add to the above One hundred and fifty Sail from Great Britain and } 150
Ireland to the Coast of Guinea, and so to the Plantations - - }
1050

Thirdly—An Estimate of the Value of the Vessels belonging to the Subjects of America, and Those belonging to Great Britain and Ireland Trading to the different Colonys &c:

1065—Ships, Snows and Brigantines belonging to the American }
Subjects trading to foreign parts, valued at a medm £1000 } 1,065,000
Sterling each is - - - - - - - }
.970—Sloops and Schooners of smaller Size and Burthen, valued }
one with the other at £400 Sterling each is - - - } .388,000
.900—Ships, Snows &c. from Great Britain and Ireland to and }
from the Plantations, valued at £1,200 each - - - } 1,080,000
.150—Ditto from Great Britain and Ireland to the Coast of }
Guinea and the Plantations, with extraordinary Outfitts } 225,000
£1500 Ea: - - - - - - - - }

3,085 Sail   £2,758,000

Fourthly—An Estimate of the Natural and Improved annuall Produce of his Majesty's American Colonys and Plantations, distinguished into each Colony or Plantation.

Newfoundland by Fish and Oyl - - - - - -	£100,000
New England and Nova Scotia by Fish, Oyl, Whalebone, Cattle, Lumber Pitch, Tarr, Turpintine, Building of Vessels &c: -	800,000
Connecticutt and Rhode Island, with the same Commoditys and Sheep, Corn, Bread, Flour, Cheese and Butter - - -	150,000
New York and the Jerseys with the same, and Tarr, Copper-Ore, Iron and Wheat - - - - - - - -	250,000
Pensylvania and the Lower Countys the Same & Tobacco - -	280,000
Maryland, in the Same - - - - - - - -	200,000
Virginia in the Same, with Pitch, Tarr, & Turpintine - -	250,000
North Carolina in the Same - - - - - -	60,000
South Carolina in Ditto with Rice, - - - - -	200,000
Bermuda, in Plett, Live-Stock, Fish, Oyl, Cabbage, Onions, & Stones for building - - - - - - -	10,000
Bahama Islands in Salt, Timber, Plank, Barke, Turtle Shell, Braz: wood & Fruit - - - - - - -	15,000
Jamaica in Sugar, Mellasses, Rum, Cotton, Limejuice, Ginger, Indico, Coffee, Alloes, Piemento, Turtle Shell, Mahogany Timber, and Plank - - - - - - - -	500,000
Antigua in the Same Commoditys - - - - -	250,000
St. Christophers - in Ditto - - - - -	220,000
Nevis - - - in Ditto - - - - - -	50,000
Mountserratt - in Ditto - - - - -	50,000
Anguilla - - in Ditto - - - - - -	15,000
Tortola - - in Ditto - - - - -	30,000
Spsh Town - - in Ditto - - - - -	15,000
Barbados - - in Ditto - - - - -	300,000
	3,745,000
Fifthly—The amount of the Value of Goods Ship't from Great Britain and Ireland to our British Plantations and the Coast of Guinea is annually by Computation - - - - -	2,550,000
Sixthly—A Calculation of the amount of Cash, Dye Woods, Druggs, Cocoa, &c: imported to the British Plantations, being the consequence of a Trade carried on to Spanish and French Dominions in America. That Trade in New England, Connecticutt and Rhode Island in Dye Woods from Honduras, Some Cash and Cacao amo': to yearly - - - - -	100,000
To New York (circa) - - - - - - -	25,000
To Bermuda - - - - - - - -	10,000
To Jamaica - - - - - - - - -	250,000
To Leeward Islands (circa) - - - - - -	20,000
To Barbados (circa) - - - - - - - -	20,000
	£425,000

It's to be observed that as this is the Produce of foreign Colony's, it's mentioned by itself to Shew the amount of that private Branch of Trade, and tho' it's carried on with Goods from Britain and Negroes, which is before considered in the Calculate, yet it's conceived, that the addition of this will not over Rate our American Trade.

Seventhly—The whole brought into an Account by which You may See the Amount of the above American Trade.

The amount of the computed Value of the Vessells trading in America, including those belonging to the Merchants of Great Britain and Ireland being 3085, which amounts to - -	2,758,000
The Amo' of the Natural and Improv'd Produce of the British Colonys, which employ the above Vessells - - - -	3,745,000
The amoᵗ of Goods from Great Britain and Ireland to the Plantations and Coast of Guinea annually - - - -	2,550,000
The Amount of a Casual Trade carried on to the Spanish and French Settlements in America annually (circa) - - -	425,000
	£9,478,000

You will please to observe that the whole Trade to and in America, belonging to his Majesty's British and American Subjects (Hudson's Bay only excepted) amounts yearly to Nine Million four hundred and seventy eight thousand pounds; This includes the Value of the whole Navigation, the annual Supplys from Great Britain and Ireland, the Naturall and Improved Produce remitted to Europe from the Plantations and Colonys, as well as the Supplys given each other by their Traffick and Commerce from one Colony or Plantation to the Other. . . .

SELECTION

Solving the Labor Problem: Indentured Servitude

The most serious economic problem the colonies had to face was the shortage of labor. Where land was so easily obtainable, few men were content to remain permanently in the status of wage laborers, and because free labor was therefore in such short supply, it was considerably more expensive than in Great Britain. For men who sought greater economic returns than they could obtain from their own and their families' efforts, the expense of free labor was almost prohibitive, and some other, cheaper kind of labor force was clearly necessary. Confronted with this problem during the very first years of settlement, the Virginia Company had tried to solve it by importing servants, who in return for their passage to the New World signed indentures by which they agreed to work for the company for a stipulated number of years. The institution quickly took hold, and servants constituted the bulk of the labor force everywhere in the continental colonies during the seventeenth century and in the northern colonies during the eighteenth century. Estimates of the number of Europeans who came to the mainland colonies as servants range as high as two-thirds of the total number of immigrants. The varieties of servants—convicts, indentured servants, and redemptioners—are described in a letter of September 20, 1770, by William Eddis, who came to Annapolis in 1769 as secretary to Governor Robert Eden of Maryland. First published in London in 1792 as part of his Letters from America, Eddis's account of the institution is basically unsympathetic. A more favorable view stressing the benefits derived by the servants and the legal arrangements established for their protection in Virginia was presented sixty-five years earlier by Robert Beverley (ca. 1673–1722), Virginia planter and historian, in The History and Present State of Virginia, *which was first published in London in 1705.*

Richard B. Morris, Government and Labor in Early America *(1946); Abbot E. Smith,* Colonists in Bondage: White Servitude and Convict Labor in America, 1607–1776 *(1947); and Marcus Wilson Jernegan,* Laboring and Dependent Classes in Colonial America, 1607–1783: Studies of the Economic, Educational, and Social Significance of Slaves, Servants, Apprentices, and Poor Folk *(1931) are the standard works on servitude.*

A. AN UNFAVORABLE VIEW: WILLIAM EDDIS, "LETTERS FROM AMERICA" (SEPT. 20, 1770)*

YOUR information relative to the situation of servants in this country, is far from being well-founded. I have now been upwards of twelve months resident in Maryland, and am thereby enabled to convey to you a tolerable idea on this subject.

Persons in a state of servitude are under four distinct denominations: negroes, who are the entire property of their respective owners: convicts, who are transported from the mother country for a limited term: indented servants, who are engaged for five years previous to their leaving England; and free-willers, who are supposed, from their situation, to possess superior advantages.

The negroes in this province are, in general, natives of the country; very few in proportion being imported from the coast of Africa. They are better cloathed, better fed, and better treated, than their unfortunate breathren, whom a more rigid fate hath subjected to slavery in our West India islands; neither are their employments so laborious, nor the acts of the legislature so partially oppressive against them. The further we proceed to the northward, the less number of people are to be found of this complexion: In the New England government, negroes are almost as scarce as on your side of the Atlantic, and but few are under actual slavery; but as we advance to the south, their multitudes astonishingly increase; and in the Carolinas they considerably exceed the number of white inhabitants.

Maryland is the only province into which convicts may be freely imported. The Virginians have inflicted very severe penalties on any masters of vessels, or others, who may attempt to introduce persons under this description into their colony. They have been influenced in this measure

---

* These excerpts are reprinted from the original edition published in London in 1792, pp. 63–78.

by an apprehension, that, from the admission of such inmates into their families, the prevalance of bad example might tend to universal depravity, in spite of every regulation, and restraining law.

Persons convicted of felony, and in consequence transported to this continent, if they are able to pay the expence of passage, are free to pursue their fortune agreeably to their inclinations or abilities. Few, however, have means to avail themselves of this advantage. These unhappy beings are, generally, consigned to an agent, who classes them suitably to their real or supposed qualifications; advertises them for sale, and disposes of them, for seven years, to planters, to mechanics, and to such as choose to retain them for domestic service. Those who survive the term of servitude, seldom establish their residence in this country: the stamp of infamy is too strong upon them to be easily erased: they either return to Europe, and renew their former practices; or, if they have fortunately imbibed habits of honesty and industry, they remove to a distant situation, where they may hope to remain unknown, and be enabled to pursue with credit every possible method of becoming useful members of society.

In your frequent excursions about the great metropolis, you cannot but observe numerous advertisements, offering the most seducing encouragement to adventurers under every possible description; to those who are disgusted with the frowns of fortune in their native land; and to those of an enterprising disposition, who are tempted to court her smiles in a distant region. These persons are referred to agents, or crimps, who represent the advantages to be obtained in America, in colours so alluring, that it is almost impossible to resist their artifices. Unwary persons are accordingly induced to enter into articles, by which they engage to become servants, agreeable to their respective qualifications, for the term of five years; every necessary accommodation being found them during the voyage; and every method taken that they may be treated with tenderness and humanity during the period of servitude; at the expiration of which they are taught to expect, that opportunities will assuredly offer to secure to the honest and industrious, a competent provision for the remainder of their days.

The generality of the inhabitants in this province are very little acquainted with those fallacious pretences, by which numbers are continually induced to embark for this continent. On the contrary, they too generally conceive an opinion that the difference is merely nominal between the indented servant and the convicted felon: nor will they readily believe that people, who had the least experience in life, and whose characters were unexceptionable, would abandon their friends and families, and their ancient connexions, for a servile situation, in a remote appendage to the British Empire. From this persuasion they rather consider the convict as the more profitable servant, his term being for seven, the latter only for five years; and, I am sorry to observe, that there are but few instances wherein they experience different treatment. Negroes being a property for life, the death of slaves, in the prime of youth or strength, is a material loss to the proprietor; they are, therefore, almost in every instance, under more comfortable circumstances than the miserable

European, over whom the rigid planter exercises an inflexible severity. They are strained to the utmost to perform their allotted labour; and, from a prepossession in many cases too justly founded, they are supposed to be receiving only the just reward which is due to repeated offences. There are doubtless many exceptions to this observation, yet, generally speaking, they groan beneath a worse than Egyptian bondage. By attempting to lighten the intolerable burthen, they often render it more insupportable. For real, or imaginary causes, these frequently attempt to escape, but very few are successful; the country being intersected with rivers, and the utmost vigilance observed in detecting persons under suspicious circumstances, who, when apprehended, are committed to close confinement, advertised, and delivered to their respective masters; the party who detects the vagrant being entitled to a reward. Other incidental charges arise. The unhappy culprit is doomed to a severe chastisement; and a prolongation of servitude is decreed in full proportion to expences incurred, and supposed inconveniences resulting from a desertion of duty.

The situation of the free-willer is, in almost every instance, more to be lamented than either that of the convict or the indented servant; the deception which is practised on those of this description being attended with circumstances of greater duplicity and cruelty. Persons under this denomination are received under express conditions that, on their arrival in America, they are to be allowed a stipulated number of days to dispose of themselves to the greatest advantage. They are told, that their services will be eagerly solicited, in proportion to their abilities; that their reward will be adequate to the hazard they encounter by courting fortune in a distant region; and that the parties with whom they engage will readily advance the sum agreed on for their passage; which, being averaged at about nine pounds sterling, they will speedily be enabled to repay, and to enjoy, in a state of liberty, a comparative situation of ease and affluence.

With these pleasing ideas they support, with cheerfulness, the hardships to which they are subjected during the voyage; and, with the most anxious sensations of delight, approach the land which they consider as the scene of future prosperity. But scarce have they contemplated the diversified objects which naturally attract attention; scarce have they yielded to the pleasing reflection, that every danger, every difficulty, is happily surmounted, before their fond hopes are cruelly blasted, and they find themselves involved in all the complicated miseries of a tedious, laborious, and unprofitable servitude.

Persons resident in America, being accustomed to procure servants for a very trifling consideration, under absolute terms, for a limited period, are not often disposed to hire adventurers, who expect to be gratified in full proportion to their acknowledged qualifications; but, as they support authority with a rigid hand, they little regard the former situation of their unhappy dependants.

This disposition, which is almost universally prevalent, is well known to the parties, who on your side of the Atlantic engage in this iniquitous and cruel commerce. It is, therefore, an article of agreement with these deluded victims, that if they are not successful in obtaining situations, on their own terms, within a certain number of days after their arrival in the country, they are then to be sold, in order to defray the charges of passage, at the discretion of the master of the vessel, or the agent to whom he is consigned in the province.

You are also to observe, that servants imported, even under this favourable description, are rarely permitted to set their feet on shore, until they have absolutely formed their respective engagements. As soon as the ship is stationed in her birth, planters, mechanics, and others, repair on board; the adventurers of both sexes are exposed to view, and very few are happy enough to make their own stipulations, some very extraordinary qualifications being absolutely requisite to obtain this distinction; and even when this is obtained, the advantages are by no means equivalent to their sanguine expectations. The residue, stung with disappointment and vexation, meet with horror the moment which dooms them, under an appearance of equity, to a limited term of slavery. Character is of little importance; their abilities not being found of a superior nature, they are sold as soon as their term of election is expired, apparel and provision being their only compensation; till, on the expiration of five tedious laborious years, they are restored to a dearly purchased freedom.

From this detail, I am persuaded, you will no longer imagine, that the servants in this country are in a better situation than those in Britain. You have heard of convicts who rather chose to undergo the severest penalties of the law, than endure the hardships which are annexed to their situation, during a state of servitude on this side the Atlantic. Indolence, accompanied with a train of vicious habits, has, doubtless, great influence on the determination of such unhappy wretches; but it is surely to be lamented that men, whose characters are unblemished, whose views are founded on honest and industrious principles, should fall a sacrifice to avarice and delusion, and indiscriminately be blended with the most profligate and abandoned of mankind.

It seems astonishing, that a circumstance so well known, particularly in this province, should not have been generally circulated through every part of the British Empire. Were the particulars of this iniquitous traffic universally divulged, those who have established offices in London, and in the principal sea-ports, for the regular conduct of this business, would be pointed out to obloquy, and their punishment would serve as a beacon to deter the ignorant and unwary from becoming victims to the insidious practices of avarice and deceit.

I am ready to admit there is every appearance of candour on the part of the agents, and their accomplices. Previous to the embarcation of any person under the respective agreements, the parties regularly comply with the requisitions of a law, wisely calculated to prevent clandestine transportation; they appear before a magistrate, and give their voluntary assent to the obligations they have mutually entered into. But are not such adventurers induced to this measure in consequence of ignorance and misrepresentation? Assuredly they are. They are industriously taught to expect advantages infinitely superior to their most sanguine views in Britain. Every lucrative incentive is delineated in the most flattering colours; and they fondly expect to acquire that independence in the revolution of a few years, which the longest life could not promise, with the exertion of their best abilities, in the bosom of their native country. . . .

B. A FAVORABLE VIEW: ROBERT BEVERLEY, "THE HISTORY AND PRESENT STATE OF VIRGINIA" (1705)*

Of the Servants and Slaves in Virginia

50. THEIR Servants, they distinguish by the Names of Slaves for Life, and Servants for a time.

Slaves are the Negroes, and their Posterity, following the condition of the Mother. . . . They are call'd Slaves, in respect of the time of their Servitude, because it is for Life.

Servants, are those which serve only for a few years, according to the time of their Indenture, or the Custom of the Country. The Custom of the Country takes place upon such as have no Indentures. The Law in this case is, that if such Servants be under Nineteen years of Age, they must be brought into Court, to have their Age adjudged; and from the Age they are judg'd to be of, they must serve until they reach four and twenty: But if they be adjudged upwards of Nineteen, they are then only to be Servants for the term of five Years.

51. The Male-Servants, and Slaves of both Sexes, are imployed together in Tilling and Manuring the Ground, in Sowing and Planting Tobacco, Corn, &c. Some Distinction indeed is made between them in their Cloaths, and Food; but the Work of both, is no other than what the Overseers, the Freemen, and the Planters themselves do.

Sufficient Distinction is also made between the Female-Servants, and Slaves; for a White Woman is rarely or never put to work in the Ground, if she be good for any thing else: And to Discourage all Planters from using any Women so, their Law imposes the heaviest Taxes upon Female-Servants working in the Ground, while it suffers all other white Women to be absolutely exempted: Whereas on the other hand, it is a common thing to work a Woman Slave out of Doors; nor does the Law make any Distinction in her Taxes, whether her Work be Abroad, or at Home.

52. Because I have heard how strangely cruel, and severe, the Service of this Country is represented in some parts of *England;* I can't forbear affirming, that the work of their Servants, and Slaves, is no other than what every common Freeman do's. Neither is any Servant requir'd to do more in a Day, than his Overseer. And I can assure you with a great deal of Truth, that generally their Slaves are not worked near so hard, nor so many Hours in a Day, as the Husbandmen, and Day-Labourers in *England.* An Overseer is a Man, that having served his time, has acquired the

* These excerpts are reprinted from the London edition, bk. IV, pp. 35–39.

Skill and Character of an experienced Planter, and is therefore intrusted with the Direction of the Servants and Slaves.

But to compleat this account of Servants, I shall give you a short Relation of the care their Laws take, that they be used as tenderly as possible.

By the Laws of their Country.

1. All Servants whatsoever, have their Complaints heard without Fee, or Reward; but if the Master be found Faulty, the charge of the Complaint is cast upon him, otherwise the business is done *ex Officio*.
2. Any Justice of Peace may receive the Complaint of a Servant, and order every thing relating thereto, till the next County-Court, where it will be finally determin'd.
3. All Masters are under the Correction, and Censure of the County-Courts, to provide for their Servants, good and wholsme Diet, Clothing, and Lodging.
4. They are always to appear, upon the first Notice given of the Complaint of their Servants, otherwise to forfeit the Service of them, until they do appear.
5. All Servants Complaints are to be receiv'd at any time in Court, without Process, and shall not be delay'd for want of Form; but the Merits of the Complaint must be immediately inquir'd into by the Justices; and if the Master cause any delay therein, the Court may remove such Servants, if they see Cause, until the Master will come to Tryal.
6. If a Master shall at any time disobey an Order of Court, made upon any Complaint of a Servant; the Court is impower'd to remove such Servant forthwith to another Master, who will be kinder; Giving to the former Master the produce only, (after Fees deducted) of what such Servants shall be sold for by Publick Outcry.
7. If a Master should be so cruel, as to use his Servant ill, that is faln Sick, or Lame in his Service, and thereby render'd unfit for Labour, he must be remov'd by the Church-Wardens out of the way of such Cruelty, and boarded in some good Planters House, till the time of his Freedom, the charge of which must be laid before the next County-Court, which has power to levy the same from time to time, upon the Goods and Chattels of the Master; After which, the charge of such Boarding is to come upon the Parish in General.
8. All hired Servants are intituled to these Priviledges.
9. No Master of a Servant, can make a new Bargain for Service, or other Matter with his Servant, without the privity and consent of a Justice of Peace, to prevent the Master's Over-reaching, or scareing such Servant into an unreasonable Complyance.
10. The property of all Money and Goods sent over thither to Servants, or caary'd in with them; is reserv'd to themselves, and remain intirely at their disposal.
11. Each Servant at his Freedom, receives of his Master fifteen Bushels of Corn, (which is sufficient for a whole year) and two new Suits of Cloaths, both Linnen and Woollen; and then becomes as free in all respects, and as much entituled to the Liberties, and Priviledges of the Country, as any other of the Inhabitants or Natives are.
12. Each Servant has then also a Right to take up fifty Acres of Land, where he can find any unpatented: But that is no great Privilege, for any one may have as good a right for a piece of Eight.

This is what the Laws prescribe in favour of Servants, by which you may find, that the Cruelties and Serverities imputed to that Country, are are an unjust Reflection. For no People more abhor the thoughts of such Usage, than the *Virginians*, nor take more precaution to prevent it.

SELECTION

Solving the Labor Problem: Slavery

During the eighteenth century Negro slavery gradually replaced servitude as the predominant form of labor in all Britain's West Indian islands and in the colonies from Maryland south to Georgia. Negro "servants" had been imported into Virginia as early as 1619. Their precise status—whether they were servants for limited periods of time or for life—is not entirely clear. By 1640, however, some Negroes were serving for life and their children were inheriting the same obligation, and by the 1660s slavery was gaining statutory recognition. But it was not until the end of the century that slaves began to be brought into the southern colonies in large numbers. By 1760, as Table A in Selection 33 indicates, nearly one-fifth of the total population of the mainland colonies was Negro. Every colony had some slaves, and they composed almost one-third of the total population of Maryland and North Carolina, one-half that of Virginia and Georgia, and two-thirds that of South Carolina. Though most slaveholders who left records of their feelings on the matter seem to have been uncomfortable about the institution of slavery, few whites opposed it openly in the colonies before the 1770s. The accepted view, expressed by Hugh Jones (ca. 1670–1760), an Anglican clergyman in Virginia and Maryland and onetime professor of mathematics at the College of William and Mary, in his Present State of Virginia *(1724), was that the Negroes were inferior to whites, that slavery was basically a beneficent institution, and that probably they were at least as well off as if they had remained in Africa. A small minority did, however, oppose slavery on moral grounds. A group of German Quakers at Germantown, Pennsylvania, went on record against it as early as 1688, as did an increasing number of Quakers in the eighteenth century. An early and extraordinarily moving condemnation of the institution,* The Selling of Joseph *(1700), was written by Samuel Sewall (1652–1730), Massachusetts merchant and diarist. Such appeals carried little weight, however, in places where slavery was so enormously profitable as it was in the southern colonies. The practical economic considerations that led to the rapid growth of the institution in the eighteenth century were made explicit in the passages printed below from* A Brief Account of the Causes That Have Retarded the Progress of the Colony

of Georgia *(1743), the work of disgruntled Georgia settlers who resented the efforts of the trustees to keep the institution out of the colony.*
The argument over the status of the first Negroes in Virginia and Maryland may be followed in Oscar Handlin and Mary F. Handlin, "Origins of the Southern Labor System," William and Mary Quarterly, *third series, volume 7 (1950), pages 199–222; Carl N. Degler, "Slavery and the Genesis of American Race Prejudice," in* Comparative Studies in Society and History *(1959), volume II, pages 49–66; and, especially, Winthrop D. Jordan, "Modern Tensions and the Origins of American Slavery,"* The Journal of Southern History, *volume 28 (1962), pages 18–30. John Hope Franklin,* From Slavery to Freedom: A History of American Negroes *(1947), contains a general survey of Negro slavery, and Ulrich B. Phillips,* American Negro Slavery: A Survey of the Supply, Employment and Control of Negro Labor as Determined by the Plantation Regime *(1918), and* Life and Labor in the Old South *(1929), are useful if allowances are made for the author's racial bias.*

A. THE BENEFITS OF SLAVERY: HUGH JONES, "PRESENT STATE OF VIRGINIA" (1724)*

THE *Negroes* live in small Cottages called *Quarters,* in about six in a *Gang,* under the Direction of an *Overseer* or *Bailiff;* who takes Care that they *tend* such Land as the Owner allots and orders, upon which they raise *Hogs* and *Cattle,* and plant *Indian Corn* (or *Maize*) and *Tobacco* for the Use of their Master; out of which the *Overseer* has a Dividend (or Share) in Proportion to the Number of *Hands* including himself; this with several Privileges is his Salary, and is an ample Recompence for his Pains, and Encouragement of his industrious Care, as to the Labour, Health, and Provision of the *Negroes.*

The *Negroes* are very numerous, some Gentlemen having Hundreds of them of all Sorts, to whom they bring great Profit; for the Sake of which they are obliged to keep them well, and not over-work, starve, or famish them, besides other Inducements to favour them; which is done in a *great Degree,* to such especially that are laborious, careful, and honest; tho' indeed some Masters, careless of their own Interest or Reputation, are too cruel and negligent.

The *Negroes* are not only encreased by fresh Supplies from *Africa* and the *West India Islands,* but also are very prolifick among themselves; and they that are born there talk *good English,* and affect our Language, Habits, and Customs; and tho' they be naturally of a barbarous and cruel Temper, yet are they kept under by severe Discipline upon Occasion, and by good Laws are prevented from running away, injuring the *English,* or neglecting their Business.

Their Work (or Chimerical hard Slavery) is not very laborious; their greatest Hardship consisting in that they and their Posterity are not at

* These excerpts are reprinted from the original London edition of 1724, pp. 36–38.

their own Liberty or Disposal, but are the Property of their Owners; and when they are free, they know not how to provide so well for themselves generally; neither did they live so plentifully nor (many of them) so easily in their own Country, where they are made Slaves to one another, or taken Captive by their Enemies.

The Children belong to the Master of the Woman that bears them; and such as are born of a *Negroe* and an *European* are called *Molattoes;* but such as are born of an *Indian* and *Negroe* are called *Mustees.*

Their Work is to take Care of the *Stock,* and plant *Corn, Tobacco, Fruits,* &c. which is not harder than *Thrashing, Hedging,* or *Ditching;* besides, tho' they are out in the violent Heat, wherein they delight, yet in wet or cold Weather there is little Occasion for their working in the Fields, in which few will let them be abroad, lest by this means they might get sick or die, which would prove a great Loss to their Owners, a good *Negroe* being sometimes worth three (nay four) Score Pounds Sterling, if he be a Tradesman; so that upon this (if upon no other Account) they are obliged not to overwork them, but to cloath and feed them sufficiently, and take Care of their Health.

Several of them are taught to be *Sawyers, Carpenters, Smiths, Coopers,* &c. and though for the most Part they be none of the aptest or nicest; yet they are by Nature cut out for hard Labour and Fatigue, and will perform tolerably well; though they fall much short of an *Indian,* that has learn'd and seen the same Things; and *those Negroes* make the best Servants, that have been *Slaves* in their *own Country;* for they that have been *Kings* and *great Men* there are generally lazy, haughty, and obstinate; whereas the others are sharper, better humoured, and more laborious.

B. THE EVILS OF SLAVERY: SAMUEL SEWALL, "THE SELLING OF JOSEPH" (1700)*

Forasmuch as Liberty *is in real value next unto* Life: *None ought to part with it themselves, or deprive others of it, but upon most mature Consideration.*

The Numerousness of Slaves at this day in the Province, and the Uneasiness of them under their Slavery, hath put many upon thinking whether the Foundation of it be firmly and well laid; so as to sustain the Vast Weight that is built upon it. It is most certain that all Men, as they are the Sons of *Adam,* are Coheirs; and have equal Right unto Liberty, and all other outward Comforts of Life. *GOD hath given the Earth* (with all its Commodities) *unto the Sons of* Adam, *Psal* 115. 16. *And hath made of One Blood, all Nations of Men, for to dwell on all the face of the Earth, and hath determined the Times before appointed, and the bounds of their habitation: That they should seek the Lord. Forasmuch then as we are*

* These excerpts are reprinted from *Massachusetts Historical Society, Collections,* 5th ser., vol. 6, pp. 16–20.

the Offstring of GOD &c. *Act* 17.26, 27, 29. Now although the Title given by the last ADAM, doth infinitely better Mens Estates, respecting GOD and themselves; and grants them a most beneficial and inviolable Lease under the Broad Seal of Heaven, who were before only Tenants at Will: Yet through the Indulgence of GOD to our First Parents after the Fall, the outward Estate of all and every of their Children, remains the same, as to one another. So that Originally, and Naturally, there is no such thing as Slavery. *Joseph* was rightfully no more a Slave to his Brethren, than they were to him: and they had no more Authority to *Sell* him, than they had to *Slay* him. And if *they* had nothing to do to Sell him; the *Ishmaelites* bargaining with them, and paying down Twenty pieces of Silver, could not make a Title. Neither could *Potiphar* have any better Interest in him than the *Ishmaelites* had. *Gen.* 37. 20, 27, 28. For he that shall in this case plead *Alteration of Property,* seems to have forfeited a great part of his own claim to Humanity. There is no proportion between Twenty Pieces of Silver, and LIBERTY. The Commodity it self is the Claimer. If *Arabian* Gold be imported in any quantities, most are afraid to meddle with it, though they might have it at easy rates; lest if it should have been wrongfully taken from the Owners, it should kindle a fire to the Consumption of their whole Estate. 'Tis pity there should be more Caution used in buying a Horse, or a little lifeless dust; than there is in purchasing Men and Women: Whenas they are the Offspring of GOD. . . .

And seeing GOD hath said, *He that Stealeth a Man and Selleth him, or if he be found in his hand, he shall surely be put to Death.* Exod. 21.16. This Law being of Everlasting Equity, wherein Man Stealing is ranked amongst the most atrocious of Capital Crimes: What louder Cry can there be made of that Celebrated Warning,

CAVEAT EMPTOR!

And all things considered, it would conduce more to the Welfare of the Province, to have White Servants for a Term of Years, than to have Slaves for Life. Few can endure to hear of a Negro's being made free; and indeed they can seldom use their freedom well; yet their continual aspiring after their forbidden Liberty, renders them Unwilling Servants. And there is such a disparity in their Conditions, Colour & Hair, that they can never embody with us, and grow up into orderly Families, to the Peopling of the Land: but still remain in our Body Politick as a kind of extravasat Blood. As many Negro men as there are among us, so many empty places there are in our Train Bands, and the places taken up of Men that might make Husbands for our Daughters. And the Sons and Daughters of *New England* would become more like *Jacob,* and *Rachel,* if this Slavery were thrust quite out of doors. Moreover it is too well known what Temptations Masters are under, to connive at the Fornication of their Slaves; lest they should be obliged to find them Wives, or pay their Fines. It seems to be practically pleaded that they might be Lawless; 'tis thought much of, that the Law should have Satisfaction for their Thefts, and other Immoralities; by which means, *Holiness to the Lord,* is more rarely engraven upon this sort of Servitude. It is likewise most lamentable to think, how in taking Negroes out of *Africa,* and Selling of them here, That which GOD has joyned together men do boldly rend asunder; Men from their Country, Husbands from their Wives, Parents from their Children. How horrible is the Uncleanness, Mortality, if not Murder, that the Ships are guilty of that bring great Crouds of these miserable Men, and Women. Methinks, when we are bemoaning the barbarous Usage of our Friends and Kinsfolk in *Africa:* it might not be unseasonable to enquire whether we are not culpable in forcing the *Africans* to become Slaves amongst our selves. And it may be a question whether all the Benefit received by *Negro* Slaves, will balance the Accompt of Cash laid out upon them; and for the Redemption of our own enslaved Friends out of *Africa.* Besides all the Persons and Estates that have perished there.

 Obj.1. *These Blackamores are of the Posterity of* Cham, *and therefore are under the Curse of Slavery.* Gen. 9. 25, 26, 27.

 Answ. Of all Offices, one would not begg this; *vis.* Uncall'd for, to be an Executioner of the Vindictive Wrath of God; the extent and duration of which is to us uncertain. If this ever was a Commission; How do we know but that it is long since out of Date? Many have found it to their Cost, that a Prophetical Denunciation of Judgment against a Person or People, would not warrant them to inflict that evil. If it would, *Hazael* might justify himself in all he did against his Master, and the *Israelites,* from 2 *Kings* 8. 10, 12.

 But it is possible that by cursory reading, this Text may have been mistaken. For *Canaan* is the Person Cursed three times over, without the mentioning of *Cham.* Good Expositors suppose the Curse entaild on him, and that this Prophesie was accomplished in the Extirpation of the *Canaanites,* and in the Servitude of the *Gibeonites. Vide Pareum.* Whereas the Blackmores are not descended of *Canaan,* but of *Cush.* Psal. 68. 31. *Princes shall come out of Egypt* [Mizraim], *Ethiopia* [Cush] *shall soon stretch out her hands unto God.* Under which Names, all *Africa* may be comprehended; and their Promised Conversion ought to be prayed for. *Jer.* 13. 13. *Can the Ethiopian change his skin?* This shows that Black Men are the Posterity of *Cush:* Who time out of mind have been distinguished by their Colour. . . .

 Obj. 2. *The* Nigers *are brought out of a Pagan Country, into places where the Gospel is Preached.*

 Answ. Evil must not be done, that good may come of it. The extraordinary and comprehensive Benefit accruing to the Church of God, and to *Joseph* personally, did not rectify his brethrens Sale of him.

 Obj. 3. *The* Africans *have Wars one with another: Our Ships bring lawful Captives taken in those Wars.*

 Answ. For ought is known, their Wars are much such as were between *Jacob's* Sons and their Brother *Joseph.* If they be between Town and Town; Provincial, or National: Every War is upon one side Unjust. An Unlawful War can't make lawful Captives. And by Receiving, we are in danger to promote, and partake in their Barbarous Cruelties. I am sure, if some Gentlemen should go down to the *Brewsters* to take the Air, and

Fish: And a stronger party from *Hull* should Surprise them, and Sell them for Slaves to a Ship outward bound: they would think themselves unjustly dealt with; both by Sellers and Buyers. And yet 'tis to be feared, we have no other kind of Title to our *Nigers. Therefore all things whatsoever ye would that men should do to you, do ye even so to them: for this is the Law and the Prophets.* Matt. 7. 12.

Obj. 4. Abraham *had Servants bought with his Money, and born in his House.*

Answ. Until the Circumstances of *Abraham's* purchase be recorded, no Argument can be drawn from it. In the mean time, Charity obliges us to conclude, that He knew it was lawful and good.

It is Observable that the *Israelites* were strictly forbidden the buying, or selling one another for Slaves. *Levit.* 25. 39. 46. *Jer.* 34 8. .... 22. And GOD gaged His Blessing in lieu of any loss they might conceipt they suffered thereby. *Deut.* 15. 18. And since the partition Wall is broken down, inordinate Self love should likewise be demolished. GOD expects that Christians should be of a more Ingenuous and benign frame of spirit. Christians should carry it to all the World, as the *Israelites* were to carry it one towards another. And for men obstinately to persist in holding their Neighbours and Brethren under the Rigor of perpetual Bondage, seems to be no proper way of gaining Assurance that God has given them Spiritual Freedom. Our Blessed Saviour has altered the Measures of the ancient Love-Song, and set it to a most Excellent New Tune, which all ought to be ambitious of Learning. *Matt.* 5. 43, 44. *John* 13. 34. These *Ethiopians,* as black as they are; seeing they are the Sons and Daughters of the First *Adam,* the Brethren and Sisters of the Last ADAM, and the Offspring of GOD; They ought to be treated with a Respect agreeable.

C. THE DEMAND FOR SLAVERY: ''BRIEF ACCOUNT OF THE CAUSES THAT HAVE RETARDED THE PROGRESS OF THE COLONY OF GEORGIA'' (1743)*

... But as if the difficulties arising from indifferent lands, and discouraging tenures, were not sufficient to humble and prepare them for the other severities they have met with, they were totally prohibited the importation, use, or even sight of negroes. In spite of all endeavors to disguise this point, it is as clear as light itself, that negroes are as essentially necessary to the cultivation of Georgia, as axes, hoes, or any other utensil of agriculture. So that if a colony was designed able but to subsist itself, their prohibition was inconsistent; if a garrison only was intended, the very inhabitants were needless: but all circumstances considered, it looked as if the assistance of human creatures, who have been called slaves, as well as subject to the treatment of such, were incongruous with a system that proceeded to confer the thing, but to spare the odium of the appellation.

* These excerpts are reprinted from *Collections of the Georgia Historical Society* (1840–   ), vol. 2, pp. 93–94.

Experience would too soon have taught them the parity of their conditions, in spite of a mere nominal difference. The only English clergymen, who were ever countenanced there, declared they never desired to see Georgia a rich, but a godly colony; and the blind subjection the poor Saltzburgers are under to the Rev. Mr. Boltzius, who has furnished such extraordinary extracts in some accounts of Georgia, published here, will be too evident from some of the annexed depositions to call for any descant.

The pretended content and satisfaction of the people of Ebenezer, without negroes, will plainly appear to be the dictates of spiritual tyranny, and only the wretched acquiescence of people, who were in truth unacquainted with the privilege of choosing for themselves.

It is acknowledged indeed that the present war, and late invasion, may furnish the enemies of the colony with the most plausible objections that could occur, against the allowance of black slaves; but these reasons have not always existed, nor have the trustees ever declared any resolution to admit them, at any other juncture. But if it plainly appears that Georgia, as a colony, cannot barely exist without them, surely an admission of them under limitations, suitable to the present situation of affairs, is absolutely necessary to its support; since want and famine must be more dreadful and insuperable invaders, than any living enemy: besides, the honorable trustees were informed by a letter from Mr. Stirling and others, of the falsehood, of the contented and comfortable situation the people of Darien were affirmed to be in; and that they were bought with a number of cattle, and extensive promises of future rewards, when they signed their petition against negroes. . . .

SELECTION

The Money Problem

Another serious economic problem was the scarcity of money. Most transatlantic business was done on credit, and some specie from the French and Spanish colonies found its way into the continental colonies through the West Indian trade. But this specie was inevitably drained off to redress a chronically unfavorable balance of trade with Great Britain, and there was never a sufficient circulating medium in the colonies to permit normal business activities, much less major internal economic expansion. To solve this problem the colonists first used barter and then paper commodity notes, each representing a certain amount of tobacco, rice, or some other product. When neither of these devices proved sufficient to meet internal currency needs, the colonies turned to government-issued paper money. First emitted in Massachusetts in 1690 to pay for an expedition against the French in King William's War, paper currency was the only kind of money the colonists could raise quickly in military emergencies. Over the next seventy-five years, during half of which time the empire was involved in war, every continental colony issued large quantities of paper to pay for both military expenses and the normal operations of government, experimenting with a number of different forms including money secured by land and, more commonly, money secured by a government promise to redeem the notes for taxes.

Whenever and wherever paper money was issued in large quantities it usually depreciated, and British merchants, fearful that colonials would attempt to pay sterling debts with depreciated paper bills, early adopted a hostile stance against colonial paper currency. Despite the fact that most paper-money experiments, especially outside New England, proved successful over the long run, imperial officials, influenced by the merchants, constantly opposed its use. In September, 1720, they issued an additional instruction forbidding governors to consent to bills for further emissions without a clause suspending them until they had received imperial approval. Although some creditors within the colonies occasionally lined up on the side of British merchants when paper was issued in too great amounts, most colonial leaders and many colonial governors were agreed on the value of controlled emissions. One of the best defenses of colonial paper money came from the pen of William Burnet (1688–1729), governor of New York and New Jersey from 1720 to 1728 and of Massachusetts from 1728 to 1729, in a letter of November 21, 1724, to the Board of Trade. With many of their own servants opposed to their policy, imperial officials clearly had little chance of enforcing it. After stronger instructions issued in 1740 also failed in their purpose, imperial officials turned to Parliament, which by the Currency Act of 1751 prohibited further legal-tender issues and required the retirement of all old issues in New England. This measure did not apply to the colonies from New York south, and during the French and Indian War they issued large amounts of paper to meet war expenses and thereby provoked demands from the British mercantile community for the extension of the 1751 act to all the colonies.

On the colonial money problem, see especially E. James Ferguson, The Power of the Purse: A History of American Public Finance, 1776–1790 *(1961).*

A. A PLEA FOR PAPER CURRENCY: GOVERNOR WILLIAM BURNET TO BOARD OF TRADE (NOV. 21, 1724)*

. . . Credit ought to be supported if it is possible, both by *reason* and *common opinion*. Reason tho ever so strong will not always do alone in the Beginning if common opinion is against it but it will carry all before

---

* These excerpts are reprinted from *New York Colonial Documents,* vol. V, pp. 736–738.

it at the long run: Common opinion or humor will generally do for a time without reason nay, against it. But then it is often attended with vast mischeif and danger—Of this we have a fatal Instance in the famous south Sea Scheme, which being left to common opinion without any restraint has produced the most terrible effects possible. If there had been a positive Law, making all Bargains for South Sea Stock above some fixed Price as 150. void and making it a legal tender at 100 all these mischeifs would have been avoided but this would have been called *compulsive Paper Credit,* yet because in Reason it is worth so much as long as the Nation stands and because the Parliament has always kept their engagements all clamors against this would soon have blown over and no enemies would have been found to it but Brokers

To make this appear it is enough to prove, that at the bottom all the present voluntary credit stands upon this very foundation at last & no other

It is very certain that there is no proportion between the Specie & the great quantity of Bank Bills and Bankers Notes. commonly current who lend their notes on the several Branches of Government Securitys and seldom at a Rate under *par* very often above *par* When the Government is safe this would do when there is any danger, Common opinion pulls down her own work & Bankers break in abundance, and the Bank itself is put to Extremitys. An Instance of this I remember at the time of the Preston affair—The Bank would have broke in a few days, if the victory there had not happened as soon as it did

And the Reason was plainly this because when they had paid away all their Specie they had nothing left but Exchequer Notes, and such other Securitys to exchange for their remaining Bank Notes and these would have been at such a discount that they must have broke, and compounded for such Payment at the Best.

Thus it is plain that the foundation in Reason of the credit of the Bank it self, not to speak of Private Goldsmiths is the Government Security remaining at *Par* and yet the Parliament is so good as to provide an interest on these Exchequer Bills, and to pay the Bank so much more per cent for circulation whereas in fact when foul weather comes the Bank is a Staff of Reed and must lean on the Government to prop itself up and so increase the load instead of easing it

And this humour keeps up the imaginary value, when there is no real accasion for it; all Government Securities being at the same time commonly above *par* But upon any ill News the like Humor beats down all voluntary credit, in the same manner as it does Exchequer Bills &c and really carries the General Discredit as much further than it ought as it had advanced credit beyond its reasonable bounds before and if once the Bank had broke, then all this would have appeared to a demonstration

But the Bank is yet a Virgin, and the exchequer was once shut up in King Charles's Reign tho' I think she has since fully made up for the Sins of her Youth by punctual Payment for thirty or forty years last past

If then instead of these secondary instruments of circulation the Parliament should think fit to make all Parliamentary Paper Credit a Tender at

Par and that it be received in all Taxes as well as paid, which is doing with private persons, as the publick is done by I can not see that it would be any injustice, nor more liable to danger, than the present methods of circulation are It may be objected that this is a french way of proceeding to declare the value of money by edict, but it is easy to answer that the Laws of a Free Government are not at all like the Edicts of an arbitrary one and that it is as unsafe in France to trust the Bankers, as the Government, for when the Government refuses to pay them, they they must break and so it would be in England,—The first Breach of Engagements in the Legislature to the Creditors of the Publick would break all the Bankers at once, and therefore what the Government does by their hands, and in which it is in effect their support it is capable of doing for itself, and if founded on Reason, tho against the present humour it will prevail in the end

I have already endeavored to shew the danger of Common Opinion in money matters, when no ways restrained by Law by the instance of the South sea.

I may add that it is the same thing with Liberty in general if Mobs are entirely left to their common opinion or humor it is well known how fatal they may be to the publick safety and if the liberty of the poor which is now grown to such a Pitch of Licentiousness as to be the greatest Tax and grievance to the Nation were regulated by as severe and as practicable Laws as in Holland it would be of great use to the Publick

From all which I beg leave to conclude, that is not the names things get for the present but the real nature of them, that will be found to hold against all events & that in the instance of Paper money where it is regulated by just Laws and where the Publick have not acted contrary to them their credit is in reason better established than the credit of any private Persons or Society and that the method used to catch the common opinion of mankind by offering them their money when they please is nothing but a fashionable Bubble which People are every day sufferers by when a Banker breaks & that even the best founded Societys can not maintain their Credit when there is the Greatest need of them. But that all Credit finally centers in the Security of the Government

I take the liberty further to observe to your Lordships on how many occasions the Government of Great Britain has found it impracticable to raise all the money wanted within the year from whence all the present debts of the nation have arisen: The same necessity lyes often upon the Plantations where frequently a sum of ready money is wanted, which it would be an intollerable Tax to raise at once, and therefore they are forced to imitate the Parliament at home, in anticipating upon remote funds. And as there is no Bank nor East India company nor even private subscribers capable of lending the Province the money they want at least without demanding the extravagant Interest of 8 Per Cent which is the common Interest here, but would ruin the publick to pay since this is a Case there is no possible way left to make distant funds provide ready money, when it is necessarily wanted, but making paper Bills to be sunk by such funds. Without this Carolina would have been ruined by their

Indian War Boston could not now support theirs nor could any of the Provinces have furnished such considerable Sums to the Expeditions against Canada Nor could at present any of the necessary repairs of this Fort be provided for, nor the arrears of the Revenue be discharged, which is done by this Act in a Tax to be levyed in 4 years nor indeed any publick Service readily and sufficiently effected

And I may add one thing more that this manner of compulsive credit does in fact keep up its value here and that it occasions much more Trade and business than would be without it and that more Specie is exported to England by reason of these Paper Bills than could be if there was no circulation but of Specie for which reason all the merchants here seem now well satisfied with it

I hope your Lordships will excuse my being so long and earnest upon this head because it is a subject of the greatest importance to all the Plantations and what I humbly conceive has been often misrepresented by the Merchants in London. . . .

B. IMPERIAL HOSTILITY TO PAPER CURRENCY

1. The Royal Instruction of (Sept. 27) 1720*

Whereas acts have been passed in some of his Majesty's plantations in America for striking bills of credit and issuing out the same in lieu of money in order to discharge their public debts and for other purposes, from whence several inconveniences have arose; it is therefore his Majesty's will and pleasure that for the future you do not give your assent to or pass any act in his Majesty's province of_____under your government whereby bills of credit may be struck or issued in lieu of money or for payment of money either to you our governor or to the commander in chief or to any of the members of his Majesty's council or of the assembly of the said province of_____, or to any other person whatsoever, without a clause be inserted in such act declaring that the same shall not take effect until the said act shall have been confirmed and approved by his Majesty, excepting acts for raising and settling a public revenue for defraying the necessary charge of the government of the said province of _____ according to the instructions already given you.

2. The Currency Act of (June 25) 1751†

WHEREAS *the act of parliment made in the sixth year of her late majesty* Queen Anne, *intituled,* An act for ascertaining the rate of foreign coins in

---

* Reprinted in full from Leonard Woods Labaree (ed.), *Royal Instructions to British Colonial Governors, 1670–1776* (1935), vol. I, p. 218.

† These excerpts are reprinted from Danby Pickering (ed.), *The Statutes at Large* (46 vols., 1762–1807), vol. XX, pp. 306–309.

her Majesty's plantations in *America, hath been entirely frustrated in his Majesty's said colonies of* Rhode Island *and* Providence *plantations,* Connecticut, *the* Massachusets Bay, *and* New Hampshire *in* America, *by their treating and issuing, from time to time, great quantities of paper bills of credit, by virtue of acts of assembly, orders, resolutions or votes, made or passed by their respective assemblies, and making legal the tender of such bills of credit in payment for debts, dues and demands which bills of credit have, for many years past, been depreciating in their value, by means whereof all debts of late years have been paid and satisfied with a much less value than was contracted for, which hath been a great discouragement and prejudice to the trade and commerce of his Majesty's subjects, by occasioning confusion in dealings, and lessening of credit in those parts;* therefore, for the more effectual preventing and remedying of the said inconveniencies . . . That from and after the twenty ninth day of *September* one thousand seven hundred and fifty one, it shall not be lawful for the governor, council or assembly for the time being, or any of them, or for the lieutenant governor, or person presiding or acting as governor or commander in chief, for the time being, within all or any of the aforesaid colonies or plantations of *Rhode Island,* and *Providence* plantations, *Connecticut,* the *Massachusets Bay,* and *New Hampshire,* to make or pass, or give his or their assent to the making or passing of any act, order, resolution, or vote, within any of the said colonies or plantations, whereby any paper bills or bills of credit, of any kind or denomination whatsoever, shall be created or issued under any pretence whatsoever; or whereby the time limited, or the provision made for the calling in, sinking or discharging of such paper bills, or bills of credit, as are already subsisting and passing in payment, within any of the said colonies or plantations, shall be protracted or postponed; or whereby any of them shall be depreciated in value, or whereby the same shall be ordered or allowed to be re-issued, or to obtain a new and further currency; and that all such acts, orders, resolutions or votes, which shall or may be passed or made, after the said twenty ninth day of *September* one thousand seven hundred and fifty one, within all or any of the said colonies or plantations, shall be, and are hereby declared to be null and void, and of no force or effect whatsoever.

II. And be it further enacted by the authority aforesaid, That all such paper bills, or bills of credit, as are now subsisting, and passing in payments . . . shall be duly and punctually called in, sunk and discharged, according to the tenor of and within the periods limited by the respective acts, orders, votes or resolutions, for creating and issuing, or continuing the same. . . .

III. Provided nevertheless, That nothing in this act contained shall extend, or be construed to extend, to restrain any governor or governors, council or assembly . . . from making or passing any act or acts of assembly in any of the said colonies or plantations, for the creating and issuing of such paper bills, or bills of credit, in lieu of, and for securing such reasonable sum or sums of money, as shall be requisite for the current service of the year. . . .

IV. ·Provided also, That nothing herein contained shall extend, or be construed to extend to restrain any governor or governors, council or assembly . . . from making or passing any act or acts of assembly, in any of the said colonies or plantations, for creating and issuing such paper bills, or bills of credit, in lieu of and for securing such reasonable sum or sums of money as shall, at any time hereafter, be necessary or expedient upon sudden and extraordinary emergencies of government, in case of war or invasion. . . .

VII. And be it further enacted by the authority aforesaid, That from and after the twenty-ninth day of *September* one thousand seven hundred and fifty-one, no paper currency, or bills of credit, of any kind or denomination, which may be made, created or issued in any of the said colonies or plantations, pursuant to the provisions herein before made in this act, shall be a legal tender in payment of any private bargains, contracts, debts, dues or demands whatsoever, within the said colonies or plantations, or any of them.

VIII. Provided, That nothing herein contained shall extend, or be construed to extend to make any of the bills now subsisting in any of the said colonies a legal tender.

IV. And be it further enacted by the authority aforesaid, That if any governor or commander in chief for the time being, in all or any of his Majesty's said colonies or plantations, whether commissioned by his Majesty, or elected by the people, shall, from and after the said twenty ninth day of *September* one thousand seven hundred and fifty one, give his assent to any act of assembly, order, resolution or vote, for the emission or issuing of any paper bills, or bills of credit, of any kind or denomination whatsoever; or for prolonging the time limited for calling in and sinking any such paper bills, or bills of credit, as are now subsisting and passing in payment; or for re issuing or depreciating the same, contrary to the true intent and meaning of this act; such act, order, resolution or vote, shall be *ipso facto* null and void, and such governor or commander in chief shall be immediately dismissed from his government, and for ever after rendered incapable of any publick office or place of trust.

The Emergence of American Society, 1713–1763: The Nature and Ideals of Society

SELECTION

The Organization of Society: Cadwallader Colden, "State of the Province of New York" (1765)

Within a generation, in every colony a few men had discovered the primary economic opportunities, successfully exploited them, and were well on their way to becoming men of wealth—the social and economic leaders of their communities. By the early eighteenth century the societies of all the colonies had assumed a definite shape and were marked by considerable social differentiation between the wealthiest families, on one hand, and the vast, almost undifferentiated body of inhabitants who lived, for the most part, modestly but comfortably and without want, on the other. What groups were at the top depended largely on available opportunities. The description of the organization of New York society in 1765 by Cadwallader Colden (1688–1776), at that time lieutenant governor of that colony, is roughly applicable to all the colonies, though it was the merchants rather than the large landholders who stood at the top of the social order in New England and Pennsylvania. Colden's description is reprinted from New York Historical Society, Collections, *volume 10 (1809–), pages 68–69. There is no comprehensive work on colonial social structure, though the conclusions of Jackson Turner Main in* The Social Structure of Revolutionary America *(1965) would seem in general to be applicable.*

The People of New York are properly Distinguished into different Ranks.

1st The Proprietors of the large Tracts of Land, who include within their claims from 100,000 acres to above one Million of acres under one Grant. Some of these remain in one single Family. Others are, by Devises & Purchases claim'd in common by considerable numbers of Persons.

2nd The Gentlemen of the Law make the second class in which properly are included both the Bench & the Bar. Both of them act on the same Principles, & are of the most distinguished Rank in the Policy of the Province.

3rd The Merchants make the third class. Many of them have rose suddenly from the lowest Rank of the People to considerable Fortunes, & chiefly by illicit Trade in the last War. They abhor every limitation of Trade and Duty on it, & therefore gladly go into every Measure whereby they hope to have Trade free.

4thly—In the last Rank may be placed the Farmers and Mechanics. Tho' the Farmers hold their Lands in fee simple, they are as to condition of Life in no way superior to the common Farmers in England; and the Mechanics such only

299

as are necessary in Domestic Life. This last Rank comprehends the bulk of the People, & in them consists the strength of the Province. They are the most usefull and the most Morall. . . .

SELECTION

The Structure of Values and the Agencies of Enforcement

The character of the New World environment and the societies that developed within it—the seemingly unlimited opportunity, the absence of perpetual poverty, the high rate of both horizontal and vertical mobility, and, especially outside New England, the isolation and loneliness of life in rural areas often on the edge of a vast wilderness—seem to have worked together to undermine the authority of traditional social institutions and to render almost inapplicable hallowed social values. By the end of the seventeenth century the family, church, and community all seemed to have lost their vigor as agencies of social control, and the old values that they were supposed to preserve were little regarded. Occasionally, during the dark days between 1670 and 1720, society in general seemed to be on the verge of complete disintegration.

At the heart of these difficulties was what seemed to be an almost universal concern for self—a lack of community spirit and a tendency to pursue selfish interests even at the expense of the interests of society at large. Acquisitive instincts of the kind illustrated by Robert Keayne earlier in the colonial period had come in time everywhere in the colonies to prevail over the social ideals of his opponents, and a society built, for the most part, upon such gross individual and antisocial behavior did not, it is clear in retrospect, correspond very closely to a value structure based on the assumption that individual considerations always had to give way before the interests of the entire society. Only dimly aware of this lack of correspondence, the new elites that began to emerge toward the end of the seventeenth century sought to counter the centrifugal tendencies in colonial society by reaffirming and cultivating the traditional social values, rather than to construct a new system of values to fit the new conditions.

The most systematic statement of these values by a colonial American in the eighteenth century was the didactic dialogue Raphael, *by Samuel Johnson (1696–1772), Anglican minister at Stratford, Connecticut, from 1723 to 1753 and president of King's College in New York from 1753 to 1763. Written around 1763 but not published until the twentieth century,* Raphael *takes the form of a conversation between the archangel Raphael (sometimes also referred to in the text as the Genius) and two mortals, the writer and his friend Publicola. In the dialogue Raphael describes the nature and operation of the ideal society with particular attention to the role of the family, religion, and education as agencies for the enforcement of community values. A less abstract endorsement of many of the same ideals was supplied by Benjamin Franklin in 1749 in his proposal to establish a college in Philadelphia. For Franklin, as for most of his contemporaries, the ultimate justification for educaton was not the benefit of individuals—that was a secondary, if important, goal—but the advantages that would accrue to the society as a whole. This emphasis is apparent in both his general remarks on the function of education and his description of the ideal curriculum.*

There is no comprehensive analysis of colonial social thought, though the chapter in Max Savelle, Seeds of Liberty *(1965), can be read with profit. On American attitudes toward education with special reference to the role of the family, see Bernard Bailyn,* Education in the Forming of American Society: Needs and Opportunities for Study *(1960). On Johnson, see Herbert Schneider and Carol Schneider (eds.),* Samuel Johnson, President of King's College: His Career and Writings *(1929).*

A. SAMUEL JOHNSON, "RAPHAEL" (CA. 1763)*

. . . every one, if he looks about him and considers, will obviously find the whole system of mankind to be so constituted as renders them on many accounts unavoidably dependent on one another for their mutual well being and happiness, as well as on Him their common Father and Lord, since in many cases they cannot do without each other's help and according as they use or abuse their rational and active powers in their conduct one towards another they are capable of doing one another a great deal of good or hurt, and by that reflecting and imagining power with which the rational nature is endured, every person is readily carried to imagine himself in the same condition in which he beholds another and by conceiving how he should expect or desire to be treated by others were the case changed, he must readily apprehend how he ought in all cases to treat others himself, because he could have no right to expect from others such treatment as he himself would naturally wish for, if he did not allow it to others in the like circumstances. Thus [. . .] inasmuch as every man has a right to call those things his own which he is possessed of by the free gift of his Maker or has acquired by his own activity and industry and that they are highly useful to his comfort and well-being, he feels a great pleasure and satisfaction in the unmolested enjoyment of them and consequently a great uneasiness and trouble in being deprived of them. Hence he must find a strong sense of injury if he be molested or abused

* These excerpts are reprinted from Herbert Schneider and Carol Schneider (eds.), *Samuel Johnson, President of King's College: His Career and Writings* (1929), vol. II, pp. 542–547, 555–560.

by others in the enjoyment of what he has, and must therefore conclude that others have as strong a sense of injury in the like case as he. This sense therefore must determine him not to do injuries to others as he would not receive any from them. He knows that he abhors to be hurt, robbed, belied, deceived, etc., and consequently since everyone must hate to be thus ill-treated as well as he, he must conclude it wrong to treat others ill in these or any the like instances, since he would not endure to be treated so himself. For the same reason therefore that he thinks it right that every one should allow him his own and treat him as being what he is and has, he must be determined to consider it as his duty and interest so to treat others. Again, every man feels a great delight in being well respected, duly valued, well-spoken of and kindly treated by others, and must therefore be led to treat others with all such acts and instances of kindness and benevolence as he would himself, in the like case, expect and take pleasure in receiving; and every one finds a great solace under pain and distress in the pity, compassion and assistance of others, and must therefore feel within himself sentiments of compassion and tenderness towards them in the like circumstances and would act unnaturally if he did not contribute all he could, consistent with his other obligations, to their ease and relief. Thus by means of this faculty of reflecting and conceiving ourselves in each other's case, our love of our selves becomes the foundation of our love of others, and of all the social passions by which we are so readily carried to yield to each one his due, to have mutual pleasure in each other's enjoyments, and mutual sympathy and fellow-feeling in each other's calamities, to take pleasure in communicating pleasure to them, and in relieving their pains, and being solicitous for them in their misfortunes; and hence spring all the social virtues of justice, truth, faithfulness, kindness and benevolence, mercy and charity, all which are in the nature of things necessary to public peace and order since the contrary necessarily lead to all manner of confusion and mischief.

Furthermore with regard to political good it is sufficiently obvious to every one that will with the least attention consider the general condition of mankind, that every man is liable to more wants and necessities than he could of himself supply without the assistance of others, and that there are abundances of the advantages and conveniences of life which cannot be provided for without the joint concurrences of many heads and hands, and the joint commerce of many and even distant nations, God having so ordered things that each different climate should produce some things peculiar to itself, which necessitates every country to have commerce with every other country, more or less, and this seems designed on purpose to promote a general acquaintance, intercourse, faith and friendship among mankind; so that all the inhabitants of the whole globe are obliged to consider themselves on many accounts as one community, throughout the whole of which it is plain that no man could be provided with the necessities and conveniences of life independent of his neighbors and the rest of mankind; hence derives the necessity of universal activity and industry, of various arts and trades and traffic with other nations, and hence buying, selling, and exchanging commodities. And as there are thus various businesses and occupations needful for the general good, so God hath given men no less various geniuses and different turns of mind, and endowed them with a wonderful diversity of faculties and inclinations; by all which, however, differing one from another, it is evident they are designed and in the best manner fitted to promote not only each one his own, but withal, every one the general good of the whole. Thus therefore while each one considers himself as depending on one neighbor for one sort of food, on another for another; on one for clothing of one kind, and on another for that of another; on one for conveniency of habitation; on another for conveniencies of furniture and utensils; on one for furnishing him with these things from home, and on another for supplying him with them by trade and commerce from abroad; on one for curing the maladies of his body; and on another for instructing and cultivating his mind; on one profession for pleading his cause and maintaining and defending his rights with respect to the things of this life, and on another to assist him in fitting himself for, and securing to himself the enjoyments of the everlasting happiness of the life to come; I say, while every one considers himself in this dependent situation with respect to the rest of his fellow-mortals; as dear as each and every of these several enjoyments and conveniencies of life are to him, so dear must the good and flourishing condition of each and every kind of business and profession be in his eye, and consequently he must be solicitous for the weal and prosperity of every one else in order to that of his own. I might add here that the condition of mankind being such that they cannot be subsisted and propagated without marriages and affinities, whence spring divers relations, natural affections and particular friendships and tendencies towards each other, which in addition to the other things above mentioned do strongly tend to bind them together and oblige them to the performance of divers relative duties; and lastly since the love of your children and care for posterity is one of your strongest passions, and since their happiness must chiefly depend upon the good order, weal and prosperity of your country with which you leave them when you go off the stage; this passion, one would think, can't but have a mighty force to engage every one to do all that he can to promote its general interests and public weal while he continues in it.

It is therefore manifest that the great Author of your beings, by all these common sentiments, necessities and interests, affections, relations and dependencies, has evidently designed to tie you together and lay you under a necessity of considering yourselves as a system or whole made up of a vast number and diversity of members, connected together in such a manner, that no one with any pretense to true wisdom can propose his own real interest, his own good and happiness, without being at the same time solicitous for the weal and advantage of every other person that is at all useful in any kind of business whatsoever. And that he that does not contrive to make himself somehow useful to the rest of his species, in proportion to his abilities and opportunities, is like a drone among the bees, a common nuisance to them, and forfeits the good will of the rest, and even the common rights of society, and deserves to be banished from among mankind. And much more he that goes into any course of life, into any vicious and mischievous practices that tend to the subversion of truth and right, of peace and order among mankind. And this leads me to add that whoever shall attentively consider the dark, weak, and depraved condition of mankind among whom the greatest part are generally so intent upon their own private good, their pleasures, profits and ambitious views, as for the sake of them to break through the eternal laws of righteousness and equity, in conformity to which the public good consists; whence many irregularities, disorders and public mischiefs can't but derive; and whoever shall consider the nature of mankind as being chiefly influenced by their hopes and fears; not only on their fears of punishment in consequence of their mischievous practices, but also on their hope of reward attending their virtuous behavior and usefulness, and that therefore those things that are necessary for promoting the public weal, such as profitable discoveries and inventions, arts, learning, and industry cannot flourish without public and honorable encouragement; I say, whoever shall duly consider these things must be readily convinced of the necessity of their subsisting under some form of government and under some sort of public agreements and compacts for maintaining of order and promoting public good according as they are divided and cantonned out into various nations and countries. In order to this some public rules or laws must be agreed upon and established in each particular community by which those things that are discovered to be for public good are commanded and the contrary are forbidden; to which laws sanctions must be annexed. The virtuous, the lovers of their country and those who have by any singular good services promoted the weal of it must be amply rewarded, and the vicious, the profligate and the mischievous must be severely punished. It is necessary to this end that the laws be duly executed, and in order to this there must be magistrates, and a various subordination of officers, all thoroughly furnished with the knowledge and inspired with the hearty love of public good, and unanimously conspiring in their several stations to promote it. Every one's duty and business must be assigned him according to their several ranks, orders and situations in the community, and the public expenses must be honorably provided for. Without such constitutions, laws and administrations as these, and the same duly reverenced, observed and obeyed, society would be a mere chaos and confusion. And lastly it is not only necessary that every community be thus provided for with means and methods for public order within itself; but it must also, from what was above observed, consider itself according as it stands variously situated in regard to other nations and countries, with which it must take care to secure its honor and interest by honorable treaties and stipulations and courageously defend itself when its honor is at any time trampled upon or its rights invaded. Many different forms of government have been devised and practised among mankind, but it may be truly said that none have ever been contrived to better advantage than that of your own nation, by which the people are abundantly secured in the enjoyment of their just liberties and properties, and in a manner sufficiently secure to the honor and dignity of government; and you can't be so happy here in any other method as in that of a firm attachment to the constitution of your mother country, and a submissive conduct towards it, in the welfare whereof and your dependence on it your own is bound up.

But after all no method or form of government can answer the ends of preserving good order and securing the public weal, without a spirit of public virtue and integrity, without a deep sense and hearty love of public good as such, and a sincere, joint, unanimous endeavor in all ranks, orders and conditions of men in their several stations and capacities to promote it, and that in spite of every temptation from any private views whatsoever. And therefore this truly divine temper, this excellent spirit and conduct is by all means to be inculcated, studied and promoted. And to this purpose I will only add here that nothing can so much tend to this as a deep sense of religion that must by all means be provided for; as you are made for a twofold state, a state of probation here and a state of retribution hereafter, provision must be made for securing your general weal in both respects. And as the former is in order to the latter, and the latter is of vastly the greatest importance to you, it concerns everyone that would study the true interest of mankind to consider things in this light and consequently how necessary it is that the public order, peace and weal of mankind respecting the present state be the more solicitously sought, that they may be under the better advantage to qualify themselves for a better state hereafter. And as God being especially intent upon the future weal of his creatures has granted them a particular revelation of His will with respect to that, their most important interest, and hath appointed an order of men to explain and enforce it; and inasmuch as the religion he hath taught and enjoined is on all accounts most friendly and advantageous to promote the temporal and political weal of mankind as well as their spiritual and eternal happiness; it ought to be a necessary article in true political wisdom to protect, encourage and honorably treat this revealed religion and the dispensers of it; for nothing can so effectually secure both fidelity and integrity in the magistrate and obedience and good order in the people as the excellent qualities and salutary effects which it is the design and tendency of the Gospel to produce in your hearts and lives. . . .

Now as there are three things which are chiefly the foundation of all that is virtuous, good and orderly among mankind, *viz.*, obedience to laws and authority, self-denial and industry, these therefore must especially be taken care of in the education of youth. The first and principal care in the education of a child should be to establish your authority over him by inflexibly insisting on reverence and obedience and therefore it is best never to require anything of him but when you intend to be peremptorily obeyed, for if you are lax and negligent in some things and at some times, he will soon expect you should be so on other occasions and always, and this will in a little time grow into an habit of disobedience. You should therefore take care to command nothing rashly and unadvisedly, nothing but what is reasonable, fit, and just, but when you have declared your will see that it be ever immediately and punctually obeyed, and let him always feel the comfort, the pleasure and advantage of an orderly, regular and obedient behavior, and let pain, shame and disgrace ever attend the contrary. And if he be thus always habitually inured by a steady conduct from the beginning to an invariable obedience and sub-mission to government this will render all your other endeavors to promote his good the more easy and successful and withal prepare him when he goes from under your care to act for himself, to be an orderly, obedient and well behaved member of the community. This, said Publicola, is what indeed needs to be much inculcated among us, for family government is grossly neglected in the country and this neglect is such a growing evil, that if it be not reformed in a little time, our youth will be utterly ruined and our commonwealth will sink into a confused jumble of untoward and ungoverned rebels.

It is no less necessary, said he, that this authority be chiefly asserted in the early practice of accustoming them to have their desires curbed, their appetites restrained, and their inclinations thwarted, for the chief occasion of stubborn, vicious habits taking early root in tender minds is their not having resolution enough to deny themselves anything they have a mind to; which when it comes to an habit, they are ready to stick at nothing however so impious or injurious that stands in the way of their gratification. If therefore you would have children virtuous, you must teach them early to deny themselves, and in order to this you must make their inclinations and appetites tame and pliable by accustoming them betimes to be easily denied and crossed. Nay you should even deny and cross them however so innocent a thing it is they desire, whenever they discover an impetuous strong and impatient inclination towards it; for though the thing itself be ever so small and inconsiderable, yet custom, the custom of being indulged on all occasions, is a great thing and draws after it a pernicious train of evil consequences. And if they have been used to have their little senses and innocent inclinations always indulged while they are young they will contract such an habit as will violently prompt them to insist on the gratification of their basest appetites and most vicious inclinations when they grow up. Let them therefore by all means be inured to self-denial, for on the other hand, if they have been used to this in obedience to your will while young, they will readily practice it in obedi-ence to the will of God and the public will, the laws and government you leave them under when they come to be adult. Of the necessity of this precept, said Publicola, we have abundant sad and deplorable evidence! When it is obvious that our youth are apace running headlong into all sorts of debauchery and uncontrolled indulgences, which I doubt not is, as you observe, chiefly owing to the fond indulgence of their parents, and their bad examples in their tender years, while they allow them every thing they ask, and deny them nothing they desire, and study to please and humor them, and even make bargains with them to purchase their obedi-ence to their wills in some things at the expense of letting them have their own wills in every thing else! This, said Raphael, is indeed a most ruinous method of managing children; but I would further add, continued he, upon your mentioning their parents' example, that it is a thing of the greatest importance that parents not only early teach them the utmost abhorence of all impurity, but also keep a strict watch over all their own words and behavior especially in the presence of their children; for there is nothing that they are so apt to be wrought upon and influenced by as the example of their parents, whether good or bad. They should therefore consider the notice and observation of their children as a strong obligation on them in addition to every other consideration, to take the strictest care of their own conduct that all their words and behavior be not only innocent and remote from everything impious, vicious and impure, but as exactly decent, virtuous and religious as possible. For it will be not only the greatest misfortune to them here to have their children take vicious courses, but also a prodigious aggravation to their punishment hereafter, when by their vices they have precipitated themselves into a state of endless misery and despair, that they have by their ill examples brought their miserable offspring into the like deplorable condition. Whereas on the contrary it must vastly add to their felicity and glory in the future state if they have by their good instructions and examples trained them up to be companions and partners with them in the endless felicities of the blessed abodes. These, said Publicola, are indeed the most moving considerations that can be suggested and would to God all parents would duly consider them lest for want of so doing they finally make both themselves and their children miserable in both worlds!

To prevent this, said the Genius, their next care should be to keep a strict eye over them, not only to prevent them from contracting vicious habits, but also when they observe them to be in danger of it, early to reclaim them by seasonable and serious admonitions and if need be, by severe reproofs and corrections. To this purpose it may be highly useful to take them alone and in a serious and dispassionate manner explain to them the mischief of any ill courses they are in danger of. And then carefully endeavor to keep them out of the way of temptation, particularly darkness and unreasonable hours of the night being the most tempting opportunities for wicked practices, let them always insist upon it that their children be at home in season and keep good hours; and since bad company is very contageous let them take care what company they keep and see that it be such as is virtuous and orderly; and lastly forasmuch as idleness is a state of perpetual temptation let them inure them to a steady course of industry, for youth are generally very active, and activity if it be rightly employed is the true perfection of the rational nature, as on the other hand if it be employed to bad purposes, it is its greatest deprivation and misery. It is therefore indispensably necessary that they be both inured to industry and diligence, and always steadily employed about something that may turn to good account; for since everything that renders mankind comfortable and happy depends upon activity and diligence in some business or other, it is absolutely necessary that youth be trained up in some steady course of business in order that they may become useful members of the commonwealth, profitable to themselves and all about them. And since your present state is unavoidably attended with many hardships, the best way to qualify them to pass successfully through the world is to inure them betimes to care, pains, labor and hardship; and besides, a lazy, idle, sauntering negligence, a trifling, luxurious, effeminate softness, are such wretched habits as can't

but be attended with a numerous train of odious and pernicious consequences, particularly gaming, intemperance and lewdness, those deadly
bains of youth, and almost unavoidable attendants of idleness. For youth
as I have said, are naturally active, and if their activity be not rightly
turned and well employed it will be apt to find employments of one
pernicious kind or other, and temptations to gaming, drinking and lewdness are always in their way, and almost sure to take hold of them, and
greater mischiefs can scarce befall them. Gaming, particularly, is a most
powerful temptation to the wasting and consumption of that precious
talent, time, which might be employed to the best purposes of ripening
and improving either their bodies by such manly exercises as would preserve their health and increase their strength and activity, or their minds
by reading histories and other books, which while they enrich them with
true and solid wisdom would at the same time give them a vastly more
rational, manly and agreeable diversion; and by these means they would
prevent a vast deal of quarrelling, swearing, cursing and other hateful
vices and mischiefs which generally attend this pernicious practice of
gaming. And then as to intemperance and lewdness, besides that they as
well as gaming are very expensive and consequently ruinous to their
estates, they weaken and enervate all the powers of soul and body; they
darken, debilitate and debase the mind and alienate it from its proper
objects and render it miserably indisposed to all that is good whether
personal or political; they fill the body with loathsome diseases, consumption and rottenness, and scarce ever fail to cut them off in the very midst
of their days. How solicitous then should parents be to keep their children
as much as possible out of the way of all temptations to these vile practices, and in order to it to keep them from the very beginning steadily and
industriously employed on something that may turn to good purpose, and
engage them in such diversions as may tend to improve either the sagacity
and virtue of their minds or the strength and activity of their bodies! And
how careful ought government to be every way and by all means to discourage and severely punish these hateful vices, idleness, gaming, intemperance and lewdness, as being the most fatal bains of virtue and public
good, and utterly subversive of every thing that is dear and amiable,
flourishing and happy among mankind. . . .

B. BENJAMIN FRANKLIN "PROPOSALS RELATING TO THE EDUCATION OF YOUTH IN PENNSYLVANIA" (1749)*

THE good education of youth has been esteemed by wise men in all ages,
as the surest foundation of the happiness both of private families and of
commonwealths. Almost all governments have therefore made it a principal object of their attention, to establish and endow with proper revenues

---

* Reprinted in full from Jared Sparks (ed.), *Works of Benjamin Franklin*
(10 vols., 1840), vol. I, pp. 569–576.

such seminaries of learning, as might supply the succeeding age with men qualified to serve the public with honor to themselves and to their country. Many of the first settlers of these provinces were men who had received a good education in Europe; and to their wisdom and good management we owe much of our present prosperity. But their hands were full, and they could not do all things. The present race are not thought to be generally of equal ability; for, though the American youth are allowed not to want capacity, yet the best capacities require cultivation; it being truly with them, as with the best ground, which, unless well tilled and sowed with profitable seed, produces only ranker weeds.

That we may obtain the advantages arising from an increase of knowledge, and prevent, as much as may be, the mischievous consequences that would attend a general ignorance among us, the following *hints* are offered towards forming a plan for the education of the youth of Pennsylvania, viz.

It is proposed,

That some persons of leisure and public spirit apply for a charter, by which they may be incorporated, with power to erect an Academy for the education of youth, to govern the same, provide masters, make rules, receive donations, purchase lands, and to add to their number, from time to time, such other persons as they shall judge suitable.

That the members of the corporation make it their pleasure, and in some degree their business, to visit the Academy often, encourage and countenance the youth, countenance and assist the masters, and by all means in their power advance the usefulness and reputation of the design; that they look on the Students as in some sort their children, treat them with familiarity and affection, and, when they have behaved well, and gone through their studies, and are to enter the world, zealously unite, and make all the interest that can be made to establish them, whether in business, offices, marriages, or any other thing for their advantage, preferably to all other persons whatsoever, even of equal merit.

And if men may, and frequently do, catch such a taste for cultivating flowers, for planting, grafting, inoculating, and the like, as to despise all other amusements for their sake, why may not we expect they should acquire a relish for that *more useful* culture of young minds. Thomson says,

'T is joy to see the human blossoms blow,
When infant reason grows apace, and calls
For the kind hand of an assiduous care.
Delightful task! to rear the tender thought,
To teach the young idea how to shoot;
To pour the fresh instruction o'er the mind,
To breathe the enlivening spirit, and to fix
The generous purpose in the glowing breast.

That a house be provided for the Academy, if not in the town, not many miles from it; the situation high and dry, and, if it may be, not far from a river, having a garden, orchard, meadow, and a field or two.

That the house be furnished with a library if in the country, (if in the town, the town libraries may serve), with maps of all countries, globes, some mathematical instruments, an apparatus for experiments in natural philosophy, and for mechanics; prints, of all kinds, prospects, buildings, and machines.

That the Rector be a man of good understanding, good morals, diligent and patient, learned in the languages and sciences, and a correct, pure speaker and writer of the English tongue; to have such tutors under him as shall be necessary.

That the boarding scholars diet together, plainly, temperately, and frugally.

That, to keep them in health, and to strengthen and render active their bodies, they be frequently exercised in running, leaping, wrestling, and swimming.

That they have peculiar habits to distinguish them from other youth, if the Academy be in or near the town; for this, among other reasons, that their behavior may be the better observed.

As to their studies, it would be well if they could be taught *every thing* that is useful, and *every thing* that is ornamental. But art is long, and their time is short. It is therefore proposed, that they learn those things that are likely to be *most useful* and *most ornamental;* regard being had to the several professions for which they are intended.

All should be taught to write a fair hand, and swift, as that is useful to all. And with it may be learned something of drawing, by imitation of prints, and some of the first principles of perspective.

Arithmetic, accounts, and some of the first principles of geometry and astronomy.

The English language might be taught by grammar; in which some of our best writers, as Tillotson, Addison, Pope, Algernon Sidney, *Cato's Letters,* &c., should be classics; the styles principally to be cultivated being the clear and the concise. Reading should also be taught, and pronouncing properly, distinctly, emphatically; not with an even tone, which *under-does,* nor a theatrical, which *over-does* nature.

To form their style, they should be put on writing letters to each other, making abstracts of what they read, or writing the same things in their own words; telling or writing stories lately read, in their own expressions. All to be revised and corrected by the tutor, who should give his reasons, and explain the force and import of words.

To form their pronunciation, they may be put on making declamations, repeating speeches, and delivering orations; the tutor assisting at the rehearsals, teaching, advising, and correcting their accent.

But if History be made a constant part of their reading, such as the translations of the Greek and Roman historians, and the modern histories of ancient Greece and Rome, may not almost all kinds of useful knowledge be that way introduced to advantage, and with pleasure to the student? As

Geography, by reading with maps, and being required to point out the places *where* the greatest actions were done, to give their old and new names, with the bounds, situation, and extent of the countries concerned.

Chronology, by the help of Helvicus or some other writer of the kind, who will enable them to tell *when* those events happened, what princes were contemporaries, and what states or famous men flourished about that time. The several principal epochas to be first well fixed in their memories.

Ancient Customs, religious and civil, being frequently mentioned in history, will give occasion for explaining them; in which the prints of medals, basso-rilievos, and ancient monuments will greatly assist.

Morality, by descanting and making continual observations on the causes of the rise or fall of any man's character, fortune, and power, mentioned in history; the advantages of temperance, order, frugality, industry, and perseverance. Indeed, the general natural tendency of reading good history must be, to fix in the minds of youth deep impressions of the beauty and usefulness of virtue of all kinds, public spirit, and fortitude.

History will show the wonderful effects of *oratory,* in governing, turning, and leading great bodies of mankind, armies, cities, nations. When the minds of youth are struck with admiration at this, then is the time to give them the principles of that art, which they will study with taste and application. Then they may be made acquainted with the best models among the ancients, their beauties being particularly pointed out to them. Modern political oratory being chiefly performed by the pen and press, its advantages over the ancient in some respects are to be shown; as that its effects are more extensive, and more lasting.

History will also afford frequent opportunities of showing the necessity of a *public religion,* from its usefulness to the public; the advantage of a religious character among private persons; the mischiefs of superstition, and the excellency of the *Christian religion* above all others, ancient or modern.

History will also give occasion to expatiate on the advantage of civil orders and constitutions; how men and their properties are protected by joining in societies and establishing government; their industry encouraged and rewarded, arts invented, and life made more comfortable; the advantages of liberty, mischiefs of licentiousness, benefits arising from good laws and a due execution of justice. Thus may the first principles of sound politics be fixed in the minds of youth.

On historical occasions, questions of right and wrong, justice and injustice, will naturally arise, and may be put to youth, which they may debate in conversation and in writing. When they ardently desire victory, for the sake of the praise attending it, they will begin to feel the want, and be sensible of the use, of *logic,* or the art of reasoning to *discover* truth, and of arguing to *defend* it, and *convince* adversaries. This would be the time to acquaint them with the principles of that art. Grotius, Puffendorff, and some other writers of the same kind, may be used on these occasions to decide their disputes. Public disputes warm the imagination, whet the industry, and strengthen the natural abilities.

When youth are told, that the great men, whose lives and actions they read in history, spoke two of the best languages that ever were, the most expressive, copious, beautiful; and that the finest writings, the most correct compositions, the most perfect productions of human wit and wisdom, are in those languages, which have endured for ages, and will endure while there are men; that no translation can do them justice, or give the pleasure found in reading the originals; that those languages contain all science; that one of them is become almost universal, being the language of learned men in all countries; and that to understand them is a distinguishing ornament; they may be thereby made desirous of learning those languages, and their industry sharpened in the acquisition of them. All intended for divinity, should be taught the Latin and Greek; for physic, the Latin, Greek, and French; for law, the Latin and French; merchants, the French, German, and Spanish; and, though all should not be compelled to learn Latin, Greek, or the modern foreign languages, yet none that have an ardent desire to learn them should be refused; their English, arithmetic, and other studies absolutely necessary, being at the same time not neglected.

If the new *Universal History* were also read, it would give a connected idea of human affairs, so far as it goes, which should be followed by the best modern histories, particularly of our mother country; then of these colonies; which should be accompanied with observations on their rise, increase, use to Great Britain, encouragements and discouragements, the means to make them flourish, and secure their liberties.

With the history of men, times, and nations, should be read at proper hours or days, some of the best *histories of nature,* which would not only be delightful to youth, and furnish them with matter for their letters, as well as other history, but would afterwards be of great use to them, whether they are merchants, handicrafts, or divines; enabling the first the better to understand many commodities and drugs, the second to improve his trade or handicraft by new mixtures and materials, and the last to adorn his discourses by beautiful comparisons, and strengthen them by new proofs of divine providence. The conversation of all will be improved by it, as occasions frequently occur of making natural observations, which are instructive, agreeable, and entertaining in almost all companies. Natural history will also afford opportunities of introducing many observations, relating to the preservation of health, which may be afterwards of great use. Arbuthnot on Air and Aliment, Sanctorius on Persperation, Lemery on Foods, and some others, may now be read, and a very little explanation will make them sufficiently intelligible to youth.

While they are reading natural history, might not a little gardening, planting, grafting, and inoculating, but taught and practised; and now and then excursions made to the neighbouring plantations of the best farmers, their methods observed and reasoned upon for the information of youth? The improvement of agriculture being useful to all, and skill in it no disparagement to any.

The *history of commerce,* of the invention of arts, rise of manufactures, progress of trade, change of its seats, with the reasons and causes, may also be made entertaining to youth, and will be useful to all. And this, with the accounts in other history of the prodigious force and effect of engines and machines used in war, will naturally introduce a desire to be instructed in mechanics, and to be informed of the principles of that art by which weak men perform such wonders, labor is saved, and manufactures expedited. This will be the time to show them prints of ancient and modern machines; to explain them, to let them be copied, and to give lectures in mechanical philosophy.

With the whole should be constantly inculcated and cultivated that *benignity of mind,* which shows itself in searching for and seizing every opportunity to serve and to oblige; and is the foundation of what is called *good breeding;* highly useful to the possessor, and most agreeable to all.

The idea of what is *true merit* should also be often presented to youth, explained and impressed on their minds, as consisting in an *inclination,* joined with an *ability,* to serve mankind, one's country, friends, and family; which ability is, with the blessing of God, to be acquired or greatly increased by *true learning;* and should, indeed, be the great *aim* and *end* of all learning.

SELECTION

Building an American Culture: Benjamin Franklin, "Proposal for Promoting Useful Knowledge among the British Plantations in America" (May 14, 1743)

With the accumulation of wealth and more leisure time, many middle- and upper-class colonials turned their attention to the creation of cultural institutions. Accordingly, in the middle decades of the eighteenth century they founded social clubs, colleges, schools, academies, libraries, musical societies, and theaters; supported newspapers and magazines; built elaborate houses and filled them with fine furnishings; and, in a few cases, dabbled in science and literature. One of their most notable accomplishments was the founding of the first learned society in the British colonies, the American Philosophical Society, at Philadelphia in 1744. Benjamin Franklin suggested it, and his proposal, first printed as a letter to his wide circle of correspondents and here reprinted from Jared Sparks (ed.), The Works of Benjamin Franklin *(ten volumes, 1840), volume VI, pages 14–17, reflects both the growing colonial interest in cultural matters and the prevailing utilitarian conception of knowledge and culture. On the cultural life of the colonies, see Louis B. Wright,* The Cultural Life of the American Colonies, 1607–1763 *(1957).*

The English are possessed of a long tract of continent, from Nova Scotia to Georgia, extending north and south through different climates, having different soils, producing different plants, mines, and minerals, and capable of different improvements, manufactures, &c.

The first drudgery of settling new colonies, which confines the attention of people to mere necessaries, is now pretty well over; and there are many in every province in circumstances, that set them at ease, and afford leisure to cultivate the finer arts, and improve the common stock of knowledge. To such of these who are men of speculation, many hints must from time to time arise, many observations occur, which if well examined, pursued, and improved, might produce discoveries to the advantage of some or all of the British plantations, or to the benefit of mankind in general.

But as, from the extent of the country, such persons are widely separated, and seldom can see and converse, or be acquainted, with each other, so that many useful particulars remain uncommunicated, die with the discoverers, and are lost to mankind; it is, to remedy this inconvenience for the future, proposed,

That one society be formed of *virtuosi* or ingenious men, residing in the several colonies, to be called *The American Philosophical Society,* who are to maintain a constant correspondence.

That Philadelphia, being the city nearest the centre of the continent colonies, communicating with all of them northward and southward by post, and with all the islands by sea, and having the advantage of a good growing library, be the centre of the Society,

That at Philadelphia there be always at least seven members, viz. a physician, a botanist, a mathematician, a chemist, a mechanician, a geographer, and a general natural philosopher, besides a president, treasurer, and secretary.

That these members meet once a month, or oftener, at their own expense, to communicate to each other their observations and experiments, to receive, read, and consider such letters, communications, or queries as shall be sent from distant members; to direct the dispersing of copies of such communications as are valuable, to other distant members, in order to procure their sentiments thereupon.

That the subjects of the correspondence be, all new-discovered plants, herbs, trees, roots, their virtues, uses, &c.; methods of propagating them, and making such as are useful, but particular to some plantations, more general; improvements of vegetable juices, as ciders, wines, &c.; new methods of curing or preventing diseases; all new-discovered fossils in different countries, as mines, minerals, and quarries; new and useful improvements in any branch of mathematics; new discoveries in chemistry, such as improvements in distillation, brewing, and assaying of ores; new mechanical inventions for saving labor, as mills and carriages, and for raising and conveying of water, draining of meadows, &c.; all new arts, trades, and manufactures, that may be proposed or thought of; surveys, maps, and charts of particular parts of the sea-coasts or inland countries; course and junction of rivers and great roads, situation of lakes and mountains, nature of the soil and productions; new methods of improving the breed of useful animals; introducing other sorts from foreign countries; new improvements in planting, gardening, and clearing land; and all philosophical experiments that let light into the nature of things, tend to increase the power of man over matter, and multiply the conveniences or pleasures of life.

That a correspondence, already begun by some intended members, shall be kept up by this Society with the ROYAL SOCIETY of London, and with the DUBLIN SOCIETY.

That every member shall have abstracts sent him quarterly, of every thing valuable communicated to the Society's Secretary at Philadelphia; free of all charge except the yearly payment hereafter mentioned.

That, by permission of the postmaster-general, such communications pass between the Secretary of the Society and the members, postage-free.

That, for defraying the expense of such experiments as the Society shall judge proper to cause to be made, and other contingent charges for the common good, every member send a piece of eight per annum to the treasurer, at Philadelphia, to form a common stock, to be disbursed by order of the President with the consent of the majority of the members that can conveniently be consulted thereupon, to such persons and places where and by whom the experiments are to be made, and otherwise as there shall be occasion; of which disbursements an exact account shall be kept, and communicated yearly to every member.

That, at the first meetings of the members at Philadelphia, such rules be formed for regulating their meetings and transactions for the general benefit, as shall be convenient and necessary; to be afterwards changed and improved as there shall be occasion, wherein due regard is to be had to the advice of distant members.

That, at the end of every year, collections be made and printed, of such experiments, discoveries, and improvements, as may be thought of public advantage; and that every member have a copy sent him.

That the business and duty of the Secretary be, to receive all letters intended for the Society, and lay them before the President and members at their meetings; to abstract, correct, and methodize such papers as require it, and as he shall be directed to do by the President, after they have been considered, debated, and digested in the Society; to enter copies thereof in the Society's books, and make out copies for distant members; to answer their letters by direction of the President, and keep records of all material transactions of the Society.

Benjamin Franklin, the writer of this Proposal, offers himself to serve the Society as their secretary, till they shall be provided with one more capable.

The Emergence of American Society, 1713–1763: Religion in Flux

SELECTION 48

The Redirection of Puritanism: Cotton Mather, "Bonfacius" (1710)

One of the notable features of colonial religious life during the first quarter of the eighteenth century was a slackening, even among the Puritans, of interest in formal theology. There was as well an acceleration of a general tendency toward Arminianism—toward an emphasis upon good works and human efforts in the process of salvation—which had been manifest in New England from the very beginnings of Massachusetts Bay. Cotton Mather (1663–1728), the most prolific writer among all the Puritan divines, was one of the key figures in the new emphasis. By advocating the redirection of Puritanism toward social charity and personal piety, his Bonifacius, *published in 1710, marked the end of primitive Puritanism and, as Perry Miller has remarked, turned the religious energies of the Puritans "from concentration upon social organization and the purely personal conscience toward a generalized concern with good works and social leadership." The excerpts below are reprinted from the Boston edition, pages 19–23. See Perry Miller,* The New England Mind: From Colony to Province *(1953), for a superb treatment of religious developments in New England during the first decades of the eighteenth century. Ralph Boas and Louise Boas,* Cotton Mather: Keeper of the Puritan Conscience *(1928), and Barrett Wendell,* Cotton Mather: The Puritan Priest *(1891), are the standard works on Mather.*

1. SUCH *Glorious Things are Spoken* in the Oracles of our Good God, concerning them who *Devise Good*, that, A BOOK OF GOOD DEVICES, may very reasonably demand Attention & Acceptance from them that have any Impressions of the most *Reasonable Religion* upon them. I am *Devising* Such a BOOK; but at the same time Offering a Sorrowful Demonstration, That if men would Set themselves to *Devise Good*, a world of *Good* might be done, more than there is, in this *Present Evil World*. It is very sure, The World has *Need Enough*. There Needs abundance to be done, That the Great GOD and His CHRIST may be more Known and Serv'd in the World; and that the *Errors* which are *Impediments* to the *Acknowledgments* wherewith men ought to Glorify their Creator and Redeemer, may be Rectified. There needs abundance to be done, That the *Evil Manners* of the World, by which men are *drowned in Perdition,* may be Reformed; and mankind rescued from the Epidemical

316

Corruption and Slavery which has overwhelmed it. There needs abundance to be done, That the *Miseries* of the World may have *Remedies* and *Abatements* provided for them; and that miserable people may be Relieved and Comforted. The world has according to the Computation of Some, above Seven hundred millions of people now Living in it. What an ample Field among all these, to *Do Good* upon! In a word, *The Kingdom of God* in the World, Calls for Innumerable *Services* from us. To Do SUCH THINGS is to DO GOOD. Those men DEVISE GOOD, who Shape any DEVICES to do Things of Such a Tendency; whether the Things be of a *Spiritual* Importance, or of a *Temporal.* You see, Sirs, the General matter, appearing as Yet, but as a *Chaos,* which is to be wrought upon. *Oh! that the Good Spirit of God may now fall upon us, and carry on the Glorious work which lies before us!*

2. TIS to be Supposed, my Readers will readily grant, That it is an Excellent, a Vertuous, a Laudable Thing to be full of *Devices,* to bring about Such *Noble Purposes.* For any man to Deride, or to Despise my Proposal, *That we Resolve and Study to Do as much Good in the World as we can,* would be to black a Character, that I am not willing to make a Supposal of it in any of those with whom I am Concerned. Let no man pretend unto the Name of, *A Christian,* who does not Approve the proposal of, *A Perpetual Endeavour to Do Good in the World.* What pretention can Such a man have to be, *A Follower of the Good One?* The Primitive *Christians* gladly accepted and improved the Name, when the Pagans by a mistake Styled them, *Chrestians;* Because it Signifyed, *Useful Ones.* The *Christians* who have no Ambition to be So, Shall be condemned by the Pagans; among whom it was a Term of the Highest Honour, to be termed, *A Benefactor;* to have *Done Good,* was accounted *Honourable.* The Philosopher being asked why Every one desired so much to look upon a Fair Object! he answered, That *it was a Question of a Blind man.* If any man ask, as wanting the Sense of it, What is it worth the while to *Do Good* in the world! I must Say, *It Sounds not like the Question of a Good man.* The Αισθησις πνευματικη as *Origen* calls it, the *Spiritual Taste* of every Good Man will make him have an unspeakable *Relish* for it. Yea, Unworthy to be discoursed as a *Man,* is he, who is not for, *Doing of Good among Men.* An *Enemy* to the Proposal, *That mankind, may be the better*

for us, deserves to be Reckoned, little better than, *A Common Enemy of Mankind*. How Cogently do I bespeak, a Good Reception of what is now designed! I produce not only *Religion*, but even *Humanity* it self, as full of a *Fiery Indignation against the Adversaries of the Design*. Excuse me, Sirs; I declare, that if I could have my choice, I would never *Eat* or *Drink*, or *Walk*, with such an one, as long as I Live; or, Look on him as any other than one by whom *Humanity* it self is Debased and Blemished. A very *Wicked Writer*, has yet found himself compell'd by the Force of *Reason*, to publish this Confession. *To Love the Publick, to Study an Universal Good, and to Promote the Interest of the whole World, as far as is in our Power, is surely the Highest of Goodness, and makes that Temper, which we call Divine.* And, he goes on. *Is the Doing of Good for Glories Sake so Divine a thing?* [Alas, Too much *Humane*, Sir!] *Or, Is it not a Diviner to Do Good, even where it may be thought Inglorious? Even unto the Ingrateful, and unto those who are wholly Insensible for the Good they receive!* A man must be far gone in *Wickedness*, who will open his Mouth, against such *Maxims* and *Actions!* A better Pen has Remark'd it; yea, the man must be much a Stranger in History, who has not made the Remark. *To Speak Truth, and to Do Good, were in the Esteem even of the Heathen World, most God-like Qualities.* God forbid, That in the Esteem of the *Christian World*, for those Qualities, there should be any Abatement!

3. I Won't yet propose the *Reward of Welldoing*, and the glorious Things which the *Mercy* and *Truth* of God will do, for them who *Devise Good;* Because I would have to do with such, as will esteem it, a Sufficient *Reward* unto it self. I will imagine that Generous Ingenuity, in my Readers, which will dispose them to count themselves *well-Rewarded* in the Things it self, if God will Accept them to *Do Good* in the World. It is an Invaluable *Honour*, To *Do Good;* It is an Incomparable *Pleasure*. A Man must Look upon himself as *Dignifyed* and *Gratifyed* by GOD, when an *Opportunity* to *Do Good* is put into his Hands. He must Embrace it with *Rapture*, as enabling him directly to answer the Great END of his being. He must manage it with *Rapturous Delight*, as a most Suitable Business, as a most Precious Priviledge. He must *Sing in those Wayes of the Lord*, wherein he cannot but find himself, while he is *Doing of Good*. As the Saint of Old Sweetly Sang, *I was glad, when they said unto me, Let us go into the House of the Lord*. Thus ought we to be *Glad*, when any *Opportunity* to *Do Good*, is offered unto us. We should need no *Arguments*, to make us Entertain the Offer; but we should *Naturally* fly into the Matter, as most agreeable to the *Divine Nature* whereof we are *made Partakers*. . . .

SELECTION

Return to the Old Faith—The Great Awakening: Jonathan Edwards, "A Faithful Narrative of the Surprising Work of God" (1737)

Beginning in the 1730s and lasting well into the 1750s, a great wave of religious enthusiasm known as the Great Awakening swept through the colonies. It appeared first in New Jersey in the 1720s among the hearers of Theodorus Frelinghuysen, a minister of the Dutch Reformed Church, and then in Northampton, Massachusetts, during the 1730s among the congregation of Jonathan Edwards (1703–1758), pastor of the Northampton Congregational Church and probably the most powerful intellect anywhere in the British American colonies in the middle of the eighteenth century. Subsequently, the movement was broadened and raised to a high pitch of intensity by a group of outstanding revivalist preachers, including Gilbert Tennent, a Presbyterian who toured the northern colonies; George Whitefield, a spellbinding young Englishman who preached up and down the Atlantic seaboard in 1739–1740; and Samuel Davies, who brought the Awakening to Virginia in the late 1740s. The message of these preachers varied greatly from individual to individual, but they all stressed the need for a sinful people to return to the ways of God, and their success can be at least in part attributed to the widespread conviction among colonials that they were in the midst of a drastic spiritual decline.

For Jonathan Edwards the ostensible source of New England's religious woes was the progress of Arminianism. He found especially alarming the Arminian notion that man was not innately sinful but capable of choosing between good and evil and capable as well, through the use of his reason, of perceiving the will of God in nature as well as in the Scriptures. This notion not only implied that man could achieve salvation simply by obeying the discernible will of God but also called into question the traditional Puritan doctrines of original sin and predestination, in the process making God both more humane and less immediately responsible for the salvation of individuals. To combat these heresies Edwards inaugurated a series of sermons at Northampton in 1734 in which he preached the impotence of man and the omnipotence of God. Salvation, he argued, could be achieved only through God's grace and not through good works. At heart, Edwards's theology bore a striking resemblance to the religious ideas of the early Puritan fathers, but he was much more than a religious reactionary, eventually erecting a theological system that managed to reconcile the traditional notions of Calvinism with the ideas of the new science of Sir Isaac Newton and John Locke. More immediately, however, his sermons stimulated a remarkable religious revival around Northampton, a surprising return to the old faith, and a reinvigoration of the spiritual life of the town. Edwards himself described the early stages of this phenomenon in 1737 in A

Faithful Narrative of the Surprising Work of God, *the introductory portions of which are reprinted below from* The Works of President Edwards *(four volumes, 1868, volume III, pages 231–241. Ultimately, Edwards proved to be too strict even for his own congregation, and his insistence upon excluding all but "visible saints" from communion led to his dismissal in 1750. Subsequently, he was a missionary to the Stockbridge Indians and very briefly, just before his death in 1758, president of the new Presbyterian College of New Jersey.*

For the general outlines of the Great Awakening, see the relevant chapters in William Warren Sweet, Religion in Colonial America *(1942). On Edwards, Perry Miller,* Jonathan Edwards *(1949), a brilliant study of Edwards's thought, and Ola Elizabeth Winslow,* Jonathan Edwards, 1703–1758 *(1940), a conventional biography, are indispensable.*

. . . The people of the county in general, I suppose are as sober, and orderly, and good sort of people, as in any part of New England; and I believe they have been preserved the freest by far, of any part of the country from error and variety of sects and opinions. Our being so far within the land, at a distance from seaports, and in a corner of the country, has doubtless been one reason why we have not been so much corrupted with vice, as most other parts. But without question the religion, and good order of the country, and their purity in doctrine, has, under God, been very much owing to the great abilities, and eminent piety, of my venerable and honored grandfather Stoddard. I suppose we have been the freest of any part of the land from unhappy divisions, and quarrels in our ecclesiastical and religious affairs, till the late lamentable Springfield contention.

We being much separated from other parts of the province, and having comparatively but little intercourse with them, have from the beginning, till now, always managed our ecclesiastical affairs within ourselves; it is the way in which the country, from its infancy, has gone by the practical agreement of all, and the way in which our peace and good order has hitherto been maintained.

The town of Northampton is of about eighty-two years standing, and has now about two hundred families; which mostly dwell more compactly together than any town of such a bigness in these parts of the country; which probably has been an occasion that both our corruptions and reformations have been from time to time, the more swiftly propagated, from one to another, through the town. Take the town in general, and so far as I can judge, they are as rational and understanding a people as most I have been acquainted with: many of them have been noted for religion, and particularly, have been remarkable for their distinct knowledge in things that relate to heart religion, and Christian experience, and their great regards thereto.

I am the third minister that has been settled in the town: the Rev. Mr. Eleazar Mather, who was the first, was ordained in July, 1669. He was one whose heart was much in his work, abundant in labors for the good of precious souls; he had the high esteem and great love of his people, and was blessed with no small success. The Rev. Mr. Stoddard, who succeeded him, came first to the town the November after his death, but was not ordained till September 11, 1672, and died February 11, 1728—9. So that he continued in the work of the ministry here from his first coming to town, near sixty years. And as he was eminent and renowned for his gifts and grace; so he was blessed, from the beginning, with extraordinary success in his ministry, in the conversion of many souls. He had five harvests as he called them: the first was about fifty-seven years ago; the second about fifty-three years; the third about forty; the fourth about twenty-four; the fifth and last about eighteen years ago. Some of these times were much more remarkable than others, and the ingathering of souls more plentiful. Those that were about fifty-three, and forty, and twenty-four years ago, were much greater than either the first or the last: but in each of them, I have heard my grandfather say, the greater part of the young people in the town, seemed to be mainly concerned for their eternal salvation.

After the last of these, came a far more degenerate time (at least among young people), I suppose, than ever before. Mr. Stoddard, indeed, had the comfort before he died, of seeing a time when there was no small appearance of a divine work amongst some, and a considerable ingathering of souls, even after I was settled with him in the ministry, which was about two years before his death; and I have reason to bless God for the great advantage I had by it. In these two years there were near twenty that Mr. Stoddard hoped to be savingly converted; but there was nothing of any general awakening. The greater part seemed to be at that time very insensible of the things of religion, and engaged in other cares and pursuits. Just after my grandfather's death, it seemed to be a time of extraordinary dullness in religion: licentiousness for some years greatly prevailed among the youth of the town; they were many of them very much addicted to night walking, and frequenting the tavern, and lewd practices, wherein some by their example exceedingly corrupted others. It was their manner very frequently to get together in conventions of both sexes, for mirth and jollity, which they called frolicks; and they would often spend the greater part of the night in them, without any regard to order in the families they belonged to: and indeed family government did too much fail in the town. It was become very customary with many of our young people to be indecent in their carriage at meeting, which doubtless would not have prevailed to such a degree, had it not been that my grandfather, through his great age (though he retained his powers surprisingly to the last), was not so able to observe them. There had also long prevailed in the town a spirit of contention between two parties, into which they had for many years been divided, by which was maintained a jealousy one of the other, and they were prepared to oppose one another in all public affairs.

But in two or three years after Mr. Stoddard's death, there began to be a sensible amendment of these evils; the young people showed more of a disposition to hearken to counsel, and by degrees left off their frolicking, and grew observably more decent in their attendance on the public worship, and there were more that manifested a religious concern than there used to be.

At the latter end of the year 1733, there appeared a very unusual flexibleness, and yielding to advice, in our young people. It had been too long their manner to make the evening after the Sabbath, and after our public lecture, to be especially the times of their mirth, and company keeping. But a sermon was now preached on the Sabbath before the lecture, to show the evil tendency of the practice, and to persuade them to reform it; and it was urged on heads of families, that it should be a thing agreed upon among them, to govern their families, and keep their children at home, at these times;—and withal it was more privately moved, that they should meet together the next day, in their several neighborhoods, to know each other's minds: which was accordingly done, and the motion complied with throughout the town. But parents found little or no occasion for the exercise of government in the case; the young people declared themselves convinced by what they had heard from the pulpit, and were willing of themselves to comply with the counsel that had been given; and it was immediately, and, I suppose, almost universally complied with; and there was a thorough reformation of these disorders thenceforward, which has continued ever since.

Presently after this, there began to appear a remarkable religious concern at a little village belonging to the congregation, called Pascommuck, where a few families were settled, at about three miles distance from the main body of the town. At this place a number of persons seemed to be savingly wrought upon. In the April following, anno 1734, there happened a very sudden and awful death of a young man in the bloom of his youth; who being violently seized with a pleurisy, and taken immediately very delirious, died in about two days; which (together with what was preached publicly on that occasion) much affected many young people. This was followed with another death of a young married woman, who had been considerably exercised in mind, about the salvation of her soul, before she was ill, and was in great distress, in the beginning of her illness; but seemed to have satisfying evidences of God's saving mercy to her, before her death; so that she died very full of comfort, in a most earnest and moving manner, warning and counselling others. This seemed much to contribute to the solemnizing of the spirits of many young persons; and there began evidently to appear more of a religious concern on people's minds.

In the fall of the year, I proposed it to the young people, that they should agree among themselves to spend the evenings after lectures, in social religion, and to that end to divide themselves into several companies to meet in various parts of the town; which was accordingly done, and those meetings have been since continued, and the example imitated by elder people. This was followed with the death of an elderly person, which was attended with many unusual circumstances, by which many were much moved and affected.

About this time began the great noise that was in this part of the country, about Arminianism, which seemed to appear with a very threatening aspect upon the interest of religion here. The friends of vital piety trembled for fear of the issue; but it seemed, contrary to their fear, strongly to be overruled for the promoting of religion. Many who looked on themselves as in a Christless condition seemed to be awakened by it, with fear that God was about to withdraw from the land, and that we should be given up to heterodoxy, and corrupt principles, and that then their opportunity for obtaining salvation would be past; and many who were brought a little to doubt about the truth of the doctrines they had hitherto been taught, seemed to have a kind of a trembling fear with their doubts, lest they should be led into by-paths, to their eternal undoing: and they seemed with much concern and engagedness of mind to inquire what was intended the way in which they must come to be accepted with God. There were then some things said publicly on that occasion, concerning justification by faith alone.

Although great fault was found with meddling with the controversy in the pulpit, by such a person, at that time, and though it was ridiculed by many elsewhere; yet it proved a word spoken in season here; and was most evidently attended with a very remarkable blessing of heaven to the souls of the people in this town. They received thence a general satisfaction with respect to the main thing in question, which they had in trembling doubts and concern about; and their minds were engaged the more earnestly to seek that they might come to be accepted of God, and saved in the way of the gospel, which had been made evident to them to be the true and only way. And then it was, in the latter part of December, that the Spirit of God began extraordinarily to set in, and wonderfully to work amongst us; and there were, very suddenly, one after another, five or six persons, who were, to all appearance, savingly converted, and some of them wrought upon in a very remarkable manner.

Particularly, I was surprised with the relation of a young woman, who had been one of the greatest company keepers in the whole town: when she came to me, I had never heard that she was become in any wise serious, but by the conversation I then had with her, it appeared to me, that what she gave an account of, was a glorious work of God's infinite power and sovereign grace; and that God had given her a new heart, truly broken and sanctified. I could not then doubt of it, and have seen much in my acquaintance with her since to confirm it.

Though the work was glorious, yet I was filled with concern about the effect it might have upon others: I was ready to conclude (though too rashly) that some would be hardened by it, in carelessness and looseness of life; and would take occasion from it to open their mouths, in reproaches of religion. But the event was the reverse, to a wonderful degree; God made it, I suppose, the greatest occasion of awakening to others, of any thing that ever came to pass in the town. I have had abundant opportunity to know the effect it had, by my private conversation with many. The news of it seemed to be almost like a flash of lightning, upon the hearts of young people, all over the town, and upon many others. Those persons amongst us, who used to be farthest from seriousness, and that I most feared would make an ill improvement of it, seemed greatly to be awakened with it; many went to talk with her, concerning what she had met with; and what appeared in her seemed to be to the satisfaction of all that did so.

Presently upon this, a great and earnest concern about the great things of religion, and the eternal world, became universal in all parts of the town, and among persons of all degrees, and all ages; the noise amongst the dry bones waxed louder and louder: all other talk but about spiritual and eternal things was soon thrown by; all the conversation in all companies, and upon all occasions, was upon these things only, unless so much as was necessary for people carrying on their ordinary secular business. Other discourse than of the things of religion, would scarcely be tolerated in any company. The minds of people were wonderfully taken off from the world; it was treated amongst us as a thing of very little consequence: they seem to follow their worldly business, more as a part of their duty, than from any disposition they had to it; the temptation now seemed to lie on that hand, to neglect worldly affairs too much, and to spend too much time in the immediate exercise of religion: which thing was exceedingly misrepresented by reports that were spread in distant parts of the land, as though the people here had wholly thrown by all worldly business, and betook themselves entirely to reading and praying, and such like religious exercises.

But though the people did not ordinarily neglect their worldly business, yet there then was the reverse of what commonly is: religion was with all sorts the great concern, and the world was a thing only by the by. The only thing in their view was to get the kingdom of heaven, and every one appeared pressing into it: the engagedness of their hearts in this great concern could not be hid; it appeared in their very countenances. It then was a dreadful thing amongst us to lie out of Christ, in danger every day of dropping into hell; and what persons' minds were intent upon was to escape for their lives, and to *fly from the wrath to come.* All would eagerly lay hold of opportunities for their souls; and were wont very often to meet together in private houses for religious purposes: and such meetings, when appointed, were wont greatly to be thronged.

There was scarcely a single person in the town, either old or young, that was left unconcerned about the great things of the eternal world. Those that were wont to be the vainest, and loosest, and those that had been most disposed to think and speak slightly of vital and experimental religion, were now generally subject to great awakenings. And the work of conversion was carried on in a most astonishing manner, and increased more and more; souls did, as it were, come by flocks to Jesus Christ. From day to day, for many months together, might be seen evident instances of sinners brought *out of darkness into marvellous light,* and delivered *out of a horrible pit, and from the miry clay, and set upon a rock,* with a *new song of praise to God in their mouths.*

This work of God, as it was carried on, and the number of true saints multiplied, soon made a glorious alteration in the town; so that in the spring and summer following, anno 1735, the town seemed to be full of the presence of God: it never was so full of love, nor so full of joy; and yet so full of distress as it was then. There were remarkable tokens of God's presence in almost every house. It was a time of joy in families on the account of salvation's being brought unto them; parents rejoicing over their children as new born, and husbands over their wives, and wives over their husbands. *The goings of God were then seen in his sanctuary, God's day was a delight, and his tabernacles were amiable.* Our public assemblies were then beautiful; the congregation was alive in God's service, every one earnestly intent on the public worship, every hearer eager to drink in the words of the minister as they came from his mouth; the assembly in general were, from time to time, in tears while the word was preached; some weeping with sorrow and distress, others with joy and love, others with pity and concern for the souls of their neighbors.

Our public praises were then greatly enlivened; God was then served in our psalmody, in some measure, in the beauty of holiness. It has been observable, that there has been scarce any part of divine worship, wherein good men amongst us have had grace so drawn forth, and their hearts so lifted up in the ways of God, as in singing his praises: our congregation excelled all that ever I knew in the external part of the duty before, the men generally carrying regularly, and well, three parts of music, and the women a part by themselves, but now they were evidently wont to sing with unusual elevation of heart and voice, which made the duty pleasant indeed.

In all companies, on other days, on whatever occasions persons met together, Christ was to be heard of, and seen in the midst of them. Our young people, when they met, were wont to spend the time in talking of the excellency and dying love of Jesus Christ, the gloriousness of the way of salvation, the wonderful, free, and sovereign grace of God, his glorious work in the conversion of a soul, the truth and certainty of the great things of God's word, the sweetness of the views of his perfections, &c. And even at weddings, which formerly were merely occasions of mirth and jollity, there was now no discourse of any thing but the things of religion, and no appearance of any but spiritual mirth.

Those amongst us that had been formerly converted, were greatly enlivened and renewed with fresh and extraordinary incomes of the Spirit of God; though some much more than others, according to the measure of the gift of Christ: many that before had labored under difficulties about their own state, had now their doubts removed by more satisfying experience, and more clear discoveries of God's love.

When this work of God first appeared, and was so extraordinarily carried on amongst us in the winter, others round about us, seemed not to know what to make of it; and there were many that scoffed at, and ridiculed it; and some compared what we called conversion to certain distempers. But it was very observable of many, that occasionally came amongst us from abroad, with disregardful hearts, that what they saw here cured them of such a temper of mind: strangers were generally surprised to find things so much beyond what they had heard, and were wont to tell others that the state of the town could not be conceived of by those that had not seen it. The notice that was taken of it by the people that came to town on occasion of the court, that sat here in the beginning of March, was very observable. And those that came from the neighborhood to our public lectures, were for the most part remarkably affected. Many that came to town, on one occasion or other, had their consciences smitten, and awakened, and went home with wounded hearts, and with those impressions that never wore off till they had hopefully a saving issue; and those that before had serious thoughts, had their awakenings and convictions greatly increased. And there were many instances of persons that came from abroad, on visits, or on business, that had not been long here before, to all appearance, they were savingly wrought upon, and partook of that shower of divine blessing that God rained down here, and went home rejoicing; till at length the same work began evidently to appear and prevail in several other towns in the county.

In the month of March, the people in South Hadley began to be seized with deep concern about the things of religion; which very soon became universal: and the work of God has been very wonderful there; not much, if any thing, short of what it has been here, in proportion to the bigness of the place. About the same time it began to break forth in the west part of Suffield (where it has also been very great), and it soon spread into all parts of the town. It next appeared at Sunderland, and soon overspread the town; and I believe was for a season, not less remarkable than it was here. About the same time it began to appear in a part of Deerfield, called Green River, and afterwards filled the town, and there has been a glorious work there: it began also to be manifest in the south part of Hatfield, in a place called the Hill, and after that the whole town, in the second week in April, seemed to be seized, as it were at once, with concern about the things of religion: and the work of God has been great there. There has been also a very general awakening at West Springfield, and Long Meadow; and in Enfield, there was, for a time, a pretty general concern amongst some that before had been very loose persons. About the same time that this appeared at Enfield, the Rev. Mr. Bull of Westfield informed me, that there had been a great alternation there, and that more had been done in one week there than in seven years before.—Something of this work likewise appeared in the first precinct in Springfield, principally in the north and south extremes of the parish. And in Hadley old town, there gradually appeared so much of a work of God on souls, as at another time would have been thought worthy of much notice. For a short time there was also a very great and general concern, of the like nature, at Northfield. And wherever this concern appeared, it seemed not to be in vain: but in every place God brought saving blessings with them, and his word attended with his Spirit (as we have all reason to think) returned not void. It might well be said at that time in all parts of the country, *Who are these that fly as a cloud, and as doves to their windows?* . . .

This remarkable pouring out of the Spirit of God, which thus extended from one end to the other of this country, was not confined to it, but many places in Connecticut have partook in the same mercy: as for instance, the first parish in Windsor, under the pastoral care of the Reverend Mr. Marsh, was thus blest about the same time, as we in Northampton, while we had no knowledge of each other's circumstances. . . .

But this shower of Divine blessing has been yet more extensive: there was no small degree of it in some parts of the Jerseys; as I was informed when I was at New-York (in a long journey I took at that time of the year for my health), by some people of the Jerseys, whom I saw: especially the Rev. Mr. William Tennent, a minister, who seemed to have such things much at heart, told me of a very great awakening of many in a place called the Mountains, under the ministry of one Mr. Cross; and of a very considerable revival of religion in another place under the ministry of his brother the Rev. Mr. Gilbert Tennent; and also at another place, under the ministry of a very pious young gentleman, a Dutch minister, whose name as I remember, was Freelinghousen.

This seems to have been a very extraordinary dispensation of Providence: God has in many respects, gone out of, and much beyond his usual and ordinary way. The work in this town, and some others about us, has been extraordinary on account of the universality of it, affecting all sorts, sober and vicious, high and low, rich and poor, wise and unwise; it reached the most considerable families and persons to all appearance, as much as others. In former stirrings of this nature, the bulk of the young people have been greatly affected; but old men and little children have been so now. Many of the last have, of their own accord, formed themselves into religious societies, in different parts of the town: a loose careless person could scarcely find a companion in the whole neighborhood; and if there was any one that seemed to remain senseless or unconcerned, it would be spoken of as a strange thing.

This dispensation has also appeared extraordinary in the numbers of those, on whom we have reason to hope it has had a saving effect: we have about six hundred and twenty communicants, which include almost all our adult persons. The church was very large before; but persons never thronged into it, as they did in the late extraordinary time. Our sacraments were eight weeks asunder, and I received into our communion about a hundred before one sacrament, and fourscore of them at one time, whose appearance, when they presented themselves together to make an open, explicit profession of Christianity, was very affecting to the congregation: I took in near sixty before the next sacrament day: and I had very sufficient evidence of the conversion of their souls, through divine grace, though it is not the custom here, as it is in many other churches in this country, to make a credible relation of their inward experiences, the ground of admission to the Lord's Supper.

I am far from pretending to be able to determine how many have lately been the subjects of such mercy; but if I may be allowed to declare any thing that appears to me probable in a thing of this nature, I hope that more than three hundred souls were savingly brought home to Christ in this town, in the space of half a year (how many more I don't guess), and about the same number of males as females; which, by what I have heard Mr. Stoddard say, was far from what has been usual in years past, for he observed that in his time, many more women were converted than men. Those of our young people that are on other accounts most likely and considerable, are mostly, as I hope, truly pious, and leading persons in the way of religion. Those that were formerly looser young persons, are generally, to all appearance, become true lovers of God and Christ, and spiritual in their dispositions. And I hope that by far the greater part of persons in this town, above sixteen years of age, are such as have the saving knowledge of Jesus Christ; and so by what I heard I suppose it is in some other places, particularly at Sunderland and South Hadley.

This has also appeared to be a very extraordinary dispensation, in that the Spirit of God has so much extended not only his awakening, but regenerating influences, both to elderly persons, and also those that are very young. It has been a thing heretofore rarely heard of, that any were converted past middle age; but now we have the same ground to think that many such have in this time been savingly changed, as that others have been so in more early years. I suppose there were upwards of fifty persons in this town above forty years of age; and more than twenty of them above fifty, and about ten of them above sixty, and two of them above seventy years of age.

It has heretofore been looked on as a strange thing, when any have seemed to be savingly wrought upon, and remarkably changed in their childhood; but now, I suppose, near thirty were to appearance so wrought upon between ten and fourteen years of age, and two between nine and ten, and one of them about four years of age; and because, I suppose, this last will be most difficultly believed, I shall hereafter give a particular account of it. The influences of God's Spirit have also been very remarkable on children in some other places, particularly at Sunderland and South Hadley, and the west part of Suffield. There are several families in this town that are all hopefully pious; yea, there are several numerous families, in which, I think, we have reason to hope that all the children are truly godly, and most of them lately become so: and there are very few houses in the whole town, into which salvation has not lately come, in one or more instances. There are several negroes, that from what was seen in them then, and what is discernible in them since, appear to have been truly born again in the late remarkable season.

God has also seemed to have gone out of his usual way in the quickness of his work, and the swift progress his Spirit has made in his operation, on the hearts of many: 'tis wonderful that persons should be so suddenly, and yet so greatly changed: many have been taken from a loose and careless way of living, and seized with strong convictions of their guilt and misery, and in a very little time old things have passed away, and all things have become new with them.

God's work has also appeared very extraordinary, in the degrees of the influences of his Spirit, both in the degree of awakening and conviction, and also in a degree of saving light, and love, and joy, that many have experienced. It has also been very extraordinary in the extent of it, and its being so swiftly propagated from town to town. In former times of the pouring out of the Spirit of God on this town, though in some of them it was very remarkable, yet it reached no further than this town, the neighboring towns all around continued unmoved.

The work of God's Spirit seemed to be at its greatest height in this town, in the former part of the spring, in March and April; at which time

God's work in the conversion of souls was carried on amongst us in so wonderful a manner, that so far as I, by looking back, can judge from the particular acquaintance I have had with souls in this work, it appears to me probable, to have been at the rate, at least of four persons in a day, or near thirty in a week, take one with another, for five or six weeks together: when God in so remarkable a manner took the work into his own hands, there was as much done in a day or two, as at ordinary times, with all endeavors that men can use, and with such a blessing as we commonly have, is done in a year.

I am very sensible how apt many would be, if they should see the account I have here given, presently to think with themselves that I am very fond of making a great many converts, and of magnifying and aggrandizing the matter; and to think that, for want of judgment, I take every religious pang, and enthusiastic conceit, for saving conversion; and I do not much wonder if they should be apt to think so: and for this reason, I have forborne to publish an account of this great work of God, though I have often been put upon it; but having now as I thought a special call to give an account of it, upon mature consideration I thought it might not be beside my duty to declare this amazing work, as it appeared to me, to be indeed divine, and to conceal no part of the glory of it, leaving it with God to take care of the credit of his own work, and running the venture of any censorious thoughts, which might be entertained of me to my disadvantage. But that distant persons may be under as great advantage as may be, to judge for themselves of this matter, I would be a little more large, and particular.

I therefore proceed to give an account of the manner of persons being wrought upon; and here there is a vast variety, perhaps as manifold as the subjects of the operation; but yet in many things there is a great analogy in all.

Persons are first awakened with a sense of their miserable condition by nature, the danger they are in of perishing eternally, and that it is of great importance to them that they speedily escape, and get into a better state. Those that before were secure and senseless, are made sensible how much they were in the way to ruin in their former courses. Some are more suddenly seized with convictions; it may be, by the news of others' conversion, or something they hear in public, or in private conference, their consciences are suddenly smitten, as if their hearts were pierced through with a dart: others have awakenings that come upon them more gradually; they begin at first to be something more thoughtful and considerate, so as to come to a conclusion in their minds, that it is their best and wisest way to delay no longer, but to improve the present opportunity; and have accordingly set themselves seriously to meditate on those things that have the most awakening tendency, on purpose to obtain convictions; and so their awakenings have increased, till a sense of their misery, by God's Spirit setting in therewith, has had fast hold of them. Others that, before this wonderful time, had been something religious and concerned for their salvation, have been awakened in a new manner, and made sensible that their slack and dull way of seeking was never like to attain their purpose, and so have been roused up to a greater violence for the kingdom of heaven.

These awakenings when they have first seized on persons, have had two effects: one was, that they have brought them immediately to quit their sinful practices, and the looser sort have been brought to forsake and dread their former vices and extravagancies. When once the Spirit of God began to be so wonderfully poured out in a general way through the town, people had soon done with their old quarrels, backbitings, and inter-meddling with other men's matters; the tavern was soon left empty, and persons kept very much at home; none went abroad unless on necessary business, or on some religious account, and every day seemed in many respects like a Sabbath day. And the other effect was, that it put them on earnest application to the means of salvation, reading, prayer, meditation, the ordinances of God's house, and private conference; their cry was, *What shall we do to be saved?* The place of resort was now altered, it was no longer the tavern, but the minister's house; that was thronged far more than ever the tavern had been wont to be.

There is a very great variety, as to the degree of fear and trouble that persons are exercised with, before they obtain any comfortable evidences of pardon and acceptance with God: some are from the beginning carried on with abundantly more encouragement and hope, than others: some have had ten times less trouble of mind than others, in whom yet the issue seems to be the same. Some have had such a sense of the displeasure of God, and the great danger they were in of damnation, that they could not sleep at nights; and many have said that when they have laid down, the thoughts of sleeping in such a condition have been frightful to them, and they have scarcely been free from terror while they have been asleep, and they have awaked with fear, heaviness, and distress still abiding on their spirits. It has been very common, that the deep and fixed concern that has been on persons' minds, has had a painful influence on their bodies, and given disturbance to animal nature.

The awful apprehensions persons have had of their misery, have for the most part been increasing, the nearer they have approached to deliverance; though they often pass through many changes, and alterations in the frame and circumstances of their minds: sometimes they think themselves wholly senseless, and fear that the Spirit of God has left them, and that they are given up to judicial hardness; yet they appear very deeply exercised about that fear, and are in great earnest to obtain convictions again.

Together with those fears, and that exercise of mind which is rational, and which they have just ground for, they have often suffered many need-less distresses of thought, in which Satan probably has a great hand, to entangle them, and block up their way; and sometimes the distemper of melancholy has been evidently mixed; of which, when it happens, the tempter seems to make great advantage, and puts an unhappy bar in the way of any good effect: one knows not how to deal with such persons; they turn every thing that is said to them the wrong way, and most to their own disadvantage: and there is nothing that the devil seems to make

so great a handle of, as a melancholy humor, unless it be the real corruption of the heart. . . .

SELECTION

The Arminian Strain: Charles Chauncy,
"The Benevolence of the Deity" (ca. 1750)

*Not everyone received the Great Awakening with enthusiasm. Although many
of the orthodox clergy at first welcomed the revival of religious zeal, they
quickly became alarmed by the excess of emotions that came with it. Their
opposition to such religious enthusiasms and their insistence upon maintaining
the tradition of a learned ministry eventually split the churches into Old Light
and New Light groups, the latter setting up their own churches and in 1746
founding the College of New Jersey (later Princeton) to train their ministers.
Paradoxically, in New England the Awakening also had the effect of quickening
the tendencies toward Arminianism that Jonathan Edwards had originally set
out to check. Although Edwards's teaching became the orthodox fare among
most of the Congregational ministers over the next century, a small and influential group of clergymen, seeking to combat the extreme emotionalism of the
Awakening, systematically set about the task of constructing a more rational
theology. Whereas Edwards had emphasized the predominance of the will
(which he identified with the emotions of liking and disliking) over understanding in man, they stressed the primacy of reason. For them God was not angry
and capricious but benevolent and well disposed toward man, and man himself,
exercising his freedom to choose between good and evil, was primarily responsible for his own salvation. One of the main leaders of the Arminian movement
was Charles Chauncy (1705–1787), minister of the First Church of Boston. In
the following selection, the preface to a much longer work written in the 1750s
but not published until 1784, he describes his conception of the deity. The
selection is reprinted from the original Boston edition, pages iii–x. For further
reading, see especially Conrad Wright, The Beginnings of Unitarianism in
America (1955).*

enevolence is that quality, in the human mind, without which we
could not be the objects of one another's esteem: Neither, were
we wholly destitute of it, could we, whatever other qualities we might be

endowed with, place that confidence in each other, upon which the well-being of the world, in so great a measure, depends. Were we possessed of power, but no benevolence, it would operate in tyranny; were we the subjects of wisdom, but no benevolence; it would be nothing better than craft: And the higher we enjoyed these properties in degree, the greater reason we should have, had we, at the same time, no benevolence, to shun one another through fear of mischief. It is *benevolence,* tempering our other qualities, and making way for their exercise in the methods of kindness, that constitutes us worthy objects of each other's love, and lays the foundation for that mutual trust between man and man, without which there could be no such thing as public happiness.

And this observation, extended to all other created intelligent agents, is equally true: Yea, it is so far true, with respect even to the uncreated Supreme Being himself, as that, if we had no idea of him as *benevolent,* we could not *esteem* him, though we might fear him: Neither could we place our *trust* in him, though we might in a servile way, do homage to him. *Benevolence* is that ingredient in his character which exhibits him to our view as *amiably* perfect, and worthy of our warmest love, and intire confidence. His other attributes, separate from this, are insufficient to inspire these affections; nor are they indeed at all suited to such a purpose. "Eternity and immensity amaze our thoughts: Infinite knowledge and wisdom fill us with admiration: Omnipotence, or irresistable power, is great and adorable; but, at the same time, if considered simply by itself, 'tis also dreadful and terrible: Dominion and majesty, clothed with perfect and impartial justice, is worthy of our highest praises; but still to *sinners* it appears rather awful and venerable, than the object of desire and love: Holiness and purity are inexpressibly beautiful and amiable perfections, but of too bright a glory for sinners to contemplate with delight. Tis goodness that finishes the idea of *God,* and represents him to us under the lovely character of the *best* as well as greatest Being in the universe. This is that attribute, which both in itself is infinitely amiable, and, as a groundwork interwoven with all the other perfections of the Divine Nature, makes every one of them also to become objects of our love, as well as of our admiration. Immense and eternal goodness, goodness all-powerful and all-wise, goodness invested with supreme dominion, and tempering the rigor of unrelenting justice: This is indeed the description of a Perfect Being; a character truely worthy of God."

But though *Benevolence* thus essentially enters into the character of the *Deity,* it has been objected to by some, and abused by others. And it may be, more objections have been levelled against, and greater reproaches cast upon, this attribute of the Divine Nature, than any of the other; though it is, in itself, the most lovely of all the perfections of God, and eminently that perfection, which, being intimately conjoined with the rest, in all their exercises, is the true and only source of all created existence, and dependent happiness, whether in present possession or future prospect.

With respect to some, their abuses of the Divine *benevolence* don't so much spring from any distinct notions they have formed of the nature of this principle, as existing in the *Deity;* or the methods, in which they conclude it ought to operate, as from a *wrong state of mind.* They are dissatisfied with their situation in the world, and quite out of humour, because they don't partake so liberally of the good things of providence, as they imagine they might do. And their discontent is still heightened if they meet with disappointments, and are reduced to suffering circumstances, though by their own folly. And being out of frame, uneasy and restless in their spirits, they find fault with their Maker, and vent themselves in reflections on his goodness; as though it were greatly defective: Otherwise, as they imagine, a more advantageous condition in life might have been alloted to them; and would have been, if the *Deity* had been as good as they can suppose him to be. These are the complaints, by which the infinitely benevolent Creator, and Governor, of all things, is abused by the less knowing and inquisitive, who are the most numerous: But, as their complaints don't so much originate in *judgment,* as a *bad temper of mind,* this chiefly needs to be rectified, and then their complaints will cease of course.

There are others, whose *objections* against the *Divine Benevolence* arises from a *vain mind,* proudly aspiring to comprehend that which is above the reach of their capacities. Some appearances, in the constitution of nature, and government of providence, are such as they can't account for, upon the plan of *infinite benevolence.* They find themselves unable to connect these, with other appearances, so as to constitute an *whole* which they distinctly and particularly perceive to be an *absolutely good* one, free'd from all difficulties: And they are therefore rather disposed to dispute the existence of an *infinitely perfect* principle of benevolence, than to call in question their own capacity to see through the whole of its operations: Though, if there be such a principle, it must be employed about the *universal system* of things; and, for that reason, require an understanding, in order to adjust its exercises, that can take in connections, and dependencies, vastly transcending the most enlarged conceptions of such imperfect creatures as we are. Nothing can be sufficient to satisfy such objectors, till they have first learnt to be modest; entertaining just apprehensions of their own weakness, and the unsearchable *greatness* and *goodness* of *God.*

There are yet others, whose *objections* against, and *abuses* of, the *benevolence* of the *Deity,* take rise from their *misconceptions* of the nature of this Divine attribute. Having formed to themselves *wrong* apprehensions of supreme absolute benevolence, and the methods of its display, they either *deny* that *God* is thus benevolent, because some detached appearances of goodness are not such as they were led, from their mistaken notions, to expect they should be: Or else, they *reproach* this glorious attribute of the Divine Being, giving false and dishonourable representations of it, conformably to the *erroneous* thoughts they have previously entertained of its *nature,* or *manner of exercise.*

Some there be who seem to have no other idea of *absolutely perfect benevolence,* than an *uncontroulable impulsive principle, necessarily* urging on to the *greatest* communication of *good,* and the total prevention of evil; its prevention so as that it should have no place in the creation, in any shape, or view whatsoever: And the constitution of nature, not falling in with this notion of goodness, they question the reality of any principle of benevolence: Not considering that benevolence if seated in an infinitely perfect mind, like *God's*, is never exerted blindly, or *necessarily*, but always under the conduct of reason and wisdom: Which thought justly pursued, will sufficiently account for all appearances, however seemingly inconsistent with goodness; as we may have occasion to shew hereafter, in its proper place: Whereas, a principle of benevolence, though of *infinite propelling force*, if not guided in its operations by *wisdom* and *intelligence*, instead of producing *nothing but good*, might, by blindly counteracting itself, produce, upon the *whole*, as the final result of its exertions, infinite confusion and disorder.

The effect of *mistaken* notions of Divine Goodness, in others, is, not their denying that God is good, infinitely good, but speaking *reproachfully* of this attribute of his nature. And, perhaps, the reflections which have been cast upon the benevolence of the *Deity,* from this cause, have been equally *malignant* with a total denyal of it, and done as much disservice to the interest of true religion, and real virtue, in the world. A more shocking idea can scarce be given of the *Deity,* than that which represents him as *arbitrarily dooming the greater part of the race of men to eternal misery.* Was he wholly destitute of goodness, yea, positively malevolent in his nature, a worse representation could not be well made of him. And yet, this is the true import of the doctrine of *absolute and unconditional reprobation,* as it has been taught, even by those who profess faith in *God* as a *benevolent,* yea, an *infinitely benevolent Being:* But they could not have taught this doctrine, it would have been impossible, if they had not first entertained *intirely wrong* conceptions of benevolence, as attributed to the *Deity.* 'Tis indeed strange that any, who feel within themselves the working of kind affection, should give in to an opinion so reproachful to the Father of mercies. To be sure their ideas of goodness in *God,* if they have any, must be totally different from all the ideas we have of goodness, as we apply the term to *ourselves,* or any created intelligent agent whatsoever. And if their ideas are thus different, and may consequently signify the same thing with what we call *cruelty* in men, or any other creatures endowed with moral agency, they can really mean nothing when they say, that God is good: And it is of no importance, of not the least significancy, whether they call him good, or not.

From those, and such like causes, be that is good so far beyond all other beings, as that it may be justly said of him, in a comparative sense, *he only is good,* has been basely traduced, either by *objections* against the existence of any principle of goodness in him, or by *such representations* of it as have tended to exhibit him, to the view of the world, rather an *odious* than a *lovely* being. An attempt therefore to remove away these *objections,* wipe off these aspersions, and set forth the *benevolence* of the *Deity,* in its *true glory,* will not be condemned as a thing needless. This is the design of the present undertaking; and I have the rather entered upon it, as I am fully persuaded, that the knowledge of God, in his amiable beauty, as an infinitely benevolent being, will lay the best and surest foundation for that sincere esteem of him, and love to him, and trust and hope in him, in which consists the sum of true religion.

I shall offer what I have to say, in prosecution of this design, under the three following general heads.

I. I shall ascertain the sense in which I attribute *perfect* and *absolute benevolence* to the *Deity*.

II. I shall look into the *natural* and *moral* world, and endeavour to make it evident, from what is there to be seen, that this is the *idea* we are most obviously and fairly led to form of *God*.

III. I shall examine those *appearances* which may be alledged as *objections* against the *supremely perfect* benevolence of the *Deity,* and show that they are no ways inconsistent herewith.

And in discoursing to those points, I shall rather apply to men's *understandings,* than their *imaginations;* endeavouring to set what I have to say in the clearest, and strongest point of rational light, that I am able. And if I should now and then be led to speak of things *abstruse* in their nature, I hope, I shall give no just occasion for complaint, that I talk so as not to be understood. And if I should be really unintelligible to an attentive reader, tolerably versed in such matters, I am willing it should be attributed, not so much to the obscurity of the things themselves, as to my own confused conception of them. For it is with me a settled point, that any man may express that clearly and intelligibly, of which he has clear and distinct ideas in his own mind, unless he is either criminally negligent, or has some design to serve by covering himself with clouds and darkness.

The Emergence of American Society, 1713–1763: Assumptions and Ideals of Politics

SELECTION

Origins and Functions of Government: John Wise, "Vindication of the Government of New-England Churches" (1717)

In politics, as in social life, colonial leaders drew heavily upon the traditions of the mother country for their assumptions and ideals, with the result that most colonial notions about politics were highly conventional. With English thinkers like John Locke, they believed that although man had originally existed in a state of nature with a high degree of liberty, he had been compelled to enter into a compact with all his fellows to establish a civil society and eventually a civil government to preside over that society. The immediate aim of government, then, was to restrain the vicious tendencies in man and thereby make it possible for men to live together in the same society. One of the most comprehensive analyses of the origins and functions of government to come out of colonial America was written by John Wise (1652–1725), pastor of the Congregational Church of Chebacco in Massachusetts. Intended primarily as a defense of the traditional New England congregational form of church government against the efforts of a powerful group of clergymen to shift to a presbyterian polity, Wise's Vindication systematically examined the nature of government in general. Although Wise took a somewhat more favorable view of man, at least in the state of nature, and had a higher opinion of democracy as a form of government than most of his contemporaries, his version of the state of nature, his view of the role of civil government, his evaluation of the various kinds of government, and his preference for a mixed form of government do not depart radically from traditional English ideas. The excerpts reprinted here are from the original Boston edition, pages 33–40, 42–51. On Wise and his ideas, see the chapter on him in Clinton Rossiter, Seedtime of the Republic: The Origin of the American Tradition of Political Liberty *(1953), and the longer, if somewhat misleading, treatment in George Allan Cook,* John Wise: Early American Democrat *(1952).*

. . . Consider Man in a state of Natural Being, as a Free-Born Subject under the Crown of Heaven, and owing Homage to none but God himself. It is certain Civil Government in General, is a very Admirable Result of Providence, and an Incomparable Benefit to Man-kind, yet must needs be acknowledged to be the Effect of Humane Free-Compacts and not of

336

Divine Institution; it is the Produce of Mans Reason, of Humane and Rational Combinations, and not from any direct Orders of Infinite Wisdom, in any positive Law wherein is drawn up this or that Scheme of Civil Government. Government [says the Lord *Warrington*] is necessary—in that no Society of Men can subsist without it; and that Particular Form of Government is necessary which best suits the Temper and Inclination of a People. Nothing can be Gods Ordinance, but what he has particularly Declared to be such; there is no particular Form of Civil Government described in Gods Word, neither does Nature prompt it. The Government of the *Jews* was changed five Times. Government is not formed by Nature, as other Births or Productions; If it were, it would be the same in all Countries; because Nature keeps the same Method, in the same thing, in all Climates. If a Common Wealth be changed into a Monarchy, is it Nature that forms, and brings forth the Monarch? Or if a Royal Family wholly Extinct [as in *Noah's* Case, being not Heir Apparent from Descent from *Adam*] is it Nature that must go to work [with the King Bees, who themselves alone preserve the Royal Race in that Empire] to Breed a Monarch before the People can have a King, or a Government sent over them? And thus we must leave Kings to Resolve which is their best Title to their Crowns, whether Natural Right, or the Constitution of Government settled by Humane Compacts, under the Direction and Conduct of Reason. But to proceed under the head of a State of Natural Being, I shall more distinctly Explain the State of Humane Nature in its Original Capacity, as Man is placed on Earth by his Maker, and Cloathed with many Investitures, and Immunities which properly belong to Man separately considered. As,

1. The Prime Immunity in Mans State, is that he is most properly the Subject of the Law of Nature. He is the Favourite Animal on Earth; in that this Part of Gods Image, *viz.* Reason is Congenate with his Nature, wherein by a Law Immutable, Instampt upon his Frame, God has provided a Rule for Men in all their Actions, obliging each one to the performance of that which is Right, not only as to Justice, but likewise as to all other Moral Vertues, the which is nothing but the Dictate of Right Reason founded in the Soul of Man. . . . That which is to be drawn from Mans

Reason, flowing from the true Current of that Faculty, when unperverted, may be said to be the Law of Nature; on which account, the Holy Scriptures declare it written on Mens hearts. For being indowed with a Soul, you may know from your self, how, and what you ought to act, Rom. 2. 14. *Those having not a Law, are a Law to themselves.* So that the meaning is, when we acknowledge the Law of Nature to be the dictate of Right Reason, we must mean that the Understanding of Man is Endowed with such a power, as to be able, from the Contemplation of humane Condition to discover a necessity of Living agreeably with this Law: And likewise to find out some Principle, by which the Precepts of it, may be clearly and solidly Demonstrated. The way to discover the Law of Nature in our own state, is by a narrow Watch, and accurate Contemplation of our Natural Condition, and propensions. Others say this is the way to find out the Law of Nature. *scil.* If a Man any ways doubts, whether what he is going to do to another Man be agreeable to the Law of Nature, then let him suppose himself to be in that other Mans Room; And by this Rule effectually Executed. A Man must be a very dull Scholar to Nature not to make Proficiency in the Knowledge of her Laws. But more Particularly in persuing our Condition for the discovery of the Law of Nature, this is very obvious to view, *viz.*

1. A Principle of Self-Love, & Self-Preservation, is very predominant in every Mans Being.

2. A Sociable Disposition.

3. An Affection or Love to Man-kind in General. And to give such Sentiments the force of a Law, we must suppose a God who takes care of all Mankind, and has thus obliged each one, as a Subject of higher Principles of Being, then meer Instincts. For that all Law properly considered, supposes a capable Subject, and a Superiour Power; And the Law of God which is Binding, is published by the Dictates of Right Reason as other ways: Therefore says *Plutarch, To follow God and obey Reason is the same thing.* But moreover that God has Established the Law of Nature, as the General Rule of Government, is further Illustrable from the many Sanctions in Providence, and from the Peace and Guilt of Conscience in them that either obey, or violate the Law of Nature. But moreover, the foundation of the Law of Nature with relation to Government, may be thus Discovered. *scil.* Man is a Creature extremely desirous of his own Preservation; of himself he is plainly Exposed to many Wants, unable to secure his own safety, and Maintenance without the Assistance of his fellows; and he is also able of returning Kindness by the furtherance of mutual Good; But yet Man is often found to be Malicious, Insolent, and easily Provoked, and as powerful in Effecting mischief, as he is ready in designing it. Now that such a Creature may be Preserved, it is necessary that he be Sociable; that is, that he be capable and disposed to unite himself to those of his own species, and to Regulate himself towards them, that they may have no fair Reason to do him harm; but rather incline to promote his Interests, and secure his Rights and Concerns. This then is a Fundamental Law of Nature, that every Man as far as in him lies, do maintain a Sociableness with others, agreeable with the main end and

disposition of humane Nature in general. For this is very apparent, that Reason and Society render Man the most potent of all Creatures. And Finally, from the Principles of Sociableness it follows as a fundamental Law of Nature, that Man is not so Wedded to his own Interest, but that he can make the Common good the mark of his Aim: And hence he becomes Capacitated to enter into a Civil State by the Law of Nature; for without this property in Nature, *viz.* Sociableness, which is for Cementing of parts, every Government would soon moulder and dissolve.

2. The Second Great Immunity of Man is an Original Liberty Instampt upon his Rational Nature. He that intrudes upon this Liberty, Violates the Law of Nature. In this Discourse I shall wave the Consideration of Mans Moral Turpitude, but shall view him Physically as a Creature which God has made and furnished essentially with many Enobling Immunities, which render him the most August Animal in the World, and still, whatever has happened since his Creation, he remains at the upper-end of Nature, and as such Is a Creature of a very Noble Character. For as to his Dominion, the whole frame of the Lower Part of the Universe is devoted to his use, and at his Command; and his Liberty under the Conduct of Right Reason, is equal with his trust. Which Liberty may be briefly Considered, Internally as to his Mind, and Externally as to his Person.

1. The Internal Native Liberty of Mans Nature in general implies, a faculty of Doing or Omitting things according to the Direction of his Judgment. But in a more special meaning, this Liberty does not consist in a loose and ungovernable Freedom, or in an unbounded Licence of Acting. Such Licence is disagreeing with the condition and dignity of Man, and would make Man of a lower and meaner Constitution then Bruit Creatures; who in all their Liberties are kept under a better and more Rational Government, by their Instincts. Therefore *as Plutarch says, Those Persons only who live in Obedience to Reason, are worthy to be accounted free: They alone live as they Will, who have Learnt what they ought to Will.* So that the true Natural Liberty of Man, such as really and truely agrees to him, must be understood, as he is Guided and Restrained by the Tyes of Reason, and Laws of Nature; all the rest is Brutal, if not worse.

2. Mans External Personal, Natural Liberty; Antecedent to all Humane parts, or Alliances must also be considered. And so every Man must be conceived to be perfectly in his own Power and disposal, and not to be controuled by the Authority of any other. And thus every Man, must be acknowledged equal to every Man, since all Subjection and all Command are equally banished on both sides; and considering all Men thus at Liberty, every Man has a Prerogative to Judge for himself, *viz.* What shall be most for his Behoof, Happiness and Well-being.

3. The Third Capital Immunity belonging to Mans Nature, is an equality amongst Men; Which is not to be denyed by the Law of Nature, till Man Resigned himself with all his Rights for the sake of a Civil State; and then his Personal Liberty and Equality is to be cherished, and preserved to the highest degree, as will consist with all just distinctions amongst Men of Honour, and shall be agreeable with the publick Good.

For Man has a high valuation of himself, and the passion seems to lay its first foundation [not in Pride, but] really in the high and admirable Frame and Constitution of Humane Nature. The Word Man, says my Author, is thought to carry somewhat of Dignity in its found; and we commonly make use of this as the most proper and prevailing Argument against a rude Insulter, *viz.: I am not a Beast or a Dog, but am a Man as well as your self.* Since then Humane Nature agrees equally with all persons; and since no one can live a Sociable Life with another that does not own or Respect him as a Man; It follows as a Command of the Law of Nature, that every Man Esteem and treat another as one who is naturally his Equal or who is a Man as well as he. There be many popular, or plausible Reasons that greatly Illustrate this Equality, *viz.* that we all Derive our Being from one stock, the same Common Father of humane Race. . . .

No Servitude or Subjection can be conceived without Inequality; and this cannot be made without Usurpation or Force in others, or Voluntary Compliance in those who Resign their freedom, and give away their degree of Natural Being. And thus we come,

2. To consider Man in a Civil State of Being; wherein we shall observe the great difference between a Natural, and Political State; for in the Latter State many Great disproportions appear, or at least many obvious distinctions are soon made amongst Men; which Doctrine is to be laid open under a few heads.

1. Every Man considered in a Natural State, must be allowed to be Free, and at his own dispose; yet to suit Mans Inclinations to Society; And in a peculiar manner to gratify the necessity he is in of publick Rule and Order, he is Impelled to enter into a Civil Community; and Divests himself of his Natural Freedom, and puts himself under Government; which amongst other things Comprehends the Power of Life and Death over Him; together with Authority to Injoyn him some things to which he has an utter Aversation, and to prohibit him other things, for which he may have as strong an Inclination; so that he may be often under this Authority, obliged to Sacrifice his Private, for the Publick Good. So that though Man is inclined to Society, yet he is driven to a Combination by great necessity. For that the true and leading Cause of forming Governments, and yielding up Natural Liberty, and throwing Mans Equality into a Common Pile to be new Cast by the Rules of fellowship; was really and truly to guard themselves against the Injuries Men were lyable to Interchangeably; for none so Good to Man, as Man, and yet none a greater Enemy. So that,

2. The first Humane Subject and Original of Civil Power is the People. For as they have a Power every Man over himself in a Natural State, so upon a Combination they can and do, bequeath this Power unto others; and settle it according as their united discretion shall Determine. For that this is very plain, that when the Subject of Sovereign Power is quite Extinct, that Power returns to the People again. And when they are free, they may set up what species of Government they please; or if they rather incline to it, they may subside into a State of Natural Being, if it be

plainly for the best. In the *Eastern* Country of the *Mogul,* we have some resemblance of the Case; for upon the Death of an absolute Monarch, they live so many days without a Civil Head; but in that *Interregnum,* those who survive the Vacancy, are glad to get into a Civil State again; and usually they are in a very Bloody Condition when they return under the Covert of a new Monarch; this project is to indear the People to a Tyranny, from the Experience they have so lately had of an Anarchy.

3. The formal Reason of Government is the Will of a Community, yielded up and surrendered to some other Subject, either of one particular Person, or more, Conveyed in the following manner.

Let us conceive in our Mind a multitude of Men, all Naturally Free & Equal; going about voluntarily, to Erect themselves into a new Common-Wealth. Now their Condition being such, to bring themselves into a Politick Body, they must needs Enter into divers Covenants.

1. They must Interchangeably each Man Covenant to joyn in one lasting Society, that they may be capable to concert the measures of their safety, by a Publick Vote.

2. A Vote or Decree must then nextly pass to set up some Particular speecies of Government over them. And if they are joyned in their first Compact upon absolute Terms to stand to the Decision of the first Vote concerning the Species of Government: Then all are bound by the Majority to acquiesce in that particular Form thereby settled, though their own private Opinion, incline them to some other Model.

3. After a Decree has specified the Particular form of Government, then there will be need of a New Covenant, whereby those on whom Sovereignty is conferred, engage to take care of the Common Peace, and Welfare. And the Subjects on the other hand, to yield them faithful Obedience. In which Covenant is Included that Submission and Union of Wills, by which a State may be conceived to be but one Person. So that the most proper Definition of a Civil State, is this. *viz.* A Civil State is a Compound Moral Person whose Will [United by those Covenants before passed] is the Will of all; to the end it may Use, and Apply the strength and riches of Private Persons towards maintaining the Common Peace, Security, and Wellbeing of all. Which may be conceived as tho' the whole State was now become but one Man; in which the aforesaid Covenants may be supposed under Gods Providence, to be the Divine. . . .

4. The Parts of Sovereignty may be considered: So,

1. As it Prescribes the Rule of Action: It is rightly termed *Legislative Power.*

2. As it determines the Controversies of Subjects by the Standard of those Rules. So is it justly Termed Judiciary Power.

3. As it Arms the Subjects against Foreigners, or forbids Hostility, so its called the Power of Peace and War.

4. As it takes in Ministers for the discharge of Business, so it is called the Right of Appointing Magistrates. So that all great Officers and Publick Servants, must needs owe their Original to the Creating Power of Sovereignty. So that those whose Right is to Create, may Dissolve the being of those who are Created, unless they cast them into an Immortal Frame.

And yet must needs be dissoluble if they justly forfeit their being to their Creators.

5. The Chief End of Civil Communities, is, that Men thus conjoyned, may be secured against the Injuries, they are lyable to from their own Kind. For if every Man could secure himself singly; It would be great folly for him, to Renounce his Natural Liberty, in which every Man is his own King and Protector.

6. The Sovereign Authority besides that it inheres in every State as in a Common and General Subject. So farther according as it resides in some One Person, or in a Council [consisting of some Select Person, or of all the Members of a Community] as in a proper and particular Subject, so it produceth different Forms of Common-wealths, *viz.* Such as are either simple and regular, or mixt.

1. The Forms of a Regular State are three only, which Forms arise from the proper and particular Subject, in which the Supream Power Resides. As,

1. A Democracy, which is when the Sovereign Power is Lodged in a Council consisting of all the Members, and where every Member has the Priviledge of a Vote. This Form of Government, appears in the greatest part of the World to have been the most Ancient. For that Reason seems to shew it to be most probable, that when Men [being Originally in a condition of Natural Freedom and Equality] had thoughts of joyning in a Civil Body, would without question be inclined to Administer their Common Affairs, by their common Judgment, and so must necessarily to gratifie that Inclination establish a Democracy; neither can it be rationally imagined, that Fathers of Families being yet Free and Independent, should in a moment, or little time take off their long delight in governing their own Affairs, & Devolve all upon some single Sovereign Commander; for that it seems to have been thought more Equitable, that what belonged to all, should be managed by all, when all had entered by Compact into one Community. The Original of our Government, says *Plato*, [speaking of the *Athenian* Commonwealth] *was taken from the Equality of our Race. Other States there are composed of different Blood, and of unequal Lives, the Consequence of which are disproportionable Soveraignty, Tyrannical or Oligarchycal Sway; under which men live in such a manner, as to Esteem themselves partly Lords, and partly Slaves to each other. But we and our Country men, being all Born Brethren of the same Mother, do not look upon our selves, to stand under so hard a Relation, as that of Lords and Slaves; but the Parity of our Descent incline up to keep up the like Parity by our Laws, and to yield the precedency to nothing but to Superiour Vertue and Wisdom.* And moreover it seems very manifest that most Civil Communities arose at first from the Union of Families, that were nearly allyed in Race and Blood. And though Ancient Story make frequent mention of Kings, yet it appears that most of them were such that had an Influence rather in perswading, then in any Power of Commanding. So *Justin* describes that Kind of Government, as the most Primitive, which *Aristotle* stiles an Heroical Kingdom. *viz.* Such as is no ways Inconsistent with a Democratical State. . . .

A democracy is then Erected, when a Number of Free Persons, do Assemble together, in Order to enter into a Covenant for Uniting themselves in a Body: And such a Preparative Assembly hath some appearance already of a Democracy; it is a Democracy in *Embrio*] properly in this Respect, that every Man hath the Priviledge freely to deliver his Opinion concerning the Common Affairs. Yet he who dissents from the Vote of the Majority, is not in the least obliged by what they determine, till by a second Covenant, a Popular Form be actually Established; for not before then can we call it a Democratical Government, *viz.* Till the Right of Determining all matters relating to the publick Safety, is actually placed in a General Assembly of the whole People; or by their own Compact and Mutual Agreement, Determine themselves the proper Subject for the Exercise of Sovereign Power. And to compleat this State, and render it capable to Exert its Power to answer the End of a Civil State: These Conditions are necessary.

1. That a certain Time and Place be Assigned for Assembling.

2. That when the Assembly be Orderly met, as to Time and Place, that then the Vote of the Majority must pass for the Vote of the whole Body.

3. That Magistrates be appointed to Exercise the Authority of the whole for the better dispatch of Business, of every days Occurrence; who also may with more Mature diligence, search into more Important Affairs; and if in case any thing happens of greater Consequence, may report it to the Assembly; and be peculiarly Serviceable in putting all Publick Decrees into Execution. Because a large Body of People is almost useless in Respect of the last Service, and of many others, as to the more Particular Application and Exercise of Power. Therefore it is most agreeable with the Law of Nature, that they Institute their Officers to act in their Name, and Stead.

2. The Second Species of Regular Government, is an Aristocracy; and this is said then to be Constituted when the People, or Assembly United by a first Covenant, and having thereby cast themselves into the first Rudiments of a State; do then by Common Decree, Devolve the Sovereign Power, on a Council consisting of some Select Members; and these having accepted of the Designation, are then properly invested with Sovereign Command; and then an Aristocracy is formed.

3. The Third Species of a Regular Government, is a Monarchy which is settled when the Sovereign Power is confered on some one worthy Person. It differs from the former, because a Monarch who is but one Person in Natural, as well as in Moral account, & so is furnished with an Immediate Power of Exercising Sovereign Command in all Instances of Government; but the fore named must needs have Particular Time and Place assigned; but the Power and Authority is Equal in each.

2. Mixt Governments, which are various and of divers kinds [not now to be Enumerated] yet possibly the fairest in the World is that which has a Regular Monarchy; [in Distinction to what is Dispotick] settled upon a Noble Democracy as its Basis. And each part of the Government is so adjusted by Pacts and Laws that renders the whole Constitution an *Elisium.* It is said of the *British* Empire, *That it is such a Monarchy, as*

*that by the necessary subordinate Concurrence of the Lords and Commons,
in the Making and Repealing all Statutes or Acts of Parliament; it hath
the main Advantages of an Aristocracy, and of a Democracy, and yet free
from the Disadvantages and Evils of either. It is such a Monarchy, as by
most Admirable Temperament affords very much to the Industry, Liberty,
and Happiness of the Subject, and reserves enough for the Majesty and
Prerogative of any King, who will own his People as Subjects, not as
Slaves. It is a Kingdom, that of all the Kingdoms of the World, is most
like to the Kingdom of Jesus Christ, whose Yoke is easie, and Burden
light. Present State of England 1st Part 64 p. . . .*

SELECTION

"Salus Populi Est Suprema Lex": Jonathan Mayhew, "A Discourse concerning Unlimited Submission and Non-resistance to the Higher Powers" (1750)

*If the immediate task of government was to protect men from one another, its
ultimate goal was to promote the happiness of society as a whole. It followed,
therefore, that in any just government the public welfare took precedence over
all other considerations. This idea was expanded upon in 1750 by Jonathan
Mayhew, Arminian pastor at West Church in Boston, in his "Discourse concerning Unlimited Submission." Delivered on the anniversary of the execution
of Charles I, this sermon took pains to deny that Rom. 13: 1–8, a favorite text
for royal absolutists, advocated unlimited obedience to civil rulers and to argue
that subjects could legitimately refuse obedience and, if ultimately necessary,
even remove a monarch, or any other governing body, that acted against the
public welfare. An excellent analysis of this sermon is in Bernard Bailyn (ed.),
Pamphlets of the American Revolution (1965), volume I, pages 204–211. A
recent life of Mayhew is Charles W. Akers, Called unto Liberty: A Life of
Jonathan Mayhew, 1720–1766 (1964). The excerpts reprinted here are from the
original Boston edition, pages 9–13, 28–31, 34–35.*

The apostle's doctrine . . . concerning the office of civil rulers, and the
duty of subjects, may be summed up in the following observations; *viz.*

THAT the end of magistracy is the good of civil society, *as such:*

THAT civil rulers, *as such,* are the ordinance and ministers of God; it being by his permission and providence that any bear rule; and agreeable to his will, that there should be *some persons* vested with authority in society, for the well-being of it.

THAT which is here said concerning civil rulers, extends to all of them in common: it relates indifferently to monarchical, republican and aristocratical government; and to all other forms which truly answer the sole end of government, the happiness of society; and to all the different degrees of authority in any particular state; to inferior officers no less than to the supreme:

THAT disobedience to civil rulers in the due exercise of their authority, is not merely a *political sin,* but an heinous *offence against God* and *religion*:

THAT the true ground and reason of our obligation to be subject to the *higher powers,* is the usefulness of magistracy (when properly exercised) to human society, and its subserviency to the general welfare:

THAT obedience to civil rulers is here equally required under all forms of government, which answer the sole end of all government, the good of society; and to every degree of authority in any state, whether supreme or subordinate: (From whence it follows,

THAT if unlimited obedience and non-resistance, be here required as a duty under any one form of government, it is also required as a duty under all other forms; and as a duty to subordinate rulers as well as to the supreme.)

AND lastly, that those civil rulers to whom the apostle injoins subjection, are the persons *in possession; the powers that be;* those who are *actually* vested with authority.

THERE is one very important and interesting point which remains to be inquired into; namely, the *extent* of that subjection *to the higher powers,* which is here enjoined as a duty upon all christians. Some have thought it warrantable and glorious, to disobey the civil powers in certain circumstances; and, in cases of very great and general oppression, when humble remonstrances fail of having any effect; and when the publick welfare cannot be otherwise provided for and secured, to rise unanimously even against the sovereign himself, in order to redress their grievances; to vindicate their natural and legal rights: to break the yoke of tyranny, and free themselves and posterity from inglorious servitude and ruin. It is upon this principle that many royal oppressors have been driven from their thrones into banishment; and many slain by the hands of their subjects. It was upon this principle that *Tarquin* was expelled from *Rome;* and *Julius Cesar,* the conqueror of the world, and the tyrant of his country, cut off in the senate house. It was upon this principle, that king *Charles* I, was beheaded before his own banqueting house. It was upon this principle, that king *James* II. was made to fly that country which he aim'd at enslaving: And upon this principle was that *revolution* brought about, which has has been so fruitful of happy consequences to *Great-Britain. . . .*

THUS, upon a careful review of the apostle's reasoning . . . it appears that his arguments to enforce submission, are of such a nature, as to conclude only in favour of submission *to such rulers as he himself describes;* i.e. such as rule for the good of society, which is the only end of their institution. Common tyrants, and public oppressors, are not intitled to obedience from their subjects, by virtue of any thing here laid down by the inspired apostle.

I NOW add, farther, that the apostle's argument is so far from proving it to be the duty of people to obey, and submit to, such rulers as act in contradiction to the public good, and so to the design of their office, that it proves *the direct contrary.* For, please to observe, that if the end of all civil government, be the good of society; if this be the thing that is aimed at in constituting civil rulers; and if the motive and argument for submission to government, be taken from the apparent usefulness of civil authority; it follows, that when no such good end can be answered by submission, there remains no argument or motive to enforce it: if instead of this good end's being brought about by submission, a *contrary end* is brought about, and the ruin and misery of society effected by it, here is a plain and positive reason against submission in all such cases, a regard to the public welfare, ought to make us with-hold from our rulers, that obedience and subjection which it would, otherwise, be our duty to render to them. If it be our duty, for example, to obey our king, merely for this reason, that he rules for the public welfare, (which is the only argument the apostle makes use of) it follows, by a parity of reason, that when he turns tyrant, and makes his subjects his prey to devour and to destroy, instead of his charge to defend and cherish, we are bound to throw off our allegiance to him, and to resist; and that according to the tenor of the apostle's argument in this passage. Not to discontinue our allegiance, in this case, would be to join with the sovereign in promoting the slavery and misery of that society, the welfare of which, we ourselves, as well as our sovereign, are indispensably obliged to secure and promote, as far as in us lies. It is true the apostle puts no case of such a tyrannical prince; but by his grounding his argument for submission wholly upon the good of civil society; it is plain he implictly authorises, and even requires us to make resistance, whenever this shall be necessary to the public safety and happiness. Let me make use of this easy and familiar *similitude* to illustrate the point in hand—Suppose God requires a family of children, to obey their father and not to resist him; and inforces his command with this argument; that the superintendence and care and authority of a just and kind parent, will contribute to the happiness of the whole family; so that they ought to obey him for their own sakes more than for his: Suppose this parent at length runs distracted, and attempts, in his mad fit, to cut all his children's throats: Now, in this case, is not the reason before assigned, why these children should obey their parent while he continued of a sound mind, namely, *their common good,* a reason equally conclusive for disobeying and resisting him, since he is become delirious, and attempts their ruin? It makes no alteration in the argument, whether this parent, properly speaking, loses his reason; or does, while he retains his understanding, that which is as fatal in its consequences, as any thing he could do, were he really deprived of it. This similitude needs no formal application. . . .

THUS it appears, that the common argument, grounded upon this passage, in favor of universal, and passive obedience, really overthrows itself, by proving too much, it if proves any thing at all; namely, that no civil officer is, in any case whatever, to be resisted, though acting in express contradition to the design of his office; which no man, in his senses, ever did, or can assert.

IF we calmly consider the nature of the thing itself, nothing can well be imagined more directly contrary to common sense, than to suppose that *millions* of people should be subjected to the arbitrary, precarious pleasure of *one single man;* (who has *naturally* no superiority over them in point of authority) so that their estates, and every thing that is valuable in life, and even their lives also, shall be absolutely at his disposal, if he happens to be wanton and capricious enough to demand them. What unprejudiced man can think, that God made ALL to be thus subservient to the lawless pleasure and phrenzy of ONE, so that it shall always be a sin to resist him! Nothing but the most plain and express revelation from heaven could make a sober impartial man believe such a monstrous, unaccountable doctrine, and, indeed, the thing itself, appears so shocking— so out of all *proportion,* that it may be questioned, whether all the *miracles* that ever were wrought, could make it credible, that this doctrine *really* came from God. At present, there is not the least syllable in scripture which gives any countenance to it. The hereditary, indefeasible, divine right of kings, and the doctrine of non-resistance, which is built upon the supposition of such a right, are altogether as fabulous and chimerical, as transubstantiation; or any of the most absurd reveries of ancient or modern visionaries. These notions are fetched neither from divine revelation; nor human reason; and if they are derived from neither of those sources, it is not much matter from *whence they come, or whither they go.* Only it is a pity that such doctrines should be propagated in society, to raise factions and rebellions, as we see they have, in fact, been both in the *last,* and in the *present,* REIGN. . . .

SELECTION

The Imperatives of Political Behavior: William Livingston, "Of Party-Divisions" and "Of Patriotism" (1753)

Because the central concern of every government was the good of the whole society it served, the men entrusted with that government—the magistrates— were expected always to act impartially in the public interest. That require-

ment meant that they could never permit themselves to become entangled with a party because parties were necessarily partial, devoted to serving the ends of a small group and not the interests of the whole. The ideal magistrate, therefore, was the patriot, the man of preeminent virtue dedicated to public service and constantly moved by nothing less than the interests of his country as a whole. Although this theoretical aversion to parties was constantly undermined by a marked tendency among colonial politicians to form and use them and although true patriots were few and far between, these ideals—the abolition of party and government by patriots—persisted as the ne plus ultra, *the highest imperatives, of colonial political life. They were elaborated on at length by William Livingston (1723–1790), lawyer and scion of an old New York family, in the two following essays from* The Independent Reflector, *a series of essays written by Livingston, William Smith, Jr., John Morin Scott, and others in New York from 1752 to 1754. The essays are reprinted here from the 1754 New York edition, pages 51–54, 91–94. For a sketch of Livingston and an analysis of* The Independent Reflector, *see the modern edition edited by Milton M. Klein and published in 1963.*

Of Party-Divisions

Factions amongst great Men, they are like Foxes; when their Heads are divided, they carry Fire in their Tails; and all the Country about them goes to Wreck for it.

—WEBSTER'S Dutchess of Malfy.

FROM the Moment that Men give themselves wholly up to a Party, they abandon their *Reason,* and are led Captive by their *Passions.* The Cause they espouse, presents such bewitching Charms, as dazzle the Judgment; and the Side they oppose, such imaginary Deformity, that no Opposition appears too violent; nor any Arts to blacken and ruin it, incapable of a specious Varnish. They follow their Leaders with an implicit Faith, and, like a Company of Dragoons, obey the Word of Command without Hesitation. Tho' perhaps they originally embark'd in the Cause with a View to the public Welfare; the calm Deliberations of Reason are imperceptibly fermented into Passion; and their Zeal for the common Good, gradually extinguished by the predominating Fervor of Faction: A disinterested Love for their Country, is succeeded by an intemperate Ardor; which naturally swells into a political Enthusiasm; and from that, easy is the Transition to perfect Frenzy. As the religious Enthusiast fathers the wild Ravings of his heated Imagination, on the Spirit of God; and is ready to knock down every Man who doubts his divine Inspiration; so the political Visionary miscalls his Party-Rage the Perfection of Patriotism; and curses the rational Lover of his Country, for his unseasonable Tepidity: The former may be reduced to his Senses, by shaving, purging, and letting of Blood; as the latter is only to be reclaim'd by Time or Preferment.

NEXT to the Duty we owe the Supreme BEING, we lie under the most indispensible Obligations, to promote the Welfare of our Country. Nor ought we to be destitute of a becoming Zeal and Fortitude, in so glorious a Cause: We should shew ourselves in earnest, resolute and intrepid. We cannot engage in a nobler Undertaking; and scandalous would be our Langour and Timidity, where the Sacrifice of our Lives, is no extravagant Oblation. Replete with such illustrious Examples, are the Annals of Antiquity, when the great Men of those heroic Ages, with a kind of glorious Emulation, exerted their Talents in the Service of their Country; and were not only contented, but pleas'd to die for the Common-Weal. Hence CURTIUS and CODRUS, with a splendid Catalogue of others, have rendered their Memories eternal, and acquired a Renown never to be obliterated. 'In Nothing (says CICERO) do we bear a stronger 'Resemblance to the Divinity, than by promoting the Happiness of our Species.' *Hontines ad Deos nulla re proprius accedunt, quam salutem hominibus dando.* But in vain doth Party-Spirit veil itself with the splendid Covering, of disinterested Patriotism: In vain usurp the Robe of Honour, to conceal its latent Motives. The Disguise may fascinate the Multitude; but appears transparent to the Unprejudiced and Judicious. With all the Eulogiums due to the Advocates for Liberty, without Success doth the self-interested Projector attempt to impose on Men of Sense, with that respectable Appellation. A Zeal for our Country is glorious, but a Spirit of Faction infamous. Nor is the incontestable Maxim of the Orator unlimited; but to be regulated by the sage Advice of the Poet,

> *Est modus in rebus: sunt certi denique sines,*
> *Quos ultrec citraque nequit consistere ratum.*
>
> —Hor.

In a Word, there's a great Difference between staring and stark-mad.

When I see a Man warm in so important an Affair as the common Interest, I either suspend my Judgment, or pass it in his Favour. But when I find him misrepresenting and vilifying his Adversaries, I take it for a shrewd Sign, that 'tis something more than the laudable Motive he pretends, which impels him with such Impetuosity and Violence.

THE great, as well as the little Vulgar, are liable to catch the Spirit of Mobbing; and cluster together to perpetrate a Riot, without knowing the Reason that set them in Motion. The genuine Consequence this, of Party-Rage and Animosity! For when once we suppress the Voice of Reason, by the Clamour of Faction, we are toss'd like a Vessel stripp'd of Sails and Rudder, at the Mercy of Wind and Tide: But 'tis a Solecism in Nature, that the best End in the World is to be attain'd by the worst Means; or that we cannot be Patriots, till we are fit for Bedlam.

A MAN of this Turn, is not half so intent upon reforming the Abuses of his own Party, as discerning the Errors of his Enemies. To view the Virtues of the Side he espouses, he uses the magnifying End of the Perspective; but inverts the Tube, when he surveys those of his Adversaries. Instead of an impartial Examination of the Principles he acts upon, or the Regularity of his Progress, he contents himself with exclaiming against the real or suppositious Faults of his Antagonists. In short, 'tis not so much the Goodness of his own Cause, as the exaggerated Badness of the other, that attaches him to his Leaders, and confirms him in his Delirium. Like a Set of Pagans, he makes the Spots in the Sun, a Reason for adoring the Moon.

THERE are some interprizing Geniuses, who love to fish in troubled Waters; and with themselves disturb the Fountain, to acquire a Reputation under Pretence of re-clarifying it to its pristine Purity. A Man who would be overlook'd, or despis'd in times of universal Tranquility, may have a Quantum of Lungs and Impudence, to make himself seem necessary when the Publick is agitated with Storms, and thrown into Convulsions. Nay, a Fellow who has deserved to be hang'd by all Laws human and divine, for his Conduct in private Life, will spring up into an important Champion at the Head of a Party.

THERE is a particular Maxim among Parties [says a fine Writer] which alone is sufficient to corrupt a whole Nation; which is to countenance, and protect the most infamous Fellows, who happen to herd amongst them. It is something shocking to common Sense, to see the Man of Honour and the Knave, the Man of Parts and the Blockhead put upon an equal Foot, which is often the Case amongst Parties. The Reason is, he that has not Sense enough to distinguish right from wrong, can make a Noise; nay, the less Sense, the more Obstinacy, especially in a bad Cause; and the greater Knave, the more obedient to his Leaders, especially when they are playing the Rogue.

Unspeakably calamitous have been the Consequences of Party-Division. It has occasioned Deluges of Blood, and subverted Kingdoms. It always introduces a Decay of publick Spirit, with the Extinction of every noble and generous Sentiment. The very Names of Things are perverted. On Fury and Violence it bestows the Appellation of Magnanimity and Opposition, and stiles Resentment and Rancour, Heroic Ardor, and Patriot-Warmth. Nor is it ever at a Loss for Pretences to bubble the Mob out of their Wits, and give its wildest Ravings a plausible Colour.

CAESAR, POMPEY, AND CRASSUS, were once the popular Party of *Rome;* and their Agent for managing the Rabble, the famous, or rather the infamous CLODIUS. Yet the first inslaved his Country, which but for him would have been inslaved by the Second; and as for CLODIUS he had Villany enough to have set *Rome* on Fire, and enjoyed the Conflagration, could he have done it with the same Impunity as NERO. CRASSUS was slain for his Avarice by the *Parthians,* who pouring down his Throat melted Gold, filled his Belly with what had ever been the Primum Mobile of *his* Party Spirit.

THAT the Heads of Parties are frequently actuated by private Views, has given great Handle to Court-Writers, who generally embrace every Opportunity to varnish the Conduct of their Employer, and argue sophistically in Proportion to his Wickedness, to triumph on so plausible a Topick, and cast an Odium on the most justifiable Opposition. Nay, they have carried their mercenary Impudence to such a Height, as to throw out sly Insinuations, that Patriotism itself is a meer Phantom, and endeavour to laugh the World out of one of the most illustrious Vertues in it. No sooner doth a Man, in the Integrity of Soul, dispute the illegal Measures of their Patron, than he is branded with the opprobrious Name of a factious Spirit, and his generous Benevolence to his Fellow Subjects, represented as a convert Project to accomplish his own Exaltation. As well might they impeach the sincerest Piety of Imposture and Hypocrisy, or infer the absolute Non-Existence of Vertue, from the World's abounding with Vice and Knavery.

THUS as the designing Party-Man always appears in the Mask of publick Spirit, and conceals the most selfish and riotous Disposition, under the venerable Pretext of asserting Liberty, and defending his Country; so the ministerial Scribbler, taking Advantage of this frequent Prostitution, gives a sinister Turn to the most laudable Views, and stigmatizes every Man who opposes the Encroachments of the Court. Hence the Necessity of our greatest Caution in siding with either Party, till by a watchful Observation in the Conduct of both, we have plainly discovered the true Patriot from the false Pretender.

ALMOST all the Mischiefs which Mankind groan under, arise from their suffering themselves to be led by the Nose, without a proper Freedom of Thought and Examination. Upon this Priestcraft has erected its stupendous Bable, and Tyranny rear'd her horrible Domination. And indeed, well may we expect, as the righteous Punishment of our Guilt, to be abandon'd by Heaven to Delusion and Error, if instead of obeying the Directions of that sacred Ray of the Divinity, in Virtue of which we claim kindred with the highest Order of Intelligences, we blindly surrender ourselves to the Guidance of any Man, or Set of Men whatever. And yet I have known Persons of good Sense, and Lovers of Liberty, so infatuated with Party, as to put a whole City and Country in Alarm, and struggle, as if it had been *pro uris et focis* to lift a Creature into a Post, who, after all the Bustle made on his Account, was fitter to guide the Tail of a Plough, than to fill an Office of Skill and Confidence: But their Breasts were inflamed with Party-Spirit, and had the Candidate been a Chimney-Sweep, or a Rope-Dancer, they would have exerted an equal Zeal and Activity.

IT must after all be allowed, that a long and uninterrupted Calm in a Government divided into separate Branches, for a Check on each other, is often presumptive, that all Things do not go well. Such is the restless and aspiring Nature of the human Mind, that a Man intrusted with Power, seldom contents himself with his due Proportion. For this Reason, an unremitted Harmony between several Persons created as a Counterpoize to each other, is suspicious. Their Union may be the Consequence of their keeping within their proper Limits, and it may be the Effect of an iniquitous Coalition. To infer, therefore, that the Liberties of the People are safe and unindanger'd, because there are no political Contests, is illogical and fallacious. Such a Tranquility may be the Result of a Confederacy in Guilt, and an Agreement between the Rulers to advance their private Interest, at the Expence of the People. But this can never be our Case. Agreable to the generous Spirit of our Constitution, we have a Right to examine into the Conduct and Proceedings of our Superiors; and upon discovering them in a Combination of Roguery, if we cannot set them together by the Ears, we can form a Party against their united Strength:

And such a Party, I hope we may never want the Spirit to form. To conclude, shou'd a future Governor give into Measures subversive of our Liberties, I hope he will meet with proper Opposition and Controul: But should a Faction be formed against him, without Law or Reason, may the Authors be branded with suitable Infamy. . . .

Of Patriotism

> *. . . Oh Greeks, respect your Fame,*
> *Let awful Virtue, patriot Warmth inspire,*
> *And catch from Breast to Breast, the noble Fire!*
> POPE'S HOMER.

PATRIOTISM, or public Spirit, is so essentially necessary to the Prosperity of Government, and the Welfare of Civil Society, that without some Portion of the *former*, the *latter*, I was going to say, cannot long exist; I will venture to say, can have no Existence.

ALL History conspires to establish this political Maxim, *That the true Dignity and Glory, the Stability and internal Tranquility of every State, were always proportionate to the Strength and Diffusiveness of Public Spirit.* The sublime Genius of the wisest Legislator, the refined Arts of the most skilful Politician, would be but *splendidæ Nugæ,* unavailing Efforts towards the Establishment of Order and Harmony, without the Assistance of Patriotism. It is this divine Principle which alone can give Vitality, Beauty, Strength and Duration to any political Body.

WHEN we consider the astonishing Grandeur, the almost incredible Victories, and that resplendent Figure which the *Grecian* and *Roman* Common-Wealths exhibited to the World, if we examine from what Sources they derived that superior Lustre, which has claimed the Admiration of all succeeding Ages, and been equalled by none; there is no Principle from whence we can with so much Justice, deduce their Glory and Renown, as from that patriot Ardor which warmed every Breast, and beamed forth with so illustrious a Blaze from their Legislators, their Heroes and Philosophers. If on the other Hand we trace them to the melancholly Periods of their Declension and Dissolution, we shall find they sunk in Proportion to their Decay of Public Spirit: And that when selfish Principles and sordid Views became predominant, lawless Ambition reared its destructive Head, generous Emulation took its Flight, and that noble disinterested Love of the Public, which had triumphed over every selfish, every partial Tie, was no longer the ruling Principle of Action. Hence they became a Prey to Tyranny, to Vice, and to abject ignominious Slavery.

IT would not be difficult to illustrate these Observations by a Deduction of Facts from the *Grecian* and *Roman* Historians, could so ample a Detail fall within the Limits of this Paper, or so fully answer its present Design. I shall therefore proceed. And

IN THE FIRST Place endeavour to prove, that ever Member of the Community, who is not actuated by a Public Spirit, or a Patriot Disposition, may and ought to be deemed an Enemy to his Country.

SECONDLY, I shall attempt to discriminate true Patriotism from its specious Appearance.

THAT we are not born for our selves alone, is the Voice of Sound Philosophy,—the Dictates of unerring Nature. Dependence and social Obligation take Place at the first Dawn of Life, and as its Threat lengthens, continually multiply and invigorate: Amongst these the Love of the Public becomes one of the Strongest. Family Affection and private Friendship, if they so engross our Hearts as to render us insensible of the general Welfare, are not only mean and unworthy Passions, but naturally hurry us into the basest, the vilest, and most immoral Conduct. The Good of the Public, includes the Life and Happiness of Thousands: And it is surely not less absurd than wicked, to give the Preference to the blind Dictates of Passion, or the narrow Ties of personal Attachment.

NOT to melt for public Calamities,—not to feel the patriot Glow of Soul, when our Country is crowned with Success, and distinguished with Honour,—to be regardless of its Fame, and unambitious in its Behalf,—to coil ourselves up within the dirty Shell of our own private Interest and Conveniency, careless of the common Good; is denying our Title to Humanity, and forfeiting the Character of rational Beings.

HE who is secured to his Country, by no Ties but those of partial Passion and private Interest, will, whenever there arises an Opposition between *that* and *those*, give the preference to the *latter*, and unrestrained by Fear, is ripe for Rebellion, Conspiracies, Rapine and Treachery. Every such Man is a concealed Mine, which only wants to be properly touched; and as far as his Influence reaches, the Fabric of public Peace, Harmony and Order, will shake and totter.

MEERLY to love the Public, to wish it well, to feel for it, in all its Vicissitudes, is not sufficient. The Man may perhaps be honest enough to do no Harm, if it should be in his Power, and may possibly be Proof against any Temptations to injure his Country. But this is by no Means fulfilling the whole of his Obligation to the Community of which he is a Member. To exemplify our Love for the Public, as far as our Ability and Sphere of Action will extend, is true Patriotism. This is the indispensible Duty of every Man, and whoever, from Indolence or Lukewarmness, neglects to advance the common Weal, when it is in his Power, is not only a bad Citizen, but a real Enemy to his Country, in Proportion to the Value and Consequence of his neglected Service. Should this Indolence and Lukewarmness universally infect a People, their Government will be unhinged, they will fall a Prey to their Enemies, and cease to be a Nation.

I GO still farther. Whoever is unstudious of the public Emolument, who denies it a Share of his thinking Hours, and refuses to exert his Head, his Heart, and his Hands in its Behalf, is a Foe to Society. Mankind have been more indebted to the patriot Zeal of Genius and Knowledge, than to the conquering Arm of Heroism. And whoso neglects to make the common Good an Object of Reflection, and to plan for its Welfare, robs it of all that Advantage which it might reap by a contrary Conduct.

I AM now to distinguish between true Patriotism, and its specious Appearance.

To shine in the first Order of Patriots, has been the Portion of few. That etherial Spark which pervades and illuminates the Breasts of the choicest Favourites of Heaven, is but sparingly shed amongst human Kind. But let us not envy those elder Sons of immortal Fame, nor murmur at our own Allowance; rather let us endeavour to improve the Talents we enjoy, than with a rash Ambition grasp at those we are not born to possess. To be in some Degree a Patriot, is in every Man's Power, and is every Man's Duty.

HE is a Patriot who prefers the Happiness of the Whole, to his own private Advantage; who, when properly called upon, is ready to rise up in its Defence, and with a manly Fortitude, shield it from Danger. He is a Patriot, the ruling Object of whose Ambition, is the public Welfare: Whose Zeal, chastised by Reflection, is calm, steady and undaunted: He whom lucrative Views cannot warp from his Duty: Whom no partial Ties can prevail on to act traiterously to the Community, and sacrifice the Interest of the *Whole* to that of a *Part:* He whom Flattery cannot seduce, nor Frowns dismay, from supporting the public Interest when it is in his Power: Who mourns for their Vices, and exerts his Abilities to work a Reformation: Who compassionates their Ignorance, and endeavours to improve their Understandings: He who aims to cultivate Urbanity and social Harmony. To conclude, he is a true Patriot whose Love for the Public is not extinguished, either by their Insensibility or Ingratitude; but goes on with unwearied Benevolence in every public-spirited Attempt.

HERE I am tempted to stop, and pay my Adorations to those exalted *Patriots,* who were the Glory, the Safe-guard, the Ornaments of their Country:—But I will repress my Emotion and keep to Order.

ONE would be apt to imagine, *Patriotism* carried such evident Marks of its native Purity, that no specious Appearance of *it* could impose upon Mankind. But if we judge of Human Nature by Experience, we shall be almost tempted to think, Men are formed to deceive and be deceived. 'Tis not in Patriotism only, but in various other Characters, that Mankind are in Masquerade, and Falsehood assumes the Air of Reality. Virtue has something so irresistably charming, that artful Vice steals her Dress, and often mimics her Air so deceitfully, that it requires more than common Penetration to discover the Delusion.

UNDER the Disguise of Patriotism, that first-rate Virtue, *Faction, Self-Interest,* and private Ambition are frequently concealed. I have found, and I own my self unequal to the Power of developing all the artificial Windings of *false Patriotism.*

BUT I may venture to pronounce, that where a benevolent Temper, does not display itself in the general Tenor of a Man's Conduct; his Pretences to Patriotism and public Spirit, are very much to be questioned. For Benevolence is the Parent of Patriotism, and where the Father has no Property, what Inheritance can the Son claim?

TRUE Patriotism cannot dwell with a mean, narrow, selfish Disposition: As easily will Figs grow upon Thorns, or Grapes upon Thistles.

THE Coward, the Flatterer, the Wretch whose sordid Soul pays

Obeysance to the splendid Insolence of Power and Fortune, can never feel the generous Warmth of honest Patriotism.

THE noisy intemperate Froth of a political Enthusiast, is as far removed from a steady Principle of Patriotism, as the Dignity of solid Understanding from the Fumes of poetical Madness.—

PARTY-Faction and personal Resentment, have often imposed themselves upon Mankind for the divine Operations of public Spirit. We shall find Hypocrites of this sort, more frequently inveighing against Men, than reasoning upon Facts: Ridicule is their favourite Engine—to mislead the Judgment by warming the Imagination, is their peculiar Art.

THE superstitious Zealot, and the religious Zealot, and the religious Bigot, have not so much as an Idea of a Public: When they presume to act the Part of Patriots, there is something so unnatural and absurd in their Manner, that they can scarcely deceive any but their own Herd.

WHEN these Characters lay Claim to Patriotism, we may be sure they are Imposters, and we should treat them as Hypocrites.

I shall close my Animadversions with an Exhortation to my Countrymen, to cultivate and display this God-like Virtue of public Spirit.

WE are, my Friends, but just emerged from the rude unpolished Condition of an Infant Colony: There is a large Field for Improvement open to us. We are set down in a Country whose Fertility will generously reward the Labours of the industrious Husbandman. The Bowels of the Earth already yield us their Treasures, and probably have more and better in Reserve. *Commerce* stretches forth its golden Arms to our Merchants; and our Situation is so pre-eminently advantageous for Navigation, that I am persuaded, it will be our own Faults, if we do not extend and increase our Trade beyond our Neighbours and Competitors. And to crown all, we are blessed with civil Liberty, and the inestimable Privilege of unprecarious Property. Without these, all our natural Advantages, would be no more than a beautiful unanimated Picture. Our Security, our Prosperity, our Duration, by a natural and necessary Connection, will be in Proportion to the Strength and Management of our Patriotism and public Spirit. We are accountable to the Supreme Beneficient Governor of the Universe, as the Donor of these Blessings: We are bound as rational active Beings to improve them, and we are answerable to Posterity for our Conduct.

LET us all then, in our respective Stations, and with our several Abilities, exert our selves as Patriots, that so a united Harmony of public Spirit may arise amongst us. Let the general Good take Place of a contracted Selfishness. Let the public Welfare triumph over private Animosity. Let us discountenance Vice, and revere *that Religion* which will make us wiser and better. Let us abhor Superstition and Bigotry, which are the Parents of Sloth and Slavery. Let us make War upon Ignorance and Barbarity of Manners. Let us invite the Arts and Sciences to reside amongst us. Let us encourage every Thing which tends to exalt and embellish our Characters. And in sine, let the Love of our Country be manifested by that which is the only true Manifestation of it, *a patriot Soul and a public Spirit. . . .*

SELECTION **54**

The Function of Representatives: Landon Carter's Report of Debates in the Virginia House of Burgesses (1754)

According to current theory in Britain in the eighteenth century, representatives to the House of Commons acted not as errand boys for their constituents but in the interests of the nation as a whole. This ideal persisted in America, though by the middle of the eighteenth century it was beginning to give way to a different conception of the function of a representative. The nature of the issue can be seen in the following report of a debate on the subject in the Virginia House of Burgesses in 1754 by Landon Carter (1710–1778), planter and member of a leading Virginia family. The report is reprinted here from Jack P. Greene (ed.), The Diary of Colonel Landon Carter of Sabine Hall, 1752–1778 (two volumes, 1965), volume I, pages 116–117. On the shifting colonial attitudes toward representation, see Richard Buel, Jr., "Democracy and the American Revolution: A Frame of Reference," William and Mary Quarterly, third series, volume 21 (1964), pages 165–190. On Landon Carter, see the introduction to Greene, The Diary of Landon Carter.

. . . Hitherto the Session was Harmonious but an affair happened to occasion great debates, vizt, the Bill for a Stint Law, which, as I imagin it will be the subject of a future Assembly, I will take but little notice of, only that it made much division amongst us. In the debates on it we had many difinitions on Casuistry and the question was Whether a Representative was obliged to follow the directions of his Constituents against his own Reason and Conscience or to be Governed by his Conscience. The Arguments for implicit obedience were that the first institution of a Representative was for the avoiding the Confusion of a Multitude in assembly. He, therefore, was to Collect the sentiments of his Constituents and whatever that Majority willed ought to be the rule of his Vote. Thus argued the favourers of Popularity, who were all headed by the Speaker, for these were nearly his own words. The Admirers of Reason and Liberty of Conscience distinguished upon it and said, where the matter related particularly to the interest of the Constituents alone, there implicit obedience ought to Govern, but, where it was to affect the whole Community, Reason and Good Conscience should direct, for it must be absurd to Suppose one part of the Community could be apprized of the good of the whole without Consulting the whole. For that Part, therefore, to order an implicit vote must be absurd and the Representative acting accordingly could only augment the Absurdity because he must suppose his people so perverse as not to be moved by Reasons ever so good that might be advanced by other parts of the Community. Many other Arguments do so naturally arise to support this last and best Opinion that I need not insert them. Be it as it will, nothing but Art could effect anything to prevent the passing of this Bill, confessedly pernicious even by most who espoused it upon the reasoning before mentioned. And by Suffering the abettors of it to Clog [it] with many gross absurdities, such as prodigious deductions from all Public tobacco and officers' fees and by moving to put off the 3d reading of it to a day known to the Proposer too far off for that session to take any farther notice of it because of the Certain Proroguations, it fell; and to palliate the thing it was ordered to be printed for the Perusal and Consideration of the Inhabitants, I hope never to Appear again. The merit of this last artifice is due to Colo. Charles Carter, Supported by Waller and, I think I may say, myself and others. . . .

The Emergence of American Society, 1713–1763:
Constitutional Tensions

The Rise of the Lower Houses of Assembly

Political opportunity was relatively broad in colonial America. At the level of local government there were myriad offices to which men could aspire, ranging from road commissioner up to town selectmen in New England or justice of the peace or sheriff in the middle and southern colonies. At the very top were the governorship and the Council, filled by appointment from above in the royal and proprietary colonies and by election in the two corporate colonies of Connecticutt and Rhode Island. Few colonials became governors in the royal or proprietary colonies, however, and the Councils never had enough room for all the men with political ambitions among the social and economic elites that everywhere emerged in the colonies during the early eighteenth century. The result was that the highest office within the reach of most politically inclined Americans was a seat in one of the lower houses of assembly, and it was largely through the lower houses that the emergent elites found an outlet for their political energies. Though Crown and proprietary officials had obviously intended the governors and Councils to be the focal point of colonial government, with the lower houses merely subordinate bodies called together when necessary to levy taxes and ratify local ordinances proposed by the executive, these lower houses—under the leadership of representatives of the new elites elected in all the colonies on the basis of a wide franchise—steadily acquired power through the last years of the seventeenth century and the early decades of the eighteenth century, until by the 1740s and 1750s they had made themselves paramount in the affairs of their respective colonies. Everywhere colonial governors complained that the lower houses had usurped most of the powers of government and had stripped them of most of their authority. Two such complaints, written within ten days of each other in October, 1748, from South Carolina and New York by Governors James Glen and George Clinton (ca. 1686–1761), respectively, reveal just how powerful the colonial lower houses had become. Glen was governor of South Carolina from 1743 to 1756, and Clinton was governor of New York from 1741 to 1753.

On the rise of the lower houses, see Jack P. Greene, The Quest for Power: The Lower Houses of Assembly in the Southern Royal Colonies, 1689–1776 *(1963), and Leonard Woods Labaree,* Royal Government in America: A Study of the British Colonial System Before 1783 *(1930).*

A. SOUTH CAROLINA: GOVERNOR JAMES GLEN TO THE BOARD OF TRADE (OCT. 10, 1748)*

[My Lords]

. . . there are other things that would add to the hapiness of this Province perhaps I might say of America in general and would make us more beneficial to our Mother Country and preserve our Dependance upon the Crown, That is, If our Constitution were modelled, or at least newly promulged, for by a long loose administration it seems to be quite forgotten, and the whole frame of Government unhinged, the political balance in which consists the strength and beauty of the British Constitution, being here entirely overturned, and all the Weights that should trim and poise it being by different Laws thrown into the Scale of the People; These evils appeared to me to be too bigg for correction during the War, and in the situation that I represented the Country about two Years ago, But my fidelty to His Majesty, makes me now lay them before Your Lordships, as well as my concern for the People, for I shall ever be of opinion, that they hurt themselves by weakening the power of the Crown, and that every deviation from the Constitution of the Mother Country, is dangerous.

I shall lay before your Lordships a few instances. Almost all the Places of either profit or trust are disposed of by the General Assembly, The Treasurer, the Person that receives and pays away all the Public money raised for his Majesty, is named by them, and cannot be displaced but by them, the present and last were most unexceptionable Men, but the one before, by making Partys in the Assembly, keept himself in 'till he broke with great Sums of the Public money in his Hands; besides the Treasurer, they appoint the Commissary, the Indian Commissioner, the Comptroller of the dutys imposed by Law upon Goods imported, the Power Receiver, (etc.).

I must also observe to your Lordships, that much of the executive part of the Government and of Administration, is by various Laws lodged in different setts of Commissioners, Thus we have Commissioners of the Market, of the Workhouse, of the Pilots, of Fortifications, and so on, without number; Nor have they stopped at civil Posts only, but all Eccles-

* These excerpts are reprinted from *Colonial Office Papers*, class 5/372, ff. 80–87 (Public Record Office, London).

iastical Preferments are in the disposal, or election of the People. Though by the King's Instructions to His Governor, the Power of collating to all Livings of which His Majesty is Patron, is invested in him, and the King is evidently Patron of all the Parishes in the Province, for the Land upon which the Churches are built, is the King's, and they have been built with money raised for his use, and the Stipends or Salarys of the Ministers (except what is paid them from Home by the Society for propagating the Gospell) arises from taxes imposed for the use of His Majesty; But here the Ministers leave their charges, and new ones are introduced in their room without the knowledge or the least notice taken of the Governor; perhaps it is owing to this that the Governor, though supream Magistrate in the Province under His Majesty, and the Representative here, is not prayed for in any Parish in the Province. This is the single instance in America where it is not done, and what makes it the more absurd, is, that the Assembly is constantly prayed for, during their sittings.

All the above Officers and most of the Commissioners are named by the General Assembly, and are answerable and accountable to them only, and let their ignorance and mistakes be never so gross, let their neglects and mismanagements be never so flagrant, A Governor has no power either to reprove them or remove them; and indeed it were to little purpose to tell them, he is displeased with them, when he cannot displace them, Thus by little and little, the People have got the whole administration into their Hands, and the Crown is by various Laws despoiled of its principal flowers and brightest Jewells. No wonder if a Governor be not cloathed with Authority, when he is stripped naked of Power, and when he can neither reward the Virtuous and Deserving, nor Displace and Punish those that offend, it must be difficult for him to keep Government in order. God Almighty in his moral Government of the World, is pleased to make use of both love and fear, of promises and also of threatenings.

It were no difficult matter to trace to their source these mistakes; and to shew how the People have been misled into such conceits and how pernicious such practices are, but, I hope, I may be excused if I pass over in silence the failings of former Governors, lest I should be thought to mention them as a foil to my own Administration; but I am to sensible of my own imperfections to attempt that. One or two instances may be necessary. I find a Message from one of my Predecessors to the Assembly to the following purpose.

> Mr. Speaker and Gentlemen, My Self and His Majesty's Council are informed, that Fort Johnstone is in a ruinous condition, We therefore desire that you may give directions to repair it.

Your Lordships will observe that this Message was not to raise money for that service, but to take the direction and ordering of the Work; such Messages tend to mislead Assemblys into a belief that they are to have the sole direction of every thing, and a Governor will not be listened to, that shall afterwards tell them, that all Castles, Forts, etc. are the King's and that they cannot be erected, repaired or demolished without proper Authority. The consequence of Assembly's intermeddling with such matters is otherwise bad and mischievous to the Public, for Sums of Money are often thrown away to little purpose; Some Years ago Two Assembly Men were by vote empowered to make a Fort at Port Royal, and for that end received about Eleven Hundred Pounds Sterling of the Public Money. It is injudiciously situated, monstrously constructed, and made of Oyster Shells and is called a Fort; but a Garden fence is as strong, It is really worse than nothing for it may tempt ignorant People to take shelter in it in case of an Enemy, and it will certainly prove a snare to those that do, whereas in case they are not able to make a stand, they may have a chance to escape, if they betake themselves to the Woods.

These things weaken the King's Prerogative, they are also hurtful to the People themselves, and it is easie to mention other matters that are prejudicial to the Mother Country, During the low price of our own Produce and the extravagant rates that British Manufactures sold for, it was impossible for me to dissuade the Inhabitants from working up Cloaths for the Wear of their Familys any other way than by convincing them that it was hurtful to themselves, and that the same Lands employed in raising Indico and the other produce of the Province would purchase these Goods better and cheaper than they could make them; and unless We encouraged Vessels to bring in these manufactures, our Produce would lye upon our Hands, but it was difficult to instill this into them after a contrary doctrine had been inculcated, and after rewards had been given of the Public money as premiums for the best cloaths made here for Sale.

Many of the above evils may be corrected if a Council will strengthen a Governor's Hands, and give a due attendance, but as they live many of them at such a great distance, it is difficult for them to do it and therefore I pray, that Your Lordships will be pleased to recommend James Graeme Esq. who resides in Charles Town to succeed Mr. Hammerton who has been now absent near Five Years, this I hope, will appear the more necessary, when I assure Your Lordships, that Mr. Hammerton wrote to Mr. Graeme some time ago, that the only thing that prevented his being named when Mr. Beaufand and Mr. Fenwick were appointed was because he was recommended by the Governor; Mr. Graeme is a Gentleman well acquainted with the Constitution, for supporting the King's Prerogative and Government, and is not of the levelling principles that prevail too much here. In former Letters I have observed to your Lordships that before my arrival the Council had entered a Resolution in their Journalls as an Upper House (though I know of nothing to warrant that name) that they would enter upon no Assembly business whatever in the Presence of the Governor or Commander in Chief, I told them that this could not be warranted from the practice of any other Province in America, and that it was contrary to the British Constitution, for that the King's Throne in the House of Peers was not placed there as an ornament to the Room, but because he had a right to be there, and Lord Coke sayes, that the Parliament is composed of two Houses, the King and House of Lords makes one House, and the House of Commons is the other, and therefore as the Governor is the King's Representative in the Province, he had a right to be present; with these and some other arguments, I obtained for the Governor the priviledge of being present, but he is not to speak one

word not even to tell them that he has an Instruction relative to any
business that they may be upon; many errors relating to the Council as
a Council, have Laws and Customes to support them, for example, The
Governor is restrained by His Commission and Instructions from calling
an Assembly or granting any of His Majesty's Lands and many other
things, but by the advice of the Council; the meaning seems mighty plain,
that the executive part is in the Governor, but that he cannot do these
things without their advice, but it has been otherwise understood here,
for the Council must sign the election Writts as well as the Governor;
and all applications and Petitions for Land are addressed to the Governor
and to the Honorable Council, so that the Governor in Council is always
interpreted to mean the Governor and the Council.

From the Council the transition is easie and natural to the Assembly;
and here many things need a reformation also; In the first place, the
election of Members is by ballot, which they vainly say, is an improvement upon their Mother Country; it is indeed different from the method
in their Mother Country, and therefore, I think, they should not be indulged in it, for the closer they confine themselves to the Customes at
Home the safer they will be, and if the greatest and wisest Men have said
in former times, We will not alter the Laws of England, much less should
a Colony be heard to say, that she has improved upon the Constitution,
But indeed I am far from thinking it an improvement, and therefore out
of tenderness to the People, I wish, it were altered as it may defeat the
very end that they propose by it, the freedome of elections; for as it is at
present managed any Person who attends the ballotting Box may, with
a very little slight of Hand, give the election to whom he pleases, I am
not insensible, that some great Men have recommended this practice in
all popular elections, but with great deference to them, I cannot be of that
opinion, because I think it has a tendency to destroy that noble generous
openess that is the characteristick of an Englishman, and to introduce a
Vile Venetian Juggle and Cunning, and I should be sorry to see the
Americans famous for wiles and deceit as the Africans were in former
ages; The Number of Members is Forty Five, but without any rule of
proportion that I know of, some Places send Five, some Four, three, two
and one, and some though equally entitled with any other, are allowed
to send none; for example the Township of Orangeburgh, where many
foreigners have settled, has petitioned the General Assembly two several
times, that they may have the power of sending Representatives, but they
have not been able to prevail; this they complain of as a Violation of the
Publick faith, for they say, that they were promised the same priviledges
with other Subjects, and they think themselves entitled to them, both
by the King's Instructions to the Governor, they having above a Hundred
House Holders in the Township; and also, as they pay their full proportion of Taxes with others, and indeed since they do bear the burden, I
think they should share the benefit equally with others; and besides the
having Representatives in Assembly, every Place or Township when it
is, as they call it, erected into a Parish, has a Minister paid by the Public,
whereas the poor People are without either Minister or Schoolmaster;
The Custome of constituting the Members by Acts of Assembly is an

evident encroachment upon the Prerogative of the Crown, and perhaps it would be more conformable to His Majesty's Instructions, if every Place in the Province that has been in use to send Members to the Assembly for a certain Number of Years (ten Years, for example) were directed to send two Members and every other Place, or Township that is within His Majesty's Instructions, so far as to have a Hundred House holders, were made a Parish, with the Power of sending one Member only 'till such time as they had also been respectively settled or in use to send Members (for a like number of Years) and from that period might send two, the Assembly would then be more equally constituted, and there would still be a Number sufficient; But the greatest evil, and what is productive of numberless ill consequences, is, that no less than Nineteen are absolutely required to be present to constitute a House, without which Number they cannot even send for an absent Member, or do the smallest act, except to adjourn; This creates many obstructions and delays; I have seen Seventeen and Eighteen attending and adjourning themselves from day to day for a Week together, and at length, it has been thought proper to prorogue them for a Month or two, but at the expiration of that time, the same inconveniencys have occurred; so that it has been necessary to dissolve them, though they could not properly be said ever to have had a being, if therefore a fourth or a third part of the whole Number might make a House, I am persuaded that Jealousy would prevent any of the Members from being absent, and Business would then no longer be protracted, but finished with chearfulness and dispatch; at present, a Party of Pleasure made by a few of the Members renders it often impossible for the rest to enter upon Business, and sometimes I Have seen a Party made to go out of Town purposely to break the House as they call it (well knowing that nothing could be transacted in their absence) and in this manner to prevent the Success of what they could not otherwise oppose. Many People here of the best Sense are of opinion that a much less Number than Nineteen would be of great Service, but it is not possible to inspire the Majority with resolution enough to make the alteration. . . .

JAMES GLEN.

B. NEW YORK: GOVERNOR GEORGE CLINTON TO THE BOARD OF TRADE (OCT. 20, 1748)*

My Lords,

    I have in my former letters inform'd Your Lordships what Incroachments the Assemblys of this Province have from time to time made on His Majesty's Prerogative & Authority in this Province in drawing an absolute dependence of all the Officers upon them for their Saleries & Reward of their services, & by their taking in effect the Nomination to all Officers, as will appear from former acts, which I formerly mentioned,

* These excerpts are reprinted from *New York Colonial Documents*, vol. VI, pp. 456–457.

and by two Acts the printed copies of which I send Your Lordships, and one Entitled "An Act to make Provision for several services &c and an Act for the payment of the salaries, services & contingencies therein mentioned &c"

That Your Lordships may the better comprehend the Methods which the Assembly have taken to draw unto themselves the executive powers of Government I must observe to Your Lordships.

1stly That the Assembly refuse to admit of any amendment to any money bill, in any part of the Bill; so that the Bill must pass as it comes from the Assembly, or all the Supplies granted for the support of Government, & the most urgent services must be lost.

2ndly It appears that they take the Payment of the Forces, passing of Muster Rolls into their own hands by naming the Commissaries for those purposes in the Act.

3rdly They by granting the Saleries to the Officers personaly by name & not to the Officer for the time being, intimate that if any person be appointed to any Office his Salery must depend upon their approbation of the Appointment.

4thly They issue the greatest part of the Money granted to His Majesty without Warrant, though by His Majesty's Commission to me it is directed that all Monies raised by Act of Assembly, shall be issued from the Treasury by my Warrant & not otherwise.

5thly They have appointed an Agent for the Colony who is to take his Directions from a Committee of Assembly (exclusive of the Council & of the Governour and to be paid by Warrant from the Speaker of the Assembly.

6thly In order to lay me under a necessity of passing the Bill for payment of the Officers Saleries & Services in the manner the Assembly had formed it, they tackt to it the payment of the Forces posted on the Frontier for the Defence thereof, so that I must either pass the Bill, or leave the Colony defenceless, & open to the Enemies incursions.

This last laid me under great difficulties, in refusing my Assent, & therefore I took the Advice of His Majesties Council for this Province, as to what may be proper for me to do on this occasion who advised me, from the present urgency of affairs, to give my assent to the Bill.

But as by the prospect of a General pacification I am in hopes to be freed from the difficulties the Assembly has from time to time (since the rupture with France) laid me under in their making Provision for the Defence of the Country: I must now referr it to Your Lordships consideration whether it be not high time to put a stop to these usurpations of the Assembly on His Majesty's Authority in this Province, and for that purpose may it not be proper that His Majesty signify his Disallowance of the Act at least for the payment of Saleries, though it have already in most parts taken its effect. There seems the more reason for this because the appointment of an Agent (exclusive of the Governour & Council) may be construed a perpetual clause, or at least may give ground for their insisting on the like clause in all future Acts of Assembly, & for their likewise insisting on the same Method of supporting the Government. And I must in General beg of Your Lordships to take under Your serious consideration what Instruction or other Method may be necessary to put a stop to these perpetually growing Incroachments of the Assemblies of this Province, on the executive Powers intrusted with me and his Majesty's other Officers. . . .

G. CLINTON.

The Constitutions of the Colonies: Divergent Views

Accompanying the rise of the lower houses was the emergence of two divergent conceptions of the constitutions of the colonies and in particular of the status of the lower houses. Despite the fact that the lower houses were yearly making important changes in their respective constitutions, imperial officials persisted in the traditional views that the colonial constitutions were static and that the lower houses were subordinate governmental agencies with only temporary and limited law-making powers. The lower houses, on the other hand, came to insist that they were the colonial counterparts of the imperial House of Commons, that they could alter the colonial constitutions by their own actions without the active consent of imperial officials, and that once such alterations were confirmed by usage they could not be countermanded by the British government. The implication of the arguments of the lower houses was that American colonists saw their constitutions as living, growing, and constantly changing organisms, a theory which was directly opposite to the imperial view. The selection by Sir William Keith (1680–1749), governor of Pennsylvania from 1717 to 1726 and erstwhile adviser to the Board of Trade on imperial matters, was written in 1726 and contains a capsule summary of the imperial view. The nature of the colonial view may be surmised from the message of the Pennsylvania Assembly to Governor Robert Hunter Morris on November 25, 1755. For further reading, see the references listed in the introduction to Selection 55.

A. THE IMPERIAL CONCEPT: SIR WILLIAM KEITH, "A SHORT DISCOURSE ON THE PRESENT STATE OF THE COLONIES IN AMERICA, WITH RESPECT TO GREAT BRITAIN (1726)*

. . . When either by Conquest or Encrease of People, Foreign Provinces are possessed, & Colonies planted abroad, it is convenient & often neces-

* These excerpts are reprinted from William Byrd, *History of the Dividing Line and Other Tracts* (2 vols., 1866), vol. II, pp. 215–216, 219–220.

sary to substitute little Dependant Governments, whose People by being enfranchised, & made Partakers of the Priviledges & Liberties belonging to the Original Mother State, are justly bound by its Laws, & become subservient to its Interests as the true End of their Incorporation.

Every Act of Dependant Provincial Governments ought therefore to Terminate in the Advantage of the Mother State, unto whom it ows its being, & Protection in all its valuable Priviledges, Hence it follows that all Advantageous Projects or Commercial Gains in any Colony, which are truly prejudicial to & inconsistent with the Interests of the Mother State, must be understood to be illegal, & the Practice of them unwarrantable, because they Contradict the End for which the Colony had a being, & are incompatible with the Terms on which the People Claim both Priviledges & Protection.

Were these Things rightly understood amongst the Inhabitants of the British Colonies in America, there wou'd be less Occasion for such Instructions & Strict Prohibitions, as are dayly sent from England to regulate their Conduct in many Points; the very Nature of the King wou'd be sufficient to direct their Choice in cultivating such Parts of Industry & Commerce only as wou'd bring some Advantage to the Interest & Trade of Great Britain, & they wou'd soon find by Experience that this was the solid & true Foundation whereon to build a real Interest in their Mother Country, & the certain Means to acquire Riches without Envy.

On the Other Hand where the Government of a Provincial Colony is well regulated, & all its business & Commerce truly adapted to the proper End, & design of its First Settlement; Such a Province like a Choice Branch, springing from the Main Root ought to be carefully nourish'd, & its just Interest well guarded; No little Partial Projector Party Gain, shou'd be Suffered to affect it, but rather it ought to be considered & weigh'd in the General Ballance of the whole State as a useful & profitable Member. . . .

From what has been said of the Nature of Colonies & the restriction that ought to be laid on their Trade, is in plain that none of the English Plantations in America can with any reason or good sence pretend to claim an Absolute Legislative Power within themselves; so that let their several Constitutions be founded on Ancient Charters, Royal Patent, Custom, Prescription or what other Legal Authority You please, yet still they cannot be possessed of any rightful Capacity to contradict or evade the force of any Act of Parliament wherewith the Wisdom of Great Britain may think fit to effect them from time to time, & in discouraging of their Legislative Power (improperly so called in a dependant Government) we are to consider them only as so many Corporations at a distance invested with Ability to make Temporary By Laws for themselves agreeable to their Respective Situations & Clymates, but no ways interfering with the Legal Prerogative of the Crown or the true Legislative Power of the Mother State.

If the Governors & General Assemblys of the Several Colonies wou'd be pleas'd to consider themselves in this Light, one wou'd think it was impossible that they wou'd be so weak as to fancy, they represented the

King, Lords & Commons of Great Britain within their little Districts; And indeed the useless or rather hurtfull & inconsistent Constitution of a Negative Council in all the Kings Provincial Governments has it is believed contributed to lead them into this mistake, For so long as the King as reserved unto himself in his Privy Council the Consideration of, & Negative upon all their Laws, the Method of appointing a few of the Richest & Proudest Men in a small Colony as an upper House, with a Negative on the Proceedings of the King's Lieutenant Governor, & the People's Representations seem not only to Cramp the natural Liberty of the Subject there, but also the Kings Just Power & Prerogative. . . .

B. THE COLONIAL CONCEPT: THE MESSAGE OF THE PENNSYLVANIA ASSEMBLY TO GOVERNOR ROBERT HUNTER MORRIS (NOV. 25, 1755)*

. . . we cannot admit of Amendments to a Money Bill like this; Amendments not founded in Reason, Justice or Equity, but in the arbitrary Pleasure of a Governor, without betraying the Trust reposed in us by our Constituents, and giving up their just Rights as Freeborn Subjects of *England*.

The Governor is pleased to tell us, "The Constitution of this Province is founded on "certain Royal and Proprietary Charters." It is true, and one of those Charters expressly says, "That the Assemblies of this Province shall have Power to chuse a Speaker, and other their Officers; and shall be Judges of the Qualifications and Elections of their own Members; sit upon their own Adjournments; appoint Committees; prepare Bills, in order to pass into Laws; impeach Criminals, and redress Grievances; and shall have OLL OTHER Powers and Privileges of an Assembly, according to the Rights of the Freeborn Subjects of *England*, and as is usual in ANY of the King's Plantations in *America*. "These very Words are also to be found in a Law of the Province, enacted in the Fourth of QUEEN ANNE, and to this Day in Force. That the "Freeborn Subjects of *England*" have a Right to grant Money by their Representatives in Parliament, in Bills that shall suffer no Amendment, the Governor does not deny; nor that it is usual in any of the King's Plantations in *America:* If therefore the Freeborn Subjects of *England* have this Right, we have it by our Charter, and our Laws. And if we had it not by our Charter and Laws, we should nevertheless have it; for the Freeborn Subjects of *England* do not lose their essential Rights by removing into the King's Plantations, extending the *British* Dominions at the Hazard of their Lives and Fortunes, and encreasing the Power, Wealth and Commerce of their Mother Country; they have, on the contrary, particular Privileges justly granted and added to their native Rights, for their Encouragement in so useful and meritorious an Undertaking.

* These excerpts are reprinted from *Pennsylvania Archives* (1852–1935), 8th ser., vol. V, pp. 4176–4177.

In the Governor's Message of *August* 12, to the late Assembly, he himself says, that by the Royal Charter the Powers of an Assembly were to be *consonant* to the Laws and Constitution of *England,* and would have them confined to that; but now he tells us, that our Constitution is *no way similar* to that of *England.* We think, however, that it will appear by the expressed as well as implied Powers of an Assembly in the *above Extract* from our Charter and Laws, that our House of Representatives is far from being *no way similar* to a *British* House of Commons in its Form and Constitution, whatever it may be in the Knowledge, Abilities and Dignity of its Members. In one Thing, indeed, it is our Misfortune, that our Constitution differs from that of *England.* The King has a natural Connection with his Subjects. The Crown descends to his Posterity; and the more his People prosper and flourish, the greater is the Power, Wealth, Strength and Security of his Family and Descendants. But Plantation Governors are frequently transient Persons, of broken Fortunes, greedy of Money, without any Regard to the People, or natural Concern for their Interests, often their Enemies, and endeavouring not only to oppress but defame them, and render them obnoxious to their Sovereign, and odious to their Fellow-Subjects.—Our present Governor not only denies us the Privileges of an *English* Constitution, but would, as far as in his Power, introduce a *French* one, by reducing our Assemblies to the Insignificance of their Parliaments, incapable of making Laws, but by Direction, or of qualifying their own Gifts and Grants, and only allowed to register his Edicts. He would even introduce a worse; he requires us to defend our Country, but will not permit us to raise the Means, unless we will give up some of those Liberties that make the Country worth defending; this is demanding *Brick without Straw,* and is so far *similar* to the *Egyptian* Constitution. He has got us indeed into *similar* Circumstances with the poor *Egyptians,* and takes the same Advantage of our Distress; for as they were to perish by Famine, so he tells us we must by the Sword, unless we will become Servants to our *Pharoah,* and make him an *absolute* Lord, as he is pleased to stile himself *absolute Proprietary.* . . .

SELECTION

The Imperial Movement for Reform

A growing awareness of the seriousness of the pretensions of the lower houses caused imperial officials to take firm steps to establish stricter controls over the colonies beginning in 1748. In that year they selected George Dunk (1716–1771), Earl of Halifax, a man of driving energy and ambition, as president of the Board of Trade. After an intensive campaign, Halifax, though he failed in his effort to establish a special secretary of state for the colonies with wide jurisdiction, secured much enlarged powers for the Board of Trade in early 1752. With its new powers the Board, under Halifax's direction, inaugurated a spirited, if piecemeal, effort to restrain the growth of the lower houses. However, the outbreak of the French and Indian War in 1754 forced Halifax to suspend his activities and prevented any further reformation of the colonial system until after the worst of the war in America was over in 1759. The new powers granted to the Board of Trade are spelled out in the instruction of April 14, 1752, and the quality of Halifax's attempted reforms of the colonial governments may be seen in the instruction to newly appointed New York governor Sir Danvers Osborne, of August 10, 1753. For further reading, see the references cited in the introduction to Selection 54.

A. ENLARGING THE POWERS OF THE BOARD OF TRADE: THE CIRCULAR INSTRUCTION OF (APR. 14) 1752 *

Whereas the governors of such of our colonies and plantations in America as are more immediately under our government are, in particular cases as well as in general, directed and required by our instructions to transmit unto us by one of our principal secretaries of state and to our Commissioners for Trade and Plantations accounts from time to time of all their proceedings and of the conditions of affairs within their respective governments; and whereas it doth appear to us that it will tend to the benefit of our said colonies and plantations, the ease and convenience of our subjects, and the greater regularity and dispatch of business if the correspondence be confined to and pass through but one channel; it is therefore our express will and pleasure that in all cases wherein by our instructions you are directed to transmit any particular or general accounts of your proceedings or of matters relative to the affairs of our province under your government, you do for the future transmit the same to our Commissioners for Trade and Plantations only, in order that they be laid before us. Provided, nevertheless, and it is our express will and pleasure that whenever any occasions shall happen within our said province under your government of such a nature and importance as may require our more immediate direction by one of our principal secretaries of state, and also upon all occasions and in all affairs whereon you may receive our orders by one of our principal secretaries of state, you shall in all such cases transmit to our said secretary only an account of all such occurrences and of your proceedings relative to such orders.

* Reprinted in full from Leonard Woods Labaree (ed.), *Royal Instructions to British Colonial Governors, 1670–1776* (1935), vol. II, pp. 748–749.

B. THE EFFORT TO LESSEN THE POWER OF THE LOWER HOUSES: INSTRUCTION TO GOVERNOR SIR DANVERS OSBORNE OF NEW YORK (AUG. 10, 1753)*

Whereas it hath been represented to us that great disputes and animosities have for some time past subsisted amongst the several branches of the legislature of our province of New York, that the peace and tranquillity of the said province has been disturbed, order and government subverted, the course of justice obstructed, and our royal prerogative and authority trampled upon and invaded in a most unwarrantable and illegal manner; and whereas the assembly of our said province have not only refused to comply with the powers and directions which we have thought it expedient to give by our commission and instructions to our governor of the said province with respect to money raised for the supply and support of government, but have also in open violation of our said commission and instructions assumed to themselves, in the laws which they have annually or occasionally passed, the disposal of public money, the nomination of all officers of government, the direction of the militia and of such other troops as have been raised for our service, and many other executive parts of government, which by our said commission and instructions we have thought proper to reserve, and which by law belong to our governor only; and whereas it likewise appears that some of our council of our said province, not regarding the duty and allegiance they owe us and the trust we have reposed in them, have joined and concurred with the assembly in these unwarrantable measures; we therefore, being extremely sensible how much all such animosities and divisions amongst the different branches of the legislature and the unwarrantable proceedings which have attended the same must affect and prove destructive of the peace and security of our said province, lessen and impair that due authority which by right belongs to us in the government thereof, and thereby alienate the hearts and affections of our loving subjects, and being determined, at the same time that we do protect all our loving subjects in the lawful enjoyment of their rights and privileges, not to permit our own authority and prerogative to be in any degree violated or unduly lessened by any encroachments whatever; it is our express will and pleasure and you are hereby strictly enjoyned and required forthwith upon your arrival to use your best endeavors in the most prudent manner to quiet the minds of our loving subjects and reconcile the unhappy differences subsisting amongst them, and having called the council and assembly of our said province together, you are to signify to them in the strongest and most solemn manner our high displeasure for their neglect and the contempt they have shown to our royal commission and instructions, by passing laws of so extraordinary a nature and by such their unwarrantable proceedings, and that we do strictly charge and enjoin them for the future to pay to our said commission and instructions due obedience, receding from all unjustifiable en-

* Reprinted in full from Labaree, *Royal Instructions to British Colonial Governors, 1670–1776,* vol. I, pp. 190–193.

croachments upon our legal authority and prerogative and demeaning themselves in their respective stations with a due regard thereto, and to the peace, security, and prosperity of the province. And whereas nothing can more effectually tend to reëstablish good order and government within our said province and promote its future peace and prosperity than the having a permanent revenue settled by law upon a solid foundation for defraying the necessary charges of government, for want of which great inconvenience and prejudice have hitherto arisen to our service and to the affairs of our said province; it is therefore our further will and pleasure that you do in the strongest manner recommend to the assembly in our name without delay to consider of a proper law to be passed for this purpose, taking care that such law shall be indefinite and without limitation, and that provision be made therein for the salary allowed by us to our captain general and governor in chief of our said province, and likewise for competent salaries to all judges, justices, and other necessary officers and ministers of government, and for repairing the fortifications and erecting such new ones as the security and safety of the province may require, for making annual presents to the Indians, and for the expense attending the same, and in general for all such other charges of government as may be fixed and ascertained. It is nevertheless our will and pleasure, and you are hereby empowered, after the passing of such law as aforesaid, to give your assent to any temporary law or laws for defraying the expenses of temporary service, provided always that the said law or laws do expire and have their full effect when the services for which such law or laws were passed shall cease and be determined, and that they be consistent with our royal prerogative and our commission and instructions to you. And it is our further will and pleasure that all money raised for the supply and support of government or upon emergencies for a temporary service, as aforesaid, shall be disposed of and applied to the service only for which it was raised, by warrant from you by and with the advice and consent of the council of our said province and not otherwise, but the assembly may nevertheless be premitted from time to time to view and examine the accounts of money disposed of by virtue of laws made by them, which you are to signify to them as there shall be occasion. And it is our further will and pleasure that if any of the members of our council or any officer holding or enjoying any place of trust or profit within our said government shall in any manner whatever give his or their assent to or in any ways advise or concure with the assembly in passing any act or vote whereby our royal prerogative may be lessened or impaired, or whereby any money shall be raised or disposed of for the public service contrary to or inconsistent with the method prescribed by these our instructions to you, you shall forthwith remove or suspend such councillor or other officer so offending, giving to our Commissioners for Trade and Plantations an immediate account thereof, in order to be laid before us.

The Emergence of American Society, 1713–1763: Aspirations, Accomplishments, and Loyalties

SELECTION **58**

The Nature of Colonial Aspirations

A soaring optimism about the future of America, a growing colonial self-consciousness, and an expanded conception of the importance of the continental colonies in the British Empire accompanied the expansion in wealth, population, and land area, the growth of cities and commerce, the emergence of economic and social elites and the achievement of a stable and well-integrated society, and the enlargement of the authority of the lower houses of assembly. On the surface and from the outside the colonies appeared to be hopelessly disunited, continually bickering, and extremely jealous of one another. How else, for instance, could the repeated refusals to cooperate with one another in the face of a common enemy during the French and Indian War be interpreted? Yet, there were important indications that this interpretation, which was almost universally accepted among colonial officials in Britain, was a serious misreading of colonial psychology. Most important of these indications was the Albany Plan of Union. Suggested by Benjamin Franklin in the summer of 1754 at a general congress of colonial delegates meeting at Albany to make a treaty with the Iroquois Indians, this plan called for a central government with delegates from all the continental colonies and with jurisdiction over Indian affairs, western lands, and defense. Although the plan was accepted with modifications by the congress, it was later rejected by the colonial legislatures and authorities in Britain. Colonial rejection of the plan can be, and at the time was, interpreted as just another sign of colonial disunity and narrow-mindedness, but the most impressive things about the Albany Plan were that it was proposed at all and that the historic divisions and chronic provincialism had been so far overcome as to permit its adoption by an intercolonial congress. The diminution of colonial provincialism can be in part attributed to the growing volume of intercolonial contact in all areas of colonial life through the middle decades of the eighteenth century, but it was also the result of a growing awareness among colonial leaders of the rising importance of the colonies. This awareness can be seen in Benjamin Franklin's proposal for colonial representation in Parliament and in his letter of December 22, 1754, to Governor William Shirley (1694–1771) of Massachusetts, in which he gives his analysis of what the relationship between the colonies and the mother country ought to have been. It is also evident in the ode to the future greatness of America by Nathaniel Ames (1708–1764), Massachusetts almanac maker, in his almanac, An Astronomical Diary for the Year 1758 *(1757). The best treatment of the rising expectations of Americans is in Richard Koebner,* Empire *(1961). Some of the centripetal tendencies forcing the colonies closer together are described in Michael Kraus,*

Intercolonial Aspects of American Culture on the Eve of the Revolution, with Special Reference to the Northern Towns *(1928)*. *Robert C. Newbold,* The Albany Congress and Plan of Union of 1754 *(1955), is the most recent study of that subject.*

A. PROPOSAL FOR UNION: THE ALBANY PLAN OF UNION (1754)*

It is proposed, that humble application be made for an act of Parliament of Great Britain, by virtue of which one general government may be formed in America, including all the said colonies, within and under which government each colony may retain its present constitution, except in the particulars wherein a change may be directed by the said act, as hereafter follows.

President-General and Grand Council

That the said general government be administered by a President-General, to be appointed and supported by the crown; and a Grand Council, to be chosen by the representatives of the people of the several colonies met in their respective Assemblies.

Election of Members

That within —— months after the passing of such act, the House of Representatives that happens to be sitting within that time, or that shall be especially for that purpose convened, may and shall choose members for the Grand Council in the following proportion—that is to say:

* Reprinted in full from Francis Newton Thorpe (ed.), *Federal and State Constitutions, Colonial Charters, and Other Organic Laws* (7 vols., 1909), vol. I, pp. 83–86.

Massachusetts Bay	7	Pennsylvania	6
New Hampshire	2	Maryland	4
Connecticut	5	Virginia	7
Rhode Island	2	North Carolina	4
New York	4	South Carolina	4
New Jersey	3		48

Place of First Meeting

—— who shall meet for the first time at the city of Philadelphia in Pennsylvania, being called by the President-General as soon as conveniently may be after his appointment.

New Election

That there shall be a new election of the members of the Grand Council every three years; and on the death or resignation of any member, his place should be supplied by a new choice at the next sitting of the Assembly of the colony he represented.

Proportion of Members after the First Three Years

That after the first three years, when the proportion of money arising out of each colony to the general treasury can be known, the number of members to be chosen for each colony shall from time to time, in all ensuing elections, be regulated by that proportion, yet so as that the number to be chosen by any one province be not more than seven, nor less than two.

Meetings of the Grand Council, and Call

That the Grand Council shall meet once in every year, and oftener if occasion require, at such time and place as they shall adjourn to at the last preceding meeting, or as they shall be called to meet by the President-General on any emergency, he having first obtained in writing the consent of seven of the members to such call, and sent due and timely notice to the whole.

Continuance

That the Grand Council have power to choose their speaker and shall neither be dissolved, prorogued, nor continued sitting longer than six weeks at one time, without their own consent or the special command of the crown.

Members' Allowance

That the members of the Grand Council shall be allowed for their service ten shillings sterling per diem during their session and journey to and from the place of meeting; twenty miles to be reckoned a day's journey.

Assent of President-General and His Duty

That the assent of the President-General be requisite to all acts of the Grand Council, and that it be his office and duty to cause them to be carried into execution.

Power of President-General and Grand Council; Treaties of Peace and War

That the President-General, with the advice of the Grand Council, hold or direct all Indian treaties in which the general interest of the colonies may be concerned; and make peace or declare war with Indian nations.

Indian Trade

That they make such laws as they judge necessary for regulating all Indian trade.

Indian Purchases

That they make all purchases, from Indians for the crown, of lands not now within the bounds of particular colonies, or that shall not be within their bounds when some of them are reduced to more convenient dimensions.

New Settlements

That they make new settlements on such purchases, by granting lands in the King's name, reserving a quit-rent to the crown for the use of the general treasury.

Laws to Govern Them

That they make laws for regulating and governing such new settlements till the crown shall think it fit to form them into particular governments.

Raise Soldiers and Equip Vessels, &C

That they raise and pay soldiers and build forts for the defence of any of the colonies, and equip vessels of force to guard the coasts and protect the trade on the ocean, lakes, or great rivers; but they shall not impress men in any colony without the consent of the legislature.

Power to Make Laws, Lay Duties, &C

That for these purposes they have power to make laws, and lay and levy such general duties, imposts, or taxes as to them shall appear most equal and just (considering the ability and other circumstances of the inhabitants in the several colonies), and such as may be collected with the least inconvenience to the people; rather discouraging luxury than loading industry with unnecessary burthens.

General Treasurer and Particular Treasurer

That they may appoint a General Treasurer and Particular Treasurer in each government, when necessary; and from time to time may order the sums in the treasuries of each government into the general treasury, or draw on them for special payments, as they find most convenient.

Money, How to Issue

Yet no money to issue but by joint orders of the President-General and Grand Council; except where sums have been appropriated to particular purposes, and the President-General is previously empowered by an act to draw such sums.

Accounts

That the general accounts shall be yearly settled and reported to the several Assemblies.

Quorum

That a Quorum of the Grand Council, empowered to act with the President-General, do consist of twenty-five members, among whom there shall be one or more from a majority of the colonies.

Laws to Be Transmitted

That the laws made by them for the purposes aforesaid shall not be repugnant, but, as near as may be, agreeable to the laws of England, and shall be transmitted to the King in Council for approbation as soon as may be after their passing; and if not disapproved within three years after presentation, to remain in force.

Death of the President-General

That in case of the death of the President-General, the Speaker of the Grand Council for the time being shall succeed, and be vested with the same powers and authorities, to continue till the King's pleasure be known.

Officers, How Appointed

That all military commission officers, whether for land or sea service, to act under this general constitution, shall be nominated by the President-General; but the approbation of the Grand Council is to be obtained before they receive their commissions. And all civil officers are to be nominated by the Grand Council, and to receive the President-General's approbation before they officiate.

Vacancies, How Supplied

But in case of vacancy by death or removal of any officer, civil or military, under this constitution, the Governor of the province in which such vacancy happens may appoint, till the pleasure of the President-General and Grand Council can be known.

Each Colony May Defend Itself On Emergency, &c. That the particular military as well as civil establishments in each colony remain in their present state, the general constitution notwithstanding; and that on sudden emergencies any colony may defend itself, and lay the accounts of expense thence arising before the President-General and General Council, who may allow and order payment of the same, as far as they judge such accounts just and reasonable.

B. AMERICA'S FUTURE IN THE EMPIRE: BENJAMIN FRANKLIN TO GOVERNOR WILLIAM SHIRLEY (DEC. 22, 1754)*

Sir,

Since the conversation your Excellency was pleased to honor me with, on the subject of *uniting the colonies* more intimately with Great Britain, by allowing them *representatives in Parliament,* I have something fur-

---

* These excerpts are reprinted from Jared Sparks (ed.), *The Works of Benjamin Franklin* (10 vols., 1840), vol. III, pp. 64–68.

ther considered that matter, and am of opinion, that such a union would be very acceptable to the colonies, provided they had a reasonable number of representatives allowed them; and that all the old acts of Parliament restraining the trade or cramping the manufactures of the colonies be at the same time repealed, and the British subjects *on this side the water* put, in those respects, on the same footing with those in Great Britain, till the new Parliament, representing the whole, shall think it for the interest of the whole to reënact some or all of them. It is not that I imagine so many representatives will be allowed the colonies, as to have any great weight by their numbers; but I think there might be sufficient to occasion those laws to be better and more impartially considered, and perhaps to overcome the interest of a petty corporation, or of any particular set of artificers or traders in England, who heretofore seem, in some instances, to have been more regarded than all the colonies, or than was consistent with the general interest, or best national good. I thing too, that the government of the colonies by a Parliament, in which they are fairly represented, would be vastly more agreeable to the people, than the method lately attempted to be introduced by royal instruction, as well as more agreeable to the nature of an English consititution, and to English liberty; and that such laws as now seem to bear hard on the colonies, would (when judged by such a Parliament for the best interest of the whole) be more cheerfully submitted to, and more easily executed.

I should hope too, that by such a union, the people of Great Britain, and the people of the colonies, would learn to consider themselves, as not belonging to different communities with different interests, but to one community with one interest; which I imagine would contribute to strengthen the whole, and greatly lessen the danger of future separations.

It is, I suppose, agreed to be the general interest of any state, that its people be numerous and rich; men enow to fight in its defence, and enow to pay sufficient taxes to defray the charge; for these circumstances tend to the security of the state, and its protection from foreign power. But it seems not of so much importance, whether the fighting be done by John or Thomas, or the tax paid by William or Charles. The iron manufacture employs and enriches British subjects, but is it of any importance to the state, whether the manufacturer lives at Birmingham, or Sheffield, or both; since they are still within its bounds, and their wealth and persons still at its command? Could the Goodwin Sands be laid dry by banks, and land equal to a large country thereby gained to England, and presently filled with English inhabitants, would it be right to deprive such inhabitants of the common privileges enjoyed by other Englishmen, the right of vending their produce in the same ports, or of making their own shoes, because a merchant or a shoemaker, living on the old land, might fancy it more for his advantage to trade or make shoes for them? Would this be right, even if the land were gained at the expense of the state? And would it not seem less right, if the charge and labor of gaining the additional territory to Britain had been borne by the settlers themselves? And would not the hardship appear yet greater, if the people of the new country should be allowed no representatives in the Parliament enacting such impositions?

Now I look on the colonies as so many countries gained to Great Britain, and more advantageous to it, than if they had been gained out of the seas around its coasts, and joined to its lands; for, being in different climates, they afford greater variety of produce, and materials for more manufactures; and, being separated by the ocean, they increase much more its shipping and seamen; and, since they are all included in the British empire, which has only extended itself by their means, and the strength and wealth of the parts are the strength and wealth of the whole, what imports it to the general state, whether a merchant, a smith, or a hatter, grows rich in Old or New England? And if, through increase of the people, two smiths are wanted for one employed before, why may not the *new* smith be allowed to live and thrive in the *new* country, as well as the *old* one in the *old?* In fine, why should the countenance of a state be *partially* afforded to its people, unless it be most in favor of those who have most merit? And if there be any difference, those who have most contributed to enlarge Britain's empire and commerce, increase her strength, her wealth, and the numbers of her people, at the risk of their own lives and private fortunes in new and strange countries, methinks ought rather to expect some preference. . . .

B. FRANKLIN.

C. THE PROMISE OF AMERICA: NATHANIEL AMES, "A THOUGHT UPON THE PAST, PRESENT, AND FUTURE STATE OF NORTH AMERICA" (1757)*

America is a subject which daily becomes more and more interesting:—I shall therefore fill these Pages with a Word upon its Past, Present and Future State.

I. First of its Past State: Time has cast a Shade upon this Scene.— Since the Creation innumerable Accidents have happened here, the bare mention of which would create Wonder and Surprize; but they are all lost in Oblivion: The ignorant Natives for Want of Letters have forgot their Stock; and know not from whence they came, or how, or when they arrived here, or what has happened since:—Who can tell what wonderful Changes have happen'd by the mighty Operations of Nature, such as Deluges, Vulcanoes, Earthquakes, &c.!—Or whether great tracts of Land were not absorbed into those vast Lakes or Inland Seas which occupy so much Space to the West of us.—But to leave the Natural, and come to the Political State: We know how the *French* have erected a Line of Forts from the *Ohio* to *Nova Scotia,* including all the inestimable Country to the West of us, into their exorbitant Claim.—This, with infinite Justice, the *English* resented, & in this Cause our Blood has been spill'd: Which brings to our Consideration,

* Reprinted in full from Samuel Briggs (ed.), *The Essays, Humor, and Poems of Nathaniel Ames* (1891), pp. 284–286.

II. Secondly, The Present State of NORTH AMERICA.—A Writer upon this present Time says, "The Parts of *North America* which may be claimed by *Great Britain* or *France* are of as much Worth as either Kingdom.—That fertile Country to the West of the Appalachian Mountains (a String of 8 or 900 Miles in Length,) between *Canada* and the *Mississippi*, is of larger Extent than all *France, Germany* and *Poland;* and all well provided with Rivers, a very fine wholesome Air, a rich Soil, capable of producing Food and Physick, and all Things necessary for the Conveniency and Delight of Life: In fine, the Garden of the World!"—Time was we might have been possess'd of it: At this Time two mighty Kings contend for this inestimable Prize:—Their respective Claims are to be measured by the Length of their Swords.—The Poet says, The Gods and Opportunity ride Post; that you must take her by the Forelock being Bald Behind.—Have we not too fondly depended upon our Numbers?—Sir *Francis Bacon* says, "The Wolf careth not how many the Sheep be:" But Numbers well spirited, with the Blessing of Heaven will do Wonders, when by military Skill and Discipline, the Commanders can actuate (as by one Soul) the most numerous bodies of arm'd People:—Our Numbers will not avail till the Colonies are united; for whilst divided, the strength of the Inhabitants is broken like the petty Kingdoms in *Africa.*—If we do not join Heart and Hand in the common Cause against our exulting Foes, but fall to disputing among ourselves, it may really happen as the Governour of *Pennsylvania* told his Assembly, "We shall have no Priviledge to dispute about, nor Country to dispute in."—

III. Thirdly, of the Future State of NORTH AMERICA—Here we find a vast Stock of proper Materials for the Art and Ingenuity of Man to work upon:—Treasures of immense Worth; conceal'd from the poor ignorant aboriginal Natives! The Curious have observ'd, that the Progress of Humane Literature (like the Sun) is from the East to the West; thus has it travelled thro' *Asia* and *Europe,* and now is arrived at the Eastern Shore of *America.* As the Cœlestial Light of the Gospel was directed here by the Finger of G O D , it will doubtless, finally drive the long! long! Night of Heathenish Darkness from *America:*—So Arts and Sciences will change the Face of Nature in their Tour from Hence over the Appalachian Mountains to the Western Ocean; and as they march thro' the vast Desert, the Residence of Wild Beasts will be broken up, and their obscene Howl cease for ever;—Instead of which the Stones and Trees will dance together at the Music of *Orpheus,*—the Rocks will disclose their hidden Gems,—and the inestimable Treasures of Gold & Silver be broken up. Huge Mountains of Iron Ore are already discovered; and vast Stores are reserved for future Generations: This Metal more useful than Gold and Silver, will imploy Millions of Hands, not only to form the martial Sword, and peaceful Share, alternately; but an Infinity of Utensils improved in the Exercise of Art, and Handicraft amongst Men. Nature thro' all her Works has stamp'd Authority on this Law, namely, "That all fit Matter shall be improved to its best Purposes."—Shall not then those vast Quarries, that teem with mechanic Stone,—those for Structure be piled into great Cities,—and those for Sculpture into Statues to perpetuate the Honor of renowned Heroes; even those who shall NOW save their Country.——O! Ye unborn Inhabitants of America! Should this Page escape its destin'd Conflagration at the Year's End, and these Alphabetical Letters remain legible,—when your Eyes behold the Sun after he has rolled the Seasons round for two or three Centuries more, you will know that in Anno Domini 1758, we dream'd of your Times.

SELECTION

The Glories of Membership in the British Empire

*The growing confidence of the colonies in their own future within the British Empire was intensified by the great British victory in the French and Indian War and by the "glorious peace" negotiated in early 1763. By the treaty signed in Paris on February 10, 1763, Britain secured possession of all North America east of the Mississippi River and significant territorial concessions in India and the West Indies. The British Empire was now the mightiest in the world and, eulogists declared, the most extensive since the days of the Roman Empire. Americans were uniformly proud to be part of it. In orations and sermons such as the one delivered in Williamsburg by James Horrocks (ca. 1734–1772), Anglican minister and later president of the College of William and Mary, they recounted the blessings of being Britons. Everywhere from Portsmouth south to Savannah local grievances against the imperial government were submerged in an orgy of patriotic sentiment, as colonials wallowed in professions of loyalty to the mother country and to the new patriot monarch, George III, who had taken the throne in 1760. Never had British nationalism been at a higher pitch in the colonies. Largely unaware that there was strong sentiment among imperial authorities to tighten up the administration of the colonies in ways that could only arouse serious protests in the colonies, colonial Americans looked forward to a bright new era of peace, prosperity, and expansion. The extent of British nationalism at the end of the French and Indian War is treated in Max Savelle, *Seeds of Liberty (1965).*

A. THE CAPSTONE OF EMPIRE: THE TREATY OF PARIS (FEB. 10, 1763)*

IV. His Most Christian Majesty renounces all pretensions which he has heretofore formed or might have formed to Nova Scotia or Acadia in all its

* These excerpts are reprinted from Charles Jenkinson (comp.), *A Collection of All the Treaties of Peace, Alliance and Commerce between Great-Britain and Other Powers* (3 vols., 1785), vol. II, pp. 181–184, 187–189.

parts, and guaranties the whole of it, and with all its dependencies, to the King of Great Britain: Moreover, his Most Christian Majesty cedes and guaranties to his said Britannick Majesty, in full right, Canada, with all its dependencies, as well as the island of Cape Breton, and all the other islands and coasts in the gulph and river of St. Lawrence, and in general, every thing that depends on the said countries, lands, islands, and coasts, with the sovereignty, property, possession, and all rights acquired by treaty, or otherwise, which the Most Christian King and the Crown of France have had till now over the said countries, lands, islands, places, coasts, and their inhabitants, so that the Most Christian King cedes and makes over the whole to the said King, and to the Crown of Great Britain, and that in the most ample manner and form, without restriction, and without any liberty to depart from the said cession and guaranty under any pretence, or to disturb Great Britain in the possessions above mentioned. His Britannick Majesty, on his side, agrees to grant the liberty of the Catholick religion to the inhabitants of Canada: he will, in consequence, give the most precise and most effectual orders, that his new Roman Catholick subjects may profess the worship of their religion according to the rites of the Romish church, as far as the laws of Great Britain permit. His Britannick Majesty farther agrees, that the French inhabitants, or others who had been subjects of the Most Christian King in Canada, may retire with all safety and freedom wherever they shall think proper, and may sell their estates, provided it be to the subjects of his Britannick Majesty, and bring away their effects as well as their persons, without being restrained in their emigration, under any pretence whatsoever, except that of debts or of criminal prosecutions: The term limited for this emigration shall be fixed to the space of eighteen months, to be computed from the day of the exchange of the ratification of the present treaty.

V. The subjects of France shall have the liberty of fishing and drying on a part of the coasts of the island of Newfoundland, such as it is specified in the XIIIth article of the treaty of Utrecht; which article is renewed and confirmed by the present treaty, (except what relates to the island of Cape Breton, as well as to the other islands and coasts in the mouth and in the gulph of St. Lawrence:) And his Britannick Majesty consents to leave to the subjects of the Most Christian King the liberty of fishing in the gulph of St. Lawrence, on condition that the subjects of France do not exercise the said fishery but at the distance of three leagues from all the coasts belonging to Great Britain, as well those of the continent as those of the islands situated in the said gulph of St. Lawrence. And as to what relates to the fishery on the coasts of the island of Cape Breton, out of the said gulph, the subjects of the Most Christian King shall not be permitted to exercise the said fishery but as the distance of fifteen leagues from the coasts of the island of Cape Breton; and the fishery on the coasts of Nova Scotia or Acadia, and every where else out of the said gulph, shall remain on the foot of former treaties.

VI. The King of Great Britain cedes the islands of St. Pierre and Macquelon, in full right, to his Most Christian Majesty, to serve as a shelter to the French fishermen; and his said Most Christian Majesty engages not to fortify the said islands; to erect no buildings upon them but merely for the conveniency of the fishery; and to keep upon them a guard of fifty men only for the police.

VII. In order to re-establish peace on solid and durable foundations, and to remove for ever all subject of dispute with regard to the limits of the British and French territories on the continent of America; it is agreed, that, for the future, the confines between the dominions of his Britannick Majesty and those of his Most Christian Majesty, in that part of the world, shall be fixed irrevocably by a line drawn along the middle of the River Mississippi, from its source to the river Iberville, and from thence, by a line drawn along the middle of this river, and the lakes Maurepas and Potchartrain to the sea; and for this purpose, the Most Christian King cedes in full right, and guaranties to his Britannick Majesty the river and port of the Mobile, and every thing which he possesses, or ought to possess, on the left side of the river Mississippi, except the town of New Orleans and the island in which it is situated, which shall remain to France, provided that the navigation of the river Mississippi shall be equally free, as well to the subjects of Great Britain as to those of France, in its whole breadth and length, from its source to the sea, and expressly that part which is between the said island of New Orleans and the right bank of that river, as well as the passage both in and out of its mouth: It is further stipulated, that the vessels belonging to the subjects of either nation shall not be stopped, visited, or subjected to the payment of any duty whatsoever. The stipulations inserted in the IVth article, in favour of the inhabitants of Canada shall also take place with regard to the inhabitants of the countries ceded by this article.

VIII. The King of Great Britain shall restore to France the islands of Guadaloupe, of Mariegalante, of Desirade, of Martinico, and of Belleisle; and the fortresses of these islands shall be restored in the same condition they were in when they were conquered by the British arms, provided that his Britannick Majesty's subjects, who shall have settled in the said islands, or those who shall have any commercial affairs to settle there or in other places restored to France by the present treaty, shall have liberty to sell their lands and their estates, to settle their affairs, to recover their debts, and to bring away their effects as well as their persons, on board vessels, which they shall be permitted to send to the said islands and other places restored as above, and which shall serve for this use only, without being restrained on account of their religion, or under any other pretence whatsoever, except that of debts or of criminal prosecutions: and for this purpose, the term of eighteen months is allowed to his Britannick Majesty's subjects, to be computed from the day of the exchange of the ratifications of the present treaty; but, as the liberty granted to his Britannick Majesty's subjects, to bring away their persons and their effects, in vessels of their nation, may be liable to abuses if precautions were not taken to prevent them; it has been expressly agreed between his Britannick Majesty and his Most Christian Majesty, that the number of English vessels which have leave to go to the said islands and places restored to France, shall be limited, as well as the number of tons of each one; that they shall go in ballast; shall set sail at a fixed time; and shall make one voyage only; all the effects belonging to the English being to be embarked at the same time. It has been farther agreed, that his Most Christian Majesty shall cause the necessary passports to be given to the said vessels; that, for the greater security, it shall be allowed to place two French clerks or guards in each of the said vessels, which shall be visited in the landing places and ports of the said islands and places restored to France, and that the merchandise which shall be found therein shall be confiscated.

IX. The Most Christian King cedes and guaranties to his Britannick Majesty, in full right, the islands of Grenada, and the Grenadines, with the same stipulations in favour of the inhabitants of this colony, inserted in the IVth article for those of Canada: And the partition of the islands called neutral, is agreed and fixed, so that those of St. Vincent, Dominico, and Tobago, shall remain in full right to Great Britain, and that of St. Lucia shall be delivered to France, to enjoy the same likewise in full right, and the high contracting parties guaranty the partition so stipulated. . . .

XIX. The King of Great Britain shall restore to Spain all the territory which he has conquered in the island of Cuba, with the fortress of the Havannah; and this fortress, as well as all the other fortresses of the said island, shall be restored in the same condition they were in when conquered by his Britannick Majesty's arms, provided that his Britannick Majesty's subjects who shall have settled in the said island, restored to Spain by the present treaty, or those who shall have any commercial affairs to settle there, shall have liberty to sell their lands and their estates, to settle their affairs, recover their debts, and to bring away their effects, as well as their persons, on board vessels which they shall be permitted to send to the said island restored as above, and which shall serve for that use only, without being restrained on account of their religion, or under any other pretence whatsoever, except that of debts or of criminal prosecutions: And for this purpose, the term of eighteen months is allowed to his Britannick Majesty's subjects, to be computed from the day of the exchange of the ratifications of the present treaty: but as the liberty granted to his Britannick Majesty's subjects, to bring away their persons and their effects, in vessels of their nation, may be liable to abuses if precautions were not taken to prevent them; it has been expressly agreed between his Britannick Majesty and his Catholick Majesty, that the number of English vessels which shall have leave to go to the said island restored to Spain shall be limited, as well as the number of tons of each one; that they shall go in ballast; shall set sail at a fixed time; and shall make one voyage only; all the effects belonging to the English being to be embarked at the same time: it has been farther agreed, that his Catholick Majesty shall cause the necessary passports to be given to the said vessels; that for the greater security, it shall be allowed to place two Spanish clerks or guards in each of the said vessels, which shall be visited in the landing places and ports of the said island restored to Spain, and that the merchandise which shall be found therein shall be confiscated.

XX. In consequence of the restitution stipulated in the preceding article, his Catholick Majesty cedes and guaranties, in full right, to his Britannick

Majesty, Florida, with Fort St. Augustin, and the Bay of Pensacola, as well as all that Spain possesses on the continent of North America, to the East or to the South East of the river Mississippi. And, in general, every thing that depends on the said countries and lands, with the sovereignty, property, possession, and all rights, acquired by treaties or otherwise, which the Catholick King and the Crown of Spain have had till now over the said countries, lands, places, and their inhabitants; so that the Catholick King cedes and makes over the whole to the said King and to the Crown of Great Britain, and that in the most ample manner and form. His Britannick Majesty agrees, on this side, to grant to the inhabitants of the countries above ceded, the liberty of the Catholick religion: he will, consequently, give the most express and the most effectual orders that his new Roman Catholic subjects may profess the worship of their religion according to the rites of the Romish church, as far as the laws of Great Britain permit. His Britannick Majesty farther agrees, that the Spanish inhabitants, or others who had been subjects of the Catholick King in the said countries, may retire, with all safety and freedom, wherever they think proper; and may sell their estates, provided it be to his Britannick Majesty's subjects, and bring away their effects, as well as their persons, without being restrained in their emigration, under any pretence whatsoever, except that of debts, or of criminal prosecutions: the term limited for this emigration being fixed to the space of eighteen months, to be computed from the day of the exchange of the ratifications of the present treaty. It is moreover stipulated, that his Catholick Majesty shall have power to cause all the effects that may belong to him, to be brought away, whether it be artillery or other things. . . .

B. THE BLESSINGS OF BEING BRITONS: JAMES HORROCKS, "UPON THE PEACE" (1763)*

He maketh Peace in thy Borders, and filleth Thee with the Flower of Wheat.

A LONG, dangerous, and expensive War now closes with an honorable Peace; and for this we are ordered to a most reasonable, pious Duty, to return our solemn Thanks to that great and good GOD, who hath taught our Hands to war and our Fingers to fight so very successfully. 'Tis this at last that completes our Joy by stopping the further Progress of War with her cruel and inseparable Attendants, Misery and Horror: For Conquerors themselves must own it ever accompanied by those ghastly Furies: The finest and most briliant Victories cost many Tears: The most blooming and verdant Laurels are ever stain'd with Blood, and even in the Day of Triumph the Cries of Bitterness and Sorrow mix themselves with the Shouts of Joy and Gladness. We may with Truth say, we have had enough of Victory, we have had enough of military Glory, and the Trophies

* These excerpts are reprinted from the original Williamsburg edition, pp. 5–7.

and the Spoils of War; or rather, enough of human Blood has been pour'd upon the Earth even to glut the ravenous Jaws of Death: We have had enough of that Success, which cannot be enjoy'd but at the Expence of the Lives of our Fellow-Creatures, and those oft the bravest and the best of Men. Therefore let us with Hearts unfeign'd and Gratitude sincere return our Thanks to Almighty GOD for restoring Peace to these Dominions, Security to Trade and Commerce, and Stability to our Religion and Church.

I shall not here take up your time in giving you a Detail of the many and great Advantages we have gain'd, the important Acquisitions made, or the signal Victories obtain'd by Sea and Land in the Course of this War, tho' such indeed might be entertaining, and agreable enough, but better seen in the Annals of the times, and I think with much more propriety read there than heard here. I shall therefore beg your Attention to what more nearly concerns you not only as a Community but as Individuals, and while I endeavour to shew you what good Use you shou'd make of these peaceable Times, I conceive I shall be offering some Things worthy your Consideration and which, if regarded, may prove of solid and lasting Benefit to you all.

The first Thing that will naturally present itself to us in our reflecting upon the happy Consequences resulting from the Blessing now given us, is the Security of our Civil Liberty, a Happiness we justly glory in; For Britons have preserv'd it pure and uncorrupted thro' all the Struggles of Ambition and the most dangerous Attacks of Power: They have set the World a fair Example that the highest Ambition of Princes shou'd be to govern a free People, and that no People can be great or happy but such as are so; whilst other Nations have bow'd their Necks to the Yoke of Power and have basely given up this indisputable Right of Man deriv'd to Him from the first Law of Nature, and daily feel that Misery, which ever waits on Slaves. Oh Liberty! Thou are the Author of every good and perfect Gift, the inexhaustible Fountain, from whence all Blessings flow. Without Thee, what avails the Sweetness of Climate, or the most delightful Situation in the World? what avail all the Riches of Nature, the various Production of the Earth, the Mine bringing forth a thousand Treasures, the Olive and the Vine blooming upon the Mountains, if Tyranny usurps the happy Plains, and proud Oppression deforms the gay-smiling face of Nature. . . .